# The Dynamics of Persuasion

*The Dynamics of Persuasion* provides a comprehensive and up-to-date introduction to persuasive communication and attitude change. Offering a thorough discussion of classic and contemporary theories of persuasion, this text explores the structure and functions of attitudes, consistency between attitude and behavior, and issues in attitude measurement.

Examining persuasion through media, interpersonal, and psychological lenses, author Richard M. Perloff systematically investigates the impact of persuasive communication on attitudes toward a variety of topics, including health, politics, and racial prejudice. In addition to presenting persuasion theory and research, he provides numerous examples of persuasion in action, demonstrating the role of persuasion research in everyday life. Written in a highly accessible and clear style, *The Dynamics of Persuasion* serves to:

- introduce the social science perspective on persuasion
- enhance understanding of persuasion theories and research
- highlight the major issues discussed in the field of persuasion research
- explore the complexities and subtleties in the dynamics of everyday persuasion
- raise awareness about the ethics of contemporary persuasion.

New to this edition are:

- 2008 election examples interspersed throughout the text
- focused discussions on compliance-gaining and negative advertising
- examples of strong attitude, such as the pros and cons of using animals in research.

Complemented by a companion website with resources for students and instructors, *The Dynamics of Persuasion* is an engaging text appropriate for advanced courses on persuasion in communication, psychology, marketing, and sociology. In its exploration of the dynamics of persuasive communication, it illuminates the powerful effects persuasion has in contemporary society and enhances understanding of this ubiquitous communicative strategy.

**Richard M. Perloff** is Professor and Director of the School of Communication at Cleveland State University. He has taught at Cleveland State University for 30 years. Prior to that, he received his Ph.D. in mass communications at the University of Wisconsin-Madison and completed a postdoctoral fellowship in social psychology and communication at Ohio State University. Dr. Perloff has written books on persuasion, political communication, and applications of social science to the AIDS crisis. A Fellow of the Midwest Association for Public Opinion Research, he is nationally known for scholarship on perceptions of media effects.

# COMMUNICATION SERIES
Jennings Bryant/Dolf Zillman, General Editors

*Fourth Edition*

# The Dynamics of Persuasion

Communication and Attitudes in the 21st Century

Richard M. Perloff

Routledge
Taylor & Francis Group

NEW YORK AND LONDON

Please visit the companion website at
www.routledge.com/textbooks/DynamicsofPersuasion4e

Acquisitions Editor: Linda Bathgate
Senior Development Editor: Nicole Solano
Editorial Assistant: Katherine Ghezzi
Production Editor: Sioned Jones

Project Manager: Fiona Isaac at Florence Production Ltd
Text Design: Susan R. Leaper at Florence Production Ltd
Copyeditor: Florence Production Ltd
Proofreader: Florence Production Ltd
Indexer: Florence Production Ltd
Cover Design: Gareth Toye
Companion Website Designer: Leon Nolan, Jr.

First edition published 1993
Second edition published 2003
by Lawrence Erlbaum Associates, Inc.
Third edition published 2007
by Routledge

This edition published 2010
by Routledge
270 Madison Avenue, New York, NY 10016

Simultaneously published in the UK
by Routledge
2 Park Square, Milton Park, Abingdon, Oxon OX14 4RN

*Routledge is an imprint of the Taylor & Francis Group, an informa business*

© 2010 Taylor & Francis

Typeset in Times New Roman PS and Futura by
Florence Production Ltd, Stoodleigh, Devon
Printed and bound in the United States of America on acid-free paper by
Edwards Brothers, Inc.

*Library of Congress Cataloging in Publication Data*
Perloff, Richard M.
    The dynamics of persuasion: communication and attitudes in the 21st
    century/Richard M. Perloff—4th ed.
        p. cm.
        Previous ed.: New York: Lawrence Erlbaum Associates, 3rd ed., c2008.
        Includes bibliographical references and indexes.
    1. Persuasion (Psychology)  2. Mass media—Psychological aspects.
    3. Attitude change.  I. Title.
    BF637.P4P39 2010
    153.8'52—dc22                                                  2009041035

ISBN10: 0–415–80567–8 (hbk)
ISBN10: 0–415–80568–6 (pbk)
ISBN10: 0–203–87032–8 (ebk)

ISBN13: 978–0–415–80567–4 (hbk)
ISBN13: 978–0–415–80568–1 (pbk)
ISBN13: 978–0–203–87032–7 (ebk)

To Timothy C. Brock:
persuasion visionary,
mentor, friend.

# Contents in Brief

# Contents

## 2 Attitudes: Definition and Structure  40

## 3 Attitudes: Functions and Consequences  80

# Preface

PERSUASION is such an endemic feature of American society that new exemplars—communicators, messages, and campaigns—emerge constantly. Just as the third edition was hitting academic bookstores, Americans found themselves in the midst of an electrifying election campaign. How could a persuasion book not touch on some of the path-breaking dimensions of the 2008 campaign? But you've just written a third edition, I told myself; isn't it a little soon? As I mulled over this question, I came across more applications: jazzy examples of product placements in entertainment programming, health campaigns migrating to the Web, unsavory mortgage companies devising persuasion ploys to manipulate home buyers, and new insights on coercion and persuasion at the Abu Ghraib prison camp in Iraq.

At the same time, new research on attitudes and persuasion continued apace. A social psychologist replicated the Milgram study! Communication scholars published interesting studies of fear-arousing messages, guilt appeals, and health campaigns. There was just enough new to refurbish the old. Why wait? With new research on the 2008 election campaign and time-honored ethical issues emerging in new contexts, there was more than enough to justify the arduous, but glorious, process of cutting and pasting, rewriting and revising. A fourth edition was hatched.

Two changes stand out, in my view. The first is the addition of political persuasion examples, chiefly from the 2008 campaign, capped off by a boxed section on negative advertising in Chapter 11. I try to show how persuasion theories help us understand campaign persuasion and strive to be scrupulously fair to all sides. Second, I have long recognized that the narrative a writer threads in a scholarly textbook leaves the impression that questions have been answered and knowledge, alas, has been obtained. But knowledge is not fixed and static, but changing. Just as a book tells you what we know, it should also tell you what we do not know or understand. In the final chapter I have added a boxed section that discusses what we do *not* know about persuasion and need to comprehend.

The book has plenty of new applications, with dozens of new citations of research. Chapter 1 features a definition of manipulation and an updated discussion of persuasion and coercion in cults. The Iraq war example that showcased attitudes in Chapter 2 has become dated. In its place is an example of a less political, but no less contentious, issue: animal research. Chapters 3 and 4 include new citations and research.

The fifth and sixth chapters include updates of research on processing and sources (including the Milgram replication in Chapter 6), as well as contemporary applications of theory to context. Chapter 7 offers a new section on guilt appeals, in-depth discussion of gain and loss effects on fear appeals, and a box on the ethics of marketing a cervical cancer vaccine. The eighth and ninth chapters are largely unchanged, save new research and examples, such as a memorable application of dissonance theory early in the chapter. Chapter 10 includes a boxed section that shows how compliance-gaining can be applied to critical communications between airline pilots. Chapter 11 contains a variety of updates, showcasing the changing world of advertising, as well as a box on negative advertising. The final chapter offers more discussion of the Web campaign context, with examples and methodological caveats. It also includes new discussions of psychological reactance, campaigns to reduce racial disparities in health care, and the box entitled, "What we do not know about persuasion."

Thus, the basics of the book remain the same, but I have added new sections and citations to keep things current.

# Acknowledgments

On a sad note, I lament the passing of two outstanding communication scholars who informed my scholarship. Michael Pfau conducted outstanding political persuasion research on inoculation and was a wonderful academic editor. Michael Salwen was a prolific scholar of the third-person effect and a researcher who contributed much to our field. Both were good, generous men who did much for the world and their families. I miss them.

Turning now to the people who helped me in so many ways with the current book, I begin with the editors and staff at Taylor and Francis. Linda Bathgate was optimistic and encouraging, always finding ways to make something positive happen. Thanks are also extended to Nicole Solano and Katherine Ghezzi for their helpful comments. I also want to thank my wonderful communication research colleagues, Julie Andsager at the University of Iowa and Fiona Chew at Syracuse University. They are always supportive of my work and do much good for our field.

Once again, I thank Sharon J. Muskin, who turned Word files into a professional and polished manuscript. This book would not have been completed as efficiently or professionally without her dedication and skills.

I also am grateful to others from Cleveland. Thanks are due to Rashelle Baker, administrative coordinator of the School of Communication, whose knowledge and wit have helped me in innumerable ways. I also thank Sandy Thorp of the Communication School for providing dependable assistance.

I appreciate the kindnesses bestowed by Jackie Carothers, Brenna Agrast, and Amy Brunkus, as well as the thoughtful comments of Joel Weisblat. The wise insights of Roknedin Safavi are also appreciated.

On a personal level, I appreciate the support and insightful comments on political persuasion, offered by my inlaws Jerry and Selma Krevans. And my parents, Robert and Evelyn Perloff, are jewels who affirm my attitudes and outlooks. And once again, Michael, Cathy, Julie, thank you for being who you are—a comedy troupe who deliver laughter and perspective. They are my faithful, stalwart supporters.

*Richard M. Perloff, Cleveland*

*Part One*  **Foundations**

# Chapter 1

# Introduction to Persuasion

W**HEN** someone mentions persuasion, what comes to mind? Powerful, charismatic leaders? Subliminal ads? News? Lawyers? Presidential campaigns? Or the Internet, perhaps, with those innumerable Web sites shamelessly promoting products and companies? That's persuasion, right? Powerful stuff—the kind of thing that has strong effects on society and spells profit for companies. But what about you? What does persuasion mean to you? Can you think of times when the media or attractive communicators changed your mind about something? Anything come to mind? "Not really," you say. You've got the canny ability to see through what other people are trying to sell you.

Well, that's perhaps what we like to think. "It's everyone else who's influenced, not me or my friends—well, maybe my friends, but not me." But wait: What about those Tommy Hilfiger jeans, Gap sweaters, or Nike sneakers you bought? Advertising had to play a role in that decision somehow. And, if you search your mind, you probably can think of times when you yielded to another's pushy persuasion, only to regret it later—the time you let yourself get talked into allowing a car repair that turned out to be unnecessary or agreed to loan a friend some money, only to discover she had no intention of paying you back.

But that's all negative. What of the positive side? Have you ever been helped by a persuasive communication—an antismoking ad or a reminder that it's not cool or safe to drink when you drive? Have you ever had a conversation with a friend who opened your eyes to new ways of seeing the world or with a teacher who said you had potential you didn't know you had?

You see, this is persuasion too. Just about anything that involves molding or shaping attitudes involves persuasion. Now there's another term that may seem foreign at first: attitudes. Attitudes? There once was a rock group that called itself that. But we've got attitudes as surely as we have arms, legs, cell phones, or personal computers. We have attitudes toward college and about music, money, sex, race, even God. We don't all share the same attitudes, and you may not care a whit about issues that intrigue your acquaintances. But we have attitudes and they shape our world in ways we don't always recognize. Persuasion is the study of attitudes and how to change them.

Persuasion calls to mind images of salespeople and manipulators, such as clever strategists on TV shows like *Survivor* and *The Apprentice.* It may also conjure up images of con artists, such as the swindlers who, just hours after the onset of Hurricane Katrina, created bogus Web sites soliciting donations for hurricane victims. Persuasion may bring to mind the unscrupulous bankers who lured prospective home buyers into purchasing mortgages they could not afford. It may also bring to mind those innumerable Web sites hoping to hoodwink people or offering questionable instruction on how to manage your money, fix your car, represent yourself in court, or live a happy life. (The British Web site VideoJug once had a link advising women to marry ugly men.) But there is another side too: persuasive communications have been used by good people to implement change. Social activists have used persuasion to change attitudes toward minorities and women. Consumer advocates have tirelessly warned people about dishonest business practices. Health communicators have launched countless campaigns to change people's thinking about cigarettes, alcohol, drugs, and unsafe sex. Political leaders have relied on persuasion when attempting to influence opinions toward policy issues or when trying to rally the country behind them during national crises. Some of our greatest leaders have been expert persuaders—Abraham Lincoln, Martin Luther King, Jr., and Franklin Delano Roosevelt come immediately to mind, as do the crop of current political persuaders, working in the thicket of the media age.

This book is about all these issues. It is about persuasive communication and the dynamics of attitudes that communicators hope to change. The text also examines applications of persuasion theories to a host of contexts, ranging from advertising to politics to physical health. On a more personal note, I try to show how you can use persuasion insights to become a more effective persuasive speaker and a more critical judge of social influence attempts.

## PERSUASION: CONSTANCIES AND CHANGES

The study and practice of persuasion are not new. Persuasion can be found in the Old Testament—for example, in Jeremiah's attempts to convince his people to repent and establish a personal relationship with God. We come across persuasion when we read about John the Baptist's exhortations for Christ. John traveled the countryside, acting as Christ's "advance man," preaching that "Christ is coming, wait till you see him, when you look in his eyes you'll know that you've met Christ the Lord" (Whalen, 1996, p. 110).

Long before professional persuaders hoped to turn a profit from books on closing a deal, traveling educators known as the Sophists paraded through ancient Greece, charging money for lectures on public speaking and the art of political eloquence. Five centuries before political consultants advised presidential candidates how to package themselves on television, the Italian diplomat Niccolo Machiavelli rocked the Renaissance world with his how-to manual for political persuaders, entitled *The Prince.* Machiavelli believed in politics and respected crafty political leaders. He offered a litany of suggestions for how politicians could maintain power through cunning and deception.

In the United States, where persuasion has played such a large role in politics and society as a whole, we find that communication campaigns are as American as media-advertised apple pie. The first crusade to change health behavior did not occur in 1970 or 1870, but in 1820. Nineteenth-century reformers expressed concern about increases in binge drinking and pushed for abstinence from alcohol. A few years later, activists committed to clean living tried to persuade Americans to quit using tobacco, exercise more, and adopt a vegetarian diet that included wheat bread, grains, fruits, and vegetables (Engs, 2000).

As they say in France: *Plus ça change, plus c'est la même chose* (the more things change, the more they remain the same). Yet, for all the similarities, there are important differences between our era of persuasion and those that preceded it. Each epoch has its own character, feeling, and rhythm. Contemporary persuasion differs from the past in the following five ways.

## The Sheer Number of Persuasive Communications Has Grown Exponentially

Advertising, public service announcements, Internet banner ads, and those daily inter-ruptions from telephone marketers are among the most salient indicators of this trend. Eons ago, you could go through a day with preciously little exposure to impersonal persuasive messages. This is no longer true during an epoch in which messages are con-veyed through mediated channels, such as radio, television, the Internet, and cell phones. And it's not just Americans who are besieged by persuasion. The reach of mass persuasion extends to tiny villages thousands of miles away. A U.S. college student traveling in remote areas of China reported that, while stranded by winter weather, he came across a group of Tibetans. After sharing their food with the student, the Tibetans began to discuss an issue that touched on matters American. "Just how," one of the Tibetans asked the young American, "was Michael Jordan doing?" (LaFeber, 1999, p. 14). More recently, another basketball superstar—LeBron James of the Cleveland Cavaliers—has become an international phenomenon. In an example of global persuasion's full-court press, James is a sensation in China, where National Basketball Association stores promote his image, his Nike commercials are seen everywhere, and sports Web sites celebrate his accomplishments (Boyer, 2006; see Box 1.1).

## Persuasive Messages Travel Faster Than Ever Before

Advertisements "move blindingly fast," one writer observes (Moore, 1993, p. B1). Ads quickly and seamlessly combine cultural celebrities (Beyoncé), symbols (success, fame, and athletic prowess), and commodity signs (the Nike swoosh). With the push of a button, political marketing specialists can send out a text message across the world. In August 2008, Barack Obama's presidential campaign spread the news that it planned to announce Obama's vice-presidential choice in a slick, contemporary fashion—via text message to supporters. The text message guaranteed favorable news coverage and provided a public relations bonanza. By signing up to receive the message, supporters and curiosity-seekers

## Box 1.1 | PERVASIVENESS OF PERSUASION

Persuasion is part of the fabric of everyday life, so much so that it is hard to escape its tentacles. One observer tried to count the number of direct attempts to influence his behavior over the course of a day. These included people asking him to do favors, countless requests to buy things, and assorted ideological appeals. "By the time I reached my office at mid-morning, I lost count somewhere around 500," he says (Rhoads, 1997).

From the Internet to television to salespeople selling . . . just about everything, our social environment is fraught with direct and indirect influence attempts. The development of an effective sales pitch is a key part of a business plan. But it's not just the commercial businesses that are after us. Consider these three very different examples of the pervasiveness of persuasion:

1. Pastor Lee McFarland is an evangelical Christian who is part marketer and part true believer. He quit a well-paying job at Microsoft to lead a church, splitting from Redmond, Washington, to a town with the unlikely name of Surprise, Arizona.

   McFarland left before completing the correspondence classes he was taking to become an evangelical pastor. Knocking on doors, sending out fliers with the help of a direct mail-company, and developing billboards that showed a smiling family next to the caption, "Isn't it time you laughed again?" McFarland plied his communication skills to attract people to a church he called Radiant. Recognizing that the young White residents of the Arizona exurbs were in search of a sense of community, McFarland built the church so that it would feel warm and inviting. The church foyer includes five plasma-screen TVs, 10 Xboxes for elementary school kids, a bookstore, and café. "We want the church to look like a mall," he says. "We want you to come in here and say, 'Dude, where's the cinema?'" (Mahler, 2005, p. 33). "If Oprah and Dr. Phil are doing it, why shouldn't we?" he adds. "We should be better at it because we have the power of God to offer" (Mahler, 2005, p. 35). Over the course of 8 years, weekly attendance at Radiant increased from 147 to 5,000, making it the fastest growing of the city's 28 churches.

   But questions remain. Some critics dismiss this new brand of religious persuasion as "Christianity lite." Scholar James B. Twitchell sees it as part of a new marketing phenomenon in which Christianity "went from in your heart to in your face." Describing a preacher who, like McFarland, aggressively markets his credo, Twitchell says, "He's not in the soul business, he's in the self business" (Blumenthal, 2006, p. B7).

2. The ad begins innocently enough, with the camera tracking a mother as she stands over a checkbook and calculator on her kitchen table. That's when her daughter, a young African-American woman, sits down and says, "Look Mom, if I decide I still want to be a doctor when I get out, I'll have had 4 years experience as a nurse or an X-ray tech. That's why I want to enlist in the military; it'll be good for my career. What do you think?" The advertisement then fades and shows the address of the Defense Department's

**Box 1.1** |

military recruitment Web site. A voiceover intones, "Make it a two-way conversation. Get the facts at *todaysmilitary.com*" (O'Brien, 2005, p. 1).

The Army spends close to $300 million annually on advertising, while at the same time pouring money into online video games geared to teenagers, leaflets (one brochure hyped the military's 30 days of annual paid vacation), and a battery of interpersonal influence techniques. Army recruiters spend several hours a day making cold calls to high school students. They show up at malls and high schools, doing whatever they can to entice young people to enlist (Cave, 2005a, 2005b). "The football team usually starts practicing in August," an Army recruiting handbook advises. "Contact the coach and volunteer to assist in leading calisthenics or calling cadence during team runs" (Herbert, 2005a, p. A29). One sergeant sounded more like a sales rep when he proclaimed to a campus group, "I mean, where else can you get paid to jump out of airplanes, shoot cool guns, blow stuff up and travel, seeing all kinds of different countries?" ("Leave No Sales Pitch Behind," 2005, p. A22).

Activities like these are perfectly legal. To many recruiters, it is a source of pride to recruit soldiers dedicated to fighting the nation's war on terrorism. But not everyone sees it this way. Columnist Bob Herbert, a relentless critic of the war in Iraq, points out that many recruiters exploit young people's vulnerabilities and present a false picture of what it is like to fight for your country. He observes:

> Recruiters desperate for warm bodies to be shipped to Iraq are prowling selected high schools and neighborhoods across the country with sales pitches that touch on everything but the possibility of being maimed or killed in combat . . . But war is not a game. Getting your face blown off is not fun . . . Potential recruits should be told the truth about what is expected of them, and what the risks are. And they should be told why it's a good idea for them to take those risks. If that results in too few people signing up for the military, the country is left with a couple of other options: Stop fighting unnecessary wars, or reinstate the draft.

(2005b, p. A17)

3. Lest you think that all persuasion today is ethically problematic, consider the truth-is-stranger-than-fiction case of Ashley Smith. On a Friday in mid-March, Brian Nichols, on trial in Atlanta for rape, seized the gun of a sheriff's deputy and fatally shot the judge in his case. On the run from police, Nichols accosted Ashley when she returned to her apartment from a late-night run to buy cigarettes. He bound her with masking tape and carried her to the bedroom, where he tied her up with more masking tape and an electrical cord.

Although most people would scream, panic, or fight back, Ashley turned the other cheek. She listened as Nichols told her what had happened in the Atlanta courthouse. She then explained that he had killed a man who was probably a father and a husband.

**Box 1.1**

She asked Nichols if he would mind if she read from a book. He agreed. She read to him from a bestselling book, *The Purpose-Driven Life*, which claims that each person's life has a divinely inspired purpose. Ashley subsequently revealed aspects of her life to Nichols. She was married and had a 5-year-old daughter. But tragedy had struck when her husband was stabbed in a fight by old friends and died in her arms. The incident set in motion a dark period for Ashley, including arrests for drunken driving and assault. She had put her life in order, crediting her recovery to faith in God. "You need to turn yourself in. No one else needs to die and you're going to die if you don't," she told him.

She asked him how he felt about what he had done and sensed a change in his demeanor. He was no longer the brazen warrior. They talked some more, she cooked him breakfast, and then called 911 on her cell phone. The police swarmed into the apartment and he surrendered. "I believe God brought him to my door so he couldn't hurt anyone else," Ashley said (Dewan & Goodstein, 2005; Rankin & Plummer, 2005, p. 2).

alike had provided Obama with their e-mails, enabling the staff to contact and mobilize them during the fall campaign. At 3 a.m. Saturday morning, August 23, Obama's advisers unleashed the announcement: *"Barack has chosen Senator Biden to be our VP nominee. Watch the first Obama-Biden rally live at 3 p.m. ET on www.BarackObama.com. Spread the word!"*

## Persuasion Has Become Institutionalized

No longer can a Thomas Jefferson dash off a Declaration of Independence. In the twenty-first century, the Declaration would be edited by committees, test marketed in typical American communities, and checked with standards departments to make sure it did not offend potential constituents.

Numerous companies are in the persuasion business. Advertising agencies, public relations firms, marketing conglomerates, lobbying groups, social activists, pollsters, speech writers, image consultants—companies big and small—are involved with various facets of persuasion. The list is long and continues to grow.

Persuasion has become a critical weapon in the arsenal of powerful companies. Tobacco companies use public relations agents to massage their images in the face of broad public criticism. Political interest groups spend millions to influence the votes of members of Congress. Energy companies hire persuasion specialists to deflate the arguments of environmentalists concerned about global warming. Wealthy, powerful organizations have more resources to use persuasion effectively than do less politically connected groups. They can depend upon networks of connections spread across society's most influential institutions.

# Persuasive Communication Has Become More Subtle and Devious

We are long past the days in which brash salespeople knocked on your door to pitch encyclopedias or hawk Avon cosmetics directly. Nowadays, salespeople know all about flattery, empathy, nonverbal communication, and likeability appeals. Walk into a Nordstrom clothing store and you see a fashionably dressed man playing a piano. Nordstrom wants you to feel like you're in a special, elite place, one that not so incidentally sells brands of clothing that jibe with this image.

Advertising no longer relies only on hard-sell, "hammer it home" appeals, but also on soft-sell messages that play on emotions. A few years back, the Benetton clothing company showed attention-grabbing pictures of a dying AIDS patient and a desperately poor Third World girl holding a White doll from a trash can. The pictures appeared with the tag line, "United Colors of Benetton." What do these images have to do with clothing? Nothing—and everything. Benetton was selling an image, not a product. It appealed to consumers' higher sensibilities, inviting them to recognize that "the world we live in is not neatly packaged and cleansed as most ads depict it . . . at Benetton we are not like others, we have vision" (Goldman & Papson, 1996, p. 52).

You can also find examples of the subtlety and deceptiveness of persuasion in the news media. Some years ago the U.S. government produced a series of 90-second TV segments that looked like news, "smelled" like news, and were broadcast by local television stations in some of the nation's largest media markets, including New York City, Chicago, and Atlanta. One report described the Bush administration's program to strengthen aviation security, calling it "one of the most remarkable campaigns in aviation history." Another segment showed Bush signing into law legislation that gave prescription drug benefits to people with Medicare health insurance. The reporter, Karen Ryan, touted the advantages of the law, but failed to mention other aspects of the story, such as prominent criticism that it was a gift to the pharmaceutical industry. What the tens of millions of Americans who watched these reports did not know was that they were prepared by public relations experts hired by the federal government and "reporters" like Karen Ryan were actually PR consultants (Barstow & Stein, 2005).

Government-produced news programming provides the White House with a positive spin on national events, offers public relations agencies a bonanza of government contracts, and gives television stations a cheap way to fill their daily news programs. The practice is a disturbing example of the subtle, increasingly devious nature of contemporary persuasion.

Political and commercial messages like these have left an imprint on the public. They have made Americans more cynical about persuasion. Bombarded by communications promoted as truth but actually misleading, as well as by blogs that dissect institutional messages, consumers have grown wary of the truthfulness of persuaders' claims. They seem to recognize that this is an age of spin in which commercial and political communicators regard the truth as just another strategy in the persuasion armamentarium.

## Persuasive Communication Is More Complex and Impersonal

Once upon a time long ago, persuaders knew their clients. Everyone lived in the same small communities. When cities developed and industrialization spread, persuaders knew fewer of their customers, but could be reasonably confident that they understood their clients because they all shared the same cultural and ethnic background. As the United States has become more culturally and racially diverse, persuaders and consumers frequently come from different sociological places. A marketer cannot assume that her client thinks the same way she does or approaches a communication encounter with the same assumptions. The intermingling of people from different cultural groups is a profoundly positive phenomenon, but it makes for more dicey and difficult interpersonal persuasion.

Technology has also increased the complexity of persuasion, blurring lines among information, entertainment, and influence. For example, a Web site intended to inform or amuse may capture the eye of a blogger, who combines it with imagery and sends the modification over the Internet. It's now a persuasive message, taking on a meaning the original communicator never intended. Such was the case with the musical group Green Day's "Wake me up when September ends," a political song about war and romance. When a blogger known as Zadi linked the song with TV news coverage of Hurricane Katrina and posted it on her Web site in September 2005, it became a musically conveyed persuasive message about society's indifference to Katrina's victims (Boxer, 2005). The pairing of lyrics like "summer has come and passed, the innocent can never last" with images of devastation created an eerie, haunting message. When combined with suggestions that the Bush administration had been callous in its response to hurricane victims, the melange conveyed a potent political message, one that might be at odds with the original Green Day song, with its more ambiguous stand toward the war in Iraq. Contemporary technologies make it possible for people to alter the content of persuasive messages, giving messages meanings they did not have and that the original communicator did not intend.

# FOUNDATIONS OF PERSUASION

Persuasion is celebrated as a quintessential human activity, but here's a subversive thought: Suppose we're not the only ones who do it? What if our friends in the higher animal kingdom also use a little homespun social influence? Frans de Waal painstakingly observed chimpanzees in a Dutch zoo and chronicled his observations in a book aptly called *Chimpanzee Politics* (1982). His conclusion: chimps use all sorts of techniques to get their way with peers. They frequently resort to violence, but not always. Chimps form coalitions, bluff each other, and even show some awareness of social reciprocity, as they seem to recognize that favors should be rewarded and disobedience punished.

Does this mean that chimpanzees are capable of persuasion? Some scientists would answer "yes" and cite as evidence chimps' subtle techniques to secure power. Indeed, there is growing evidence that apes can form images, use symbols, and employ deception

(Angier, 2008; Miles, 1993). To some scientists, the difference between human and animal persuasion is one of degree, not kind.

Wait a minute. Do we really think that chimpanzees persuade their peers? Perhaps they persuade in the *Godfather* sense of making people an offer they can't refuse. However, this is not persuasion so much as it is coercion.

As we will see, persuasion involves the persuader's awareness that he or she is trying to influence someone else. It also requires that the "persuadee" make a conscious or unconscious decision to change his mind about something. With this definition in mind, chimpanzees' behavior is better described as social influence or coercion than persuasion. "Okay," you animal lovers say, "but let me tell you about my cat." "She sits sweetly in her favorite spot on my sofa when I return from school," one feline-loving student told me, "then curls up in my arms, and purrs softly until I go to the kitchen and fetch her some milk. Isn't that persuasion?" Well—no. Your cat may be trying to curry your favor, but she has not performed an act of persuasion. The cat is not cognizant that she is trying to "influence" you. What's more, she does not appreciate that you have a mental state— let alone a belief—that she wants to change. Some animals, like apes, do have cognitive abilities. For example, they are aware of themselves; they can recognize that a reflected image in a mirror is of them (Fountain, 2006). But there is no evidence they have beliefs or attitudes; nor do their attempts to influence humans appear directed at changing human attitudes.

There is one other reason why it does not make sense to say that animals engage in persuasion. Persuasion has moral components; individuals choose to engage in morally beneficent or morally reprehensible actions. However, as philosopher Carl Cohen (Cohen & Regan, 2001) points out, "with all the varied capacities of animals granted, it remains absolutely impossible for them to act *morally*, to be members of a moral community. . . A being subject to genuinely moral judgment must be capable of grasping the *maxim* of an act and capable, too, of grasping the *generality* of an ethical premise in a moral argument" (p. 38). Even granting that animals have mental and emotional capacities, they most assuredly cannot function as moral creatures who consciously make moral (or immoral) communicative decisions. In short, persuasion matters and strikes to the core of our lives as human beings. This means that we must define what we mean by persuasion and differentiate it from related terms.

## DEFINING PERSUASION

Scholars have defined persuasion in different ways. I list the following major definitions to show you how different researchers approach the topic. Persuasion, according to communication scholars, is:

- a communication process in which the communicator seeks to elicit a desired response from his receiver (Andersen, 1971, p. 6);
- a conscious attempt by one individual to change the attitudes, beliefs, or behavior of another individual or group of individuals through the transmission of some message (Bettinghaus & Cody, 1987, p. 3);

- a symbolic activity whose purpose is to effect the internalization or voluntary acceptance of new cognitive states or patterns of overt behavior through the exchange of messages (Smith, 1982, p. 7); and
- a successful intentional effort at influencing another's mental state through communication in a circumstance in which the persuadee has some measure of freedom (O'Keefe, 1990, p. 17).

All of these definitions have strengths. Boiling down the main components into one unified perspective (and adding a little of my own recipe), I define persuasion as *a symbolic process in which communicators try to convince other people to change their attitudes or behaviors regarding an issue through the transmission of a message in an atmosphere of free choice.* There are five components of the definition.

## Persuasion Is a Symbolic Process

Contrary to popular opinion, persuasion does not happen with the flick of a switch. You don't just change people's minds—snap, crackle, pop. On the contrary, persuasion takes time, consists of a number of steps, and actively involves the recipient of the message. As Mark Twain quipped, "Habit is habit, and not to be flung out of the window, but coaxed downstairs a step at a time" (cited in Prochaska, Redding, Harlow, Rossi, & Velicer, 1994, p. 471).

Many of us view persuasion in macho, "John Wayne" terms. Persuaders are seen as tough-talking salespeople, strongly stating their position, hitting people over the head with arguments, and pushing the deal to a close. But this oversimplifies matters. It assumes that persuasion is a boxing match, won by the fiercest competitor. In fact, persuasion is different. It's more like teaching than boxing. Think of a persuader as a teacher, moving people step by step to a solution, helping them appreciate why the advocated position solves the problem best.

Persuasion also involves the use of symbols, with messages transmitted primarily through language with its rich, cultural meanings. Symbols include words like freedom, justice, and equality; nonverbal signs like the flag, Star of David, or Holy Cross; and images that are instantly recognized and processed like the Nike swoosh or McDonald's golden arches. Symbols are persuaders' tools, harnessed to change attitudes and mold opinions.

## Persuasion Involves an Attempt to Influence

Persuasion does not automatically or inevitably succeed. Like companies that go out of business soon after they open, persuasive communications often fail to reach or influence their targets. However, persuasion does involve a deliberate attempt to influence another person. Persuaders must intend to change another individual's attitude or behavior and must be aware (at least at some level) that they are trying to accomplish this goal.

For this reason it does not make sense to say that chimpanzees persuade each other. As noted earlier, chimps, smart as they are, do not seem to possess high-level awareness that they are trying to change another primate, let alone modify a fellow chimp's mind. Indeed, it is unlikely that they can conceptualize that the other animal has a mind that they seek to change, let alone an attitude that they would like to modify.

In a similar fashion, we should not make the claim that very young children are capable of persuasion. True, a mother responds to an infant's cry for milk by dashing to the refrigerator (or lending her breast, if that's her feeding preference). Yes, we have all shopped in toy stores and watched as 2-year-olds point to toys seen on television and scream, "I want that." And we have been witness to the pitiful sight of parents, who pride themselves on being competent professionals, helplessly yielding to prevent any further embarrassment.

Yet the baby's cry for milk and the toddler's demand for toys do not qualify as persuasion. These youngsters have not reached the point where they are aware that they are trying to change another person's mental state. Their actions are better described as coercive social influence than persuasion. In order for children to practice persuasion, they must understand that other people can have desires and beliefs; recognize that the persuadee has a mental state that is susceptible to change; demonstrate a primitive awareness that they intend to influence another person; and realize that the persuadee has a perspective different from theirs, even if they cannot put all this into words (Bartsch & London, 2000). As children grow, they appreciate these things, rely less on coercive social influence attempts than on persuasion, and develop the ability to persuade others more effectively (Kline & Clinton, 1998).

The main point here is that persuasion represents a conscious attempt to influence the other party, along with an accompanying awareness that the persuadee has a mental state that is susceptible to change. It is a type of social influence. Social influence is the broad process in which the behavior of one person alters the thoughts or actions of another. Social influence can occur when receivers act on cues or messages that were not necessarily intended for their consumption (Dudczak, 2001). Persuasion occurs within a context of intentional messages that are initiated by a communicator in the hope of influencing the recipient. This is pretty heady stuff, but it is important because, if you include every possible influence attempt under the persuasion heading, you count every communication as persuasion. That would make for a very long book.

The larger question is whether persuasion should be defined from the perspective of the audience member or of the communicator. If you define it from the audience member's point of view, then every message that attempts to change someone's attitude gets counted as persuasion. This is democratic, but unwieldy. It means that communication and persuasion are the same thing. Yet people do a lot of communicating—talking, gossiping, disclosing things about themselves—that are not attempts to persuade. This is why it is more useful to stipulate that persuasion involves some sort of intentional effort to change another person's mind.

## People Persuade Themselves

One of the great myths of persuasion is that persuaders convince us to do things we really don't want to do. They supposedly overwhelm us with so many arguments or such verbal ammunition that we acquiesce. They force us to give in. This overlooks an important point: people persuade themselves to change attitudes or behavior. Communicators provide the arguments. They set up the bait. We make the change, or refuse to yield. As D. Joel Whalen puts it:

> You can't force people to be persuaded—you can only activate their desire and show them the logic behind your ideas. You can't move a string by pushing it, you have to pull it. People are the same. Their devotion and total commitment to an idea come only when they fully understand and buy in with their total being.
>
> (1996, p. 5)

You can understand the power of self-persuasion by considering an activity that does not at first blush seem to involve persuasive communication: therapy. Therapists undoubtedly help people make changes in their lives. But have you ever heard someone say, "My therapist persuaded me"? On the contrary, people who seek psychological help look into themselves, consider what ails them, and decide how best to cope. The therapist offers suggestions and provides an environment in which healing can take place (Kassan, 1999). But if progress occurs, it is the client who makes the change and it is the client who is responsible for making sure that there is no regression to the old ways of doing things.

Of course, not every self-persuasion is therapeutic. Self-persuasion can be benevolent or malevolent. An ethical communicator will plant the seeds for healthy self-influence. A dishonest, evil persuader convinces a person to change her mind in a way that is personally or socially destructive. Note also that persuasion typically involves change. It does not focus on forming attitudes, but on inducing people to alter attitudes they already possess. This can involve shaping, molding, or reinforcing attitudes, as is discussed later in the chapter.

## Persuasion Involves the Transmission of a Message

The message may be verbal or nonverbal. It can be relayed interpersonally, through mass media, or via the Internet. It may be reasonable or unreasonable, factual or emotional. The message can consist of arguments or simple cues, like music in an advertisement that brings pleasant memories to mind. Persuasion is a communicative activity; thus, there must be a message for persuasion, as opposed to other forms of social influence, to occur.

Life is packed with messages that change or influence attitudes. In addition to the usual contexts that come to mind when you think of persuasion—advertising, political campaigns, and interpersonal sales—there are other domains that contain attitude-altering messages. News unquestionably shapes attitudes and beliefs (McCombs & Reynolds, 2002). Talk to older Americans who watched TV coverage of White policemen beating Blacks in the South or chat with people who viewed television coverage of the Vietnam War, and you will gain firsthand evidence of how television news can shake up people's worldviews. News of more recent events—the tsunami in Indochina, Hurricane Katrina, the tragedy of September 11—have left indelible impressions on people's views of global issues and America.

Art—books, movies, plays, and songs—also has a strong influence on how we think and feel about life. Artistic portrayals can transport people into different realities, changing the way they see life (Green & Brock, 2005). If you think for a moment, I'm sure you can call to mind books, movies, and songs that shook you up and pushed you to rethink your assumptions. Dostoyevsky's discussions of the human condition, a Picasso painting, movies like *Hotel Rwanda* or *Fahrenheit 9/11*, *The Simpsons* television show, a folk melody or rap song—these can all influence and change people's worldviews.

Yet, although news and art contain messages that change attitudes, they are not pure exemplars of persuasion. Recall that persuasion is defined as an attempt to convince others to change their attitudes or behavior. In many cases, journalists are not trying to change people's attitudes toward a topic. They are describing events to provide people with information, offer new perspectives, or entice viewers to watch their programs. In the same fashion, most artists do not create art to change the world. They write, paint, or compose songs to express important personal concerns, articulate vexing problems of life, or soothe, uplift, or agitate people. In a sense, it demeans art to claim that artists attempt only to change our attitudes. Thus, art and news are best viewed as borderline cases of persuasion. Their messages can powerfully influence our worldviews, but because the intent of these communicators is broader and more complex than attitude change, news and art are best viewed as lying along the border of persuasion and the large domain of social influence.

For example, you can easily think of movies that have a clearly persuasive purpose. Michael Moore definitely hoped that *Fahrenheit 9/11* would convince Americans to change their attitudes toward former President Bush and the war in Iraq. Director Gus Van Sant seems to have hoped that *Milk*, the story of the first openly-gay man to be elected to public office in California, would serve some educational functions, teaching people about the political plight of gay Americans. But other directors' motives are less clear-cut. It seems unlikely that Paul Haggis wrote *Crash* to promote a liberal or conservative agenda. Instead, he seems to have had grander, more complex purposes that in all likelihood centered on inducing viewers to think more deeply about the complex ways that prejudice insinuates its way into everyday American life. Was Haggis trying to persuade viewers or, more likely, was he trying to nudge them to look at life through different lenses?

## Persuasion Requires Free Choice

If, as noted earlier, self-persuasion is the key to successful influence, then an individual must be free to alter his own behavior or to do what he wishes in a communication setting. But what does it mean to be free? Philosophers have debated this question for centuries, and if you took a philosophy course, you may recall those famous debates about free will versus determinism.

There are more than 200 definitions of freedom, and, as we will see, it's hard to say precisely when coercion ends and persuasion begins. I suggest that a person is free when he has the ability to act otherwise—to do other than what the persuader suggests—or to reflect critically on his choices in a situation (Smythe, 1999). Even so, it is important to remember that people do not have absolute freedom, even in a democratic society like ours that enshrines human rights. Americans do not have the same access to international media, such as the Middle East television network Al Jazeera, that offer critical portraits of U.S. policies, as they do to American media that provide a more positive picture. Are Americans free to sample all media? Theoretically, yes, but practically, no. From an early age, American children are exposed to advertisements that tout the blessings of commercial products, but have virtually no exposure to communications that question the virtues of the capitalist system. Given the powers of socialization, how free are these individuals to reject the trappings of capitalism when they become adults? In America, girls and boys learn (partly through advertising) that diamond rings symbolize marital bliss and that marriage is a desirable life-pursuit. What is the likelihood that, as adults, these individuals could reject wedding rings and marriage after, say, reading articles that criticize the spiritual emptiness of material possessions and the rigidities of marital roles?

I ask these questions not to argue that wedding rings or marriage are without value, but to suggest that none of it is as free as we think—not in America or in any other culture, and that the concept of freedom that underlies persuasion is a relative, not an absolute, concept.

I have defined persuasion and identified its main features. But this tells us only half the story. To appreciate persuasion, you have to understand what it is not—that is, how it differs from related ideas.

## PERSUASION VERSUS COERCION

How does persuasion differ from coercion? The answer may seem simple at first. Persuasion deals with reason and verbal appeals, while coercion employs force, you suggest. It's not a bad start, but there are subtle relationships between the terms—fascinating overlaps—that you might not ordinarily think of. Consider these scenarios:

- Tom works for a social service agency that receives some of its funding from United Way. At the end of each year, United Way asks employees to contribute to the charity. Tom would like to donate, but he needs every penny of his salary to support his family. One year, his boss, Anne, sends out a memo strongly urging employees to give to United Way. Anne doesn't threaten, but the implicit message is: I expect you to donate, and I'll know who did and who didn't. Tom opts to contribute money to United Way. Was he coerced or persuaded?

- Debbie, a college senior, makes an appointment with her favorite English professor, Dr. Stanley Hayes, to get advice on where to apply for graduate school. Hayes compliments Debbie on her writing style, tells her she is one of the best students he has had in 20 years of teaching, and reflects back on his own experiences as a youthful graduate student in American literature. The two chat for a bit, and Hayes asks if she would mind dropping by his house for dessert and coffee to discuss this further. "Evening's best for me," Hayes adds. Debbie respects Professor Hayes and knows she needs his recommendation for graduate school, but she wonders about his intentions. She accepts the offer. Was she persuaded or coerced?

■ Elizabeth, a high school junior, has been a football fan since grade school and throughout middle school. Waiting eagerly for the homecoming game to start, she glances at the field, catching a glimpse of the senior class president as he strides out to the 50-yard line. Much to her surprise, the class president asks the crowd to stand and join him in prayer. Elizabeth is squeamish. She is not religious and suspects that she's an atheist. She notices that everyone around her is standing, nodding their heads, and reciting the Lord's Prayer. She glances to her left and sees four popular girls shooting nasty looks at her and shaking their heads. Without thinking, Elizabeth rises and nervously begins to speak the words herself. Was she coerced or persuaded?

Before we can answer these questions, we must know what is meant by coercion. Philosophers define coercion as a technique for forcing people to act as the coercer wants them to act—presumably contrary to their preferences. It usually employs a threat of some dire consequence if the actor does not do what the coercer demands (Feinberg, 1998, p. 387). Tom's boss, Debbie's professor, and Elizabeth's classmates pushed them to act in ways that were contrary to their preferences. The communicators employed a direct or veiled threat. It appears that they employed coercion.

Things get murkier when you look at scholarly definitions that compare coercion with persuasion. Mary J. Smith (1982) takes a relativist perspective, emphasizing the role of perception. According to this view, it's all a matter of how people perceive things. Smith argues that when people believe that they are free to reject the communicator's position, as a practical matter they are free, and the influence attempt falls under the persuasion umbrella. When individuals perceive that they have no choice but to comply, the influence attempt is better viewed as coercive.

Assume now that Tom, Debbie, and Elizabeth are all confident, strong-minded individuals. Tom feels that he can say no to his employer. Debbie, undaunted by Professor Hayes's flirtatiousness, believes that she is capable of rejecting his overtures. Elizabeth feels that she is free to do as she pleases at the football game. In this case, we would say that the influence agents persuaded the students to comply.

On the other hand, suppose Tom, Debbie, and Elizabeth lack confidence in themselves and don't believe that they can resist these communicators. In this case, we might say that these individuals perceived that they had little choice but to comply. We would conclude that coercion, not persuasion, had occurred.

You can now appreciate how difficult it is to differentiate persuasion and coercion. Scholars differ on where they draw the line between the two terms. Some would say that the three influence agents used a little bit of both. (My own view is that the first case is the clearest instance of coercion. The communicator employed a veiled threat. What's more, Tom's boss wielded power over him, leading to the reasonable perception that Tom had little choice but to comply. The other two scenarios are more ambiguous; arguably, they are more persuasion than coercion because most people would probably assume that they could resist the communicators' appeals. In addition, no direct threats of any kind were employed in these cases.) More generally, the point to remember here is that persuasion and coercion are not polar opposites, but rather overlapping concepts.

One gains useful perspective on the overlap in the terms by considering another contemporary issue: terrorism. Terrorism is unquestionably a coercive act: it employs threats of dire consequence and physical force to compel individuals to behave as the coercer wants them to behave. But terrorists also have persuasive goals. "The point of terrorism," Louise Richardson notes, "is not to defeat the enemy but to send a message . . . Victims are used as a means of altering the behavior of a larger audience" (2006, pp. 4–5). Terrorists commit violent acts to gain attention and sympathy for their cause. They may kill dozens of innocent people to influence millions of others. They attempt to provoke a reaction, hoping to scare people, convince them to change their lifestyles, or demonstrate that the terrorist organization remains capable of communicating a message. Persuasion and coercion are sometimes inextricable, more difficult to unravel than commonly assumed.

One sees this all too clearly in the controversial abuses of Iraqi prisoners at the Abu Ghraib prison (Zimbardo, 2007). During the war in Iraq, a handful of American soldiers humiliated and tortured Iraqi prisoners—for example, leaving a detainee naked in his cell and forcing him to bark like a dog and crawl on his stomach as soldiers urinated and spat on him. He was later sodomized by a police stick while two female military police officers threw a ball at his genitals. Even those who supported the war in Iraq and sympathized with the terrible pressures soldiers faced from attacks from insurgents acknowledged that the soldiers' behavior was unethical. Were the soldiers coerced or persuaded? It is hard to separate the two forms of social influence. Coercion clearly was at work. During the early phases of the war, senior military commanders made it clear that they wanted intelligence information about Iraqi prisoners. This in turn placed pressure on lower level officers to take whatever steps were necessary to obtain this information (Schmitt, 2004). The White House had declared that Al Qaeda and the Taliban were outside the purview of the Geneva Convention's restrictions on torture. Thus, it seems plausible that Pentagon officials implicitly conveyed acceptance of torture as a way to get information and that this attitude filtered down the chain of command.

By the same token, the soldiers who committed the abuses do not appear to have been ordered to perform these specific actions. Private Lynndie England—who held a leash around the neck of a naked Iraqi prisoner and gleefully posed next to naked Iraqi men who had been forced to simulate masturbation—told a military court she knew this was wrong. Pleading guilty to seven criminal counts, she admitted that she went along because her former lover, Sergeant Charles Graner, "asked me to." "Could you have chosen to walk away?" the judge asked her. "I could have," Private England said. "I was yielding to peer pressure" (Levy, 2005). Acknowledging her personal freedom, England sounds like she was acquiescing to a persuasive influence attempt.

It is easy to criticize England and Graner, but none of us knows what we would have done if we had faced the same pressures that these two soldiers experienced in Iraq. Social influence—coercion and persuasion—exerts powerful, not always positive, effects on human behavior. The line between persuasion and coercion is rarely clear and is even murkier in situations like Abu Ghraib (see Figures 1.1 and 1.2, and Box 1.2). Difficult as it is to make absolute demarcations, it is important to differentiate the terms clearly.

Those who say it all comes down to perception must wrestle with the ambiguity (unsatisfactory in a court of law) that an influence attempt can be persuasion for one person (if he claims to be free to reject the communicator's position), yet coercive for another (if she claims she has no choice but to comply). This means that two individuals could be influenced by the same message, but one (who claimed it was persuasion) would be held accountable for his actions, while the other (who perceived coercion) could be exonerated on the grounds that she lacked the freedom to reject the message. This is clearly unsatisfactory. Interesting as the perceptual approach is, it does not provide a clear boundary line between persuasion and coercion. A more concrete approach is needed.

Based on contemporary approaches, we can say that coercion occurs when the influence agent: (a) delivers a threat of some consequence, (b) attempts to induce the individual to act contrary to her preferences, and (c) deprives the individual of some measure of freedom or autonomy (Feinberg, 1998; Rosenbaum, 1986). Persuasion, by contrast, occurs in an atmosphere of free choice: it assumes the individual is capable of resisting an influence attempt or of willingly persuading him or herself to alter an attitude about an issue.

## THE BAD BOYS OF PERSUASION

We're not done yet! There are two additional terms that are bandied about when social influence and persuasion are discussed: *propaganda* and *manipulation*. Propaganda overlaps with persuasion, as both are invoked to describe powerful instances of social influence. However, there are key differences between the terms.

First, propaganda is typically invoked to describe mass influence through mass media. Persuasion, by contrast, occurs in mediated settings, but also in interpersonal and organizational contexts.

---

Coercion_____Persuasion


        Nature of Psychological Threat
        Ability to Do Otherwise
        Perception of Free Choice



Coercion and persuasion are not polar opposites. They are better viewed as lying along a continuum of social influence.

---

**FIGURE 1.1** | Coercion and persuasion.

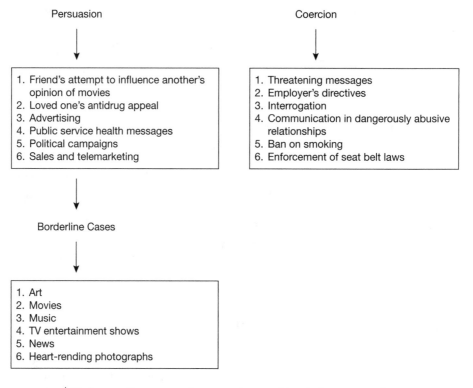

**FIGURE 1.2** | Understanding persuasion, coercion, and borderline cases of persuasion.

Note that coercion can be negative, or positive (as in smoking bans and enforcement of seat belt laws). Borderline cases focus on persuasion rather than coercion. They lie just outside the boundary of persuasion because the intent of the communicator is not to explicitly change an individual's attitude toward the issue, but is, instead, broader and more complex (Gass & Seiter, 2003).

Second, propaganda is covert. Some years ago, the Pentagon planted articles in Iraqi newspapers. The articles put a positive spin on the Iraqi economy and the country's political future in an effort to win the hearts and minds of the Iraqi people (Gerth & Shane, 2005). Pentagon officials figured Iraqis would be more persuaded if they perceived the stories to be bona fide news rather than what they were—stories written by an American public relations firm hired by the Defense Department. Neither the true source nor intent of the communications could be discerned by audience members, pointing up another characteristic of propaganda.

Third, propaganda refers to instances in which a group has total control over the transmission of information—for example, Hitler in Nazi Germany, the Chinese Communists during the Chinese Revolution, Saddam Hussein in Iraq, and violent religious cults. Persuasion can be slanted and one-sided, but it ordinarily allows for a free flow of information; in persuasion situations, people can ordinarily question the persuader or offer contrasting opinions.

## Box 1.2 | THE CULT OF PERSUASION

Edison Jessop, a resident of the Yearning for Zion Ranch in west Texas, had no complaints. "We've got 300 pounds of cabbage out of there already, and a couple hundred more coming," he said, as he drove by a garden (Kovach, 2008). Jessop regarded the ranch, home to followers of the Fundamentalist Church of Latter Day Saints, as a wonderful place to raise children. However, the church was also a polygamist community that followed the strict teachings of leader Rulon Jeffs and his son, Warren. Television and Internet were forbidden. Laughter was against the law. All the women wore old-fashioned "Little House on the Prairie Dresses." Some of the men had as many as five wives. Warren Jeffs is believed to have fathered more than 100 children (Atlas, Dodd, Lang, Bane, & Levy, 2008). Most disturbingly, there was evidence of possible sexual abuse. When a 16-year-old girl called a domestic abuse hotline, claiming she had been abused by her 50-year-old husband, state authorities raided the compound. Although there was disagreement about the merits—and legality—of the state's action, there was little doubt that the church bore the earmarks of a religious cult.

It was hardly the first time that a religious cult attracted national attention. In March 1997, the nation learned the tragic fate of the 39 members of Heaven's Gate Cult, all of whom committed suicide. Many wondered why 39 intelligent, committed men and women willingly took their own lives, joyfully announcing their decision in a farewell videotape and statement on their Web site. The suicide was timed to coincide with the arrival of the Hale–Bopp comet. Believing that a flying saucer was traveling behind the comet, members chose to leave their bodies behind to gain redemption in a Kingdom of Heaven (Robinson, 1998). To many people, this provided yet another example of the powerful, but mysterious, technique called brainwashing. The cult leader, Marshall Applewhite, known to his followers as "Do," supposedly brainwashed cult members into committing mass suicide in their home in Rancho Santa Fe, California. Although Heaven's Gate was the first Internet cult tragedy, one that drove millions of curiosity seekers to the group's Web site, it was only the most recent in a series of bizarre cult occurrences that observers could describe only as brainwashing. In one of the most famous of these tragic tales, over 900 members of the People's Temple followed leader Jim Jones's directive to drink cyanide-spiked Kool-Aid at the cult's home in Guyana, South America, back in 1978. Other cases, including the violent story of David Koresh's Branch Davidians in Waco, Texas (circa 1993), continue to fascinate and disturb. Searching for a simple answer, people assume that charismatic leaders *brainwash* followers into submission.

Famous though it may be, brainwashing is not a satisfactory explanation for what happens in cults. It does not tell us why ordinary people choose to join and actively participate in cults. It does not explain how leaders wield influence or are able to induce followers to engage in self-destructive behavior. Instead, the brainwashing term condemns people and points fingers.

How can we explain the cult phenomenon? First, we need to define a cult. *A cult is a group of individuals who are: (a) excessively devoted to a charismatic leader, himself or herself "the object of worship"; (b) effectively isolated from the rest of society; (c) denied access to alternative*

**Box 1.2** |

*points of view; and (d) subjected to exploitative social influence techniques* (see Lifton, 2003, p. xii). To appreciate how cults influence individuals, we need to consider the dynamics of persuasion and coercion. As an example, consider the case of one young person who fell into the Heaven's Gate cult and, by crook or the hook of social influence, could not get out. Her name was Gail Maeder, and she was one of the unlucky 39 who ended her life on that unhappy March day.

Gail, a soft-hearted soul, adored animals. The lanky 27-year-old also loved trees, so much so that she tried not to use much paper. Searching for something—maybe adventure, possibly herself—she left suburban New York for California. Traveling again, this time in the Southwest, she met some friendly folks in a van—members of Heaven's Gate, it turns out. Gail joined the group and told her parents not to worry. She was very happy.

If you look at Gail's picture in *People*, taken when she was 14, you see a bubbly all-American girl with braces, smiling as her brother touches her affectionately (Hewitt, Fields-Meyer, Frankel, Jewel, Lambert, O'Neill, & Plummer, 1997). Your heart breaks when you see the photo, knowing what will happen when she becomes an adult. People join cults—or sects, the less pejorative term—for many reasons. They are lonely and confused, and the cult provides a loving home. Simple religious answers beckon and offer a reason for living. Isolated from parents and friends, young people come to depend more on the cult for social rewards. The cult leader is charismatic and claims to have supernatural powers. He gains followers' trust and devotion. Purposelessness is relieved; order replaces chaos. The more people participate in the group's activities, the better they feel; the better they feel, the more committed they become; and the more committed they are, the more difficult it is to leave.

Initially, cult leaders employ persuasive appeals. Over time they rely increasingly on coercive techniques. Heaven's Gate leaders told followers that they must learn to deny their desires and defer to the group. At Heaven's Gate, it was considered an infraction if members put themselves first, expressed too much curiosity, showed sexual attraction, trusted their own judgment, or had private thoughts. Everyone woke at the same time to pray, ate the same food, wore short haircuts and nondescript clothing, and sported identical wedding rings on their fingers to symbolize marriage to each other. Individual identity was replaced by group identity. Autonomy gave way, slowly replaced by the peacefulness of groupthink (Goodstein, 1997). Once this happens—and it occurs slowly—cult members no longer have free choice; they are psychologically unable to say no to leaders' demands. Coercion replaces persuasion. Conformity overtakes dissent. Persuasion and coercion coexist, shading into one another. Simple demarcations are hard to make.

Gail Maeder wasn't street smart, her father said. "She just got sucked in and couldn't get out" (Hewitt et al., 1997, p. 47).

Events like Heaven's Gate are deeply troubling. It is comforting to affix blame on charismatic cult leaders like Applewhite. It is easy to say that they brainwashed people into submission. But this ignores the powerful role that coercive social influence and

**Box 1.2** |

persuasive communication play in cults. And it tragically underplays the psychological needs of people like Gail, folks who persuaded themselves that a doomsday cult provided the answer to their problems.

It would be a happy ending if Heaven's Gate were the last cult that exploited individuals' vulnerabilities. However, in recent years, we have witnessed the growth of cross-national terrorist cults composed of men who are convinced that America is the enemy of Islam and are willing to kill innocent people or themselves, if directed by their *maulanas* or masters (Goldberg, 2000). It is tempting to view these individuals as victims of terrorist brainwashing—automatons directed into action by receipt of an e-mail message. Once again, the brainwashing metaphor simplifies and distorts. These individuals have frequently joined Muslim religious schools out of their own volition. Bereft of meaning and purpose in a changing world, grasping for an outlet to express decades-long simmering hate, and seeking a way to exact revenge or seek recognition, they join terrorist cells. There they are groomed, influenced, even coerced by "teachers" and assorted leaders of an international political-religious cult (Zakaria, 2001).

"These are poor and impressionable boys kept entirely ignorant of the world and, for that matter, largely ignorant of all but one interpretation of Islam," notes journalist Jeffrey Goldberg (2000, p. 71). "They are the perfect jihad machines."

Individuals are hardly brainwashed into becoming suicide bombers. They are coerced or more likely persuaded, ultimately convincing themselves that their lives will take on grand meaning if they carry out an action on behalf of their brethren. Terrorist groups employ a host of persuasive techniques, not unlike those used by religious cults. Working in isolation, preying on young men's vulnerabilities, and telling them that those who do not follow the extremist path are infidels, terrorists break down recruits' resistance. They convince individuals to commit suicide bombings in the name of Islam. As one recruit put it, "We were taught that . . . everyone else, including our families, was going to hell . . . And I wanted to be one of the select few who made it into heaven" (Ambah, 2006, C4).

Terrorist cults persuade members to buy into their mission by controlling the flow of information. Only information that confirms terrorists' view of reality is permitted; dissent is stifled. The enemy is demonized and hostile motives are ascribed to those outside the cult. Training videos that perpetrate a sense of victimization and humility reinforce the message. Messages emphasize that Muslims are victims and the West is the oppressor (Sunstein, 2003, pp. 115–117). This, along with a strong sense of male bonding, peer pressure, and duty to do jihad, strengthens commitment to Al Qaeda and other terrorist cells. Self-sacrifice becomes the order of the day, prized and valued. The terrorist group becomes worthy of self-sacrifice. What was once a vague desire to join a terrorist group becomes commitment to the death. This is not brainwashing—but cunning persuasion and coercion. If democratic societies are to guide young people tempted by terrorism to adopt more humane alternatives, they need to understand that violent groups are engaging in clever persuasion. Democratic leaders need to design compelling communications that appeal to strongly-held democratic values.

The final difference lies in the connotation or meaning of the terms. Propaganda has a negative connotation; it is associated with bad things or evil forces. Persuasion, by contrast, is viewed as a more positive force, one that can produce beneficial outcomes. Subjectively, we use the term propaganda to refer to *a persuasive communication with which one disagrees and to which the individual attributes hostile intent.* Liberals claim that the news is unadulterated propaganda for Republicans; conservatives contend that the news is propaganda for the Left. Both use the propaganda term to disparage the news. When you hear people call a persuasive communication propaganda, beware. The speakers are using language to denounce a message with which they disagree.

A related term, frequently used synonymously with persuasion, is manipulation. People frequently use the term to criticize persuaders for employing underhanded techniques. "She's so manipulative," someone charges. "That's another example of media manipulation," a friend observes. Is manipulation the same as persuasion? Is all persuasion manipulative? Although the terms overlap, there are key differences. *Manipulation is a persuasion technique that occurs when a communicator disguises his or her true persuasive goals, hoping to mislead the recipient by delivering an overt message that belies its true intent.* Flattery, sweet talk, and false promises are manipulative techniques.

All persuasion is not manipulative. A persuader whose motives are honest and transparent is not employing manipulation. At the same time, message recipients can naively trust a communicator, failing to notice that the persuader is disguising more sinister intentions. A trusting receiver may fall prey to manipulative con artists, who run the gamut from sweet-talking salesmen promising infirmed elderly individuals "miracle" pain products at exorbitant prices to the celebrated case of financier Bernard Madoff, who bilked thousands of trusting clients of their life-savings in a $50 billion scam.

## UNDERSTANDING PERSUASIVE COMMUNICATION EFFECTS

The discussion thus far has emphasized the differences between persuasion and related terms. However, there are different kinds of persuasive communications, and they have different types of effects. Some messages dramatically influence attitudes; others exert smaller or more subtle impacts. Taking note of this, Miller (1980) proposed that communications exert three different persuasive effects: shaping, reinforcing, and changing responses.

**Shaping.** Today everyone has heard of the Nike "swoosh." You've seen it on hundreds of ads and on the clothing of celebrity athletes. It's a symbol that resonates and has helped make Nike a leader in the athletic shoe business. The now-classic ad campaigns featuring Michael Jordan and Bo Jackson helped mold attitudes toward Nike by linking Nike with movement, speed, and superhuman athletic achievement.

A nastier example is cigarette marketing. Tobacco companies spend millions to shape people's attitudes toward cigarettes, hoping they can entice young people to take a pleasurable, but deadly, puff. Marketers shape attitudes by associating cigarettes with beautiful women and virile men. They appeal to teenage girls searching for a way to rebel against boyfriends or parents by suggesting that smoking can make them appear defiant and strong willed. ("I always take the driver's seat. That way I'm never taken for a ride," says one Virginia Slims ad.)

On a more positive level, socialization counts as an example of attitude shaping or formation. Influential social agents model a variety of pro-social values and attitudes, such as self-discipline, altruism, and religion.

**Reinforcing.** Contrary to popular opinion, many persuasive communications are not designed to convert people, but rather to reinforce a position they already hold. As discussed in Chapter 2, people have strong attitudes toward a variety of topics, and these attitudes are hard to change. Thus, persuaders try to join 'em, not beat 'em.

In political campaigns, candidates try to bolster party supporters' commitment to their cause. Democratic standard-bearers have made late-campaign appeals to African-American voters, the overwhelming majority of whom are registered Democrats. Republican candidates have won elections by appealing to religious conservatives. Increasingly, political consultants argue that elections are not about winning over undecided voters, but rather about concentrating on the base.

In a similar fashion, health education experts try to reinforce individuals' decisions to quit smoking or to abstain from drinking in excess. Persuaders recognize that people can easily relapse under stress, and they design messages to help individuals maintain their commitment to give up unhealthy substances.

**Changing.** This is perhaps the most important persuasive impact and the one that comes most frequently to mind when we think of persuasion. Communications can and do change attitudes. Just think how far this country has come in the last 50 years on the subject of race. In the 1950s and 1960s, Blacks were lynched for being in the wrong place at the wrong time, many southerners openly opposed school desegregation, and northern Whites steered clear of socializing with Black friends or colleagues. This changed as civil rights campaigns, heart-rending media stories, and increased dialogue between Blacks and Whites led Whites to rethink their prejudiced attitudes toward African-Americans (Thernstrom & Thernstrom, 1997). In 1948, 4 percent of Americans favored marriage between Blacks and Whites. Nearly a half century later, the percentage in agreement had increased 18-fold, to 72 percent (Grimes, 2005).

Other political attitudes have changed as well. Two decades ago, the idea that a woman could be president of the United States was a feminist pipe dream. But times have changed, as indicated by Hillary Clinton's success in the 2008 Democratic presidential primaries and Governor Sarah Palin's Republican vice-presidential candidacy. Americans have changed their attitudes on a host of other topics as well, ranging from the environment to fatty fast food to exercise. Persuasive communications have had strong, desirable effects on these issues. They have influenced attitudes and behavior.

Important as these effects are, they rarely occur overnight. Persuasion is a process; change can be slow and painstaking. A bigot does not become more open-minded after one persuasive encounter. It takes many years of exposure to people of color, rethinking of prejudices, and self-insight. Persuasion is a process. It happens over time, step by step, with each step counting as an instance of self-persuasion.

## HISTORICAL REVIEW OF PERSUASION SCHOLARSHIP

It is now time to put persuasion scholarship in perspective. It's not a new field—not by a long shot. The area has a long, distinguished history, dating back to ancient Greece. This section reviews the history of persuasion scholarship, offering an overview of major trends and the distinctive features of contemporary research on persuasion.

You may wonder why I review ancient history. There are many reasons, but here are two. Historical overviews help us appreciate origins of ideas. They remind us that we are not the first to ponder persuasion or the first to wrestle with persuasion dilemmas. Second, an historical approach helps us see continuities from past to present to future. It helps us take note of what is unique about our era and how today's scholarship builds on the shoulders of giants.

### Ancient Greece: "It's All Sophos to Me"

"If any one group of people could be said to have invented rhetoric," James L. Golden and colleagues note, "it would be the ancient Greeks" (Golden, Berquist, & Coleman, 2000, p. 1). The Greeks loved public speech. Trophies were awarded for skill in oratory. Citizens frequently acted as prosecutor and defense attorney in lawsuits that were daily occurrences in the Athenian city-state (Golden et al., 2000). Before long, citizens expressed interest in obtaining training in rhetoric (the art of public persuasion).

To meet the demand, a group of teachers decided to offer courses in rhetoric, as well as in other academic areas. The teachers were called *Sophists*, after the Greek word *sophos* for knowledge. The Sophists traveled from city to city, pedaling their intellectual wares for a fee—the Sophists were dedicated to their craft but needed to make a living. Two of the traveling teachers—Gorgias and Isocrates—taught classes on oratory, placing considerable emphasis on style.

The Sophists attracted a following, but not everyone who followed them liked what they saw. *Plato*, the great Greek philosopher, denounced their work in his dialogues. To Plato, truth was a supreme value. Yet the Sophists sacrificed truth at the altar of persuasion, in Plato's view. Thus, he lamented that "he who would be an orator has nothing to do with true justice, but only that which is likely to be approved by the many who sit in judgment" (Golden et al., 2000, p. 19). The Sophists, he charged, were not interested in discovering truth or advancing rational, "laborious, painstaking" arguments, but rather in "the quick, neat, and stylish argument that wins immediate approval—even if this argument has some hidden flaw" (Chappell, 1998, p. 516). To Plato, rhetoric was like cosmetics or flattery: not philosophy and therefore not deserving of respect.

The Sophists, for their part, saw persuasion differently. They surely believed that they were rocking the foundations of the educational establishment by giving people practical knowledge rather than "highfalutin" truth. They also were democrats, willing to teach any citizen who could afford their tuition.

Why do we care about the differences of opinion between Plato and the Sophists some 2,500 years later? We care because the same issues bedevil us today. Plato is the friend of all those who hate advertisements because they "lie" or stretch the truth. He is on the side of everyone who turns off the television during elections to stop the flow of "political speak," or candidates making any argument they can to win election. The Sophists address those practical persuaders—advertisers, politicians, salespeople—who have to make a living, need practical knowledge to promote their products, and are suspicious of "shadowy" abstract concepts like truth (Kennedy, 1963). The Sophists and Plato offer divergent, dueling perspectives on persuasive communication. Indeed, one of the themes of this book is that there are *dual approaches* to thinking about persuasion: one that emphasizes platonic thinking and cogent arguments and the other focusing on style, oratory, and simpler persuasive appeals that date back to some of the Sophist writers.

## The First Scientist of Persuasion

Plato's greatest contribution to persuasion—or rhetoric, as it was then called—may not have been the works he created, but rather his intellectual offspring. His best student—a Renaissance person before there was a Renaissance, a theorist before "theories" gained adherents—was *Aristotle*. Aristotle lived in the fourth century BC and wrote 170 works, including books on rhetoric. His treatise, "Rhetoric," is regarded as "the most significant work on persuasion ever written" (Golden et al., 2000, p. 2).

Aristotle's great insight was that both Plato and the Sophists had a point. Plato was right about truth being important, and the Sophists were correct that persuasive communication is a very useful tool. Aristotle, to some degree, took the best from both schools of thought, arguing that rhetoric is not designed to persuade people but to discover scientific principles of persuasion. Aristotle's great contribution was to recognize that rhetoric could be viewed in scientific terms—as a phenomenon that could be described with precise concepts and by invoking probabilities (Golden et al., 2000; McCroskey, 1997). Drawing on his training in biology, Aristotle developed the first scientific approach to persuasion.

Rather than dismissing persuasion, as did Plato, the more practical Aristotle embraced it. "Aristotle said the goal of rhetoric wasn't so much finding the truth of a matter as convincing an audience to make the best decision about that matter," note Martha D. Cooper and William L. Nothstine (1998, p. 25). Aristotle proceeded to articulate a host of specific concepts on the nature of argumentation and the role of style in persuasion. He proposed methods by which persuasion occurred, described contexts in which it operated, and made ethics a centerpiece of his approach. During an era in which Plato was railing against the Sophists' pseudo-oratory, teachers were running around Greece offering short courses on rhetoric, and great orators made fortunes by serving as ghostwriters for the wealthy, Aristotle toiled tirelessly on the scientific front, developing the first scientific perspective on persuasion.

Aristotle proposed that persuasion had three main ingredients: *ethos* (the nature of the communicator), *pathos* (emotional state of the audience), and *logos* (message arguments). Aristotle was also an early student of psychology, recognizing that speakers had to adapt to their audiences by considering in their speeches those factors that were most persuasive to an audience member.

Aristotle's Greece was a mecca for the study and practice of persuasion. Yet it was not always pretty or just. Women were assumed to be innately unfit for engaging in persuasive public speaking; they were denied citizenship and excluded from the teaching professions (Waggenspack, 2000). When Greek civilization gave way to Rome, the messengers were lost, but not the message. The practical Romans preserved much of Athenian civilization, adapting classic rhetorical works to Roman culture.

## A Breezy Tour of Rome and the Centuries That Followed

Roman rhetorical theorists Cicero and Quintilian wrote treatises on the art of oratory. Cicero refined Greek theories of rhetoric, emphasizing the power of emotional appeals. Quintilian developed recommendations for the ideal orator. Their work reminds us that concerns with public persuasion and inclusion of emotional arguments date back to early Rome and probably earlier if you consider the Sophists.

With the decline of Roman civilization, rhetoric became a less important feature of European society. Earth-shattering events occurred over the ensuing centuries: growth of Christianity, Italian Renaissance, Black Death, European wars. Nonetheless, Aristotle's and Cicero's works survived and influenced the thinking of rhetorical theorists of their times. Some of these writers' works made their way west, to the intellectual vineyards of the New World.

## Rhetorical Developments in the United States

Like Athens, colonial and eighteenth-century America was a persuader's paradise, with merchants, lawyers, politicians, and newspaper editors crafting arguments to influence people and mold public opinion. Great rhetorical works emerged in the eighteenth and nineteenth centuries, including the Declaration of Independence and Lincoln's Gettysburg Address. Yet, like ancient Greece, the public paradise was closed to slaves and women. But, unlike Greece, legal limits did not stifle protest voices. Frederick Douglass and, later, W. E. B. DuBois became eloquent spokesmen for disenfranchised African-Americans. Elizabeth Cady Stanton and Susan B. Anthony used rhetorical strategies derived from Cicero in their efforts to gain equality for women (Waggenspack, 2000).

Over the course of the twentieth century, numerous rhetoricians have written insightful books. Richard Weaver (1953) argued that all language contains values. Kenneth Burke (1950), calling on philosophy and psychoanalysis, showed how good and evil communicators persuade people by identifying their views with the audience. Marshall McLuhan (1967), using the catchy phrase "the medium is the message," startled and then captivated people by alerting them to the ways in which the medium—television, radio, print—was more important than the content of a communicator's speech. Subsequently, radical scholars argued that the field of rhetoric could itself be studied and critiqued. Michel Foucault controversially questioned the notion that there is such a thing as true knowledge. Instead, he claimed, knowledge and truth are interwoven with power; those who rule a society define what is true and what counts as knowledge (Golden et al., 2000). Feminist critics like Karlyn Kohrs Campbell (1989) pointed out that rhetorical history has been dominated by men and that women were barred from speaking in many supposedly great eras of rhetorical eloquence.

Rhetorical theorists continue to enlighten us with their work. However, their mission has been supplemented and to some degree replaced by legions of social scientists. The social science approach to persuasion now dominates academia. The history of this perspective is summarized next.

## Origins of the Social Scientific Approach

Social scientific studies of persuasion began in the 1930s with research on attitudes (Allport, 1935). Scholarship got a boost in World War II when the U.S. War Department commissioned a group of researchers to explore the effects of a series of documentary films. The movies were designed to educate Allied soldiers on the Nazi threat and to boost morale. The War Department asked Frank Capra, who had previously directed such classics as *Mr. Smith Goes to Washington*, to direct the films. They were called simply *Why We Fight*.

Asked to evaluate the effects of the wartime documentaries, the social scientists got the added benefit of working, albeit indirectly, with Capra. It must have been a heady experience, assessing the effects of a Hollywood director's films on beliefs and attitudes. The studies offered some of the first hard evidence that communications influenced attitudes, albeit complexly (Hovland, Lumsdaine, & Sheffield, 1949). The experiments showed that persuasion research could be harnessed by government for its own ends—in this case, beneficial ones, but certainly not value-neutral objectives.

Several of the researchers working on the *Why We Fight* research went on to do important research in the fields of psychology and communication. One of them, Carl Hovland, seized the moment, brilliantly combining experimental research methodology with the ideas of an old persuasion sage, the first scientist of persuasion, the A-man: Aristotle. Working in a university setting, Hovland painstakingly conducted a series of experiments on persuasive communication effects. He and his colleagues took concepts invented by Aristotle—ethos, pathos, and logos—and systematically examined their effects, using newly refined techniques of scientific experimentation (Hovland, Janis, & Kelley, 1953). What the researchers discovered—for example, that credible sources influenced attitudes—was less important than how they went about their investigations. Hovland and colleagues devised hypotheses, developed elaborate procedures to test predictions, employed statistical procedures to determine whether predictions held true, and reported findings in scientific journals that could be scrutinized by critical observers.

Hovland died young, but his scientific approach to persuasion survived and proved to be an enduring legacy. A host of other social scientists, armed with theories, predictions, and questionnaires, began to follow suit. These included psychologists William J. McGuire and Milton Rokeach, and communication scholar Gerald R. Miller. The list of persuasion pioneers also includes Gordon Allport, the luminary psychologist who did so much to define and elaborate on the concept of attitude.

From an historical perspective, the distinctive element of the persuasion approach that began in the mid-twentieth century and continues today is its empirical foundation. Knowledge is gleaned from observation and evidence rather than armchair philosophizing. Researchers devise scientific theories, tease out hypotheses, and dream up ways of testing them in real-world settings. No one—not the Greeks, Romans, or twentieth-century Western rhetorical theorists—had taken this approach. Capitalizing on the development of a scientific approach to behavior, new techniques for measuring attitudes, advances in statistics, and American pragmatism, early researchers were able to forge ahead, asking new questions and finding answers.

Scholarly activity continued apace from the 1960s onward, producing a wealth of persuasion concepts far surpassing those put forth by Aristotle and classical rhetoricians. These terms include attitude, belief, cognitive processing, cognitive dissonance, social judgments, and interpersonal compliance. We also have a body of knowledge—thousands of studies, books, and review pieces on persuasion. More articles and books on persuasion have been published over the past 50 years than in the previous 2,500 years.

What once was a small field that broke off from philosophy has blossomed into a multidisciplinary field of study. Different scholars carve out different parts of the pie. *Social psychologists* focus on the individual, exploring people's attitudes and susceptibility to persuasion. *Communication scholars* cast a broader net, looking at persuasion in two-person units, called dyads, and examining influences of media on health and politics. *Marketing scholars* examine consumer attitudes and influences of advertising on buying behavior. If you look up "persuasion" under PsycINFO or in Communication Abstracts, you will find thousands of studies, journal articles, and books.

What's more, research plays a critical role in everyday persuasion activities. Advertising agencies spend millions on research. When Nike plans campaigns geared to young people (with ads resembling music videos), company executives plug in facts gleaned from marketing research. Antismoking campaigns hire academic researchers to probe teenagers' attitudes toward smoking. Campaigners want to understand why kids smoke and which significant others are most apt to endorse smoking in order to design messages that change teens' attitudes. In the political sphere, the White House launched a worldwide marketing campaign after September 11 in an effort to change Muslims' negative perceptions of the United States.

Plato, the purist, would be horrified by these developments. Aristotle, the practical theorist, might worry about ethics, but would be generally pleased. Both would be amazed by the sheer volume of persuasion research and its numerous applications to everyday life. Who knows? Maybe they'll be talking about our age 500 years from now! So, sit back and enjoy. You're about to embark on an exciting intellectual journey.

# THE CONTEMPORARY STUDY OF PERSUASION

Contemporary scholars approach persuasion from a social science point of view. This may seem strange. After all, you may think of persuasion as an art. When someone mentions the word "persuasion," you may think of such things as "the gift of gab," "manipulation," or "subliminal seduction." You may feel that by approaching persuasion from the vantage point of contemporary social science, we are reducing the area to something antiseptic. However, this is far from the truth. Social scientists are curious about the same phenomena that everybody else is: for example, what makes a person persuasive, what types of persuasive messages are most effective, and why people go along with the recommendations put forth by powerful persuaders. The difference between the scientist's approach and that of the layperson is that the scientist formulates theories about attitudes and persuasion, derives hypotheses from these theories, and puts the hypotheses to empirical test. By empirical test, I mean that hypotheses are evaluated on the basis of evidence and data collected from the real world.

Theory plays a major role in the social scientific enterprise. A theory is a large, umbrella conceptualization of a phenomenon that contains hypotheses, proposes linkages between variables, explains events, and offers predictions. It may seem strange to study something as dynamic as persuasion by focusing on abstract theories. But theories contain ideas that yield insights about communication effects. These ideas provide the impetus for change. They are the pen that is mightier than the sword.

In fact, we all have theories about human nature and about persuasion (Roskos-Ewoldsen, 1997a; Stiff, 1994). We may believe that people are basically good, parents have a major impact on kids' personalities, or men are more competitive than women. We also have theories about persuasion. Consider these propositions:

- *Advertising exploits people.*

- *You can't persuade people by scaring them.*

- *The key to being persuasive is physical appeal.*

At some level these are theoretical statements—propositions that contain interesting, testable ideas about persuasive communication. But there are problems with the statements from a scientific perspective. They are not bona fide theories of persuasion.

The first statement is problematic because it uses a value-laden term, *exploit*. Exploitation evokes negative images. Perhaps advertising doesn't exploit so much as guide consumers toward outcomes they sincerely want. The first rule of good theorizing is to state propositions in value-free language.

The second statement—you can't persuade people by merely scaring them—sounds reasonable until you start thinking about it from another point of view. One could argue that giving people a jolt of fear is just what is needed to get them to rethink dangerous behaviors like drug abuse or binge drinking. You could suggest that appeals to fear motivate people to take steps to protect themselves from dangerous outcomes.

The third statement—that physical appeal is the key to persuasion—can also be viewed with a critical eye. Perhaps attractive speakers turn audiences off because people resent their good looks or assume they made it because of their bodies, not their brains. I am sure you can think of communicators who are trustworthy and credible, but aren't so physically attractive.

Yet, at first blush, the three statements made sense. They could even be called intuitive "theories" of persuasion. But intuitive theories—our homegrown notions of what makes persuasion tick—are problematic. They lack objectivity. They are inextricably linked with our own biases of human nature (Stiff, 1994). What's more, they can't be scientifically tested or disconfirmed. By contrast, scientific theories are stated with sufficient precision that they can be empirically tested (through real-world research). They also contain formal explanations, hypotheses, and corollaries. Researchers take formal theories, derive hypotheses, and test them in real-world experiments or surveys. If the hypotheses are supported over and over again, to a point of absolute confidence, we no longer call them theories, but rather laws of human behavior. We have preciously few of these in social science. (Darwinian evolution counts as a theory whose hypotheses have been proven to the point that we can call it a law.) At the same time, there are many useful social science theories that can forecast behavior, shed light on people's actions, and suggest strategies for social change.

The beauty of research is that it provides us with a yardstick for evaluating the truth value of ideas that at first blush seem intuitively correct. It lets us know whether our gut feelings about persuasion—for example, regarding fear or good looks—amount to a hill of beans in the real world. Moreover, research provides a mechanism for determining which notions of persuasion hold water, which ones leak water (are no good), and, in general, which ideas about persuasive communication are most accurate, compelling, and predictive of human action in everyday life.

Researchers study persuasion in primarily two ways. They conduct *experiments*, or controlled studies that take place in artificial settings. Experiments provide convincing evidence that one variable causes changes in another. Because experiments typically are conducted in university settings and primarily involve college students, they don't tell us about persuasion that occurs in everyday life among diverse population groups. For this reason, researchers conduct *surveys*. Surveys are questionnaire studies that examine the relationship between one factor (for example, exposure to a media antismoking campaign) and another (e.g., reduced smoking). Surveys do not provide unequivocal evidence of causation.

In the preceding example, it is possible that people may reduce smoking shortly after a media campaign, but the effects may have nothing to do with the campaign. Smokers may have decided to quit because friends bugged them or they wanted to save money on cigarette costs.

Most studies of persuasive communication effects are experiments. Studies of attitudes and applications of persuasion are more likely to be surveys. Both experiments and surveys are useful, although they make different contributions (Hovland, 1959).

Research, the focus of this book, is important because it clarifies concepts, builds knowledge, and helps solve practical problems. One must not lose sight of the big picture: the role persuasion plays in society and the fundamental ethics of persuasive communication. The final section of the chapter, building on the preceding discussion, examines these broader concerns. The next portion provides an overall perspective on persuasion's strengths and its contributions to contemporary life. The final portion examines ethics.

## SEEING THE BIG PICTURE

Persuasion is so pervasive that we often don't ask the question: What sort of world would it be if there were no persuasive communications? It would be a quieter world, that's for sure—one with less buzz, especially around dinnertime when telemarketers phone! But, without persuasion, people would have to resort to different means to get their way. Many would resort to verbal abuse, threats, and coercion to accomplish personal and political goals. Argument would be devalued or nonexistent. Force—either physical or psychological—would carry the day.

Persuasion, by contrast, is a profoundly civilizing influence. It prizes oratory and argument. It says that disagreements between people can be resolved through logic, empathy-based appeals, and the rough-and-tumble banter of group discussion. Persuasion provides us with a constructive mechanism for advancing our claims and trying to change institutions. It offers a way for disgruntled and disenfranchised people to influence society. Persuasion provides a mechanism for everybody—from kids promoting Web sites to Wall Street brokers selling stocks—to advance in life and achieve their goals.

Persuasion is not always pretty. It can be mean, vociferous, and ugly. Persuasion, as Winston Churchill might say, is the worst way to exert influence—except for all the others. Were there no persuasion, George W. Bush and Al Gore would not have settled their dispute about the 2000 election vote in the courtroom, but on the battlefield. Conversely, if persuasion were the accepted way to resolve problems in Iraq and among terrorist militia operating in the Middle East, peace, not deadly violence, would reign supreme.

Persuasion is not analogous to truth. As Aristotle recognized, persuasive communications are designed to influence, rather than uncover, universal truths (Cooper & Nothstine, 1998). In fact, persuaders sometimes hide truth, mislead, or lie outright in the service of their aims or clients. The field of ethics is concerned with determining when it is morally appropriate to deviate from truth and when such deviations are ethically indefensible. Persuasion researchers do not pretend to know the answers to these questions. Instead, like everyone else, we do the best we can, seeking guidance from philosophers, wise people, and theologians. Hopefully, reading this book will give you insight into your own values, and will help you develop rules of thumb for what constitute ethical and unethical social influence attempts.

Persuasion assumes without question that people have free choice—that they can do other than what the persuader suggests. This has an important consequence. It means that people are responsible for the decisions they make in response to persuasive messages. Naturally, people can't foresee every possible consequence of choices that they make. They cannot be held accountable for outcomes that could not reasonably have been foreseen.

*Foundations*  But one of the essential aspects of life is choice—necessarily based on incomplete, and sometimes inaccurate, information. Provided that individuals have freedom of choice, a foundation of persuasion, they are responsible for the decisions they make.

Persuaders also make choices. They must decide how best to appeal to audiences. They necessarily must choose between ethical and unethical modes of persuasion. Persuaders who advance their claims in ethical ways deserve our respect. Those who employ unethical persuasion ploys should be held accountable for their choices. This raises an important question: Just what do we mean by ethical and unethical persuasion? The final portion of the chapter addresses this issue.

## PERSUASION AND ETHICS

Is persuasion ethical? This simple question has engaged scholars and practitioners alike. Aristotle and Plato discussed it. Machiavelli touched on it. So have contemporary communication scholars and social psychologists. And you can bet that practitioners— Tommy Hilfiger, Phil Knight, Donna Karan, even Tiger Woods—have given it a passing thought, no doubt on the way to the bank.

Yet persuasion ethics demand consideration. As human beings, we want to be treated with respect, and we value communications that treat others as an ends, not a means, to use Immanuel Kant's famous phrase. At the same time, we are practical creatures, who want to achieve our goals, whether they be financial, social, emotional, or spiritual. The attainment of goals—money, prestige, love, or religious fulfillment—requires that we influence others in some fashion somewhere along the way. Is the need to influence *incompatible* with the ethical treatment of human beings?

Some scholars would say it invariably is. Plato, who regarded truth as "the only reality in life," was offended by persuasive communication (Golden et al., 2000, p. 17). As noted earlier, he regarded rhetoric as a form of flattery that appealed to people's worst instincts. Although Plato did believe in an ideal rhetoric admirably composed of truth and morality, he did not think that ordinary persuasion measured up to this standard.

The German philosopher Immanuel Kant would view persuasion as immoral for a different reason: in his view, it uses people, treating them as means to the persuader's end, not as valued ends in themselves (Borchert & Stewart, 1986). This violates Kant's ethical principles. In a similar fashion, Thomas Nilsen (1974) has argued that persuasion is immoral because a communicator is trying to induce someone to do something that is in the communicator's best interest, but not necessarily in the best interest of the individual receiving the message.

As thoughtful as these perspectives are, they set up a rather high bar for human communication to reach. What's more, these authors tend to lump all persuasive communication together. Some communications are indeed false, designed to manipulate people by appealing to base emotions, or are in the interest of the sender and not the receiver. But others are not. Some messages make very intelligent appeals, based on logic and evidence. In addition, not all persuaders treat people as a means. Therapists and health professionals ordinarily accord clients a great deal of respect. The best counselors treat each person as unique, a mysterious treasure to be deciphered and understood. Many people who do volunteer work—such as those who counsel teens in trouble or AIDS victims—do not receive great financial benefit from their work. Their communications can be very much in the best interest of those receiving the message.

On the other extreme are philosophers who argue that persuasion is fundamentally moral. Noting that people are free to accept or reject a communicator's message, conservative thinkers tend to embrace persuasion. Believing that people are sufficiently rational to distinguish between truth and falsehood, libertarian scholars argue that society is best served by diverse persuasive communications that run the gamut from entirely truthful to totally fallacious (Siebert, Peterson, & Schramm, 1956). Persuasion, they say, is better than coercion, and people are in any event free to accept or reject the communicator's message.

There is some wisdom in this perspective. However, to say that persuasion is inherently moral is an extreme, absolute statement. To assume that people are capable of maturely rejecting manipulative communicators' messages naively neglects cases in which trusted but evil people exploit others' vulnerability. What of men who trick or seduce women and then take advantage of their dependence to demand additional sexual and emotional favors? Perhaps we would argue that the women chose to get involved with the men—they're persuaded, not coerced—but it would be heartless to suggest that such persuasion is moral.

Consider also those nasty car salespeople who stretch the truth or lie outright to make a sale (Robin Williams skillfully played one of these some years back in the movie *Cadillac Man*). Throw in the tobacco companies, which waged campaigns to hook people into smoking even though they knew that smoking was addictive. Don't forget history's legions of con men—the snake oil salesmen of the nineteenth century who promised that new nutritional cures would work magic on those who purchased them, and their modern counterparts, the hosts of infomercials who tell you that vitamin supplements will boost sales and sex. It defies credulity to argue that persuasion is inherently ethical.

This brings up a third viewpoint, which comes closest to truth. Persuasion can be used for good or bad purposes, with ethical and unethical intentions. Aristotle endorsed this view. He argued that persuasion could be used by anyone: "by a good person or a bad person, by a person seeking worthy ends or unworthy ends" (McCroskey, 1997, p. 9). Thus, charisma can be employed by a Hitler or a Martin Luther King, by a bin Laden or a Ghandi. Step-by-step persuasion techniques that begin with a small request and hook the person into larger and larger commitments have been used by North Korean captors of American soldiers during the Korean War and by religious cult leaders—but also by Alcoholics Anonymous.

What determines whether a particular persuasive act is ethical or unethical? How do we decide if a communicator has behaved in a moral or immoral fashion? In order to answer these questions, we must turn to moral philosophy. Philosophers have offered many perspectives on these issues, beginning with Plato and continuing to the present day.

One prominent view emphasizes the consequences of an action. Called *utilitarianism*, it suggests that actions should be judged based on whether they produce more good than evil. If a message leads to positive ends, helping more people than it hurts, it's good; if it produces primarily negative consequences, it's bad. For example, an antismoking campaign is good if it convinces many young people to quit. It is bad if it boomerangs, leading more people to take up the habit.

*Deontological* philosophers, who emphasize duty and obligation, object to this view. They argue that a successful antismoking campaign sponsored by the tobacco industry is not as morally good as an equally successful program produced by activists committed to helping young people preserve their health (Frankena, 1963). These philosophers frequently emphasize intentions, or the motives of the persuader. James C. McCroskey is a proponent of intention-based morality. He argues, "If the communicator seeks to improve the well-being of his audience through his act of communication, he is committing a moral act. If he seeks to produce harm for his audience, the communicator is guilty of an immoral act" (1972, p. 270). Yet even those who agree that morality should be based on intentions acknowledge that it is difficult to arrive at objective criteria for judging another's intention.

Still other approaches to ethics have been proposed. Feminist theorists advocate an ethics of caring, empathy, and mutual respect (Jaggar, 2000). Persuasion is viewed as something one does with another rather than to another (Reardon, 1991). Another useful approach is existentialism, which emphasizes freedom and responsibility. People are free to choose what they want in life, but are responsible for their choices. "There are no excuses, for there is no one to blame for our actions but ourselves," existentialists argue (Fox & DeMarco, 1990, p. 159).

One choice people have is not to be ethical at all, to pursue self-interest at any cost. Philosophers cannot persuade people to make ethical judgments; they cannot convince unsavory characters to behave in humane ways or to use morally acceptable strategies to influence others. One can give many arguments on behalf of ethical persuasion, from the Golden Rule to moral duty to "you'll be more effective if you're honest," which originated with Aristotle. The best argument is that ethical persuasion is one of the requirements of being a decent and beneficent human being. Ethical persuaders advance arguments forcefully, but not aggressively. They affirm the dignity of each person, treat audience members as free and autonomous agents, present facts and opinions fairly, and provide different perspectives on an issue to enable people to make the most thoughtful decision possible (e.g., Wallace, 1967). Perhaps as you read this book and think about persuasion ethics, you will discover more reasons to practice ethical persuasive communication.

## THE PRESENT APPROACH

There are thousands of books on persuasion, hundreds of thousands of articles, probably more. "How to persuade" books, audios, and Web sites proliferate. No surprise here: a search for the keys to persuasion is surely among the most basic of human desires.

Who among us has not entertained the thought that somewhere out there lies the secret to persuasion? Who has not dreamed that he or she might, with luck or perseverance, find the simple trick or magic elixir that contains the formula for social influence?

We may yet find the secret to persuasion or, failing that, we may someday understand perfectly why people need to believe that simple solutions exist. But you won't find a simple formula here. Instead, you will discover intriguing theories, bundles of evidence, creative methodologies, and rich applications of research to everyday life. This book, focusing on academic scholarship on persuasion, attempts to increase your knowledge of attitudes and persuasion. Specifically, I hope that the book will provide you with:

- greater understanding of persuasion theory and research;
- deeper appreciation of just how communications change attitudes;
- increased insight into your own persuasion styles, strengths, and biases;
- greater tolerance of others' attitudes;
- more skill in resisting unwanted influence attempts;
- enhanced understanding of persuasion as it occurs in twenty-first-century society; and
- new insights on how to be a more effective and ethical persuader.

The book is divided into three sections. The first part examines the foundations of persuasion: basic terminology, attitude definitions and structure, attitude functions, consistency, and measurement (Chapters 1, 2, 3, and 4). The second part focuses on persuasion theory and communication effects, beginning with an exploration of contemporary cognitive approaches in Chapter 5. Chapter 6 examines the communicator in persuasion, discussing such factors as credibility and attractiveness. Chapter 7 focuses on the message, particularly emotional appeals and language. Chapter 8 explores personality and whether certain people are more susceptible to persuasion than others. Chapter 9 discusses the granddaddy of attitude and persuasion approaches: cognitive dissonance theory. Chapter 10 explores interpersonal persuasion and compliance. The third section, focusing on persuasion in American society, examines advertising (Chapter 11) and communication campaigns (Chapter 12). Throughout, I explore what it means to persuade and be persuaded, the contexts in which this occurs, and the social implications of persuasive communications.

Certain themes predominate and run through the book: the central role persuasion plays in contemporary life (from mass marketing to interpersonal politicking); the need to dissect persuasive communication effects carefully; the critical role that people's thinking and cognitive processing play in persuasion effects; the ability of persuasion to manipulate but also soothe and comfort people; the fact that we persuade ourselves and are responsible for outcomes that occur; and the incredible complexity of human behavior, a fact that makes the study of persuasion fascinating and never ending.

## CONCLUSIONS

Persuasion is a ubiquitous part of contemporary life. If you search the term on the Web, you find hundreds of topics, ranging from "brainwashing controversies" to "marketing" to "how to get people to like you." The Internet is a persuader's paradise, with Web sites promoting millions of products and services. However, persuasion has more personal components. We can all think of times when we yielded to other people's influence attempts, tried to persuade friends to go along with us, or scratched our heads to figure out ways we could have done a better job of getting a colleague to buy our plan.

Persuasion is an ancient art. It dates back to the Bible and ancient Greece. Yet there are important aspects of contemporary persuasion that are unique to this era. They include the volume, speed, subtlety, and complexity of modern messages.

Persuasion is defined as a symbolic process in which communicators try to convince other people to change their attitudes or behavior regarding an issue through the transmission of a message, in an atmosphere of free choice. A key aspect of persuasion is self-persuasion. Communicators do not change people's minds; people decide to alter their own attitudes or to resist persuasion. There is something liberating about self-persuasion. It says that we are free to change our lives in any way that we wish. We have the power to become what we want to become—to stop smoking, lose weight, modify dysfunctional behavior patterns, change career paths, or discover how to become a dynamic public speaker. Obviously, we can't do everything: there are limits set by both our cognitive skills and society. But in saying that people ultimately persuade themselves, I suggest that we are partly responsible if we let ourselves get conned by dishonest persuaders. I argue that people are capable of throwing off the shackles of dangerous messages and finding positive ways to live their lives.

Of course, this is not always easy. The tools of self-persuasion can be harnessed by both beneficent and malevolent communicators. Persuaders can be honest and truthful, appealing to the best angels in the message recipient. Or they can be dishonest and manipulative, trying to pull the wool over people's eyes. Trying to see the best in a persuader or hoping against hope that a persuader's ministrations will bring forth money, love, or happiness, people can coax themselves into accepting messages advanced by unsavory communicators.

Social influence is a powerful phenomenon. It can be viewed as a continuum, with coercion lying on one end and persuasion at the other. There are not always black-and-white differences between persuasion and coercion. They can overlap, as in situations involving authority, religious cults, and terrorism. Still, with clear definitions we can disentangle coercion and persuasion. Coercion occurs when the influence agent delivers a threat of some consequence, attempts to induce the individual to act contrary to his or her preferences, and deprives the individual of some measure of freedom or autonomy. Persuasion occurs in an atmosphere of free choice, where the individual is autonomous, capable of saying no, and able to change his or her mind about the issue.

Persuasion is a strong exemplar of social influence, but not the only force. Applied ethically and conscientiously, it can solve interpersonal and political dilemmas, but it can't solve every human problem. (If this only were the case!) Unfortunately, when human understanding and tolerance reach limits, coercive influence is employed. Coercion can be an instrument of good, as when communities ban smoking or even trans fats in restaurant cooking, but also a force of evil in the case of unnecessary wars or ethnic cleansing.

Ethical precepts determine the morality of coercive influence, in the same way as they determine the moral rightness of persuasion.

Persuasive communications have been studied for thousands of years, beginning with the early Greeks. Plato criticized the Sophists' rhetoric, and Aristotle developed the first scientific approach to persuasion. Since then, numerous rhetorical books have been written, spanning oratory, language, identification, and mass media. Contemporary approaches emphasize the usefulness of social science theories and methods.

A persistent theme in persuasion scholarship—from Plato to the present era—is ethics. The rub is that persuasive communication can be used with great effectiveness by both moral and immoral persuaders. This does not mean that persuasion is amoral, as is sometimes believed. There is ethical and unethical persuasion.

Persuasive communications must be judged by the consequences of the act, the intentions of the persuader, the morality of the message, and the context in which persuasion occurs. There are many reasons to practice ethical persuasion, not the least of which is that it is one of the requirements of being a good, beneficent human being. In this book I will explore the many facets of persuasion, introducing you to the techniques persuaders employ, the impact of communications on individuals and society, and the psychology behind their effects. By gaining a greater appreciation for persuasion processes and effects, as well as for its ethical foundations, we can hopefully wield this powerful instrument in more influential and beneficent ways.

# Chapter 2

# Attitudes: Definition and Structure

Cʟɪᴄᴋ onto a Web site for gay rights, religion, poverty, gun control, or capital punishment. Or if you prefer cultural venues, check out sites for hip hop music, body piercing, tattoos, sports, or cars. If you prefer the older, traditional media, you can peruse books or letters to the editor, or you can tune in to a radio talk show. You will find them there.

What you will locate are attitudes—strong, deeply felt attitudes, as well as ambivalent, complex ones. You see, even today, when we communicate through Skype, cell phones, and laptops, attitudes are ubiquitous. To illustrate the depth and strength of attitudes, I examined a topic that arouses strong feelings among some people: animal rights. By reading these viewpoints (pro and con) on the merits of conducting research on animals, you can appreciate the power of attitudes.

> Do you approve of the scientific experiments using animals that have in fact resulted in the protection of millions of human beings, probably including yourself and your children, from diphtheria, hepatitis, measles, rabies, rubella, and tetanus? Do you believe that the scientific studies now in progress to combat AIDS, lyme disease, Alzheimer's disease, heart disease, diabetes, and cancer—almost all of those studies relying essentially on the use of animals—are morally justifiable? Probably, you do. I surely do, with all my heart.
>
> (Cohen & Regan, 2001, p. 25)

> We humans kill billions of animals every year, just in the United States. Frequently what we do causes them intense physical pain; often they are made to live in deplorable conditions; in many, possibly the majority of cases, they go to their deaths without having had the opportunity to satisfy many of their most basic desires . . . (Imagine) a mugger has pushed you to the ground and stolen your money; you are left with a number of cuts and bruises—minor to be sure, but still painful. Next, let us try to imagine the pain felt by the dogs who were vivisected by the scientists . . . the dogs who, without the benefit of anesthetic, had their four paws nailed to boards before being slit open. Are we to say that your minor pain is qualitatively

worse than the much greater pain experienced by the dogs, because your pain is the pain of a human being, the dogs' pain not?

(Cohen & Regan, 2001, pp. 135, 291)

Animal research has contributed to 70% of the Nobel prizes for physiology or medicine; many award-winning scientists say they could not have made their discoveries without animals. Polio would still be claiming hundreds of lives a year in Britain if it wasn't for animal research by the Nobel laureate Albert Sabin. "There could have been no oral polio vaccine without the use of innumerable animals," he once said.

(Pigilito says, 2006)

The small, shivering cat huddles against the corner of her tiny cage, trying to sleep but kept awake by the ever-present pain in her head and body. She has been awake for 43 hours now, undergoing experimental research . . . Sleep-deprived and dazed with pain, she is barely conscious . . . Worldwide, 100 to 300 million animals die each year in laboratory experiments, experiments whose methods are unnecessarily cruel and whose results are often inconclusive. Animal experimentation is unethical and impractical.

(Without-Feathers.com)

Attitudes—not always this strong or vitriolic, but an indispensable part of our psychological makeup—are the subject of this chapter and the one that follows. Attitudes and their close cousins (beliefs and values) have been the focus of much research over the past 50 years. They are the stuff of persuasion—materials persuaders try to change, possessions we cling to tenaciously, badges that define us, categories that organize us, and constructs that marketers want to measure and manipulate. The first portion of the chapter defines attitude and discusses its main components. The second section focuses on the structure of attitude, ambivalence, and how people cope with inconsistency. The third portion of the chapter examines the psychology of strong, deeply held attitudes.

# THE CONCEPT OF ATTITUDE

"She's got an attitude problem," someone says, telegraphing familiarity with the term *attitude*. But being familiar with a term does not mean one can necessarily articulate a clear, comprehensive definition. This is a task that we look to scholars to perform, and social scientists have offered a litany of definitions of attitude, dating back to the nineteenth century. Darwin regarded attitude as a motor concept (a scowling face signifies a "hostile attitude"; see Petty, Ostrom, & Brock, 1981a). Freud, by contrast, "endowed [attitudes] with vitality, identifying them with longing, hatred and love, with passion and prejudice" (Allport, 1935, p. 801). Early twentieth-century sociologists Thomas and Znaniecki placed attitude in a social context, defining it as a "state of mind of the individual toward a value" (Allport, 1935).

Their view resonated with a growing belief that the social environment influenced individuals, but then-contemporary terms like *custom* and *social force* were too vague and impersonal to capture the complex dynamics by which this occurred. *Attitude*, which referred to a force or quality of mind, seemed much more appropriate. By the 1930s, as researchers began to study the development of racial stereotypes, Gordon Allport (1935) declared that attitude was the most indispensable concept in contemporary social psychology.

Over the past century, attitude research has flourished. Social scientists have conducted surveys of people's attitudes, examining political, religious, and sex-role attitudes, to name but a few. They have explored the structure and functions of attitudes and documented relationships between attitudes and behavior. "A recent search for the term *attitude* in the American Psychological Association's comprehensive index to psychological and related literature (PsycINFO) yielded 180,910 references," Dolores Albarracín and colleagues observed (Albarracín, Johnson, & Zanna, 2005, p. vii).

Attitude is a psychological construct. It is a mental and emotional entity that inheres in, or characterizes, the person. It has also been called a "hypothetical construct," a concept that cannot be observed directly but can only be inferred from people's actions. An exemplar of this approach is the Michigan psychology professor who ran through the halls of his department shouting (in jest), "I found it. I found it. I found the attitude." His comment illustrates that attitudes are different from the raw materials that other scientific disciplines examine—materials that can be touched or clearly seen, such as a rock, plant cell, or an organ in the human body.

Although in some sense we do infer a person's attitude from what he or she says or does, it would be a mistake to assume that for this reason attitudes are not real or are "mere mental constructs." This is a fallacy of behaviorism, the scientific theory that argues that all human activity can be reduced to behavioral units. Contemporary scholars reject this notion. They note that people have thoughts, cognitive structures, and a variety of emotions, all of which lose their essential qualities when viewed exclusively as behaviors. Moreover, they argue that an entity that is mental or emotional is no less real than a physical behavior. As Allport noted perceptively:

> Attitudes are never directly observed, but, unless they are admitted, through inference, as real and substantial ingredients in human nature, it becomes impossible to account satisfactorily either for the consistency of any individual's behavior, or for the stability of any society.
>
> (1935, p. 839)

Over the past century, numerous definitions of attitude have been proposed. The following views of attitude are representative of the population of definitions. According to scholars, an attitude is:

- an association between a given object and a given evaluation (Fazio, 1989, p. 155);
- a psychological tendency that is expressed by evaluating a particular entity with some degree of favor or disfavor (Eagly & Chaiken, 1993, p. 1);

■ a learned predisposition to respond in a consistently favorable or unfavorable manner with respect to a given object (Fishbein & Ajzen, 1975, p. 6); or

■ a more or less permanently enduring state of readiness of mental organization which predisposes an individual to react in a characteristic way to any object or situation with which it is related (Cantril, quoted in Allport, 1935, p. 804).

Notice that these definitions emphasize different aspects of the attitude concept. Fazio focuses simply on the mental association of an object and a feeling. Eagly and Chaiken stress that attitudes involve a person's evaluation of an issue. Fishbein and Ajzen, as well as Cantril, take a behavioral view, suggesting that attitudes predispose people to behave in a particular way. Which is right, you ask? Which definition is the correct one? There are no objective answers to these questions. As was the case with the definition of persuasion, scholars differ in how they view a particular phenomenon. You can't say that one definition is more correct than another because defining things is a logical, not empirical, exercise. If you find the lack of certainty frustrating, you're not alone. But take heart! Science has to start somewhere, someone has to come up with a workable definition of a term before the empirical explorations can begin. Science requires a leap of faith. Yet this does not mean that one must settle with definitions that are inadequate or incomplete. Definitions are evaluated on the basis of their clarity, cogency, and comprehensiveness. The above definitions of attitude are erudite and perceptive. So which definition is correct? All are, in varying degrees. In this, a textbook that offers multiple approaches, I offer an integrative approach that combines these definitions and emphasizes commonalities. Attitude is defined here as: *a learned, global evaluation of an object (person, place, or issue) that influences thought and action.* Psychologically, an attitude is not a behavior, though it may consist of acquired patterns of reacting to social stimuli. It is not pure affect, though it is most assuredly emotional. It is a predisposition, a tendency, a state of readiness that guides and steers behavior in certain predictable, though not always rational, ways. The next section reviews the different components of the definition of attitude.

## CHARACTERISTICS OF ATTITUDES

### Attitudes Are Learned

People are not born with attitudes. They acquire attitudes over the course of socialization in childhood and adolescence. This has important implications. It means, first, that no one is born prejudiced. Children don't naturally discriminate against kids with different skin color or religious preferences. Over time, kids acquire prejudiced attitudes. Or to be more blunt, they learn to hate.

Fortunately, not all attitudes are so negative. Think about the rush you get when "The Star-Spangled Banner" is played after a U.S. victory at the Olympics. People have positive sentiments toward all sorts of things—hometown sports teams, teachers who lift our spirits, children, pets, cool cars—you get the drift. People's attitudes vary widely.

They depend to a considerable degree on what individuals have learned in their course of cultural and social upbringing. Do you think abortion should be legal? Do you feel that homosexuality should be accepted or discouraged by society? Your attitude depends in part on your religious background. Twenty percent of Americans who belong to mainstream Protestant churches believe that abortion should be legal in all cases; however, only 8 percent of Mormons feel this way. Sixty-four percent of Evangelical Christians believed that homosexuality should be discouraged by society, in contrast to 15 percent of Jews who espouse this position (Pew Forum, 2008). Attitudes vary as a function of religion, social upbringing, even the cultural landscape in which an individual was raised. People tend to cluster with those who share their attitudes (Bishop, 2008). This is why they are frequently surprised to learn that people from different groups have vastly different outlooks on social issues than they do.

Given the powerful role attitudes play in our lives, some researchers have speculated that attitudes contain a genetic component. Tesser (1993) acknowledged that there is not "a gene for attitudes toward jazz in the same way as there is a gene for eye color" (p. 139). But he argued that inherited physical differences in taste and hearing might influence attitudes toward food and loud rock music. Perhaps those who are born with higher activity levels gravitate to vigorous exercise or sports.

These are reasonable, very interesting claims. In light of growing evidence that genes can influence behavior, it is certainly possible that we may someday discover that people's genetic makeup predisposes them to approach certain activities and avoid others. At present, though, there is insufficient evidence to conclude that attitudes have a genetic foundation. Moreover, even if Tesser's claims turned out to be true, it would not mean that genes cause certain attitudes to develop. The environment will always have a large impact in shaping our responses and modes of seeing the world. For example, a person might be genetically predisposed to like pineapple, but if pineapple is not available (or affordable), she cannot develop a positive attitude toward the fruit. In addition, if the first time she tastes pineapple she develops a rash or gets bitten by a dog, she is bound to evaluate pineapple negatively.

Thus, even if attitudes have genetic antecedents, these inherited preferences are not equivalent to attitudes. Attitudes develop through encounters with social objects. "Individuals do not have an attitude until they first encounter the attitude object (or information about it) and respond evaluatively to it," Alice H. Eagly and Shelly Chaiken declare (1998, p. 270).

## Attitudes Are Global, Typically Emotional, Evaluations

Attitudes are, first and foremost, evaluations. Having an attitude means that you have categorized something and made a judgment of its net value or worth. It means that you are no longer neutral about the topic. That doesn't mean you can't have mixed feelings, but your view on the issue is no longer bland or without color.

Attitudes invariably involve affect and emotions. "Attitudes express passions and hates, attractions and repulsions, likes and dislikes," note Eagly and Chaiken (1998, p. 269).

Affect usually plays an important part in how attitudes are formed or experienced. I say "usually" because some attitudes may develop more intellectually, by absorbing information, while others are acquired through reward and punishment of previous behavior (Dillard, 1993; Zanna & Rempel, 1988). Attitudes are complex. They have different components and are formed in different ways. A classic tripartite model emphasizes that attitudes can be expressed through thoughts, feelings, and behavior (Breckler, 1984). Our attitudes are not always internally consistent, and you may have contradictory attitudes toward the same issue.

Attitudes can be regarded as large summary evaluations of issues and people. (They are global, or macro, not micro.) Your attitude toward men's and women's roles is a large, complex entity composed of beliefs, affect, and perhaps intentions to behave one way or another. For this reason, researchers speak of "attitude systems" that consist of several subcomponents. Attitudes encompass beliefs, feelings, intentions to behave, and behavior itself.

## Attitudes Influence Thought and Action

Attitudes (and values) organize our social world. They allow us to categorize people, places, and events quickly and to figure out what's going on. They're like notebook dividers or labels you use to categorize your collection of favorite books. Attitudes shape perceptions and influence judgments. If you're a Republican, you probably evaluate Republican political leaders favorably and have a negative, gut-level reaction to Democratic politicians. And vice versa if you're a Democrat. On the other hand, if you hate politics and distrust politicians, you filter the political world through a skeptical set of lenses.

Attitudes also influence behavior. They guide our actions and steer us in the direction of doing what we believe. In our society, consistency between attitude and behavior is valued, so people try hard to "practice what they preach." As will be discussed, people usually translate attitudes into behavior, but not always.

Attitudes come in different shapes and sizes. Some attitudes are strong; others are weaker and susceptible to influence. Still others contain inconsistent elements. Some attitudes exert a stronger impact on thought and behavior than others. In sum: attitudes are complex, dynamic entities—like people. Persuasion scholar Muzafer Sherif put it best:

> When we talk about attitudes, we are talking about what a person has learned in the process of becoming a member of a family, a member of a group, and of society that makes him react to his social world in a *consistent and characteristic* way, instead of a transitory and haphazard way. We are talking about the fact that he is no longer neutral in sizing up the world around him; he is *attracted* or *repelled, for* or *against, favorable* or *unfavorable.*
>
> (1967, p. 2)

# VALUES AND BELIEFS

What do you value? What do you believe about life and society? To answer these questions, it helps to define value and belief clearly. Both concepts play an important role in persuasion. Like attitudes, values and beliefs are learned and shape the ways we interpret information.

*Values* are ideals, "guiding principles in one's life," or overarching goals that people strive to obtain (Maio & Olson, 1998). They are our "conceptions of the desirable means and ends of action" (Kluckhohn, 1951). More comprehensively, values are *"desirable end states or behaviors that transcend specific situations, guide selection or evaluation of behavior and events, and are ordered by relative importance"* (see Schwartz & Bilsky, 1987, p. 551). Values can either transcend or celebrate selfish concerns. Freedom, equality, and a world of beauty are universal values that extend beyond individual interests (Rokeach, 1973; Schwartz, 1996). Self-fulfillment, excitement, and recognition express strong desires to enrich our own lives. Power and achievement are self-enhancement values. Warm relationships with others and a sense of belonging emphasize love and security (Kahle, 1996).

In everyday life, values conflict and collide. "Difficult choices are unavoidable," observe Philip E. Tetlock and colleagues (Tetlock, Peterson, & Lerner, 1996, p. 25; see Box 2.1). Values are large macro constructs that underlie attitudes. Recall the divergent attitudes people hold toward research on animals. Those who support scientific research on animals place a greater value on human life, arguing that we owe humans obligations that we do not owe animals. Those who strenuously oppose animal research retort that this wreaks of "specism." They accord equal value to all living sentient beings, whether animals or humans. Your attitude toward animal research derives from your more general values. In contrast to values, beliefs are more specific and cognitive. Freedom encompasses attitudes toward censorship, entrepreneurship, political correctness, and smoking in public. People have hundreds of attitudes, but dozens of values (e.g., Rokeach, 1973). Even more than attitudes, values strike to the core of our self-concepts. Values are more global and abstract than attitudes.

In contrast, beliefs are more specific and cognitive. Beliefs number in the hundreds, perhaps thousands. These are typical:

- Girls talk more about relationships than do guys.
- Maintaining a vegetarian diet improves your state of mind.
- Video games are addictive.
- College students drink too much.
- A daily dose of religion uplifts the spirits.

Beliefs are more cognitive than values or attitudes. Beliefs are cognitions about the world—subjective probabilities that an object has a particular attribute or that an action will lead to a particular outcome (Fishbein & Ajzen, 1975).

People frequently confuse beliefs with facts. Just because we fervently believe something to be true does not make it so. Almost half of the American public does not accept the theory of evolution, believing instead that God created human beings in their present form (Collins, 2006). Yet more than a century's worth of scientific studies offers incontrovertible support for evolution and principles such as natural selection and adaptation (Dennett, 2005; Scott, 2004). In the political realm, despite news stories stating that weapons of mass destruction had not been discovered in Iraq, nearly a fourth of the public believed that the United States had located such weapons (Kull, Ramsay, & Lewis, 2003).

Beliefs can be patently and unequivocally false. A Taliban leader from Afghanistan claimed that in America, parents do not show love to their children and the only good thing to come out of the United States is candy (Goldberg, 2000). Unfortunately, beliefs like these are tenaciously held and highly resistant to change.

Other beliefs can be strongly held, but impossible to verify. Sixty-eight percent of Americans believe in life after death, 62 percent believe in hell, and 59 percent believe in the devil (Schott, 2008).

Attitudes are complex components of beliefs and affect. Beliefs can also be categorized into different subtypes. *Descriptive beliefs*, such as those previously discussed, are perceptions or hypotheses about the world that people carry around in their heads. *Prescriptive beliefs* are "ought" or "should" statements that express conceptions of preferred end-states. Prescriptive beliefs, such as "People should vote in every election" or "The minimum wage should be increased," cannot be tested by empirical research. They are part of people's world views. Some scholars regard prescriptive beliefs as components of values.

Certain beliefs can appear rational to the believer but, in fact, may be highly irrational and even delusional. Other beliefs may seem irrational, but have a strong rational foundation. After Hurricane Katrina hit New Orleans, some Blacks suspected that the levees had been deliberately blown (Remnick, 2005). While recognizing the dubious nature of the proposition, they nonetheless harbored the belief because it resonated so powerfully with racist historical events, such as Whites' refusal to rescue African-Americans during a terrible 1927 New Orleans flood; an engineer's idea at the time to order several hundred Blacks to lie on top of a levee to prevent further overflow of water; and, of course, the notorious Tuskegee experiments that used Black men as guinea pigs in a study of syphilis. "Perception is reality, and their reality is terrible," explained Jim Amoss, the editor of a New Orleans newspaper. "We are talking about people who are very poor and have a precondition to accept this belief . . . They are isolated in shelters and they know a thing or two about victimization. It fits well into a system of belief" (Remnick, 2005, p. 56). Thus, beliefs that seemed uncanny to many Whites had a rational foundation to many African-Americans, one that squared with actual historical events.

Beliefs and values are fascinating and important. Yet they have been the focus of somewhat less empirical research study than attitudes. This is because historically the attitude concept helped bridge behaviorist and cognitive approaches to psychology. It explained how people could be influenced by society, yet also internalize what they learned. It articulated a process by which social forces could affect behavior and not merely stamp their response on the organism.

## Box 2.1 | THE VALUE OF COMPLEXITIES

The following is a list of things that some people look for or want out of life. Please study the list carefully and then rate each thing on how important it is in your daily life, where 1 = important to me and 9 = extremely important to me.

1. Sense of belonging (to be accepted and needed by our family, friends, and community):

   1 2 3 4 5 6 7 8 9

2. Excitement (to experience stimulation and thrills):

   1 2 3 4 5 6 7 8 9

3. Warm relationships with others (to have close companionships and intimate friendships):

   1 2 3 4 5 6 7 8 9

4. Self-fulfillment (to find peace of mind and to make the best use of your talents):

   1 2 3 4 5 6 7 8 9

5. Being well respected (to be admired by others and to receive recognition):

   1 2 3 4 5 6 7 8 9

(Adapted from Kahle, 1996)

This is one way that psychologists measure people's values. Lynn Kahle (1996), who developed this scale, has found that there are countless individual differences in values. For example, fashion leaders value fun and enjoyment in life more than other people. Women favor a sense of belonging and warm relationships with others more than men do.

Values may also predict whether people stay together. Perhaps couples who share values when they are forging a relationship, as when both want stimulation and excitement, break up when their values diverge. Having satiated the need for excitement, one partner wants self-fulfillment, while the other still craves ever more exciting encounters.

People face intrapersonal, as well as interpersonal, value conflicts. When a choice pits two cherished, universal values against one another, individuals weigh each option carefully, realizing that neither alternative will make them totally happy. Such gut-wrenching decisions are common in government, where policymakers must adjudicate between values of diverse constituent groups. Tetlock discusses this in his value–pluralism model, which looks at how people wrestle with difficult ideological choices (Tetlock et al., 1996).

Consider, for example, that a decision to regulate Internet pornography upholds the value of preventing harm to others, but undermines freedom of choice. Former New York Mayor Rudolph Giuliani's policy of stopping and frisking suspicious people violated civil liberties, but reduced crime. Affirmative action presents a choice between two "good" values:

**Box 2.1** |

promoting diversity and allocating rewards based on merit. The issue is so complicated that philosophers do not agree on what constitutes a fair or just policy.

Abortion is even more daunting. It pits the value of sanctity of life against freedom of choice. Partisans see these issues very differently. Conservative opponents of abortion cannot comprehend how liberals, who are pro-choice, can at the same time oppose capital punishment. In the conservative's view, liberals favor murder of a fetus but oppose execution of a hardened criminal. Liberals wonder how people who oppose abortion can favor capital punishment. How, they wonder, could someone who views abortion as killing babies favor the death penalty (Seligman & Katz, 1996, p. 53)?

George Lakoff, a cognitive linguist sensitive to the meaning of words and power of conceptual systems, wrote a book that explores such apparent contradictions in belief systems. To Lakoff (1996), a liberal does not experience a contradiction in taking a pro-choice position and opposing capital punishment, and a conservative is equally comfortable opposing abortion but favoring the death penalty. Here's why:

A strict conservative has an absolute view of right and wrong. Aborting a baby is morally wrong (of course, the choice of the word "baby" to describe abortion is critical, an issue taken up in Chapter 7). A conservative, adhering to a value of self-discipline and responsibility, puts the onus on (for example) the unmarried teenage girl who consented to sex in the first place. She engaged in immoral behavior and should at least have the guts to take responsibility for her actions. Capital punishment fits into a somewhat different cognitive category. Believing that morality involves retribution (punishment for sins committed), conservatives feel strongly that capital punishment is an acceptable method to punish crime.

A pure liberal, by contrast, puts considerable value on protecting rights and extending compassion to those in need. Arguing that abortion does not involve a human life, but rather destruction of an embryo or fetus, liberals gravitate to protecting the freedom of the pregnant woman to choose whether or not to have a baby. In addition, guided by values of compassion and nurturance, liberals look with empathy at the teenage girl's predicament. She made a mistake, they acknowledge, but she is not old enough to be a mother; forcing her to have a child when she is not psychologically ready to be a mom will only hurt her child in the long run. When it comes to capital punishment, liberals note that "nurturance itself implies a reverence for life" but that "the death penalty denies such a reverence for life" and so is inconsistent with liberal values (Lakoff, 1996, pp. 208–209).

There is merit in both liberal and conservative values. Both are grounded in deep commitments to morality, yet liberals and conservatives view morality in different ways. Unfortunately, many people react to labels in knee-jerk ways when someone from the other camp discusses an issue. "You're just a bleeding heart liberal," a conservative shrieks. "He's a real conservative," a liberal moans, as if "conservative" were an obscenity.

# STRUCTURE OF ATTITUDES

Suppose we could glimpse an attitude up close. Let's say we could handle it, feel its shape and texture, and then inspect it carefully. What would we see?

We cannot observe attitudes with the same exactitude that scientists employ when examining molecules under electron microscopes. We lack the attitudinal equivalent to the human genome, the long strand of DNA that contains our twenty-three critical chromosome pairs. Instead, we infer attitudes from what people do or say, and what they report on carefully constructed survey instruments. This does not make attitudes any less real than chemicals on the periodic table, the 30,000 human genes, rocks, plants, or any other material that scientists scrutinize. It simply makes our job of uncovering their basic content more challenging and perhaps more subject to human fallibility.

Just as the human genome and physical substances have structure, attitudes also possess a certain organization. How are attitudes organized? What are their major components? Social scientists have proposed several models to help answer these questions.

## Expectancy–Value Approach

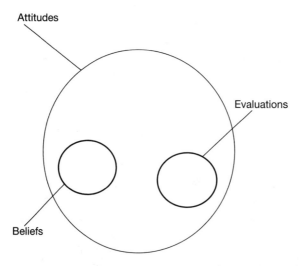

**FIGURE 2.1** | Expectancy–value approach to attitudes.

The expectancy–value perspective asserts that attitudes have two components: cognition and affect (or head and heart). Your attitude is a combination of what you believe or expect of a certain object and how you feel about (evaluate) these expectations. The theory was developed by Martin Fishbein and Icek Ajzen in 1975 and is still going strong today! According to Fishbein and Ajzen, attitude is a multiplicative combination of (a) strength of beliefs that an object has certain attributes and (b) evaluations of these attributes (see Figure 2.1). The prediction is represented by the following mathematical formula:

$A = \text{sum } b(i) \times e(i)$

where $b(i)$ = each belief and $e(i)$ = each evaluation.

Formulas like these are helpful because they allow for more precise tests of hypotheses. There is abundant evidence that attitudes can be accurately estimated by combining beliefs and evaluations. Fishbein and Ajzen showed that beliefs (particularly personally important ones) and evaluations accurately estimate attitudes toward a host of topics, ranging from politics to sex roles (Fishbein & Ajzen, 1975; Ajzen & Fishbein, 2008). Beliefs are the centerpiece of attitude and have provided researchers with rich insights into the dynamics of attitudes and behaviors.

Diane M. Morrison and colleagues (Morrison, Gillmore, Simpson, Wells, & Hoppe, 1996) systematically examined beliefs about smoking in an elaborate study of elementary school children's decisions to smoke cigarettes. They measured *beliefs* about smoking by asking kids whether they thought that smoking cigarettes would:

- hurt your lungs;
- give you bad breath;
- make your friends like you better;
- make you feel more grown up; or
- taste good.

The researchers assessed *evaluations* by asking children if they felt that these attributes (e.g., hurting your lungs, making your friends like you better) were good or bad. An evaluation was measured in this general fashion:

Do you think that making your friends like you better is: *very good, good, not good or bad, bad, or very bad?*

Morrison and colleagues gained rich insights into the dynamics of children's attitudes toward smoking. Had they just measured attitude, they would have only discovered how kids evaluated cigarette smoking. By focusing on beliefs, they identified specific reasons why some children felt positively toward smoking. By assessing evaluations, the researchers tapped into the affect associated with these attributes. Their analysis indicated that two children could hold different attitudes about smoking because they had different beliefs about smoking's consequences or because they held the same beliefs but evaluated the consequences differently.

Morrison and colleagues' findings shed light on the underpinnings of attitudes toward smoking. Some children evaluate smoking favorably because they believe that their friends will like them better if they smoke or that smoking makes them feel grown up. Kids who value these outcomes may be particularly inclined to start smoking before they hit adolescence. This information is clearly useful to health educators who design antismoking information campaigns.

**Affect, Symbols, and Ideologies**

A second perspective on attitude structure places emotion and symbols at center stage. According to the symbolic approach, attitudes—particularly political ones—are characterized by emotional reactions, sweeping sentiments, and powerful prejudices. These, rather than molecular beliefs, are believed to lie at the core of people's evaluations of social issues.

Consider racism, sexism, or attitudes toward abortion. These evaluations are rife with symbols and charged with affect. According to David O. Sears, people acquire affective responses to symbols early in life from parents, peers, and mass media (Sears & Funk, 1991). Symbols include the flag, religious ornaments, and code words associated with minority groups.

As a result of early learning experiences, people develop strong attitudes toward their country, as well as religious values, ethnic loyalties, and racial prejudices. These "symbolic predispositions," as they are called, lie at the core of people's attitudes toward social issues. Two examples may be helpful here.

Back in the 1970s, many Whites opposed school busing to achieve racial integration. Some observers suggested that one reason Whites reacted this way was because they were personally affected by busing. Their kids would have to be bused, perhaps taking the bus for a considerable distance. But this turned out not to be the case. In fact, the best predictor of Whites' opposition to busing was racial prejudice, a symbolic predisposition (Sears, Henry, & Kosterman, 2000; Sears, Lau, Tyler, & Allen, 1980).

A more recent example involves AIDS. Although Americans have become more empathic toward the plight of AIDS victims in recent years, many still harbor prejudice toward those who have contracted the AIDS virus. John Pryor and Glenn Reeder offer the following explanation:

> HIV/AIDS may have acquired a symbolic meaning in our culture. As a symbol or a metaphor, it represents things like homosexual promiscuity, moral decadence, and the wrath of God for moral transgressions . . . So, when people react negatively to someone with AIDS (or HIV), they may be expressing their feelings about the symbol. This analysis could explain why those strongly opposed to homosexuality react negatively to nonhomosexuals with HIV. Even the infected child bears the symbol of homosexual promiscuity.
>
> (1993, p. 279)

Pryor and Reeder argue that we cognitively represent people and ideas in certain ways. A person with AIDS (called a person node) is not a neutral entity, but is connected with all sorts of other ideas and emotions that come to mind when we think about AIDS. AIDS (or HIV) may be associated in an individual's mind with homosexuals, drug users, minorities, promiscuous sex, even death. All of these entities are charged with emotion or affect. These emotions become powerfully associated with a person with AIDS (see Figure 2.2).

The symbolic attitude perspective goes a long way toward helping us deconstruct people's views on contemporary issues. It calls attention to the role that associations play in attitude structure (as well as the effect of more elaborated beliefs; Sears et al., 2000).

**STRUCTURE OF ATTITUDES**

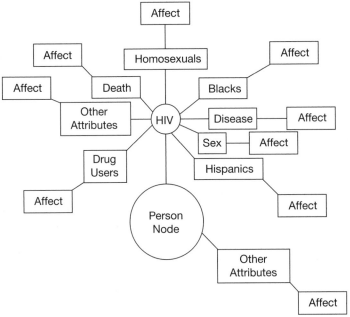

**FIGURE 2.2** | A symbolic view of attitudes toward HIV/AIDS.

From Pryor, J. B., & Reeder, G. D. (1993). Collective and individual representations of HIV/AIDS stigma. In J. B. Pryor & G. D. Reeder (Eds.), *The social psychology of HIV infection* (p. 271). Hillsdale, NJ: Lawrence Erlbaum Associates.

In fairness, although the model has done much to clarify the dynamics of racially prejudiced and homophobic attitudes, it has not been applied to the study of other equally strong attitudes, such as those held by religious extremists. Presumably, symbolic predispositions are at the foundation of a variety of affect-based social and political attitudes that we encounter in everyday life.

## The Role of Ideology

A third view of attitude organization emphasizes ideology, or world view. Some people's attitudes are guided by broad ideological principles. These individuals typically forge stronger connections among diverse political attitudes than those who don't think much about ideology. For example, conservatives, whose world views emphasize self-reliance, responsibility, and reward for hard work, typically oppose welfare because it gives money to those who don't hold down jobs. Conservatives support across-the-board tax cuts because they reward with tax refunds those who have earned the most money (Lakoff, 1996). Attitudes toward welfare and taxes, flowing from a conservative ideology, are therefore interrelated.

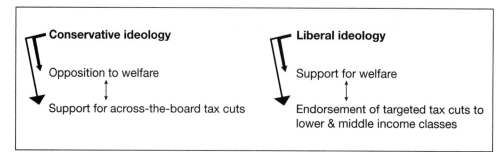

**FIGURE 2.3** | Large arrow depicts influence of ideology on attitudes. Smaller arrow denotes association between two attitudes.

By contrast, liberals—who value nurturance, fairness, and compassion for the disadvantaged—favor welfare because it helps indigent individuals who have been left behind by society. Liberal thinkers also oppose across-the-board tax cuts because (in their view) they favor the rich; liberals prefer targeted tax cuts that redistribute money to low- and middle-income people. Attitudes toward welfare and tax cuts go together—are correlated—in liberals' minds (see Figure 2.3).

As a general rule, ideologues view social and political issues differently than ordinary citizens do. Unlike many people, who respond to issues primarily on the basis of simple symbolic predispositions, ideologues begin with an ideology, and their attitudes flow from this (see Lavine, Thomsen, & Gonzales, 1997).

The ideological approach to attitudes asserts that attitudes are organized "top-down." That is, attitudes flow from the hierarchy of principles (or predispositions) that individuals have acquired and developed.

A shortcoming with this approach is that it assumes people operate on the basis of one set of ideological beliefs. In fact, individuals frequently call on a variety of prescriptive beliefs when thinking about social issues (Conover & Feldman, 1984). For instance, a student might be a social liberal, believing affirmative action is needed to redress societal wrongs. She could also be an economic conservative, believing that government should not excessively regulate private companies. The student might also have strong religious convictions and a deep belief in a Supreme Being. Her social attitudes are thus structured by a variety of belief systems (sometimes called schema), rather than by one singular ideological set of principles.

## ATTITUDE STRUCTURE AND PERSUASION

These perspectives on attitude structure contain insights about the underlying dynamics of people's attitudes. They also are of interest to communicators who hope to change attitudes. For example, suppose you were asked to develop a campaign to increase Americans' support for gay marriage, currently a contentious issue in American life. The expectancy–value approach suggests you should first explore beliefs about gay marriage, such as biased perceptions that gay people who want to have children would be poor parents. You would then find information to counteract these beliefs.

The symbolic approach would focus on the affective basis of attitudes—chiefly the negative feelings some Americans experience when linking the storied institution of marriage with gay men and women. Communications might warmly depict a gay parent frolicking in loving ways with his or her children. This could produce a more positive association between marriage and gay individuals.

The ideological approach would locate the bedrock principle underlying a particular ideological perspective. For instance, when targeting conservatives, who put a premium on self-reliance and responsibility, the campaign might emphasize that gay parents are just as apt as heterosexual parents to demand independence, discipline, and personal responsibility from their kids.

# ARE ATTITUDES INTERNALLY CONSISTENT?

As we have seen, expectations, symbols, and ideology influence attitudes and persuasion. This raises a new question, one filled with intriguing dimensions. Given that attitudes are complex macromolecules with so many different components, are they in harmony or in disarray? Are attitudes at peace or ready to ignite due to the combustible combination of cognitions, affect, and behavior? In other words, when we have an attitude toward an issue, are we all of one mind, consistent in our thoughts and feelings, or are we divided and ambivalent? These are questions that many of us have probably asked in one way or another. We have heard people say, "Intellectually, I agree, but emotionally I don't," or "You're a hypocrite; you say one thing and do another."

Social scientists have explored these issues, guided by theories and empirical methods. This section examines internal consistency of attitudes, and the next chapter focuses on the larger issue of attitude and behavior congruency.

## Intra-Attitudinal Consistency

It's pleasant when we are all of one mind on an issue—when our general attitude is in sync with specific beliefs about the topic or has the same "electrical charge" as our feelings. However, life does not always grant us this pleasure. We are ambivalent about many issues. Ambivalence occurs when we feel both positively and negatively about a person or issue (Thompson, Zanna, & Griffin, 1995). Ambivalence is characterized by uncertainty or conflict between attitude elements.

One type of ambivalence occurs when we hold seemingly incompatible beliefs. Many people evaluate their own doctor positively, but view the health system negatively. They believe their family is healthy, but American families are in trouble. And they frequently have kind things to say about their own representative to Congress, but disparage "the bums in Washington" (Perloff, 1996). One source for this discrepancy is the mass media, which typically focus on the seamy side of political life. An effect is an ambivalence about the issue in question.

Perhaps the most common type of ambivalence is the head versus heart variety—our cognitions take us one way, but our feelings pull us somewhere else. Expectancy–value theory deals with this when it stipulates that people can have strong beliefs about two or more outcomes, but evaluate the outcomes very differently. For example, a student may believe that her professor taught her a lot about physiology, but at the same time kept her waiting in his office. She evaluates knowledge gain positively, but time misspent negatively. A more dramatic example involves the ambivalent attitudes many young women harbor toward safer sex. For example, many women (correctly) believe that using condoms can prevent AIDS, and they evaluate AIDS prevention positively. They also believe that requesting condoms will upset their boyfriends and place a negative value on this outcome. "My boyfriend hates them," one young woman said, adding, "Frankly, I can't blame him. For me it certainly puts a crimp on what I would like to do to satisfy him" (Perloff, 2001, p. 13). Persuaders face a challenge in cases like this one. To change this woman's attitude toward safer sex, they must help her rethink her fear of offending her boyfriend.

Sex roles are unquestionably an area in which many people feel a great deal of ambivalence. Some of this stems from conflict between early socialization and later experiences, in which individuals realize that some of the attitudes learned as children don't fit reality. As children, girls traditionally learn that they should get married, have children, and center their lives around caring for others. Boys develop an orientation toward careers, viewing women as trophies to acquire along the way. When girls grow up and come to value independence of mind, and boys view women in a more egalitarian light, they realize that their symbolic upbringing is at odds with their newly acquired beliefs. But old ideas die hard, and the result is conflict between childhood affect and grown-up cognition.

Ambivalence can frequently be found among young women who love the power and responsibility that comes with high-powered corporate jobs, yet also worry that their commitment to a career will compromise their chances of raising a family when they reach their 30s. Writer Peggy Orenstein (2000) documented this, interviewing scores of women across the country, asking them to share their feelings about careers, relationships, and future plans to become a mom and raise a family. Some of the 20-something women Orenstein interviewed worried that "having a child 'too soon' would be a disaster: it would cut short their quest for identity and destroy their career prospects" (pp. 33–34). At the same time, these women felt pressure not to have kids too late, noting that women have more difficulty conceiving a child when they reach their late 30s. On the other side of the career track, educated women who "mommy-tracked" their aspirations to raise families also experienced mixed feelings. These women found enormous gratification in being a mom, yet at the same time lamented, as one woman put it, that "I don't really have a career and I feel crummy about that" (p. 224). "Ambivalence may be the only sane response to motherhood at this juncture in history, to the schism it creates in women's lives," Orenstein concluded (p. 141).

Ambivalence is also a reasonable response to the complex issues women face in another arena: abortion. In contrast to the us versus them and pro-life versus pro-choice polarities that characterize the media debate, in reality, most women find themselves on shakier ground, balancing moral values against practical realities, "weighing religious, ethical, practical, sentimental and financial imperatives that [are] often in conflict" (Leland, 2005, p. 29). Women who learn that a child has a strong chance of having Down syndrome must balance their fear of raising a child with this condition against a religious belief in the sanctity of life. Poor women who received abortions at an Arkansas medical clinic readily admitted their ambivalence and pain. "I know it's against God," said Tammy, who works in a coffee shop in Tennessee:

> But you have three kids, you want to raise them good. My friends and sister-in-law say, "You care about money problems but don't care about what God will do," I believe it's wrong. I pray to God to forgive me. This will be the last one. Never, never again.
>
> (Leland, p. 29)

## Balancing Things Out

Ambivalence drives some people berserk. They will do anything to resolve it. More generally, psychologists argue that individuals dislike inconsistency among cognitive elements and are motivated to reconfigure things mentally so as to achieve a harmonious state of mind. Fritz Heider (1958) proposed an algebraic model of attitudes, called *balance theory*. Heider's model involves a triad of relationships: a person or perceiver (P), another person (O), and an issue (X). Heider argued that people prefer a balanced relationship among P, O, and X.

Borrowing from chemistry, Heider suggested that cognitive elements have a positive or negative valence (or charge). A positive relationship, in which P likes O or X, is symbolized with a plus sign. A negative relationship, in which P dislikes O or X, is assigned a minus sign. A visual thinker, Heider diagrammed his model with a series of triangles. Each of the three relationships (P,O; P,X; and O,X) is assigned a plus or minus. Attitudes are in harmony when the signs multiplied together yield a plus. If you remember your elementary arithmetic, you recall that a plus × a plus is a plus, a minus × a minus is a plus, and a plus × a minus yields a minus. Let's see how this works in real life to understand how people cope with inconsistency among attitudinal elements.

Consider for a moment the contemporary quandary of an individual—let's call him Sam—who believes in evolution. A religious friend, Samantha, a devotee of intelligent design, believes God created human beings in their present form. She questions the validity of Darwinian evolution. Sam's belief in evolution is symbolized by a + in the model. Sam's liking of Samantha is conveyed by a +. Samantha's disagreement with evolution is symbolized by a –. Multiplying the three terms, one gets a minus, suggesting that Sam's attitude is imbalanced, or not entirely consistent (see Figure 2.4a). Presumably, Sam would find the inconsistency uncomfortable and would feel impelled to restore mental harmony. Balance theory says that he has several options. He could change his attitude toward evolution and question the notion that human beings evolved from earlier species of animals (Figure 2.4b). Or he could alter his attitude toward Samantha, deciding that he can't be friendly with someone who harbors such opinions (Figure 2.4c).

(a)

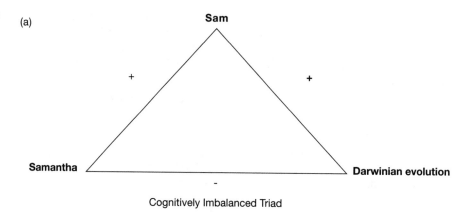

Cognitively Imbalanced Triad

(b)

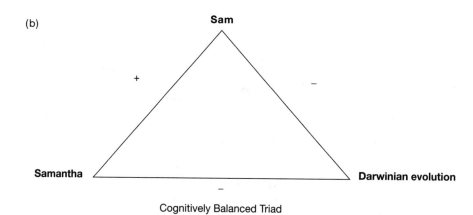

Cognitively Balanced Triad

(c)

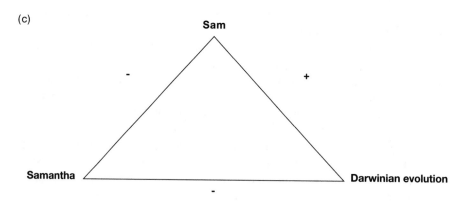

Cognitively Balanced Triad

**FIGURE 2.4** | Balance theory analysis of Sam's attitudes toward Darwinian evolution and those of a friend who does not believe in evolution ("+" indicates positive sentiments; "−" shows negative ones).

Balance theory helps us understand many situations in which people face cognitive inconsistency. For example, one anti-abortion activist told a researcher that she could not be a friend with somebody who disagreed with her on abortion (Granberg, 1993). Unfortunately, balance theory does not describe many subtleties in people's judgments. It also fails to describe those situations in which people manage to like people with whom they disagree (Milburn, 1991). For example, during the Clinton impeachment, many Democrats did not reduce their liking of President Clinton after they found out about his affair. Nor did they change their negative attitude toward his sexual relationship with Monica Lewinsky. Most Democrats continued to give high marks to Clinton's performance as president, while disapproving of his liaison with Lewinsky. This is not entirely consistent with balance theory. Thus, we need another approach to explain how people grapple with inconsistency. A model proposed by Robert P. Abelson (1959) is more helpful. Abelson suggested that people resolve cognitive conflict in four ways: (a) denial, (b) bolstering, (c) differentiation, and (d) transcendence.

Consider how this could work in the following example:

*Denial.* Sam could try to forget about the inconsistency between his support of evolution and Samantha's feeling that evolution flies in the face of a belief that God created *humans in their present form.*

*Bolstering.* Sam could add mental elements to his attitude, noting that there is strong empirical support for the idea of natural selection and no scientific challenge to the notion that human beings evolved from earlier species of animals. In this way, he might feel more strongly about the belief, thereby reducing cognitive imbalance.

*Differentiation.* He might differentiate his liking of Samantha from her disbelief in evolution. In effect, Sam could agree to disagree with Samantha, noting they have been long-time friends and agree about other issues.

*Transcendence.* Sam could acknowledge, as some scientists have, that there is no contradiction between belief in evolution and belief in God. He might conclude that God started the process by which humans evolved from earlier animal species. Science explains how human beings evolved; religion explains why humans developed in the first place. By transcending the conflict, he might reconcile his belief in evolution with Samantha's theist principles.

## THE PSYCHOLOGY OF STRONG ATTITUDES

Flag burning. Abortion. Capital punishment. Gun control. These are what typically come to mind when we think of attitudes. As suggested earlier, not all attitudes are this strong or are based as exclusively in affect. However, strong attitudes like these seem to have profound influences on thoughts and behavior. From the French Revolution to violence perpetrated against doctors who perform abortion, "the incidents that attract our attention are often those associated with strong sentiments," Jon A. Krosnick and Richard E. Petty note (1995, p. 1). Intrigued by the dynamics of such attitudes, social psychologists have embarked on a series of studies exploring strong attitude characteristics and effects (see Figure 2.5).

**FIGURE 2.5** | People frequently display strong political attitudes in public. These attitudes are involving, emotional, and invariably complex.
Photograph by William C. Rieter.

This might all seem obvious at first blush. People with strong attitudes have lots of passion and care a lot; isn't that what one would expect? Yes—but remember that persuasion scholars take a scientific approach. They want to understand what a strong attitude looks like, what it means psychologically to feel deeply about an issue, how strong attitudes differ from weaker or more ambivalent ones, and the effects of such attitudes on behavior. Remember also that people have done terrible things in the name of strong attitudes. They have killed innocent people and destroyed themselves. The more we can understand such attitudes, the more likely it is that we can devise ways to convince troubled or violent people to rethink their approaches to life.

Attitudes by definition influence thought and action. But strong attitudes are particularly likely to: (a) persist over time, (b) affect judgments, (c) guide behavior, and (d) prove resistant to change (Krosnick & Petty, 1995). Why is this so? Why are strong attitudes stable? According to Maureen Wang Erber and colleagues:

> First, strong attitudes are probably anchored by other beliefs and values, making them more resistant to change. If people were to change their basic religious beliefs, for example, many other attitudes and values linked to these beliefs would have to be changed as well. Second, people are likely to know more about issues they feel strongly about, making them more resistant to counterarguments. Third, people are

likely to associate with others who feel similarly on important issues, and these people help maintain and support these attitudes. Fourth, strong attitudes are often more elaborated and accessible, making it more likely that they will be at the tip of the tongue when people are asked how they feel on different occasions. Fifth, people with strong attitudes are likely to attend to and seek out information relevant to the topic, arming them with still more arguments with which to resist attempts to change their minds.

(Wang Erber, Hodges, & Wilson, 1995, pp. 437–438)

Think for a moment about something you feel strongly about. Your attitude might concern one of those issues we have discussed in the book: politics, race, sex roles, abortion. Or it could be about something quite different—a vegetarian diet, jogging, the stock market, music. Now think of something you feel less strongly or personally about. How does the first attitude differ from the second? We gain insights from perspectives discussed in this chapter.

The symbolic approach suggests that people acquire strong attitudes at an early age. They are learned, reinforced, and associated with positive aspects of a child's upbringing. Consider the example of a sportsman who has a staunchly favorable (yet complicated) attitude toward hunting. Hunter Steve Tuttle explained how he acquired his attitude:

I remember the first time I ever killed something. It was a rabbit, and I was about 12 years old. I put my gun to my shoulder and aimed—taking care to lead the target— and pulled the trigger. The animal seemed to tumble end over end in slow motion . . . My father . . . looked up at me and said, "Good shot, boy!" and handed me the rabbit. I was proud and devastated all at once . . . The other men in the hunting party came over and slapped me on the back. Little did they know that I would have given anything to bring that rabbit back to life. I would feel sad about it for weeks . . . I went on to shoot a lot more game over the years, but none ever had the same emotional impact, nor did I ever get teary-eyed at the moment of the kill. In my culture, in the rural America of western Virginia, that was the day I began to change from boy to man.

(2006, pp. 50–51)

The ideological approach takes another tack, emphasizing that strong attitudes are likely to be organized around principles and values. For example, pro-life partisans anchor their opposition to abortion in religious convictions. Pro-choice activists derive their support for a woman's right to choose on human beings' inalienable right to make choices about issues that confront them.

Social psychologists who study strong attitudes offer additional insights. They emphasize that there is not just one way that a strong attitude differs from a weaker one. Attitude strength is a multifaceted concept. Thus, there are a variety of elements that differentiate strong from weak attitudes (Holbrook, Berent, Krosnick, Visser, & Boninger, 2005; Krosnick, Boninger, Chuang, Berent, & Carnot, 1993; Petrocelli, Tormala, & Rucker, 2007). Strong attitudes are characterized by:

- importance (we care deeply about the issue);
- ego involvement (the attitude is linked to core values or the self);
- extremity (the attitude deviates significantly from neutrality);
- certainty (we are convinced that our attitude is correct);
- accessibility (the attitude comes quickly to mind);
- knowledge (we are highly informed about the topic); and
- hierarchical organization (the attitude is internally consistent and embedded in an elaborate attitudinal structure).

Note that a particular strong attitude may not possess all of these characteristics. You could regard an attitude as important, but not link it up to your self-concept (Boninger, Krosnick, Berent, & Fabrigar, 1995). You could know a lot about an issue, but not be certain that your knowledge is correct. An attitude could come quickly to mind, but it might not be embedded in an extensive internal structure. The upshot of all this is that certain attitudes may be strong, but they are not likely to be simple.

# ATTITUDES AND INFORMATION PROCESSING

Strong attitudes influence message evaluations and judgments of communications. Two theories shed light on how this occurs: social judgment theory and the attitude accessibility approach.

## Social Judgment Theory

On the eve of a Subway Series between the New York Yankees and New York Mets a few years back, a reporter filed this tongue-in-cheek report on how Yankee and Mets fans saw each other, based on interviews with New York baseball fans:

> "Yankee fans are much more highly educated," [Allen Sherman, a Yankee fan] said. "... We have to be. It's harder to spell Yankees than Mets. And we can curse in so many different languages. We earn more, so when we throw a beer can it's those high-priced beer cans ..." Fred Sayed, 26, a technical support manager from Queens and a Mets fan, was able to be pretty explicit himself in defining Yankee fans: "All Yankee fans are just flat-out stupid."
>
> (Kleinfield, 2000, p. A1)

Ask a baseball pitcher why so many home runs are hit these days and you will hear an impassioned speech from a member of an oppressed minority. You will hear how umpires are calling a fist-size strike zone (*They're sticking it to us!*), ... the mounds are lower (*They won't give us any edge!*) and, of course, the baseball is different ... (*We're throwing golf balls out there!*). Ask an infielder, an outfielder or any player except a pitcher about the inordinate increase in home runs and a royal smirk often precedes the response. (*The answers are pretty obvious, aren't they?*)

**FIGURE 2.6** | This painting, *Hand with Reflecting Globe*, by the artist M. C. Escher, illustrates a central principle of social judgment theory. It highlights the notion that people are consumed by their own attitudes toward a topic. They cannot escape their own perspectives on the issue.

From M. C. Escher's *Hand with Reflecting Sphere* © 2007 The M. C. Escher Company—Holland. www.mescher.com. With permission.

You are informed the hitters are stronger than they used to be . . . , train daily (*I am a machine!*) and capitalize on modern technology (*We study videotape between at-bats and recognize the weaknesses in all pitchers*).

(Olney, 2000, p. 38)

These anecdotes show that some people have very strong attitudes toward baseball. But they tell more than that. They speak to the biases individuals have when they harbor strong feelings about a topic, and, in this way, illustrate the social judgment approach to attitudes. Pioneered by Muzafer Sherif and Carolyn Sherif (1967), social judgment theory emphasizes that people evaluate issues based on where they stand on the topic. As Sherif and Sherif noted:

The basic information for predicting a person's reaction to a communication is *where* he places its position and the communicator relative to himself. The way that a person appraises a communication and perceives its position relative to his own stand affects his reaction to it and what he will do as a result.

(p. 129)

Thus, social judgment theory emphasizes that receivers do not evaluate a message purely on the merits of the arguments. Instead, the theory stipulates that people compare the advocated position with their attitude and then determine whether they should accept the position advocated in the message. Like Narcissus preoccupied with his reflection in the water, receivers are consumed with their own attitudes toward the topic. They can never escape their own points of view (see Figure 2.6).

Social judgment theory, so named because it emphasizes people's subjective judgments about social issues, articulates several core concepts. These are: (a) latitudes of acceptance, rejection, and non-commitment; (b) assimilation and contrast; and (c) ego-involvement.

**Latitudes.** Attitudes consist of a continuum of evaluations—a range of acceptable and unacceptable positions, as well as positions toward which the individual has no strong commitment. The *latitude of acceptance* consists of all those positions on an issue that an individual finds acceptable, including the most acceptable position. The *latitude of rejection* includes those positions that the individual finds objectionable, including the most objectionable position. Lying between these two regions is the *latitude of non-commitment*, which consists of those positions on which the individual has preferred to remain noncommittal. This is the arena of the "don't know," "not sure," and "haven't made up my mind" responses (see Figure 2.7).

Early research focused on the relationship between extreme attitudes and size of the latitudes. Studies indicated that extremity of position influenced the size of the latitudes of rejection and acceptance (Sherif, Sherif, & Nebergall, 1965). Individuals with strong—in particular, extreme—views on a topic have large latitudes of rejection. They reject nearly all opposing arguments and accept only statements that are adjacent to their own stands on the issue. This is one reason why it is hard to change these folks' minds.

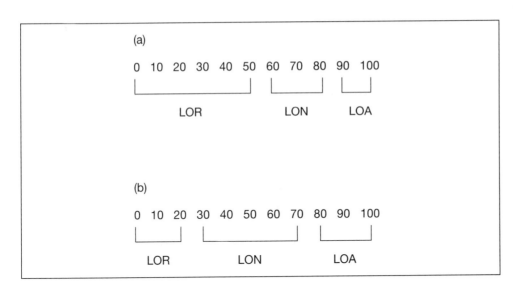

FIGURE 2.7 | Latitude of rejection (LOR), latitude of noncommitment (LON), and latitude of acceptance (LOA) of individuals with strong and moderate attitudes on an issue. Panel (a) illustrates latitudes of an individual with a strong attitude. Panel (b) shows latitudes of an individual with a moderate attitude. Hypothetical scale goes from 0 to 100, where 100 indicates a message in total agreement with an individual's position and 0 indicates a position in total disagreement.

**Assimilation/contrast.** One way to appreciate these terms is to focus on an entirely different issue for a moment: the weather. For example, if the weather is unseasonably warm in Chicago one December (say, 60°), people will yak on and on about how hot it is. Expecting the temperature to register 30°, they are pleasantly surprised. This is a *contrast* effect, in which we focus on how different reality is from expectation. On the other hand, if the thermometer reads 38° in December, people think nothing of it. Expecting the temperature to be in the 30s, they are hardly surprised. They *assimilate* the temperature to what they expected, neglecting the fact that 38° is somewhat warmer than average.

Assimilation and contrast are perceptual mistakes, distortions that result from the tendency to perceive phenomena from the standpoint of a personal reference point or anchor. People judge message positions not objectively, but rather subjectively. Their initial attitude serves as the reference point. In assimilation, people pull a somewhat congenial message toward their own attitude, assuming the message is more similar to their attitude than it really is. They overestimate the similarity between a speaker's attitude and their own. In the case of contrast, individuals push a somewhat disagreeable message away from their attitude, assuming it is more different than it really is. They overestimate the difference between the communicator's attitude and their own (Granberg, 1993).

Assimilation and contrast are part of everyday life. We assimilate our friends' attitudes toward our own, assuming their views are more similar to ours than they really are. This is one reason why people who fall in love are so shocked at their first disagreement. At the same time, we contrast our foes, exaggerating the degree to which their attitudes are different from ours. "You mean, we actually agree," we jokingly say to an opponent at the office.

Assimilation and contrast effects show up frequently in politics. This makes sense when you consider two important facts: (a) politicians frequently make ambiguous statements so that they will not offend key constituents, and (b) social judgment theory says that assimilation/contrast will only occur when communications are ambiguous (Granberg, 1993). (When a message is clear cut, no one has any doubt as to where the communicator stands on the issue.) Thus, American voters end up doing a lot of assimilating and contrasting in presidential elections. Not being that interested in politics to begin with, many just assume that their favored candidate shares their position on education or health care, and tell themselves that the person they're not voting for takes sharply different positions from their own. After the election, voters are sometimes surprised to discover that the candidate for whom they voted does not share all their viewpoints and that the opposing candidate was not as different as they feared.

**Ego-involvement.** If you had to say which concept from social judgment theory exerted the greatest influence on research, it would be involvement. Social scientists have found involvement fascinating because it seems to have such a strong impact on latitudes and assimilation/contrast. Practitioners have been intrigued because of its many implications for intractable conflict on social and political issues.

Ego-involvement is "the arousal, singly or in combination, of the individual's commitments or stands in the context of appropriate situations" (Sherif et al., 1965, p. 65). People are ego-involved when they perceive that the issue touches on their self-concepts or core values. Highly involved individuals differ from less involved persons in three ways. First, when people are involved in or care deeply about a social issue, they have larger latitudes of rejection relative to their latitudes of acceptance and non-commitment. This means that they reject just about any position that is not in sync with their own. Second, and in a related vein, they contrast mildly disagreeable messages from their attitudes more frequently than folks who aren't as invested in the issue. Third, when concerned deeply about an issue, people are apt to assimilate ambiguous messages only when the arguments are generally consistent with their preconceived attitudes (Sherif et al., 1965). Individuals with ego-involved stands are hard to persuade: they are stubborn or resilient, depending on your point of view (see Figure 2.7).

There has been much research exploring the psychology of ego-involved attitudes. Studies have shown that when individuals are ego-involved in an issue (as people frequently are with the environment, religion, or animal rights), they engage in what is known as *selective perception*. They perceive events so that they fit their preconceived beliefs and attitudes. Two 1950s-era studies documented this tendency. The research was distinctive because the investigators tested hypotheses by locating people with strong views on an issue and then asking them to indicate their perceptions of a message.

Hovland, Harvey, and Sherif (1957), focusing on repeal of a law prohibiting sale of alcoholic beverages in Oklahoma, found that both those opposed to alcoholic beverages and those in favor of drinking thought that a message that by and large agreed with their point of view was fair, but one that disputed it was biased. Hastorf and Cantril (1954) asked Princeton and Dartmouth students to view a film of a football game between their colleges that featured lots of rough play and rule infractions. Students interpreted the game in light of their biases: Princeton and Dartmouth students each saw a game in which their squad was "the good guys" and the other team the "bad guys." Thus, where we "stand" on an issue depends on where we "sit" psychologically.

Flash back to the baseball examples that introduced this section. Yankee and Mets fans' strong attitudes colored their views of the other team. Ball players' explanations of increases in home runs differed, depending on whether they were pitchers or hitters.

Newer research, flowing out of the "oldy but goody" tradition of Sherif and Hastorf, has documented that people with strong, ego-involved attitudes still perceive messages in biased ways (Edwards & Smith, 1996; Miller, McHoskey, Bane, & Dowd, 1993; Newman, Duff, Schnopp-Wyatt, Brock, & Hoffman, 1997; Thompson, 1995; see Box 2.2). An intriguing study by Charles Lord and colleagues (Lord, Ross, & Lepper, 1979) provides a snapshot on current thinking on this issue. The study was conducted over a quarter century ago, but is regarded as a classic in the field.

Focusing on attitudes toward capital punishment, the investigators followed the Sherif and Hastorf tradition of locating individuals with strong views on an issue. They focused on two groups of students. One group favored the death penalty, believing it to be an effective deterrent against crime. The second group opposed it, maintaining that capital punishment was inhumane or an ineffective deterrent. Individuals from each group read brief descriptions of two purported investigations of the death penalty's deterrent effects. One study always reported evidence that the death penalty was effective (e.g., "in 11 of the 14 states, murder rates were *lower* after adoption of the death penalty"). The other study used similar statistics to make the opposite point—that the death penalty was an ineffective deterrent against crime (e.g., in 8 of the 10 states, "murder rates were *higher* in the state *with* capital punishment").

Students evaluated the studies and indicated whether they had changed their attitude toward capital punishment. Thus, students read one study that supported and one study that opposed their position on the death penalty. The evidence in support of the death penalty's deterrent effect was virtually the same as the evidence that questioned its impact.

If people were objective and fair, they would acknowledge that the evidence for both sides was equally strong. But that is not how these ego-involved partisans responded. Proponents of capital punishment found the pro-death-penalty study more convincing, and opponents found the anti-death-penalty study more persuasive. For example, a supporter of capital punishment said this about a study favoring the death penalty:

"The experiment was well thought out, the data collected was valid, and they were able to come up with responses to all criticisms."

The same person reacted to the anti-capital-punishment study by remarking that:

"There were too many flaws in the picking of the states and too many variables involved in the experiment as a whole to change my opinion."

## Box 2.2 | WHAT'S THE RIGHT THING?

You may have heard of Spike Lee's classic movie, *Do the Right Thing*. It's a disturbing, controversial portrait of relationships among Blacks, Whites, and Hispanics in the New York City neighborhood of Bedford–Stuyvesant. But did you know that Black and White viewers sometimes react to the movie in diametrically opposite ways? That, at least, is the conclusion reached by Brenda Cooper (1998), who studied the ways that White and African-American students interpreted the film. Her study provides additional evidence that ego-involvement influences social judgments. Psychologists have made this point for years, but now comes evidence that the same processes operate when people watch blockbuster movies.

The film is set in New York City on a hot summer day. The movie examines the experiences of Black and Hispanic residents and their tense relationship with Sal, an Italian-American owner of the neighborhood pizza joint. Mookie, the main Black character, earns $250 a week delivering Sal's pizzas to neighborhood residents. The film edges toward the climax when:

> Buggin' Out, one of Mookie's friends, complains to Sal that all of the pictures on the pizzeria's "Wall of Fame" are of Italian Americans, yet most of his customers are Blacks ... Buggin' Out enlists another Black man, Radio Raheem, in his boycott of Sal's pizzeria to protest the absence of pictures of African Americans on the "Wall of Fame." The two men confront Sal, and when Radio Raheem refuses to lower the volume of his boom box, Sal smashes his radio with a baseball bat, calls his customers "niggers," and a brawl begins.
>
> (Cooper, pp. 205–206)

Subsequently, the police arrive, Radio Raheem is killed, Mookie hurls a garbage can through the window, and the pizzeria goes up in flames. Researcher Cooper, noting that people interpret mass media differently depending on their cultural experiences, predicted that Blacks and Whites would experience the film in dramatically different ways. She asked a group of predominately White and Black students to describe their reactions to the movie. As social judgment theory would predict, the perceptions of Whites differed considerably from those of Blacks. Here is how Whites perceived the film:

> Sal's character was a loving, hardworking man and he treated Mookie like one of his own sons ... Sal was not racist and I believe he tried to do what was right ... Sal, despite his hard-hitting attitude, genuinely cared for the people of the community ... If a Black man would have owned that pizzeria, and had pictures of just Black men, none of this would have started. I also don't think that a White man would ever ask a Black person who owned something, to put up pictures of some White guy who Blacks neither like nor know what that person did ... The guys who came in breaking Sal's rules incited Sal to react negatively ... Even though the Black boy with the radio was killed by the White cops, I do not believe that justifies the cruel act of destroying a man's business.
>
> (pp. 212, 214)

**Box 2.2**

African-American respondents saw things differently:

> Sal's interactions with the different characters were strictly business. He considered himself to be king of the block and the African Americans were his servants . . . I saw his [—Buggin' Out's] point when he made the statement that if 99% of your business comes from Blacks, then why aren't there any Blacks on the wall? . . . In my community I see exactly what Spike filmed—Whites operate their businesses in Black neighborhoods and yet they do not live in that neighborhood . . . Sal destroyed his radio—which meant that Sal destroyed a part of Raheem . . . We received a clear picture of brutality when one of Mookie's friends is killed by the White police. This incident showed us that a Black man was convicted before he was tried . . . Mookie did the right thing by throwing the garbage can through Sal's window . . . It helped everyone to channel their anger on Sal's property rather than to allow the crowd to continue to attack Sal in revenge for Radio's death.
>
> (pp. 212, 215)

Social judgment theorists could find plenty of examples in these comments of assimilation, contrast, and selective perception. On a general level, there is a similarity among predictions made by social judgment theory, a social psychological account, and qualitative, "postmodern" perspectives cited by Cooper. If there is a moral in these approaches and Cooper's findings, it is that we should appreciate that what we "see" in messages reflects our own cultural perspective. Someday, historians may discover that our "view" was indeed correct. But until that time, tolerance and understanding seem like useful prescriptions to follow.

An opponent of capital punishment said this of a study opposing capital punishment:

> "The states were chosen at random, so the results show the average effect capital punishment has across the nation. The fact that 8 out of 10 states show a rise in murders stands as good evidence."

The opponent reacted in this way to the pro-capital-punishment study:

> "The study was taken only 1 year before and 1 year after capital punishment was reinstated. To be a more effective study they should have taken data from at least 10 years before and as many years as possible after."
>
> (Lord et al., 1979, p. 2103)

Individuals processed information very selectively, exhibiting what the authors called *biased assimilation*. They assimilated ambiguous information to their point of view, believing that it was consistent with their position on capital punishment. What's more, proponents and opponents managed to feel even more strongly about the issue by the study's conclusion. Proponents reported that they were more in favor of the death penalty than they had been at the study's start. Opponents indicated that they were more opposed than they had been at the beginning of the experiment. Reading the arguments did not reduce biased perceptions; it caused partisans to become even more polarized, more convinced that they were right.

Fascinated by the cognitive underpinnings of such perceptions, social psychologists have tried to piece together what happens inside an individual's mind when he or she is faced with conflicting evidence on an issue. They have suggested that people with strong attitudes have no intention of mentally searching for information that might prove their position wrong. On the contrary, they engage in a "biased memory search" at the get-go; convinced that their position is correct, they search memory for facts that support their view of the world, conveniently overlooking or rejecting evidence on the other side that might call their ideas into question (Edwards & Smith, 1996).

Another factor that plays into all this is the way that involved observers visualize the problem. When thinking about welfare, conservatives see a lazy, fat mother thumbing her nose at those who want her to work. Liberals envision a needy, frail person, marginalized by society, doing her best to raise her kids on her own. On the issue of capital punishment, those who favor the death penalty think first about the victims of the murderer's horrific act. Or, when thinking of the killer, they call to mind a depraved, sadistic person who kills for sheer pleasure. Death penalty opponents visualize the sadistic execution of a human being, turned from a person to charred human remains. These cognitive representations powerfully influence thinking, and help explain why involved individuals on different sides of the political fence process the same information so differently (Lord, Desforges, Fein, Pugh, & Lepper, 1994).

Interestingly, ego-involved partisans are not necessarily uninformed about the positions advocated by their opponents. In some cases they know their foes' arguments excruciatingly well, probably better than neutral observers (Pratkanis, 1989). Early social judgment research probably oversimplified the dynamics of social attitudes, suggesting that people shun or quickly forget information that disputes their point of view. Recent studies show that people do not deliberately avoid information that is inconsistent with their viewpoint. Nor do they remember facts congenial with their point of view better than those that are inconsistent with their preexisting attitude (Eagly, Chen, Chaiken, & Shaw-Barnes, 1999). On the contrary, when people are ego-involved in an issue, they sometimes scrutinize facts from the other side carefully, and remember them remarkably well, even though they are not persuaded in the least by the position advocated in the message (Eagly, Kulesa, Chen, & Chaiken, 2001). Individuals with strong viewpoints may find it useful to know arguments from the other side, perhaps to develop stronger counterarguments, or they may be intrigued by the entire issue and therefore motivated to find out as much as they can about both sides. Whatever the reasons, it is fair to say that ego-involved partisans have more complex attitude structures than nonpartisans. Unfortunately, this does not make them more objective or open to considering alternative points of view (see Box 2.3).

## Box 2.3 | ON STRONG ATTITUDES AND POLITICAL SEGREGATION

It was November 2000. Democratic nominee Al Gore led Republican George W. Bush in Electoral College votes, but Bush held a 1,784-vote lead in Florida. If Bush won Florida, he would gain enough electoral votes to win the presidency. Gore's supporters challenged the outcome, citing the time-honored rule that when an election is in doubt, you count the votes by hand. Republican partisans filed a lawsuit, arguing that manual recounts are notoriously subjective.

An automatic voting-machine-conducted recount, more objective in Bush team's eyes, had reduced Bush's margin, but still showed him the victor. Hordes of celebrity lawyers, politicians, public relations specialists, and activists streamed into Florida, trying to win the battle for public opinion.

Strong attitudes reigned supreme. Eighty-nine percent of Bush voters believed the results that proclaimed Bush the winner were a fair and accurate count. Democrats saw a different verdict: 83 percent of Gore voters perceived that the results were neither a fair nor accurate rendering of the vote (Berke & Elder, 2000). Political biases are so strong that they can even manifest themselves in brain activity. A group of psychologists asked supporters of President Bush and Democratic opponent John Kerry in 2004 to consider dissonant or consonant information about the candidates. Partisans processed the information while being monitored by magnetic resonance imaging. The reasoning arenas of their brains "shut down" when they were considering information inconsistent with their political positions, and the emotional areas lit up brightly when processing consonant information (Westen, Blagov, Harenski, Kilts, & Hamann, 2006; see also Tavris & Aronson, 2007). We do not know how pervasive these tendencies are or the causal connection between the brain and mental processing. However, the findings suggest that selective perception is a fundamental aspect of human psychology.

*Selective exposure* is also pervasive. Selective exposure is the tendency to seek out communications that embrace one's world view. To be sure, there are situations in which people deliberately look for information that contradicts their position, as when they are trying to make an important financial or medical decision and realize that they need both sides to make an informed choice (Frey, 1986). However, in subtle ways, selective exposure is a norm. People select social worlds—neighborhoods, friends, even Web sites and blogs—that reinforce their preexisting viewpoints (Iyengar & Hahn, 2009). Many of us grew up in neighborhoods peopled by individuals who shared our social attitudes and lifestyles. People tend to cluster or segregate by attitudes, so that voters are most likely to live and talk with those who share their political points of view (Bishop, 2008; Mutz, 2006). This selectivity even extends to preference for controversial movies.

In 2004, Mel Gibson's *The Passion of the Christ* and Michael Moore's *Fahrenheit 9/11* grossed hundreds of millions at the box office. But there was a striking political schism.

**Box 2.3** |

The top theaters for *Passion* were typically located in Republican strongholds: suburbs and in the West, Southwest, and South. The highest grossing theaters for *Fahrenheit* were located in urban, traditionally Democratic areas, such as New York City, Los Angeles, and San Francisco (Waxman, 2004; see Stroud, 2007 for more empirical support). This exemplifies what one writer called "political segregation"—people's tendency to prefer media that support their side and live with people like themselves.

As columnist David Brooks (2004) observed:

> Once you've joined a side, the information age makes it easier for you to surround yourself with people like yourself. And if there is one thing we have learned over the past generation, it's that we are really into self-validation. We don't only want radio programs and Web sites from members of our side—we want to live near people like ourselves . . . The information age was supposed to make distance dead, but because of clustering, geography becomes more important. The political result is that Republican places become more Republican and Democratic places become more Democratic . . . When we find ourselves in such communities, our views shift even further in the dominant direction.

(p. A27)

One final point: it may seem as if this discussion applies only to those strong-minded, ego-involved partisans out there—individuals driven to protest and agitate. Nothing could be farther from the truth. Everybody—me, you, our friends—have strong attitudes on certain topics. It may not be global warming or animal research or electoral politics. It could be fashion, Facebook, football, or video games. There are certain issues on which we all are biased and psychologically intransigent. Social judgment research leaves no doubt that when we encounter messages on these topics, we will selectively perceive information, reject viewpoints that actually might be congenial to our own, even assume the communicator harbors hostile intentions. Not me, you gently protest; I'm a reasonable person. Yes, you, I am afraid — and me too. Such is the power of strong social attitudes. Once one recognizes this, one can take steps to counteract selective biases—for example, by considering that the other individual has a legitimate point of view and that one's own perspective may blind one to the cogent arguments in the other's position.

## Attitude Accessibility

The event happened years ago, but we still remember it. On September 11, 2001, Americans received a massive, tragic jolt from their quiescence. The terrorist attacks on the World Trade Center and Pentagon had an enormous impact on the country. A particularly dramatic effect was the outpouring of patriotism that the events unleashed. Flags flew everywhere. They could be seen on houses, cars, clothing, book bags, even tattoos. People sang the national anthem and "America the Beautiful" proudly and with feeling, not mumbling the words in private embarrassment. Feelings of patriotism, long moribund, came out in waves, as Americans came to appreciate how deeply they felt about the nation's basic values—independence, freedom, liberty, and equality—and how much they loved their country.

Tragically, the events of September 11 accessed attitudes toward America. They thus provide a poignant introduction to the concept of attitude accessibility, a helpful approach to attitude dynamics developed by Russell H. Fazio. Fazio (1995) views attitude as an association between an object (person, place, or issue) and an evaluation. It's a linkage between a country (United States) and a great feeling; an ethnic identity (Black, Hispanic, Asian) and feelings of pride; or a product (Nike tennis shoes) and exhilaration. Prejudiced attitudes, by contrast, are associations between the object and feelings of disgust or hatred.

Attitudes vary along a continuum of strength. Weak attitudes are characterized by a familiarity with the object, but a lukewarm evaluation of its net worth. Your attitudes toward Denmark, Eskimos, and an infrequently advertised brand of sneakers probably fall under the weak label. You have heard of the entities, but don't have particularly positive or negative feelings toward them. You can retrieve your attitude toward these objects, but not automatically or without effort. Strong attitudes—toward country, an ethnic group, a celebrity, or favorite product—are characterized by well-learned associations between the object and your evaluation. These attitudes are so strong and enduring that we can activate them automatically from memory. Simply reading the name of the object in print will trigger the association and call the attitude to mind. (Thought experiment: look at the word "Denmark" and observe what comes to mind. Now try "U.S.A." What thoughts leap to mind? What emotions do you feel? According to accessibility theory, a global feeling about America should come to mind when you see the word on the page; see Figure 2.8).

The key constructs of the theory are accessibility and association. *Accessibility* means the degree to which attitude is automatically activated from memory. If you want a simple colloquial phrase, think of accessibility as "getting in touch with your feelings." *Associations* are links among different components of the attitude. The stronger the linkages are, the stronger is the attitude. Accessibility theory calls on a cognitive model of associative networks to explain attitude strength. It's a complex model, so an example may help you appreciate the associative notion.

Consider attitude toward America, mentioned previously. Imagine the attitude is located somewhere in your mind, with "pathways" or "roads" connecting different components of the attitude. Each component is linked with a positive or negative evaluation. Fourth of July is associated with positive affect, which radiates out (in red, white, and blue) to fireworks and hot dogs, also evaluated positively. Other components of the America concept could be freedom of speech, Thomas Jefferson, the "Star-Spangled Banner," baseball, land of opportunity, and rock 'n' roll. Many people have good feelings about these concepts. The stronger the association between the overall concept, America, and a positive evaluation is, the more likely it is that a strong, favorable attitude will come quickly to mind when people see the word "America."

Needless to say, not everyone loves America. Some Americans have a negative attitude toward their country. Racial prejudice, school violence, and poverty might be

**FIGURE 2.8** | The American flag evokes strong sentiments, typically pride and reverence for country. What comes to mind when you see these flags?
Photograph by William C. Rieter.

images of the United States that these individuals have conjured up many times. Having learned to strongly associate America with negative feelings, they have a strongly unfavorable attitude that would come automatically to mind when they encounter the name of their country (see Figure 2.9).

You see how powerful accessing can be. Associations among ideas and feelings, learned early in childhood, can form the bulwark of our attitudes. Strong attitudes can be accessed at the drop of a hat—or powerful symbol—triggering a variety of mental and behavioral reactions. (In this sense, accessibility theory resembles the symbolic attitude approach discussed earlier in the chapter.)

Stimulated by the accessibility notion, researchers have conducted numerous experiments over the past decade. They have examined factors that make it more likely that we are "in touch with" our attitudes. They also have explored the influence of

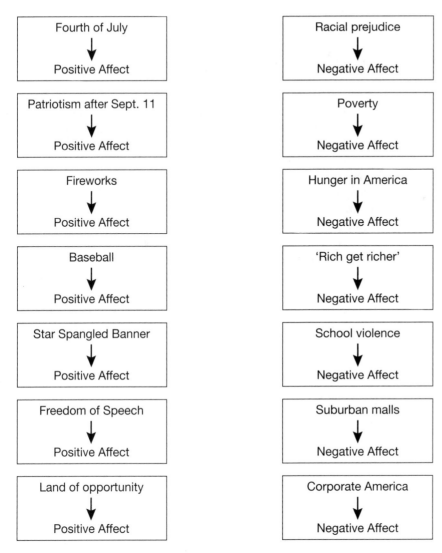

**FIGURE 2.9** | Associations and accessibility. An associative network for an individual with a positive attitude toward America (left) and negative attitude toward America (right). When attitudes are strong, they can be accessed immediately—in this case, as soon as individuals see the word "America."

accessibility on processing information (Fazio, 1990, 2000; Roskos-Ewoldsen, 1997b; Roskos-Ewoldsen, Arpan-Ralstin, & St. Pierre, 2002). In order to measure this deep-seated construct, researchers have used reaction time procedures. Participants in the study view the name or picture of an attitude object on a computer screen and indicate whether they like or dislike the object. The speed with which they push a button on the computer indexes accessibility. The quicker their response time is, the more accessible the attitude is. Guided by this and related procedures, psychologists have learned a great deal about attitude accessibility. Key findings include:

- *The more frequently that people mentally rehearse the association between an object and evaluation, the stronger the connection will be.* Thus, prejudice, on the negative side, and love, on the positive side, are strong attitudes. People have come over time to associate the object of prejudice or love with bad or good feelings. These attitudes come quickly to mind and can influence our behavior, sometimes without our being aware of it. The same processes occur with attitudes toward country, as in the example of America previously discussed.
- *Objects toward which we have accessible attitudes are more likely to capture attention* (Roskos-Ewoldsen & Fazio, 1992). Objects that are strongly associated in memory with good or bad feelings are more likely to get noticed. This has interesting implications for advertising, as is discussed in Chapter 11.
- *Accessible attitudes serve as filters for processing information.* People are more likely to process issues in a biased manner if they can access their attitudes from memory (or call them to mind in a situation). An attitude cannot influence thinking if people cannot call it to mind, and attitudes based on strong linkages between the issue and feelings are more apt to be activated when people encounter the issue in real life. An individual may have an extreme position on an issue, but unless he is in touch with his feelings on the topic, it will not influence his judgments.

Attitude accessibility, pioneered over 20 years ago, has become such a popular staple in social psychology that it has generated criticism as well as praise. Although intrigued by the concept, some researchers question whether accessibility has the strong effects Fazio attributes to it (Doll & Ajzen, 1992). Others have suggested that accessibility is less important than other aspects of attitude strength, such as the ways in which attitudes are mentally structured (Eagly & Chaiken, 1995). These are complex issues. Some researchers, like Fazio, believe that accessibility is the key aspect of attitude strength. Other researchers maintain that personal importance of the attitude is what differentiates strong from weak attitudes; still other scholars believe that ego-involvement is critical. (And you thought strong attitudes were simple!) Despite their differences, social psychologists agree that accessibility is an intriguing construct, with fascinating implications for information processing and persuasion. We access more of these applications in Chapter 3.

## IMPLICIT ATTITUDES

Some strong attitudes are characterized by a feature not discussed thus far in the book: they are outside conscious awareness. In other words, we are not consciously aware that we harbor certain feelings about the person or issue. Consider prejudiced attitudes—instances in which people blindly hate other people from different racial, ethnic, or religious groups. Prejudiced persons do not give the despised group member much chance; the mere thought or sight of the other elicits a volcanically negative response. For example, in a much publicized incident, comedian Michael Richards accessed prejudiced attitudes when he unleashed a visceral, racist series of insults against several Black men who heckled his comedy routine. Or consider the case of Amadou Diallo, which attracted considerable national attention some years back.

Diallo, born in Guinea, worked in 1999 as a peddler selling videotapes on a sidewalk in lower Manhattan. While he was standing on the steps of his apartment building one February night, his behavior aroused the suspicion of four White plainclothes police officers wearing sweatshirts and baseball caps.

Convinced that Diallo fit the description of a serial rapist who had stalked the neighborhood a year ago, one of the policemen confronted Diallo and asked to have a word with him. Frightened, Diallo ran into a nearby building. The police followed, demanding that he take his hands out of his pockets. His hand on the door knob, Diallo began slowly pulling an object from his pocket, an object that looked unmistakably to the officers like the slide of a black gun. Fearing for their lives, the officers opened fire. It was only when they examined Diallo's dead body and looked at his open palm that they could see the object up-close. It was a wallet. Diallo, the dark-skinned immigrant, perhaps thinking the police wanted to see his ID, had reached for a wallet.

Had the policemen, in that split second when impressions are formed and attitudes jell, misperceived Diallo based on stereotypes of his race? Had they categorized him as Black and therefore, at lightning-quick speed, accessed a negative attitude that led them to infer he was a criminal ready to gun them down? Perhaps.

This tragic case points up the potential power of implicit attitudes. Implicit attitudes are defined as:

> evaluations that (a) have an unknown origin (i.e., people are unaware of the basis of their evaluation); (b) are activated automatically; and (c) influence implicit responses, namely uncontrollable responses and ones that people do not view as an expression of their attitude and thus do not attempt to control.
>
> (Wilson, Lindsey, & Schooler, 2000, p. 104)

Implicit attitudes are habitual; they emerge automatically, in the absence of conscious thought. Such attitudes may be formed at an early age. As early as 6 years of age, White children display a pro-White, anti-Black evaluation (Baron & Banaji, 2006). In fairness, as children grow up, they learn about the prejudice African-Americans faced in this country and are exposed to egalitarian role models. This encourages the development of favorable attitudes toward people of different racial groups. What happens to the implicit, negative evaluation acquired at an early age? Some psychologists argue that it persists, even coexists, with a positive attitude toward the ethnic group.

Timothy D. Wilson and colleagues (2000) argue that people have *dual attitudes*: an explicit attitude that operates on a conscious level and guides much everyday behavior, and an implicit attitude that influences nonverbal behaviors and other responses over which we lack total control. The implicit attitude can be activated automatically, perhaps in highly charged emotional situations in which the individual is not able to keep feelings at bay. This may have happened to the police officers who confronted Amadou Diallo that cold February night.

There is much discussion about these issues in the academic journals. Critics note that all attitudes may not have dual components; a moderately held pro-environmental attitude may operate only on the conscious level. It may lack the preconscious primitive dimension. It is also possible that people don't have dual attitudes at all, but instead have one rather complex attitude that contains aspects they are aware of and others that elude conscious awareness. In addition, there are instances in which people are fully and proudly conscious that they hold virulently negative attitudes. One thinks of bigots who get drunk and brag about their racist, anti-Semitic, or homophobic attitudes. Finally, an implicit attitude need not always be negative; it can be positive, as are attitudes toward one's country, religion, or God. This affect can help the person cope, offering an emotional compass in times of confusion or stress.

There is much that we need to know about implicit attitudes and how dual attitudes operate. For now, these new approaches provide new insights on strong attitudes. They suggest that when people harbor highly prejudiced attitudes, the negative, gut-level feelings acquired at a young age can overwhelm or override social norms or positive attitudes acquired later. Hateful attitudes may be impervious to influence because they are so much a part of the individual or because the person is not aware of the depths of prejudice. This raises troubling questions for those of us who believe in persuasion. To what degree can prejudice be unlearned? Can a positive attitude override the negative feelings learned at a young age? Can an individual learn to focus on their higher ideals and cultivate the tolerant attitudes that are part of a more mature self? Or, when stereo-types turn to prejudice and prejudice morphs into hate, is argumentation powerless? Can people who hate ever change their minds?

## CONCLUSIONS

Attitudes—emotional, evaluative, frequently formed at a young age—are a core dimension of persuasion. Attitudes, after all, are the entities that communicators seek to shape, reinforce, mold, and change. An attitude is defined as a learned, global evaluation of an object (person, place, or issue) that influences thought and action.

Attitudes dovetail with values, defined as conceptions of desirable means and ends, and beliefs, which are defined as cognitions about the world. Beliefs can theoretically be tested to determine if they are true, although people frequently assume their beliefs are equivalent to facts. (They're not.)

One of the interesting questions about attitudes concerns their structure or organization. Expectancy–value theory says that attitudes are composed of expectations (beliefs) and evaluations of these beliefs. It emphasizes the role that salient, or psychologically relevant, beliefs play in shaping attitudes. Expectancy–value theory helps break down the macroconcept of attitude into component parts, yielding rich information about the human mind. The symbolic attitude approach argues that symbolic predispositions, like prejudice and deep-seated values, lie at the heart of attitudes. It calls attention to the many affective attributes that are associated with the attitude object. An ideological perspective contends that attitudes are organized around ideological principles, like liberalism–conservatism. Because people are complex, attitudes are not always internally consistent. Individuals frequently experience ambivalence, feeling both positively and negatively about a person or issue. Preferring harmony to discord, people strive to reduce inconsistency among cognitive elements. Balance theory and other cognitive consistency models describe ways that individuals can restore mental harmony. We don't always succeed in this endeavor, and inconsistency is inevitably a fact of life. A particularly noteworthy aspect of attitudes is their strength. Strong attitudes are characterized by personal importance, accessibility, and hierarchical organization. Social judgment theory provides many insights into the nature of strong attitudes, calling attention to ways that ego-involved partisans assimilate and contrast messages so as to maintain their original perspective on the issue.

Another factor that influences message processing is attitude accessibility. Strong attitudes are typically more accessible than weaker ones, characterized as they are by strong associations between feelings and the object (person, place, or political issue). Attitudes that come readily to mind—and are steeped in powerful emotional associations—are likely to lead to biased thinking about persuasive messages. Biased thinking is also likely when people harbor strong implicit attitudes or those excluded from awareness. Some prejudiced attitudes may operate at this level, making them resistant to persuasion.

Theory and research on strong attitudes help us understand why partisans disagree so vehemently about contemporary social issues. They size up the problem differently, perceive matters in a biased manner, and tend to be resistant to persuasive communication. Ethicists suggest that if we could just supply people with the facts, they would put aside opinions and act rationally (Frankena, 1963). Unfortunately, there are no such things as pure facts. Partisans come to the table with different interpretations of the facts. Just bringing people from different sides together cannot guarantee that they will reach agreement. This is why negotiations on issues ranging from labor–management disputes to the Middle East frequently fail.

This fact—that objective facts frequently elude us and biased perceptions are the order of the day—has become a ubiquitous part of contemporary culture. Comedian Stephen Colbert calls it "truthiness." "I'm not a fan of facts," he remarked satirically. "You see, facts can change, but my opinion will never change, no matter what the facts are" (Peyser, 2006).

All this raises the specter that one can never change strong attitudes. And, to be sure, people with strong attitudes are loath to change them, as a result of selective perception and the host of social judgment biases discussed in this chapter. But pessimists do not always have the last word. Communications have changed strongly held attitudes on a host of topics, from global warming to ethnic prejudice. Persuasion research holds out a key. Persuaders may be able to nudge people into changing their attitudes if they understand the structure, functions, and underlying dynamics of these attitudes. There is no guarantee that change will occur, but it is certainly more likely if communicators appreciate the psychology of the individuals they hope to influence.

# Chapter 3

# Attitudes: Functions and Consequences

LESLIE Maltz regards herself as a California housewife, "virtually a byword for conventionality," as a magazine reporter put it (Adler, 1999, p. 76). But a while back she did something a little different. She had her navel pierced and put "a diamond-studded horseshoe through it." As a result, she no longer regards herself as a housewife. "I feel like a sex symbol," she says (Adler, p. 76).

Leslie's bodacious decision illustrates a theme of this chapter: attitudes serve functions for people, and people must decide whether and how to translate attitudes into behavior. As we will see, the issues of attitude functions and attitude–behavior consistency are intricate, complicated, and filled with implications for persuasion. This chapter continues the exploration of attitudes launched in Chapter 2, focusing first on attitude function theory and research. The second section examines the venerable issue of attitude–behavior consistency, more colloquially expressed as: Do people practice what they preach?

## FUNCTIONS OF ATTITUDES

### Overview

Functional theories of attitude examine why people hold the attitudes they do. These approaches explore the needs that attitudes fulfill and motives they serve. Functional approaches turn attitudes on their head. Instead of taking attitudes as a given and looking at their structure, they ask: "Just what benefits do attitudes provide? What if people did not have attitudes? What then?" Bombarded by numerous stimuli and faced with countless choices about issues and products, individuals would be forced to painstakingly assess the costs and benefits of each particular choice in each of hundreds of daily decisions (Fazio, 2000). Deprived of general attitudes to help structure the environment and position individuals in certain directions, human beings would find daily life arduous. Noting that this is not the case, theorists conclude that attitudes help people manage and cope with life. In a word, attitudes are functional.

The beauty of functional theory is that it helps us understand why people hold attitudes. This not only is interesting to theorists, but also appeals to the people-watcher in us all. Ever wonder why certain people are driven to dedicate their lives to helping others, why other individuals buy fancy sports cars at the zenith of their midlives, or why younger folks, in a carefree moment, decide to get themselves tattooed? Attitude function theories shed light on these decisions.

Researchers have catalogued the main functions of attitudes or the primary *benefits* that attitudes provide (Katz, 1960; Maio & Olson, 2000a; Smith, Bruner, & White, 1956). These include:

**Knowledge.** Attitudes help people make sense of the world and explain baffling events. They provide an overarching framework, one that assists individuals in cognitively coming to terms with the array of ambiguous and sometimes scary stimuli they face in everyday life. Religious attitudes fulfill this function for many people, particularly those who have experienced personal tragedies. For example, relatives of people who were killed in the September 11 attacks found comfort in "religious certainty of a hereafter. 'A plan of exultation, a plan of salvation: they both are in a better place,'" said Margaret Wahlstrom, whose mother-in-law died at the World Trade Center (Clines, 2001, p. B8). In a similar fashion, the Kennedy family, which has experienced great highs but also crushing lows, has found solace in the Catholic religion. Religion seems to offer comfort to family members who experienced inexplicably tragic events, ranging from the assassinations of John and Bobby to the deaths of John Jr. in a plane crash and Michael in a skiing accident.

**Utilitarian.** On a more material level, attitudes help people obtain rewards and avoid punishments. Smart, but mathematically challenged students say that it is functional to develop a positive attitude toward statistics courses. They figure that if they show enthusiasm, the professor will like them more. They also recognize that if they look on the bright side of the course, they can more easily muster the motivation to study. On the other hand, if they decide at the outset to blow off the course because it's too hard, they will deprive themselves of the chance to prove themselves up to the task. In a similar vein, athletes find it functional to develop a positive—rather than hostile—attitude toward a tough coach. A positive attitude can help them get along with the "drill sergeant type," thereby minimizing the chances they will earn the coach's wrath.

**Social adjustive.** We all like to be accepted by others. Attitudes help us "adjust to" reference groups. People sometimes adopt attitudes not because they truly agree with the advocated position, but rather because they believe they will be more accepted by others if they take this side. For example, a student who wants to get along with a musically hip group of friends may find it functional to adopt a more favorable attitude toward new hip-hop bands. During the 1960s and early 1970s, political attitudes served a social adjustive function for some students. Although many young people marched in rallies to express strong attitudes (e.g., opposition to the Vietnam War), not all participated for this reason. Some students attended rallies for social adjustive purposes—to prove to others or themselves that they were "with it," or meshed with the prevailing groove of the time.

One 1970 rally in Michigan seemed to have served this function for students, as the following account from a university newspaper of the era suggests (I wrote this myself, a student reporter at the time):

> Grab your coat, you'll need it tonight. Get your gloves, find a hat; take out the contacts—tear gas can be dangerous. All right, it's 8:30, let's go. All these people, are they headed for [campus]? They are. They're laughing, chanting . . . Can't miss any of the action . . . What are we fighting? The system, I suppose, yeah, we're battling the system . . . The march is a free for all, it doesn't matter what you protest, just as long as you're here. Got to protest, just got to protest. Gotta be here, man, gotta be here . . . We're at the dorms now. "Join us, join us," someone's got music, let's dance, in the streets. What'd he say? "Everybody must get stoned." Yeah, march and get stoned. Outtasight!
>
> (Perloff, 1971, p. 24)

Although the pressures of the protest years may have pushed some students into adopting attitudes for social adjustive reasons, there is no reason to believe that the need to belong does not operate equally strongly in today's era, with its own tensions and undercurrents.

**Social identity.** People hold attitudes to communicate who they are and what that they aspire to be (Shavitt & Nelson, 2000). This is one reason people buy certain products; they hope that by displaying the product in their homes (or on their bodies), they will communicate something special about themselves. Women wear perfumes like Obsession and men don Polo cologne to communicate that they have money and brains (Twitchell, 1999). Others buy T-shirts with the names of brand-name stores (Hard Rock Café) or dates of rock band tours to tell passersby something of their identity ("I'm not just an ordinary student; I'm with the band. See my shirt?").

Other people get tattooed to express a social identity. Patriotic symbols, mythological creatures, animals, arm bands, and flowers are among the many designs people have inked on their bodies to express a group identity or enhance their sense of uniqueness. As one woman said,

> I see tattooing as crafting your body into a piece of moving art. Look at my arms . . . what is naturally attractive about a blank arm? Place a beautiful piece of art on your arm and it becomes something unique . . . Tattooing might be our generation's call to be aware of artistic bodies.
>
> (Atkinson, 2004, p. 133)

Products other than tattoos, T-shirts, and perfume can fulfill social identity functions. Electronic products can do this too. One study found that men use cell phones "to advertise to females their worth, status and desirability" (Angier, 2000a, p. D5). On our campus I have observed women holding cell phones like they are prized possessions, objects that lift these students from the pedestrian realm of test taking to the lofty arena of transacting deals or settling interpersonal dilemmas. For some men and women, attitudes toward cell phones serve a social identity function.

**Value-expressive.** An important reason people hold attitudes is to express core values and cherished beliefs. According to Maio and Olson,

> [Some individuals] claim that they favor capital punishment because they value law and order; they support affirmative action programs as a means of promoting equality; they support recycling programs because they value the environment . . . and they frown on cheating because it is dishonest.
>
> (2000b, p. 249)

The value-expressive function is pervasive. Some young people pierce their nose, tongue, belly button, or . . . well, other body parts to express a variety of values, including autonomy and independence from parents. Parents might have merely pierced a left earlobe in an age when that showcased rebelliousness. Today, ear piercings are viewed as "sooo . . . boring" by some avant-garde teens (see Figure 3.1).

**Ego-defensive.** Attitudes can serve as a "defense" against unpleasant emotions people do not want to consciously acknowledge. People adopt attitudes to shield them from psychologically uncomfortable truths. Let's say a young woman decides to break up with her boyfriend, realizing that the relationship is not going anywhere and fearing he will dump her when they go their separate ways after college. She still has feelings for her soon-to-be-ex, but to defend against these feelings and to make her position known to him clearly and with conviction, she declares in no uncertain terms that their relationship is over, kaput. Adopting a hostile attitude toward her boyfriend is functional because it helps her muster the strength she needs to call off the romance.

## ATTITUDES AND PERSUASION

A central principle of functional theory is that the same attitudes can serve different functions for different people. In other words, different people can hold the same attitude toward a person, product, or issue; however, they may harbor this view for very different reasons.

Consider attitudes toward shopping. Some people shop for utilitarian reasons. They trek to the mall to happily purchase presents for loved ones and go home once the presents are paid for. Others shop for ego-defensive reasons, to help them forget about their problems or relieve stress. Recent immigrants to America sometimes shop to satisfy value-expressive needs. To these folks, America symbolizes the freedom to do as they wish. For those who grew up in economically and socially impoverished dictatorships, the notion that you can "buy what you want when and where you want it" is one of the great appeals of the United States (Twitchell, 1999, p. 23).

**FIGURE 3.1** | Body piercing is popular among young people. It does different things for different people, or fulfills diverse psychological functions.

Photograph by William C. Rieter.

For native-born American teenagers, shopping fulfills entirely different functions. Some teens shop to reinforce a social identity. Stores like Gap, Limited, and Record Town are like "countries for the young." They offer teens a territory in which they are king and queen and can rule the roost. Malls provide adolescents with space to strut about and to shop for products that define them as distinctive and important. (Of course, critics view this somewhat differently. James B. Twitchell says that "the mall approaches a totalitarian Eden into which the innocent and the oppressed enter eagerly, lured by the dream of riches" (1999, p. 299).)

It's not just attitudes toward products that serve diverse psychological functions. People can be deeply religious for different reasons, become active in politics to satisfy different needs, even pursue identical career paths for vastly different motivations. It's fascinating to discover just how different individuals can be once you peel away the superficial attribute of attitude similarity. Such an insight emerges with particular clarity in Mark Snyder's research on the psychology of volunteerism.

Millions of Americans—as many as 89 million—annually volunteer their time and services to help sick, needy, homeless, and psychologically troubled individuals (Snyder, Clary, & Stukas, 2000). They work in soup kitchens on weekends, participate in AIDS walkathons, offer counseling to depressed youth, aid victims of disasters, and try mightily to cheer the spirits of kids who have incurable cancer. A functional theorist, moved by people's willingness to help others in need, asks why. Why do people give so generously of themselves? Do different people have different motives? Snyder and colleagues found that people volunteer for very different reasons. Their reasons include:

- expressing values related to altruistic and humanitarian concern for others;
- satisfying intellectual curiosity about the world, learning about people different from themselves;
- coping with inner conflicts (reducing guilt about being more fortunate than other people);
- providing opportunities to participate in activities valued by important others; and
- providing career-related benefits, such as new skills and professional contacts. (Snyder et al., 2000, pp. 370–371)

These functions are intriguing. They also suggest ideas for how to promote provolunteering attitudes and behavior. Functional theory suggests that *a persuasive message is most likely to change an individual's attitude when the message is directed at the underlying function the attitude serves. Messages that match the function served by an attitude should be more compelling than those that are not relevant to the function addressed by the attitude.* The more that a persuasive appeal can explain how the advocated position satisfies needs important to the individual, the greater its impact is.

Thus, if you want to recruit volunteers or persuade people to continue engaging in volunteer activities, you must appreciate why individuals chose to volunteer in the first place. One message will not fit all. The message must match the motivational function served by volunteering.

E. Gil Clary, Mark Snyder, and their colleagues dreamed up a study to test this hypothesis. They asked students to rate the importance of a series of reasons for volunteering. Reasons or functions included knowledge ("I can learn useful skills"), utilitarian ("I can gain prestige at school or work"), value-expressive ("I believe someone would help me if I were ever in a similar situation"), and ego-defensive ("Good things happen to people who do good deeds") (Clary, Snyder, Ridge, Miene, & Haugen, 1994, p. 1133). The researchers then computed each student's responses to identify the volunteering function that was most and least important to him or her. Armed with this information, Clary and colleagues assigned individuals to watch a videotaped message that recommended involvement in volunteer activities. The message targeted a student's most important volunteer function (*matched* condition) or his or her least important function (*mismatched* condition). Each student watched either a matched or mismatched videotape.

For example, if a student said that volunteering mostly served a utilitarian function, he would watch a matched videotape that contained a utilitarian appeal: "You know, what

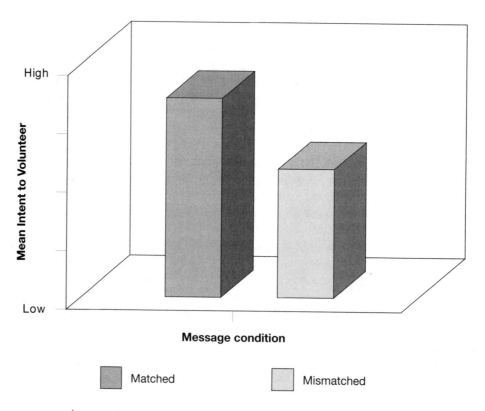

**FIGURE 3.2** | Mean intent to volunteer as a function of match of message with personal motivations.

From Clary, E. G., Snyder, M., Ridge, R. D., Miene, P. K., & Haugen, J. A. (1994). Matching messages to motives in persuasion: A functional approach to promoting volunteerism. *Journal of Applied Social Psychology, 24*, 1129–1149.

I really like about all this is that I can make myself more marketable to employers and be a volunteer at the same time." If another student indicated that volunteering primarily fulfilled a value-expressive need, she would view a matched value-expressive video that noted: "By volunteering I get to turn my concerns into actions and make a difference in someone else's life" (Clary et al., 1994, pp. 1147–1148). Other students received *mismatched* videos (e.g., a student who volunteered for value-expressive reasons watched the utilitarian video).

Students then rated the effectiveness of the videotape. The results showed that matched messages were more persuasive than mismatched ones. Videotapes that targeted students' most important volunteering functions were more appealing than those that were directed at less important functions (see Figure 3.2). The implications are intriguing: they suggest that if we know the motives that volunteering fulfills, we can promote positive attitudes toward helping others. For a person who volunteers for value-expressive reasons, the message should emphasize how volunteering can relieve suffering or contribute to the social good. But a message like this will not cut it with an individual who pursues utilitarian goals. For this person, the message should emphasize how volunteering can enhance career skills. Idealists would find it heartless that a utilitarian message is more persuasive than an altruistic appeal. They may have a point, but such is the nature of human attitudes. To change an attitude, one must understand the function it serves and direct the message to the underlying function. This works for volunteering and other attitudes as well (Hullett, 2004, 2006; Julka & Marsh, 2005).

**Attitude dysfunctions.** There is, unfortunately, a dark side to attitude functions. An attitude that helps an individual satisfy certain needs can be detrimental in another respect. An attitude can assist the person in coping with one problem, while exerting a more harmful or dysfunctional effect in another area of the person's life. Consider, for example, the teenager who "hangs" at the mall, shops constantly with friends, and gains self-identity from shopping. There's nothing wrong with shopping—it's an American pastime. But if the teen neglects studying or athletics, we could say that shopping is dysfunctional, producing negative effects on grades or performance in sports.

Consider attitudes toward body piercing. *The New York Times* reported the story of a 15-year-old named David, who had his tongue pierced over the objections of his father (Brody, 2000). The tongue pierce may have fulfilled a value-expressive function for David, a way to stake out his autonomy from his dad. But the stud in the tongue quickly became dysfunctional when David found that "for more than a week, he could hardly talk and could eat little other than mush." David now warns: "Think of the consequences and things that might happen afterward. When one says that the first five or six days is close to hell, you won't fully understand it until you get a tongue-pierce" (Brody, p. D8).

Complicating matters is the fact that attitudes can be functional for one individual, but dysfunctional for others. Talking on a cell phone can serve social identity needs for a phone buff, but try listening to someone rant and rave over the phone while you wait in line at the drugstore! Harboring prejudiced attitudes may serve an ego-defensive function for a bigot. ("It's not my fault. It's them—those blankety blank others.") However, prejudice is not exactly functional for those at the other end of the hate monger's stick.

The foregoing discussion alerts us to several problems with the functional approach. It is hard to know whether an attitude is primarily functional or dysfunctional. If it helps the individual satisfy a need, do we call it functional, even if it leads to negative consequences? How do we weigh the benefits the attitude provides the individual with negative consequences on others? It can also be difficult to identify clearly the function that an attitude serves. People may not know why they hold an attitude or may not want to admit the truth. However, no theory is perfect, and on balance the functional approach is more functional than dysfunctional for persuasion scholarship! It contains hypotheses for study and generates useful insights for everyday life. These include the following nuggets:

■ *People are deep and complicated creatures.* We often do things that appear inexplicable or strange, until we probe deeper and understand the needs they satisfy.

- *We should extend tolerance to others.* People have many reasons for holding an attitude. These may not be our motivations, but they can be subjectively important to that particular person.
- *Persuaders must be acutely sensitive to the functions attitude serve.* "What warms one ego, chills another," Gordon Allport observed (1945, p. 127). A message can only change attitudes if it connects with people's needs. One may totally disagree with a person's attitude, believing it to be immoral. However, condemning the other may be less useful than probing why the individual feels the way he or she does and gently nudging the individual toward change.

## ATTITUDES AND BEHAVIOR

- Kelly has strong values, but you wouldn't guess this by observing her in everyday situations. She is charming, likable, and adept at getting along with different kinds of people. Her friends sometimes call her a chameleon. Yet Kelly has strong views on certain issues, notably the environment and protecting endangered species. At a party, conversation turns to politics and several people advocate drilling for oil in the Arctic National Wildlife Refuge. Will Kelly take issue with their position?
- Susan is an agnostic, a skeptic who has doubts about the existence of God, and believes religion is of little use in today's society. She is a strong believer in Darwinian evolution, a forceful critic of creationist philosophy. At the same time, Susan has a soft spot for religion because it means a lot to her dad. An old friend of her dad's calls one day. He's been teaching Sunday school, but will be out of town next week when the class is scheduled to discuss the beauty of God's creation of the universe. He asks whether Susan would mind filling in for him just this once. Will Susan agree?

What's your best guess? Do these anecdotes remind you of people you know or conflicts you've experienced? These two examples are fictitious, but are based on factors studied in actual psychological experiments. They also focus on a central issue in attitude research—the connection between attitudes and behavior. The question is of theoretical and practical importance.

Theoretically, attitudes are assumed to predispose people to behave in certain ways. For example, suppose we found that attitudes had no impact on behavior. There would be less reason to study attitudes in depth. We would be better advised to spend our time exploring behavior. From a practitioner's perspective, attitudes are important only if they predict behavior. Who cares what consumers think about fast food or fast cars if their attitudes don't forecast what they buy? On the other hand, if attitudes do forecast behavior, it becomes useful for marketers to understand people's attitudes toward commercial products. Then there's us. The people watcher—intuitive psychologist—in us all is intrigued by the attitude–behavior relationship. We can all think of times when we didn't quite practice what we preached. You probably know people who frequently say one thing and do another. The research discussed in this section sheds light on these issues.

The discussion that follows examines conditions under which people are likely to display attitude–behavior consistency. A subsequent section introduces theories of the attitude–behavior relationship. The final part of the chapter views consistency in a larger perspective.

## Historical Background

It is morning in America, 1933. President Roosevelt is hard at work in Washington, DC, trying to harness the forces of government to get the country moving again. It's a daunting task. Depression and frustration are adrift in the land. People are unemployed, and some take out their anger on minorities. A psychologist, Richard LaPiere, is aware of the prejudice that one ethnic group, located in his home state of California, faces. He decides to examine the relationship between behavior and attitudes toward the Chinese.

Accompanied by a personable Chinese couple, LaPiere stops at restaurants and hotels across America. Much to his surprise, the group is served at all but one of the restaurants or hotels. But when he sends out questionnaires asking if owners would accept members of the Chinese race as guests in their establishments, over 91 percent of those surveyed reply, "No" (LaPiere, 1934).

The findings surprise LaPiere and attract the attention of scholars. It appears as if behavior (serving the Chinese) is out of whack with attitude (questionnaire responses). For years, LaPiere's findings dominate the field. Researchers conclude that attitudes do not predict behavior, and some researchers recommend that we discard the term attitude entirely (Wicker, 1969).

But hold the cell phone! It turns out that LaPiere's study had a number of problems. First, the people who waited on the Chinese couple were not those who filled out the questionnaires. Second, the survey probed intention to serve a Chinese couple, but the behavioral measure involved serving a personable Chinese couple accompanied by an educated Caucasian man.

What is more, when researchers systematically examined the relationship between attitude and behavior over the ensuing decades, they found that LaPiere's study was an anomaly. Most surveys reported significant correlations between attitudes and behavior (Fishbein & Ajzen, 1975; Kim & Hunter, 1993).

But give the early scholars their due. They correctly observed that attitudes do not *always* predict behavior. They called attention to the fact that attitudes do not forecast action nearly as well as one might assume on the basis of common sense. But they threw out the attitudinal baby with the dirty behavioral bath water! Sure, attitudes don't always predict what we will do. But that doesn't mean they aren't useful guides or aren't reasonable predictors, given the incredible complexity of everyday life. The consensus of opinion today is that attitudes do influence action; they predispose people toward certain behavioral choices, but not all the time. Under some conditions, attitudes forecast behavior; in other circumstances they do not. The relationship between attitude and behavior is exquisitely complex.

Now here's the good news: we can identify the factors that moderate the attitude–behavior relationship. Key variables are: (a) aspects of the situation, (b) characteristics of the person, and (c) qualities of the attitude (Fazio & Roskos-Ewoldsen, 1994; Zanna & Fazio, 1982).

## Situational Factors

The context—the situation we're in—exerts a powerful impact on behavior. We are not always aware of how our behavior is subtly constrained by norms, roles, and a desire to do the socially correct thing. A norm is an individual's belief about the appropriate behavior in a situation. Roles are parts we perform in everyday life, socially prescribed functions like professor, student, parent, child, and friend.

**Norms and roles.** Individuals may hold an attitude, but choose not to express the attitude because it would violate a social norm. You may not like an acquaintance at work, but realize that it violates conventional norms to criticize the person to his face. Someone may harbor prejudice toward co-workers, but be savvy enough to know that she had better hold her tongue lest she get in trouble on the job (Kiesler, Collins, & Miller, 1969).

Norms vary across cultures. In traditional Middle Eastern societies, friendly, outgoing behavior is held in low repute. Gregarious behavior that is regarded positively in the United States ("Hey, how ya' doin'?") is viewed negatively in Middle Eastern countries. Instead, the norm is to be serious, even somber in public (Yousef, 1982). Thus, a person may hide her affection for a colleague when seeing him at work. Attitude fails to predict behavior because the public display of attitude runs counter to cultural norms.

Roles also influence the attitude–behavior relationship. When people take on professional roles, they have to act the part, putting their biases aside. This helps explain why reporters, who have strong political beliefs, rarely display biases in their professional activity at newspapers or television stations. For example, many Washington reporters are liberal Democrats, but their news stories go right down the middle, offering criticism of Democrat and Republican politicians (Perloff, 1998). One of the requirements of news is that it show no favoritism to either side—that it be perceived as fair and objective. Journalists know that if they write biased news stories, they will quickly lose their jobs or will be viewed as unprofessional by colleagues. Thus, liberal political attitudes do not reliably predict reporters' public behavior.

**Scripts.** To illustrate the concept of script, I ask that you imagine you face a term paper deadline and are hard at work at your word processor. A phone rings; it's a telemarketer, the tenth to call this week. She's asking for money for injured war veterans, a cause you normally support because a relative got hurt while serving in the Iraq war. Not thinking and mindlessly putting on your "I'm busy, leave me alone" hat, you cut the volunteer off, telling her in no uncertain terms that you have work to do. Trying to be cute, you use the line from the old television quiz show: "You're the weakest link; goodbye."

Your attitude obviously didn't come into play here. If it had, you would have promised a donation. Instead, you invoked a script: an "organized bundle of expectations about an event sequence" or an activity (Abelson, 1982, p. 134). Like an actor who has memorized his lines and says them on cue, you call on well-learned rules about how to handle pushy telemarketers interrupting your day. Your expectations of how the transaction with the telemarketer is going to proceed—the overly pleasant intro, follow-up for money, plea to keep you on the phone—set the tone for the conversation, and you mindlessly follow the script rather than taking the time to consult your attitude toward veterans.

## Characteristics of the Person

Individuals differ in the extent to which they display consistency between attitudes and behavior. Some people are remarkably consistent; others are more variable. Social psychological research has helped pinpoint the ways in which personal factors moderate the attitude–behavior relationship. Two moderating factors are self-monitoring and direct experience.

**Self-monitoring.** Social psychologist Mark Snyder, whose research we glimpsed before, confidently believes people can be divided into two categories. A first group consists of individuals who are concerned with displaying appropriate behavior in social situations. Adept at reading situational cues and figuring out the expected behavior at a given place and time, these individuals adjust their behavior to fit the situation. When filling out Snyder's (1974) scale, they agree that "in different situations and with different people, I often act like very different persons." These individuals are called high self-monitors because they "*monitor* the public appearances of self they display in social situations" (Snyder, 1987, pp. 4–5).

A second group is less concerned with fitting into a situation or displaying socially correct behavior. Rather than looking to the situation to figure out how to behave, they consult their inner feelings and attitudes. "My behavior is usually an expression of my true inner feelings, attitudes, and beliefs," they proudly declare, strongly agreeing with this item in the self-monitoring scale. These individuals are called low self-monitors.

High and low self-monitors differ in plenty of ways (see Chapter 8). One relevant difference is that high self-monitors exhibit less attitude–behavior consistency than do low self-monitors (Snyder & Kendzierski, 1982; Snyder & Tanke, 1976). High self-monitors look to the situation to decide how to act; as "actor types" who enjoy doing the socially correct thing, they don't view each and every situation in life as a test of character. If a situation requires that they put their attitudes aside for a moment, they happily do so. Low self-monitors strongly disagree. Living by the credo, "To thine own self be true," low self-monitors place value on practicing what they preach and main-taining congruence between attitude and behavior. Not to do so would violate a personal canon for low self-monitors.

In the example given earlier, Kelly—the outgoing, chameleon-like young woman who has strong attitudes toward wildlife preservation—would be in a pickle if acquaintances at a party began taking an anti-environmental stand. Her personality description suggests she is a high self-monitor. If so, she would be unlikely to challenge her acquaintances. Instead, she might smile sweetly, nod her head, and resolve to talk up the environmental issue in situations where she could make a difference. Needless to say, a low self-monitor who shared Kelly's values would be foaming at the mouth when her friends began saying that we should drill for oil in the National Wildlife Refuge. She probably wouldn't hesitate to tell them how she felt.

**Direct experience.** Experience also moderates the attitude–behavior relationship. Some of our attitudes are based on direct experience with an issue; we have encountered the problem in real life, it has evoked strong feelings, or led us to think through the implications of behaving in a certain way. Other attitudes are formed indirectly—from listening to parents or peers, reading books, watching television, or partaking in Internet chat rooms. Attitudes formed through direct experience "are more clearly defined, held with greater certainty, more stable over time, and more resistant to counter influence" than attitudes formed through indirect experience (Fazio & Zanna, 1981, p. 185; see also Millar & Millar, 1996). Attitudes produced by direct experience also come more quickly to mind than attitudes acquired through indirect experiences. For these reasons, people are more apt to translate attitude into behavior when the attitude has been formed through direct experiences in real-world situations (Fazio & Zanna, 1978).

Consider a contemporary issue, but one most people don't like to talk about much: safe sex. Two teenagers may both have positive attitudes toward safe sex practices. However, one may have formed her attitude through unpleasant experiences—trying to convince a boyfriend to put on a condom—only to find him intransigent, getting scared, and then resolving to assert herself more forcefully next time around. Another young woman may have read articles about safer sex in *Cosmopolitan* and heard the condom rap from parents on different occasions. Then comes the time to decide whether to put the attitude into practice: a relationship blossoms, spring is in the air, passions lead to sex, then the excitement is broken by an awkward silence. Can you see why the teenager who developed a positive attitude toward safe sex from direct (albeit unpleasant) experience would be more likely to broach the topic of condoms than the second young woman? In the first case, the attitude would be more clearly defined and therefore be easier to call to mind at the moment of decision.

Sex is by no means the only arena in which experience moderates attitude–behavior consistency. Consider any issue about which people feel strongly, but differ in their experience: politics, education, cigarette smoking, drug use. You will invariably find that those with direct experience on an issue will be more likely to behave in accord with their attitudes. Those with less experience are apt to look to other factors to help them decide what to do. They may, therefore, be particularly likely to yield to persuasive communicators, some of whom are adept at manipulating inexperienced young people.

## Characteristics of the Attitude

As noted in Chapter 2, attitudes differ in their structure and strength. The nature of an attitude moderates the relationship between attitudes and behavior.

*General versus specific attitudes.* Ajzen and Fishbein (1977) distinguished between *general* and *highly specific* attitudes. A general attitude, the focus of discussion up to this point, is the global evaluation that cuts across different situations. A specific attitude, called *attitude toward a behavior*, is evaluation of a single act, or specific behavior that takes place in a particular context at a particular time. For example, consider the issue of predicting religious behavior from religious attitudes. The general attitude is the individual's attitude toward religion. This is the sum total of the person's evaluations of many religious behaviors, such as praying, attending religious services, partaking in holiday rituals, talking about religion in everyday life, and donating money to religious causes. The specific attitude is the attitude toward one of these behaviors at a particular place and time.

A general attitude, sometimes called *attitude toward the object*, will not predict each and every religious behavior. A Ph.D. student who is deeply religious may attend only a handful of religious services over the course of 6 months—not because he has abandoned religion, but because he is immersed in doctoral comprehensive exams and realizes he must forsake this part of his religious identity for a time. (To compensate, the student may regularly devote time to reading inspirational portions of the Bible.) The student harbors a favorable attitude toward religion, but rarely, it seems, translates attitude into behavior.

But here's the rub: if you take the dozens of other religious behaviors in which the student could (and does) partake (from praying to Bible reading), and include them in your equation, you will discover that attitude predicts behavior rather handsomely.

This is the conclusion that Fishbein and Ajzen reached in an exhaustive review of this topic. In a 1974 study—old but still good—the investigators asked people to indicate their general religious attitude, as well as how frequently they participated in each of 100 specific religious behaviors. The correlation, or association, between general attitude toward religion and any specific action was 0.15. This is a very small correlation; it means that attitude toward religion is not closely related to a particular behavior in a given situation. But when Fishbein and Ajzen looked at the overall behavior pattern, focusing not on one situation but rather on the sum total, they discovered that the relationship between attitude toward religion and religious behavior was substantial. The correlation was 0.71, approaching 1 (the latter a perfect correlation).

Other researchers, focusing on different behaviors, have obtained similar findings. For example, Weigel and Newman (1976) found that individuals who had favorable attitudes toward environmental preservation were more likely than those with less positive attitudes to participate in a variety of environmental protection projects. The projects included signing petitions opposing construction of nuclear power plants, distributing petitions to family members and friends, and taking part in a roadside litter pickup. The more positive individuals' environmental attitudes were, the more likely they were to engage in a broad range of pro-environmental activities.

However, harboring a positive attitude toward the environment did not lead people to participate in each and every environmental cause. For example, one woman who scored high on the environmental attitude scale declined to participate in a litter pickup project. Her husband asked her not to do so. Apparently, the man was also an environmentalist, and as luck would have it, planned to organize a local Boy Scout troop in a similar project. He feared that his wife's litter pickup project might interfere with his plans. His wife, either because she agreed with him or chose to be deferent, opted not to participate in the pickup project.

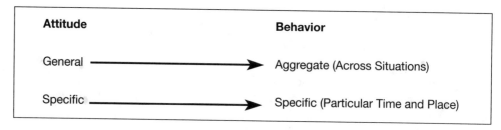

**FIGURE 3.3** | Compatibility principle. Arrows denote strong relationships between attitude and behavior. General attitude will not predict specific behavior, and a specific attitude will not forecast behavior in the aggregate.

Again, it was not that the woman had displayed marked inconsistency between attitude and behavior, for she apparently translated her environmental attitude into action across most other domains (signing petitions, distributing them, and so forth). It was that, as often happens in life, something else came up. If you wished to predict the woman's behavior in particular circumstances, you would be better advised, Fishbein and Ajzen say, to consider her *specific attitude* toward participating in the environmental project in question.

These ideas are an outgrowth of what Ajzen and Fishbein (1977) call *the compatibility principle*. A strong relationship between attitude and behavior is possible only if the attitudinal predictor corresponds with the behavioral criteria. "Corresponds with" means that the attitudinal and behavioral entities are measured at the same level of specificity. Thus, specific attitudes toward a behavior predict highly specific acts. General attitudes predict broad classes of behavior that cut across different situations (see Figure 3.3).

**Attitude strength.** Another moderator of the attitude–behavior relationship is the strength of the individual's attitude. Strong attitudes are particularly likely to forecast behavior (Lord, Lepper, & Mackie, 1984). This makes sense psychologically and resonates with ordinary experience. Those with strong convictions on issues ranging from abortion to gay rights are the ones who are out there on the picket lines or are lobbying Congress to pass legislation favorable to their groups.

It gets more complicated when you consider those instances when we're ambivalent about issues. When people have strong feelings on both sides of an issue or are torn between head and heart, they are less apt to translate attitude into behavior (Armitage & Conner, 2000; Lavine, Thomsen, Zanna, & Borgida, 1998). Different feelings push people in different behavioral directions. Alternatively, the affective aspect of an attitude (feelings) can propel people toward one choice, while the cognitive dimension (beliefs) can push them in a different direction. Faced with these cross-pressures, individuals may behave in accord with their attitude in one situation, but not so much in another.

Consider the case of Susan, the agnostic who believes strongly in evolution, but has a soft spot for religion because it means a lot to her dad. Asked to teach a Sunday school class in which she has to take a creationist position on evolution, Susan is likely to have mixed feelings. Her negative views toward religion should propel her to reject the request. (Fishbein and Ajzen's model suggests that her specific negative evaluation of teaching creationism should also push her in that direction.) However, cognition clashes with affect: Susan's relationship with her dad means a lot, and the call from an old friend of her father evokes fond memories. If heart governs head and feelings overpower thoughts, she is likely to agree to teach the class. If she opts to base her decision on logic, she will politely decline. Much depends on what information comes to mind at the moment of decision, and how she goes about deciding which course to take (Wang Erber, Hodges, & Wilson, 1995).

Consider another example: many women are ambivalent about abortion, believing that it is wrong but also fearing the consequences of bringing an unwanted child into the world. "People will come into my office in tears and say they've been against abortion their whole lives, but they'll make an exception for themselves," one obstetrician said (Harmon, 2004, p. 19). Critics would call such women hypocrites, but a persuasion scholar would be more forgiving, noting that consistency is not likely when people have positive and negative beliefs about an issue; values pull them one way and affect pushes them another.

# MODELS OF ATTITUDE–BEHAVIOR RELATIONS

As we have seen, people are complex. They can be consistent, practicing what they preach, or they can surprise you, doing things that you would not expect based on their attitudes. Research sheds light on these phenomena. We know that attitudes frequently guide behavior, though under some circumstances, for some individuals, and with some attitudes more than others. The studies offer a patchwork—a pastiche—of conditions under which attitudes are more or less likely to influence action. Social scientists prefer more organized frameworks, such as models that explain and predict behavior. Three models of attitude–behavior relations have been proposed: the theory of reasoned action, the theory of planned behavior, and the accessibility model.

## Theory of Reasoned Action

Fishbein and Ajzen, who brought you the precision of the compatibility principle, also formulated a major model of attitude–behavior consistency: the theory of reasoned action (Fishbein & Ajzen, 1975). The model assumes that people rationally calculate the costs and benefits of engaging in a particular action and think carefully about how important others will view the behavior under consideration. The hallmark of the model is its emphasis on conscious deliberation.

There are four components of the theory. The first is *attitude toward the behavior* ("the person's judgment that performing the behavior is good or bad"); the second is *subjective norm* ("the person's perceptions of the social pressures put on him to perform or not perform the behavior in question"; Ajzen & Fishbein, 1980, p. 6). The third component is *behavioral intention*, the intent or plan to perform the behavior. The final aspect is behavior itself—action in a particular situation (see Figure 3.4). Although the terms in the model are abstract, the theory has many practical applications.

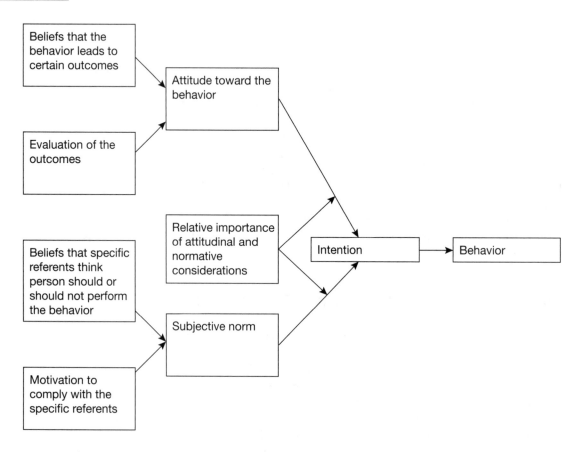

**FIGURE 3.4** | The theory of reasoned action.

Consider this example: after you graduate, you land a job with the American Cancer Society. Your task is to explore why some young people succeed in quitting smoking and why others fail. You recall that the theory of reasoned action is a major model of attitude–behavior relations and focus your empirical efforts on the reasoned action approach. It's a smart choice. The theory offers precise strategies for assessing attitudes and has an excellent track record in forecasting actual behavior (Sutton, 1998). Let's examine the model and its applications to smoking in detail next.

**Attitude.** Attitude toward the behavior is a highly specific attitude. It consists of two subcomponents: behavioral beliefs (beliefs about consequences of the behavior) and outcome evaluations (evaluations of the consequences). These two elements are combined, as they were in the simple expectancy–value model described in Chapter 2. Each behavioral belief is multiplied by the corresponding evaluation, and results are summed across items. Beliefs and evaluations regarding quitting smoking could be measured in the following way:

*Behavioral beliefs*

1.  Quitting smoking will increase my physical endurance.

    (Likely)   1   2   3   4   5   6   7   (Unlikely)

2.  Quitting smoking will cause me to gain weight.

    (Likely)   1   2   3   4   5   6   7   (Unlikely)

*Outcome evaluations*

1.  Increasing my physical endurance is:

    (Good)   1   2   3   4   5   6   7   (Bad)

2.  Gaining weight is:

    (Good)   1   2   3   4   5   6   7   (Bad)

**Subjective norm.** This factor also consists of two components: normative beliefs ("the person's beliefs that specific individuals or groups think he should or should not perform the behavior") and motivation to comply (the individual's motivation to go along with these significant others) (Ajzen & Fishbein, 1980). Subjective norms are calculated by multiplying the normative belief score by the corresponding motivation to comply and then summing across all items.

*Normative beliefs*

1.  My mom thinks:

    (I definitely                    (I definitely
    should quit   1   2   3   4   5   6   7   should not quit
    smoking)                         smoking)

2.  My girlfriend/boyfriend thinks:

    (I definitely                    (I definitely
    should quit   1   2   3   4   5   6   7   should not quit
    smoking)                         smoking)

*Motivation to comply*

In general, how much do you care about what each of the following thinks you should do:

1.  My mom:

    (Care                            (Do not
    very much)   1   2   3   4   5   6   7   care at all)

2. My girlfriend/boyfriend:

(Care
very much)   1  2  3  4  5  6  7  (Do not
care at all)

**Behavioral intention.** As the name suggests, behavioral intention is the intention to perform a particular behavior, a plan to put behavior into effect. Intention to quit smoking, measured as specifically as possible, could be assessed in this way:

I intend to quit smoking tomorrow.

(Likely)  1  2  3  4  5  6  7  (Unlikely)

Intention is a function of attitude toward the behavior and subjective norm. For example, if I have a strong, favorable attitude toward quitting and everyone around me wants me to quit, I am apt to say that I will give quitting a try. I am likely to formulate a plan to quit smoking cigarettes.

The model uses a mathematical formula to combine attitude and norm. It relies on empirically derived criteria that take into account the particular situation in which the behavior occurs.

**Behavior.** Fishbein and Ajzen argue that most social behavior is under the individual's control. Thus, intention to perform a particular behavior should predict the actual performance of the act. However, intention is most likely to predict behavior when it corresponds with—is identical to—the behavior in key ways. If you want to predict whether teenagers will quit smoking high-tar cigarettes tomorrow, you should ask them if they intend to quit smoking such cigarettes tomorrow. Asking them if they plan to stop smoking or stop engaging in risky behavior is too general and would not predict this specific behavior.

**Predicting behavior from attitude.** The theory of reasoned action allows us to specify the precise impact that attitudes exert on behavior. In the present case, young people who strongly believe that quitting smoking will lead to positive outcomes should be especially likely to intend to quit smoking. In the same fashion, teenagers who find smoking satisfying—those who hold a negative attitude toward quitting—should not plan to quit smoking. These individuals may believe that if they quit smoking, they will gain weight— a highly undesirable outcome. In either case, attitude predicts behavior.

In some cases, though, attitude will not forecast action. An adolescent might positively evaluate smoking, but decide to quit because significant others keep bugging her to give up the habit. In this case, attitude is less important than subjective norm. Social pressures trump attitude.

Thus, the theory offers a framework for predicting behavior from attitudes. While earlier researchers might have thrown up their hands when they discovered attitudes do not always predict action, concluding that behavior is ultimately not predictable, Fishbein and Ajzen offer a calmer, more reasoned approach. They caution that behavior can be predicted, but you need to consider both likes and dislikes (attitudes) and people's natural propensity to want to please others (norms).

The theory has an excellent track record in predicting behavior. Numerous studies have tested its propositions. They have found that attitudes and subjective norms forecast intentions, and intentions help predict behavior (Ajzen & Fishbein, 2005; Hale, House-holder, & Greene, 2002; Sheeran, Abraham, & Orbell, 1999; Sutton, 1998; Wallace, Paulson, Lord, & Bond, 2005). For example, attitudes and subjective norms forecast:

- intentions to eat meals in fast-food restaurants (Brinberg & Durand, 1983);
- women's occupational orientations (Sperber, Fishbein, & Ajzen, 1980);
- condom use among high-risk heterosexual adults (Morrison, Gillmore, & Baker, 1995); and
- breast-feeding or bottle-feeding infants (Manstead, Proffitt, & Smart, 1983).

Over the years, Fishbein has extended the theory, adding a component and applying it to different domains. He has expanded subjective norm to include not only perceptions of what important others think the individual should do, but also perceptions of what the others are actually doing. For example, researchers studying healthy eating behavior might ask respondents to indicate the degree to which significant others think they should or should not eat five servings of fruits and vegetables most days over the course of a year (the traditional measure) and the extent to which important others actually ate five or more servings of vegetables and fruits most days over the past year. Fishbein and colleagues believe that the use of both measures can enhance the ability to predict intentions and behaviors (Fishbein, 2000; Smith-McLallen & Fishbein, 2008).

**Shortcomings.** Although it has a good batting average for predicting behavior, and particularly intention, reasoned action theory (like all approaches) has limitations. Some scholars protest that attitude and behavioral intention measures are virtually the same, making predictions obvious and not so interesting. Others note that contrary to the assumption that the impact of attitudes on behavior is mediated by intentions, attitudes exert a direct impact on behavior (Bentler & Speckhart, 1979; Fazio, Powell, & Williams, 1989). The main shortcoming of the model, though, is that it assumes that people have control over their behavior—in other words, that they are psychologically capable of acting on their attitude or carrying out their intentions. In some cases, this assumption is not tenable. What happens when people lack control or perceive that they can't control their behavior? For example, what of the person who wants to lose weight, but can't muster the psychological strength; the individual who wants to stop binge drinking but can't; or the woman who wants to say no to unsafe sex, but in the heat of the moment, finds herself psychologically unable to reject her boyfriend's advances? In such cases, the theory of reasoned action breaks down: people don't act on attitude or norm. They do not do what they intend.

Noting the problem, Icek Ajzen, one of the architects of the reasoned action model, proposed an alternative approach. Like a rock star who drops out of a big band to sing songs solo, Ajzen had his own message to impart. While clearly showing respect for the Fishbein–Ajzen model, Ajzen argued that another theory might do a better job of forecasting behavior.

## Theory of Planned Behavior

Ajzen (1991) developed a theory of planned behavior that adds another component to the reasoned action model: perceived behavioral control. Ajzen argues that behavioral intention is determined by three factors: attitude, subjective norm, and perceptions of behavioral control. Perceived behavioral control is the individual's perception of how much control he or she has over the behavior; it is a subjective estimate of how easy or difficult it will be to perform the behavior. The more I perceive that I can perform the action, the more successful I should be in translating intention into behavior (see Figure 3.5).

Like the reasoned action approach, the theory of planned behavior has an excellent track record in predicting behavior (Conner & Armitage, 1998; Sutton, 1998). If you want to predict whether someone is going to quit smoking, you would definitely want to consider the planned behavior model. If you've smoked and tried unsuccessfully to quit, you can appreciate the important role that personal control plays in your efforts to break the habit. Perceived behavioral control could be measured in the following way:

> Now this is just a "what if" question, but if you decided you were going to quit
> smoking tomorrow, how sure are you that you could?
>
> (Extremely sure    1  2  3  4  5  6  7    (Extremely sure
> I could)                                 I could not)

**Summary.** Despite their differences, planned behavior and reasoned action theories both emphasize that attitudes can predict behavior under certain circumstances. They also

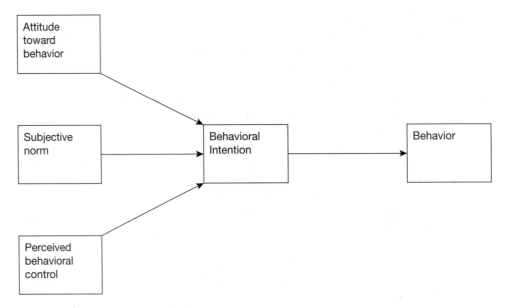

**FIGURE 3.5** | Theory of planned behavior.

acknowledge that attitudes will not predict behavior when subjective norms apply, or when people lack the psychological ability to translate attitude into action. When strong social pressures are present, attitudes do not accurately forecast behavior (Wallace et al., 2005). When individuals fear that peers or an authority figure will disapprove of their behavior, they do not always practice what they preach. Their attitudes do not forecast behavior.

In addition, when people unconsciously harbor negative feelings toward ethnic groups, they may indicate on a questionnaire that they are unprejudiced, but viscerally behave negatively toward a member of the group. When they hold a strong implicit prejudice, their conscious expression of the attitude on the survey will not predict negative body language toward a member of the disliked group (Ajzen & Fishbein, 2005).

Neither reasoned action nor planned behavior says that attitudes always predict behavior, only that attitudes are a reasonably accurate indicator of what people will do, provided certain conditions are met. There will always be circumstances in which people, being complex, will behave on the basis of factors other than attitude.

## Accessibility Theory

It's a humid summer day, and you feel like a cold one. Glancing over the usual suspects—Miller Lite, Coors, Michelob, Bud Lite—your mouth watering, you want to make a quick choice of which six-pack to buy at the convenience store. Suddenly, the expression "Whazzup?" from an advertisement of some years back leaps into your mind. You smile, and reach for the Budweiser.

According to Fazio's accessibility model (see Chapter 2), your attitude toward Budweiser is accessible, or capable of being quickly activated from memory. Your favorable attitude toward Bud Lite predicts your purchase behavior. Now if we wanted, we could measure your behavioral beliefs, normative beliefs, perceptions of behavioral control, and other variables from the models previously discussed. However, all this would be beside the point and far too laborious a process, according to accessibility theory. The core notion of accessibility theory is that attitudes will predict behavior if they can be activated from memory at the time of a decision. If a person is in touch with her attitudes, she will act on them. If not, she will be swayed by salient aspects of the situation.

This captures the gist of the model, but the core notions are more complicated. In reality, two things must transpire for an attitude to influence behavior. First, the attitude must come spontaneously to mind in a situation. That is, it must be activated from memory. Second, the attitude must influence perceptions of an issue or person, serving "as a filter through which the object is viewed" (Fazio & Roskos-Ewoldsen, 1994, p. 85). These perceptions should then color the way people define the situation, pushing them to behave in sync with their attitude. (If people do not call up their attitude from memory, they will be susceptible to influence from other factors in the situation, such as norms or eye-catching stimuli; see Figure 3.6).

In short: you can harbor an attitude toward a person or issue, but unless the attitude comes to mind when you encounter the other person or issue, you cannot act on the attitude in a particular situation. This is one reason why it's good to be in touch with your attitudes: you can act on them when important issues come up in life.

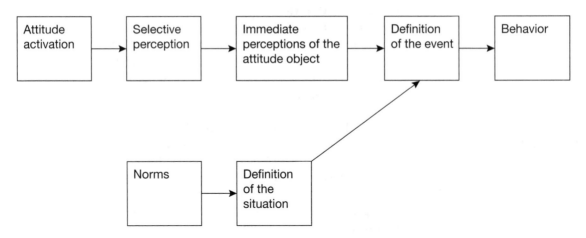

**FIGURE 3.6** | Fazio's attitude-to-behavior process model.

From Fazio, R. H., & Roskos-Ewoldsen, D. R. (1994). Acting as we feel: When and how attitudes guide behavior. In S. Shavitt & T. C. Brock (Eds.), *Persuasion: Psychological insights and perspectives* (pp. 71–93). Boston: Allyn and Bacon.

Accessibility theory complements the reasoned action/planned behavior approach. Fazio argues that under some conditions people behave like Fishbein and Ajzen (1975) suggest: they carefully consider the consequences of behaving in a particular fashion and deliberate about pros and cons of doing x or y. But when people lack the motivation or opportunity to deliberate in this fashion, they act more spontaneously. In such situations, attitude can guide behavior if people automatically call up attitudes from memory.

Research supports these propositions (Kraus, 1995). One study found that individuals who were "in touch" with attitudes toward then-President Reagan were more likely to vote for Reagan than those who could not quickly access their favorable assessment of Reagan (Fazio & Williams, 1986; see also Bassili, 1995). In a similar vein, students who could immediately call to mind a favorable attitude toward food products were more inclined to select these products as a free gift than those with less accessible attitudes (Fazio et al., 1989). Interestingly, two students might have equally favorable attitudes toward Snickers candy bar. The student who was more "in touch" with her feelings about Snickers—who could say immediately that she loved Snickers—was more likely to select Snickers than a fellow student who had to think a little before recognizing how much she adored Snickers.

## IMPLICATIONS FOR PERSUASION

Research on attitude–behavior consistency tells us a great deal about attitudes. But what does it say about persuasion? Quite a bit, as it turns out. Ultimately, most persuaders want to change behavior, and they hope to do so by influencing attitudes. The more researchers know about when and how attitudes influence behavior, the more useful their recommendations are to real-life persuaders. Imagine that as a follow-up to your work for the American Cancer Society you are asked to devise a media campaign to convince teenagers to quit smoking. The three theories discussed suggest different types of campaign strategies. First, the theory of reasoned action suggests that as a campaign coordinator, you should:

- *Target relevant beliefs.* You should probe teens' salient or relevant beliefs to discover what would induce them to give up smoking. Don't assume reasons that apply to you also apply to adolescents. Teenagers might tell you that they are least concerned with dying (they think they will live forever), but believe that smoking causes body odors or leads others to think smokers are uncool. Use this information to devise campaign messages.
- *Locate relevant reference groups.* Teens may be more influenced by peers than by the surgeon general, but the particular peers will differ depending on the subculture.

Planned behavior theory, by contrast, suggests that you convince young people that they are psychologically capable of quitting. Messages could remind young people that they, not their parents or friends, are the ones lighting up cigarettes, and that they have the power to quit (Parker, Stradling, & Manstead, 1996). Accessibility theory takes a different tack. It suggests that campaign planners put teenagers in touch with their desire to quit smoking. Teens might draw a self-portrait of what they look and feel like when they have smoked too many cigarettes. They could carry the picture in their wallets and look at it whenever they are tempted to take a puff. This might remind them of their commitment to give up smoking.

## JUDGING CONSISTENCY

**Hypocrite**. This term frequently gets bandied about when people observe inconsistencies between attitudes and behavior. It reflects an ethical concern, the belief that an individual is not living up to prescribed standards. Now that you have an appreciation for the complex underpinnings of attitude–behavior consistency, we can proceed to this more controversial aspect of the consistency issue.

Every day, it seems, we hear of famous men or women behaving badly and subsequently earning the wrath of observers, who call them hypocrites. Thomas Jefferson is the classic example. The egalitarian author of the Declaration of Independence, who penned that "all men are created equal," owned more than 100 slaves and believed that Blacks are inferior in mind and body to Whites. Was Jefferson a hypocrite, or a complicated man who harbored both revolutionary and prejudiced attitudes? A more recent example of alleged hypocrisy in a president involves Bill Clinton's relationship with Monica Lewinsky.

During his first term and while running for re-election in 1996, Clinton championed family values, telegraphing what appeared to be a positive attitude toward marriage and monogamy. Yet he behaved quite differently, cheating on his wife and engaging in a long, sordid affair with Lewinsky. Critics pointed to the blatant contradictions between Clinton's words and actions (Bennett, 1998). Others viewed the situation differently. We should be wary of "judging a complex being by a simple standard," one psychoanalyst said of the Clinton quandary. "To equate consistency with moral (and political) virtue, and then to demand consistency of people," wrote Adam Phillips, "can only cultivate people's sense of personal failure" (1998, p. A27). In other words, we should not ask people to be consistent. To do so is to set people up for failure, as none of us is perfect in this regard.

Consider the case of Reverend Jesse Jackson, who preached religious values, commitment to Biblical commandments like "Thou shalt not commit adultery," and counseled President Clinton regarding his sexual sins. In early 2001, the public learned that Jackson fathered a child out of wedlock. Was Jackson a hypocrite? He would seem to be, if one consults the Webster's dictionary definition. A hypocrite, the dictionary tells us, is one who pretends to be what he or she is not, or harbors principles or beliefs that he or she does not have. However, critic Michael Eric Dyson, taking a different view of hypocrisy, viewed Jackson differently. Dyson argued:

> It is not hypocritical to fail to achieve the moral standards that one believes are correct. Hypocrisy comes when leaders conjure moral standards that they refuse to apply to themselves and when they do not accept the same consequences they imagine for others who offend moral standards.
>
> (2001, p. A23)

Noting that Jackson accepted responsibility for his behavior, Dyson said he was not a hypocrite.

More recently, critics accused Governor Sarah Palin, the 2008 Republican vice-presidential candidate, of hypocrisy. As a family-values conservative, she publicly supported abstinence-until-marriage education in schools. However, her unmarried 17-year-old daughter, Bristol, became pregnant, suggesting to some that she had not practiced what she preached when it came to her own family. Others were more tolerant. "The media is already trying to spin this as evidence that Governor Palin is a hypocrite," noted James Dobson, the founder of Focus on the Family. "But all it really means is that she and her family are human" (Nagourney, 2008, p. A18).

Thus, the term "hypocrite" is subject to different readings and different points of view. In trying to decide if someone behaved in a hypocritical fashion, a variety of issues emerge. What criteria do we use to say that someone is a hypocrite? Is it enough for the individual to display one inconsistency between attitude and behavior? Or is that too harsh a criterion? How many inconsistencies must the person commit before the hypocrite label fits? Do certain inconsistencies get more weight than others? Does a blatant violation of an individual's deeply held values cut more to the heart of hypocrisy than other inconsistencies? Are certain kinds of attitude–behavior inconsistencies (e.g., violations of marital oaths) more ethically problematic and therefore more deserving of the hypocrite label than others? Is hypocrisy culturally relative, with certain kinds of inconsistencies more apt to be regarded as hypocritical in one culture than in another? Does application of the label "hypocrite" tell us more about the observer than the person being judged?

There are no absolute answers to these questions. Like other issues in the psychology of persuasion, they are complex, controversial, and shaded in gray rather than black or white.

## CONCLUSIONS

Attitude research sheds light on the reasons people hold the attitudes they do and the degree to which attitudes predict behavior.

Functional theory stipulates that people would not hold attitudes unless they satisfied core human needs. Attitudes help people cope, serving knowledge, utilitarian, social adjustive, social identity, value-expressive, and ego-defense functions. Two people can hold the same attitude for different reasons, and an attitude that is functional for one person may be dysfunctional for someone else. An attitude can help a person function nicely in one part of his or her life, while leading to negative consequences in another domain. Attitude function research also suggests strategies for attitude change. It emphasizes that persuaders should probe the function a particular attitude serves for an individual and design the message so that it matches this need.

The bottom-line question for attitude researchers is whether attitudes forecast behavior. Decades of research have made it abundantly clear that attitudes do not always predict behavior and people are not entirely consistent. People are especially unlikely to translate attitude into behavior when norms and scripts operate, they are ambivalent about the issue, or they regard themselves as high self-monitors. Under a variety of other conditions, attitudes predict behavior handsomely. When attitudes and behavior are measured at the same level of specificity, attitudes forecast behavior. Attitudes guide and influence behavior, but not in every life situation.

Three models of attitude–behavior consistency—theory of reasoned action, theory of planned behavior, and accessibility theory—offer rich insights into attitude–behavior relations. The models tell us that under some conditions people will deliberate on attitudes, thoughtfully considering their implications for behavior, while in other circumstances individuals spontaneously use their feelings as a guide for action. These models and empirical research help us understand when and why people are consistent.

There is a tension between the theories' reasoned predictions and the ultimate unpredictability of humans in everyday life. An individual may recognize the benefits of staying calm in the heat of an argument with an acquaintance, yet lash out physically against the other person. You may positively evaluate safe sex, but in the passion of the moment, conveniently forget about the condom sitting on the dresser. A co-worker may feel that it is important to complete assignments on time. However, feeling lonely and frustrated, she gets drunk the night before and fails to turn in the assignment until after the deadline has passed. People are not always consistent. Theories strive to capture the complexity of human behavior, but do not always succeed because of the many factors that come into play. Still, attitude–behavior models have done much to help shed light on the circumstances under which attitudes forecast behavior. They remind us that, even if you can't predict all the people all the time, you can do a much better job of accounting for human behavior if you take attitudes, norms, and intentions into account.

Consistency between attitude and behavior—or practicing what you preach—remains a core aspect of human character, the essence of integrity. But because we are human beings, the promise of rewards or desire to fit in can thwart attempts of the best of us to act on what we know to be our attitude or moral values. As the noted military leader Norman Schwarzkopf said, "The truth of the matter is that you always know the right thing to do. The hard part is doing it" (Dowd, 2006a, p. A23).

# Chapter 4

# Attitude Measurement

Pollsters do it with precision. Theorists do it with conceptual flair. Survey researchers do it for a living. "It," of course, is designing questionnaires to measure attitudes!

Puns and double entendres aside, attitude measurement plays a critical role in the study and practice of persuasion. It is the practical side of the field, the down-to-earth domain that provides the instrumentation to test hypotheses and to track changes in attitudes and beliefs. If there were no reliable scientific techniques to measure attitudes, we would not know how people evaluated social and political issues. We would not know the impact that persuasive communications had on people's feelings and thoughts. Documenting the effects of large-scale media campaigns would permanently elude us.

This chapter explores the main themes in attitude measurement. It describes scales used to tap attitudes, as well as the pitfalls and challenges researchers face when trying to assess attitudes empirically. After reading this chapter, you should know more about how to write good attitude questions and how to locate valid surveys that measure specific attitudes.

## OVERVIEW

Attitude questionnaires date back to 1928. It was in this year that psychologist Louis Thurstone published an article titled "Attitudes Can Be Measured." Thurstone proposed an elaborate procedure to assess people's views on social issues. Although measurement techniques have been streamlined over the years, Thurstone "started the fire." We now have established methodologies for assessing attitudes. What's more, thousands of questionnaires have been developed to tap beliefs and attitudes on countless issues.

Are you interested in attitudes toward race or affirmative action? You can find dozens of surveys, such as those developed by McConahay (1986) and Schmermund, Sellers, Mueller, and Crosby (2001). Do you want to explore attitudes toward the homeless? Aberson and McVean (2008) developed a scale to measure biases toward homeless individuals. Are you curious where the public stands on same-sex marriage and civil unions? If so, you can check out questionnaire measures appearing in Brewer and Wilcox (2005). Did a recent trip to Las Vegas whet your intellectual appetite toward gambling? If so, you can find a valid scale tapping gambling passion in an article by Rousseau and associates (2002). There are questionnaires tapping attitudes on hundreds of issues, including religion, abortion, environmental pollution, prejudice against fat people, adulation of thin models, sex, sex roles, basking in the glory of sports teams, political activism, even cloning human beings.

It is not easy to write good attitude questions. You can appreciate this if you have ever tried to dream up questions assessing views on one or another issue. Administering your survey to others, you may have found respondents scratching their heads and asking, "What do you mean by this question?" Devising reliable attitude items is not as easy as it looks.

There are people who do this for a living—folks who are so proficient at devising questions that they work for professional research centers or advertising firms. There is a science to writing attitude questions, one that calls on principles of measurement, statistics, and cognitive psychology (Hippler, Schwarz, & Sudman, 1987; Tourangeau & Rasinski, 1988). It all flows from an underlying belief—core assumption—that one can measure phenomena by assigning numbers to objects on the basis of rules or guidelines (Stevens, 1950; see Figure 4.1).

Perhaps the simplest way to assess attitudes is to ask people if they like or dislike the attitude object. Gallup polls tap Americans' attitudes toward the president by asking if they approve or disapprove of the way the chief executive is handling the job of president. However, there are two problems with this procedure. First, the agree–disagree scale offers people only two choices. It does not allow for shades of gray. Second, it measures attitudes with only one item. This puts all the researcher's eggs in one basket. If the item is ambiguous or the respondent misunderstands the question, then all hope of accurately measuring the attitude disappears. In addition, by relying on only one item, the researcher misses the opportunity to tap complex, even contradictory, components of the attitude.

For these reasons, researchers prefer to include many survey items and to assess attitudes along a numerical continuum. Questionnaires that employ these procedures are called scales. There are three standard attitude scales: (a) Likert, (b) Guttman, and (c) the semantic differential.

## QUESTIONNAIRE MEASURES OF ATTITUDE

### Likert Scale

The nice thing about being the first to do something is that they name it after you.

A psychologist named Rensis Likert refined Thurstone's procedures in 1932. Likert recommended that researchers devise a series of opinion statements and ask individuals to indicate their agreement or disagreement with each statement along a numerical scale. A Likert scale assumes that each item taps the same underlying attitude and there are significant interrelationships among items. It also presumes that there are equal intervals

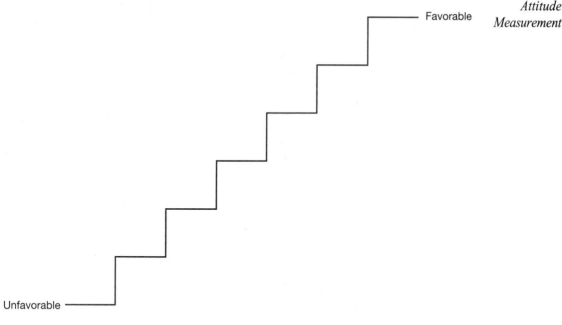

Favorable

Unfavorable

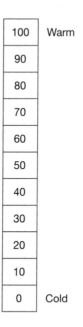

| | |
|---|---|
| 100 | Warm |
| 90 | |
| 80 | |
| 70 | |
| 60 | |
| 50 | |
| 40 | |
| 30 | |
| 20 | |
| 10 | |
| 0 | Cold |

**FIGURE 4.1** │ Two different types of numerical attitude scales.

Adapted from Ostrom, T. M., Bond, C. F., Jr., Krosnick, J. A., & Sedikides, C. (1994). Attitude scales: How we measure the unmeasurable. In S. Shavitt & T. C. Brock (Eds.), *Persuasion: Psychological insights and perspectives* (pp. 15–42). Boston: Allyn and Bacon.

between categories. For example, on a 5-point (*strongly agree, somewhat agree, neutral, somewhat disagree, strongly disagree*) scale, researchers assume that the psychological difference between strongly agree and somewhat agree is the same as that between strongly disagree and somewhat disagree.

Likert scales are commonplace today. No doubt you've completed dozens of these strongly agree–strongly disagree surveys. An example is the course evaluation question-naire students complete on the last day of class. (You know, the day your professor acts oh-so-nice to you and bakes those fudge brownies!) Students indicate how much they agree or disagree with statements regarding the prof's teaching abilities and the course content.

Likert scales can proceed from 1 to 5, as noted previously. They can also go from 1 to 7, 1 to 9, or 1 to 100. Most researchers prefer 5- or 7-point scales because they allow respondents to indicate shades of gray in their opinions, but do not provide so many categories that people feel overwhelmed by choices. A sample Likert scale, measuring attitudes toward sex roles, appears in Table 4.1. You might enjoy completing it to see how you feel about this issue.

**TABLE 4.1** | Likert scale for sex role attitudes

Please indicate whether you Strongly Agree (SA), Agree (A), are Neutral (N), Disagree (D), or Strongly Disagree (SD) with each of these statements.

| | | SA | A | N | D | SD |
|---|---|---|---|---|---|---|
| 1. | Women are more emotional than men | 1 | 2 | 3 | 4 | 5 |
| 2. | Swearing and obscenity are more repulsive in the speech of a woman than of a man | 1 | 2 | 3 | 4 | 5 |
| 3. | When two people go out on a date, the man should be the one to pay the check | 1 | 2 | 3 | 4 | 5 |
| 4. | When a couple is going somewhere by car, it's better for the man to do most of the driving | 1 | 2 | 3 | 4 | 5 |
| 5. | If both husband and wife work full-time, her career should be just as important as his in determining where the family lives | 1 | 2 | 3 | 4 | 5 |
| 6. | Most women interpret innocent remarks or acts as being sexist | 1 | 2 | 3 | 4 | 5 |
| 7. | Society has reached the point where women and men have equal opportunities for achievement | 1 | 2 | 3 | 4 | 5 |
| 8. | Many women have a quality of purity that few men possess | 1 | 2 | 3 | 4 | 5 |
| 9. | Women should be cherished and protected by men | 1 | 2 | 3 | 4 | 5 |

Sources: Statement 2 is from Spence, J. T., Helmreich, R., & Stapp, J. (1973), *Bulletin of the Psychonomic Society*, 2, 219–220. Statements 4 and 5 are from Peplau, L. A., Hill, C. T., & Rubin, Z. (1993), *Journal of Social Issues*, 49(3), 31–52. Items 6, 8, and 9 are from Glick, P. & Fiske, S. T. (1996). *Journal of Personality and Social Psychology*, 70, 491–512. Statement 7 is from Swim, J. K., Aikin, K. J., Hall, W. S., & Hunter, B. A. (1995), *Journal of Personality and Social Psychology*, 68, 199–214. Note: Items 1, 2, 6, 7, and 8 can be regarded as descriptive beliefs; statements 3, 4, 5, and 9 are prescriptive beliefs.

**TABLE 4.2** | Guttman scale for sex roles

| | | |
|---|---|---|
| Least Difficult to Accept | 1. | Fathers should spend some of their leisure time helping to care for the children |
| | 2. | Fathers should share in infant care responsibilities, such as getting up when the baby cries at night and changing diapers |
| | 3. | If both parents work, the father and mother should divide up equally the task of staying at home when children get sick |
| Most Difficult to Accept | 4. | If both parents work, the father and mother should divide up equally the task of raising the children |

## Guttman Scale

Sometimes it seems that the person with the strongest attitude toward a topic is the one willing to take the most difficult stands, those that require the greatest gumption. One may not agree with these positions, but one is hard pressed to deny that these are difficult positions to endorse. A Guttman scale (named after Louis Guttman) takes this approach to measuring attitudes (Guttman, 1944).

The scale progresses from items easiest to accept to those most difficult to endorse. Those who get a high score on a Guttman scale agree with all items. Those with moderate attitudes agree with questions that are easy and moderately difficult to endorse, and those with mildly positive attitudes agree only with items that are easy to accept. A Guttman scale for sex roles appears in Table 4.2.

Guttman scales are hard to construct. They are not as easy to administer as Likert scales. However, they can be useful in tapping attitudes on sensitive topics like prejudice. People might be willing to take liberal stands on items that are relatively easy to accept, such as favoring enforcement of fair housing laws, endorsing efforts to hire minorities in professions that have been historically hostile, and supporting the idea of interracial marriage. However, prejudice might surface on items more difficult to accept, such as encouraging one's own child to date someone from another race or accepting without argument a son or daughter's decision to marry a same-sex partner.

## Semantic Differential

Charles Osgood and colleagues do not have a scale that bears their name. But they succeeded in developing one of the most frequently used scales in the attitude business. Osgood, Suci, and Tannenbaum (1957) chose not to assess beliefs or agreement with opinion statements. Instead, they explored the meanings that people attach to social objects, focusing on the emotional aspect of attitude. The term *semantic* is used because their instrument asks people to indicate feelings about an object on a pair of bipolar, adjective scales. The term *differential* comes from the fact that the scale assesses the different meanings people ascribe to a person or issue.

**TABLE 4.3** | Semantic differential for sex roles

| | | | FEMINISM | | | | | |
|---|---|---|---|---|---|---|---|---|
| Good | — | — | — | — | — | — | — | Bad |
| Pleasant | — | — | — | — | — | — | — | Unpleasant |
| Strong | — | — | — | — | — | — | — | Weak |
| Heavy | — | — | — | — | — | — | — | Light |
| Active | — | — | — | — | — | — | — | Passive |
| Wholesome | — | — | — | — | — | — | — | Unhealthy |
| Valuable | — | — | — | — | — | — | — | Worthless |

Note. Numbers do not appear underneath the dashes. For each item, a response is assigned a score from 3 to 3, with a 3 assigned to the blank closest to the positive pole and a 3 to the blank nearest the negative pole.

Participants rate a concept using bipolar adjectives: one adjective lies at one end of the scale; its opposite is at the other end. Osgood and colleagues discovered that people typically employ three dimensions to rate concepts: evaluation (Is it good or bad for me?), potency (Is it strong or weak?), and activity (Is it active or passive?) (Osgood, 1974). A semantic differential scale for sex roles appears in Table 4.3. You could also use this scale to tap attitudes toward female politicians, corporate leaders, or media stars. Any come to mind?

## PITFALLS IN ATTITUDE MEASUREMENT

There is no perfect attitude scale. Even the best scales can fail to measure attitudes accurately. Inaccuracies result from such factors as: (a) respondent carelessness in answering the questions, (b) people's desire to say the socially appropriate thing rather than what they truly believe, and (c) a tendency to agree with items regardless of their content (Dawes & Smith, 1985). Although these problems can be reduced through adroit survey measurement techniques (see next section), some inaccuracy in responses to attitude scales is inevitable.

A particularly gnawing problem in survey research involves the format and wording of questions. The way the researcher words the question and designs the questionnaire can elicit from the respondent answers that may not reflect the individual's true attitude (Schuman & Presser, 1981; Schwarz, 1999). The manner in which the question is asked can influence the response that the researcher receives. It reminds one of what writer Gertrude Stein reportedly said on her death bed. With death near, a friend in search of the guiding principle of life asked Stein, "What is the answer?" to which she famously replied, "What is the question?"

Two key survey design factors that can influence—or bias—attitude responses are survey context and wording.

**Context.** Survey questions appear one after another on a piece of paper, computer screen, or in an interview administered over the telephone. Questions occurring early in the survey can influence responses to later questions. This is because thoughts triggered by earlier questions can shape subsequent responses. The answers that individuals supply may thus be artifacts of the "context" of the survey instrument rather than reflections of their actual attitudes.

For instance, respondents asked to evaluate the morality of American business leaders might respond differently if they heard Bernard Madoff's name at the beginning rather than at the end of a list (e.g., Schwarz & Bless, 1992). Madoff bilked thousands of investors of their fortunes and life savings in a $50 billion scam. With Madoff as an anchor or standard of comparison respondents might give other business leaders favorable ratings, noting that they had at least not cheated people out of their hard-earned money. But if Madoff's name did not appear until the end of the list, respondents would have no reason to base evaluations of other business leaders on comparisons with Madoff's morally inscrupulous behavior. As a result, business leaders might receive comparatively less positive ratings.

Howard Schuman and Stanley Presser (1981) documented question order effects in a classic study of Americans' attitudes toward abortion. Naturally, abortion attitudes were complex, but a majority supported legalized abortion. When asked, "Do you think it should be possible for a pregnant woman to obtain a legal abortion if she is married and does not want any more children?" over 60 percent said "Yes." However, support dropped when the following question was asked first: *Do you think it should be possible for a pregnant woman to obtain a legal abortion if there is a strong chance of serious defect in the baby?*

In this case, only 48 percent agreed that a married woman should be able to obtain a legal abortion if she did not want any more children. To be sure, these attitudes are controversial and would outrage those who oppose abortion in all instances. But the point here is methodological, not ideological. The order of questions influenced evaluations of abortion. Something of a contrast effect appears to have emerged.

When asked to consider the question of legal abortion for married women, pro-choice respondents had no anchor other than their support for a woman's right to choose. A substantial majority came out in favor of abortion in this case. But after considering the gut-wrenching issue of aborting a fetus with a medical defect and deciding in favor of this option, a second group of respondents now mulled over the question of abortion for married women who did not want any more children. In comparison to the birth defect choice, this seemed relatively unsubstantial, perhaps trivial. Using the birth defect case as the standard for comparison, the idea that a woman should get a legal abortion if she did not want any more children seemed not to measure up to these individuals' moral criterion for abortion. Not surprisingly, fewer individuals supported abortion in this case.

It is also possible that, in light of the ambivalence many pro-choice supporters feel toward abortion, those who supported abortion in the case of a serious defect in the baby felt guilty. To reduce guilt, some may have shifted their position on abortion for married women, saying they opposed abortion in this less taxing situation. Whatever the explanation, it seems clear that the order in which the questions appeared influenced respondents' reports of their attitudes. Another example involves measurement of happiness and dating. When students are asked first to say how happy they are and then to indicate how often they are dating, there is no relationship between happiness and dating. However, when the questions are reversed something interesting happens. When the first question is "How often are you dating?" and the second is, "How happy are you?," responses to the questions are highly correlated. Students who date a lot say they are happy and those who do not date very much claim they are unhappy. Presumably, some students think to themselves, "I have been dating a lot. I must be pretty happy about that." Others may ruminate that, "Gosh, I can't recall when I went on a date. I must be truly unhappy" (Thaler & Sunstein, 2008; see also self-perception theory, Chapter 9). The difference in perceptions is not real, but has everything to do with the order in which questions were asked.

**Wording.** As writers have long known, language is full of meaning, capable of conveying powerful sentiments. It should, therefore, come as no surprise that the way a question is worded can influence respondents' evaluations of the issue.

This has become abundantly clear on the topic of affirmative action (Kinder & Sanders, 1990). A *New York Times*/CBS News poll probed Americans' attitudes toward racial diversity, using a variety of questions to tap beliefs. When asked their opinion of programs that *"give preferential treatment to racial minorities,"* just 26 percent of respondents indicated they would favor such programs. But when asked their views of programs that *"make special efforts to help minorities get ahead,"* significantly more Americans (55 percent) expressed approval (Verhovek, 1997).

A more recent example emerged during polling about health reform in late 2009. While just about everybody agreed that the nation's health-care system needed overhaul, there were sharp disagreements among political leaders about just what type of health plan was best for America. In such a situation, public opinion exerted a pivotal influence on the debate, and the way opinion poll questions were phrased produced vastly different results. When a national poll asked respondents whether they would favor or oppose *"creating a public health care plan administered by the federal government that would compete directly with private health insurance companies,"* only 48 percent indicated they would support such a plan. However, when individuals were asked how important they felt it was *"to give people a choice of both a public plan administered by the federal government and a private plan for their health insurance,"* 72 percent said they believed this was very important (Connelly, 2009, p. A17). The wording in the first question emphasizes competition with private health insurance companies, while the second focuses on choice, a positive value to Americans.

Perhaps the most striking example of wording effects came from polls probing an even more emotional issue: Americans' belief that the Holocaust actually occurred. With some anti-Semitic groups arguing that the Holocaust had never happened and was a figment of Jews' imagination, the Roper polling organization launched a national survey to see how many Americans actually bought into this false belief. In 1992, Roper probed Americans' attitudes toward the Holocaust, tapping beliefs with this key question:

*The term Holocaust usually refers to the killing of millions of Jews in Nazi death camps during World War II. Does it seem possible or does it seem impossible to you that the Nazi extermination of the Jews never happened?*

Amazingly, 22 percent of respondents said it was "possible" that the mass executions never happened, about 12 percent claimed they "didn't know," and 65 percent said it was "impossible" that the event had not happened. "The fact that nearly one fourth of U.S. adults denied that the Holocaust had happened . . . raised serious questions about the quality of knowledge about recent history," observed Carroll J. Glynn and colleagues (Glynn, Herbst, O'Keefe, & Shapiro, 1999, p. 76). It also raised the possibility that large numbers of Americans consciously or unconsciously subscribed to an anti-Semitic ideology.

Public opinion researchers suspected the problem, once again, was not ideological, but methodological. They suggested that the Roper question was misleading and the double negative had confused people. Several polling organizations, including Roper, conducted new surveys, this time with clearer questions like: *"Does it seem possible to you that the Nazi extermination of the Jews never happened, or do you feel certain that it happened?"*

This time, 91 percent said they were certain it happened. Just 1 percent of the public said it was possible the Holocaust never happened, and 8 percent did not know (Smith, 1995).

The results restored faith in the public's knowledge and good sense. They also revealed the strong influence that question wording has on reports of attitudes.

## POLICY IMPLICATIONS

Question wording is not just of interest to academic researchers. It is of considerable importance to policymakers, who recognize that the way a question is worded or framed can shape the contours of policy debates. Consider the case of polling on embryonic stem cell research.

This research is controversial because initiating a line of stem cells typically involves destruction of the human embryo. Opponents argue that this is morally wrong and it is immoral to use embryos for research purposes. Supporters say the embryos would be discarded anyway and the stem cells have the potential to produce life-saving cures for a host of medical conditions, such as spinal cord injuries and Parkinson's disease. With the White House weighing ethical and political dimensions, opinion polls have been a factor in presidential decisions.

Polls have obtained strikingly different results, depending on the way questions have been framed. A partisan poll sponsored by a national Catholic organization stated that *"live embryos would be destroyed in their first week of development to obtain these cells."* When the question was worded this way, 70 percent of the public opposed using federal tax dollars for stem cell experiments. The results gratified the Catholic group, which opposes stem cell research on religious grounds. But when nonpartisan polls conducted by news and professional opinion research organizations framed the issue in terms of utilitarian benefits of such research, the results were dramatically different. For example, an NBC News/*Wall Street Journal* poll gave opponents' side and supporters' position, noting that the research "*could lead to breakthrough cures for many diseases, such as cancer, Alzheimer's, Parkinson's, and spinal cord injuries, and this research uses only embryos that otherwise would be discarded*." When the question was worded this way," 69 percent of respondents favored stem cell research (Bishop, 2005, pp. 42–44).

Partisan lobbyists seize upon supportive findings such as these and distribute them to lawmakers. Manipulation of statistical information is a routine and accepted way of doing the business of political persuasion in a democracy. Yet it can be troublesome when the goals of persuasion clash with larger interests of the country.

An example that resonates with those concerned with America's long-term energy policies concerns beliefs about a gasoline tax. Experts argue that U.S. dependence on foreign oil is self-defeating because oil profits go to countries (like Iran and Saudi Arabia) that support terrorist groups determined to attack this country. The only way to solve the problem, some say, is to raise the gasoline tax. This would discourage consumers from driving cars as frequently, which in turn would encourage Detroit to develop more fuel-efficient hybrid automobiles (Friedman, 2006). As a consequence, over the long haul, despots in the Middle East would have less oil money and would need to broker deals with Western powers.

Enter opinion poll findings. When Americans are asked simply if they favor a gasoline tax, 85 percent say they do not. However, when pollsters frame the gas tax issue in more specific terms—such as a way to reduce the country's dependence on foreign oil—55 percent favor it. Even more Americans (59 percent) support the tax when it is described as a way to reduce global warming (Friedman, 2006). "Sadly," columnist Thomas L. Friedman notes, "both sides fear the other will smear them if they run on this issue. O.K., say you're running for Congress and you propose a gas tax, but your opponent denounces you as a wimpy, tree-hugging, girlie-man, a tax-and-spender" (p. A25). Fearing such silly but politically consequential labels, politicians are apt to run for cover. A simple way to justify their refusal to support a gas tax is to point to polls showing that 85 percent of the public opposes the tax. In this way, political leaders can use polls to rationalize a reluctance to embrace bold measures for social change.

**Psychological issues.** Wording and context effects have stimulated much discussion among researchers. In addition to raising questions about political manipulation of poll findings, researchers have elucidated more scholarly concerns. Some theorists have suggested that the reason that question wording exerts such strong effects is not just that people are sensitive to subtle variations in language, but because in many cases they don't have full-blown attitudes at all. Instead, these researchers suggest, individuals construct their attitudes on the spot, based on what happens to be on their minds at the time or on thoughts triggered by survey questions (Bishop, 2005; Wilson, LaFleur, & Anderson, 1996; Zaller, 1992). In support of this position, research has found that large numbers of people volunteer opinions on fictitious issues, those that the pollster has invented for the purposes of the survey. For example, over 50 percent of respondents gave their opinion of the Monetary Control Bill, legislation dreamed up by survey researchers (Bishop, Tuchfarber, & Oldendick, 1986)!

People *do* construct attitudes on the spot in response to pollsters' questions. We should not assume that this is the norm, however. It pushes the envelope to argue that people lack attitudes; clearly, people harbor attitudes when the issue touches on strong values, is the product of socialization, or has been mentally worked through. At the same time, there are plenty of policy issues in which people lack firm beliefs or opinions. In such cases, their attitudes can be swayed by pollsters' questions, a fact that has not been lost on savvy marketers hoping to manipulate public opinion (see Box 4.1).

## Box 4.1 | SKEWING THE SURVEY RESULTS

You've probably heard television advertisements that claim that "a majority of people interviewed in a major survey" said such-and-such about the product. The results make it sound like a scientific study proved that people prefer Crest to Colgate, Coke to Pepsi, Burger King to McDonald's, or Google to its competitors. As you listened, you no doubt thought to yourself, "Is this research real, or what?"

"Or what" is the appropriate answer. Some of the research that companies cite in their behalf is based on questionable methods. It is a powerful example of how marketing researchers can cook the data to fit the client, or design surveys that assure that companies will receive the answers they desire. Reporter Cynthia Crossen (1991) discussed this trend in *The Wall Street Journal*. She reported that:

- When Levi Strauss & Co. asked students which clothes would be most popular this year, 90 percent said Levi's 501 jeans. They were the only jeans on the list.

- A survey for Black Flag said: "A roach disk . . . poisons a roach slowly. The dying roach returns to the nest and after it dies is eaten by other roaches. In turn these roaches become poisoned and die. How effective do you think this type of product would be in killing roaches?" Not surprisingly, 79 percent said effective.

- An obviously-dated Chrysler study showing its cars were preferred to Toyota's included just 100 people in each of two tests. But more important, none of the people surveyed owned a foreign car, so they may well have been predisposed to U.S.-made vehicles.
  (pp. A1, A7)

Summarizing her report on the use of marketing research, Crossen acknowledged that some studies use valid measurement techniques. But many surveys are filled with loaded questions and are designed to prove a point rather than investigate one. "There's been a slow sliding in ethics," said Eric Miller, who reviewed thousands of marketing studies as editor of a research newsletter. "The scary part is, people make decisions based on this stuff. It may be an invisible crime, but it's not a victimless one" (Crossen, p. A1).

# ASKING GOOD QUESTIONS

As long as surveys are constructed by human beings and administered to human beings, we will never totally eliminate order or wording effects. You have to put your questions in a certain order and use particular words to communicate meaning. These are bound to influence respondents. Nonetheless, we can minimize the impact of context factors by taking precautions when designing the survey. More generally, there are many things researchers can do to improve the quality of attitude questions (Sudman & Bradburn, 1982). The next time you are asked to develop a self-report survey, you might consider these suggestions:

1. Use words that all respondents can comprehend.
2. Write specific and unambiguous items.
3. Avoid double negatives.
4. Pretest items to make sure people understand your questions.
5. If you think order of questions will influence respondents, ask questions in different sequences to check out order effects.
6. Avoid politically correct phrases that encourage socially desirable responses.
7. Write items so that they take both the positive and negative sides of an issue (to reduce respondents' tendency to always agree).
8. Consider whether your questions deal with sensitive, threatening issues (sex, drugs, antisocial behavior). If so, ask these questions at the end of the survey, once trust has been established.
9. Allow people to say "I don't know." This will eliminate responses based on guesses or desire to please the interviewer.
10. Include many questions to tap different aspects of the attitude.

You can also save yourself some time—and improve the quality of your questionnaire—by turning to established attitude scales. You don't have to reinvent the wheel if someone else has developed a scale on the topic you're researching. To paraphrase the lyrics of an old folk song, "You can get anything you want at Alice's Restaurant"—you can get pretty much any scale you want, if you do a thorough search! There are many standardized scales out there that tap attitudes very effectively. The advantage of using someone else's scale (other than that it frees you up to relax!) is that the scale has passed scientific muster—it is reliable, valid, and comprehensible to respondents. You can find scales from computerized databases, such as PsycINFO, Health and Psychosocial Instruments, and Communication Abstracts, or in specialized books (for example, Robinson, Shaver, & Wrightsman, 1999; Rubin, Palmgreen, & Sypher, 1994). Of course, if you're researching a new issue or want to cook up your own questions, you will have to devise your own questionnaire.

As you construct your survey, just remember that people are complex and that you will need good questions to tap their attitudes.

## Open-Ended Measures

The main advantage of attitude scales—that they offer an efficient way to measure social attitudes accurately—is their main drawback. Scales do not always shed light on the underlying dynamics of attitudes—the rich underbelly of cognitions and emotions. These components can be measured through more open-ended, free-form techniques. Open-ended measures complement the structured attitude scales that have been discussed thus far. They are like essay questions.

One open-ended technique involves assessing cognitive responses to communications (Petty, Ostrom, & Brock, 1981b). Individuals typically read or view a message and list their cognitive reactions (i.e., thoughts). For example, if you wanted to measure people's cognitive responses regarding sex roles, you might have them view a sexist advertisement and ask them to write down the first ideas that come to mind. These responses could be subsequently categorized by researchers according to specific criteria (Cacioppo, Harkins, & Petty, 1981).

*Affect* can also be assessed in an open-ended way. People can be asked to write down 10 emotions that they ordinarily feel toward members of a group, organization, or nation (Eagly, Mladinic, & Otto, 1994; see also Crites, Fabrigar, & Petty, 1994).

Combining open-ended measures with traditional attitude scales increases the odds that researchers will tap attitudes accurately and completely. Of course, this does not guarantee success. Even the best survey researchers err. Some years ago pollster Richard Morin listed "the worst of the worst"—the most terrible questions ever asked in a poll. One of them appeared in a 1953 Gallup Poll: *"If you were taking a new job and had your choice of a boss, would you prefer to work under a man or a woman?"* (1997, p. 35).

## INDIRECT METHODS TO MEASURE ATTITUDES

In light of such doozies (the question just cited) and the methodological problems noted earlier, some researchers recommend measuring attitude through ways other than questionnaires. They advocate the use of a variety of indirect techniques to assess attitudes. Although not without their problems, indirect measures can be useful when it is physically difficult to administer attitude scales or when people are reluctant to acknowledge what they really believe on a questionnaire. Key indirect measures include the following:

**Unobtrusive measures.** Researchers can observe individuals unobtrusively or without their knowledge. Behavior is used as a surrogate for attitude.

Unobtrusive measures can be useful in cases where it is not possible to administer self-report scales or one fears individuals will not accurately report attitudes (Webb, Campbell, Schwartz, & Sechrest, 1966). For example, if investigators wanted to assess attitudes toward American music in a dictatorship, they might examine the amount of wear and tear on rock and roll CDs or check out the number of hits on hip-hop musicians'

Web sites. Useful as these techniques could be, the obvious problem is that they might not tap liking of the music so much as interest or idle curiosity.

**Physiological measurements.** Did you ever sweat a little when you asked someone out for a date? Do you know anyone whose pupils seem to get bigger when they are talking about something they really care about? Have you ever noticed how some people's facial muscles—eyebrows and cheeks—can telegraph what they are feeling? If so, you are intimately aware of the physiology of attitudes. Physiological measures can provide useful indirect assessments of attitudes.

A physiological approach to attitudes has gained adherents in recent years as researchers have recognized that attitudes have a motor or bodily component (Cacioppo, Priester, & Berntson, 1993). There are a host of ways of tapping attitudes through physiological techniques. These include (a) *galvanic skin response*, a change in the electrical resistance of the skin (e.g., measurements of sweating); (b) *pupil dilation* (precise assessments of expansion of the pupils); and (c) *facial electromyographic (EMG) techniques* that tap movements of facial muscles, particularly in the brow, cheek, and eye regions. The latter can provide a particularly sensitive reading of attitudes. In one study, students imagined they were reading an editorial with which they agreed or disagreed. Findings showed that students displayed more EMG activity over the brow region when imagining they were reading an article they disliked than one they liked (Cacioppo, Petty, & Marshall-Goodell, 1984).

Physiological measures can be useful in tapping feelings people are not aware they have, or which they might choose to disguise on a questionnaire. Marketing firms have used galvanic skin response measures to test advertising copy (LaBarbera & Tucciarone, 1995). Advertising researchers have found that facial electromyographic techniques can provide a more sensitive measure of emotional responses to ads than self-reports (Hazlett & Hazlett, 1999). Pupil dilation measures can shed light on abnormal sexual attitudes (Atwood & Howell, 1971).

Useful as these devices are, they can unfortunately tap responses other than attitudes. Sweating, pupil dilation, and facial muscle activity can occur because people are interested in or perplexed about the attitude object. Physiological reactions do not always provide a sensitive indication of the directionality (pro vs. con) of people's feelings. It is also frequently impractical or expensive to use physiological techniques. In addition, wide use of physiological measurements has been hampered by the jargon-based language that is frequently used to communicate physiological findings.

**Response time.** These measures assess the latency or length of time it takes people to indicate if they agree or disagree with a statement. For example, individuals may sit before a computer screen and read a question (e.g., "Do you favor capital punishment?"). They are instructed to hit a button to indicate whether they do or don't favor capital punishment. Researchers do not focus on whether individuals are pro or con, or favorable or unfavorable to the attitude object. Their primary interest is in how long it takes individuals to make their selection (Fazio, 1995). The assumption is that the longer it takes people to access their attitude, the less well developed or strong the attitude is. Conversely, the more quickly people punch a button to indicate their attitude, the stronger the attitude is presumed to be.

The most popular response-time-based measure is the Implicit Association Test (IAT), developed by Anthony Greenwald and colleagues (Greenwald, McGhee, & Schwartz, 1998). The IAT has been a godsend to researchers seeking to measure deep-seated attitudes, particularly implicit attitudes that operate unconsciously. Such attitudes, especially when they involve prejudices, are notoriously hard to uncover on paper-and-pencil questionnaires. People do not like to admit they harbor prejudices or may not be conscious of their biases. The IAT can tap such prejudices because it involves a less obtrusive methodology.

Individuals taking the IAT are presented with a series of items. If the item belongs to a category in the left-hand column, they might push the letter *e*. If it belongs to the category in the right-hand column, they might push the letter *i*. In the race IAT, the category White American could appear on the left and African-American on the right. The practice rounds are easy. When you see a photograph of a White person, you push the letter *e* and when you view a Black person, you push *i*. The test begins when the racial category appears along with a label, either "good" or "bad." The labels could be: (a) White American or good; (b) African-American or bad; (c) White American or bad; and (d) African-American or good. You then see pictures of Whites and Blacks again. How long does it take to classify the photograph of a White person when the category is "White American or good," and how long to classify a Black when the category is "African-American or bad?" Now the counter-stereotypic case: *How long does it take to classify the photograph of the White person when the category is "White American or bad" and a Black when the category is "African-American or good?"* Writer Malcolm Gladwell described what happened when the latter scenario occurred:

> Immediately, something strange happened to me. The task of putting the . . . faces in the right categories suddenly became more difficult. I found myself slowing down. I had to think. Sometimes I assigned something to one category when I really meant to assign it to the other category.
>
> (2005, pp. 82–83)

The IAT provides a measure of the strength of association between an attribute, such as race, and positive or negative feelings. It assumes that the less time it takes a respondent to punch the appropriate key, the stronger the attitude. Presumably, if the attitude is strong and well learned, the individual should push a key (or letter on the keyboard) immediately without having to think about the issue. For example, someone with a prejudiced attitude toward Blacks should take less time to push the key when the photograph of a White appears with "White American or good" than with "White American or bad." The same person should take less time to push the key when the photograph of a Black appears with "African-American or bad" than with "African-American or good." "When there's a strong prior association, people answer in between four hundred and six hundred milliseconds," researcher Greenwald says. "When there isn't, they might take two hundred to three hundred milliseconds longer than that—which in the realm of these kinds of effects is huge" (Gladwell, 2005, p. 81).

There is debate about the validity of the IAT (Arkes & Tetlock, 2004; Olson & Fazio, 2004). Critics argue that that the test does not measure individuals' attitudes so much as the cultural associations they have learned. I may have learned that White is linked with "good" in our culture, but this does not mean I personally harbor a pro-White/anti-Black attitude. It is also not clear that responding more quickly to certain words on a computer test means that an individual harbors latent prejudices or deep-seated hostility toward members of minority groups. Critics worry that unfairly labeling individuals as prejudiced, based on a computerized test, can itself have dysfunctional effects on race relations (Tetlock & Arkes, 2004).

## CONCLUSIONS

Attitude measurement plays a critical role in persuasion research. Persuasion is a science, as well as an art, and we need valid instruments to assess attitudes. Three venerable scales are typically employed: Likert, Guttman, and the semantic differential. The Likert scale is used most frequently because it taps beliefs and can be constructed easily. Open-ended measures, such as cognitive responses, can supplement closed-ended, structured scales.

There are a variety of problems in measuring attitudes through self-reports, including survey context and wording effects. To minimize these problems, researchers have devised strategies to improve questionnaire quality that focus on asking questions clearly and thoughtfully. Supplementing self-report surveys are several indirect techniques to assess attitudes, such as unobtrusive, physiological, and response time measures. Indirect techniques can shed light on sensitive issues or topics where a forthright response could betray a socially undesirable response. In the end, as Jon Krosnick and colleagues point out, "Both traditional self-report and more indirect attitude measures will continue to be used. The goal is not to come up with a single 'best' attitude measure, but rather to measure attitudes in all their complexity and all their manifestations" (Krosnick, Judd, & Wittenbrink, 2005, p. 63).

*Part Two*

# Changing Attitudes and Behavior

# Chapter 5

# Processing Persuasive Communications

K<small>ATE</small> and Ben, recently married, delightfully employed, and happy to be on their own after 4 long years of college, are embarking on a major decision—a happy one, but an important one. They're buying a car. They have some money saved up from the wedding and have decided that, the way the stock market has been going, they'd be better off spending it than losing cash on some risky Internet investment.

Sitting in their living room one Thursday night watching TV, they find that they are tuning in more closely to the car commercials than the sitcoms. "That's a sign we're an old married couple," Kate jokes. Ben nods in agreement.

The next day after work, at Kate's request they click onto the *Consumer Reports* Web site and print out information about compact cars. On Saturday they brave the car dealerships, get the lowdown from car salesmen, and take spins in the cars. Kate, armed with her incredible memory for detail and ten 3 × 5 cards, hurls questions at the car salesmen, while Ben, shirt hanging out, eyes glazed, looks dreamily at the sports cars he knows he can't afford.

By early the next week, they have narrowed down the choices to a Honda Accord and a Hyundai Sonata. Her desk covered with papers, printouts, and stacks of warranties and brochures from the dealerships, Kate is thinking at a feverish pace; she pauses, then shares her conclusions with her husband: "Okay, this is it. The Honda gets more miles per gallon and handles great on the highway. But *Consumer Reports* gives the new Sonata better ratings on safety on account of their anti-lock brakes and traction control, which is important. The Sonata also has a better repair record than the Accord. But the big thing is we get a stronger warranty with the Hyundai dealer and, Ben, the Sonata is a thousand bucks cheaper. Soooo . . . what do you think?"

Ben looks up. "Well, you know, I'm not into all this technical stuff like you are. I say if the Sonata gets better ratings from *Consumer Reports*, go for it. I also think the Sonata salesman made a lot of good points—real nice guy. The Honda guy basically blew us off when we told him we needed the weekend to think it over."

"There's also the other thing," says Kate, sporting a grin.

"What?"

"The name."

"It's true," says Ben a bit sheepishly. "The name 'Sonata' is cool. I like it."

"What am I going to do with you?" Kate asks, with a smile and a deliberately exaggerated sigh.

"How about, take me to the Hyundai dealer, so we can buy our new car?" Ben says, gently running his hands through the $3 \times 5$ cards as he walks out the front door.

The story is fiction—but perhaps not too far from everyday experience. It is based on interviews with consumers and observations of people buying cars. The example illustrates two very different styles of processing information: careful consideration of message arguments (Kate) and superficial examination of information and a focus on simple cues (Ben). These two ways of processing information are the main elements of contemporary theories of persuasion and form the centerpiece of the present chapter.

This chapter launches the second part of the book, which examines theory and research on the effects of persuasive communication. The chapter describes guiding models of attitude and behavior change—approaches that underlie much of the research and applications that follow. The cornerstone of these theoretical approaches is a focus on *process*. Scholars believe that if they can understand *how* people cognitively process messages, they can better explicate the impact that communications have on attitudes. They believe that the better they comprehend individuals' modes of processing information, the more accurately they can explain the diverse effects messages have on attitudes. This is what scholars mean when they say you cannot understand the effects of communications on people without knowing how people process the message.

Contemporary models evolved from earlier perspectives on persuasion—notably Hovland's path-breaking work and research conducted in the 1960s. It is important to describe these programs of research because they contributed helpful insights and also laid the groundwork for current theorizing. The first section of the chapter provides an overview of these approaches. The second portion of the chapter describes a major cognitive processing model of persuasion, the Elaboration Likelihood Model (see p. 130), along with evidence that backs it up. Subsequent sections focus on real-life applications, fine points of the model, intellectual criticisms, and the model's contributions to persuasion.

## HISTORICAL FOUNDATIONS

As noted in Chapter 1, Carl Hovland and colleagues at Yale University conducted the first detailed, empirical research on the effects of persuasive communications. The Yale attitude change approach was distinctive because it provided facts about the effects on attitudes of the communicator's credibility, message appeals, and audience members' personality traits. Convinced by theory and their generation's experience with World War II persuasion campaigns that communications had strong effects on attitudes, the researchers set out to examine who says what to whom with what effect (Hovland, Janis, & Kelley, 1953; Smith, Lasswell, & Casey, 1946).

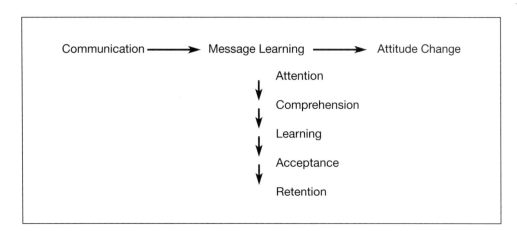

FIGURE 5.1 | The Hovland/Yale model of persuasion.

Although Hovland and colleagues' findings were interesting, it was their theory-driven approach and commitment to testing hypotheses that proved enduring. The Yale researchers were also interested in understanding why messages changed attitudes. Working in an era dominated by reward-based learning theories and research on rats' mastery of mazes, Hovland naturally gravitated to explanations that focused on learning and motivation. He emphasized that persuasion entailed learning message arguments and noted that attitude change occurred in a series of steps. To be persuaded, individuals had to attend to, comprehend, learn, accept, and retain the message (see Figure 5.1).

It sounds logical enough. Indeed there is considerable evidence that learning is a component of persuasion—the more people learn and comprehend message arguments, the more likely they are to accept the advocated positions (Chaiken, Wood, & Eagly, 1996). However, the thesis misses the mark in an important respect. It assumes that people are sponge-like creatures who passively take in information they receive. In fact, as Leon Festinger and Nathan Maccoby noted, an audience member:

> does not sit there listening and absorbing what is said without any counteraction on his part. Indeed, it is more likely that under such circumstances, while he is listening to the persuasive communication, he is very actively, inside his own mind, counter-arguing, derogating the points the communicator makes and derogating the communicator himself.
>
> (1964, p. 360)

Think of how you react to a persuasive message. Do you sit there, taking in everything the speaker says? Are you so mesmerized by the communicator that you stifle any thoughts or mental arguments? Hardly. You actively think about the speaker, message, or persuasion context. You may remember message arguments, yet probably recall with greater accuracy your own criticisms of the speaker's point of view. This view of

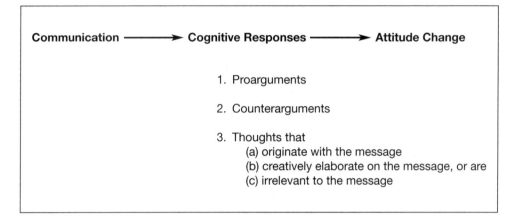

FIGURE 5.2 │ The cognitive response model of persuasion.

persuasion developed in the years that followed the publication of Hovland's research and is known as the *cognitive response approach* to persuasion. The approach asserts that people's own mental reactions to a message play a critical role in the persuasion process, typically a more important role than the message itself (Brock, 1967; Greenwald, 1968; Petty, Ostrom, & Brock, 1981b). Cognitive responses include thoughts that are favorable to the position advocated in the message (*proarguments*) and those that criticize the message (*counterarguments*). Persuasion occurs if the communicator induces the audience member to generate favorable cognitive responses regarding the communicator or message.

The cognitive response view says that people play an active role in the persuasion process. It emphasizes that people's *own* thoughts about a message are more important factors in persuasion than memory of message arguments (Perloff & Brock, 1980; see Figure 5.2). There is a good deal of evidence to substantiate this view. In fact, it may seem obvious that thoughts matter in persuasion. But remember that what is obvious at one point in time is not always apparent in an earlier era. During the 1950s and early 1960s, animal learning models of human behavior dominated psychology, and, on a broader level, Americans were assumed to follow lock, stock, and barrel the dictates of government and free-enterprise capitalism. It only seemed natural to theorize that persuasion was primarily a passive process of learning and reinforcement.

With the advent of the 1960s, all this changed. Cognitive models emphasizing active thought processes gained adherents. It became clear that older views, while useful, needed to be supplemented by approaches that afforded more respect to the individual and assigned more emphasis to dynamics of the gray matter inside the brain.

"Feed your head," the rock group Jefferson Airplane belted out during this decade. The cognitive response approach echoed the refrain. It stimulated research, bottled old scholarly wine in new explanations, and helped pave the way for new theories of attitude change. By calling attention to the role thoughts play in persuasion, the cognitive response approach illuminated scholarly understanding of persuasion. Consider the following examples.

The first involves *forewarning*, which occurs when a persuader warns people that they will soon be exposed to a persuasive communication. This is a common occurrence in life, and research has explored what happens when people are warned that they are going to receive a message with which they will staunchly disagree. Cognitive response studies have clarified just what happens inside people's minds when this occurs. Individuals generate a large number of counterarguments, strengthening their opposition to the advocated position (Petty & Cacioppo, 1977). An old expression, "Forewarned is forearmed," describes this phenomenon, but sheds no light on why it occurs. Cognitive response analysis helps us understand it better. When a close friend marches out of the house in the middle of an argument, vowing, "We'll talk about this when I get home," you are likely to intensify your resolve not to give in. Generating arguments on your behalf and persuading yourself that you are right, you arm yourself with a battering ram of justifications that you invoke when your friend returns. In fact, as cognitive response research predicts, forewarning someone in this general fashion significantly reduces the likelihood that a subsequent persuasive communication will succeed. "Forewarning an audience to expect a persuasive message tends to make that message less persuasive," William L. Benoit concludes after studying this issue (1998, p. 146).

Another way of saying this is that forewarnings stiffen resistance to persuasion. Arming individuals to resist harmful communications is important, given that people are frequently tempted to yield to peers' requests that they smoke, drink when they drive, or take drugs (Quinn & Wood, 2004). Forewarnings can instill resistance, provided they get people to think long and hard about the issue and the arguments contained in the message.

Cognitive responses also help explain an off-beat persuasion effect called *distraction*. Sometimes people are distracted from paying attention to a communication with which they disagree. Other people may be talking, or music may be blaring at a party at precisely the moment when someone chooses to explain why she disagrees with a position one holds on an issue. In other cases, communicators intentionally distract receivers from paying attention to a message. Advertisers do this all the time, using humor, music, and sex to take people's attention away from the message. In such circumstances, people can be highly susceptible to persuasion. The distraction hypothesis holds that distraction facilitates persuasion by blocking the dominant cognitive response to a message (Petty, Wells, & Brock, 1976). If I listen to a message with which I disagree, my normal response is probably to counterargue with the communicator in my head. But if my mind is elsewhere—I'm grooving to the music or am laughing at a joke—I am not able to formulate arguments against the message. I, therefore, have fewer mental objections to the advocated position. As a result, I end up moving somewhat closer to the communicator's point of view than I would have if I had not been distracted in this way.

Notice what is going on here. It's not the distraction from the message that counts; rather, it's the distraction from our own arguments regarding the message (Osterhouse & Brock, 1970). Recognizing that people are primed to contest advertisements in their own minds, advertisers resort to all sorts of clever distractions (see Chapter 11). Sometimes they even seem to be aware that we mentally take issue with ads that appear on television, as they try to tease us into not taking the ad so seriously. This too can be distracting and can facilitate persuasion. Mind you—distraction does not always succeed, and it does not always work by inhibiting counterargument production. Indeed, David B. Buller and John R. Hall (1998) present an array of evidence that challenges the counterargument disruption thesis. However, the distraction research caught researchers' eyes by raising the possibility that cognitive responses could influence attitude change. This in turn stimulated scholarship and suggested new ideas for everyday persuasion (see, for example, Boxes 5.1 and 5.2).

# ELABORATION LIKELIHOOD MODEL

There is little doubt that the cognitive response approach advanced knowledge of persuasion. It also provided a method to measure cognitive aspects of attitudes creatively. After a time, though, researchers realized that the approach had two limitations. First, it assumed that people think carefully about messages. Yet there are many times when people turn their minds off to persuasive communications, making decisions based on mental shortcuts. Second, the cognitive response approach failed to shed much light on the ways that messages influence people. It did not explain how we can utilize cognitive responses to devise messages to change attitudes or behavior. In order to rectify these problems, scholars proceeded to develop process-based models of persuasion.

Two models currently dominate the field. The first, devised by Shelly Chaiken and Alice H. Eagly, is called the Heuristic–Systematic Model (HSM) (Chaiken, Liberman, & Eagly, 1989; Todorov, Chaiken, & Henderson, 2002). The second, formulated by Richard E. Petty and John T. Cacioppo, is the Elaboration Likelihood Model (ELM) (Petty & Cacioppo, 1986; Petty & Wegener, 1999; Petty, Wheeler, & Tormala, 2003). Both approaches emphasize that you cannot understand communication effects without appreciating the underlying processes by which messages influence attitudes. Both are *dual-process models* in that they claim that there are two different mechanisms by which communications affect attitudes. This chapter focuses on the ELM because it has generated more research on persuasive communication and offers a more comprehensive framework for understanding communication effects.

## Main Principles

The first question students may have when reading about an ELM of persuasion is: "Just what does the term 'Elaboration Likelihood' mean?" This is a reasonable question. *Elaboration* refers to the extent to which the individual thinks about or mentally modifies arguments contained in the communication. *Likelihood*, referring to the probability that an event will occur, is used to point out the fact that elaboration can be either likely or unlikely. Elaboration is assumed to fall along a continuum, with one end characterized by considerable rumination on the central merits of an issue and the other by relatively little mental activity. The model tells us when people should be particularly likely to elaborate, or not elaborate, on persuasive messages.

## Box 5.1 | INOCULATION THEORY

Persuasion not only involves changing attitudes. It also centers on convincing people not to fall prey to unethical or undesirable influence attempts. Communicators frequently attempt to persuade individuals to resist social and political messages that are regarded as unhealthy or unwise. For example, health campaigns urge young people to "say no" to drugs, smoking, drinking when driving, and unsafe sex. In the political domain, candidates attempt to persuade wavering voters to resist the temptation to bolt their party and vote for the opposing party candidate or a third-party contender.

A variety of techniques have been developed to strengthen resistance to persuasion. The techniques work by triggering counterarguments that, along with other factors, help individuals resist persuasive appeals. One of the most famous strategies evolved from a biological analogy and is known as inoculation theory. The theory is an ingenious effort to draw a comparison between the body's mechanisms to ward off disease and the mind's ways of defending itself against verbal onslaughts. In his statement of the theory, William McGuire noted that doctors increase resistance to disease by injecting the person with a small dose of the attacking virus, as in a flu shot (McGuire & Papageorgis, 1961). Pre-exposure to the virus in a weakened form stimulates the body's defenses: it leads to production of antibodies, which help the body fight off disease. In the same fashion, exposure to a weak dose of opposition arguments, "strong enough to stimulate his defenses, but not strong enough to overwhelm him," should produce the mental equivalent of antibodies—counterarguments (McGuire, 1970, p. 37). Counterarguing the oppositional message in one's own mind should lead to strengthening of initial attitude and increased resistance to persuasion.

One of the hallmarks of inoculation research is the creativity with which it has been tested. McGuire and colleagues chose to expose people to attacks against attitudes that had been rarely if ever criticized: cultural truisms, or beliefs individuals learn through socialization. Cultural truisms include: "You should brush your teeth three times a day" and "People should get a yearly checkup." In essence, participants in the experiments received either a supportive defense—arguments defending the truism—or an inoculation defense (for example, arguments against the notion that you should brush your teeth three times a day, along with refutation of these arguments). Individuals who received the inoculation defense were more likely to resist subsequent attacks on a brush-your-teeth-three-times-a-day type truism than those who just received supportive arguments (McGuire & Papageorgis, 1961). Presumably, the attack and refutation stimulated individuals to formulate arguments why the truism was indeed correct. They were apparently more motivated than those who heard the usual "rah-rah, it's true" supportive arguments.

These findings provided the first support for inoculation theory. The theory fundamentally stipulates that resistance to persuasion can be induced by exposing individuals to a small dose of arguments against a particular idea, coupled with appropriate criticism of these arguments. In essence, inoculation works by introducing a threat to a person's belief system

**Box 5.1** |

and then providing a way for individuals to cope with the threat (that is, by refuting the counterattitudinal message). As the insightful scholar Michael Pfau points out, "By motivating receivers, and then preemptively refuting one or more potential counterarguments, inoculation spreads a broad blanket of protection both against specific counterarguments raised in refutational preemption and against those counterarguments not raised" (1997, pp. 137–138).

Other explanations of inoculation have also been advanced. Some researchers suggest that inoculation confers resistance to persuasion by providing the persuader with an opportunity to reframe the arguments before the opposition gets to them (Williams & Dolnik, 2001). Michael Pfau and colleagues (2003) have shown that inoculations make attitudes more accessible and stronger, and therefore more resistant to attack. Pfau has also found that inoculations bolster the structure of attitudes, increasing connections among cognitive and affective elements. This in turn renders attitudes more resistant to subsequent attack (Pfau, Ivanov, Houston, Haigh, Sims, Gilchrist, Russell, Wigley, Eckstein, & Richert, 2005). Although there is healthy debate about just which processes account best for inoculation effects, there is little doubt that inoculation provides a useful way to encourage resistance to persuasive communications (Benoit, 1991; Lim & Ki, 2007; Pfau, 1997; Szabo & Pfau, 2002).

Indeed, inoculation theory has stimulated considerable research over the years, usefully transcending its initial focus on cultural truisms, explored exclusively in laboratory settings. Communication scholars have taken the concept to the real world, examining its applications to commercial advertising, political campaigns, and health (Pfau, Van Bockern, & Kang, 1992; see Chapter 12). A number of practical conclusions have emerged from this research. They include the following:

1. **Inoculation can be a potent weapon in politics**. Politicians can anticipate the opposition's attacks and preempt them by using inoculation techniques (Pfau & Burgoon, 1988; Pfau & Kenski, 1990). Barack Obama used the technique in the 2008 election, trying to build voter resistance to Republican opponent John McCain. Obama first acknowledged McCain's service to his country. "Now let there be no doubt. The Republican nominee, John McCain, has worn the uniform of our country with bravery and distinction, and for that we owe him our gratitude and respect. And we'll also hear about those occasions when he's broken with his party as evidence that he can deliver the change that we need." He then proffered the counterargument. "But the record's clear: John McCain has voted with George Bush 90 percent of the time. Senator McCain likes to talk about judgment, but, really, what does it say about your judgment when you think George Bush was right more than 90 percent of the time? I don't know about you, but I'm not ready to take a 10 percent change on change." The crowd roared. Obama's staffers undoubtedly hoped that their candidate had successfully inoculated Americans who heard snippets of the speech on television at home. (Of course, McCain's advisers hoped the inoculation attempt would fail and voters would assign weight to McCain's foreign affairs experience.)

The ELM stipulates that there are two distinct ways people process communications.
These are called routes, suggesting that two different highways crisscross the mind,
transporting thoughts and reactions to messages. The term *route* is a metaphor: we do
not know for sure that these routes exist (any more than we know with absolute certainty
that any mental construct exists in precisely the way theorists use it). Social scientists
employ terms like "processing route" (or attitude) to describe complex cognitive and
behavioral phenomena. As with attitude, the term "processing route" makes eminent sense
and is supported by a great deal of empirical evidence. The ELM refers to the two routes
to persuasion as the *central* and *peripheral routes*, or central and peripheral processes.

The central route is characterized by considerable cognitive elaboration. It occurs
when individuals focus in depth on the central features of the issue, person, or message.
When people process information centrally, they carefully evaluate message arguments,
ponder implications of the communicator's ideas, and relate information to their own
knowledge and values. This is the thinking person's route to persuasion.

The peripheral route is entirely different. Rather than examining issue-relevant
arguments, people examine the message quickly or focus on simple cues to help them
decide whether to accept the position advocated in the message. Factors that are peripheral
to message arguments carry the day. These can include a communicator's physical
appeal, glib speaking style, or pleasant association between the message and music
playing in the background. When processing peripherally, people invariably rely on simple
decision-making rules or heuristics. For example, an individual may invoke the heuristic
that "experts are to be believed" and, for this reason (and this reason only), accept the
speaker's recommendation. In a similar fashion, people employ a "bandwagon heuristic,"
illustrated by the belief that "if other people think this is good, then it probably is." You
see this all the time on social networking sites, as when one infers an individual's
popularity from the number of friends she has on Facebook, judges a song to be desirable
based on song download rankings, or decides to purchase a book based on consumer
ratings on Amazon (Schmierbach, Xu, Bellur-Thandaveshwara, Ash, Oeldorf-Hirsch,
& Kegerise, 2009).

Thus, the ELM says that people can be simple information processors—"cognitive
misers" as they are sometimes called (Taylor, 1981)—or deep, detailed thinkers. Under

## Box 5.2 | THE POWER OF THOUGHT

There is nothing either good or bad, but thinking makes it so.—Shakespeare, *Hamlet*

The mind is its own place, and in itself can make a heaven of hell, a hell of heaven.—John Milton

Shakespeare and Milton may have been two of the earliest proponents of the cognitive response approach. Milton—and perhaps Shakespeare too—would also have endorsed the idea that thinking plays a critical role in mental and physical problems. Centuries after Milton and Shakespeare penned their epic works, we have evidence that generating favorable thoughts can have positive implications for mental and physical health. Christopher D. Ratcliff and colleagues (1999) explored the power of thought in a study of academic success.

Noting that "the majority of couch potatoes admit that their health would benefit from greater exercise [and] the majority of students recognize that their grades and career chances would be enhanced if they spent more time studying," Ratcliff and his associates argued that one way to help these individuals achieve their goals is to encourage them to think about the positive results of these activities (p. 994). Ratcliff and colleagues asked students to think about actions that might make studying enjoyable. They found that, compared to students in other experimental conditions, these students reported more positive intentions to spend time studying. Thinking of the benefits of studying may have strengthened attitudes toward studying, as well as perceptions that one could actually achieve this goal.

Thinking and positive cognitive responses also play a part in the well-known placebo effect—the tendency of patients to get better not because of the actual effects of a medical treatment, but rather due to a belief that the treatment will cure them. There is evidence from pain studies that placebos (dummy pills that do not actually control pain) are about 60 percent as effective as active medications like aspirin and codeine (Blakeslee, 1998). Patients suffering pain after getting a wisdom tooth extracted feel just as much relief from a fake ultrasound application as from a real one, provided both patient and doctor believe the ultrasound machine is on. Researchers have reported that they could successfully dilate asthmatics' airways by simply telling them they were inhaling a bronchodilator, even though they actually were not (Talbot, 2000).

Naturally, there are many reasons why placebos work, and of course they don't work in each and every circumstance (Kolata, 2001). However, thinking you are going to get better and rehearsing these thoughts to yourself as the doctor gives you the treatment may actually help you to achieve the desired result.

some conditions (when processing superperipherally), they are susceptible to slick persuaders—and can be thus characterized by the saying attributed to P. T. Barnum: "There's a sucker born every minute!" In other circumstances (when processing centrally), individuals are akin to Plato's ideal students—seeking truth and dutifully considering logical arguments—or to Aristotelian thinkers, persuaded only by cogent arguments (logos). The model says people are neither suckers nor deep thinkers. Complex creatures that we are, we are both peripheral and central, heuristic and systematic, processors. The critical questions are when people process centrally, when they prefer the peripheral pathway, and the implications for persuasion. The nifty thing about the ELM is that it answers these questions, laying out conditions under which central or peripheral processing is most likely, and the effects of such processing on attitude change.

The key factors that determine processing strategy are *motivation* and *ability*. When people are *motivated* to consider the message seriously, they process centrally. They also pursue the central route when they are cognitively able to ponder message arguments. Situations can limit or enhance people's ability to process centrally and so too can personal characteristics. On the other hand, when people lack the motivation or ability to process a message carefully, they opt for a simpler strategy. They process superficially.

It is frequently neither possible nor functional to process every message carefully. "Just imagine if you thought carefully about every television or radio commercial you heard or ad you came across in newspapers or magazines," note Richard Petty and colleagues. "If you ever made it out of the house in the morning, you probably would be too mentally exhausted to do anything else!" (Petty, Cacioppo, Strathman, & Priester, 1994, p. 118). Contemporary society, with its multiple stimuli, unfathomably complex issues, and relentless social change, makes it inevitable that people will rely on mental shortcuts much of the time.

In addition to spelling out factors that make peripheral processing most likely, the ELM contains hypotheses about the impact that such processing exerts on persuasion. Different persuasive appeals are effective, depending on the processing route. These appeals also differ in their long-term effects on attitudes (see Figure 5.3).

## Motivation to Process

**Involvement.** Can you think of an issue that has important implications for your own life? Perhaps it is a university proposal to raise tuition, a plan to change requirements in your major, or even a proposal to ban cell phoning while driving. Now think of an issue that has little impact on your day-to-day routines. This could be a proposal to strengthen the graduation requirements at local high schools or a plan to use a different weed spray in farming communities. You will certainly process the first issues differently than the second. Different persuasive appeals are likely to be effective in these two circumstances as well.

The topics just cited differ in their level of personal involvement, or the degree to which they are perceived to be personally relevant to individuals. *Individuals are high in involvement when they perceive that an issue is personally relevant or bears directly on their own lives. They are low in involvement when they believe that an issue has little or no impact on their own lives.*

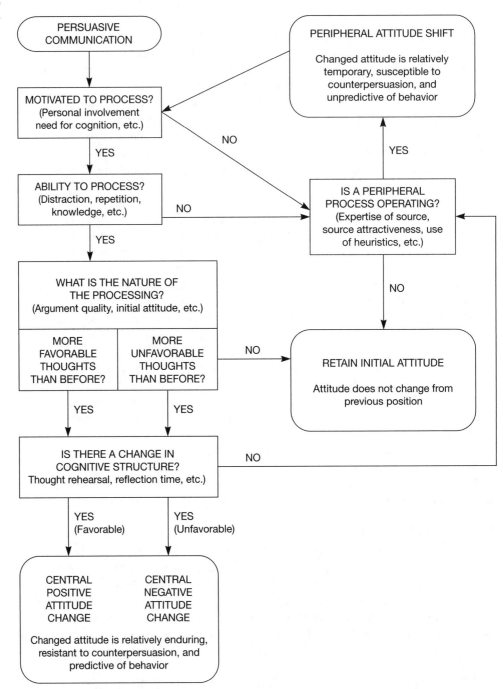

**FIGURE 5.3** | The Elaboration Likelihood Model of persuasion.

Adapted from Petty, R. E., & Wegener, D. T. (1999). The Elaboration Likelihood Model: Current status and controversies. In S. Chaiken & Y. Trope (Eds.), *Dual-process theories in social psychology* (pp. 41–72). New York: Guilford.

The ELM stipulates that when individuals are high in involvement, they will be motivated to engage in issue-relevant thinking. They will recognize that it is in their best interest to consider the arguments in the message carefully. Even if they oppose the position advocated in the message, they may change their attitudes if the arguments are sufficiently compelling to persuade them that they will benefit by adopting the advocated position. Under high involvement, people should process messages through the central route, systematically scrutinizing message arguments.

By contrast, under low involvement, people have little motivation to focus on message arguments. The issue is of little personal consequence; therefore, it doesn't pay to spend much time thinking about the message. As a result, people look for mental shortcuts to help them decide whether to accept the communicator's position. They process the message peripherally, unconcerned with the substance of the communication.

These predictions are intriguing, but how do we know if they hold water in the real world? In order to discover if hypotheses are correct, researchers test them empirically. Petty, Cacioppo, and Goldman (1981) examined these hypotheses in a now-classic study. To help you appreciate the procedures, I ask that you imagine that the experiment was being conducted again today using equivalent methods and materials. Here is how it would work:

You first enter a small room in a university building, take a seat, and wait for the experimenter. When the experimenter arrives, she tells you that the university is currently reevaluating its academic programs and is soliciting feedback about possible changes in policy. One proposal concerns a requirement that seniors take a comprehensive exam in their major area of study.

If randomly assigned to the high-involvement condition, you would be told that the comprehensive exam requirement could begin next year. That's clearly involving as it bears directly on your educational plans. How would you feel if you learned that you might have to take a big exam in your major—communication, psychology, marketing, or whatever it happened to be? You would probably feel nervous, angry, worried, or curious. Whichever emotion you felt, you clearly would be concerned about the issue.

If, on the other hand, you had been assigned to the low-involvement condition, you would be told that the exam requirement would not take effect for 10 years. That clearly is low involvement. Even if you're on the laid-back, two-classes-a-semester plan, you do not envision being in college 10 years from now! Realizing the message is of little personal consequence, you would gently switch gears from high energy to autopilot.

Regardless of involvement level, you would be asked now to listen to one of two messages delivered by one of two communicators. The particular message and source would be determined by lot, or random assignment.

You would listen to either strong or weak arguments on behalf of the exam. Strong arguments employ statistics and evidence ("Institution of the exams had led to a reversal in the declining scores on standardized achievement tests at other universities"). They offer cogent arguments on behalf of the exam requirement. Weak arguments are shoddy and unpersuasive (for example, "A friend of the author's had to take a comprehensive exam and now has a prestigious academic position").

Lastly, you would be led to believe that the comprehensive exam proposal had been prepared by either a communicator high or low in expertise. If assigned to the high-expertise group, you would be told that the report had been developed by the Carnegie Commission on Higher Education, which had been chaired by an education professor at Princeton University. If randomly assigned to the low-expertise communicator, you would be informed that the proposal had been prepared by a class at a local high school. You would then indicate your overall evaluation of the exam.

This constituted the basic design of the study. In formal terms, there were three conditions: involvement (high or low), argument quality (strong or weak), and expertise (high or low). Petty and colleagues found that the impact of arguments and expertise depended to a considerable degree on level of involvement.

Under high involvement, argument quality exerted a significant impact on attitudes toward the comprehensive exam. Regardless of whether a high school class or Princeton professor was the source of the message, strong arguments led to more attitude change than did weak arguments. Under low involvement, the opposite pattern of results emerged. A highly expert source induced more attitude change than did a low-expert source, regardless of whether the arguments were strong or weak (see Figure 5.4).

The ELM provides a parsimonious explanation of the findings. Under high involvement, students believed that the senior exam would affect them directly. This heightened motivation to pay careful attention to the quality of the arguments. Processing the arguments carefully through the central route, students naturally were more swayed by strong than by weak arguments.

Imagine how you would react if you had been in this condition. Although you would hardly be overjoyed at the prospect of an exam in your major area of study, the idea would grab your attention, and you would think carefully about the arguments. After reading them, you would not be 100 percent in favor of the comprehensive exam—but having thought through the ideas and noted the benefits the exam provided, you might be more sympathetic to the idea than you would have been at the outset and certainly more favorable than if you had listened to weak arguments on behalf of the exam.

Now imagine you had been assigned to the low-involvement–high expertise group. You'd be on autopilot because the exam would not take place until long after you graduated. Blasé about the whole thing, feeling little motivation to think carefully about the issue, you would understandably have little incentive to pay close attention to the quality of arguments.

You would focus on one salient cue—a factor that might help you decide what to do about this issue so that you could complete the assignment and get on with your day. The fact that the communicator was from Princeton might capture your attention and offer a compelling reason to go along with the message. "If this Princeton prof. thinks it's a good idea, it's fine with me," you might think. Click-whirr—just like that, you would go along with the message (Cialdini, 2001).

As we will see, these findings have intriguing implications for everyday persuasion.

Looking back on the study findings, it may seem as if the main principle is that under high involvement, "what is said" is most important, and under low involvement, "who says it" is the key. There is some truth to this, but it greatly oversimplifies matters.

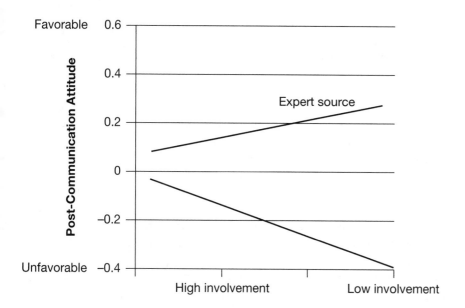

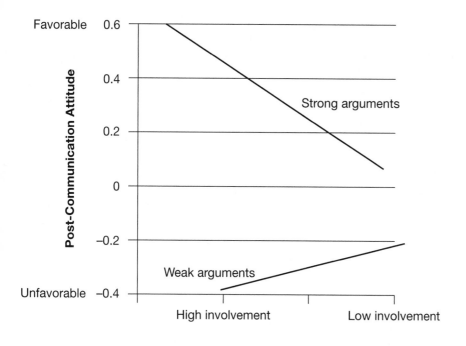

**FIGURE 5.4** | Effects of involvement, source expertise, and argument quality on attitudes.
From Petty, R. E., Cacioppo, J. T., & Goldman, R. (1981). Personal involvement as a determinant of argument-based persuasion. *Journal of Personality and Social Psychology, 41*, 847–855.

The key point is not that message appeals are more effective under high involvement and communicator appeals are more compelling under low involvement. Instead, the core issue is that people engage in issue-relevant thinking under high involvement, but under low involvement, they focus on simple cues that are peripheral to the main issues. In fact, there are times when a peripheral aspect of the message can carry the day under low involvement.

Case in point: number of message arguments. This attribute is absolutely irrelevant, or peripheral, to the quality of the message. A speaker can have nine shoddy arguments or one extremely cogent appeal. However, the number of arguments can signify quality of argumentation in the minds of perceivers. If people would rather not think too deeply about an issue, they may fall into the trap of assuming that the more arguments a message has, the more convincing it is. This is exactly what Petty and Cacioppo (1984) discovered. When students were evaluating a proposal to institute senior comprehensive exams at their own school 10 years in the future, they were more influenced by a message that had nine arguments. It didn't matter if all of them were weak. However, when contemplating a senior exam policy that would take place next year, they were naturally more motivated to devote energy to thinking about the issue. They processed arguments centrally, seeing through the shoddy ones and accepting the message only if arguments were strong.

**Other motivational factors.** Critical as it is, personal involvement is not the only factor that influences message processing. If you expect to deliver a message to an audience, you should be highly motivated to expend cognitive effort processing the message (Boninger, Brock, Cook, Gruder, & Romer, 1990). If you are concerned with making a good impression on others when giving your pitch, you should also be motivated to systematically scrutinize the arguments you are going to discuss (see Leippe & Elkin, 1987; Nienhuis, Manstead, & Spears, 2001).

There is one other motivational factor that influences processing, and it is a particularly interesting one. It is a personality characteristic: *the need for cognition—* a need to understand the world and to employ thinking to accomplish this goal. People who score high in need for cognition "prefer complex to simple problems" and "enjoy a task that involves coming up with new solutions to problems" (Cacioppo & Petty, 1982, pp. 120–121). These individuals tend to prefer central to peripheral processing. The types of persuasive appeals that work on people high in need for cognition are different from those that work on people low in cognitive needs. These issues are taken up in Chapter 8.

### Ability

A second determinant of processing strategy (besides motivation) is the person's ability to process the message. Situations can enhance or hamper individuals' ability to process a message. For example, people are less able to process a message when they are distracted, resulting in persuasive effects discussed earlier. More interestingly, we centrally or peripherally process messages depending on our cognitive ability, or knowledge.

Knowledge is a particularly important factor. When people know a lot about an issue, they process information carefully and skillfully. They are better able to separate the rhetorical wheat from the chaff than those with little knowledge of the issue. They are more capable of evaluating the cogency of information and are adept at identifying shortcomings in message arguments. It doesn't matter what the issue is: it could be nuclear physics, baseball, or roof repair. Knowledgeable people process information centrally and are ordinarily tough nuts for persuaders to crack (Wood, Rhodes, & Biek, 1995). By contrast, people with minimal knowledge on a topic lack the background to differentiate strong from weak arguments. They also may lack confidence in their opinions. They are the peripheral processors, more susceptible to persuasion in most situations.

As an example, think of an issue you know a lot about—let's say, contemporary movies. Now conjure up a topic about which you know little—let's say, computer scanners. The ELM says that you will process persuasive messages on these topics very differently and that persuaders should use different techniques to change your mind on these topics. Given your expertise on modern films (you know all about different film techniques and the strengths and weaknesses of famous directors), there is every reason to believe you would centrally process a message that claims 1960s movies are superior to those of today. The message would grab your attention and could change your attitudes—provided it contained strong, compelling arguments.

A "rational" approach like this would be stunningly ineffective on the subject of scanners that digitize photos and convert words on a printed page into word-processing files. Given your ignorance of scanners, you would have difficulty processing technical arguments about optical character recognition, driver software, or high-resolution scans. On the other hand, the salesperson who used a peripheral approach might be highly effective. A salesperson who said she had been in the business 10 years or who furnished 10 arguments why Canon was superior to Epson might easily connect with you, perhaps changing your attitude or inducing you to buy a Canon scanner. Consistent with this logic, Wood, Kallgren, and Preisler (1985) found that argument quality had a stronger impact on attitudes among individuals with a great deal of knowledge on an issue, but message length exerted a stronger influence on those with little knowledge of the issue.

## PERIPHERAL PROCESSING IN REAL LIFE

There is nothing as practical as a good theory, Kurt Lewin famously said. This is abundantly apparent in the case of the ELM. Once you appreciate the model, you begin to find all sorts of examples of how it is employed in everyday life. Four examples of peripheral processing follow, and in the next section implications of central processes are discussed.

### The Oprah Book Club Effect

Over the years, tens of millions of Americans have watched "Oprah's Book Club," a monthly segment of *The Oprah Winfrey Show* that featured engaging discussions of recently published novels. Book club shows involved a discussion among Winfrey, the author, and several viewers, who discuss the book and its relationship to their own lives. "The show receives as many as 10,000 letters each month from people eager to participate," a reporter related,

> By the time the segment appears, 500,000 viewers have read at least part of the novel. Nearly as many buy the book in the weeks that follow . . . Oprah's Book Club has been responsible for 28 consecutive best sellers. It has sold more than 20 million books and made many of its authors millionaires.
>
> (Max, 1999, pp. 36–37)

"Oprah's Book Club" has been a great thing for books and publishing. It is also an example of peripheral processing in action. What convinces hundreds of thousands of people to buy these novels? What persuades them to purchase Wally Lamb's *She's Come Undone*, the story of an intelligent, overweight woman who overcomes problems stemming from sexual abuse, rather than an equally compelling novel about abuse and redemption? The answer, in a word, is Oprah. Her credibility, warmth, and celebrity status suggest to viewers that the book is worth a try. It's not that audience members are meticulously comparing one book to another and integrate Oprah's advice with their literary assessments of the plot and character development. They lack motivation and perhaps ability. So, they rely on Oprah's advice and purchase the book, much to the delight of the publishing house and struggling novelist.

Oprah as peripheral cue can also work to the detriment of an author. When she criticizes an author, as she did after discovering that James Frey had fabricated much of *A Million Little Pieces*—a book once touted on her book club—sales of the book plummet. As one critic put it, "Fool millions, make millions. Fool Oprah, lord help you" (Carr, 2006, p. C1). With Winfrey's decision to end her nationally syndicated program in September, 2011, the publishing industry appears to have lost a powerful brand, one that has served as a powerful peripheral cue over the years. But it is likely that her impact on audiences will not end, but will simply move to a new platform as she launches a new cable television network.

## The Electoral Road Show

To many Americans, politics is like a traveling road show, a circus that the media cover every 4 years, complete with clowns, midgets, and daredevils who will do just about anything to win the crowd's approval. Politics does not affect them personally—or so many believe. About half of the electorate votes in presidential elections, and many are cynical about the political process (Doppelt & Shearer, 1999). "We have no control over what's going on," one disconnected citizen told researchers Jack Doppelt and Ellen Shearer (1999). Another said, "I don't really think any of the candidates are interested in the issues that I am [interested in]" (p. 16).

Feeling cynical about politics and blasé about their participation, large numbers of voters put little mental energy into the vote decision. Instead, they process politics peripherally, if at all. When it comes time to cast their vote, low-involved voters consider such peripheral cues as:

- *Candidate appearance.* Although people hate to admit it, they are influenced by candidates' physical appeal (Budesheim & DePaola, 1994; Rosenberg & McCafferty, 1987). Voters look at a physically attractive candidate, feel positively, and connect their positive affect with the candidate when it comes time to cast their vote.
- *Endorsements.* Political ads frequently contain long lists of endorsements. Names of well-known groups—for example, the American Bar Association, Fraternal Order of Police, and National Organization for Women—as well as not-so-famous organizations appear on a television screen, while the voice-over praises the candidate. The list serves as a peripheral cue, inviting the inference that "if all these groups endorse that candidate, he's got to be qualified."
- *Names.* In low-involving elections, the name of the candidate can make a difference. Voters prefer candidates whose names they have heard many times, in part because such names have positive associations (Grush, McKeough, & Ahlering, 1978). In an Illinois primary election, two candidates with relatively smooth-sounding names (Fairchild and Hart) defeated candidates with less euphonious names (Sangmeister and Pucinksi). Many voters were probably shocked to discover that Mark Fairchild and Janice Hart were followers of the extremist and unconventional political candidate Lyndon LaRouche (O'Sullivan, Chen, Mohapatra, Sigelman, & Lewis, 1988)!

Candidates are not exactly oblivious to these points. They appreciate the psychology of low-involvement voting, and they develop persuasive messages to reach these voters. They hire image consultants, who advise them on what to wear and how to present themselves positively in public.

Some years back, during the 2000 election, Al Gore was counseled to take on a more macho appearance by releasing his "inner-alphamale" (Bellafante, 2000). In one political debate, he showed up wearing a three-button suit, a French blue shirt, and a horizontally striped tie. Although he looked more like a movie producer than a candidate, he hoped this would resonate with Democrats dissatisfied with his personae.

At other times, candidates rely on slogans. Candidates who use catchwords that resonate with voters—"social justice" for Democrats, "family values" for Republicans—can elicit positive perceptions from individuals who lack motivation to consider issue positions (Garst & Bodenhausen, 1996). Hearing the "right" words may be all it takes to convince these individuals to cast their vote for the candidate.

What do attractiveness, slogans, endorsements, and name sound have to do with a candidate's qualifications for office? Not too much: they are peripheral to the main issues of the campaign. Yet low-involved voters often rely on these cues and can be swayed by superficial appeals. This in turn raises troubling questions about the role communications play in contemporary democracy.

## Jargon

Has this ever happened to you? Your car engine is on the blink; you take the auto to the mechanic; he (they're usually guys) looks at you with an expression that says, "You're clueless about cars, aren't you?" and then puts his hands to his hips and begins to talk in tongues—invoking the most complicated car jargon you have ever heard. Impressed by the verbiage and afraid to admit you don't know much about cars, you acquiesce to his appeal.

Tom and Ray Magliozzi, hosts of the National Public Radio show "Car Talk," echoed this point in a humorous, but telling, article. Asked by an interviewer how someone could fake being a car mechanic, they recommend a heavy use of jargon (Nitze, 2001). Use words like "the torque wrench and torquing," Tom says. Ray replies, "Torquing always sounds good." Tom adds, "I'll bet you, you could walk into some party and mention the expression 'negative torque,' there would be nobody who would have the guts to ask you what that meant. A pro included" (p. 38).

This fits right in with the ELM. Individuals with little knowledge about car mechanics have trouble following explanations involving torque or car computer systems. When a mechanic begins using the jargon, they invoke the heuristic, "Mechanics who talk this way know their stuff; if they say this, it must be so." And, just like that, the mechanic persuades these customers to make the purchase. (A similar example comes from the movie *My Cousin Vinny*, when the character played by Marisa Tomei wows a judge and jury, using jargon comprehensible only to car experts to prove that a getaway car could not possibly have been driven by the two men accused of the crime.)

## Seduced by a Quick Fix

How were countless Americans lured into purchasing mortgages they could not afford? Over the course of a decade—from about 1998 to 2008—home buyers across the country signed their names on legally binding documents, committing themselves to purchase homes at prices that were too good to be true. With details complicated and technical terms (like variable rate loans and adjustable rate mortgages) reeling in their minds, many buyers put their trust in lenders. Big mistake.

The ELM reminds us that when individuals lack ability on an issue, they resort to the peripheral route, accepting a message because a credible source recommends it. Unfortunately, some credible bank loan officers were all too eager to pitch crooked messages. Under pressure from their bosses to approve mortgages so that the bank could amass huge profits, the lending agents frequently pulled out all stops, offering loans to buyers who they knew could not afford the monthly payments. Executives at one bank, Washington Mutual, were particularly eager to exploit (they would say "convince") borrowers who lacked adequate credit.

Washington Mutual relied heavily on adjustable rate mortgages that functioned as the financial equivalent of smoke and mirrors. Unschooled in the fine points of adjustable mortgages, home buyers were enticed by the promise that they could decide how much their house payment would cost each month. There was a catch: borrowers who chose to make small monthly payments were underpaying interest due on the loan, while adding to the principal—the actual amount of money lent by the bank. In the long run, this caused loan payments to skyrocket (Goodman & Morgenson, 2008, p. A21). One elderly couple found their housing costs rose from about $1,000 to $3,000 a month, leading them to fall behind in their monthly payments.

On the other hand, no one put a gun to borrowers' heads. They freely chose to accept the terms of the loan, relying on peripheral credibility cues, while discounting their responsibility to study payment arrangements. Yet bank executives knew they were making shaky loans and encouraged loan officers to ignore their fiduciary responsibilities.

"If you were alive, they would give you a loan. Actually, I think if you were dead, they would still give you a loan," one banking expert said (Goodman & Morgenson, 2008).

## CENTRAL PROCESSING

Peripheral processing is a persuader's paradise. It allows communicators to devise simplistic—sometimes deceptive—appeals to influence individuals. Tempting as it is to conclude that this is the basis for all contemporary persuasion, the fact is that much persuasion also involves careful, thoughtful consideration of message arguments. As discussed earlier, when people are motivated or able to process messages, they don't rely exclusively on peripheral cues or necessarily fall for a persuader's ploys. Instead, they attend closely to the communicator's arguments. In these situations, persuasion flows through the central route, and appeals are necessarily crafted at a higher intellectual level.

Thus, when people typically buy big-ticket items like stereo systems, computers, and, of course, houses, they respond to cogent arguments in support of the particular product in question. In politics, when voters are out of work or concerned about the economy, they listen closely to candidates' plans to revitalize the nation's finances. For example, in 1980, with the country reeling from double-digit inflation, Ronald Reagan made the economy a centerpiece of his campaign against then-president Jimmy Carter. "Are you better off than you were 4 years ago?" he asked Americans in a presidential debate. Reagan went on to suggest that many folks were worse off than they had been prior to Carter taking office. In posing the question this way, Reagan induced people to think seriously about their own economic situations and at the same time to give his challenge to an incumbent president dutiful consideration. His appeals apparently worked, for Reagan handily defeated Carter in the November election (Ritter & Henry, 1994).

Arguments, however, do not always carry the day in persuasion. Cogent arguments can fall on deaf ears when they run counter to an individual's strong attitudes or values. Recall the discussion in Chapter 2 of how passionate supporters and opponents of the death penalty reacted to evidence that questioned their position. They did not alter their attitudes. On the contrary, they criticized data that disputed their point of view, praised evidence that supported their position, and emerged with renewed confidence that their view on capital punishment was correct. How could this be, one wonders, if people are supposed to consider arguments rationally when they are interested in the issue in question?

The answer points to a complexity in the ELM. All central-route processing is not rational and free of bias. Human beings are not objective thinkers. The key is the degree to which the issue touches on an individual's strong attitudes, values, or ego-entrenched positions. It is useful to distinguish between issues that are of interest because they bear on important outcomes in the individual's life—comprehensive exams, tuition increases, the economy—and those that bear on values or deep-seated attitudes. When the message focuses on a personally relevant outcome, people process arguments rationally, putting aside their biases as best they can, focusing on the merits of issue arguments. However, when the issue touches on core values or *ego-involved* schema, individuals can be extremely biased and selective in how they approach the issue.

Make no mistake: in both cases, they process centrally, engaging in considerable thinking and evaluating the basic ideas contained in the message. However, when thinking about outcomes (a comprehensive exam), they are open to cogent arguments. When considering a message that touches on core values (capital punishment, abortion), they attend to the opponent's arguments, but usually reject them (Johnson & Eagly, 1989; Wood et al., 1985, though see Park, Levine, Kingsley Westerman, Orfgen, & Foregger, 2007). Highly knowledgeable people with strong attitudes will muster all sorts of sophisticated reasons why the opponent's plan is a bad one. They will impress you with their ability to remember the other side's arguments, but in the end they will prove to be just as biased as anyone else.

In these situations, people behave like ostriches, stubbornly rejecting ideas that are inconsistent with their attitude and sticking only with communications that fall into the latitude of acceptance. How do communicators persuade people in such situations? With great difficulty and care, to be sure. Social judgment theory (see Chapter 2) suggests that when trying to persuade people about issues that touch on core values, persuaders must strive to do two things. First, they should encourage individuals to assimilate the issue, or candidate, to their position. That is, they want people—or voters, applying this to a political context—to perceive that the candidate shares their position on the issue. The goal is not to change the voter's position on abortion, defense spending, the environment, or affirmative action. Instead, the idea is to convince voters that the candidate shares *their* positions on the issue and is sympathetic with *their* concerns (Schwartz, 1973).

At the same time, a communicator wants to make sure that people do not come away from the persuasive encounter perceiving that they are in sharp disagreement with the communicator on the issue (Kaplowitz & Fink, 1997). If voters *contrast* their position from a politician's and assume that the politician takes a very different position on a key issue, the candidate is in deep do-do, as former president George H. W. Bush liked to say. For these reasons, candidates are frequently careful not to take strong positions on hot-button issues like abortion, gun control, capital punishment, and racial quotas. They are fearful of alienating undecided voters—of pushing voters' contrast effect buttons. If this happens, these folks may vote for the opposing candidate or stay home. Thus, there is a practical reason why candidates take "fuzzy" positions on hot-button issues. Yet this points up a troubling ethical issue. Candidates must camouflage or moderate their positions to get elected (Granberg & Seidel, 1976). However, in so doing they risk compromising their integrity or turning off voters who suspect the worst in politicians. Yet if they admirably stick to their guns and take strong positions, they alienate middle-of-the-roaders and end up being right—not president.

Senator John McCain faced this quandary when he ran for president in 2008. The long-time Republican senator from Arizona had run as a maverick reformist in the 2000

Republican primaries, promising "straight talk" and keeping his distance from the party's religious conservatives. McCain lost the 2000 Republican nomination after a bruising South Carolina primary, in which underground political groups smeared his character and family. Chastened by his loss and recognizing that he needed the support of evangelical Christians, he broke bread with religious conservatives, hoping to gain their support in 2008. Already unpopular with conservatives for taking a liberal position on immigration and opposing a federal ban on same-sex marriage, he switched gears, emphasizing his pro-life stance and endorsing the Bush tax cuts he had once opposed.

McCain seemed to recognize that, in the realm of strong attitudes, a candidate cannot risk taking positions that are in voters' latitudes of rejection. Instead, candidates must make statements that fall squarely in voters' latitudes of acceptance, encouraging them to assimilate the candidate's positions to their own. McCain hoped voters would centrally process his positions, perceiving them as consonant with their own attitudes.

In politics, central processing frequently leads to reinforcement or strengthening of existing attitudes. However, central processing can also produce profound *changes* in attitudes, alterations that extend beyond hardening of preexisting sentiments. Americans radically changed their attitudes toward smoking, health, and exercise, in part due to central processing. In this way, the ELM explains how people modify their attitudes under high-involvement conditions. Individuals reconsider earlier positions, gradually alter their assessments of the issue, think deeply about the matter (sometimes through painful reassessment of themselves and their values), and over time link up the new attitude with other aspects of themselves. This leads to the attitude becoming a more permanent fixture of individuals' self-systems.

Attitudes changed through deep, central route thinking are more likely to persist over time than those formed through short-circuited thinking or peripheral cues (Petty, Haugtvedt, & Smith, 1995). The hopeful side of this is that prejudice and dysfunctional attitudes can be changed. Once modified, such changes can also persist and lead to improvements in the person's overall mental state.

## COMPLICATIONS AND CRITICISMS

In the many years that have elapsed since the ELM was first introduced, the theory has been discussed, criticized, clarified, extended, and, yes, elaborated on in a variety of ways. In this section, I review these intellectual developments, hoping to illuminate the fine points of cognitive theorizing about persuasion.

A key issue involves the ability of a particular variable to do different things or serve diverse functions. Consider physical attractiveness. If you had to describe the role physical attractiveness plays in persuasion based on the earlier discussion, you might suggest that it serves as a peripheral cue. You might speculate that when people do not care much about an issue or lack ability to process the message, they fall back on the physical appeal of the speaker. Opting not to process the message carefully, they let themselves get carried away a bit by the speaker's good looks. The pleasant association of the communicator with the communication pushes individuals toward accepting the message. This analysis of attractiveness is indeed in sync with the ELM as it has been discussed thus far. Attractiveness frequently has just this effect, serving as a cue for peripheral processing.

Unfortunately, matters become more complicated when we examine other persuasion settings. For example, suppose a young woman is looking for a beauty product, flips through the pages of *Glamour* magazine, and sees models promoting L'Oreal and Cover Girl lipcolors. The models' good looks represent key selling points for the products. Isn't a model's attractiveness central to the decision regarding the product, not peripheral? Couldn't the physical appeal of the model—the fact that she is beautiful and uses this product—serve as a compelling reason to purchase the particular facial cream, lipcolor, or makeup? Weren't endorsements by Jessica Simpson and other models central arguments that buttressed the case for purchasing the acne medicine, Proactiv? The answer to these questions is "Yes."

The ELM argues that, theoretically, a particular variable can serve in one of three capacities. It can function as a: (a) *persuasive argument*, (b) *peripheral cue*, or (c) *factor that influences thinking about the person or issue*. Thus, for someone trying to decide whether to purchase a beauty product or shampoo, the communicator's attractiveness can serve as an argument for the product (Kahle & Homer, 1985). In another context—electoral politics—attractiveness can function as a *peripheral cue*, as when people decide to vote for candidates because they think they're cute.

Now consider a third situation involving a different aspect of politics. Let's say a person has mixed feelings on environmental and energy issues. She believes that the United States needs to locate alternative sources of fuel, but also feels it is important to preserve breathtakingly beautiful wildlife refuges. When an attractive source like actor Robert Redford (2001) criticizes policies to drill for oil in the Arctic National Wildlife Refuge, she may find herself *devoting more cognitive energy* to the communicator's arguments. She may picture Redford in her mind, link up his attractive appearance with the beauty of the wilderness, and therefore give his arguments more thought than if a less attractive communicator had advanced these positions.

Or consider another environmental issue: global warming. Some Americans are unaware of evidence that the world is hotter now than it has been at any point in the last 2,000 years. Suppose a reputable Web site called "Feeling the Heat" presents a list of credible scientists who declare that there is incontrovertible evidence that significant global warming is occurring (Easterbrook, 2006). The Web site has the imprimatur of the National Academy of Sciences. The opinions of scientists on this issue can be influential. What does the ELM say about the role played by credibility here?

The model offers up a complicated prediction (Petty & Wegener, 1999). It says the scientists' expertise can serve as a peripheral cue for people low in concern or knowledge about environmental issues. These folks may say to themselves, "Who knows what's going on with the environment these days? It's beyond me. I'll go with what the scientists say. If they say this, it must be right."

For those with considerable knowledge and concern about the environment, the scientists' views may actually function as an argument. These highly involved individuals may think:

I know the scientific community had been reluctant to declare that temperatures are artificially rising or that carbon dioxide emissions are responsible for global warming. If scientists have changed their tune now, it must be that there is strong evidence that global warming effects are real.

To other individuals, with moderate knowledge or involvement, the scientists' proclamations about global warming may stimulate issue-relevant thinking. They may consider the issue more carefully now that the National Academy of Sciences, as well as scientific academies across the world, have concluded that significant global warming is occurring across the planet. They may not change their minds, especially if they have strong views on this issue. However, the highly credible-source endorsement might catalyze their thinking, leading them to develop more detailed arguments on global warming or increasing their confidence in particular beliefs.

Note that the same processes could work on the opposite side of the issue. Suppose that a publisher released a new book by Freeman Dyson, an internationally-renowned scientist who has publicly *challenged* the validity of global warming. His book could serve as a peripheral cue for the low-involved, a persuasive argument for highly-involved individuals, and an intellectual catalyst for those with moderate knowledge or interest in the issue.

In this way, a particular variable can serve multiple functions. Just as an attitude can serve different functions for different people, so too a persuasion factor can play different roles in different situations.

## CRITICISMS AND RECONCILIATIONS

Any persuasion model that stimulates research will generate criticism. This is as it should be: theories are meant to be criticized and subjected to empirical scrutiny. Knowledge advances from the dueling of conflicting scholarly guns. New ideas emerge from the critical exchange of points of view.

The ELM has elicited its share of criticism, with bullets targeted at the multiple functions notion previously discussed. Critics have lamented the lack of clarity of this notion. They have argued that the ELM position permits it "to explain all possible outcomes," making it impossible in principle to prove the model wrong (Stiff & Boster, 1987, p. 251). "A persuader can conduct a post mortem to find out what happened but cannot forecast the impact of a particular message," Allen and Preiss contend (1997a, pp. 117–118).

Proponents of the ELM have thundered back, arguing that critics fail to appreciate the model's strengths (Petty, Cacioppo, Kasmer, & Haugtvedt, 1987; Petty, Wegener, Fabrigar, Priester, & Cacioppo, 1993). As a general rule, proponents note, individuals will be more likely to elaborate on messages when they are high in motivation or ability, and more inclined to focus on peripheral cues when they are lower in ability or motivation. What's more, they say, if you understand the particular variable under investigation and the situation in which it operates, you can make clear predictions about the influences of persuasion factors on attitudes (Haugtvedt & Wegener, 1994; Petty & Wegener, 1998). Persuasion and human behavior are so complex, ELM proponents assert, that it is not possible to make precise predictions for every variable in each and every situation. On balance, they maintain, the ELM offers a highly useful framework for understanding how persuasion works in the panoply of situations in which it occurs in everyday life.

Both sides have a point. The multiple functions notion discussed earlier is intriguing, but it points to a problematic ambiguity in the model: the ELM is so all inclusive that it is difficult to prove the model incorrect. We want hypotheses to be capable of being proven right—and wrong. And yet for all the criticisms, the ELM has many compensating virtues, as both critics and proponents acknowledge. It offers a comprehensive theory of cognitive processing. It helps us understand the dynamics of thinking about persuasive messages. These are important contributions, ones that should not be minimized.

Before the ELM (and the HSM: see Box 5.3) was invented, there were few in-depth approaches to understanding cognition and persuasive communication. There was a hodgepodge of results—findings about this type of communicator, that type of message, and this kind of message recipient. It was like a jigsaw puzzle that didn't quite fit together. The ELM has helped provide us with a unified framework to understand the blooming, buzzing confusion of persuasion. For example, it helps explain why certain attitudes persist longer and predict behavior better than others (the former are elaborated on, accessed more, and linked up to a greater degree with other mental elements).

To be sure, the model has imperfections. It understates the role emotion plays in persuasion. It also does not clearly specify the type of message that persuaders should employ under high involvement. The only advice the model offers is that communicators should induce audience members to generate positive thoughts on behalf of the message. But what type of message should you employ? How should you frame your message to get people thinking positively? Just what constitutes a high-quality, strong argument in the ELM (Frymier & Nadler, 2007). The model is silent on these matters (see Johnson, Maio, & Smith-McLallen, 2005).

Nevertheless, no theory is perfect, and the ELM has done much for the field of persuasion research. It has helped illuminate the psychological reasons why communications can powerfully influence audiences. It linked cognitive processes to communication effects in a coherent way. It has provided a framework for understanding the psychology of persuasive communication, helping to explain why different messages are effective in different circumstances and on different individuals. More than two decades after it was proposed, the ELM continues to stimulate insights, with scholars exploring how new cognitive mechanisms, such as the mere perception of processing, influence attitudes (Barden & Petty, 2008).

In the end, as several scholarly critics note, it would be difficult to overstate the model's contribution to our knowledge of persuasive communication (Kruglanski, Thompson, & Spiegel, 1999, p. 294; see also Booth-Butterfield & Welbourne, 2002; Slater, 2002). It has, in short, emphasized the interdependence of the message and the mind in persuasion. You cannot understand the mind without appreciating how messages influence attitudes. You cannot develop persuasive messages without understanding the features of the human mind.

## Box 5.3 | HEURISTIC AND SYSTEMATIC THINKING

The HSM complements the ELM. It too has generated a great deal of research. No discussion on persuasion would be complete without discussing its main features.

Like the ELM, the HSM emphasizes that there are two processes by which persuasion occurs. Instead of calling the routes central and peripheral, it speaks of systematic and heuristic processing. Systematic processing entails comprehensive examination of issue-relevant arguments. Heuristic processing, discussed earlier in this chapter, involves the use of cognitive shortcuts. People invoke heuristics, or simple rules of thumb that enable them to evaluate message arguments without much cognitive effort. For example, the notion that "experts are always right" is a cognitive heuristic.

Like the ELM, the HSM says that motivation and ability determine processing strategy. It emphasizes that people can be motivated by a need to hold accurate attitudes, defensive needs to maintain attitudes that bear on the self-concept, or desire to make a positive impression on others (Chen & Chaiken, 1999).

The HSM interestingly emphasizes that heuristic and systematic processes are not mutually exclusive. Instead, it says that, under certain circumstances, people can rely on heuristics and systematically process a message (Eagly & Chaiken, 1993; Todorov et al., 2002).

A major contribution of the HSM is its suggestion that simple decision rules or heuristics play an important role in attitude change. People are viewed as "minimalist information processors" who are unwilling to devote much effort to processing persuasive arguments (Stiff, 1994). They like their shortcuts and they use them frequently in everyday life. Even so, there are some conditions under which people will gravitate to a systematic processing mode, and individuals seek a balance between relying on shortcuts and carefully processing a message.

Despite the differences in approach, both models emphasize that there are two fundamentally different ways to process a persuasive message. They maintain that people use one of these two routes, depending on how much they care about the issue and how capable they are of understanding the topic at hand. Although most researchers like the idea of two different routes to persuasion, there are dissenters. Arie W. Kruglanski and Erik P. Thompson (1999) have argued that it's easier to think of just one pathway to persuasion; the key is how extensively people process information. However, they too emphasize that you can't appreciate the effects of persuasion without understanding the process. Or you can't understand the message without appreciating the mind.

# CONCLUSIONS

We can trace dual-process models to ancient Greece. Plato's ideal thinkers epitomized systematic, deep processing of persuasive messages; some of the Sophist writers (at least as depicted by Plato) embodied the colorful, stylistic appeals we associate with the peripheral route. Contemporary models, attempting to explain a very different world of persuasion than that which bedeviled the Greeks, hark back to the duality that preoccupied Plato in the fourth century BC.

Contemporary models stipulate that there are two routes to persuasion—one thoughtful, focusing on the main arguments in the message, the other superficial and short circuited, characterized by an attempt to make a quick choice, an easy fix. The ELM and HSM, building on the Yale attitude change and cognitive response approaches, offer insights about how people process messages in many situations. Motivation and ability determine processing strategy. Processing route, in turn, determines the type of message appeal that is maximally effective in a particular context, as well as the long-term effects of the message on attitudes. In other words, if you understand the factors impinging on someone and how he or she thinks about a persuasive message, you have a good chance of devising a message that will target the individual's attitudes.

Complications arise when we consider that persuasion factors perform multiple functions. A given factor can serve as a cue, an argument, or catalyst to thought, depending on the person and situation. The multiple functions notion helps explain a variety of persuasion effects; however, its ambiguity can frustrate attempts to derive clear applications of the ELM to real-life situations. Taken as a whole, however, the model offers scholars a framework for understanding persuasion and provides practitioners with ideas for designing effective appeals (see Box 5.4). In essence, the model tells persuaders—in areas ranging from politics to health—to understand how their audiences approach and process messages. The ELM cautions against confrontation. Instead, it instructs communicators to tailor their arguments to audience members' motives and abilities.

The model has shed light on the mental processes that underlie persuasive communication effects. For all its contributions, it, like other psychological approaches, does not always offer a clear explanation of how an understanding of people's thought processes can help persuaders generate specific messages. It also has trouble explaining how persuaders should change views that are not governed so much by conscious thought, such as implicit prejudiced attitudes (Rydell & McConnell, 2006). Hopefully, the next generation of persuasion models will provide crisper linkages between the subtle psychology of the mind and communication of the persuasive message. From an ethical perspective, the model is value neutral. Reliance on peripheral or central cues can be functional or dysfunctional. Messages containing peripheral cues can take advantage of audiences' lack of motivation to consider issues under low involvement; centrally processed arguments can be cogent, but deceptive. As a psychological theory of persuasion, the model is silent as to whether people's motivation to process issues carefully under high involvement balances out their susceptibility to manipulation under low involvement. The most reasonable answer to these conundrums is that individuals are

## Box 5.4 | PERSUASION TIPS

One of the nifty things about the ELM is that it contains practical, as well as theoretical, suggestions. Here are several suggestions for everyday persuasion, gleaned from the model:

1.  As you prepare a presentation, ask yourself if the topic is one that engages the audience or is one of little consequence. Does the audience care a lot about the issue? Or is it of little personal relevance? If it is a high-involvement issue, you should make sure you prepare strong arguments and get the audience thinking. If it is a low-involvement matter, you should emphasize peripheral cues, simple strategies, and ways to bolster the audience's confidence that you know your stuff. But in either case, make sure you deliver your message ethically and with respect for moral values.

2.  Next time you are trying to convince someone of something, you should ask yourself: What is central, or most critical, to my attempt to change the other's mind? What type of appeal will serve my goal best? For example, people are frequently scared of giving a public speech and assume that the most important thing is to look nice— buy fancy clothes, put on lots of makeup, and so forth. This can be an important aspect of persuasion, but it may be peripheral to the task. If you are trying to make a sale, you need compelling arguments that the purchase is in the client's interest. If you are trying to convince people to get more exercise, you must show them that exercise can help them achieve their goals.

3.  By the same token, remember that something that appears peripheral to you may be of considerable importance to the person you are trying to convince (Soldat, Sinclair, & Mark, 1997). You may spend a lot of time coming up with great arguments to convince neighbors to sign a petition against McDonald's building a new franchise near a beautiful park located down the block. But if your memo has a couple of typos or your Web site containing the message is overloaded with information, people may think a little less of you. They may jump to the conclusion that your arguments are flawed. To you, the typos or abundance of information is of much less consequence than the cogency of your arguments. And you may be right. But what is peripheral to you can be central to someone else. Put yourself in the minds of those receiving your message, and consider how they will react to what you say and how you package your message.

4.  When you are on the other end of the persuasion stick and are receiving the message, ask a couple of questions. First, is this something I really care about, or is it a low-involvement issue to me? Second, can I figure out what the persuader is promoting, or is this beyond me? If it is a high-involvement issue or you can understand where the persuader is coming from, you will probably scrutinize the message carefully and make a good decision. If you decide it's a low-involvement issue or you lack knowledge on the topic, you may find yourself turning to peripheral cues or relying on mental

**Box 5.4** |

shortcuts. You may search for the easy way to make up your mind. There is nothing wrong with this, but it can lead you to place more trust in a persuader than perhaps you should. You could get snookered as a result!

To protect yourself, always ask yourself if you're trying to go for the quick fix, either because you don't care or don't know much about the issue. If you recognize that you are relying on mental shortcuts, take the opposite tack. Spend more time than you ordinarily would on the decision. Think about the issue. You may find it's more interesting or less difficult than you thought. The extra few minutes you spend thinking may help prevent you from making a costly or embarrassing mistake.

responsible for the persuasive decisions they make. It is our responsibility to recognize that we like to take mental shortcuts when we care or know little about an issue and persuaders will try to take advantage of this tendency. In the short and long runs, it is our responsibility to protect ourselves from being taken in by the peripheral persuaders of the world.

# Chapter 6

# "Who Says It": Source Factors in Persuasion

CHARISMA. It's a word that comes to mind frequently when people speak of persuasion. You probably think of great speakers, a certain magnetic quality, or perhaps people you know who seem to embody this trait. Charisma is also one of those "god-terms" in persuasion (Weaver, 1953)—concepts that have positive connotations, but have been used for good and evil purposes. We can glimpse this in the tumultuous events of the twentieth century, events that were shaped in no small measure by the power of charismatic leaders. We can also observe this in speeches delivered by orators in the twenty-first century, speeches that influenced political history. For example:

On July 27, 2004, a little-known state senator from Illinois, Barack Obama, rocked the Democratic national convention in Boston, delivering a keynote speech that propelled him to his party's nomination 4 years later and sent ripples of change through the system. He spoke forcefully and with poise. His syntax, sentence structure, and clever turns of a phrase captured the delegates' attention. "His height, his prominent sober head, (and) his long arms" lent him "a commanding aura." His voice, "with its oratorical cadences," boomed (Messud, 2008, p. 49). Calling on time-honored myths rooted deeply in the American experience and harnessing the power of language, Obama transported the audience to a higher place. After paying tribute to American individualism, he spoke of "another ingredient in the American saga, a belief that we are all connected as one people." Offering up several emotional examples, he intoned:

> Now even as we speak, there are those who are preparing to divide us, the spin masters and negative ad peddlers who embrace the politics of anything goes. Well, I say to them tonight, there's not a liberal America and a conservative America; there's the United States of America. There's not a Black America and White America and Latino America and Asian America; there's the United States of America. The pundits, the pundits like to slice and dice our country into red states and blue states; red states for Republicans, blue states for Democrats. But I've got news for them, too. We worship an awesome God in the blue states, and we don't like federal agents poking around our libraries in the red states. We coach Little

League in the blue states and, yes, we've got some gay friends in the red states. There are patriots who opposed the war in Iraq, and there are patriots who supported the war in Iraq. We are one people, all of us pledging allegiance to the stars and stripes, all of us defending the United States of America.

Obama followed in the footsteps of another charismatic orator, Reverend Martin Luther King, Jr., whose words had inspired a movement. On August 28, 1963, King delivered his most famous address.

On that day, hundreds of thousands of people converged on Washington, DC, protesting racial prejudice and hoping to place pressure on Congress to pass a civil rights bill. The protesters marched from the Washington Monument to the Lincoln Memorial, listening to a litany of distinguished speakers, but waiting patiently for King to address the crowd. King had worked all night on his speech, a sermonic address that would prove to be among the most moving of all delivered on American soil. He alluded to Abraham Lincoln, called on Old Testament prophets, and presented "an entire inventory of patriotic themes and images typical of Fourth of July oratory," captivating the audience with his exclamation, repeated time and again, that "I have a dream" (Miller, 1992, p. 143). King's wife, Coretta Scott King, recalls the pantheon:

> Two hundred and fifty thousand people applauded thunderously, and voiced in a sort of chant, Martin Luther King . . . He started out with the written speech, delivering it with great eloquence . . . When he got to the rhythmic part of demanding freedom now, and wanting jobs now, the crowd caught the timing and shouted now in a cadence. Their response lifted Martin in a surge of emotion to new heights of inspiration. Abandoning his written speech, forgetting time, he spoke from his heart, his voice soaring magnificently out over that great crowd and over to all the world. It seemed to all of us there that day that his words flowed from some higher place, through Martin, to the weary people before him. Yea—Heaven itself opened up and we all seemed transformed.
>
> (1969, pp. 238–239)

Charisma also was in force some 60 years earlier, at a different place, during a different time. In cities like Nuremberg and Berlin, to audiences of Germans—young, old, educated, uneducated, cultured, and uncultured—Adolf Hitler spoke, using words and exploiting symbols, bringing audiences to their feet "with his overwhelming, hysterical passion, shouting the same message they had heard over and over again, that they had been done in by traitors, by conspirators . . . , by Communists, plutocrats, and Jews" (Davidson, 1977, p. 183). Like King's, Hitler's oratory moved people and appealed to their hopes and dreams. But his speeches malevolently twisted hope into some gnarled ghastly entity and appealed to Germans' latent, darkest prejudices. Here is how a journalist who carefully observed Hitler described the Fuhrer's charismatic skill:

> With unerring sureness, Hitler expressed the speechless panic of the masses faced by an invisible enemy and gave the nameless specter a name. He was a pure fragment

of the modern mass soul, unclouded by any personal qualities. One scarcely need ask with what arts he conquered the masses; he did not conquer them, he portrayed and represented them. His speeches are daydreams of this mass soul; they are chaotic, full of contradictions, if their words are taken literally, often senseless as dreams are, and yet charged with deeper meaning . . . The speeches always begin with deep pessimism, and end in overjoyed redemption, a triumphant, happy ending, often they can be refuted by reason, but they follow the far mightier logic of the subconscious, which no refutation can touch. Hitler has given speech to the speechless terror of the modern mass, and to the nameless fear he has given a name. That makes him the greatest mass orator of the mass age.

(quoted in Burleigh, 2000, pp. 100–101)

Charisma—exploited for evil purposes by Hitler, used to lift human spirits by Martin Luther King—describes the power of so many forceful speakers, including (in the political realm), John F. Kennedy, Ronald Reagan, Bill Clinton, and Barack Obama; Malcolm X and Jesse Jackson in the domain of race and civil rights; and Nelson Mandela and Mahatma Ghandi in the international domain of human rights.

Regrettably, it also describes a legion of cult leaders, who enchanted, then deceived, dozens, even hundreds of starry-eyed followers. The list of charismatic cult leaders includes Charles Manson; Jim Jones, who induced 900 people to commit suicide in Guyana; David Koresh, leader of the ill-fated Branch Davidians in Waco, Texas; Marshall Applewhite, who led 38 members of the Heaven's Gate cult to commit suicide in 1997; and, most recently, Osama bin Laden, who masterminded the September 11 attacks and, to many, is the personification of evil.

Charismatic sociopaths such as these fascinate people. "Everything that deceives," Plato declared, "may be said to enchant."

What is charisma? How is it defined? Coined over a century ago by German sociologist Max Weber (1968), charisma is "*a certain quality of the individual personality by virtue of which he is set apart from ordinary men and treated as endowed with supernatural, superhuman, or at least exceptional powers and qualities*" (p. 241). Scholars who have studied charisma acknowledge the powerful influence it can have over ordinary people. Yet they also are quick to identify its limits. Charismatic individuals, after all, are not superhuman, but are seen in this light by their followers. Followers, for their part, influence the self-perception of leaders. As Ronald E. Riggio notes, "The charismatic leader inspires the crowd, but he also becomes charged by the emotions of the followers. Thus, there is an interplay between leader and followers that helps to build a strong union between them" (1987, p. 76).

Charisma is also bound and bracketed by history. A person who has charisma in one era might not wield the same influences on audiences in another historical period. The chemistry between speaker and audience is a product of a particular set of circumstances, psychological needs, and social conditions. Martin Luther King might not be charismatic in today's more complex multicultural era, which involves increased tolerance for racial diversity but also wariness of the costs of worthy social experiments like affirmative action. Franklin Delano Roosevelt, a grand and majestic speaker on radio, might not move millions of television viewers, who would watch a crippled president clutch his wheelchair for support. Even John F. Kennedy, who was captivating on television, might be charismatically challenged on YouTube, a medium that prizes technological manipulations—elegantly-designed videos, cutaways, exquisite cinematography—that were unheard of in his era.

Charisma, a powerful force in the twentieth century, is not likely to disappear. People need to believe in the power of myth, and charismatic leaders feed—and can exploit—this motivation. Charismatic leaders in the twenty-first century will exude qualities different from those of orators of previous eras. They will adapt their styles to the conditions and media of their times.

What more can be said of charisma? What role does it play in everyday persuasion? These questions are more difficult to answer. Charisma is an intriguing factor in persuasion, but an elusive one, to be sure. Granted, charisma involves a persuader's ability to command and compel an audience, but what specific traits are involved? The communicator's sociability? Attractiveness? Power? Or is it an attribute of the message: the words, metaphors, or nonverbal communication (hand motions and eye contact, for example)? Or does charisma have more to do with the audience—individuals' own vulnerability and need to believe that a communicator has certain qualities they yearn for in life? These questions point to the difficulty of defining charisma with sufficient precision that it can be studied in social scientific settings. There is no question that charisma exists and has been a powerful force in persuasion. On a practical level, it is difficult to study the concept and to determine just how it works and why.

Thus, those who wish to understand why the Martin Luther Kings and Hitlers of the world have profoundly affected audiences must take a different tack. They must either study political history or take a more finely tuned, social scientific approach to examining communicator effects.

More generally, those of us who want to comprehend how persuaders persuade are advised to chip away at the question by examining the different pieces of the puzzle. A key piece of the puzzle—a core aspect of charisma—is the communicator. His or her qualities, and the ways in which these characteristics interact with the audience, can strongly influence attitudes. The chapters that follow explore other noteworthy aspects of this jigsaw puzzle of persuasive communication effects: the message (Chapter 7) and the psychology of the audience (Chapters 8 and 9).

The present chapter begins with an overview of communicator (or source) factors. It then discusses key factors in depth, applying them to contemporary life.

## UNDERSTANDING THE COMMUNICATOR

Just as there is not one type of charismatic leader (Ronald Reagan differed vastly from Jesse Jackson), there is not one defining characteristic of effective communicators. Communicators have different attributes and influence audiences through different processes.

159

*"Who
Says It":
Source
Factors in
Persuasion*

There are three fundamental communicator characteristics: authority, credibility, and social attractiveness. Authorities, credible communicators, and attractive ones produce attitude change through different mechanisms (Kelman, 1958).

Authorities frequently influence others through compliance. Individuals adopt a particular behavior not because they agree with its content, but rather because they expect "to gain specific rewards or approval and avoid specific punishments or disapproval by conforming" (Kelman, 1958, p. 53). In other words, people go along with authority figures because they hope to obtain rewards or avoid punishment.

Credible communicators, by contrast, influence attitudes through internalization. We accept recommendations advanced by credible communicators because they are congruent with our values or attitudes.

Attractive communicators—likable and physically appealing ones—seem to achieve influence through more affective processes, such as identification. People go along with attractive speakers because they identify with them, or want to establish a positive relationship with the communicators (Kelman, 1958).

Although Kelman's analysis oversimplifies matters to some degree, it provides a useful framework for understanding communicator effects. The next sections examine the impact of authority, credibility, and social attractiveness on persuasion.

## Authority

It was an amazing study—unique in its time, bold, yet controversial, an attempt to create a laboratory analogue for the worst conformity in twentieth-century history and one of the most graphic cases of criminal obedience in the history of humankind. Legendary psychologist Gordon W. Allport called the program of research "the Eichmann experiment" because it attempted to explain the subhuman behavior of Nazis like Adolf Eichmann: after ordering the slaughter of 6 million Jews, Eichmann said, "It was unthinkable that I would not follow orders" (Cohen, 1999, p. A1). More generally, the research was designed to shed light on the power that authorities hold over ordinary people, and how they are able to induce individuals to obey their directives, sometimes in ways that violate human decency.

You may have heard of the research program called the Milgram experiments after psychologist Stanley Milgram who conceptualized and directed them. They are described in social psychology and social influence texts. A documentary film depicting the studies has been shown in thousands of college classrooms (you may have seen it). Milgram's 1974 book, *Obedience to Authority*, has been translated into 11 languages. A rock musician of the 1980s, Peter Gabriel, called on the research in his song, "We Do What We're Told—Milgram's 37."

### Experimental Procedures and Results

Milgram conducted his research—it was actually not one study, but a series of experiments —from 1960 to 1963 at Yale University and nearby Bridgeport, Connecticut. The basic procedure follows.

Each individual receives $4.50 for participating in the experiment, billed as a study of memory and learning. At the laboratory, participants are joined by a man introduced as a fellow subject in the study, who is actually working for the researcher.

At this point the participants are told that they will draw slips of paper to determine who will serve as the "teacher" and who will take the "learner" role. The drawing is rigged so that the naive subject is always selected to be the teacher.

The experimenter tells teacher and learner that the study concerns the effects of punishment on learning. The teacher watches as an experimenter escorts the learner to a room, seats him in a chair, straps his arms to prevent too much movement, and attaches an electrode to his wrist. The learner is told that he must learn a list of word pairs. When he makes a mistake, he will receive electric shocks, the intensity increasing with each error committed.

The teacher then is seated before a shock generator that contains a horizontal line of 30 switches varying from 15 to 450 volts and descriptions ranging from SLIGHT SHOCK to DANGER—SEVERE SHOCK. The experimenter instructs the teacher to read the word pairs to the learner, located in the next room. When the learner responds incorrectly, the teacher is to administer an electric shock, starting at the mildest level (15 volts) and increasing in 15-volt increments. After a series of shocks have been administered, the learner begins to express pain, grunting, complaining, screaming at 285 volts, and then remaining silent. Each time the teacher expresses misgivings about administering a shock, the experimenter orders him or her to continue, saying, "It is absolutely essential that you continue."

In reality, of course, the learner is not getting shocked. The experiment does not concern the effect of punishment on learning, but instead is designed to determine how far people will go in obeying an authority's directives to inflict harm on a protesting victim (Milgram, 1974). Although the shocks are not real, they seem quite authentic to individuals participating in the study. Participants frequently experience considerable tension, torn between sympathy for a suffering compatriot and perceived duty to comply with authority. As Milgram notes:

> I observed a mature and initially poised businessman enter the laboratory smiling and confident. Within 20 minutes he was reduced to a twitching, stuttering wreck, who was rapidly approaching a point of nervous collapse . . . At one point he pushed his fist into his forehead and muttered: "Oh God, let's stop it." And yet he continued to respond to every word of the experimenter, and obeyed to the end.
>
> (1963, p. 377)

The businessman was the norm, not the exception. Although a group of psychiatrists predicted that only 1 in 1,000 individuals would administer the highest shock on the shock generator, as many as 65 percent went this far. Large numbers of individuals were perfectly content to go along with the experimenter's orders.

The Milgram studies are one of many investigations of the effects of authority on behavior. There is an entire research literature on this topic (Kelman & Hamilton, 1989).

The Milgram research provides a useful framework for understanding these effects—it is a window on the role authority plays in persuading individuals to comply with diverse requests.

Milgram's interest was in obedience, but not typical obedience in everyday life, like obeying traffic signs or laws prohibiting shoplifting. This obedience is not objectionable. Milgram's focus was obedience to malevolent authority, obedience that violates moral judgments, what Kelman and Hamilton call "crimes of obedience." Authority—the concept that preoccupied Milgram—is assumed to emanate not from personal qualities, *"but from (the person's) perceived position in a social structure"* (Milgram, 1974, p. 139). A legitimate authority is someone who is presumed to have "the right to prescribe behavior" for others (Milgram, 1974, pp. 142–143). In the experimental drama of the Milgram studies, the experimenter exploited his authority and led many people to administer shocks to a helpless victim.

## Explanations

Why? Why would normal, upstanding human beings ignore their consciences and administer what they thought were electric shocks to a middle-aged learner? The explanation must lie in part with the power that situations can exert on human behavior, particularly the effects of the aura—or trappings—of authority. Interpretations of the Milgram findings include:

- *Early socialization.* People are socialized to obey authority, and they get rewarded for doing so. Success in school, on sports teams, in corporate organizations, and even in Hollywood movies requires complying with the requests of authorities. "We learn to value obedience, even if what ensues in its name is unpleasant," Arthur G. Miller and colleagues note. "We also trust the legitimacy of the many authorities in our lives," they remark (Miller, Collins, & Brief, 1995, p. 9).
- *Trappings of authority.* Various aspects of the experimental situation contributed to its majesty, or "aura of legitimacy" (Kelman & Hamilton, 1989, p. 151). These included: (a) status of the institution, Yale University; (b) complex, expensive scientific equipment in the room; (c) the experimenter's clothing (his lab coat served as a symbol of scientific expertise); and (d) the experimenter's gender—men are accorded more prestige "simply by virtue of being male" (Rudman & Kilianski, 2000, p. 1315). These trappings of authority could have served as peripheral cues, calling up the rule of thumb that "you do what authorities ask."
- *Binding forces.* The experiment set in motion powerful psychological forces that "locked" participants into compliance. Participants did not want to harm the learner, and probably harbored doubts about the necessity of administering severe electric shocks to advance scientific knowledge of memory. Still, they were reluctant to mention these concerns. Believing they lacked the knowledge or expertise to challenge the experimenter's requests, afraid of what would happen if they confronted the experimenter, concerned that he might implicitly indict them for failing to serve the noble goals of science and Yale University, they knuckled under. "To refuse to go on meant to challenge the experimenter's authority," Kelman and Hamilton note

(1989, p. 153). While some people were willing to undertake this challenge, most did not. They did not perceive that they had the right or ability to question the experimenter, and thus opted to accept his view of the situation.

The Milgram experiments illustrate the powerful impact that social influence can exert on behavior. To some degree, the experiments straddle the line between coercion and persuasion. There is a coercive aspect to the studies in that the experimenter was pushing individuals to act contrary to their preferences, and participants may have experienced the authority's directives as a threat. But the bottom line is that no one was holding a gun to participants' heads; they were free to stop the shocks whenever they wanted, and some individuals did. The experimenter set up the bait, but individuals persuaded themselves to go along with his commands.

## Additional Issues

Milgram conducted a variety of studies of obedience, varying aspects of the experimental situation. He found that obedience was more likely to occur under certain conditions than others. For example, substantially more individuals obeyed when the experimenter sat a few feet from the teacher than when he left the room and relayed orders by telephone. In one experiment, three individuals served as teachers. Unbeknownst to the subject, two worked for the experimenter. When the two individuals refused to shock the learner, obedience dropped sharply. This is the most hopeful aspect of the research. It suggests that authorities lose their grip if enough people resist.

Over the years, Milgram's studies have generated considerable discussion in the academic community. It would be ironic if academics accepted Milgram's findings lock, stock, and barrel—if they marched to Milgram's music in unison, just as his subjects followed the experimenter's order. I am happy to report that this is not what has occurred. Milgram's studies have been endlessly debated, criticized, and praised (Miller, 1986; Orne & Holland, 1968).

Critics have pointed out that the study involved the use of archaic, physical violence; yet much violence involves verbal or psychological abuse (Meeus & Raaijmakers, 1986). Scholars have also suggested that individuals' obedience was not as nasty as Milgram suggested. "Subjects take it for granted that the experimenter is familiar with the shock generator and that he knows that the shocks are not fatal," two researchers contended (Meeus & Raaijmakers, p. 312). In response, Milgram has noted that research participants —the teachers—perceived that the experimental situation was very real—not a game. They believed that the shocks had inflicted pain.

Others have objected to the experiments on ethical grounds, arguing that Milgram had no right to play God. They suggest that it was immoral to leave participants with knowledge that they could be cruel, slavishly obedient creatures (Baumrind, 1964). The ethical critique has stimulated much discussion, with Milgram (1974) pointing out that participants in his studies had been debriefed, had not suffered harm, and actually viewed the experiment as enlightening. Yet even if one shares Milgram's positive assessment of the research, there is still something unsettling about deceiving people in the name of science.

Granting these deontological objections, there are strong utilitarian reasons to evaluate the experiment positively. It has generated rich insights about human behavior, illuminating dark sides of persuasion that continue to intrigue students and scholars today. What's more, knowledge of the findings can help people take steps to protect themselves against engaging in unethical obedience.

## Revisiting Milgram: The 2009 Replication Article

For decades, persuasion students have wondered if Milgram's findings would be obtained today. Some scholars argued that obedience is a universal feature of the human condition. Others countered that the obedience experiments were period pieces, studies conducted nearly a half century ago in a profoundly different time when authorities were revered and citizens were compliant. The debate has raged over the years, with some researchers contending the findings would not hold up in our more irreverent era and others pointing to recent studies that report disturbing evidence of contemporary obedience, albeit to orders that were milder than those administered by Milgram's experimenter (see Blass, 1992; Meeus & Raaijmakers, 1986). Researchers have been unable to replicate Milgram's study, in light of strong ethical proscriptions—guidelines to protect human subjects from harm—that were implemented as a result of concerns about Milgram's research.

In January 2009, the flagship journal of the American Psychological Association published a major article by Jerry M. Burger that caught the attention of persuasion scholars and others across the world who were familiar with Milgram's classic study. Burger had done what thousands of researchers had dreamed of doing. He had conducted a study that employed many of the same procedures Milgram had used, but took necessary ethical precautions. He had convinced the institutional review board at his university that the experiment satisfied guidelines designed to protect human subjects from stress and psychological harm. Burger had designed an experiment that allowed researchers to answer the time-honored question: "Would people still obey today" (Burger, 2009).

In order to protect individuals' welfare, Burger informed participants that they could leave the experiment at any juncture and still keep the money they had been paid for participating in the experiment. They were told the confederate (the learner) had been given the same assurance. Berger also screened participants prior to the study, eliminating those who reported that they suffered from anxiety or depression. Moreover, Burger stopped the experiment when subjects administered a shock of 150 volts, rather than allowing them to continue to the stressful 450-volt level.

Did participants behave as their counterparts had some 40 years earlier? Or did they choose to disobey?

Burger found that the rate of obedience paralleled that obtained in Milgram's experiments. Seventy percent of participants in Burger's replication delivered 150-volt shocks, compared to 82.5 percent in a comparable condition in Milgram's study. Although there was more obedience a half-century ago, the difference between the proportion that obeyed was not statistically significant. Obedience seems not to have meaningfully decreased over the span of four decades.

Questions remain, of course: Would the same findings emerge with different ethnic groups? (A majority of Burger's participants were White, and, in line with Milgram's study, the learner was also Caucasian.) Non-White racial groups might have different norms governing conformity. Suppose the teacher was White and the learner of a different race? Would this attenuate or increase obedience? These questions remain interesting issues to pursue and are worthwhile topics for scholarly investigation. They do not reduce the significance of Burger's findings. His replication (supported as it is by conceptually similar work over the years) showed that Milgram's experiment stands the test of time. Participants in a laboratory study of obedience readily comply with the unethical directives of an authority figure.

## Applications

The Milgram experiments are classic studies in the psychology of persuasion. They have emerged, as one scholar put it, as "one of the most singular, most penetrating, and most disturbing inquiries into human conduct that modern psychology has produced" (quoted in Blass, 1999, p. 957). They provide an explanation—not the only one, but a powerful one—for the Holocaust of the Jews. Many German soldiers and civilians slavishly conformed to the orders of Nazi authorities. The findings also illuminate more recent war-time atrocities, such as in Korea, Vietnam and Iraq, as when U.S. soldiers— responding to orders by higher-ups and peer pressure—tortured prisoners at the Abu Ghraib, Iraq, prison.

Consider Private Lynndie England, who was photographed holding a naked prisoner with a strap around his neck, like it was a leash. Lynndie grew up in a trailer park in a small town in West Virginia. As a girl, she wore her hair short, played softball, and participated in Future Farmers of America. She quit her job at a chicken-processing plant because she objected to the management's decision to send unhealthy chicken parts down the factory line (McKelvey, 2007). It was therefore ironic that she ended up doing the bidding of her commanders at Abu Ghraib, particularly Sergeant Charles A. Graner, Jr., the crude and violent man with whom she was infatuated. Brigadier General Janis L. Karpinski, who supervised detainee operations at Abu Ghraib, ventured an explanation:

> "You have to understand that it builds into a crescendo . . . You're being mortared every night. You are breathing dust and broken concrete. It's hot. You feel dehumanized. You're drained of every bit of compassion you have. She did it because she wanted to come back from this godforsaken war and say, 'We did this for the government.'. . . She was made to believe this was of such importance to national security. It was, you know, 'You stick with me, kid, and you might even win a medal.'"
>
> (McKelvey, pp. 238–239)

Thus do ordinary people, who are not cruel by nature, find themselves engaged in extraordinarily violent acts. England and others were justly punished for their actions, justly as they chose to perform them. Yet the higher-ups who created the conditions under which these behaviors were normative emerged scot-free. No high-ranking Army officer or general served prison time. No Defense Department or administration official was charged with torture or war crimes. England and others succumbed to the pressure of authorities and were punished for their compliance.

The Milgram findings not only shed light on compliance to authorities during war time, but on conformity in a variety of political and organizational contexts. They help us understand why White House aides have followed presidents' commands to cover up illegal acts, lie about them, or stonewall the press. Events such as these occurred during Watergate (Kelman & Hamilton, 1989) and, to some degree, during the Clinton–Lewinsky scandal. The Milgram studies also explain actions taken in health maintenance organizations (HMOs), as when doctors slavishly follow HMO authorities' orders to have special medical procedures performed only at the HMO. Some years back, a physician found that a patient's appendix was inflamed, but told her she would have to wait over a week to have an exam performed by the HMO staff. While waiting for her appointment, the patient's appendix burst, leading to a complicated medical situation (Greenhouse, 1999). Had the physician not followed orders, she might have found a way out of the logjam.

The Milgram study also helps explain a much different, but no less stressful, situation: the distress many professional secretaries experience when their bosses ask them to commit unethical acts. Eighty-eight percent of administrative professionals admitted they had told a "little white lie" for a supervisor (Romano, 1998). Some have done worse, like the secretary for a school district who routinely complied with her boss's requests to inflate grades of college-bound students. "What am I supposed to do?" the 48-year-old woman, a single mother of two children, said to reporter Lois Romano. "I have to put food on the table. I need the benefits and so I am forced to do things I know are not correct. I have nowhere to go" (Romano, p. 29).

The woman's comments illustrate the tension people feel when faced with having to carry out orders they know are wrong. The secretary is frank about her problem, but mistaken in one respect, I maintain.

She says she has nowhere to go. Yet people always have places to go. There are always choices in life, and people can usually find a way to reconcile conscience with survival needs. The secretary may not have been able to quit her job, but she could have blown the whistle on the boss by asking a newspaper reporter to investigate the issue. Failing that, she could have kept a diary, and at a later time in life—when she could afford to leave the job or had retired—could reveal all. Or, realizing she had to put bread on the table, she might have thought through her predicament, redefined the situation as one in which her compliance was required but did not reflect her true personality, and resolved to do morally upstanding things in other aspects of her life.

The point is: there is always a way to respect conscience and resist exploitive authorities, in some way, shape, or form. If ever you are faced with a situation in which you must choose between your morals and the tempting desire to follow the crowd or a boss, remember the Milgram results.

Ask yourself: What do I believe? Is this something I really want to do? How will I feel tomorrow when I realize I could have respected my own beliefs? If you ask these questions, you will be less likely to acquiesce to authority and more inclined to do something that will sit well with your inner convictions.

## Credibility

Take a deep breath. We're about to shift gears now, moving from the transcendental moral issues of authority to everyday questions of credibility. Credibility is one of the "big 3" communicator factors—along with authority and social attractiveness. It dates back to Aristotle, who coined the term *ethos* to describe qualities of the source that facilitated persuasion. Hovland explored it in his early research, communication researchers deconstructed credibility in the 1960s and 1970s, and the concept continues to fascinate scholars today. Of course, corporate managers, salespeople, and politicians are very interested in what makes someone credible. Nowadays, consultants offer pointers to clients who want to improve the credibility of their commercial Web sites. D. Joel Whalen, in a book on persuasive business communication, says that credibility is "the single biggest variable under the speaker's control during the presentation" (1996, p. 97). Jay A. Conger, writing about the role persuasion plays in business, observes that "credibility is the cornerstone of effective persuading; without it, a persuader won't be given the time of day" (1998, p. 90).

So, what is credibility? First, let's say what it is *not*. It is not the same as authority, although the two are frequently confused. Authority emanates from a person's position in a social structure. It involves the ability to dispense rewards and punishments. Credibility is a psychological or interpersonal communication construct. You can be an authority, but lack credibility. Parents can be authority figures to their kids, but have zero credibility in their children's eyes due their hypocrisy or indifference. In politics, a president is the nation's commander-in-chief—the top political authority. However, a president can lack credibility in the nation's eyes if he (or she) ignores the nation's economic problems or gets embroiled in a scandal. Dictators can do as they please; they have total, supreme authority. But ask their citizens in private what they think of these people and you will quickly discover that authority does not translate into credibility.

Credibility is defined as *"the attitude toward a source of communication held at a given time by a receiver"* (McCroskey, 1997, p. 87). It is an audience member's perceptions of the communicator's qualities. Although we commonly think of credibility as something a communicator has, it is more complex. As Roderick Hart and colleagues note: "Credibility is *not a thing*. It is not some sort of overcoat that we put on and take off at will. Rather, it is a perception of us that lies inside of the people to whom we talk" (Hart, Friedrich, & Brummett, 1983, p. 204).

Credibility is more than a psychological characteristic. It is also a communication variable. It is part of the two-way interaction between communicator and message recipients—a dynamic entity that emerges from the transaction between source and audience member. This means that communicators are not guaranteed credibility by virtue of who they are, their title, or academic pedigree. As Hart reminds us, credibility "is not something we can be assured of keeping once gotten. Credibility can only be earned by paying the price of effective communication" (Hart et al., 1983, pp. 204–205). There is something democratic about credibility. It says that communicators have to enter the rough-and-tumble realm of persuasion. They must meet and greet—either interpersonally or electronically—those they seek to influence. They must earn an audience's respect and win its credibility.

## Core Characteristics

What are the main attributes of credibility? What does it mean to be a credible speaker?

Communication researchers have explored these time-honored questions, using empirical methodologies and survey research. Scholars asked people to evaluate the believability of famous people, giving speeches on various topics, and to rate friends or supervisors on semantic differential scales. They found that credibility is not a simple, unitary concept: it has more than one dimension, more than a single layer. Credible communicators are perceived as having expertise, trustworthiness, goodwill, dynamism, extroversion, sociability, and composure (e.g., Berlo, Lemert, & Mertz, 1969; McCroskey & Young, 1981).

By far the most important characteristics—the ones that have emerged in study after study or generated the greatest theoretical interest—are (a) expertise, (b) trustworthiness, and (c) goodwill.

Expertise and trustworthiness have emerged with greatest regularity, and goodwill has been uncovered in systematic research by James McCroskey (McCroskey & Teven, 1999). Based on the studies as a whole, one can say that a credible communicator is one who is seen as an expert, is regarded as trustworthy, and displays goodwill toward audience members. Each quality is important and deserves brief discussion.

*Expertise* is the knowledge or ability ascribed to the communicator. It is the belief that the communicator has special skills or know-how. You see experts used all the time in commercials. Lawyers pay for experts to testify for their side in courtroom trials. There is abundant evidence that experts are perceived as credible and can influence attitudes (Petty & Wegener, 1998). However, expertise has limits. For instance, if you are trying to reach inner city drug abusers, you might think twice about calling on the surgeon general. True, he is a recognized expert on health, but he also is seen as a member of the ruling class. It would be better to employ a former drug user who has seen the error of his or her ways and can communicate on the same wavelength as the inner city audience (Levine & Valle, 1975). The former drug user also inspires trust, which is an important attribute of credibility.

*Trustworthiness*, the next core credibility component, refers to the communicator's perceived honesty, character, and safety. A speaker may lack expertise, but can be seen as an individual of integrity and character. This can work wonders in persuasion. Some years ago, Ross Perot, the billionaire businessman turned politician, declared on a television talk show that he would be willing to run for president if citizens worked steadfastly in his behalf. His declaration stimulated a flood of support from ordinary Americans who liked his persona and plans to reduce the deficit. Within months he had an army of loyal campaign workers. Legions of reporters trailed him everywhere, and he became a major force in the 1992 election campaign. Perot was no political expert; he had never held political office, although he was widely known to the public for his committed political stances. Many Americans perceived Perot as a man of integrity, someone who said what he meant and meant what he said. Finding this refreshing, they supported Perot—and he led the polls for a time, in mid-June (Abramson, Aldrich, & Rohde, 1994).

*Goodwill* or perceived caring, is the final core communicator factor. Communicators who display goodwill convey that they have listeners' interests at heart, show understanding of others' ideas, and are empathic toward their audiences' problems (McCroskey & Teven, 1999). You can probably think of a doctor who knows her stuff and is honest, but seems preoccupied or uninterested in you when you complain about medical problems. The physician undoubtedly gets low marks on your credibility scale, and her advice probably has little impact on you.

On the positive side, communicators who show us they care can gain our trust and inspire us. Goodwill is an element of charisma, as embodied by leaders like Gandhi and Martin Luther King. It also is a quality that can help persuaders achieve practical goals. Salespeople who understand their clients' needs can tailor their appeals to suit their clients. This can help them achieve day-to-day success on the job (McBane, 1995). Goodwill also has important implications for medical communication, particularly between physicians and patients. Doctors who convey empathy with patients' needs can enhance patients' satisfaction and compliance with medical recommendations (Kim, Kaplowitz, & Johnston, 2004).

## Role of Context

Expertise, trustworthiness, and goodwill are the primary attributes of credibility. Communicators who are credible have all or at least one of these qualities. There is a complicating factor, however: context. As anyone who has worked in telemarketing, politics, or community organizing can tell you, the situation you are in can potently influence persuasion. This means that different facets of credibility will be influential in different social situations. This conclusion emerged from early academic studies of credibility, which found that results varied, depending on the ways in which researchers probed credibility and circumstances in which the speeches were delivered (Cronkhite & Liska, 1976). Critical situational factors include audience size, communicator role, and cultural dynamics.

**Audience size.** Do you remember those big lecture classes where no one knows anyone else and you have to listen to a professor talk or present material via PowerPoint for an hour? It's hard to impart information in these contexts, and if I were in charge of American universities, I'd get rid of them immediately! Unfortunately, mass lectures are here to stay because they allow universities to educate thousands of students efficiently and at low cost. And, in fairness, some lecture classes can be pretty interesting, even entertaining. That brings me to the point. If a prof. hopes to gain credibility in a large lecture, he or she must be dynamic and extroverted. These qualities are necessary to capture students' attention.

**169**

*"Who
Says It":
Source
Factors in
Persuasion*

Now consider a small seminar. A professor who is bold and talkative, hams it up, and booms out lecture material in a loud voice may be perceived as insensitive or "incredible" in a small seminar. In this context, students want a teacher to listen, share information, and help them relate personally to the course. A more empathic, caring style of communicating may be perceived as more credible in this situation.

**Communicator role.** In a similar vein, the role a communicator plays—or functions he or she performs for the individual—can determine the particular aspect of credibility that is most important. In the case of a therapist, credibility involves composure, poise, character, and goodwill.

Yet, if a communicator is addressing cognitive aspects of attitudes—for example, beliefs about a far-reaching issue—he or she is better advised to dramatize a different aspect of credibility. A scientist speaking to an audience about global warming should convey expertise—that is, intelligence and knowledge of the technical aspects of this subject.

**Culture.** National and political culture can play an important role in credibility judgments. American students evaluate political leaders on the basis of competence and character, while Japanese students sometimes employ two additional attributes: consideration and appearance (King, Minami, & Samovar, 1985). What's more, the particular type of credibility that is important can depend on the particular time and political place. In some national elections, expertise can be the key attribute that Americans value in a president.

A long time ago, in 1972, Richard Nixon emphasized his political experience. Realizing that he was not a particularly likable guy but had vastly more expertise than his opponent, his consultants urged Nixon to stress his qualifications and experience. Nixon defeated George McGovern by a landslide in 1972.

What a difference 4 years makes! After Nixon's blatant lies to the public during the Watergate affair, the nation yearned for a more honest political leader. Along came Jimmy Carter riding on a white horse and striking many as a "John Boy Walton" character (after the popular television show of the 1970s). Carter promised he would never lie to the American people, thereby stressing trustworthiness and integrity. Carter defeated incumbent Gerald Ford in a close election.

Fast-forward to the 1990s, and you find candidate Bill Clinton exuding compassion and sensitivity, trying to distance himself from the incumbent president, George Bush. Many Americans perceived Bush as out of touch with their problems and insufficiently concerned with the economic recession (Denton, 1994). Showing goodwill and empathy toward the plight of ordinary Americans, Clinton gained in stature and credibility. This helped him defeat Bush in the 1992 election.

Trustworthiness was in vogue again in 2000, especially among voters displeased with Clinton's sexual shenanigans and lies under oath during the Lewinsky scandal. Democratic candidate Al Gore and Republican nominee George W. Bush tripped over themselves to show that they could be trusted not to violate family values that Americans held dear. Expertise was back in fashion in 2004 when George W. Bush sought to emphasize that, in these dangerous times, America could ill afford to elect a candidate who lacked experience combating terrorism. At the same time, trustworthiness, in the form of candidate authenticity, remained salient. Bush's folksy language appealed to voters wary of poll-tested phrases and opponent John Kerry's highfalutin oratory.

Four years later, in 2008, with the economy in tailspin and voters concerned about their pocketbooks, candidates' credibility on economic issues become a salient factor in voters' decisions. Republican candidate John McCain had enormous credibility on foreign affairs, but, unfortunately for McCain, this was not relevant to voters in 2008. Instead, the economy was the main issue in the campaign. Democrat Barack Obama conveyed goodwill by empathizing with Americans' financial woes. He enhanced his credibility by criticizing McCain for suggesting that "the fundamentals of the economy are strong" during the nation's worst economic crisis since the Great Depression.

In sum, candidate credibility plays a prominent role in presidential campaigns, with voters attending to credibility cues. The lesson for persuasion students is that the particular type of credibility communicators emphasize depends on the time and political place. Certain components are more consequential, with effects varying as a function of economic, political, and psychological circumstances.

If there is an overarching lesson in this, it is that we need to adopt a flexible approach to credibility. If credibility were a key, it would have to be adapted to fit the particular persuasion door in question. If credibility were a recipe, chefs would have to take the main ingredients and season them to suit the tastes of the folks at the restaurant. Smart persuaders know how to adapt their traits to fit the situation. They apply persuasion knowledge to the context in question, selecting the particular style of expertise, trust-worthiness, and goodwill that best suits the audience and circumstances. In politics, as in so many other contexts, there is an ineffable quality to the ways in which these features are combined in situations. Credible, and especially charismatic, political leaders have a way of connecting with voters, making contact with gut-level values and pressing human concerns. Obama did this in 2008, as did Clinton in the 1990s and Reagan in the '80s. It is a cardinal feature of persuasion.

## A Theoretical Account

As noted earlier in the book, social scientists attempt to develop theories to explain and predict events. In the case of credibility, researchers have devised a model that assumes people are canny, skeptical observers of persuaders. Eagly, Wood, and Chaiken (1978) argue that people figure persuaders have their own motives for saying what they do. What's more, audience members attribute persuaders' statements to various factors. The attribution that individuals make can exert an important influence on credibility judgments and persuasion.

Eagly and colleagues point out that individuals make predictions—or develop expectations—about what a particular communicator will say, based on what they know about him or her, and the situation. For instance, if you were told that a member of the college track team was going to talk about exercise, you probably would assume he was going to explain why running is healthy. Or, to take a political example, if informed that a candidate was speaking to a pro-environmental group, you might assume he or she was going to sing the praises of conservation.

Expectations can be confirmed—it turns out you are correct—or disconfirmed—you end up being wrong. When a speaker disconfirms your expectation, you scratch your head and want to figure out why this occurred. In such cases, you may (as we will see) conclude that the communicator is a credible source. The underpinnings for this lie in two psychological concepts: *knowledge bias* and *reporting bias*.

**Knowledge bias.** Suppose you were told that a young female professor was scheduled to give a lecture on affirmative action. If you ventured a prediction about what she was going to say, you might guess that, being young and a professor (and, therefore you assume, liberal), she would advocate affirmative action programs for women. If the speaker confirmed your prediction, you might conclude that she possessed what is called a knowledge bias. *A knowledge bias is the presumption that a communicator has a biased view of an issue.* It is an audience member's belief that the speaker's background—gender, ethnicity, religion, or age—has prevented him or her from looking objectively at the various sides of the issue. The audience member concludes that the communicator has a limited base of knowledge, produced by a need to view an issue in accord with the dominant views of her social group. "Oh, she's a modern woman; of course she'd see things that way," you might say, meaning no disrespect. Communicators who are perceived to harbor knowledge biases lack credibility and do not change attitudes (Eagly et al., 1978).

Now suppose that the speaker took the unexpected position and spoke out against affirmative action programs for women. The theory says that individuals might be taken aback by this and would feel a need to explain why the communicator defied expectation. Unable to attribute her position to gender or background, they would have to conclude that something else was operating. They might reasonably infer that the arguments against affirmative action were so compelling that they persuaded the young professor to go against the grain and take an unpopular stand. Or they might conclude that the communicator was a bit of an iconoclast, someone who defied the norm. Both these interpretations could enhance the speaker's credibility and increase the odds that she would change audience attitudes. As a general rule, when communicators are perceived to violate the knowledge bias, they gain in credibility (see Figure 6.1a).

Knowledge bias is admittedly a different way of looking at communicators and so it takes some getting used to. But once you appreciate the idea, it becomes an appealing way to explain seemingly paradoxical situations in everyday life. Consider the following examples:

- Some years back, the American Civil Liberties Union (ACLU), a group with many Jewish members, spoke out in favor of the right of American Nazis to hold a rally in Skokie, Illinois. Skokie had many Jewish residents, some of whom had survived the Holocaust, and for these individuals the rally was an odious reminder of the horrific past. One might expect that a group with Jewish leaders would oppose the rally. By defying expectation, the ACLU probably enhanced its credibility.
- African-American lawyer David P. Baugh defended Barry E. Black, a White member of the Ku Klux Klan accused of burning a cross. The case was intriguing because

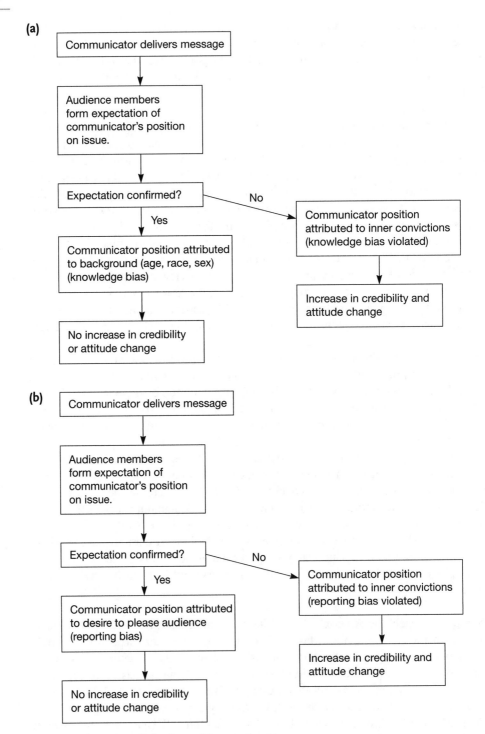

**FIGURE 6.1** | (a) Knowledge bias; (b) reporting bias.

of "the paradox of an African-American defending a white supremacist, who, if he had his way, would oppress his lawyer because of his race" (Holmes, 1998, p. A14). Arguing that the principle of free speech overwhelmed any discomfort he had about the defendant's actions, the lawyer violated the knowledge bias and may have enhanced his credibility in the case.

- Long-time advocates of capital punishment with law and order credentials have increasingly raised questions about the ethics of the death penalty. For example, an Illinois governor who for years supported capital punishment imposed a moratorium on the death penalty, after discovering that the system was error ridden and had come close to taking innocent lives (Johnson, 2000). When long-time death penalty proponents support a moratorium, it defies expectation and may therefore carry more weight than when liberals or pacifists take this position.

- At the 50th anniversary of the *Brown v. Board of Education* school desegregation decision, Bill Cosby lambasted African-Americans who don't speak proper English, saying, "You can't land a plane with 'why you ain't' . . . You can't be a doctor with that kind of crap coming out of your mouth." He blamed Black parents for failing to take responsibility for their children's moral transgressions, criticizing those who buy their kids $500 sneakers, but refuse to "spend $250 on Hooked on Phonics" (Dyson, 2005, pp. 57–58). Cosby's comments resonated with many (though not all) middle-class Black adults. Defying expectation, they were precisely the opposite of what one expected to hear on this occasion from a trailblazing Black entertainer who had been a tireless fighter for racial justice. If Bill Cosby is so outraged by Black parenting, people likely thought to themselves, then perhaps there is merit in his criticisms.

- Some of the country's wealthiest Americans, including Warren Buffet and David Rockefeller, Jr., urged Congress not to repeal federal taxes on estates. Although they would benefit from repeal of the tax, since they own lavish estates, Buffet, Rockefeller, and other billionaires said repealing the tax "would enrich the heirs of America's millionaires and billionaires while hurting families who struggle to make ends meet" (Johnston, 2001, p. A1). This is not what you would expect these rich people to say and, for this reason, their statements may enhance their credibility.

- Before the bygone era of Jerry Springer and assorted hosts of "shock" TV, there was Morton Downey, Jr., a pioneer of "in your face" TV talk shows. Downey smoked five packs a day and died of lung cancer some years ago. While still alive and informed he had cancer, Downey changed his tune and became a passionate anti-smoking advocate. Violating the knowledge bias (you wouldn't expect a chain smoker to become a leading advocate of nonsmoking), Downey attracted a following, gaining credibility for his position. Downey is an example of a convert communicator, an individual who has converted from one lifestyle or ideology to a totally opposite set of beliefs. Such communicators can be credible spokespersons for their causes (Levine & Valle, 1975). Other examples include former drug-using rock musicians (like the legendary David Crosby of Crosby, Stills, Nash and Young) who lecture young people about the terrible effects of drugs. Another exemplar is Jane Roe, the pseudonym for the famous plaintiff in Roe v. Wade, the Supreme Court decision that legalized abortion. Roe, whose real name is Norma McCorvey, switched sides in 1995 after long conversations with pro-life supporters and conversion to Christianity. She became a strong anti-abortion activist. Converts are not always persuasive though. If audiences perceive that the convert has not freely changed his or her mind, credibility goes out the window. A Mafia hit man who testifies against the crime syndicate and lectures about the evils of crime may be "incredible" if people believe he is doing these things to get his sentence reduced. An ex-producer of pornographic Web sites who preaches about the healing power of Christ may not be credible if people believe he is doing this to pedal his latest book.

**Reporting bias**. When judging communicators, audience members also examine the extent to which speakers are taking the position merely to make points with the audience. If they believe the communicator is brownnosing the group, they assume that the speech reflects a situational pressure to say the socially correct thing. They conclude that the communicator has withheld—or chosen not to report—facts that would upset the group. *This is the reporting bias, the perception that the communicator has opted not to report or disclose certain facts or points of view.* When individuals believe that speakers are guilty of a reporting bias, they downgrade their credibility. For example, consider a political candidate who told an audience that held somewhat favorable attitudes toward the environment that she favored harsh penalties for polluters. "I figured she'd tell them that to get their votes," an audience member might say. The politician would not be seen as particularly credible.

On the other hand, when audience members' expectations are violated—the communicator says something that is inconsistent with group values—the speaker is seen as credible and convincing. Individuals figure that anyone who has the courage to go against the grain must truly believe what he or she is saying. They figure that the position must be so compelling and cogent that it led the speaker to ignore social conventions and adopt the position as her own. A communicator who told a moderately pro-environmental group that the United States needed to worry less about preserving the environment and more about finding alternative sources of energy would be perceived as credible and (at least in theory) could influence observers' attitudes (Eagly et al., 1978; see Figure 6.1b).

The reporting bias helps us understand why voters greet maverick candidates like Ralph Nader and contemporary third-party contenders with enthusiasm. The candidates violate the reporting bias and are seen as having the guts to challenge the status quo. Unfortunately their positions do not resonate with the bulk of the public. Violating the reporting bias will not change attitudes if, as discussed in Chapter 2, attitudes are deeply felt or strongly held.

## Social Attractiveness

Credibility is an important factor in persuasion. But it is not the only communicator characteristic that influences attitudes. Socially attractive communicators—those who are likable, similar to message recipients, and physically appealing—can also induce attitude change. Let's see how.

## Likability

Do you know someone who is just so nice and appealing you can't reject what he says? This person may score high on likability. There is evidence that likable communicators can change attitudes (Rhoads & Cialdini, 2002; Sharma, 1999). There are several reasons for this. First, a likable person makes you feel good, and the positive feelings become transferred to the message. Second, a likable persuader puts you in a good mood, which helps you access positive thoughts about the product the persuader is pedaling. Third, a likable speaker may convey that she has your interest at heart, which communicates goodwill.

Sometimes we make persuasion too complicated. Just being likable can help a communicator achieve his or her goals. Case in point: Ross Perot, the Texas billionaire who ran for president in 1992. Although Perot had never run for office before and was not a drop-dead gorgeous politician (quite the contrary, with ears that talk show comics parodied), he led the national polls for a time. There were several reasons for this, some having to do with the sensibility of Perot's ideas; however, one reason Perot fared so well is that he displayed an "aw-shucks" down-home charm, a likability that resonated with voters.

Sixteen years later, likability entered the political fray again, this time in the 2008 Democratic primary campaign. At a Democratic candidate debate two days before the New Hampshire primary, a reporter asked Hillary Clinton about her likability, noting that many voters did not find her particularly likable. Responding with apparent sincerity, Clinton said "Well, that hurts my feelings, but I'll try to go on. I don't think I'm that bad." The audience responded positively. A couple of days later, Clinton teared up in response to a question about the strains and stresses of the campaign. "It's not easy," she said. "And I couldn't do it if I didn't passionately believe it was the right thing to do ... Some people think elections are a game, lots of who's up or who's down. It's about our country. It's about our kids' futures. And it's really about all of us together." Critics said the tears were phony, a manipulative attempt to manufacture emotion.

Manufactured or not, Clinton's emotional displays proved politically effective. They showed a more human side to the frequently-brittle Hillary Clinton, enhanced her likability in voters' eyes, and seemed to have contributed to her surprise victory over Obama in the 2008 New Hampshire primary (Healy, 2008).

Likability effects appear in a variety of public arenas—not just politics. One context in which likability matters is one that probably would not occur to you initially: tipping waiters and waitresses. Restaurant servers who are likable get bigger tips (e.g. Rind & Bordia, 1995). What's more, there are several techniques that waiters and waitresses can use to make themselves more likable; these, in turn, have been found to increase the amount of money customers leave on the table. If anyone reading this book is currently waiting tables, he or she may find these strategies lucrative, or at least useful! Research indicates that the following techniques increase tip size (suggestions culled from Crusco & Wetzel, 1984; Lynn & Mynier, 1993; Leodoro & Lynn, 2007; and Rind & Bordia, 1995, 1996):

- writing "thank you" on the back of the check;
- drawing a happy, smiling face on the back of checks before giving them to customers;

- squatting down next to tables; and
- touching the diner's palm or shoulder (waitresses only; sorry, guys).

As this discussion suggests, a communicator's *nonverbal behaviors* can enhance liking. For example, a persuader who touches a message recipient lightly on the upper arm or shoulder while making a request is more likely to gain compliance than a communicator who does not touch the target (Segrin, 1993). Making eye contact and standing closer to a target can also enhance persuasion. As you might expect, a host of contextual factors come into play, such as the nature of the touch or gaze, the relationship between communicator and recipient, and gender.

## Similarity

Is a communicator who shares your values or perspective or dresses like you do more apt to change attitudes than one who does not? The answer is yes, especially under some conditions.

Similarity between source and receiver can facilitate persuasion in business (Brock, 1965), on social issues (Berscheid, 1966), and for health problems. For example, research indicates that African-American women are more likely to feel positively toward performing a breast self-exam and to getting tested for HIV when the message is delivered by an African-American female (Anderson & McMillion, 1995; Kalichman & Coley, 1995).

There is also anecdotal support for the influence of similarity on attitudes. Think back to Ashley Smith, the Atlanta woman kidnapped by an accused rapist, who talked the man into turning himself in (see Box 1.1). Ashley called on her own hard-scrabble background, her own arrests for drunk driving, and redemption through discovery of God. "She felt the sadness and she felt the aloneness—she could relate," her aunt said later. "I don't think a socialite or a squeaky clean could have done that," she said (Dewan & Goodstein, 2005, p. A11).

Similarity works for some of the same reasons that likability succeeds. It induces positive affect and promotes favorable cognitive responses. In addition, people compare themselves to similar others. I may infer that if someone who is similar to me endorses a position, it's a good bet that the proposal will work for me as well.

Similarity is particularly likely to succeed if the similarity is relevant to the message (Berscheid, 1966). People selling DVDs and compact discs are more likely to make a sale if they emphasize that they share the customer's taste in music than if they confess that they too like to play golf on Saturday afternoons. However, similarity may fail if it suggests to the receiver that the persuader is "just like I am" and is therefore no expert. In this case, the persuader is believed to lack expertise and the recommendation is rejected.

This raises the knotty question of when communicators should stress similarity and when they should emphasize expertise. There are no quick and easy answers. Research suggests that similarity is more effective when people must make personal and emotional decisions (Goethals & Nelson, 1973). In these cases we feel a kinship with the similar other and assume that the similar communicator is more apt to empathize with our

**177**

*"Who
Says It":
Source
Factors in
Persuasion*

concerns than a dissimilar speaker. By contrast, when the issue concerns factual matters, experts' intellectual knowledge may carry the day.

The question of whether a communicator should emphasize expertise or similarity comes up in many real-life persuasion situations. Politicians, advertisers, and salespeople are often faced with deciding whether to emphasize their experience or the fact that they are "just plain folks." Increasingly, it seems, companies are putting a premium on similarity, particularly similarity in appearance. Many businesses, finding that formal attire can turn off clients dressed in jeans or simple pants suits, are telling employees to dress like their clients (Puente, 1999). Indeed, it would seem as if the buttoned-down business announcement has gone out of style. Few who watched the two casually dressed, youthful founders of YouTube announce in a video clip that they had sold their company to Google for $1.65 billion thought twice about their informal attire.

Steve Constanides, an owner of a computer graphics firm, exemplifies this trend. "When you went on a sales call, you definitely got a cooler reaction if you showed up in a nice suit, because the clients would see you as just a salesman," Constanides related. "If I came in more casual attire, all of a sudden I'm like them. And it's easier to get a project," he said (Puente, 1999, p. 2D). However, if his computer graphics sales staff abandoned expertise entirely and talked just like the clients—saying, "Hey, what's up dude?" or "Man, that's awesome!"—they would probably not sell much high-tech equipment!

Political candidates also have to juggle between appeals to similarity and expertise. During her 2008 presidential campaign, Republican vice-presidential candidate Sarah Palin chose the former over the latter. In her acceptance speech at the Republican convention, Palin introduced her children, one-by-one: a son bound for military duty in Iraq, her three daughters, including the pregnant Bristol, her infant son with Downs syndrome, and her husband Todd ("he's still my guy"). She was just a gal who hunted on the North slopes of Alaska, your "average hockey mom." Pausing, and using a deadpan with devastating effect, she said, "You know, (what) they say the difference between a hockey mom and a pit bull (is)? Lipstick." The audience howled. (Research suggests that her humor deflected counterarguments among some members of the audience, perhaps enhancing positive perceptions; see Nabi, Moyer-Guse, & Byrne, 2007 and Skalski, Tamborini, Glazer, & Smith, 2009.)

Palin portrayed herself as an ordinary American, reared with good, small-town values, unimpressed by media elites, a modern-day Harry Truman, a twenty-first-century female incarnate of Jimmy Stewart's Mr. Smith in *Mr. Smith Goes to Washington*. Many female voters said they could relate to her.

"She's me," confessed Tana Krueger, a 58-year-old mother of six from Wisconsin. "I can just really relate to everything in her life, children with disabilities, teenage pregnancy" (Bumiller & Zeleny, 2008, p. 11). Other women, while acknowledging the appeal of similarity, worried about her expertise. Donna Davis, a New Yorker, noted that women looked at Palin, holding her infant, talking about being an average hockey mom, and felt that she understood their experiences. "The question for them," Davis asked, is: "'Am I ready to be vice president of the United States?'" (Davis, 2008, A28).

As it turned out, opinion polls taken during the 2008 election revealed that many Americans doubted Palin's qualifications to be president. It seems as if she would have been better served had she talked up expertise rather than similarity.

## Physical Attractiveness

Flip through any issue of *GQ* magazine and you will come across advertisements featuring sensationally attractive male models sporting a fashionably tailored suit or sport coat. Turn on the TV and you will see beautiful female models promoting perfume or a new brand of clothing for women. Advertisers obviously believe that attractiveness sells products. So do most of us. We buy new clothes, get our hair done, and buy contact lenses to make a good impression in persuasive presentations.

Does attractiveness change attitudes? You could argue that it does because people are fascinated by beauty. Or you could say that it doesn't because people resent extremely attractive people—or assume they're dumb. To decide which of these is correct and how attractiveness plays out in persuasion, researchers conduct experiments and articulate theories. Most studies find that attractiveness does change attitudes. In a nifty study, Chaiken (1979) recruited individuals who were high and low in physical appeal and instructed them to approach students on a university campus. Attractive and not-so-attractive communicators gave a spiel, advocating that the university stop serving meat at breakfast and lunch at the campus dining hall. Students who heard the message from the attractive speakers were more inclined to agree that meat should not be served than were students exposed to the less-attractive communicators. The arguments that both sets of speakers gave were exactly the same; the only difference was that one group of communicators was nicer looking than the other. Yet this peripheral factor carried the day, inducing students to change their minds on the topic.

Why does attractiveness influence attitudes? First, people are more likely to pay attention to an attractive speaker, and this can increase the odds that they will remember message arguments. Second, attractiveness becomes associated with the message. The pleasant affect one feels when gazing at a pretty woman or handsome guy gets merged with the message, resulting in an overall favorable evaluation of the topic. Third, people like and identify with attractive communicators. At some level, perhaps unconscious, we feel we can improve our own standing in life if we do what attractive people suggest. Fourth, attractive individuals may simply be better public speakers. As psychologist Susan Fiske explains, "if you're beautiful or handsome, people laugh at your jokes and interact with you in such a way that it's easy to be socially skilled" (Belluck, 2009, p. 8).

**Contextual factors**. A communicator's physical appeal can add sweetness and value to a product. Attractive communicators seem to be more effective than their less attractive counterparts, everything else being equal. But everything else is never totally equal. Attractiveness influences attitudes more under certain conditions than others.

First, attractiveness can help form attitudes. One reason people begin buying certain perfumes or toothpastes is that they link the product with attractive models, and develop a favorable attitude toward the product. Unfortunately, the same process can work with unhealthy products like cigarettes, which is one reason why cigarette advertisements feature attractive-looking smokers.

Second, attractiveness can be effective when the communicator's goal is to capture attention. This is one reason why advertisers use drop-dead gorgeous models. They want to break through the clutter and get people to notice the product. Once that is accomplished, they rely on other strategies to convince people to purchase the good or service.

Third, attractiveness can be effective under low involvement, as when people are trying to decide which of two advertised convenience store products to buy or for whom to vote in a low-level election. In these cases, physical appeal acts as a peripheral cue.

Fourth, on the other extreme, attractiveness can be a deciding factor when the communicator's physical appeal is relevant to the product. In cases of beauty products or expensive clothing lines, a model's or salesperson's good looks can swing the sale. Physical appeal serves as an argument for the product, as the ELM suggests.

Fifth, attractiveness can influence opinions when it violates expectations. Consider the true story of Rebekka Armstrong, former *Playboy* playmate who contracted HIV from intercourse with a male model. After years of suffering, denial, and drug abuse, Armstrong went public with her story, trying to teach young people the dangers of unprotected sex. She has spoken to capacity university crowds and has her own Web site (Perloff, 2001). Why might she be effective?

Your image—or schema—of a *Playboy* model does not include contracting HIV. This disconfirms your expectation, and you have to think about it to put things back together mentally. As one listens to an attractive model like Armstrong talk, one discovers that she is arguing for these positions not because of a knowledge or reporting bias— but because she truly believes people must take precautions against AIDS. Thus, when attractive communicators say or do unexpected things that seem out of sync with their good looks and these events can be attributed to inner convictions, these speakers can influence attitudes.

When doesn't attractiveness make a difference?

Physical appeal cannot change deeply felt attitudes. Listening to an attractive speaker explain why abortion is necessary is not going to change the mind of a staunch pro-life advocate. Attractiveness is rarely enough to close a deal when the issue is personally consequential or stimulates considerable thinking.

Just as attractiveness can work when it positively violates expectations, it can fail when it negatively violates expectations of what is appropriate for a particular job or role (Burgoon, 1989). You would not expect your family doctor to be sensationally attractive. If the doctor accentuates his or her physical attributes, this could interfere with processing the message or lead you to derogate the doctor. "Patients and colleagues may dismiss a young doctor's skills and knowledge or feel their concerns aren't being taken seriously when the doctor is dressed in a manner more suitable for the gym or a night on the town," one medical expert noted (Marcus, 2006, p. D5). (On the other hand, some might argue that patients display a subtle prejudice when they reject an expert *because* she is good-looking.)

Finally, attractiveness effects tend to be rather short-lived. As a primarily peripheral cue, it tends not to be integrated with the person's overall attitude. The person may feel positively toward the communicator, but fail to do the cognitive work necessary to develop a strong, lasting attitude toward the issue.

Beauty, in sum, has always fascinated us. It always will. Attractiveness is commonly assumed to weave a magical spell on people. Its effects are more psychological than astrological, and are inevitably due to individuals letting themselves be bowled over by an attractive person or allowing themselves to fantasize about what will happen if they go along with the communicator's recommendations.

Real-world persuaders have long recognized that attractiveness sells, even if they are less familiar with the psychological trappings of attractiveness effects. Advertisers use physical appeal as a peripheral cue to sell many products and as a central argument for beauty products. Drug companies hire former college cheerleaders to sell pharmaceutical products to doctors. In an article headlined, "Gimme an Rx! Cheerleaders Pep Up Drug Sales," a *New York Times* reporter describes how ex-cheerleaders, including a former Miss Florida USA, traipse into physicians' offices promoting pharmaceutical products. They combine physical appeal, charm, and likability to influence the nation's doctors, who are mostly men. "There's a saying that you'll never meet an ugly drug rep," one physician said (Saul, 2005, p. A1).

Discriminating *in favor* of physically attractive women is not against the law in the United States. And handsome, athletic men are also apt to be hired as pharmaceutical reps and lobbyists. Attractiveness raises ethical issues when individuals are hired solely on the basis of their physical appeal or someone less attractive is fired, as has happened with older female newscasters. The pursuit of beauty also raises moral issues when advertisements featuring unrealistically thin models tempt adolescent girls to starve themselves and adopt dangerously unhealthy diets (see Box 6.1).

## Box 6.1 | PHYSICAL ATTRACTIVENESS AND CULTURE

Is attractiveness relative?

Is physical beauty culturally relative, or are standards of beauty universal phenomena? It's an interesting question, with relevance for attractiveness effects in persuasion.

Some scholars argue that signs of youth, such as cleanliness, clear skin, and absence of disease, are universally perceived as attractive. They note that there is consensus across cultures that symmetrical faces are attractive (Buss & Kenrick, 1998). Perhaps—but culture leaves its imprint in a host of other ways.

In the United States, thin is in. Lean, ever-skinnier female models define the culture's standard for beauty in women. There has been a significant reduction in body measurements of *Playboy* centerfolds and beauty pageant contestants in recent years (see Harrison & Cantor, 1997). Cosmetic plastic surgery has increased dramatically, with tummy tucks

181

*"Who
Says It":
Source
Factors in
Persuasion*

**Box 6.1** |

up by over 140 percent since 1997 (Kuczynski, 2006). Yet thinness in women—propelled by the fashion industry, advertising, and young girls' desire to emulate sometimes dangerously thin models—is a relatively new cultural invention. In earlier eras, voluptuous body shapes were regarded as sexy. "The concept of beauty has never been static," researcher April Fallon reports (1990, p. 84).

Going a long, long way back in time, one finds that, between 1400 and 1700, "fat was considered both erotic and fashionable . . . Women were desired for their procreative value and were often either pregnant or nursing. The beautiful woman was portrayed as a plump matron with full, nurturant breasts" (Fallon, 1990, p. 85). The art of Botticelli and Rubens reflects this ideal.

There are also subcultural variations in what is regarded as beautiful in the United States. Research shows that African-American women are less likely than White women to be preoccupied with body weight (Angier, 2000b). "It's a cultural thing," observed Roneice Weaver, a coauthor of *Slim Down Sister*, a weight-loss book for Black women. She said that Black men don't judge women's physical appeal by their waist size (Angier, p. D2).

The attractiveness of other body features also varies with culture. In America, breast size is linked with beauty, as indicated by the popularity of bras that pad and surgical breast implants. Yet in Brazil, large breasts are viewed as déclassé, "a libido killer," and in Japan bosoms are less enchanting than the nape of the neck, which is seen as an erotic zone (Kaufman, 2000, p. 3). In Peru, big ears are considered beautiful, and Mexican women regard low foreheads as an indication of beauty (de Botton, 2000).

Standards for male attractiveness also vary across cultures and historical periods. Macho guys like Humphrey Bogart and Marlon Brando have been replaced by softer looking icons of attractiveness, like Leonardo DiCaprio, Justin Timberlake, Robert Pattinson, the controversial Tiger Woods, and music stars just breaking into the mainstream (Fitzpatrick, 2000).

To be sure, there are some universals in physical appeal. Yet culture still powerfully influences standards of physical appeal. Increasingly, the American emphasis on hourglass Barbie-like figures has insinuated itself into other cultures (including Brazil), which historically valued plumper physiques (Rohter, 2007). As Fallon notes, "Culturally bound and consensually validated definitions of what is desirable and attractive play an important part in the development of body image" (1990, p. 80). Our standards for what is beautiful are acquired and molded through culture, with the mass media playing an influential role in transmitting and shaping cultural norms. Technological innovations exert insidious influences. "On the covers of magazines, all the beautiful women are photoshopped, their skin is cleaned up. Everybody does it," notes a beauty specialist at a San Francisco advertising firm (Williams, 2008, p. 12). In this way young women acquire unrealistic and false notions of attractiveness. Thus, culture leaves a strong imprint on conceptions of physical attractiveness, and we apply these—consciously and unconsciously—in evaluating everyday persuaders.

# CONCLUSIONS

This chapter has focused on the communicator—a key feature of persuasion. The concept of charisma comes to mind when we think about the communicator, and for good reason: charismatic speakers have seemed to magnetize audiences, influencing attitudes in benevolent and malevolent ways. Charisma involves a host of characteristics, not well understood, and for this reason scholars have tried to break down the term into constituent parts. Preferring a scientific approach to this topic, researchers have focused painstakingly on three core communicator qualities: authority, credibility, and social attractiveness.

Authority, epitomized by the Milgram study of obedience, can influence behaviors through a process of compliance. Participants in the Milgram study obeyed a legitimate authority significantly more than experts predicted—a testament to the role of early socialization, authority's trappings, and binding psychological forces. Although Milgram's experiments raised questions about the ethics of deception in research, they nonetheless shed light on continuing crimes of obedience in society.

Credibility, a distant cousin of authority, is a critical communicator factor, the cornerstone of effective persuasion. Research suggests that expertise, trustworthiness, and goodwill are the three core dimensions of credibility. (Expertise and trustworthiness have emerged with greater regularity, and goodwill has been uncovered in more recent research.)

Each of these factors is important in its own right, and can interact with contextual factors, such as audience size, communicator role, and historical epoch.

Major theoretical approaches to credibility include the ELM and an expectancy–violation model. The latter assumes that communicators gain in credibility to the degree that they take unexpected positions on issues—stands that audiences cannot attribute to their background or situation.

Social attractiveness consists of three elements: likability, similarity, and physical appeal. All three factors can influence attitudes under particular conditions and have intriguing implications for everyday persuasive communication (see Box 6.2).

Interestingly, credibility and social attractiveness translate easily to the interactive environment.

You have probably come across Web sites that convey credibility or lack thereof. You've seen visually attractive sites that invite exploration and make you feel positively toward the sponsoring organization. Research shows that expertise is conveyed by comprehensiveness of information listed on the site, as well as by sponsor credentials (Dutta-Bergman, 2004a; Metzger, Flanagin, Eyal, Lemus, & McCann, 2003). Trustworthiness is enhanced by including explicit policy statements and by lack of advertising. Social attractiveness is conveyed by layout, colorful pictures, and perceived beauty. These features can also be used to mislead or bamboozle consumers. But once again, we see that "who says it" and the nature of the source are fundamental facets of persuasion, as critical to effective persuasion today as they were in Aristotle's age of oral communication. Messages and channels have changed, but, as the song from *Casablanca* puts it, the fundamental things apply.

183

*"Who
Says It":
Source
Factors in
Persuasion*

## Box 6.2 | COMMUNICATOR TIPS

Can research and theory offer practical suggestions on how to be a more effective communicator? You bet! Here are five ideas, gleaned from persuasion concepts and experiments:

1. If you are delivering a speech and have technical knowledge about the topic, you should let your audience know this at the outset. Don't blow your horn too much or you will come off as obnoxious. Instead, discreetly note your credentials. If, on the other hand, you are new on the job and have not accumulated much technical knowledge, don't mention this before you give the talk. There is some evidence that this could reduce your credibility in the audience's eyes (Greenberg & Miller, 1966). Instead, demonstrate your qualifications as you discuss your ideas (Whalen, 1996).

2. Show your audience you care about both the topic and your role as a persuader. Goodwill counts for a great deal in persuasion, as discussed earlier. People forgive a lot if they believe you have their interests at heart. You should be true to yourself here: don't fake deep caring if you don't feel it. Instead, identify one or two areas that you are legitimately interested in imparting, and focus on these.

3. Try to get the audience to like you. Likability can enhance persuasion (Sharma, 1999), so you should find a feature of your personality that you are comfortable with and let this shine through during your talk. It may be your serenity, sensitivity, gregariousness, or sense of humor. Use this as a way to connect with the audience.

4. Find out as much as you can about your audience's tastes, attitudes, and familiarity with the issues under discussion. The ELM emphasizes that persuasion works best when it is attuned to the processing style of the audience. If working in an organization, "you should make a concerted effort to meet one-on-one with all the key people you plan to persuade," Conger advises (1998, p. 89). This will provide you with the range of viewpoints on the issue and help you gear your presentation accordingly.

5. When it comes to attractiveness, keep in mind Aristotle's emphasis on moderation and balance (Golden, Berquist, & Coleman, 2000). You want to look nice because it can enhance persuasion, especially in some situations. What's more, you may develop a positive view of yourself if you are well groomed and well dressed. This positive self-perception can lead you to feel better about yourself, which can increase your persuasive power. But unless you are working in the fashion industry, attractiveness is of limited value. Prior to a presentation, some people spend a lot of time worrying about their wardrobe or trying to make a smashing physical appearance. But what worked for Erin Brockovich or Julia Roberts in the movie of this name may not work for you. What's more, if you look like you're preoccupied with appearance, audience members may conclude you are not concerned with them, which can reduce your credibility. Better to spend that valuable pre-presentation time honing your arguments and figuring out ways to present your ideas in a cogent, interesting fashion.

# Chapter 7

# Message Factors

THE message has fascinated scholars for centuries. Aristotle emphasized that deductive syllogisms are the bases of rhetorical arguments. Twentieth-century rhetoricians, building on Aristotle's foundations, identified key components of valid, cogent arguments (Toulmin, 1958). Contemporary scholars assume as a first principle that messages cannot be understood without appreciating the psychology of the audience. They have explored the influences of different message factors on receivers, trying to understand which components have the most impact and why. This chapter examines the time-honored factor of the persuasive message, a key component of persuasion and a critical consideration for communication practitioners.

## UNDERSTANDING THE MESSAGE

It seems pretty obvious.

The message—what you say and how you say it—influences people. Uh-huh, an intelligent person impatient with intellectual theories might think; now can we move on? Persuasion scholars would like to move on too—they have books to write, students to teach, and families to feed. But they—and you too, no doubt—recognize that the message construct is so big and unwieldy that it needs to be broken down, decomposed, and analyzed in terms of content and process. Communication scholars, taking note of this issue, have seized on a concept that fascinated ancient philosophers and deconstructed it. Their research offers us a wealth of insights about communication effects.

There are three types of message factors. The first concerns the structure of the message—how it is prepared and organized. The second is the content of the communication—its appeals and arguments. The third factor is language—how communicators use words and symbols to persuade an audience (see Table 7.1).

**TABLE 7.1** | Key message factors

**Message Structure**

1. Message sidedness

2. Conclusion drawing

3. Order of presentation (primacy vs. recency)*

**Message Content**

1. Evidence

2. Case histories

3. Fear

4. Guilt

**Language**

1. Speed of speech

2. Powerless versus powerful language

3. Intense language

4. Political language

* Primacy occurs when an argument presented early in a message, or the first of two opposing messages, is most persuasive. Recency occurs when an argument presented later in a message, or the second of two opposing messages, is most compelling. There is no conclusive evidence in favor of either primacy or recency. Effects depend on situational factors, such as amount of time that elapses between messages, and audience involvement.

# MESSAGE STRUCTURE

How should you package your message? What is the best way to organize your arguments? These are practical questions, ones that have attracted research interest since Hovland's path-breaking studies of the 1950s. There are two particularly interesting issues here. The first concerns whether communicators should present both sides of the issue or just their own. The second focuses on the most persuasive way to conclude the message.

## One or Two Sides?

A *one-sided message* presents one perspective on the issue. A *two-sided communication* offers arguments on behalf of both the persuader's position and the opposition. Which is more persuasive?

You might argue that it is best to ignore the other side and hammer home your perspective. After all, this lets you spend precious time detailing reasons why your side is correct. On the other hand, if you overlook opposition arguments with which everyone is familiar, you look like you have something to hide. For example, let's say you staunchly oppose people talking on cell phones when they drive and have decided, after years of frustration, to take this issue to the city council. Should you present one or both sides of this issue to council members?

A review of message sidedness research provides an answer to this question. Two communication scholars conducted *meta-analyses* of research on one- and two-sided messages. A meta-analysis is a study of other studies. A researcher locates all the investigations of a phenomenon and uses statistical procedures to determine the strength of the findings. After exhaustively reviewing the many studies in this area, researchers Mike Allen (1998) and Daniel J. O'Keefe (1999) reached the same conclusion, something that does not always happen in social science research! Researchers O'Keefe and Allen concluded *that two-sided messages influence attitudes more than one-sided messages, provided one very important condition is met: the message refutes opposition arguments.* When the communication mentions, but not does demolish, an opponent's viewpoint, a two-sided message is actually less compelling than a one-sided message.

Refutational two-sided messages, as they are called, gain their persuasive advantage by (a) enhancing the credibility of the speaker (he or she is perceived as honest enough to discuss both sides of the coin), and (b) providing cogent reasons why opposing arguments are wrong.

This has obvious implications for your speech urging a ban on talking on a cell phone while driving. You should present arguments for your side (talking on a handheld cell phone while driving is a dangerous distractor) and the other position (there are other distractors, like putting a CD in the disc player or applying makeup, that should also be banned if government is going to restrict cell phone use). You should then refute the other side, citing evidence that talking on a cell phone while driving has caused large numbers of automobile accidents; cell phone use causes more serious accidents than other distractors because it interferes with visual processing skills; and talking on the phone is a prolonged, not temporary, distraction from the road.

On a more philosophical level, the sidedness research leaves us with a reassuring finding about human nature. It tells us that communicators can change attitudes when they are fair, mention both sides, and offer cogent arguments in support of their position. The results celebrate values most of us would affirm: honesty and intellectual rigor.

## Conclusion Drawing

Should persuaders *explicitly* draw the conclusion? Should they wrap things up for listeners in an unambiguous, forceful fashion, making it 100 percent clear which path they want audience members to pursue? Or should they be more circumspect and indirect, letting audience members put things together for themselves? These questions point to the question of explicit versus implicit conclusion drawing. Arguments can be made for both sides. Perhaps, since audience attention wanders, it is best to present a detailed and forceful conclusion. On the other hand, people might prefer that persuaders not tell them explicitly what to do, but instead allow them to believe they arrived at the conclusion on their own.

A meta-analysis of research provides us with an answer to this dilemma. O'Keefe (1997) found that messages clearly or explicitly articulating an overall conclusion are more persuasive than those that omit a conclusion. As McGuire bluntly observed: "In communication, it appears, it is not sufficient to lead the horse to the water; one must also push his head underneath to get him to drink" (1969, p. 209). Making the conclusion explicit minimizes the chances that individuals will be confused about where the communicator stands. It also helps people comprehend the message, which in turn enhances source evaluations and persuasion (Cruz, 1998).

## Continuing Issues

There is little doubt that message organization influences attitudes. Certain methods are more effective than others. But message organization does not work in a vacuum. Context and modality matter. For example, in politics, communicators organize messages around negative arguments. Negative advertising spots—featuring criticisms of the other candidate, sometimes with great gusto—are commonplace, and can be remarkably effective (West, 1997). Voters expect politicians to run negative campaigns, and to some degree people want to be told the shortcomings of opposing candidates. Try the same technique in an organizational setting—lambasting your office rival in a group discussion—and see how far it gets you. The requirements and expectations of organizational persuasion are much different from those of politics.

In the same fashion, messages delivered interpersonally should be structured differently than those relayed over television and via the Internet. The Web, with its nonlinear approach to communication, presents persuaders with opportunities and challenges. They can use graphics, links, and navigational aids to help organize message arguments. Advocacy Web pages do this all the time, and persuaders are becoming increasingly adept at effectively structuring Web-based communications (Alexander & Tate, 1999).

The remainder of the chapter focuses on other message factors: the content of the message (evidence, case histories, fear appeals, and guilt appeals) and language.

## EVIDENCE

- Passive smoking is a major cause of lung cancer. A husband or wife who has never smoked has an approximately 16 percent increased chance of contracting lung cancer if he or she lives with a smoker.
- A United Nations panel of experts on climate change has concluded that global warming is occurring at a faster rate than previously believed. Twenty of the twenty-one hottest years measured since 1860 have occurred within the past quarter-century.
- Herbal medicines contain tonics that strengthen the nervous system, making it more resilient to everyday stressors. Studies show that these over-the-counter herbal products offer a regular supply of the neurotransmitters needed to ward off serious physical and mental ailments.
- Ballistic tests conducted by the prosecutor's office prove that the bullet that killed Kenneth Lewis could not have been fired from the gun owned by the defendant.

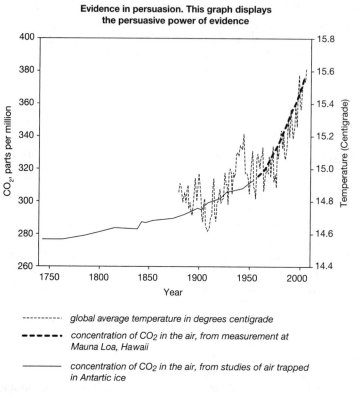

**Evidence in persuasion. This graph displays
the persuasive power of evidence**

---------- *global average temperature in degrees centigrade*

▬ ▬ ▬ ▬ ▪ *concentration of CO2 in the air, from measurement at
Mauna Loa, Hawaii*

———— *concentration of CO2 in the air, from studies of air trapped
in Antartic ice*

**FIGURE 7.1** | The amount of carbon dioxide in the air has risen about 35 percent since the
beginning of the Industrial Revolution in the 1700s. During this same period, the global average
temperature has risen about 0.7°C. Scientists attribute this to human activities, like the burning of fossil fuels.

Data from Carbon Dioxide Information Analysis Center, Oakridge National Laboratory, and the National
Climatic Data Center, National Oceanographic & Atmospheric Administration. Graph supplied, courtesy
of Paul B. Shepson.

These diverse arguments have one thing in common: they use evidence to substantiate their claims. Evidence is employed by persuaders working in a variety of settings,
including advertising, health, and politics. Evidence, John C. Reinard notes, is a classic
"building block of arguments," or "information used as proof" (1991, p. 102). Evidence
is a broad term, McCroskey observes. He defines it as: *"factual statements originating
from a source other than the speaker, objects not created by the speaker, and opinions
of persons other than the speaker that are offered in support of the speaker's claims"*
(1969, p. 170).

Evidence consists of factual assertions, quantitative information (like statistics; see
Figure 7.1), eyewitness statements, testimonials, or opinions advanced by credible sources.
We're all familiar with evidence and have witnessed its use many times. Communication

researchers, also intrigued by evidence, have conducted numerous studies over a 50-year period, probing the effects of evidence on attitudes. Does evidence change attitudes?

You bet.

"The use of evidence produces more attitude change than the use of no evidence," Rodney A. Reynolds and J. Lynn Reynolds declare after reviewing the many studies in the area (2002, p. 428). Reinard goes further, observing that "there actually may be more consistency in evidence research than can be found in almost any other area of persuasion. Evidence appears to produce general persuasive effects that appear surprisingly stable" (1988, p. 46).

Evidence is especially persuasive when attributed to a highly credible source—an outgrowth of principles discussed in the previous two chapters. Evidence is also more apt to change attitudes, the more plausible and novel it is (Morley & Walker, 1987).

Persuaders must do more than simply mention evidence: audience members must recognize that evidence has been offered in support of a proposition and perceive the evidence to be legitimate (Parrott, Silk, Dorgan, Condit, & Harris, 2005; Reynolds & Reynolds, 2002). If individuals are dozing off and don't hear the evidence, or they dispute the legitimacy of the factual assertions, the evidence presented has less impact on attitudes.

Evidence, in short, must be processed. The ELM reminds us that the ways in which evidence is elaborated determine its effect on persuasion. When people are highly involved in or knowledgeable about the issue, evidence will be processed centrally. Under these circumstances, quality of evidence matters. Cogent evidence can change people's minds. But remember: even the most compelling evidence is unlikely to change strong attitudes—those that touch on the self-concept or core values.

Evidence can have striking effects under low involvement, but it works through different processes. When people lack motivation or ability to decipher the issue, they rely on peripheral cues. They may go along with arguments that sound impressive because the communicator cites many facts, uses highfalutin statistics, or throws in testimonial statements. The trappings of evidence are more important than the legal or statistical quality of the facts. Evidence operates more as a cue than an argument when people aren't motivated or knowledgeable about the issue. In such cases, communicators can use evidence truthfully, or they can lie with statistics (Huff, 1954).

Persuaders can also err by citing too much evidence. In ELM terms, they can use evidence as an *argument* rather than a *cue*, thereby failing to connect with low- or modest-involvement audience members. Presidential candidates who have used too much evidence—trying to bowl over voters with numbers and mastery of facts—have tended to lose presidential debates (Levasseur & Dean, 1996). "Instead of appearing as a 'man with the facts,' a candidate is more likely to appear as one who creates confusion," two researchers concluded (Levasseur & Dean, p. 136).

The winning formula in political debates, and many other contexts in which audiences are modestly interested in the issue, is to use evidence in such a way that it enhances, rather than reduces, credibility. Evidence should be used to buttress arguments rather than distract audiences from the communicator or the message. John F. Kennedy succeeded in using evidence in this manner in the now-classic first 1960 debate, linking data with claims and repeating phrases to hammer in his arguments ("I'm not satisfied to have 50 percent of our steel mill capacity unused. I'm not satisfied when the United States had last year the lowest rate of economic growth of any major industrialized society in the world"). By using evidence in this way, Kennedy achieved the goal that all persuaders wish to achieve: he appeared like a "farsighted leader" with vision rather than a boring policy wonk (Levasseur & Dean, 1996).

## The Other Side of Evidence: The Case of Case Histories

Has this ever happened to you? You are trying to decide whether to add a course at the beginning of the semester. You're tempted to take the class because a variety of people you spoke with recommended it, and the class received positive ratings in course evaluation data posted on the student government Web site. The day before the drop–add deadline you ask a friend what she thinks and she says in no uncertain terms, without even flinching or hesitating, "The prof sucks. That was the worst class I've ever taken. You don't want to take that course with him." You don't add the course.

This example illustrates the power that vivid case studies or narratives exert on persuasion. Your friend's evidence was attention grabbing and emotional, the information from course evaluations pallid and abstract. Yet the course evaluation data were more representative of student opinion toward the course since they drew on a larger and more diverse cross-section of course enrollees. By contrast, your friend could be an outlier— someone whose views lay outside the distribution of student opinion, shaped perhaps by an idiosyncratic response to the professor.

Social psychologists argue that people are frequently more influenced by concrete, emotionally interesting information than by "dry, statistical data that are dear to the hearts of scientists and policy planners" (Nisbett, Borgida, Crandall, & Reed, 1976, p. 132). Vivid case histories—also called personalized stories or narratives—exert particularly strong effects on attitudes (Taylor & Thompson, 1982). What is meant by vivid case histories or narratives? These are emotionally engaging (not purely factual) stories of an individual's experiences with a problem in life. They are gripping anecdotes of how one person or a handful of people have coped with an issue. These cases engage the imagination, but are not necessarily representative of the larger population.

The mass media are filled with stories about how one person battled cancer, another died tragically in a car crash when she was hit by a drunk driver, or others had their lives cut short by AIDS. Persuaders—running the gamut from attorneys to advocacy groups to health practitioners—frequently call on vivid anecdotes, hoping these will tug at our heartstrings and influence beliefs (see Box 7.1).

Some scholars argue this is a stunningly effective strategy. They contend that when it comes to persuasion, graphic narratives are more compelling than statistics. Never mind that narratives frequently are based on the experience of just one person and statistics derive from the experience of hundreds, maybe thousands. Vivid case histories evoke stronger mental images than abstractly presented information, are easier to access from memory, and are therefore more likely to influence attitudes when the individual is trying

## Box 7.1 | A VIVID NARRATIVE ON DRINKING AND DRIVING

Mothers Against Drunk Driving and Students Against Drug Driving frequently rely on vivid anecdotes—commonly a part of narratives—to convey their arguments. They undoubtedly regard these as more persuasive than gray statistics about the number of deaths caused by drunk drivers. Here is one particularly gripping example, supplied by a student. She read it during high school prom week, the narrative poem made an indelible impression, and she kept it over the years. As you read it over, ask yourself if you find this persuasive—and if so, why?

> I went to a party, Mom, I remembered what you said.
> You told me not to drink, Mom, so I drank a coke instead . . .
> I know I did the right thing, Mom, I know you're always right.
> Now the party is finally ending, Mom, as everyone drives out of sight . . .
> I started to drive away, Mom, but as I pulled onto the road,
> The other car didn't see me, Mom, it hit me like a load.
> As I lay here on the pavement, Mom, I hear the policeman say
> The other guy is drunk, Mom, and I'm the one who'll pay.
> I'm lying here dying, Mom, I wish you'd get here soon.
> How come this happened to me, Mom? My life burst like a balloon . . .
> The guy who hit me, Mom, is walking. I don't think that's fair.
> I'm lying here dying, Mom, while all he can do is stare . . .
> Someone should have told him, Mom, not to drink and drive.
> If only they would have taken the time, Mom, I would still be alive.
> My breath is getting shorter, Mom. I'm becoming very scared . . .
> Please don't cry for me Mom, because when I needed you, you were always there.
> I have one last question, Mom, before I say goodbye,
> I didn't ever drink, Mom, so why am I to die?

to decide whether to accept message recommendations (Rook, 1987). Narratives are—let's face it—more interesting than statistical evidence (Green & Brock, 2000). As stories, they engage the imagination and are "intuitively appealing to humans, as we are all essentially storytellers and avid story recipients" (Kopfman, Smith, Ah Yun, & Hodges, 1998, p. 281).

An alternative view, put forth by other scholars, is that vivid information can be so distracting that it interferes with reception of the message. When this occurs, people fail to process message arguments or neglect to connect the evidence with the position advocated in the communication (Frey & Eagly, 1993). According to this view, statistical evidence, dull though it may be, has the upper hand in persuasion. Statistics also can evoke heuristics like "an argument backed by numbers is probably correct."

With such strong logic on the sides of both narratives and statistical evidence, it should come as no surprise that both have been found to influence attitudes (Allen, Bruflat,

Fucilla, Kramer, McKellips, Ryan, & Spiegelhoff, 2000; Kazoleas, 1993). Some scholars believe that vivid narratives are more compelling; others contend that statistics are more persuasive than narratives (Allen & Preiss, 1997b; Baesler & Burgoon, 1994). Still other researchers say that it depends on the persuader's purpose: narratives may be more effective when communicators are trying to shake up people who strongly disagree with the message; statistics carry more weight when persuaders are trying to influence cognitions or beliefs (Kopfman et al., 1998; Slater & Rouner, 1996).

The optimum strategy is to use both evidence and narrative. When artfully combined, they pack a powerful punch. One glimpses this in Al Gore's (2006) book and movie, *An Inconvenient Truth*. Gore provided charts and factual evidence to show how global warming has led to sharp increases over time in the number of floods and hurricanes. He presented heart-rending images of the human devastation wrought by Hurricane Katrina. Gore used numerical evidence to show that there has been a sharp decrease over time in the number of days a year that the Alaskan tundra is frozen solidly enough to drive on. He then presented vivid images of scenic glaciers in the Alps in the early twentieth century and the snow-capped peak of Mount Kilimanjaro in 1970, only to follow these up with images of the same sites today. The glaciers are nonexistent and the mountaintop has far less snow. By weaving evidence and memorable pictures together in a narrative focused on his commitment to environmental preservation, Gore used the film medium to influence attitudes (see Box 7.2 for a discussion of the narrative effect of films and other media).

## Summary

Simple and prosaic as it sounds, evidence enhances persuasion. If you use evidence in your public or electronic presentations, you are apt to influence attitudes or at least to increase your credibility. Things quickly become more complex when we try to discover why evidence works (central and peripheral processes are important), and the types of evidence that are most influential in particular contexts (the issue of narratives vs. statistics surfaces). Evidence does not stamp its imprint on receivers, but must be recognized and processed to influence attitudes. What's more, evidence does not, as commonly assumed, automatically fall into the category of a rational message factor. Contrary to common beliefs, which suggest that certain factors like evidence are rational and others, like fear or guilt, are emotional, evidence can be viewed as rational or emotional. It is rational when people appreciate high-quality evidence in a message and change their attitudes because they recognize that the weight of evidence favors a certain option. But evidence can also be an emotional factor when individuals go along with evidence-based messages for affective reasons (as when they tell themselves that "any argument with that many numbers has got to be right") or feel terribly sad after reading statistics about the spread of AIDS in Africa and decide on the spot to donate $50 to AIDS research.

By the same token, factors that seem oh-so-emotional, like fear, have cognitive as well as affective aspects. Classifying message content factors as rational or emotional is a tempting way to differentiate message factors. It turns out that messages and people are too complex to permit this simple dichotomy. Messages change attitudes because they

## Box 7.2 | NARRATIVE PERSUASION

You leave a movie theater in a daze, your mind transfixed by the scenes and sadness you witnessed. The plot plays out in your mind for days as you mull over the social dilemmas the movie raises.

A friend relates that she cannot stop thinking about a novel she read. The characters' struggles, the inability of the protagonist to defy the stigmas society has put in his path, and the author's mordant criticisms of contemporary culture unnerve her. She finds herself questioning assumptions she once easily made.

Novels, short stories, films, and an array of other art forms influence our attitudes in subtle and profound ways. As discussed in Chapter 1, these communications fall into the category of borderline persuasion because the intent of the communicator is not necessarily to change attitudes so much as to enlighten or agitate. And yet, as Timothy C. Brock and colleagues note, "*Public narratives*—the stories we hear everyday in the news media and the stories that we consume in books, films, plays, soap operas, and so forth—command a large share of our waking attention" (Brock, Strange, & Green, 2002, p. 1). What's more, social narratives in books and movies have profoundly affected society. Charles Dickens's descriptions of life in nineteenth-century England awakened people to the plight of children working in dangerous factories. Novels about race (Harriet Beecher Stowe's *Uncle Tom's Cabin*, James Baldwin's *The Fire Next Time*) helped build social movements that led to the Civil War in the nineteenth century and the civil rights protests of the 1960s. The list of movies that have influenced beliefs and attitudes is seemingly endless. One thinks of *Schindler's List*, *Saving Private Ryan*, *Milk*, *The Passion of the Christ*, and even *Super Size Me*. You can probably list many other films that affected your outlook toward social issues.

The academic literature on persuasion neglected the impact of public narrative on attitudes, emphasizing instead the effects of advocacy messages deliberately designed to change attitudes. Scholars have pointed out that advocacy messages influence attitudes through processes different from those of fictional narratives. Advocacy communications (blogs, advertisements, speeches, political campaigns) work through central and peripheral processes, by activating beliefs, evoking social norms, and arousing inconsistencies. Fiction does its work by arousing the emotions, transporting people to different psychological places, and causing them to become absorbed in different realities (Green & Brock, 2002; Green, Kass, Carey, Herzig, Feeney, & Sabini, 2008). As one scholar puts it, great novels "transport" people to different mental arenas—the world of the author's imagination; "the traveler returns to the world of origin, somewhat changed by the journey" (Gerrig, 1993, p. 11).

Melanie C. Green and Timothy C. Brock (2000) devised a nifty way to study these issues empirically. They developed a scale to measure individuals' tendency to become absorbed psychologically by stories or transported to the narrative world created by the author. Their scale includes items like: "The narrative affected me emotionally," "I was mentally involved in the narrative while reading it," and "I could picture myself in the scene of the events described in the narrative." Green and Brock asked research participants to read an

**Box 7.2**

evocative story, "Murder at the Mall," about a college student whose younger sister is brutally murdered by a psychiatric patient at the mall. The researchers then asked participants a series of questions about the story and characters.

In order to determine the impact of being "transported" into a narrative world, the researchers analyzed participants' responses to questions like those just mentioned. Those who strongly agreed with these and similar questions were considered to be high in transportation; those who disagreed were regarded as low in transportation. Highly transported individuals were more influenced by the story, reporting more beliefs consistent with the narrative. For example, they were more likely than low-transported participants to believe that the world was less just and psychiatric patients' freedoms should be restricted. They were less likely to doubt the story, viewing it as more authentic than did those low in transportation.

Narrative is not limited to books and movies. Contemporary narratives can appear on a host of interactive technologies, such as movies shown on Web sites, video games, and virtual reality. Research on narrative effects has important social implications. It suggests that change agents concerned with issues ranging from prejudice to AIDS might complement traditional advocacy messages by writing compelling stories, conveyed through different modalities (Kincaid, 2002; Slater, 2002; Smith, Downs, & Witte, 2007). By transporting individuals to social realms located in the human imagination, stories can induce them to look at everyday problems through a new set of lenses.

stimulate thought, arouse affect, and mesh with receivers' motivations and needs. In the next section, I discuss another major message factor—fear, a concept rich in intellectual and practical content.

## FEAR APPEALS

Several years back, Maureen Coyne, a college senior enrolled in a persuasion class, ruminated about a question her professor asked: Think of a time when you tried to change someone's attitude about an issue. How did you go about accomplishing this task? After thinking for a few moments, Maureen recalled a series of events from her childhood, salient incidents in which she mightily tried to influence loved ones' attitudes. "My entire life," she related, "I have been trying to persuade my lovely parents to quit smoking. It started with the smell of smoke," she said, recollecting:

> I would go to school and kids could smell it on me to the extent that they would ask me if my parents smoked. It was humiliating. Then the lessons began from the teachers. They vehemently expressed how unhealthy this habit was through videos,

books, and even puppet shows. In my head, the case against smoking was building. From my perspective, smoking was hurting my parents, my younger brothers, and me. With this in mind, it is understandable that a young, energetic, opinionated child would try and do something to rid her life of this nasty habit. Well, try I did. I educated them constantly about the dangers of first- and second-hand smoke, with help from class assignments. I would tell them about the cancers, carbon monoxide, etc., and remind them every time I saw something on TV or in the paper about smoking statistics. I begged and begged and begged (and then cried a little). I explained how much it hurt my brothers and me. I reminded them that they should practice what they preach (they told us not to smoke).

(Coyne, 2000)

Although Maureen's valiant persuasive efforts ultimately failed (her parents disregarded her loving advice), she showed a knack for devising a compelling fear appeal to influence attitudes toward smoking. Maureen is hardly alone in trying to scare people into changing a dysfunctional attitude or behavior. Fear appeals are ubiquitous. Consider the following:

- Hoping to deter juvenile criminals from a life of crime, a New Jersey prison adopted a novel approach in the late 1970s. Teenagers who had been arrested for crimes like robbery were carted off to Rahway State Prison to participate in a communication experiment. The teens were seated before a group of lifers, men who had been sentenced to life imprisonment for murder and armed robbery. The men, bruising, brawling criminals, intimidated the youngsters, swearing at them and threatening to hurt them. At the same time, they used obscene and intense language to scare the youngsters into changing their ways. The program, *Scared Straight*, was videotaped and broadcast on national television numerous times over the ensuing decades (Finckenauer, 1982).
- Public service announcements (PSAs) in magazines, on television, and on Web sites regularly arouse fear in hopes of convincing young people to stop smoking, quit using dangerous drugs like methamphetamine, and avoid binge-drinking episodes. Some PSAs have become world famous, like the Partnership for a Drug-Free America's "brain on drugs" ad. ("This is your brain. This is drugs. This is your brain on drugs. Any questions?")
- Advertisers, who exploited fears long before public-health specialists devised health PSAs, continue to appeal to consumers' fears in television spots. Toothpaste and deodorant ads suggest that if you don't buy their products, you will be shunned by friends who smell your bad breath or body odor. Liquid bleach commercials warn that a baby's clothing can breed germs that cause diaper rash or other skin irritations. To avoid these consequences—and the larger humiliation of being viewed as a bad parent —you only need plunk down some money to buy Clorox or another liquid bleach.
- Parents use fear, from the get-go, to discourage children from approaching dangerous objects and people. They warn toddlers that they can choke and die if they put small parts of toys in their mouths. School-age kids are warned what can happen if they

don't buckle up safety belts or wear bicycle helmets, or if they play with firearms. When they reach adolescence, youngsters are told of the dangers of risqué Web sites, promiscuous peers, and unsafe sex.

Fear appeals evoke different reactions in people. They remind some individuals of the worst moments of adolescence, when parents warned them that every pleasurable activity would end up haunting them in later life. Others, noting that life is full of dangers, approve of and appreciate these communications. Still other observers wonder why we must resort to fear; why can't we just give people the facts?

Appealing to people's fears is, to a considerable degree, a negative communication strategy. The communicator must arouse a little pain in the individual, hoping it will produce gain. The persuader may have to go further than the facts of the situation warrant, raising specters and scenarios that may be rather unlikely to occur even if the individual continues to engage in the dysfunctional behavior. In an ideal world, it would not be necessary to arouse fear. Communicators could simply present the facts, and logic would carry the day. But this is not an ideal world; people are emotional, as well as cognitive, creatures, and they do not always do what is best for them. People are tempted by all sorts of demons—objects, choices, and substances that seem appealing but actually can cause quite a bit of harm. Thus, fear appeals are a necessary persuasive strategy, useful in a variety of arenas of life.

## The Psychology of Fear

Before discussing the role that fear plays in persuasion, it is instructive to define our terms. What is fear? What is a fear appeal? Social scientists define the terms in the following ways:

- *Fear*: an internal emotional reaction composed of psychological and physiological dimensions that may be aroused when a serious and personally relevant threat is perceived (Witte, Meyer, & Martell, 2001, p. 20).
- *Fear appeal*: a persuasive communication that tries to scare people into changing their attitudes by conjuring up negative consequences that will occur if they do not comply with the message recommendations.

Over the past half-century, researchers have conducted numerous studies of fear-arousing messages. As a result of this research, we know a great deal about the psychology of fear and the impact of fear appeals on attitudes. The research has also done much to clarify common-sense notions—in some cases misconceptions—of fear message effects.

At first glance, it probably seems like it is very easy to scare people. According to popular belief, all persuaders need do is conjure up really terrible outcomes, get the person feeling jittery and anxious, and wait as fear drives the individual to follow the recommended action. There are two misconceptions here: first, that fear appeals invariably work, and second, that fear acts as a simple drive. Let's see how these notions oversimplify matters.

Contrary to what you may have heard, it is not easy to scare people successfully. Arousing fear does not always produce attitude change. After reviewing the research in this area, Franklin J. Boster and Paul Mongeau concluded that "manipulating fear does not appear to be an easy task. What appears to be a highly-arousing persuasive message to the experimenter may not induce much fear into the recipient of the persuasive message" (1984, p. 375).

More generally, persuaders frequently assume that a message scares audience members. However, they may be surprised to discover that individuals either are not frightened or did not tune in to the message because it was irrelevant to their needs. This has been a recurring problem with automobile safety videos—those designed to persuade people to wear seat belts or not drink when they drive. Message designers undoubtedly have the best of intentions, but their persuasive videos are often seen by audience members as hokey, far-fetched, or just plain silly (Robertson, Kelley, O'Neill, Wixom, Eiswirth, & Haddon, 1974).

Not only can fear appeals fail because they arouse too little fear, but they can also backfire if they scare individuals too much (Morris & Swann, 1996). Fear messages invariably suggest that bad things will happen if individuals continue engaging in dangerous behaviors, like smoking or excessive drinking. None of us like to admit that these outcomes will happen to us, so we deny or defensively distort the communicator's message. There is considerable evidence that people perceive that bad things are less likely to happen to them than to others (Weinstein, 1980, 1993). In a classic study, Neil D. Weinstein (1980) asked college students to estimate how much their own chances of experiencing negative life events differed from the chances of their peers. Students perceived that they were significantly less likely than others to experience a host of outcomes, including:

- dropping out of college;
- getting divorced a few years after getting married;
- being fired from a job;
- having a drinking problem;
- getting lung cancer; and
- contracting venereal disease.

It is not just students who harbor perceptions. A national survey found that close to half of all respondents believe that talking on a cell phone constitutes the most dangerous driving distraction. However, 98 percent of individuals who have used a cell phone while driving regard *themselves* as safe drivers (Richtel, 2009).

The belief that one is less likely to experience negative life events than others is known as *unrealistic optimism* or *the illusion of invulnerability*. People harbor such illusions for three reasons. First, they do not want to admit that life's misfortunes can befall them. For instance, many young people routinely accept medications like Ritalin from friends, switch from Paxil to Prozac based on the recommendation of an e-mail acquaintance, or trade Ativan for Ambien (Harmon, 2005). Youthful, assured, and confident of their knowledge, they minimize the risks involved in taking drugs for which they do not have a prescription.

A second reason people harbor an illusion of invulnerability is that they maintain a stereotype of the typical victim of negative events and blithely maintain that they do not fit the mold. For example, in the case of cigarette smoking, they may assume that the typical smoker who gets lung cancer is a thin, nervous, jittery, middle-aged man who smokes like a chimney. Noting that they smoke but do not fit the prototype, individuals conclude they are not at risk. This overlooks the fact that few of those who get cancer from smoking actually match the stereotype.

A third reason is that people, enjoying the pleasures of risky choices, decide to offload the costs of these pleasures to the more mature adults they will become in the future (Holt, 2006). In essence, an individual separates out her present and future selves, then rationalizes pursuit of a risky behavior in the here and now, "making the future self suffer for the pleasure of the moment" (Holt, pp. 16–17). In so doing the individual minimizes the long-term consequences that she will endure as an adult (see Box 7.3).

The illusion of invulnerability is a major barrier to fear appeals' success. If I don't believe or don't want to believe that I am susceptible to danger, then I am unlikely to accept the persuader's advice.

The second misconception of fear appeals follows from this tendency. Fear is commonly thought to be a simple drive that propels people to do as the persuader requests. According to this notion (popularized by early theorists), fear is an unpleasant psychological state, one that people are motivated to reduce. Supposedly, when the message provides recommendations that alleviate fear, people accept the recommendations and change their behavior (Hovland, Janis, & Kelley, 1953). To be sure, fear is an unpleasant emotional state, but contrary to early theorists, people do not behave in a simple, animal-like manner to rid themselves of painful sensations. Fear is more complicated.

A message can scare someone, but fail to change attitudes because it does not connect with the person's beliefs about the problem, or neglects to provide a solution to the difficulty that ails the individual. The drive model puts a premium on fear. It says that if you scare someone and then reassure them, you can change a dysfunctional behavior. However, we now know that persuaders must do more than arouse fear to change an individual's attitude or behavior. They must convince message recipients that they are susceptible to negative outcomes and that the recommended response will alleviate the threat. Messages must work on a cognitive, as well as affective, level. They must help individuals appreciate the problem and, through the power of words and suggestions, encourage people to come to grips with the danger at hand.

## A Theory of Fear Appeals

Devising an effective fear appeal is, to some extent, an art, but it's an art that requires a scientist's appreciation for the intricacies of human behavior. For this reason, theoretical approaches to fear messages are particularly important to develop, and there has been no shortage of these over the years (Dillard, 1994; Rogers, 1975). The most comprehensive is Kim Witte's Extended Parallel Process Model (EPPM). As the name suggests, the

## Box 7.3 | ILLUSIONS OF INVULNERABILITY

"I never thought I needed to worry about AIDS," confessed Jana. "I thought it only happened to big-city people, not people like me who are tucked away in the Midwest. But 18 months ago, I was diagnosed with the virus that causes AIDS. Now I live in fear of this deadly illness every single day of my life," she told a writer from *Cosmopolitan* (Ziv, 1998).

Born in a small Midwestern town, Jana had an unhappy childhood: broken home, deadbeat dad, life in foster homes. After moving to a city and completing vocational training, Jana met a good-looking 22-year-old man, who flattered her with compliments, told her he loved her, and seemed like the answer to her prayers. They soon became sexually intimate. "We had sex, on average, four times a week," Jana recalled. "We didn't talk about using condoms or getting tested, and I wasn't worried about using protection. We used condoms only when we had any lying around." Fearing Jana might get pregnant, her boyfriend coaxed her into having anal sex, which they performed 10 times, never with a condom.

One day in July, Jana decided to get an AIDS test. The test confirmed her worst fears: she was HIV-positive and had been infected by her boyfriend. He had tested positive years earlier, but never bothered to tell Jana. Although she knew the dangers of unprotected sex, Jana felt invulnerable. "I was one of those girls who thought, *AIDS won't happen to me*," Jana said (Ziv, 1998, p. 241).

What crosses your mind when you read this story? That it's sad and tragic? That Jana took risks, ones your friends or you wouldn't take? That she's not like you, with her checkered past and desperate need for companionship? Perhaps you didn't have such thoughts at all—but if you did, if you tried to psychologically distance yourself from Jana or told yourself her situation is much different from yours or silently whispered, "This couldn't happen to me because . . .," you've revealed something important. You've shown yourself a mite susceptible to what psychologists call the illusion of invulnerability.

How forcefully the illusion of invulnerability operates in the arena of HIV and AIDS! The rate of HIV infection has risen sharply among young people (DiClemente, 1992). Sexually transmitted diseases are common among adolescents (about one in every seven reports an STD), and the presence of STDs increases susceptibility to HIV. Yet college students perceive they are less susceptible to HIV infection than are other persons; they underestimate their own susceptibility to HIV, while overestimating other students' risks.

What's more, although students know that condom use helps prevent HIV, they frequently engage in unprotected sex. Sexually active college students report that they used condoms less than 50 percent of the time when they had sex over the past year (Thompson, Anderson, Freedman, & Swan, 1996). But wait a minute. The overwhelming number of AIDS cases in America are found among gay men and injecting drug users. "Heterosexual AIDS in North America and Europe is, and will remain, rare," Robert Root-Bernstein notes, observing that "the chances that a healthy, drug-free heterosexual will contract AIDS from another heterosexual are so small they are hardly worth worrying about" (1993, pp. 312–313). Experts across the scientific and political spectrum agree with this analysis.

**Box 7.3** |

And yet, bad things do happen to innocent people: healthy individuals like you and me get cancer or contract viruses we never heard of (the odds of this happening are one in a million, but I bet you can think of someone, one person, you know personally who suddenly got very sick or died young). Although middle-class, heterosexual American high school and college students are not primarily at risk for HIV infection, handfuls of young people from these backgrounds will fall prey to HIV in the coming years. Sexually transmitted diseases like chlamydia and herpes are spreading at alarming rates, particularly among adolescents (Stolberg, 1998). Sexually transmitted diseases produce lesions, which offer the HIV convenient access to an individual's bloodstream. Although sexually transmitted infections don't cause HIV infection, they can increase the odds that a person will contract the AIDS virus (adapted from Perloff, 2001).

model extends previous work on fear appeals, synthesizing different research strands and sharpening predictions. It also emphasizes two parallel processes, or two different mechanisms by which fear appeals can influence attitudes. Like the ELM, the EPPM is a process model, one that calls attention to the ways in which people think and feel about persuasive messages. Reasoning that fear is a complex emotion, Witte (1998) invokes specific terms. She talks about fear, but recognizes that we need to consider other subtle aspects of fear-arousing messages if we are to understand their effects on attitudes.

A fear-arousing message contains two basic elements: *threat and efficacy information*, or a problem and solution. A message must first threaten the individual, convincing him or her that dangers lurk in the environment. To do this, a message must contain the following elements:

1. *Severity information*: information about the seriousness or magnitude of the threat ("Consumption of fatty food can lead to heart disease.").
2. *Susceptibility information*: information about the likelihood that the threatening outcomes will occur ("People who eat a junk-food diet put themselves at risk for getting a heart attack before the age of 40.").

After threatening or scaring the person, the message must provide a recommended response—a way the individual can avert the threat. It must contain efficacy information or facts about effective ways to cope with the danger at hand. Efficacy consists of two components, which result in two additional elements of a fear appeal:

3. *Response efficacy*: information about the effectiveness of the recommended action ("Maintaining a diet high in fruits and vegetables, but low in saturated fat, can reduce the incidence of heart disease.").
4. *Self-efficacy information*: arguments that the individual is capable of performing the recommended action. ("You can change your diet. Millions have.")

Each of these message components theoretically triggers a cognitive reaction in the person. Severity and susceptibility information should convince the individual that the threat is serious and likely to occur, provided no change is made in the problematic behavior. Response efficacy and self-efficacy information should persuade the individual that these outcomes can be avoided if the recommended actions are internalized and believed.

The operative word is *should*. There is no guarantee a fear appeal will work in exactly this way. Much depends on which of the two parallel processes the message unleashes. The two cognitive processes at the core of the model are *danger control* and *fear control* (see Figure 7.2). Danger control occurs when people perceive that they are capable of averting the threat by undertaking the recommended action. They turn their attention outward, appraise the external danger, and adopt strategies to cope with the problem. Fear control occurs when people face a serious threat, but focus inwardly on the fear, rather than the problem at hand. They concentrate on ways of containing their fear and keeping it at bay, rather than on developing strategies to ward off the danger. Witte and colleagues invite us to consider how the processes might work:

> Think of a situation in which you were faced with a grave threat. Sometimes, you may have tried to control the danger by thinking about your risk of experiencing the threat and ways to avoid it. If you did this, you engaged in the danger control process.

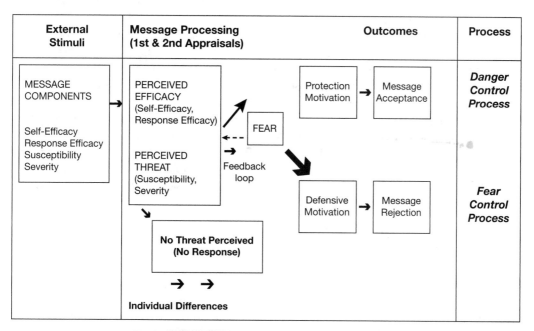

FIGURE 7.2 | Extended Parallel Process Model.

From Witte, K. (1998). Fear as motivator, fear as inhibitor: Using the Extended Parallel Process Model to explain fear appeal successes and failures. In P. A. Andersen & L. K. Guerrero (Eds.), *Handbook of communication and emotion: Research, theory, applications, and contexts* (pp. 423–450). San Diego: Academic Press.

*Message Factors*

Now, think of times when your fear was so overwhelming that you didn't even think of the threat. Instead, you focused on ways to calm down your racing heart, your sweaty palms, and your nervousness. You may have taken some deep breaths, drunk some water, or smoked a cigarette. These all are fear control strategies. You were controlling your fear, but without any thought of the actual danger facing you.

(2001, pp. 14–15)

In essence, a fear appeal works if it nudges the person into danger control. It fails if it pushes the individual into fear control. If the message convinces people that they can cope, it can change attitudes. If people are bowled over by their fear and paralyzed by the severity of the threat, the message backfires. Indeed, when people possess unusually high levels of fear, scaring them can be counterproductive. When individuals are terrified about a social problem, scaring them can increase anxiety and render fear appeals ineffective (Muthusamy, Levine, & Weber, 2009).

Witte and colleagues (2001), attempting to develop a more precise formulation to help theorists and practitioners, emphasize that if perceived efficacy exceeds perceived threat, individuals engage in danger control and adopt recommendations to avert the danger. They feel motivated to protect themselves from danger (protection motivation in the model) and take necessary steps to deal with the problem at hand. However, if perceived threat exceeds perceived efficacy, people shift into fear control mode, obsess about the fear, defensively process the message, and do nothing to alter their behavior. For example, an antismoking campaign succeeds if it convinces the person that the risk of cancer can be averted if he quits smoking now and begins chewing Nicorette gum instead of smoking Camels. The campaign fails if it gets the individual so worried that he will get cancer that he begins smoking cigarettes just to calm down!

What role does fear play in all this? Fear is probably a necessary condition for messages to succeed. People have to be scared, and messages that arouse high levels of fear can produce significant attitude change (Boster & Mongeau, 1984; Mongeau, 1998). But fear is not enough. In order to change attitudes, a message must harness fear and channel it into a constructive (danger control) direction. This entails "pushing all the right buttons" or, more precisely, convincing people that the threat is severe and real, but that there is something they can do to ward off the danger (see Figure 7.3).

## Applying Theory to the Real World

Fear appeal theories like Witte's have generated many studies, mostly experiments. Researchers have randomly assigned one group of subjects to a video or DVD that contains a very threatening message. They have exposed an equivalent group to a message that raises milder threats. Experimenters have also varied other aspects of the message, such as the effectiveness of the recommended response or self-efficacy. A variety of studies support the thrust of Witte's model. For example, in one study smokers who were led to believe that there was a high probability that smoking causes cancer indicated an intention to quit only if they believed that the recommended practice (quitting smoking) was highly effective (Rogers & Mewborn, 1976).

**FIGURE 7.3** | One way to convince smokers to quit is to scare the heck out of them. However, fear is a dicey weapon in the persuasion arsenal and works only if it is used deftly and sensitively.

Photograph by William C. Rieter.

Particularly compelling support for the model was offered in an experiment on gun safety. Firearms represent the second leading cause of fatal injury in the United States, even surpassing car accidents in several states to become the primary cause of fatal injuries. Concerned about this problem, researcher Anthony J. Roberto and colleagues developed a graphic videotape to influence attitudes toward gun safety (Roberto, Meyer, Johnson, & Atkin, 2000). Guided by the EPPM, they organized the videotape so that it presented susceptibility, severity, response efficacy, and self-efficacy information.

The video presents heart-rending statements by young men whose physical and emotional lives were shattered by gun accidents. For example, Andy, a 29-year-old Michigan native, relates that one night he was cleaning his gun and accidentally shot himself in the leg. Severely wounded, Andy crawled about 50 feet to his home to get help. Although doctors saved Andy's life, his leg was amputated below the knee.

In the video you are introduced to other young people who were severely injured by gun accidents. They talk openly about what happened and how the accident could have been prevented.

Severity information is persuasively communicated by comments like this one: "If you get shot in the head, there is an 80 percent chance you will die. If you get shot in the body, there is a 90 percent chance you will need surgery."

Susceptibility is displayed through comments like this one, spoken by Andy: "I've been around guns all my life. I knew gun safety. I was always careful. I never thought that I could have an accident with a gun."

Response efficacy is relayed by statements like: "If I just had a trigger lock on the gun, none of this would have happened." Self-efficacy information is relayed by statements like: "A gun safety class takes only a few hours to complete."

In Michigan, 175 individuals enrolled in hunter safety classes participated in the experiment. Participants in the experimental group watched the video and filled out a survey probing perceptions of gun safety. Individuals in the control group answered the gun safety questions first and then watched the video. In dramatic support of the EPPM, experimental group participants (a) perceived that gun injuries resulted in more severe consequences, (b) believed that they were more susceptible to accidental gun injuries, and (c) listed more recommended gun safety practices, such as always using a trigger lock, than individuals in the control group (Roberto et al., 2000).

As we have seen with other models, the EPPM is not perfect. There remain important questions about what happens psychologically when perceived threat exceeds perceived efficacy. The ways in which mental, emotional, and physiological processes combine and collide when fear is aroused are not entirely understood (e.g., Dillard & Anderson, 2004; Nabi, 2002; Rimal & Real, 2003). The model also does not provide a precise recipe for how to design the optimum fear appeal (O'Keefe, 2003). Nevertheless, the EPPM has shed considerable light on the psychology of fear appeals and the ways that fear messages change attitudes. It helps explain diverse findings on fear message effects (Witte & Allen, 2000; Wong & Cappella, 2009). The EPPM also offers a framework for discussing fear appeal effects, an important contribution given the large number of situations in which it is necessary to scare people into making life changes. As human beings, we take risks, underestimate our vulnerability to misfortune, do stupid things, deny we're at risk, and bury our heads in the sand when it comes time to do something to rectify the situation. We need fear appeals. Theories such as the EPPM offer general guidelines for designing health risk communications. Following are four practical suggestions that emerge from theory and research.

1. *Communicators must scare the heck out of recipients.* We are frequently tempted to go easy on others, trying not to hurt their feelings. Research suggests that fear enhances persuasion and that high-fear appeals are more effective than low-fear appeals (Boster & Mongeau, 1984). "Adding additional fear-arousing content to a persuasive message is likely to generate greater levels of persuasion," Paul A. Mongeau concluded after reviewing the research in the area (1998, p. 64). As an example, consider text-messaging while driving, a behavior that is twice as dangerous as driving while drunk. If you want to convince people to quit texting when they drive, you should tell them straight out what the dangers are, graphically depicting deadly accidents caused by drivers who text-messaged as they drove. In most situations, it is best not to beat around the bush.

2. *Persuaders must discuss solutions, as well as problems.* Communicators must offer hope, telling individuals that they can avert the dangers graphically laid out earlier in the message. Witte notes that "after you scare someone about terrible outcomes and make them feel vulnerable to negative consequences, you must tell them clearly and explicitly how to prevent this outcome from occurring" (1997, p. 151). Communications must

"get 'em well" after they "get 'em sick." They must teach, as well as scare. They should also make sure that solutions are communicated cogently and vividly so that they put people in touch with their attitudes toward the issue (Roskos-Ewoldsen, Yu, & Rhodes, 2004).

3. *Efficacy recommendations should emphasize costs of not taking precautionary actions, as well as benefits of undertaking the activity.* Persuaders frequently must decide how to frame, or position, the message. They must decide whether to emphasize benefits of adopting a behavior ("a diet high in fruits and vegetables, but low in fat, can keep you healthy") or costs of not performing the requested action ("a diet low in fruits and vegetables, but high in fat, can lead to cancer") (Salovey & Wegener, 2002). Messages that emphasize benefits of adopting a behavior are gain-framed; those that present the costs of not adopting the behavior are loss-framed.

Fear messages have usually been couched in terms of gain, but they also can be framed on the basis of losses. It may seem strange to emphasize what people lose from not performing a behavior until you consider that negative information—losses linked with inaction—can be more memorable than benefits associated with action. Beth E. Meyerowitz and Shelly Chaiken (1987) demonstrated this in a study of persuasive communication and breast self-examination, a simple behavior that can help diagnose breast cancer but is performed by remarkably few women.

Some undergraduate female subjects in the study read gain-framed arguments ("by doing breast self-examination now, you can learn what your normal, healthy breasts feel like so that you will be better prepared to notice any small, abnormal changes that might occur as you get older"). Others read loss-oriented arguments ("by not doing breast self-examination now, you will not learn what your normal, healthy breasts feel like, so you will be ill prepared to notice any small, abnormal changes that might occur as you get older"; Meyerowitz & Chaiken, p. 506). Women who read the loss-framed arguments held more positive attitudes toward breast self-exams and were more likely than gain-oriented subjects to report performing this behavior at a four-month follow-up.

Behavior being complex, there are also cases in which gain-framed arguments are more compelling. Alexander J. Rothman and colleagues (Rothman, Salovey, Antone, Keough, & Martin, 1993) compared the effects of gain-and loss-framed pamphlets regarding skin cancer prevention. The gain-framed message emphasized benefits rather than costs, and focused on positive aspects of displaying concern about skin cancer ("regular use of sunscreen products can protect you against the sun's harmful rays"). The loss-framed message stressed risks, rather than benefits ("If you don't use sunscreen products regularly, you won't be protected against the sun's harmful rays"). Of those who read the positive, gain-framed message, 71 percent requested sunscreen with an appropriate sun protection factor. Only 46 percent of those who read the loss-framed pamphlet asked for sunscreen with an appropriate sun-protection level (see also Reinhart, Marshall, Feeley, & Tutzauer, 2007).

Some researchers have argued that gain-framed messages are more effective in promoting *health-affirming (disease prevention) behaviors*. These are behaviors where gains or benefits are obvious, such as sunscreen use or physical exercise. They also theorize that loss-framed messages are more effective in influencing *illness-detection behaviors*, where uncertainty and risks are noteworthy. These include obtaining a mammogram, performing monthly breast self-exams, and getting tested for HIV, where there are significant consequences of non-compliance, or *not* getting screened (Salovey, Schneider, & Apanovitch, 2002). Research provides some support for these predictions. But stay with me, as there are complexities.

Gain-framed messages are more influential than loss-framed appeals for disease-prevention behaviors. However, loss-framed messages are not more persuasive for encouraging illness-detection behaviors (O'Keefe & Jensen, 2006; see also O'Keefe & Jensen, 2009). Yet loss-framed messages may be effective in other contexts. One context is when individuals feel vulnerable. In these situations, people focus on negative aspects of the issue, leading them to be more susceptible to the negatively-oriented, loss-framed communications.

Hyunyi Cho and Franklin J. Boster (2008) obtained evidence consistent with this view. They reported that loss-framed antidrug ads that emphasized the *disadvantages* of doing drugs exerted a stronger impact on teenagers who reported their friends used drugs than did gain-framed ads that focused on the *benefits* of not doing drugs. If your friends do drugs, you would probably feel anxious or nervous about doing drugs yourself, but worried that your friends may reject you if you don't partake. With negative issues salient in adolescents' minds, loss-framed messages carried greater weight. Taken together, these findings suggest that gain- and loss-framed communications are more likely to change attitudes when they fit the health orientation of the audience member (Cesario, Grant, & Higgins, 2004; see also Nan, 2007).

4. Finally, and in related fashion, *threats and recommendations should be salient—or relevant—to the target audience.* You cannot assume that what scares you also terrifies your target audience. Different fears are salient to different groups. If you want to scare middle-class high school girls into practicing safer sex, you should stress that they might get pregnant. These teens don't want to have a baby; pregnancy represents a serious threat. However, if your target audience is poor ethnic women, you should rethink this appeal. To many of these women, pregnancy is a positive, rather than negative, consequence of sexual intercourse. It produces a human being who depends on them and loves them to bits; it also, at least in the best of worlds, shows that they have a loving, trusting, relationship with a man, which provides status and emotional fulfillment (Sobo, 1995; Witte et al., 2001).

Surprisingly, perhaps, the main drawback of getting pregnant, in the view of inner-city teenage girls, is that you get fat and lose your friends (Witte et al., 2001). Thus, a campaign to promote abstinence or safer sex among inner-city teenagers should emphasize how much weight you gain when you're pregnant. It should also explain that you can lose your friends if you have to spend time taking care of a baby rather than hanging with them (Witte et al., 2001). As is discussed in Chapter 12, campaign specialists must carefully consider the needs and values of the target audience before developing their communications.

## Summary

Fear appeals are among the diciest weapons in the persuader's arsenal. This is because they evoke fear, a strong emotion with physiological correlates, touch on ego-involved issues, and attempt to change dysfunctional behaviors that are difficult to extinguish. To succeed, fear-arousing messages must trigger the right emotional reaction, lest they push the message recipient into fear control mode. Kathryn A. Morris and William B. Swann aptly observed that health risk communications must "walk the whisker-thin line between too little and too much—between making targets of persuasive communications care enough to attend to the message but not dismiss the message through denial processes" (1996, p. 70). The campaign communication floor is littered with examples of fear appeals that failed because they did not maintain the proper balance between fear and danger, or threat and efficacy.

Yet for all their problems, fear appeals that take context into account, put theoretical factors into play, and are of high-aesthetic quality can influence attitudes. It's tough to scare people effectively, but it can be done. Although one would rather not resort to fear, given its negative and volatile qualities, it can't be ignored in a risky world where people don't always do as they should and often put themselves and loved ones in harm's way (see also Box 7.4).

## GUILT APPEALS

Charitable organizations frequently depict graphic appeals of deprived children, portraying them as abused, undernourished and in desperate need of attention. The pictures haunt you—the child's gaunt face, sad eyes, mournful expression. These televised messages—you have watched them many times—are unabashed guilt appeals, attempts to arouse guilt in an effort to induce people to donate money to charitable groups. Do these appeals work?

Like fear, guilt is a negative emotional response, one that has affective and cognitive components. Guilt, however, involves "ought" and "should" dimensions. "*It occurs when an individual notes with remorse that s/he failed to do what s/he 'ought to' or 'should' do— for example, when s/he violates some social custom, ethical or moral principle, or legal regulation,*" explain Debra Basil and colleagues (Basil, Ridgway, & Basil, 2008, p. 3).

Basil and colleagues proposed a model of guilt and giving derived from the EPPM. They argue that the two key processes are empathy and efficacy. Just as a fear appeal contains a threat to motivate people to act, a guilt appeal arouses empathy to induce individuals to perform a particular helping behavior. Empathizing with the plight of deprived children should remind people of a cultural norm to assist the less fortunate. This in turn should arouse guilt, an unpleasant feeling people are motivated to reduce— ideally, by donating to charity. Guilt is not a sufficient condition. Basil's model stipulates that people will donate to a charitable organization only if guilt is combined with efficacy, the perception that one can effectively engage in the advocated action. Televised messages frequently contain self-efficacy messages, such as "for less than a $1 a day you can save a child's life."

## Box 7.4 | POLITICS OF FEAR

In contemporary society, where fear appeals and communication campaigns are commonplace, fear messages can become embroiled in controversy. These controversies inevitably raise troubling ethical issues. Consider a recent campaign on behalf of two vaccines designed to ward off cervical cancer. A number of physicians and state legislators, concerned about the devastating consequences of cervical cancer, recommended that middle-school girls receive vaccinations that offer protection against the cancer. Television advertisements, which directed viewers to a Web site replete with patients' stories, have employed fear-based appeals, like a hip woman in her 20s saying "I chose to get vaccinated because my dreams don't include cervical cancer" (Rosenthal, 2008, p. A18). The state of Virginia recently required that all sixth-grade girls receive the vaccine.

Not everybody is convinced. Some medical experts object that the vaccine's long-term side effects have not been assessed. Others worry that the vaccine may not be necessary because at least, in Western countries, cervical cancer almost always can be prevented through regular Pap smears. Most disturbingly, claims on behalf of the drugs have originated from the two major pharmaceutical companies that stand to profit from their sale. The companies, including the pharmaceutical giant, Merck, have been pushing the vaccines, developing high-priced marketing campaigns. (Critics would refer to them as propaganda.) Drug companies have recruited doctors to give talks on behalf of the vaccines and have lobbied politicians. In Virginia, where the vaccine is now mandated, there were uncomfortable ties between the pharmaceutical firm, Merck, and leaders in state government. Although it is widely acknowledged that the vaccine can offer benefits, critics worry that fears were aroused as much for marketing as to advance health education.

In experiments to examine guilt appeal effects, Basil and colleagues devised messages to prod individuals to donate to charity. Research participants were randomly assigned to read messages high or low in guilt, empathy, and efficacy. For example, the following message was designed to induce both empathy and guilt:

*You are Lilia.* You are eight, and curious about books and pens, things that you knew for a few months in your school before it burned. Before your mother became sick, and lost the resources within her care to care adequately for a child. And before you reached the point where you stopped drawing pictures in the dirt with sticks, because you are so tired from doing your mother's job.

 As a citizen of the most privileged country in the world, your life couldn't be more different from Lilia's. Not only do you live in America, you also get to go to college. So not having access to elementary education is difficult to imagine. But it's frighteningly common. Please help. Childreach needs your donation.

(Basil, Ridgway, & Basil, 2006, p. 1052)

There is evidence that guilt appeals like these have positive effects. In line with their model, Basil and colleagues (2008) found that a message promoting empathy with deprived children induced guilt, which in turn led to an increase in intent to donate to a charitable organization. Self-efficacy also spurred donation intentions. Many of us have viewed heart-rending televised messages such as the one above, yet have not donated a dime. How could this be, if experiments demonstrate that guilt appeals work? There are many reasons. First, the televised appeals may be less impactful than the laboratory messages; they may fail to induce empathy or guilt. Second, the study shows only that people intend to donate; many factors determine whether people make good on their intentions, such as external constraints and availability of significant others who endorse the norm of giving (Fishbein & Ajzen, 1975). Third, people may distrust charitable organizations, suspecting that they are inefficient or corrupt. Fourth, individuals may not believe it is their responsibility to improve the lives of needy children.

Like fear appeals, guilt communications are effective only if certain conditions are met. Basil's research suggests that charitable appeals can work if the message induces empathy, reminds individuals that inaction is inconsistent with their moral standards, and convinces them that a donation can reduce feelings of guilt. However, guilt is a complex emotion, and there have been only a handful of studies of its effects on persuasion (O'Keefe, 2002). We know that people frequently employ guilt appeals in interpersonal conversations, particularly when relationships are close. But guilt messages do not always persuade message recipients to change their attitude or comply with a request. They can backfire when recipients perceive that the speaker is applying inappropriate pressure to induce them to comply, as when someone complains that "she's laying on a guilt trip." Nonetheless, when used appropriately, guilt has salutary effects. It can promote helping behavior and enhance maturity. Appeals to guilt—frequently referred to as the "sinking feeling in the stomach" —can build character (Tierney, 2009, p. D1).

# LANGUAGE

Great persuaders have long known that how you say it can be as important as what you say. Persuasion scholars and speakers alike recognize that the words persuaders choose can influence attitudes. But just what impact does language have? How can we get beyond the generalities to hone in on the specific features of language that matter most? Can language backfire and cause audience members to reject a communicator's message, possibly because it is too strident or obscene? How can you use language more effectively yourself in your efforts to convince people to go along with what you recommend?

These are social scientific questions—specific inquiries that allow us to explore theories and see how they play out in everyday life. They aren't the big, gigantic questions that people frequently ask about language and persuasion—queries like "What sorts of language make someone charismatic?" and "Do cult leaders like Charles Manson brainwash people with language?" These are difficult questions to answer—in some cases impossible because the terminology (e.g., brainwashing) obfuscates and defies clear explication. However, the queries mentioned in the preceding paragraph have intrigued persuasion scholars and generated interesting insights about language and attitude change.

## Speed of Speech

Ever since America mythologized the fast-talking salesman, people have assumed that fast speakers are more compelling than slow ones. The character Harold Hill in the American classic, *The Music Man*, epitomizes our stereotype of the fast-talking peddler of wares. Since then, movies, videos, and songs have rhapsodized about the supposed persuasive effects of fast-talking persuaders.

Leave it to social scientists to study the phenomenon! Does speed of speech enhance persuasion? Early studies suggested it did (Miller, Maruyama, Beaber, & Valone, 1976; Street & Brady, 1982). However, more recent studies have cast doubt on this glib conclusion. Researchers have discovered that speech rate does not inevitably change attitudes and, under some conditions, may not exert a particularly strong impact on attitudes or beliefs (Buller, LePoire, Aune, & Eloy, 1992). Just as you can hypothesize that faster speech should be persuasive because it acts as a credibility cue, you can also reason that it should reduce persuasion if it interferes with message processing or annoys the audience ("Don't y'all know we don't speak as fast as you Yankees down here in ol' Alabama?").

Thus, there are both theoretical and practical reasons to argue that speech rate does not have a uniformly positive or negative effect on persuasion. Instead, the most reasonable conclusion is that effects depend on the context. Several contextual factors are important.

Speech rate enhances persuasion when the goal of the persuader is to capture attention or to be perceived as competent. Speaking quickly can suggest that the communicator is credible, knowledgeable, or possesses expertise. Moderately fast and fast speakers are seen as more intelligent, confident, and effective than their slower speaking counterparts. These effects are particularly likely when audience members are low in involvement (Smith & Shaffer, 1995). Under low involvement, speech rate can serve as a peripheral cue. Invoking the heuristic or cultural stereotype that "fast talkers know their stuff," audience members may go along with fast speakers because they assume they are credible or correct. Fast speech may be a facade, employed to disguise a lack of knowledge, but by the time message recipients discover this, they may have already plunked down their money to purchase the product.

Speech rate can also enhance persuasion when it is relevant to the message topic. A now-famous advertisement for Federal Express depicted a harried businessman, facing an urgent deadline. The man barked out orders to a subordinate and spoke in a staccato voice at lightning-quick speed:

*Businessman:* You did a bang up job. I'm putting you in charge of Pittsburgh.
*Employee:* Pittsburgh's perfect.
*Businessman:* I know it's perfect, Peter. That's why I picked Pittsburgh. Pittsburgh's perfect, Peter. Can I call you Pete?
*Employee*: Call me Pete.

This ear-catching ad helped make FedEx a household name. Its success was due in part to the nice symmetry between the theme of the ad—speed of speech—and the product being sold, a mail delivery service that promised to be there "absolutely, positively, overnight."

Under other conditions, fast speech is not so likely to enhance credibility or persuasion. When the message concerns sensitive or intimate issues, a faster speaker may communicate insensitivity or coldness (Giles & Street, 1994; Ray, Ray, & Zahn, 1991). When a message focuses on medical problems, safer sex, or a personal dilemma, slow speech may be preferable. In these situations, slow speech may convey communicator concern, empathy, and goodwill.

This plays out on a national political level as well. When citizens are experiencing a national crisis, they may respond more positively to a slower speaker, whose slower pace conveys calm and reassurance. During the 1930s and 1940s, when Americans faced the Depression and World War II, they found solace in the slow speech—and melodious voice—of President Franklin Delano Roosevelt (Winfield, 1994). Had FDR spoken quickly, he might have made people nervous; his pace might have reminded them of the succession of problems that faced them on a daily basis.

Thus, one of the intriguing lessons of speech-rate research is that faster speech is not inherently more effective than slow speech. Instead, persuaders must appreciate context, and the audience's motivation and ability to process the message. It would be nice if we could offer a simple prescription, like one your doctor gives the pharmacist. The reality is that speech rate effects are more complex. This also makes them a lot more interesting and challenging to explore.

## Powerless Versus Powerful Speech

Has this ever happened to you? You're sitting in class when a student raises his hand and says, "I know this sounds like a stupid question, but . . ." and proceeds to ask the professor his question. You cringe as you hear him introduce his query in this manner; you feel embarrassed for your classmate and bothered that someone is about to waste your time with a dumb question. Something interesting has just happened. The student has deliberately undercut his own credibility by suggesting to the class that a query that may be perfectly intelligent is somehow less than adequate. The words preceding the question—not the question itself—have produced these effects, providing another example of the subtle role language plays in communication.

The linguistic form at work here is *powerless speech*. It is a constellation of characteristics that may suggest to a message receiver that the communicator is less than powerful or is not so confident. In contrast, *powerful speech* is marked by the conspicuous absence of these features.

The primary components of powerless speech are:

*Hesitation forms.* "Uh" and "well, you know" communicate lack of certainty or confidence.

*Hedges.* "Sort of," "kinda," and "I guess" are phrases that reduce the definitiveness of a persuader's assertion.

*Tag questions.* The communicator "tags" a declarative statement with a question, as in, "That plan will cost us too much, don't you think?" A tag is "a declarative statement without the assumption that the statement will be believed by the receiver" (Bradley, 1981, p. 77).

*Disclaimers.* "This may sound a little out of the ordinary, but" or "I'm no expert, of course" are introductory expressions that ask the listener to show understanding or to make allowances.

Researchers have examined the effects of powerless and powerful speech on persuasion. Studies overwhelmingly show that powerless speech is perceived as less persuasive and credible than powerful speech (Burrell & Koper, 1998; Hosman, 2002). Communicators who use powerless speech are perceived to be less competent, dynamic, and attractive than those who speak in a powerful fashion (e.g., Adkins & Brashers, 1995; Erickson, Lind, Johnson, & O'Barr, 1978; Haleta, 1996; Holtgraves & Lasky, 1999; Hosman, 1989). There are several reasons why powerless communicators are downgraded. Their use of hedges, hesitations, and qualifiers communicates uncertainty or lack of confidence. Powerless speech may also serve as a low-credibility cue, a culturally learned heuristic that suggests the speaker is not intelligent or knowledgeable (Sparks & Areni, 2008). In addition, powerless speech distracts audience members, which reduces their ability to attend to message arguments.

This research has abundant practical applications. It suggests that, when giving a talk or preparing a written address, you should speak concisely and directly. Avoid qualifiers, hedges, tag questions, and hesitations. If you are nervous or uncertain, think through the reasons why you feel that way and try to enhance your confidence. You may feel better by sharing your uncertainty with your audience, but the powerlessness you convey will reduce your persuasiveness.

Another application of powerless speech research has been to courtroom presentations. Two experts in the psychology of law argue, based on research evidence, that "the attorney should, whenever possible, come directly to the point and not hedge his points with extensive qualifications" (Linz & Penrod, 1984, pp. 44–45). Witnesses, they add, should be encouraged to answer attorneys' questions as directly and with as few hesitations and qualifiers as possible.

In some instances, attorneys or consultants may work with witnesses to help them project confidence. Take Monica Lewinsky, the woman who had "sexual relations" with President Clinton in 1995 and became the focal point of the impeachment scandal of 1998. When she first graced the nation's airwaves, she seemed naive and vulnerable, and in her conversations with people at the Clinton White House, tentative and girlish. But when Lewinsky addressed the Senate impeachment trial of Clinton in 1999, "her appearance, voice and vocabulary said she was all grown up" (Henneberger, 1999, p. 1). "Ms. Lewinsky was well-spoken, used no slang and showed only trace evidence of the Valley Girl of her taped phone conversations with Linda R. Tripp. Even her voice seemed different now, more modulated, less high-pitched and breathy," a reporter noted (Henneberger, p. 1). It is likely that Lewinsky was extensively coached for her Senate performance.

Her use of powerful speech seems to have enhanced her credibility, perhaps leading some in the audience to place more trust in her story and others to feel more positively toward her version of events.

Although powerful speech is usually more persuasive than powerless language, there is one context in which powerless speech can be effective. When communicators wish to generate goodwill rather than project expertise, certain types of unassertive speech can work to their advantage. Let's say that an authority figure wants to humanize herself and appear more down-to-earth in message recipients' eyes. She may find it useful to end some statements with a question. Physicians and therapists frequently use tags to gain rapport with clients. Tag questions such as "You've been here before, haven't you?"; "That's the last straw, isn't it?"; and "That must have made you feel angry, right?" can show empathy with patients' concerns (Harres, 1998). As researcher Annette Harres observed, after studying physicians' use of language devices, "Affective tag questions were a very effective way of showing that the doctor was genuinely concerned about the patient's physical and psychological well-being . . . They can indicate to patients that their concerns are taken seriously" (Harres, pp. 122–123).

## Language Intensity

This is the aspect of language that most people think of when they free-associate about language effects. Language intensity includes metaphors, strong and vivid language, and emotionally charged words. It is the province of political rhetoric, social activism, hate speech, and eloquent public address. You can read intense language if you click onto Web sites for pro-life and pro-choice abortion groups, supporters and opponents of cloning human embryos, animal rights activists, environmentalists, and the National Rifle Association, among others. You can hear intense language in the speeches of charismatic leaders, political activists, and presidents of the United States.

One prominent feature of language intensity is the metaphor. A *metaphor* is "a linguistic phrase of the form 'A is B,' such that a comparison is suggested between the two terms leading to a transfer of attributes associated with B to A" (Sopory & Dillard, 2002, p. 407). For example, former president Ronald Reagan liked to describe America as "a torch shedding light to all the hopeless of the world." The metaphor consists of two parts: A (America) and B ("torch shedding light to all the hopeless of the world"). It suggests a comparison between A and B, such that the properties associated with a torch shedding light to the world's hopeless are transferred to America. There are many other metaphors. Civil rights activists were fond of using "eyes on the prize" to symbolize Blacks' quest for success in America. Opponents of nuclear weapons use terms like "holocaust," "nuclear winter," and "republic of insects and grass" to describe the consequences of global nuclear war (Schell, 1982). Abortion opponents liken abortion to the bloody killing of innocent human beings. More benignly, political partisans of all stripes and colors are fond of using gridlock on the roadways as a metaphor for political gridlock, or the inability of Congress to bridge differences and pass legislation.

Persuaders in all walks of life employ metaphor as a technique to alter attitudes. Do they have this effect? Researchers Pradeep Sopory and James P. Dillard (2002) conducted a meta-analytic review of the empirical research on metaphor and persuasion. They concluded that messages containing metaphors produce somewhat greater attitude change than do communications without metaphors. They proposed several explanations for this effect:

> Metaphorical language creates greater interest in a message than does literal language, thereby increasing motivation to more systematically process the message ... A metaphor helps to better structure and organize the arguments of a persuasive message relative to literal language. A metaphor evokes a greater number of semantic associations, and the different arguments, when consistent with the metaphor, get connected together more coherently via the many available semantic pathways. In addition, the links to the metaphor "highlight" the arguments making them more salient.
>
> (p. 417)

Powerful as metaphors are, they are not the only component of intense language (Bowers, 1964; Hamilton & Hunter, 1998; Hosman, 2002). Intense language includes specific, graphic language. It also encompasses emotion-laden words like "freedom" and "beauty," as well as "suffering" and "death." Intense language can also reflect the extremity of the communicator's issue position. A communicator who describes efforts to clone human beings as "disgusting" is using more intense language than one who calls such research "inappropriate." The first speaker's language also points up a more extreme position on the cloning issue.

What impact does such language have on attitudes? Should persuaders deploy vivid, graphic terms? The answer depends on the persuader's goal, his or her credibility, and the audience's involvement in the issue. If the goal is to enhance your dynamism—to convince the audience you are a dynamic speaker—intense language can help you achieve this goal. But intense language will not change the minds of audience members who oppose your position and are ego-involved in the issue (Hamilton & Hunter, 1998; Hosman, 2002). They are too stuck in their ways, too committed to the position for mere word choice to change their minds. By contrast, if the audience disagrees with your position, but is less personally involved in the issue, it is likely to respond to intense language. The only hitch is that you need to be perceived as credible by those who hear or read your speech. *Intense language can goad an audience into changing its attitude toward an issue, provided it is not terribly ego-involved in the matter, the communicator possesses considerable credibility, and the speaker's use of such language is seen as appropriate or suitable in the particular context.* Under these conditions, graphic, emotional language can cause people to pay more attention to the message, which in turn can produce more favorable evaluations of the persuader's position (see Hamilton & Hunter, 1998, for more complex discussions of these issues).

Unfortunately, this all may seem abstract or removed from everyday life. In fact these research findings have intriguing applications to real-life situations. Social activists are adept at choosing metaphors that can galvanize support for their cause. They recognize that the way they frame the issue—and the linguistic terms they select—can strongly influence attitudes. Language intensity may have particularly strong effects when people do not have well-developed attitudes on the issue, are low in involvement, and are exposed to appeals from credible spokespersons. Case in point: the appeals made by opponents and supporters of abortion.

Abortion foes chose the metaphor "pro-life" to describe their heartfelt opposition to abortion in the United States. Just about everyone loves life. By linking a fetus with life, activists succeeded in making a powerful symbolic statement. It placed those who did not believe that a fetus constituted a full, living human being on the defensive. What's more, pro-life activists deployed vivid visual metaphors to make their case. They developed brochures and movies that depicted powerful images—for example, "a fetus floating in amniotic fluid, tiny fetal feet dangled by a pair of adult hands, [and] a mutilated, bloodied, aborted fetus with a misshapen head and a missing arm" (Lavin, 2001, p. 144). These visual images became the centerpiece of a national anti-abortion campaign that began in the 1960s and 1970s. As Celeste Condit recalled:

> Thousands of picture packets were distributed, and television ads as well as billboards focused on the human-like features of the physical appearance of the fetus. Most Americans had no idea what a fetus looked like at any stage of development . . . Thus, visual display and supporting scientific argument worked together to characterize the fetus as a human being.
>
> (1990, p. 61)

Over the ensuing decades, the language became more intense, the rhetoric fiercer. Pro-life activists spent much linguistic energy condemning a specific late-term abortion procedure, called partial-birth abortion. The procedure is unpleasant and controversial, and pro-life supporters have gained rhetorical punch by promoting the name "partial-birth abortion" rather than employing the formal medical term, intact dilation and evacuation.

Appreciating the power of language, pro-life advocates have been adept at describing the entity that is removed from the womb as a "baby" rather than a "fetus." The linguistic frame matters. In one study, individuals who read an article on a ban on partial-birth abortion that used the term "baby" registered more opposition to legalizing partial-birth abortion than those who read the same article with the term "fetus" (Simon & Jerit, 2007).

On the other side of the abortion divide, women's groups that favor abortion rights have also exploited the symbolic power of language and pictures. They used a coat hanger dripping blood as a metaphor for "the horrid means and consequences of the illegal abortions that occur when legal abortion is banned" (Condit, 1990, p. 92). They argued that the fetus should be characterized as a lump of tissues rather than a baby. They went to lengths to stress that they did not so much favor abortion as a woman's right to choose. One popular pro-choice pamphlet presented the Statue of Liberty, with the line that "there are no pictures in this pamphlet, because you can't take a picture of liberty." Condit notes that "the statue—as a woman, a symbol of the downtrodden, and a symbol of Freedom, Liberty, and home—embodied the ideal American representation of Choice or Repro-ductive Freedom" (1990, pp. 93–94).

Pro-choice activists' intense language hardly changed the minds of abortion foes. Nor did the strident imagery of pro-life Web sites alter attitudes of women committed to choice. But language-intensity research suggests that the language influenced those who were less ego-involved in the issue, particularly when communications were delivered by credible spokespersons. Many citizens fall into this category—they have opinions on abortion, but are not emotionally invested in the issue or are profoundly ambivalent. The ways that pro-life and pro-choice persuaders framed the issue undoubtedly had an impact on these individuals' views on abortion, in some cases producing major shifts in public sentiments (Condit, 1990).

Although pro-choice appeals to values like freedom helped to shift the focus of the abortion debate, it did not eliminate the rhetorical power of visual images, like mangled fetuses. The coat hanger packs less rhetorical punch than a bloody fetus, and the choice metaphor loses out in the language-intensity war when pitted against graphic images of "aborted babies." As one abortion advocate conceded, "When someone holds up a model of a 6-month-old fetus and a pair of surgical scissors, we say 'choice,' and we lose" (Klusendorf, 2001). One can acknowledge that some pro-life activists have nothing but pure motives in using this imagery, while also lamenting that it has led to a "visualization of the abortion debate" that has polarized both sides, made compromise more difficult, and in some cases sparked violent and deadly confrontation (Lavin, 2001).

Intense language has also been a persuasive weapon in the ongoing debates over cloning and embryonic stem cell research. Ever since University of Wisconsin researchers isolated stem cells from human embryos, the stem cell issue has become a scientific and political cause célèbre. Stem cells, once extracted from embryos, have the potential to grow into human tissues, which can be used to replace damaged cells that cause such diseases as Alzheimer's, diabetes, and cancer (Stolberg, 2001). Nothing comes without a price, however. Extracting stem cells results in the destruction of the embryo, a centerpiece of human life. This deeply offends religious conservatives, who have likened embryonic stem cell research to murder. Proponents of stem cell research use different language. They couch the discussion in terms of "the dawning of a medical revolution" and the ability of research to save lives. Borrowing from abortion opponents' strategic playbook, research proponents argue that "there is more than one way to be pro-life" (President Bush Waffles, 2001).

Proponents and opponents are battling for public opinion. They are trying to change people's attitudes. This is a complex issue. There are many facets, angles, scientific layers, and moral perspectives. As you read about this topic over the coming years, you should take note of the ways in which activists frame the issue. Listen to the words they use. Be cognizant of the words you select to describe the issue to others. Words matter. They can subtly influence the way we think about social issues.

In some instances, persuasion involves a deft appreciation of the sensitivity of linguistic meanings. When the New Jersey Supreme Court ruled that gay couples are entitled to the same rights and benefits as heterosexual couples, it danced around the use of the contentious and socially explosive term "gay marriage." The court said the question of what to call same-sex unions—civil union, marriage, or another name—was best decided by the state legislature (Chen, 2006). Had the court ruled that unions could be called gay marriage, religious conservatives would have been outraged. Had it said gay unions could never be called marriage, liberals would have been furious. The ruling was legally and psychologically ingenious. It gave new freedoms to gay couples, while appreciating the psychology of social judgments discussed in Chapter 2. If the gay marriage terminology had been made an explicit part of the ruling, partisans would have selectively perceived and contrasted the judgment from their own attitudes. By deftly avoiding the term, the court advanced civil rights, while also providing time and linguistic space for both sides to move toward reconciliation. This appears to have happened over the past several years, as the schism separating those who support and oppose gay marriage has become less intense.

## Political Language

"When Aeschines spoke, they said, 'How well he speaks.' But when Demosthenes spoke, they said, 'Let us march . . .'."

As this legendary quote illustrates, political oratory has been prized for centuries. In this country, some of the most gifted persuaders have been political leaders. One thinks of Abraham Lincoln's speeches during the Civil War and Franklin D. Roosevelt's fireside chats in the 1930s. During the late twentieth century, Ronald Reagan became known as "the great communicator" for his ability to speak simply and persuasively. Political language includes linguistic features discussed earlier: powerful speech, metaphors, and intensity. Its goal is to influence public attitudes and shape political agendas. In an era of mediated communication, the most effective way that leaders can reach citizens is through the media and Internet. What leaders say and how well they say it is a fundamental ingredient of contemporary political leadership.

One important aspect of political speech is *simplicity*. As an example, consider the contrast between presidents Jimmy Carter and Ronald Reagan. As a thinker, strategist, and peacemaker, Carter was brilliant, a gifted politician who could think outside normal political boundaries. But Carter failed to inspire the American public. He was a dreary, lugubrious speaker whose language confused and dispirited the public. Roderick Hart notes:

Only a person intent on political suicide would, on national television and radio, use a sentence like the following: "To help curtail the excessive uses of credit and by dampening inflation, they (his new policies) should, along with the budget measures that I have described, speed prospects for reducing the strains which presently exist in our financial markets."

(1984, p. 180)

The rhetorical opposite of Carter, Reagan spoke plainly and clearly. He adapted his language to the demands of television, speaking in short sentences not loaded down by modifying structures. A cabdriver said, "He's the only politician I can understand." In addition, Reagan spoke positively. Drawing shamelessly on American values, he delivered a simple, optimistic message (Perloff, 1998). Consider the following, typical of Reagan's speech:

> We have every right to dream heroic dreams. Those who say that we're in a time when there are no heroes, they just don't know where to look. You can see heroes every day, going in and out of factory gates. Others, a handful in number, produce enough food to feed all of us and then the world beyond. You meet heroes across a counter. And they're on both sides of that counter . . . Their patriotism is deep. Their values sustain our national life.
>
> (Hart, 1984, p. 228)

The same words would come off as schmaltzy and trite in another speaker.

In Reagan, they played well because he believed what he said and felt what he believed. They also fit the rhetorical demands of the 1980s, an era in which most Americans sought a leader who could restore their faith that America could tackle any problem, whatever its complexity and wherever its geographic origin.

As an actor, Reagan had another card to play. He persuasively conveyed political emotions. Through compelling use of his facial expressions, Reagan communicated anger and happiness in ways that resonated with the public.

Bill Clinton displayed a similar skill, moving audiences to laughter and tears in ways that even his opponents had to admire. "He's unpredictable," noted Republican consultant Frank Luntz. "When he drapes his hands over the podium and looks at you, there's this aw-shucks demeanor. He's completely unpredictable, and so you listen. I say this to Republicans all the time, and they nod their heads" (Hernandez, 2006, p. A19).

Both Clinton and Reagan, when at their best, used language and nonverbal cues to connect with the public. In this way they conveyed leadership through communication.

In addition to conveying verbal and nonverbal information persuasively, politicians manipulate another dimension of language, one touched on earlier: *the frame*. A frame is the "*central organizing idea for making sense of relevant events and suggesting what is at issue*" (Gamson, 1989, p. 157). By framing an issue in one way rather than another, candidates make certain aspects of an issue salient or promote one way of looking at a problem rather than another. Consider the issue of cutting taxes. For years Republicans framed the issue as lowering the tax burden and Democrats counterargued that tax cuts reduce the money government has available to provide needed social services. Both views were plausible; thus, the debate produced no political winners. Then the Republicans got the bright idea of framing the issue not as tax cuts, but as tax relief. Linguist George Lakoff explains why this was persuasive:

> Think of the framing for *relief*. For there to be relief there must be an affliction, an afflicted party, and a reliever who removes the affliction and is therefore a hero. And if people try to stop the hero, those people are villains for trying to prevent relief.

When the word *tax* is added to *relief*, the result is a metaphor: Taxation is an affliction. And the person who takes it away is a hero, and anyone who tries to stop him is a bad guy.

(2004, pp. 3–4)

Republicans used frames to their advantage on other issues. They dramatized opposition to the estate tax—a tax placed on the net value of a large estate at the time of the property owner's death—by calling it a *"death tax"* rather than an *"estate tax."* People ordinarily view an estate tax positively as a tax on fat cats' property. A death tax conjures up negative feelings, suggesting a mean-spirited attempt to extract money at the moment a person takes the last breath of life. By calling it a death tax, Republicans marshaled opposition to the tax on large estates.

Frames make issues salient, activate beliefs, and lead individuals to place more weight on certain considerations than others (Nelson, Oxley, & Clawson, 1997). Lakoff points out that people think in terms of frames and just providing them with the facts will not change attitudes. "To be accepted, the truth must fit people's frames. If the facts do not fit a frame, the frame stays and the facts bounce off," he notes (2004, p. 17).

There are two ethical perspectives on this issue. One view is that frames are useful devices that derive from a coherent political philosophy. When Democrats frame issues in terms of caring or community and Republicans emphasize strength and discipline, they are calling on core values. By emphasizing one frame over another, a candidate employs language to convey ideas. The second school of thought holds that frames are word games. Rather than developing a coherent message, politicians use catch phrases, test-marketing their language so that it sounds authentic, employing words that resonate with voters in hopes of snaring their votes.

## CONCLUSIONS

This chapter has focused on different facets of the persuasive message. Scholarship on the message dates back to Aristotle and the early Sophist writers. Contemporary research builds on the shoulders of giants. We ask the same questions as our forefathers and foremothers: Which types of appeals are most effective? Is logic more persuasive than emotion? How far should persuaders go in arousing the audience's emotions before the message backfires, producing effects opposite to those intended? There are no simple answers to these questions. Contemporary scholarship has offered more specific answers than earlier work, yielding more clarity. But it has not eliminated complexity or ambiguity.

We can divide the message into three components: structure, content, and language appeals. With regard to structure, we know that: (a) two-sided messages are more persuasive than one-sided messages, provided they refute the opposing side; and (b) it is typically better to draw the conclusion explicitly than implicitly. The content domain—evidence, fear, and framing—has generated numerous theoretical and practical insights. Evidence enhances persuasion, with different types of evidence effective under different psychological conditions. If you want to persuade someone, you are usually better off

## Box 7.5 | THE SLEEPER EFFECT

McDonald's hamburgers have ground worms.

Girl Scout cookies have been mixed with hashish.

A subliminal message is embedded on the pack of Camel cigarettes.

These statements have been bandied about for years, and some people (more than you would think) assume they are true (Perloff, 2001; Reinard, 1991). But these assertions are false. How do people come to develop false beliefs? There are many explanations, but one, relevant to this chapter, is this: these messages were relayed by communicators who initially inspired little trust or respect. As time elapsed, people forgot the source of the message, but continued to remember—and believe—the message itself.

This illustrates *the sleeper effect*: the notion that the effects of a persuasive communication increase with the passage of time. As Allen and Stiff note, "The term 'sleeper' derives from an expectation that the long-term effect is larger than the short-term effect in some manner (the effect is asleep but awakes to be effective later)" (1998, p. 176).

The core thesis is that a message initially discounted by message receivers comes to be accepted over time. The message is initially accompanied by a discounting cue that leads individuals to question or reject the advocated position. At Time 1, individuals recognize that the message is persuasive, but are bowled over by the discounting cue, such as information that the source is not an expert (Gruder, Cook, Hennigan, Flay, Alessis, & Halamaj, 1978). They therefore reject the message. Over time the cue (low-credibility source) becomes disassociated from the message. Individuals forget the source of the message, but remember the message arguments, perhaps because the arguments are more extensively processed and more accessible in memory than the source cue (Hannah & Sternthal, 1984).

A vexing part of the sleeper effect is that a message delivered by a highly credible source becomes less persuasive over time, while the same message, transmitted by a low-credible source, becomes more convincing. How can this be? What may occur is that message recipients agree with the message initially because the source is credible. The credibility of the source sells them on the message. Over time, source and message become disassociated, and people forget the key selling proposition—the source's credibility. Because this was what sold them on the message, its disappearance from memory reduces the persuasiveness of the message. By contrast, a message delivered by a low-credible communicator can gain in acceptance over time, having never been accepted exclusively on the basis of the credibility of the source.

Keep in mind that sleeper effects are not the norm in persuasion. Highly credible sources are invariably more effective, particularly in the short term. It is certainly better for persuaders to strive to have high rather than low credibility. Nonetheless, there are contexts in which sleeper effects occur (Kumkale & Albarracín, 2004), and these effects have intriguing implications for politics and marketing. Unfortunately, these applications have not been lost on unsavory marketing specialists.

## Box 7.5 |

False messages disseminated by low-credible communicators can come to be viewed as true over time, particularly if they are memorable. Dishonest and opportunistic political consultants exploit the sleeper effect when they try to implant misleading or negative information about their opponents into the public mind. They attempt to do this through push-polls, or telephone surveys in which an interviewer working for a political candidate (Candidate A) slips false and negative information about Candidate B into the poll, and asks respondents whether that would change their opinion of Candidate B. The questions are designed to push voters away from one candidate and *pull* them toward the candidate financing the poll (Sabato & Simpson, 1996).

In some cases, pollsters have deliberately exploited voter prejudices, hoping this would push individuals away from their preferred candidates. Interviewers have fabricated information, in one case claiming that an Alaska Democrat supported gay marriage when he had never endorsed marriage between homosexuals. In another case, an unmarried Democratic Congressman from Ohio kept receiving reports about push-polls that would ask his supporters, "Would you still vote for him if you knew he was gay?" The candidate noted that he was not gay, but acknowledged the tactic placed him in a "catch-22." "What do you do?" he asked. "Do you hold a press conference and say, 'I'm not gay!'?" (Sabato & Simpson, 1996, p. 265).

The candidate did not hold a press conference. He also did not get reelected to Congress.

The sleeper effect provides one explanation for those outcomes. The push-pollsters' negative messages about opposing candidates were persuasive, encouraging cognitive elaboration (Priester, Wegener, Petty, & Fabrigar, 1999). The pollster was a low-credible source, a discounting cue. Over time, the cue became disassociated from the message. The message was deeply processed and memorable. At a later point in time, the message awoke and influenced attitudes toward the candidates.

A sleeper effect may also underlie the widely-reported perception during the 2008 presidential campaign that Barack Obama was Muslim. Thirteen percent of registered voters insisted that Obama was a Muslim. They asked columnist Nicholas Kristof questions like "*That Obama—is he really a Christian? Isn't he a Muslim or something?*" (Kristof, 2008, p. 9). In fact, Obama is a Christian and this was widely pointed out. These beliefs had a variety of sources, but one source may have been viral attacks—vicious Internet messages claiming Obama was Muslim. A sleeper effect may have been operating, with people remembering the negative message but forgetting the low-credible source that conveyed it.

In fairness, other election-year Web sites also spread rumors on the other candidates, such as those suggesting that Republican vice-presidential nominee Sarah Palin had faked her pregnancy or others that made false claims about Republican presidential nominee John McCain's Vietnam background. These sites also may have produced sleeper effects.

citing evidence; in some situations, presenting narratives (telling stories, offering gripping anecdotes) can be remarkably effective. (Evidence can also have an increased effect with the passage of time; see Box 7.5 for a discussion.)

One of the most intriguing areas of message research has centered on fear—whether you should scare someone and if so, how you should go about it. Fear appeals are common in everyday life, from toothpaste commercials to drunk-driving PSAs to warnings about sexual exploitation on the Internet. Social scientists have advanced knowledge of fear messages by devising theories of fear arousal and testing hypotheses. The EPPM stipulates that fear appeals must contain threat and efficacy components and are most likely to work if they convince the person that he or she is capable of undertaking a protective action that will avert the threat. The "magic point" at which efficacy exceeds threat is not easy to reach. Consequently, fear appeals can fail to change attitudes. However, sounding a more optimistic note, fear messages derived from theory and research have been shown to exert substantial effects in communication campaigns (see Chapter 12).

Guilt appeals call on some of the same processes as fear messages. However, guilt calls on a host of emotions arising from the perception that one violated a moral norm. There is some evidence that guilt messages are effective when they combine empathy and self-efficacy appeals. Guilt, like fear, is a volatile weapon in the persuader's arsenal because it can trigger an array of strong feelings that push people in the opposite direction to the advocated message.

Language appeals, among the most interesting of all message factors, emphasize speech rate, powerful speech, and language intensity. Speaking quickly, powerfully, and with intensity can increase a communicator's credibility, and this in turn can enhance persuasion. But it is difficult to tick off specific rules that tell you which factor to use in a given situation. This is because context and audience expectations of a speaker exert important effects on persuasion (Burgoon, Denning, & Roberts, 2002; see Box 7.6.) Intelligent speakers take the audience's expectations into account ("Do they expect me to wow them with big words? Will they be offended if I throw in a four-letter word?") when they deliver persuasive messages.

These language factors play out with particular gusto in the political context. Good leaders use simple language, vivid metaphors, and compelling frames. Ineffective leaders stumble over language and frame issues in unappealing ways. Frames are complex: they can convey meaningful ideas or function as mere word games designed to snare votes.

The message remains a centerpiece of persuasion—a complex, fascinating one, to be sure. It revolves around arguments, but arguments are diverse entities. They can be logical, statistical, anecdotal, or highly emotional (as in the case of the fetus-as-baby metaphor). People do respond to emotional arguments, and there is debate about whether these are as legitimate as "purely logical" ones. There is also debate about the time-honored issue of whether you should accommodate or confront your audience. It is frequently best to accommodate your audience—using evidence that audience members find persuasive, devising appeals that mesh with cultural norms, speaking quickly if the audience speaks at a rapid clip (Giles & Street, 1994). On the other hand, if persuaders accommodate their audiences too much, they can be accused of pandering, or being so in need of audience approval that they don't raise ethically important issues. Moreover,

## Box 7.6 | LANGUAGE TIPS

How can you use language to spruce up your persuasive communications? Here are several suggestions, based on research and theory:

1.  Avoid "uh," "um," and other non-influences.

2.  Don't use disclaimers ("I'm no expert, but . . ."). Just make your point.

3.  Vary your pitch as much as possible. Avoid the boring monotone.

4.  Accommodate your speech to listeners' language style. If your audience speaks quickly (and your talk does not concern intimate issues), speak at a faster clip.

5.  Accommodate to audience language style, but don't pander. One African-American student related a story of a White speaker who addressed her high school class. Trying to be hip, he infused his talk with Black lingo (using phrases of the "yo, what's poppin'?" variety). The students laughed, seeing through his insincere attempt to appeal to them.

6.  Be careful about using intense, obscene speech. Intense language can work, particularly when the communicator is credible and the topic is of low ego-involvement. Obscenities can be effective, if listeners expect the speaker to use four-letter words. In his heyday, radio DJ Howard Stern's fans expected him to use obscene speech, and when he used it, he may have positively influenced attitudes. Obscenity can be the norm in certain neighborhoods; thus, if speakers don't swear, they will be disregarded. But in most instances, obscene speech is risky; it violates audience expectations of what is appropriate and can offend key constituents.

7.  Be aware of your nonverbal expressions. About 65 percent of the meaning in an interpersonal interaction is communicated nonverbally (Burgoon, 1994). Thus, you may know your stuff, but if you look like you're not happy to be speaking—because you're frowning or clenching your fists—you can trump the positive effects of expertise. Use facial expressions and a posture that you're comfortable with. And unless you're communicating bad news, smile.

in some cases, it is necessary to confront audience members—by scaring them or using intense language—so that they consider problematic personal or social issues.

The message remains a work in progress—a critical persuasion factor about which we know a lot, but that changes as new ideas, technologies, and norms spread through society. Next time you hear a persuasive message, you might examine whether it contains the key features discussed in this chapter. And when you are on the other side of the persuasion ledger, you should ask yourself if you have done all you can to build the most compelling aspects of the message into your persuasive communication.

# Chapter 8

# Personality and Persuasion

**A**RE certain people more gullible than others? What differentiates the gullible from the canny? Should communicators take personality into account when devising messages?

These questions are the ones typically asked when we think about the role personality plays in persuasion. It is commonly believed that certain people are more susceptible to persuaders' wiles than others. When you read about schemes to defraud the elderly, Internet credit card hoaxes, and religious cults' success in attracting new recruits, you may suspect that certain people are more vulnerable to persuasion than others. This issue has intrigued researchers and is the focus of this chapter. As has been true of other topics, the myths surrounding the issue of personality and persuasion are plentiful. The first section of the chapter reviews, then debunks, simplistic notions of personality and susceptibility to persuasion.

Subsequent sections focus on personality factors—stable aspects of an individual's character—that influence persuasibility, or susceptibility to persuasive communications.

## THE MYTH OF THE VULNERABLE OTHER

We commonly assume there is a certain class of people who are most susceptible to persuasive communications. Researchers have tried mightily to discover just who these people are. Initially, researchers speculated that people low in *self-esteem* might be especially inclined to acquiesce to persuasive communicators. They argued, in essence, that if individuals were "down on themselves" or doubted their abilities, they should be highly likely to yield to others, particularly experts. However, this hypothesis has not received much empirical support. Individuals with low self-esteem are not invariably more suggestible than those who are high in self-regard (Petty & Wegener, 1998). At first blush, this seems surprising. Wouldn't individuals with a poor self-image be particularly likely to succumb to others' suggestions? It seems like only common sense, right?

Well, what seems to be "only common sense" has a way of turning out to be far more complicated than was initially assumed. After carefully considering the issue,

McGuire (1968) concluded that there are good reasons to doubt that low-self-esteem individuals will inevitably follow persuaders' recommendations. McGuire noted that persuasion consists of a series of steps, including attending to a message, comprehending it, and yielding to the communicator. Individuals low in self-esteem are preoccupied with their own problems and worried about themselves. Dwelling on their own predicaments, they do not pay attention to or comprehend the message. As a result, cogent message arguments never get through; they're not processed by low-self-esteem individuals.

It works just the opposite for individuals who are high in self-esteem, McGuire (1968) argued. They tune into the message, directing attention outward (to the communication) rather than inward (toward their own thoughts and feelings). A cogent, well-reasoned series of arguments is processed and comprehended by high-self-esteem individuals. However, precisely because they are high in self-esteem, they are not so easily swayed. They understand the communicator's arguments, but refuse to yield. When low- and high-self-esteem individuals' responses are lumped together, something unusual happens. They cancel each other out. At the low end of the self-esteem scale, individuals do not process the message, so they can't be influenced; at the high end, individuals don't yield, so their attitudes can't change either. The result? Those most susceptible to persuasion are those in the middle—individuals with moderate self-esteem (Rhodes & Wood, 1992). But this is a large, heterogeneous group, so big and diverse that it is difficult to identify a specific type of person who is most vulnerable to persuasion.

Another factor that could help us classify people is *intelligence*. We don't like to say it publicly, but perhaps individuals with less innate cognitive ability are the ones most susceptible to persuasion. Some researchers make precisely this case (Rhodes & Wood, 1992). The problem is that intelligence is not a simple, one-dimensional concept. Gardner (1993) has argued that there are different types of intelligence, including verbal skills, mathematical abilities, body-kinesthetic skills, musical skills, and interpersonal skills. Someone high in verbal intelligence might be more skeptical of written arguments than others. However, this individual might be highly susceptible to interpersonal manipulation. Thus, it is difficult to make blanket statements about the effects of intelligence on persuasion.

A final factor that has been bandied about is *gender*. In bygone eras when sexism reigned and women were relegated to housework, researchers suspected that females would be more susceptible to persuasion than males. Women, 1950s-style scholars gently suspected, were the weaker sex. Others argued that it wasn't nature, but nurture. The female role emphasizes submissiveness and passivity, Middlebrook (1974) observed; thus, girls learn that they are expected to yield to persuaders' requests. However, this hypothesis is not supported by the facts. There are few strong sex differences in persuasibility (Eagly & Carli, 1981). When Eagly and Carli performed a meta-analysis of the gender and persuasion research, they discovered that only 1 percent of the variability in influence-ability was accounted for by gender. There are more differences within the same gender than between men and women.

And yet, one intriguing piece of evidence did emerge that suggested the sex differences idea should not be totally discarded. When the investigators looked at research on group pressure situations—in which people are faced with the task of deciding whether to go along with a position advocated by members of a group—they found that women were more likely than men to yield to the advocated viewpoint. When subjects had to decide whether to yield to the group position and believed that other group members would see or hear their responses, women were more likely than men to acquiesce. One possibility is that women are more insecure about their opinions in group settings than men are. However, it is also possible that women yield not because they are bowled over by group opinion, but rather because "they are especially concerned with maintaining social harmony and insuring smooth interpersonal relations" (Eagly, 1978, p. 103). Yielding helps the conversation proceed and ensures that the group can continue with its business. Perhaps men are more concerned with showing independence and women with showing that they are helpful (Tannen, 1990).

Thus, although the final chapter on sex differences in persuasion has not been written—and never will be, as gender roles are in a state of flux—the once-common myth that women are more gullible than men is not supported by research. Like most things, gender effects on persuasibility are more complex than is commonly assumed.

## Summary

Someday, perhaps, as psychological studies and genetic research advance, we will discover the prototypical gullible human being. More likely, given the complexity of human behavior, we will continue to discover that no personality trait is reliably associated with susceptibility to persuasion. Individuals may be more open to influence—by benign and (I'm afraid) manipulative persuaders—at certain times in their life, perhaps when they are young and lack experience with the issue (Fazio & Zanna, 1978).

Contemporary scholars emphasize that personality influences persuasibility, but not in the way ordinarily assumed. Individuals with a particular personality trait are not necessarily more gullible than others with a different trait. Instead, individuals with different personal characteristics are apt to be influenced by rather different persuasive appeals. To illustrate, I discuss three intriguing personality characteristics: need for cognition, self-monitoring, and dogmatism.

## NEED FOR COGNITION

Do you enjoy thinking? Or do you only think as hard as you have to? Do you prefer complex to simple problems? Or do you gravitate to tasks that are important, but don't require much thought?

These questions focus on the need for cognition, a personality characteristic studied by Cohen, Stotland, and Wolfe (1955) and later by Cacioppo and his associates. Need for cognition (NFC) is "a stable individual difference in people's tendency to engage in and enjoy effortful cognitive activity" (Cacioppo, Petty, Feinstein, & Jarvis, 1996, p. 198). People high in need for cognition enjoy thinking abstractly. Those low in NFC say thinking is not their idea of fun, and they only think as hard as they have to (see Box 8.1).

Need for cognition is not the same as intelligence. The two are related: you have to be somewhat intelligent to enjoy contemplating issues; thus, there is a modest relationship

## Box **8.1** | NEED FOR COGNITION SCALE

1. I would prefer complex to simple problems.

2. I like to have the responsibility of handling a situation that requires a lot of thinking.

3. Thinking is not my idea of fun.

4. I would rather do something that requires little thought than something that is sure to challenge my cognitive abilities.

5. I try to anticipate and avoid situations where there is a likely chance I will have to think in depth about something.

6. I find satisfaction in deliberating hard and for long hours.

7. I only think as hard as I have to.

8. I prefer to think about small, daily projects than long-term ones.

9. I like tasks that require little thought once I've learned them.

10. The idea of relying on thought to make my way to the top appeals to me.

11. I really enjoy a task that involves coming up with new solutions to problems.

12. Learning new ways to think doesn't excite me very much.

13. I prefer my life to be filled with puzzles that I must solve.

14. The notion of thinking abstractly is appealing to me.

15. I would prefer a task that is intellectual, difficult, and important to one that is somewhat important but does not require much thought.

16. I feel relief rather than satisfaction after completing a task that required a lot of mental effort.

17. It's enough for me that something gets the job done; I don't care how or why it works.

18. I usually end up deliberating about issues even when they do not affect me personally.

*Note:* Individuals indicate the extent to which each statement is characteristic of them on a 5-point scale: 1 means the item is extremely uncharacteristic of oneself; 5 means that it is extremely characteristic.

*High-NFC individuals agree with items 1, 2, 6, 10, 11, 13, 14, 15, and 18, but disagree with items 3, 4, 5, 7, 8, 9, 12, 16 and 17. This is a short form of the Need for Cognition Scale. See Cacioppo, Petty, and Kao (1984); see also Cacioppo and Petty (1982) for a report on the original NFC scale.*

between verbal intelligence and need for cognition. However, two people could score high on verbal intelligence tests, yet one individual could find abstract thinking appealing, while the other could find it monotonous. Need for cognition is a motive, not an ability.

What does need for cognition have to do with persuasion? Plenty. Individuals high in need for cognition recall more message arguments, generate a greater number of issue-relevant thoughts, and seek more information about complex issues than those low in NFC (Briñol & Petty, 2005; Cacioppo et al., 1996). Given that people high in need for cognition like to think, they should be more influenced by quality of message arguments than those low in NFC. And in fact cogent issue arguments do carry more weight with high-NFC individuals. By contrast, those low in NFC are more influenced by cues that save them from effortful thought. They are frequently swayed more by such simple cues as source credibility, communicator attractiveness, and celebrity endorsements (Cacioppo et al., 1996; Haugtvedt, Petty, & Cacioppo, 1992; Kaufman, Stasson, & Hart, 1999; Priester & Petty, 1995). Of course, there are times when individuals who are low in need for cognition will pay close attention to the message. For example, when the issue bears on their personal lives, low-NFC folks will process arguments centrally.

These findings have interesting practical implications. They suggest that if persuaders are targeting messages to individuals they know are high in need for cognition, they should make certain they employ strong arguments or make cogent appeals to respondents' values. If, on the other hand, the message is directed at low-NFC respondents, persuaders should develop appeals that don't tax these folks' mental capacities. Simple, clear appeals—the simpler, the better—are probably advisable. For example, Bakker (1999), in a study of AIDS prevention messages geared to low-NFC individuals, found that simple, visual safer-sex messages were highly effective. Similar findings in different health contexts have also been reported (Braverman, 2008; Vidrine, Simmons, & Brandon, 2007; Williams-Piehota, Schneider, Pizarro, Mowad, & Salovey, 2003).

Research also points to the intriguing possibility that people low and high in need for cognition are persuaded by different media. Green and her associates (2008) found that individuals with a low need for cognition were more transported into a narrative conveyed by film, a medium that ordinarily requires less cognitive effort than print. High need for cognition individuals were more transported by print, which seemed to match their preference for expending mental energy. Might film be a more effective modality to influence individuals low in need for cognition, while print might be better suited for those high in NFC? On the other hand, could there be instances where mentally-demanding films would be more effective with people high in NFC, and simpler print narratives would carry more weight with those low in NFC? These remain intriguing questions for research.

One cautionary note: it is easy to breeze through this and (on a personal level) conclude that it is better to be high than low in need for cognition. That is not necessarily so. You can be high in NFC, enjoy thinking abstractly, but puzzle so long about a simple issue that you lose the forest for the trees. One could be low in need for cognition and get straight to the heart of the issue, without getting bogged down in excessive detail. The key for persuaders is to accept individuals for what and who they are. Communicators are more apt to be successful if they match messages to individuals' personality styles.

Individuals who enjoy thinking are more likely to change their minds when they receive cogent messages that stimulate central processing. By contrast, people who make decisions based on intuition and gut feelings may be more swayed by messages that sketch a vision or tug at the heartstrings (Aune & Reynolds, 1994; Smith, 1993).

## SELF-MONITORING

Self-monitoring, a fascinating personality variable discussed in Chapter 3, has intriguing implications for persuasion. As noted earlier, high self-monitors put a premium on displaying appropriate behavior in social situations. Adept at reading situational cues and figuring out the expected behavior in a given place and time, they adjust their behavior to fit the situation. By contrast, low self-monitors are less concerned with playing a role or displaying socially appropriate behavior. They prefer to "be themselves," and consequently they look to their inner attitudes and feelings when trying to decide how to behave. Attitudes are more likely to predict behavior for low than for high self-monitors.

What implications does self-monitoring have for persuasion? You might guess that high self-monitors are more susceptible to persuasion because they want to impress people or are nervous about how they come across with others. One might also speculate that low self-monitors are resistant to persuasion because they stubbornly insist on being themselves. It turns out that both high and low self-monitors are susceptible to influence, but are swayed by different psychological appeals.

The core notion is attitude function. Chapter 3 describes the different functions that attitudes perform for people, including helping people fit into social situations (social-adjustive function) and aiding them in expressing key values (value-expressive function). Theorists argue that attitudes are more apt to serve a social-adjustive function for high self-monitors, concerned as they are with doing the socially appropriate thing. In the case of low self-monitors, attitudes should serve a value-expressive function, as they help these individuals fulfill the all-important need of being themselves (DeBono, 1987).

Kenneth G. DeBono tested this hypothesis in a study of attitudes toward treating the mentally ill in state hospitals and institutions. Tests conducted prior to the experiment revealed that most students opposed institutionalizing the mentally ill. Thus, the stage was set for determining whether social-adjustive and value-expressive appeals on this issue had different effects on high and low self-monitors.

High and low self-monitors listened to a social-adjustive or value-expressive argument in favor of institutionalizing the mentally ill. The social-adjustive message emphasized that the majority of students polled favored treating the mentally ill in hospitals and institutions, thereby providing information on the "socially correct" thing to do. The value-expressive communication stressed that the values of responsibility and loving (values that most students had previously rated as important) underlined favorable attitudes toward institutionalizing the mentally ill.

High self-monitors became more favorable toward institutionalizing the mentally ill after hearing the social-adjustive message. Low self-monitors were more influenced by the value-expressive appeal. Appeals that matched the individual's personality style—

or meshed with the appropriate attitude function—were more likely to influence individuals' attitudes on the topic.

Interesting as these findings are, we need to be careful not to over-generalize from the results of one study. The topic was modestly involving at best. It did not touch on deep personal concerns or bear directly on issues in individuals' personal lives. It is likely that if we picked an issue that was deeply important to high self-monitors, they would be influenced by value-based arguments. Similarly, if the issue were one in which even low self-monitors felt concerned about being ostracized, we could sway them by appealing to social norms. Yet there are numerous issues that are of only modest or low interest to people, and in these situations, social-conformity appeals are apt to carry greater weight with high self-monitors, while value-expressive messages should exert a greater influence on low self-monitors.

Different sources can also have different effects on high and low self-monitors. High self-monitors, concerned as they are with social appearances, devote a great deal of cognitive energy to processing a message when it is delivered by a prestigious, attractive, and popular source. By contrast, low self-monitors, focused as they are on "bottom-line values," are highly attentive when the message comes from an expert (DeBono & Harnish, 1988).

There is much we need to learn about self-monitoring and persuasion. Self-monitoring is a fascinating, as well as complex, concept (see Briggs & Cheek, 1988).

Undoubtedly, self-monitoring has different effects on attitudes in different situations, an issue worthy of future research. There are also apt to be striking cultural differences in self-monitoring effects. The self-monitoring scale (see Box 8.2) has been employed in hundreds of communication experiments, and you may want to see where you fall on the scale. Self-monitoring is one of those persuasion factors that lends itself to both beneficent and malevolent applications. High self-monitoring politicians who can adapt their arguments to different audiences display versatility and sensitivity. Unctuous salespeople who change their attitudes at will to broker a deal give all persuaders a bad name.

## DOGMATISM

An additional personality variable that influences persuasion focuses on people's tendency to close off their minds to new ideas and accept only the opinions of conventional, established authorities. Highly dogmatic individuals fit this mold (Rokeach, 1960). Low-dogmatic individuals, by contrast, are open-minded, receptive to new ideas, and willing to consider good arguments on behalf of a position. Highly dogmatic individuals agree with statements like, "Of all the different philosophies that exist in the world, there is probably only one which is correct," and "In this complicated world of ours the only way we can know what's going on is to rely on leaders or experts who can be trusted" (Rokeach, 1960). Low-dogmatic individuals naturally disagree with these items.

Individuals high in dogmatism find it difficult to come up with evidence that contradicts their beliefs (Davies, 1998). They also are willing to accept the views of an

# Box 8.2 | THE SELF-MONITORING SCALE

1. I find it hard to imitate the behavior of other people.
2. My behavior is usually an expression of my true inner feelings, attitudes, and beliefs.
3. At parties and social gatherings, I do not attempt to do or say things that others will like.
4. I can only argue for ideas which I already believe.
5. I can make impromptu speeches even on topics about which I have almost no information.
6. I guess I put on a show to impress or entertain people.
7. When I am uncertain how to act in a social situation, I look to the behavior of others for cues.
8. I would probably make a good actor.
9. I rarely seek advice of my friends to choose movies, books, or music.
10. I sometimes appear to others to be experiencing deeper emotions than I actually am.
11. I laugh more when I watch a comedy with others than when alone.
12. In a group of people I am rarely the center of attention.
13. In different situations and with different people, I often act like very different persons.
14. I am not particularly good at making other people like me.
15. Even if I am not enjoying myself, I often pretend to be having a good time.
16. I'm not always the person I appear to be.
17. I would not change my opinions (or the way I do things) in order to please someone else or win their favor.
18. I have considered being an entertainer.
19. In order to get along and be liked, I tend to be what people expect me to be rather than anything else.
20. I have never been good at games like charades or improvisational acting.
21. I have trouble changing my behavior to suit different people and different situations.
22. At a party I let others keep the jokes and stories going.
23. I feel a bit awkward in company and do not show up quite so well as I should.
24. I can look anyone in the eye and tell a lie with a straight face (if for a right end).
25. I may deceive people by being friendly when I really dislike them.

*Note:* You answer each question True or False. High self-monitors would answer questions in this way: 1 (F); 2 (F); 3 (F); 4 (F); 5 (T); 6 (T); 7 (T); 8 (T) 9 (F); 10 (T); 11 (T); 12 (F); 13 (T); 14 (F); 15 (T); 16 (T); 17 (F); 18 (T); 19 (T); 20 (F); 21 (F); 22 (F); 23 (F); 24 (T); 25 (T). Low self-monitors would give the opposite response to each question. (From Snyder, M., 1987, *Public appearances/private realities: The psychology of self-monitoring.* New York: W. H. Freeman.)

expert, even when he or she uses weak arguments to support the position (DeBono & Klein, 1993). Highly dogmatic individuals tend to be defensive and insecure; accepting the views of a recognized expert provides them with confidence and a sense of superiority.

Low-dogmatic individuals, feeling more motivated by a need to know than a desire to conform, are more willing to acknowledge shortcomings in their arguments. Strong arguments carry more weight with them than does the status of the communicator (DeBono & Klein, 1993).

It is hard to convince high-dogmatic individuals of anything. But you can make some headway if the communicator is a recognized expert. Low-dogmatic individuals are more open to persuasion, particularly from strong arguments. This highlights a point made earlier in the book: there are cases in which receptivity to communication is a good thing, the mark of a healthy, flexible person.

## ADDITIONAL ISSUES

Given that personality factors influence persuasion, it is appropriate to examine the "how" question, or the processes by which a particular personality trait affects attitude change. The ELM provides a clue. A personality trait can affect attitudes by influencing the amount of thinking people engage in when considering the issue. Individuals high in need for cognition tend to think a lot about issues, so they may process arguments deeply and carefully. A personality trait can also influence persuasion by getting people to rely on simple peripheral cues. Highly dogmatic individuals do this, going along with a message solely because an expert says it is right. A third way a personality characteristic could influence persuasion is by bolstering or undermining the confidence people have in their assessments of the message (Briñol & Petty, 2005). For example, people high in self-esteem may be more confident about the quality of their thoughts and may rely on them when evaluating the message. Others may give little credence to their thoughts, perhaps disregarding them and relying instead on the opinions of a trusted—but dishonest—persuader.

## OTHER PERSONALITY FACTORS

Research on personality and persuasion is a work in progress. Scholars are continuing to identify personality traits that have implications for attitudes and persuasion. For example, *the need to evaluate* taps people's tendency to evaluate social experiences as either good or bad. People high in this need are prone to form opinions about people and issues. They have lots of opinions, prefer to take extreme stands, and enjoy strongly liking or disliking new products or issues (Jarvis & Petty, 1996). By contrast, individuals low in this need are less inclined to take strong positions and probably less likely to make judgments about people they encounter.

*The need for affect* focuses on a need to tune in to—or tune out—emotional events (Maio & Esses, 2001). People high in this need feel that it is important to be in touch with their feelings. They believe that strong emotions are beneficial, and emotions help people function well in life. If the need for cognition taps a preference for intellectual thought, the need for affect taps a preference for experiencing and acting on emotions.

*The need for closure* involves a preference for getting a definitive answer on an issue and a discomfort with ambiguity (Holbert & Hansen, 2006; Webster & Kruglanski, 1994). Under some conditions, individuals high in need for closure may be less motivated to process persuasive messages carefully. Individuals low in closure might be more inclined to work patiently through an ambiguous social problem. By the same token, they might also drive you crazy because they would never want to come up with a definitive solution to the dilemma. As is always the case, there are good and bad points about each of these personality styles. It is interesting to discover how different people are and how differently they approach attitudes and attitude change.

## CONCLUSIONS

Most of us assume that certain types of people are gullible and susceptible to manipulation.

It turns out that the relationship between personality and persuasibility is more complex than this. The usual (and old-fashioned) suspects—low-self-esteem individuals, people low in intelligence, and women—turn out to be innocent of the charge that they are gullible. Adopting a more focused approach to the message and the person, researchers have found that need for cognition and self-monitoring are important personality variables. Appeals that match an individual's cognitive needs and self-monitoring tendency are more apt to be successful than those that are not in sync with the individual's cognitive motivation or self-monitoring orientation. The greater the degree that a communicator can fulfill an individual's psychological needs, the more likely it is that the message will change attitudes (see Figure 8.1).

We don't know as much about personality traits that stiffen resistance to persuasion, although some speculate that argumentativeness has this effect (Infante & Rancer, 1996). We also lack knowledge about the particular situations in which personality traits such as self-monitoring and need for cognition are most likely to influence persuasibility. Personality traits may have predictable influences on behavior, but they are apt to have stronger effects in certain contexts than others.

Although most research has examined the effect of personality on vulnerability to persuasion, personality can also influence techniques individuals use when they are working the other side of the street—that is, when they are trying to change audience members' minds. People who enjoy arguing and regard it as an intellectual challenge are perceived as credible communicators and experience success in social influence (see Box 8.3). Arguing gets a bad reputation, but in reality this ancient art has personal and professional benefits.

This chapter began with the question: "Are certain people more gullible than others?" Although interesting theories have been advanced, the fact is that we still do not have an adequate answer to this question. Why do certain individuals join religious cults while others resist? Why do some people succumb to deceptive financial Ponzi schemes, or sign on to real-estate deals that they know are too good to be true? More than a half-century since research on these issues began, we have made headway in understanding individual differences in persuasibility, but we still cannot pinpoint the psychological variables that explain why some people yield to, and others reject, persuaders' ministrations. Alas, the impact of personality on persuasion remains a work in progress.

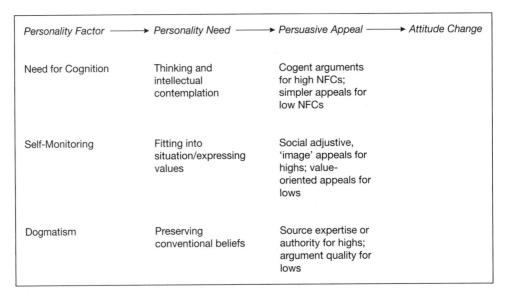

**FIGURE 8.1** | Personality, psychology, and attitude change.

## Box 8.3 | PERSONALITY AND ARGUMENTATION

"Early Sophists roamed ancient Greece fulfilling a great need in the city-states and fledgling democracies—they taught citizens how to argue effectively," Dominic A. Infante and Andrew S. Rancer observe. "Arguing," they note, "was an essential skill for success" (1996, p. 319). The art of argumentation, long prized in communication, has fallen on hard times. Debate classes are no longer required. Students receive preciously little training in developing cogent, logical arguments. The term "argument" has a negative connotation, calling to mind obstinate, unpleasant, even aggressive individuals. Yet skill in arguing is an important ability to cultivate. It can sharpen the mind and help people appreciate the value of sound, logical thinking. Skill in argumentation can also lead to professional success, as arguments and discussions are a critical aspect of just about any job you can think of. Argumentative skill can also help negotiators defuse interpersonal and ethnic conflicts.

Argumentativeness is defined as "a generally stable trait which predisposes individuals in communication situations to advocate positions on controversial issues and to attack verbally the positions which other people hold on these issues" (Infante & Rancer, 1982,

## Box **8.3** |

p. 72). Infante and Rancer (1982) developed a reliable, valid 20-item scale to tap argumentativeness. If you are an argumentative person (which can be viewed as a positive trait), you would agree with items like these:

- I enjoy a good argument over a controversial issue.
- I have a pleasant, good feeling when I win a point in an argument.
- I consider an argument an exciting intellectual challenge.
- I enjoy defending my point of view on an issue.

Research shows that contrary to stereotype, argumentativeness confers social benefits. Individuals high in argumentativeness are viewed as more credible persuaders than those low in this trait, and are more inclined to employ a greater range of influence strategies. They also encourage others to give their opinions on controversial matters and are judged as more capable communicators (Infante & Rancer, 1996; Rancer, 1998). Interestingly, argumentative individuals are less apt to use their power to goad others into accepting their positions.

Argumentative individuals are not necessarily verbally aggressive, a point scholars emphasize. "When individuals engage in argumentativeness, they attack the positions that others take or hold on controversial issues," Rancer notes. "When individuals engage in verbal aggressiveness they attack the self-concept of the other," he adds (1998, p. 152). Verbal aggressiveness includes insults, ridicule, and the universal put-down. It can be the province of the desperate communicator, the one who runs out of arguments and resorts to personal attacks. Do you know people who are verbally aggressive? They would be likely to agree with statements like these:

- When individuals are very stubborn, I use insults to soften the stubbornness.
- When I am not able to refute others' positions, I try to make them feel defensive in order to weaken their positions.
- If individuals I am trying to influence really deserve it, I attack their character.
- When people simply will not budge on a matter of importance, I lose my temper and say rather strong things to them (Infante & Wigley, 1986).

Verbal aggressiveness reduces the persuader's credibility and overall communication effectiveness (Infante & Rancer, 1996; Wigley, 1998). It produces destructive, rather than constructive, outcomes. Rather than helping or convincing people, one ends up hurting their feelings or feeling guilty oneself.

Scholars are quick to point out that both argumentativeness and verbal aggressiveness are more likely to be activated in certain situations than others, such as when the message concerns ego-involving issues. Noting the negative effects of verbal aggressiveness and the virtues of argumentativeness, researchers have developed training programs to teach individuals to argue constructively and to avoid getting enmeshed in destructive communication spirals (Rancer, Whitecap, Kosberg, & Avtgis, 1997).

# Chapter 9

# Cognitive Dissonance Theory

■ EDWARD Yourdon was nothing if not prepared. Fully expecting computers, cash machines, and VCRs to fail on January 1, 2000, the 55-year-old computer programmer took elaborate precautions. He relied on a backup computer to log onto the Internet. He stocked tuna fish and rice in a New Mexico home he built partly due to Y2K concerns, dividing his time between Taos and an apartment in New York. When the much ballyhooed electronic problems failed to materialize on New Year's Day, few would have been surprised if Mr. Yourdon expressed shame or embarrassment. Instead, the bulky computer programmer stuck by his predictions. "There is going to be another opportunity for bugs [on January 3]," he insisted. "It is possible that bugs will manifest themselves in coming days and weeks," he said, apparently undaunted by reports that Y2K had arrived without serious incident (Brooke, 2000).

■ When Litesa Wallace packed her bags for college at Western Illinois University some years back, she never harbored any doubt that she would pledge a sorority. The initiation rites for Delta Sigma Theta turned out to be a tad more severe than Litesa expected: doing 3,000 sit-ups, drinking hot sauce and vinegar, and swallowing her own vomit. While some might have quit at this point, Litesa endured the hardship. "She wanted to be in the sorority very badly. It's very prestigious, and she believed that it would be beneficial to her life," her attorney explained. Attorney? That's right: Ms. Wallace sued the sorority for hazing after she was hospitalized for injuries sustained during the initiation period. Yet, even as she awaited the outcome of her suit, Litesa remained a Delta, apparently feeling considerable loyalty to the sorority (Pharnor, 1999).

■ Movies strike resonant chords in many people, and the following conversation from the 1982 movie *The Big Chill* sheds light on a phenomenon that many have probably experienced in everyday life:

*Sam:* Why is it what you just said strikes me as a mass of rationalizations?

*Michael:* Don't knock rationalizations. Where would we be without it? I don't know anyone who could get through the day without two or three juicy rationalizations. They're more important than sex.

*Sam:* Ah, come on. Nothin's more important than sex.

*Michael:* Oh yeah? You ever gone a week without a rationalization?

(Steele, 1988)

■ A week after the 9/11 attacks, a strange development occurred. Five anthrax-laced envelopes were mailed to major media outlets in New York City. Three weeks later, two anthrax-laden envelopes were sent to the offices of two U.S. senators. The anthrax-laden materials ultimately killed five people, caused 17 others to become sick, and led to widespread national panic.

Over a 7-year period, FBI investigators conducted more than 9,000 interviews and close to 100 searches, in the most intricate criminal investigation in FBI history. But the emotional costs were high. Federal officials pegged Dr. Kenneth Berry, an emergency room doctor concerned about bioterrorism problems, as a suspect. In August, 2004, agents, clothed in protective outfits, raided his western New York home. Scenes of authorities leaving his house, carting away computers, books, and papers, were played over and over again on local television. Although Berry turned out not to be the culprit, the stress took a toll on his career and marriage.

Dr. Steven Hatfill, a physician and former Army researcher, became the focus of the FBI investigation in 2002. FBI agents informed the woman he was living with that he was a murderer, threatening her if she did not talk. Although Hatfill claimed he was innocent, the FBI trailed him for a year and raided his home. Prominent news articles associated him with the case. He sued the U.S. Department of Justice and *The New York Times*. He was subsequently cleared and received $4.6 million from the U.S. government.

Despite all this, authorities steadfastly denied they did anything wrong. Federal officials rejected criticisms from government colleagues, voicing neither regret nor remorse. "I do not apologize for any aspect of the investigation," FBI director Robert Mueller III said. It is incorrect to "say there were mistakes" (Broad & Shane, 2008, p. 17).

What do these different examples have in common? They illustrate the powerful role that a phenomenon called cognitive dissonance plays in everyday life. You may have heard the term "cognitive dissonance." No surprise: it has become part of the popular lexicon. Writers, politicians, therapists, and ordinary folks use the words to describe conflict or negative feelings about issues. But what exactly does dissonance mean? Why did one psychologist call it the greatest achievement of social psychology? (See Aron & Aron, 1989.) How can dissonance principles be harnessed in the service of persuasion? And what insights can cognitive dissonance theory contribute to everyday life? This chapter examines these issues.

# FOUNDATIONS

Cognitive dissonance is a bona fide theory, one of the oldies but goodies. It contains definitions, hypotheses, explanations, and theoretical statements. It has generated numerous studies, as well as disagreements among scholars as to just why a particular finding has emerged. It is a psychological theory, one of a wave of 1950s-style approaches that assumed people have an overarching need for cognitive consistency or balance. Leon Festinger developed the theory in 1957, conducted some of the major experiments on dissonance effects, and then departed from the social psychology scene to pursue studies of human perception. That was dissonant—or inconsistent—with what you would expect an established, successful theorist to do. But in a way it was typical of dissonance theory: a counterintuitive "reverse psychology" sort of approach that turned ideas on their head, but in a fashion that stimulated and intrigued scholars across the world.

So what do we mean by cognitive dissonance? Dissonance means discord, incongruity, or strife. Thus, cognitive dissonance means incongruity among thoughts or mental elements. Two cognitions are in a dissonant relationship when the opposite of one cognitive element follows from the other. For example, the idea that "eating junk food is bad for your heart" is ordinarily dissonant with the cognition that "I love junk food." The cognition "I just plunked down $20,000 for a car" is dissonant with the observation that "I just found out you can't accelerate past 60 on the highway in this piece of junk." The cognitions "My boyfriend gets abusive when he's mad" and "I love him and want to stay with him always" are also dissonant. Finally, and most gravely, the cognition "The world is a beautiful and wonderful place" is dissonant with the realization that "evil people can kill thousands of innocent people in a single day."

Dissonance, as these examples suggest, cuts across contexts. It is specifically and formally defined as *"a negative, unpleasant state that occurs whenever a person holds two cognitions that are psychologically inconsistent"* (Aronson, 1968, p. 6). Notice that I say "psychologically inconsistent." Two thoughts can be psychologically—but not logically—inconsistent. The cognition "I love junk food" is not logically inconsistent with the belief that "eating junk food is bad for your heart." Knowing that a junk-food diet increases the risk of heart disease does not make it illogical to eat burgers, fries, and nuggets. However, the two cognitions arouse dissonance because, psychologically, it does not make sense—at least for most people—to engage in a behavior that increases the risk of disease.

Dissonance is a complex theory with many hypotheses. It has been refined many times over the years. Its core components remain the following:

1.  Dissonance is psychologically uncomfortable, physiologically arousing, and drives individuals to take steps to reduce it.
2.  Dissonance occurs when an individual: (a) holds two clearly incongruent thoughts, (b) freely performs a behavior that is inconsistent with an attitude, (c) makes a decision that rules out a desirable alternative, (d) expends effort to participate in what turns out to be a less than ideal activity, or (e) in general is unable to find sufficient psychological justification for an attitude or behavior he or she adopts.

3. The magnitude of dissonance depends on a host of factors, including the number of dissonant elements and the importance of the issue.
4. People are motivated to take steps to reduce dissonance, including changing their attitude in response to a persuasive message.
5. Different people employ different strategies to reduce dissonance. Some people are better at coping with dissonance than others.
6. People may not always succeed in alleviating dissonance, but they are motivated to try.

Dissonance theory is intriguing in an important respect. The theories discussed up to this point have emphasized that changes in attitude lead to changes in behavior. Dissonance theory suggests that the opposite can occur—changes in behavior can produce changes in attitude (Cooper & Scher, 1994). For this to happen, a critical requirement of persuasion must be satisfied: people must persuade themselves to adopt a new attitude on the topic. Dissonance theory, as one would expect from a theory of persuasion, assigns central importance to the power of self-persuasion.

## DISSONANCE AND DECISION MAKING

Life is filled with decisions, and decisions (as a general rule) arouse dissonance. For example, suppose you had to decide whether to accept a job in a stunningly beautiful area of the country or to turn down the job so that you could be near friends and family. Either way, you would experience dissonance. If you took the job, you would miss loved ones; if you turned down the job, you would pine for the breathtaking mountains, luscious waterfalls, and great evening sunsets. Both alternatives have their good and bad points. The rub is that making a decision cuts off the possibility that you can enjoy the advantages of the unchosen alternative. It also ensures that you must accept the negative elements of the choice you make.

When trying to make up their minds, people frequently experience difficulty, confusion, and conflict. It's only after the decision is made that they experience the particular stress known as dissonance (Aronson, 1968). At this point, they truly are faced with two incompatible cognitions: I chose Alternative A, but this means I must forego the benefits of Alternative B (or C or D, for that matter). We don't experience dissonance after each and every decision. It's the ones that are the most important and least amenable to change that seem to trigger the greatest amount of cognitive dissonance (Simon, Greenberg, & Brehm, 1995; Wicklund & Brehm, 1976). Thus, choosing between two equally desirable paper towels should ordinarily produce less dissonance than selecting between two attractive and similarly priced apartments. In addition, if you can revise your decision—take it back, so to speak—you should have less dissonance than if you have signed the deal on the dotted line and cannot revisit your choice, except with considerable psychological or financial pain. If you suddenly discover, after you signed your lease, that the apartment you're renting is located in a dwelling built with asbestos, you're apt to experience a good deal of cognitive dissonance.

Just how this would feel would depend on you and how you deal with decisional stress. But there is little doubt that it wouldn't feel good! Scholars have actually studied how dissonance "feels," and they conclude it's a complex amalgamation of physiological arousal, negative affect, and mental anguish (Cooper & Fazio, 1984; Elkin & Leippe, 1986; Elliot & Devine, 1994).

So how do people cope with this discomfort we call dissonance? Theorists argue that they employ a variety of different techniques. To illustrate, consider this example: you invite a close friend to a movie that has garnered favorable reviews. The movie, obligatory popcorn, and soft drinks are expensive, so you hope the film will pan out. It doesn't; the movie turns out to be a real loser, and you find yourself sitting there, hoping it will get better. Hope springs eternal; nevertheless, the movie stinks.

You're in a state of cognitive dissonance. The cognition "I spent a lot of money on this movie" is dissonant with the knowledge that the movie is no good. Or, the thought that "I'm personally responsible for ruining my friend's evening" is dissonant with your positive self-concept or your desire to look good in your friend's eyes. How can you reduce dissonance? Research suggests you will try one or several of these techniques:

1. *Change your attitude.* Convince yourself it's a great flick, on balance—this may be hard if the movie is really bad.
2. *Add consonant cognitions.* Note how cool the cinematography is or decide that one of the actors delivered an especially convincing portrayal.
3. *Derogate the unchosen alternative.* Tell yourself that going to a movie beats sitting at home, listening to and shuffling eternally through your iPod.
4. *Spread apart the alternatives.* Let's assume that before you made the choice, you felt just as positively about going to a movie as you did about spending the evening at home. In effect, the two choices were "tied" at 4 on a 5-point scale in your mind. You would spread apart the alternatives by figuratively pushing the movie up to a 4.5 and dropping staying at home to a 3. This would work until it became clear the movie was a disappointment.
5. *Alter the importance of the cognitive elements.* Trivialize the decision by telling yourself that it's only a movie, just 2 hours of your life.
6. *Suppress thoughts.* Deny the problem and just try to get into the movie as much as you can.
7. *Communicate.* Talk up the movie with your friend, using the conversation to convince yourself it was a good decision.
8. Alter the behavior. Leave.

It's amazing how few people seem to avail themselves of the last option. Don't we frequently sit through a bad movie, spending our valuable cognitive energy justifying and rationalizing instead of saving ourselves the hardship by walking out? Yet this is consistent with dissonance theory. Dissonance theorists emphasize that people prefer easier to harder ways of changing cognitive elements (Simon et al., 1995). It's hard to alter behavior. Behavior is well learned and can be costly to modify. Walking out could be embarrassing. You might also be wrong; the movie might have become really good at precisely the moment you left. Of course, sticking through a lemon of a movie is not necessarily rational; it's an example of what psychologists call a sunk cost (Garland, 1990). You are not going to get the money back, no matter how much you convince yourself that it was a great film. However, as dissonance theorists are fond of reminding us, human beings are not *rational* animals, but, rather, rationalizing animals, seeking "to appear rational, both to others and [themselves]" (Aronson, 1968, p. 6). As Benjamin Franklin observed, people can devise a rationalization for anything they wish to do. Rather than admit they are wrong, people rationalize. They deny and distort reality, refusing to acknowledge that they made a mistake. As Carol Tavris and Elliott Aronson (2007) note, "most people, when directly confronted by evidence that they are wrong, do not change their point of view or course of action but justify it even more tenaciously" (p. 2).

How apt a description of human decision making! Immediately after people make up their minds to embark on one course rather than another, they bear an uncanny resemblance to the proverbial ostrich, sticking their heads in the sand to avoid perspectives that might conflict with the option they chose, doing all they can to reaffirm the wisdom of their decision. If you chose the Hyundai instead of the Honda (Chapter 5) and then suddenly learned that the Hyundai's engine is not as well constructed as the Honda's, your first impulse might be to deny this, then perhaps to counterargue it, or to focus on areas in which the Hyundai is clearly superior to the Honda. Or, to take another example, let's say a friend of yours smokes a pack a day. If you asked her why she smokes, you would hear a long list of rationalizations speaking to the power of dissonance reduction. Her reasons might include: "I know I should quit, but I've got too much stress right now to go through quitting again"; "I guess I'd rather smoke than pig out and end up looking like a blimp"; and "Hey, we're all going to die anyway. I'd rather do what I enjoy." All these reasons make great sense to your friend; they help restore consonance, but they prevent her from taking the steps needed to preserve her health. Such is the power of cognitive dissonance.

## DISSONANCE AND EXPENDITURE OF EFFORT

Have you ever wondered why fraternity pledges come to like a fraternity more after they have undergone a severe initiation procedure? Ever been curious why law students who have survived the torturous experience of being asked to cite legal precedent before a class of hundreds come to think positively of their law school professors? Or why medical interns who work 30-hour shifts, with barely any sleep, vigorously defend the system, sometimes viewing it as a grand way to learn the practice of medicine (Kleinfield, 1999)? An explanation of these phenomena can be found in the application of dissonance theory to the expenditure of effort.

The core notion here is quite simple, as Aronson and Mills explained:

No matter how attractive a group is to a person it is rarely completely positive; i.e., usually there are some aspects of the group that the individual does not like. If he has undergone an unpleasant initiation to gain admission to the group, his cognition that he has gone through an unpleasant experience for the sake of membership is dissonant with the cognition that there are things about the group that he does not like.

(1959, p. 177)

One way to reduce dissonance is to convince oneself that the group has many positive characteristics that justify the expenditure of effort.

Elliot Aronson and Judson Mills tested this hypothesis long ago—in 1959. Yet their findings have been replicated by other experimenters, and continue to shed light on events occurring today. Like many researchers of their era, they preferred to set up a contrived procedure to study dissonance and effort. Believing that they needed to provide a pure test of the hypothesis, they devised an experiment in which female college students were told they would be participating in several group discussions on the psychology of sex. Informed that the group had been meeting for several weeks and they would be replacing a woman who dropped out due to scheduling conflicts, women in the experimental condition were told they would be screened before gaining formal admission to the group. (The experimenters deliberately chose women, perhaps because they felt that the sexual words they would ask women to read would have a stronger effect on these 1950s coeds than on male students. Researchers conducting the study in today's savvy college environment would no doubt employ a different procedure.)

Students assigned to the severe initiation condition read aloud twelve obscene words and two graphic descriptions of sexual activity from contemporary novels. Women in the mild initiation condition read five sex-related words that were not obscene. Subjects in both conditions were then informed they had performed satisfactorily and had been admitted into the group. All the women subsequently listened to a tape-recorded discussion of a group meeting. The discussion was made to seem dull and banal, with group members speaking dryly and contradicting each other.

The discussion was set up this way to arouse dissonance. Female participants in the study had to confront the fact that they had undergone a humiliating experience, reading sexual words in front of some guy they had never met, for the sake of membership in a group that seemed boring and dull.

You might think that women in the severe initiation condition would dislike the group. Indeed, simple learning models would suggest that the unpleasant experience these women underwent would increase antipathy to the group. However, dissonance theory made the opposite prediction. It predicted that women in the severe initiation treatment would evaluate the group most positively. They had the most dissonance, and one way to reduce it would be to rationalize the unpleasant initiation by convincing themselves that the group discussion was not as bad as it seemed and was, in some sense, worth the pain they endured. This is what happened: women in the severe initiation condition gave the group discussion higher ratings than other subjects did.

Although Aronson and Mills' study was intriguing, it did not convince all researchers. Some suggested that perhaps the severe initiation procedure did not embarrass the women at all, but aroused them sexually! If this were true, women in the severe initiation condition would have liked the group more because they associated the pleasant arousal with the group experience (Chapanis & Chapanis, 1964). To rule out this and other alternative explanations, researchers conducted a different test of the effort justification hypothesis, one that involved not a sexual embarrassment test but, rather, different initiation procedures. Using these operationalizations, experimenters found additional support for the Aronson and Mills findings (Cooper & Axsom, 1982; Gerard & Mathewson, 1966).

## Applications

We must be careful not to apply these findings glibly to the real world. People do not always rationalize effort by changing their attitude toward the group; they may reduce dissonance in other ways—for example, by trivializing the initiation rite. In some cases, the effort expended is so enormous and the initiation ceremony so humiliating that people cannot convince themselves that the group is worth it. This helps explain why Litesa Wallace, the young woman mentioned at the beginning of the chapter, sued her sorority (while still remaining a Delta). (In response to such egregious cases, anti-hazing Web sites have cropped up in recent years.)

Yet the effort-justification notion sheds light on numerous real-life situations. It helps explain why fraternities and sororities still demand that pledges undergo stressful initiation ceremonies. Seniors who underwent the initiation procedure as freshmen rationalize the effort expended, develop a favorable attitude to the group, and derive gratification from passing on this tradition to new recruits (Marklein, 2000; see Figure 9.1).

Effort justification also helps us understand other phenomena. It explains why U.S. leaders continued to defend problematic ventures, like the wars in Iraq and Vietnam. Having expended so much effort, so many resources, and so much human blood, leaders can reduce dissonance by arguing that the cause was worth it. To acknowledge error would create immense dissonance and psychological pain. Antiwar critics would be quick to point out that if leaders acknowledged the dissonance, they could reverse course and save countless lives. But dissonance theory argues that people are loath to do this, particularly when an acknowledgment has serious emotional and political repercussions.

Effort justification has other applications. For example, Jewish children spend numerous Saturdays and Sundays learning Hebrew and reciting the Torah in preparation for their Bar and Bat Mitzvahs. The time spent is dissonant with the knowledge they could be having more fun doing other things, but in the end the need to reduce dissonance pushes them to evaluate the experience positively. This enables the ritual—and religion—to get passed on to future generations, thus preserving time-honored traditions.

## INDUCED COMPLIANCE

What happens if a person is coaxed to argue publicly for a position he or she does not privately accept? Further, what if the individual is paid a paltry sum to take this position? Suppose you gave a speech that advocated banning cell phone use in cars, although you privately disagreed with this position? Let's say someone paid you a dollar to take this

**FIGURE 9.1** | Why do fraternities like this one frequently require individuals to undergo challenging —even stressful—initiation ceremonies? Dissonance theory offfers a compelling explanation.

Photograph by William C. Rieter.

stand. Dissonance theory makes the unusual prediction that, under these circumstances, you would actually come to evaluate the proposal favorably.

This prediction is part of a phenomenon known as induced compliance. The name comes from the fact that a person has been induced—gently persuaded—to comply with a persuader's request. The person freely chooses to perform an action that is inconsistent with his or her beliefs or attitude. Such actions are called counterattitudinal. When individuals perform a counterattitudinal behavior and cannot rationalize the act—as they could if they had received a large reward—they are in a state of dissonance. One way to reduce dissonance is to change one's attitude so that it is consistent with the behavior— that is, convince oneself that one really agrees with the discrepant message.

This hypothesis was elegantly tested and supported by Leon Festinger and J. Merrill Carlsmith in 1959. Students were asked to perform two tasks that were phenomenally boring: (1) placing spools on a tray, emptying the tray, and refilling it with spools; and (2) turning each of 48 pegs on a peg board a quarter turn clockwise, then another quarter

**TABLE 9.1** | Results of Festinger and Carlsmith study

| Question | Experimental condition | | |
|---|---|---|---|
| | $1 | $20 | Control |
| How enjoyable were tasks? (rated from −5 to +5) | 1.35 | −.05 | −.45 |
| Were tasks scientifically important? (rated from 0 to 10) | 6.45 | 5.18 | 5.60 |
| Are you willing to participate in similar experiments? (rated from −5 to +5) | 1.20 | −.25 | −.62 |

Source: Festinger, L. & Carlsmith, J. M., 1959, *Journal of Abnormal and Social Psychology*, 58, 203–210.

turn, and so on for half an hour. In what could have been an episode from the old TV show, *Spy TV*, the experimenter then asked students to do him a favor: tell the next participant in the study that this monotonous experiment had been enjoyable, exciting, and a lot of fun. You see, the experimenter suggested, the person who usually does this couldn't do it today, and we're looking for someone we could hire to do it for us. The whole thing was a ruse: there was no other person who usually performed the task. The intent was to induce students to say that a boring task was enjoyable—a dissonant act. There was also a twist.

Some students were paid $20 for telling the lie, others were paid $1, and those in a control condition didn't tell a lie at all. Participants then rated the enjoyableness of the tasks. As it turned out, those paid $1 said they liked the tasks more and displayed greater willingness to participate in similar experiments in the future than did other students (see Table 9.1).

How can we explain the findings? According to theory, the cognition that "the spool-removing and peg-turning tasks were really boring" was dissonant with the cognition that "I just told someone it was lots of fun." The $20 provided students with external justification for telling the lie. It helped them justify why they said one thing (the tasks were exciting), yet believed another (they were really boring). They received $20; that helped them feel good about the whole thing, and they had no need to change their attitude to restore consonance. Like a stiff drink that helps people forget their sorrows, the $20 helped erase the dissonance, or sufficiently so that students didn't feel any need to change their attitude toward the tasks.

For students paid $1, it was a different matter. Lacking a sufficient external justification for the inconsistency, they had to turn inward to get one. They needed to bring their private attitude in line with their public behavior. One way to do this was to change their attitude toward the tasks. By convincing themselves that "the thing with the spools wasn't so bad; it gave me a chance to do something, perfect my hand–eye coordination—yeah, that's the ticket," they could comfortably believe that the statement they made to fellow students ("I had a lot of fun") actually reflected their inner feelings. Dissonance was thus resolved; they had restored cognitive harmony.

Note that these findings are exactly the opposite of what you might expect based on common sense and classic learning theory. Both would suggest that people paid more money would like something more. Reward leads to liking, right? Not according to dissonance theory. Indeed, the negative relationship between reward and liking, consistent with cognitive dissonance theory, has held up in other studies conceptually replicating the Festinger and Carlsmith experiment (Harmon-Jones, 2002; Preiss & Allen, 1998).

The early research had exciting theoretical implications. As researcher Elliot Aronson observed:

> As a community we have yet to recover from the impact of this research—fortunately! ... Because the finding departed from the general orientation accepted either tacitly or explicitly by most social psychologists in the 1950s: [that] high reward—never low reward—is accompanied by greater learning, greater conformity, greater performance, greater satisfaction, greater persuasion ... [But in Festinger and Carlsmith] either reward theory made no prediction at all or the opposite prediction. These results represented a striking and convincing act of liberation from the dominance of a general reward-reinforcement theory.
>
> (quoted in Aron & Aron, 1989, p. 116)

More generally, the results of this strange—but elegantly conducted—experiment suggested that people could not be counted on to slavishly do as experts predicted. They were not mere automatons whose thoughts could be controlled by behavioral engineering or psychologists' rewards. Like Dostoyevsky's underground man, who celebrated his emotion and spontaneity, dissonance researchers rejoiced in the study's findings, for they spoke to the subjectivity and inner-directedness of human beings.

## Applications

The great contribution of induced compliance research is theoretical, in suggesting new ways to think about human attitudes and persuasion. However, the research does have practical applications. The negative incentive effect—paying people less changes their attitudes more—can be applied to the problem of motivating individuals to engage in positive, healthy acts they would rather not perform. For example, consider the case of a parent who wants to convince a couch-potato child to exercise more. Should the parent pay the kid each time she or he jogs, plays tennis, or swims laps? Dissonance theory says no. It stipulates that children frequently face dissonance after engaging in vigorous physical exercise—for example, "*I just ran a mile, but, geez, did that hurt*"; "*I just ran five laps, but I could have been watching a DVD.*" By paying sons or daughters money for exercising, parents remove children's motivation to change their attitudes. The money provides strong external justification, erasing the dissonance: the child no longer feels a need to change an anti-exercise attitude so that it is compatible with behavior (jogging a mile a day). Instead, the money bridges thought and action and becomes the main thing the child gets out of the event. Thus, the same old negative attitude toward exercise persists.

By contrast, if parents don't pay their children a hefty sum (or give them only a paltry reward), children must reduce the dissonance on their own. To be sure, kids may not restore consonance by developing a positive attitude toward exercise (they could blame their parents for "forcing" them to work up a sweat or just complain about how sore their bodies feel). But it is entirely possible—and I've seen examples of this with parents in my neighborhood, to say nothing of research that backs it up (Deci, 1975)—that children will change their attitude to fit their behavior. They develop a positive attitude toward exercise to justify their behavior. Once this happens, their attitude "grows legs" (Cialdini, 2001). Exercise becomes a positive, not a negative, force in their lives; it becomes associated with pleasant activities; and the attitude motivates, then triggers behavior. The child begins to exercise spontaneously, on his or her own, without parental prodding.

## EXPLANATIONS AND CONTROVERSIES

When a theory is developed, researchers test it to determine if it holds water. If hypotheses generated from the theory are empirically supported, researchers are elated: they have come upon a concept that yields new insights, and they have landed a way to publish studies that enhance their professional reputations. But once all this happens, the question, "What have you done for me lately?" comes to mind. The ideas become rather familiar. What's more, scholars begin wondering just why the theory works and come to recognize that it may hold only under particular conditions. These new questions lead to revisions of the theory and advance science. They also help to "keep the theory young" by forcing tests in new eras, with new generations of scholars and different social values.

Dissonance theory fits this trajectory. After the studies of the 1950s and 1960s were completed (yes, they were conducted that long ago!), scholars began asking deeper questions about dissonance theory. They began to wonder just why dissonance leads to attitude change and whether there weren't other reasons why individuals seek to restore dissonance than those Festinger posited. Many theorists proposed alternative accounts of dissonance and tested their ideas. These studies were published from the 1970s through the 1990s, and they continue to fill journals and books today (Harmon-Jones, 2002; Mills, 1999).

The catalyst for this research was the Festinger and Carlsmith boring-task study previously discussed. Like a Rorschach projection test, it has been interpreted in different ways by different scholars. Their research suggests that when people engage in counter-attitudinal behavior, there is more going on than you might think. Four explanations of the study have been advanced. Each offers a different perspective on human nature and persuasion. Yet all four agree on one point: Festinger's thesis—people are driven by an overarching need to reduce inconsistency—is not the only psychological engine that leads to dissonance reduction. Students in the boring-task study may have been bothered by the inconsistency between attitude toward the task and behavior (telling others it was enjoyable). However, there were other reasons why they changed their attitude than the mere discomfort inconsistency causes. Let's review these four perspectives on cognitive dissonance.

## Unpleasant Consequences + Responsibility = Dissonance

What really bothered students in Festinger and Carlsmith's experiment, researcher Joel Cooper has suggested, is that they might be personally responsible for having caused unpleasant consequences (Scher & Cooper, 1989). By leading an innocent person to believe that a monotonous study was enjoyable, they had arguably caused a fellow student to develop an expectation that would not be met by reality. This realization caused them discomfort. To alleviate the pain, they convinced themselves that the task was really interesting. Thus, it was not inconsistency per se, but rather "the desire to avoid feeling personally responsible for producing the aversive consequence of having harmed the other participant" that motivated attitude change (Harmon-Jones & Mills, 1999, p. 14).

## Dissonance Occurs When You Are Concerned That You Look Bad in Front of Others

This view emphasizes people's need to manage impressions or present themselves positively in front of other people (Tedeschi, Schlenker, & Bonoma, 1971). Theorists argue that students in Festinger and Carlsmith's study did not really change their attitudes, but only marked down on the questionnaire that they liked the task to avoid being viewed negatively by the experimenter. Concerned that the experimenter would look down on them for being willing to breach their ethics for the reward of $1, students in the $1 condition strategically changed their attitude so that it looked as if they really liked the task. Thus, they could not be accused of selling their souls for a trivial sum of money (Cooper & Fazio, 1984). In addition, students in the $1 condition may not have wanted to appear inconsistent in the experimenter's eyes (i.e., telling a fellow student the tasks were fun and then marking down on the survey that they were boring). Perceiving that people think more favorably of you when you are consistent, they indicated on the survey that they liked the task, thus giving the impression that they exhibited consistency between attitude and behavior.

## Dissonance Involves a Threat to Self-Esteem

The self-concept is at the center of this interpretation. In Aronson's view, students in Festinger and Carlsmith's study experienced dissonance between the cognition "I am a good and moral person" and the knowledge that "I just lied to someone, and I won't have a chance to 'set him straight' because I probably won't see him again" (1968, p. 24). Students were not bothered by the mere inconsistency between thoughts, but rather by the fact that their behavior was inconsistent with—or violated—their positive self-concept. Of course, lying is not dissonant to a pathological liar; yet it was assumed that for most people, telling a fib would be moderately dissonant with their views of themselves as honest individuals. The self-concept is at the center of other contemporary views of dissonance reduction, such as Steele's theory (1988), which takes a slightly different approach to the issue.

## It's Not Dissonance, but Self-Perception

Daryl J. Bem (1970) argued that effects observed in experiments like Festinger and Carlsmith's had nothing to do with cognitive dissonance, but were due to an entirely different psychological process. Unlike the three explanations just discussed, Bem's theory dismisses dissonance entirely. Arguing that people aren't so much neurotic rationalizers as dispassionate, cool observers of their own behavior, Bem suggests that people look to their own behavior when they want to understand their attitudes. Behavior leads to attitude, Bem (1972) argues, but not because people want to bring attitude in line with behavior to gain consistency. Instead, behavior causes attitude because people infer their attitudes from observing their behavior. For example, according to Bem, a young woman forms her attitude toward vegetarian food by observing her behavior: "I'm always eating noodles and pasta—I never order meat from restaurants anymore. I must really like veggie food." Or a guy decides he likes a girl, not on the basis of his positive thoughts, but rather because he observes that "I'm always calling her on the phone and am excited when she calls. I must really like her."

Applying this analysis to Festinger and Carlsmith's classic experiment, Bem argued that students paid $20 to say a boring task was interesting quickly looked to the situation, asked themselves why they would do this, and observed that they had just been paid $20 to make the statement. "Oh, I must have done it for the money," they concluded. Having reached this judgment, there was not the slightest reason for them to assume that their behavior reflected an attitude.

Subjects paid $1 looked dispassionately at their behavior to help decide why they told the other student the task was fun. Noting that they had received only a buck to lie, they concluded, "I sure didn't do this for the money." Seeking to further understand why they behaved as they did, the $1 subjects then asked themselves, "Now why would I have told the experimenter the tasks were interesting? I didn't get any big external reward for saying this." Then came the explanation, obvious and plausible: "I must have really liked those tasks. Why else would I have agreed to make the statements?" These inferences —rather than rationalizations—led to the $1 students' forming a favorable attitude toward the tasks.

## THE DISSONANCE DEBATE: INTELLECTUAL ISSUES

Who's right? Who's wrong? Which view has the most support or the most adherents? What's the right answer?

These questions probably occur to you as you read the different views of dissonance. However, there is usually not one correct interpretation of a complex phenomenon, but many. Thus, there are various reasons why low rewards or counterattitudinal advocacy leads to attitude change. Inconsistency between cognitions, feeling responsible for producing negative consequences, discomfort at looking bad in front of others, perceiving that one has engaged in behavior that is incongruent with one's sense of self, and subsequent self-perceptions all motivate individuals to change attitudes to fit behavior.

Theorists continue to debate which theory does the best job of explaining the research on cognitive dissonance.

There is currently an intellectual tug-of-war going on between those who believe dissonance occurs when one feels responsible for having caused aversive consequences (the first interpretation discussed earlier) and others who believe dissonance is a broader phenomenon, one that occurs even when counterattitudinal behavior does not lead to especially negative outcomes (Harmon-Jones, Brehm, Greenberg, Simon, & Nelson, 1996). The second interpretation, impression management, remains viable, but has been undercut to some degree by evidence that dissonance reduction occurs in private settings, in which impressing others is less salient (Harmon-Jones & Mills, 1999). Skipping to the fourth view, self-perception, I note that Bem's theory has stimulated much discussion and has many interesting implications for persuasion (see Chapter 10). However, research shows that self-perception can't explain away all dissonance phenomena. Individuals aren't always dispassionate observers of their own behavior, but rather are motivated to rationalize, justify, and persuade themselves, particularly after they have committed actions that bother them greatly (Elliot & Devine, 1994; Harmon-Jones & Mills, 1999). Contrary to Bem's theory, we don't just sit back and observe our behavior like neutral spectators. We're concerned when our behavior has adverse personal or social consequences, and we are motivated to redress the cognitive dissonance.

The third interpretation, focusing on the self-concept, continues to intrigue researchers, probably because it centers on that quintessential human attribute: the ego (Mailer, 1999).

Researchers disagree on several technical points. For example, some scholars emphasize that people are bothered when they perform an action that is inconsistent with their self-concepts (Aronson, 1999). Others from the self-concept school argue that people are less concerned with maintaining consistency between self and behavior than in engaging in actions that affirm their global sense of self (Aronson, Cohen, & Nail, 1999; Steele, 1988). According to this view, individuals can reduce dissonance that arises from taking a counterattitudinal position by performing an action that restores global self-integrity, even if it is not related to the issue in question (see Box 9.1). The self-concept approach to the self is intriguing and continues to generate intellectual dialogue among researchers (Stone, Wiegand, Cooper, & Aronson, 1997).

## SUMMARY

If you can think of a time you performed a behavior that caused harm to someone else, violated your self-concept, embarrassed you, or was just plain inconsistent with what you believe, you can appreciate the power of cognitive dissonance. About half a century after Festinger invented the concept, the idea is still going strong; it continues to stimulate dialogue among scholars. There is no question that dissonance produces genuine, abiding changes in attitudes, beliefs, and behavior. It has particularly powerful effects when the issue is important to the individual and touches on the self-concept. What's more, the person must have freely chosen to perform the advocated behavior. Dissonance does not

## Box 9.1 | DISSONANCE AND MENTAL HEALTH

One of the great things about dissonance theory is that over half a century after it was formulated, it continues to contain enlightening ideas about everyday life. Some of these ideas have interesting implications for mental health. Here are five suggestions, culled from theory and research, for how to harness dissonance in the service of a happier, healthier life:

1.  *Expect to experience dissonance after a decision.* Don't expect life to be clean and free of stress. If you choose one product or side of the issue instead of another and the selection was difficult, there is bound to be discomfort.

2.  *Don't feel you have to eliminate the dissonance immediately.* Some people, uncomfortable with dissonance, mentally decree that no unpleasant thoughts about the decision should enter their mind. But sometimes the more we try to suppress something, the more apt it is to return to consciousness (Wegner, Schneider, Carter, & White, 1987). Dissonance can present us with a learning experience; it can help us come to grips with aspects of decisions we didn't like or positions that have more of a gray area than we believed at the outset. The thinking that dissonance stimulates can help us make better decisions, or deliver more compelling persuasive communication next time around. Of course, it is perfectly natural to want to reduce dissonance that follows a decision or performance of a behavior. However, we should also be open to the possibility that dissonance can be a teaching tool, as well as an annoyance—a phenomenon that can deepen our understanding of human experience.

3.  *Don't feel bound to each and every commitment you make.* Dissonance research indicates that once people make a public commitment, they are loath to change their minds, for fear of looking bad or having to confront the fact that they made a mistake, and so on. But there are times—such as undergoing a cruel initiation rite to join a sorority—when backing out of a commitment may be the healthy thing to do.

    Naturally, we should try to honor our commitments as much as possible, but we also should not feel obligated to do something unhealthy or unethical just because we sunk a lot of time into the project.

4.  *Recognize that some people need consistency more than others.* Robert B. Cialdini and colleagues report that there are intriguing individual differences in preference for consistency. Some people are more apt than others to agree with statements like: "I get uncomfortable when I find my behavior contradicts my beliefs," "I make an effort to appear consistent to others," and "I'm uncomfortable holding two beliefs that are inconsistent" (Cialdini, Trost, & Newsom, 1995, p. 328). We're not all cut from the same consistency cloth, and we're apt to have more pleasant interactions with others if we accept that they may need more or less consistency than we do.

**Box 9.1** |

5.  *Admit your mistakes.* Most of us are loath to admit we made a mistake. Fearing that the mistake would reflect negatively on their self-concept or arouse other dissonant elements, people cling tenaciously to their original decision. But this is not always a mature or helpful response. Understanding why a decision caused dissonance and learning from mistakes can help us grow and avoid similar errors in the future. The Chinese philosopher Lao Tzu said: "A great nation is like a great man: when he makes a mistake, he realizes it. Having realized it, he admits it. Having admitted it, he corrects it. He considers those who point out his faults as his most benevolent teachers" (Tavris & Aronson, 2007).

6.  *Be creative in your attempts to reduce dissonance.* You may not be able to reduce all the dissonance that results from a decision or performance of behavior. A young woman who smokes, quits for a while, and then starts up again is apt to feel dissonance. A deadbeat dad may finally feel guilt or discomfort after years of leaving and neglecting his kids. According to Claude M. Steele and colleagues, these individuals feel dissonant because they have performed actions that call into question their self-worth or sense of themselves as competent, good people (Aronson et al., 1999; Steele, 1988). Given that this is the root of dissonance, these folks can alleviate dissonance by doing things that help them look good in their own eyes, Steele argues. Although the smoker can't reduce all the dissonance aroused by her failure to quit, she might restore a sense of self-competence by completing important projects at work or doing other things that show she can follow up on personal promises she makes. Realistically, the deadbeat dad may have alienated his kids so much he can't do much to regain their trust. However, he might be able to restore a positive sense of self by at least celebrating their major accomplishments, or by taking the radically different step of spending time with other children in need.

    The same processes can work at the national level. Millions of Americans felt waves of pain and dissonance after the September 11 attacks. (The dissonance was complex, an outgrowth of a realization that America was now vulnerable, as well as recognition that the belief in a good and just world had been shattered more deeply than before.) Knowing they could not bring these beliefs back to life (anymore than they could bring back the lives of the people killed that September morning), they sought to restore consonance by volunteering—sending money and food to victims, giving blood, even helping rescue workers at the World Trade Center. Collectively, these actions may have restored pride in America and reaffirmed a strong belief in the fundamental decency of human beings.

produce attitude change when behavior is coerced; in such situations, the person feels no internal need to rationalize the behavior. Dissonance, like persuasion, occurs under situations of free choice.

This brings us to the final issue in this chapter—an important one for this book: implications of dissonance theory for attitude change. The next section explores ways in which communication experts can use dissonance theory to influence attitudes in a variety of real-life settings.

## DISSONANCE AND PERSUASION

Dissonance theorists take a decidedly different approach to persuasion than approaches reviewed in earlier chapters. Rather than trying to accommodate the other person's thinking or speech style, like the ELM or speech accommodation, dissonance theory is confrontational. It suggests that persuaders deliberately arouse cognitive dissonance and then let psychology do its work. Once dissonance is evoked, individuals should be motivated to reduce the discomfort. One way they can do this is to change their attitude in the direction the persuader recommends.

Calling on the major implications of the approaches previously discussed, we can suggest some concrete ways that persuaders can use dissonance theory to change attitudes.

**Make a commitment public.** When we commit ourselves publicly to an action, something interesting happens. We put pressure on ourselves to translate intention into action. If we fail to make good on a promise that others expect us to keep, we face opprobrium from strangers or friends; we also risk a very public blow to our self-esteem. In order to forestall such negative consequences, dissonant as they are, people find it psychologically easier to make good on their commitments (see Cialdini, 2001). In our era, individuals frequently make commitments public by posting details on Web sites and blogs. A 29-year-old woman who called herself Tricia noticed that she owed more than $22,000 in credit card bills. Ashamed of her indebtedness but determined to make things right, Tricia posted details of her finances on the Web. She noted that her net worth was a minus $38,691 and shared how much of her financial debt she had succeeded in paying down (Ariely, 2008). Presumably by announcing her determination to pay down her debt publicly, she placed psychological pressure on herself to make good on her commitment. That, at least, was Tricia's hope. We don't know if she succeeded, but, given the right circumstance and appropriate dose of motivation, public commitments can strengthen individuals' resolve to translate thought into action.

**Encourage people to publicly advocate a position with which they disagree.** If someone who harbors a prejudiced attitude toward minorities or gays can be coaxed into making a tolerant statement in public, she may feel cognitive dissonance. She privately harbors a negative attitude, but has now made an accepting speech in public. This may heighten the dissonance and, in some instances, motivate the individual to bring her attitude in line with public behavior. In a study that tested this hypothesis, Michael R. Leippe and Donna Eisenstadt (1994) gave White students an opportunity to write essays endorsing a scholarship policy that would significantly increase money available to Blacks, presumably at the expense of Whites. White students who believed their essays could be made public became more favorable toward both the policy and African-Americans (see also Eisenstadt, Leippe, Stambush, Rauch, & Rivers, 2005).

Interestingly, a judge used a variant of this procedure on a bigot who burned a Black doll and a cross in Black residents' yards. In addition to using coercive punishments—such as sentencing him to jail—the judge ordered the man to go to the library to research the impact of cross burnings (Martin, 2001). Studying the issue in a public setting might lead the man to think through and come to grips with his racist attitudes, perhaps inducing attitude change.

**Confront people with their own hypocrisy.** Jeff Stone and colleagues employed this procedure in an engaging study of safe sex. They recognized that most students believe they should use condoms to prevent the spread of AIDS, but do not always practice what they preach. Stone and colleagues argued that, if they reminded individuals of this fact, "the resulting inconsistency between [students'] public commitment and the increased awareness of their current risky sexual behavior should cause dissonance" (Stone, Aronson, Crain, Winslow, & Fried, 1994, p. 117). To alleviate dissonance, students might begin to practice safer sex.

Participants in the study were led to believe they were helping design an AIDS prevention program for use at the high school level. Experimental group subjects wrote a persuasive speech about safer sex and delivered it in front of a video camera. Some students read about circumstances that made it difficult for people to use condoms. They also made a list of reasons why they had not used condoms in the past. This was designed to provoke inconsistency or induce hypocrisy. (Control group subjects did not list these reasons or make the safer-sex speech before a video camera.)

All students were given an opportunity to buy condoms, using the $4 they had earned for participating in the study. As predicted, more students in the hypocrisy condition purchased condoms and bought more condoms than students in the control condition. Their behavior was apparently motivated by the discomfort and guilt they experienced when they recognized they did not always practice what they preached (O'Keefe, 2000).

As intriguing as Stone and colleagues' findings are, we need to be cautious about glibly endorsing hypocrisy induction as a method for safer-sex induction. First, making people feel hypocritical may make them angry and that may cause the treatment to boomerang. Second, safer-sex requests in real-world situations meet up against a variety of roadblocks, including the pleasures of sex, reluctance to offend a partner by proposing condom use, and even anxiety about being physically assaulted if one suggests using a condom. Hypocrisy induction may change attitudes in the short term, but may not influence behavior that occurs in such high-pressure sexual situations. Still, it's an important start.

More generally, letting people know that a behavior they perform or position they endorse is incompatible with an important component of their self-concepts can make them feel uncomfortable (Takaku, 2006). Telling someone straight-out that she has made a prejudiced remark can reduce the likelihood that this person will behave in a stereotyped

## Box **9.2** | **90210** DISSONANCE

This story is about a father and teenage son who live in the 90210 zip code region of the United States. You know where that is: Beverly Hills. All too ordinary in some respects, the story concerns a high school student who was heavily dependent on drugs, and a dad who found out and tried to do something about it. The story, originally broadcast on the National Public Radio program *This American Life* on January 16, 1998, would not be relevant to this chapter except for one small but important fact: the father used dissonance theory to try to convince his son to quit doing drugs. His dad probably had never heard of cognitive dissonance, but his persuasive effort is a moving testament to the ways that dissonance can be used in family crisis situations. Here is what happened:

Joshua, a student at plush Beverly Hills High School, got involved with drugs in a big way. "I failed English. I failed P.E. even, which is difficult to do, unless, you're, you know, running off getting stoned whenever you're supposed to be running around the track. And I just, you know, I just did whatever I wanted to do whenever I wanted to do it," he told an interviewer. He stole money from his parents regularly to finance his drug habit.

Joshua had no reason to suspect his parents knew. But strange things began to happen. His dad started to punish him, grounding him on the eve of a weekend he planned to do LSD, offering no reason for the punishment. Claiming there was going to be a drug bust at Beverly Hills High, Josh's dad revealed the names of students who were doing drugs. How could his father know this? Josh wondered.

About a month later, Josh and a buddy were hanging out in his backyard. The night before, there had been a big wind storm. It ripped off a panel from the side of the house. He and his friend were smoking a joint, like they did every day after school, when his buddy, noticing the downed panel, suddenly said, "Dude, what is this? Come here, dude. Come here, dude. Look at this." Josh saw only a strange piece of machinery inside a wall when his buddy shocked him. "Dude, your parents are taping your calls."

Suddenly, Josh understood. That explained his dad's punishments and knowledge of the high school drug group. At this point, the radio program switched to Josh's dad, who revealed what had happened. He said he became upset when Josh's grades plunged and his son "started acting like a complete fool." Concerned and noticing that Josh spent a lot of time on the phone, he decided to tape-record Josh's phone calls. The ethical aspects of this appeared not to bother the father.

Aware his dad was taping him, Josh made a decision. He would not quit drugs—that was too great a change—but would tell his friends that he was going straight when they talked on the phone. This worked for a while until Josh felt guilty about lying to his father. He valued his relationship with his dad and decided to talk to him. He cornered his dad at a party and told him that he knew he had been taping his phone calls.

**Box 9.2** |

In a dramatic admission, his father conceded he had been tape-recording Josh's conversations and said he was not going to do it anymore. He then told his son that there was something he didn't know yet, and perhaps would not understand. "Josh", he said, "you think that because I'm your father and I am in this role of the disciplinarian, that it's between you and me. What you haven't realized yet is that your actions have far more impact on your own life than they will on mine." He told Josh that he was going to take out the tape recorder the following day. At this point, Josh was waiting for a punishment— a severe punitive action, he assumed, perhaps military school. "I'll take the tape recorder out tomorrow," his dad said, "and there is only one thing I want you to do. I have about 40 tapes. I am going to give them to you, and I want you to listen to them, and that's all I ask."

With this statement, Josh's dad hoped to unleash cognitive dissonance in his son. He wanted Josh to hear how he sounded on the tapes—his redundant, frequently incoherent conversations, non sequiturs, his treatment of other people. Clearly, his dad wanted to provoke an inconsistency between Josh's self-concept and his behavior on the tapes. And this was exactly what occurred. Josh was embarrassed—appalled—by the conversations that he heard. He listened to a call from his girlfriend, upset that he had ignored her and that he treated her coldly and with indifference. He showed the same indifference with his friends.

"I had no idea what I sounded like and I didn't like what I sounded like at all," Josh said. "I was very self-centered and egotistical and uncaring of other people. It was about me. I was the star of my own stage and everybody else could basically, you know, go to hell as far as I was concerned. I had never realized that aspect of my personality. I didn't know how mean in that sense I had gotten."

After listening to the tapes over time, Josh changed his attitudes toward drugs, stopped lying, and altered his life's course. His father—who instigated the radical plan—was amazed. "He understood the entire thing that he was doing," he said proudly.

way in the future (Czopp, Monteith, & Mark, 2006). Gently confronting individuals with an instance of their prejudice or self-incongruent behavior can be just the right psychological medicine to goad them into changing their attitudes (see Box 9.2).

## CONCLUSIONS

Cognitive dissonance remains an important, intriguing psychological theory with numerous implications for persuasion. Dissonance is an uncomfortable state that arises when individuals hold psychologically inconsistent cognitions. As revised and reconceptualized over the years, dissonance also refers to feeling personally responsible for unpleasant consequences, and experiencing stress over actions that reflect negatively on the self. There are different views of dissonance and diverse explanations as to why it exerts the impact that it does on attitudes.

There is little doubt that dissonance influences attitudes and cognitions. Its effects fan out to influence decision making, justification of effort, compliance under low reward, and advocating a position with which one disagrees. The theory also helps us understand why people commit themselves to causes—both good and bad ones. It offers suggestions for how to help people remain committed to good causes and how to aid individuals in quitting dysfunctional groups. The theory also has intriguing implications for persuasion. Departing from conventional strategies that emphasize accommodating people or meeting them halfway, dissonance theory recommends that persuaders provoke inconsistencies in individuals. Dissonance then serves as the engine that motivates attitude change. In this sense, dissonance is a powerful theory of persuasive communication, emphasizing, as it does, the central role that self-persuasion plays in attitude change.

# Chapter 10

# Interpersonal Persuasion

**B**ERNAE Gunderson, a paralegal specialist from St. Paul, has no difficulty deciphering the fine print of legal documents. Still, she was puzzled by materials she received from her mortgage company. They didn't jibe with the home equity loan she and her husband had been promised. Mrs. Gunderson called the company, First Alliance Corporation, asked questions about monthly payments and fees, and was promptly reassured that her understanding of the loan was indeed correct. What Mrs. Gunderson was not told—but soon would discover—was that First Alliance had tacked on $13,000 in fees to the loan, and the interest rate rose a full percentage point every 6 months (Henriques & Bergman, 2000).

First Alliance, it turned out, used deceptive sales procedures to promote its services. Sued by regulators in five states, the company recruited unsuspecting borrowers using a high-level con game and elaborate sales pitch that was designed to snooker people into paying higher fees and interest rates than were justified by market factors. The company's loan officers were required to memorize a 27-page selling routine that included the following gambits:

- Establish rapport and a common bond. Initiate a conversation about jobs, children, or pets. Say something funny to get them laughing.

- To soften the financial blow, when talking about dollar amounts, say "merely," "simply," or "only."

- If the customer asks questions about fees, just reply, "May I ignore your concern about the rate and costs if I can show you that these are minor issues in a loan?"

- If all else fails and the sale appears to be lost, say, "I want to apologize for being so inept a loan officer. I want you to know that it's all my fault, and I'm truly sorry. Just so I don't make the same mistake again, would you mind telling me what I did that was wrong? Didn't I cover that? (And get right back into it.) (Henriques & Bergman, 2000, p. C12).

There is nothing wrong with using persuasion techniques to make a sale. The problem is that First Alliance trained its loan officers to deceive customers about its services. They lied about the terms of home equity loans and refused to come clean when people like Bernae Gunderson raised questions. They were experts in using strategies of interpersonal persuasion. Unfortunately, they exploited their knowledge, manipulating individuals into signing off on deals that were unduly expensive and unfair.

Interpersonal persuasion, the centerpiece of First Alliance's promotional campaign and subject of this chapter, offers a glimpse into a realm of persuasion that is somewhat different from those discussed so far in the book. Unlike purely psychological approaches, it focuses on the dyad, or two-person unit (persuader and persuadee). In contrast to attitude-based research, it centers on changing behavior—on inducing people to comply with the persuader's requests. Unlike message-oriented persuasion research, which focuses on modifying views about political or social issues, it explores techniques people employ to accomplish interpersonal objectives—for example, how they "sell themselves" to others.

Drawing on the fields of interpersonal communication, social psychology, and marketing, interpersonal persuasion research examines the strategies people use to gain compliance. It looks at how individuals try to get their way with others (something we all want to do). It examines techniques businesses use to convince customers to sign on the dotted line, strategies charities employ to gain donations, and methods that health practitioners use to convince people to take better care of their health. To gain insight into these practical issues, interpersonal persuasion scholars develop theories and conduct empirical studies—both experiments and surveys. In some ways, this is the most practical, down-to-earth chapter in the book; in other ways, it is the most complicated because it calls on taxonomies and cognitive concepts applied to the dynamic dance of interpersonal communication.

The first portion of the chapter looks at a variety of techniques that have amusing sales pitch names like foot-in-the-door and door-in-the-face. These persuasive tactics are known as *sequential influence techniques*. Influence in such cases "often proceeds in stages, each of which establishes the foundation for further changes in beliefs or behavior. Individuals slowly come to embrace new opinions, and actors often induce others to gradually comply with target requests" (Seibold, Cantrill, & Meyers, 1994, p. 560). The second section of the chapter focuses more directly on the communication aspect of interpersonal persuasion. It looks at the strategies that people—you, me, our friends, and parents—use to gain compliance, how researchers study this, and the many factors that influence compliance-gaining.

## FOOT-IN-THE-DOOR

This classic persuasion strategy dates back to the days when salespeople knocked on doors and plied all tricks of the trade to maneuver their way into residents' homes. If they could just overcome initial resistance—get a "foot in the door" of the domicile—they felt they could surmount subsequent obstacles and make the sale of an Avon perfume, a vacuum cleaner, or a set of encyclopedias. Going door to door is out of date, but starting small and moving to a larger request is still in vogue. The foot-in-the-door technique stipulates that an individual is more likely to comply with a second, larger request if he or she has agreed to perform a small initial request.

Many studies have found support for the foot-in-the-door (FITD) procedure. Researchers typically ask individuals in an experimental group to perform a small favor, one to which almost everyone agrees. Experimenters next ask these folks to comply with a second, larger request, the one in which the experimenter is actually interested. Participants in the control condition receive only the second request. Experimental group participants are typically more likely than control subjects to comply with the second request. For example:

- In a classic study, Freedman and Fraser (1966) arranged for experimenters working for a local traffic safety committee to ask California residents if they would mind putting a 3-inch "Be a safe driver" sign in their cars. Two weeks later, residents were asked if they would place a large, unattractive "Drive Carefully" sign on their front lawns. Homeowners in a control condition were asked only the second request. Seventeen percent of control group residents agreed to put the large sign on their lawns. However, 76 percent of those who agreed to the initial request or had been approached the first time complied with the second request.
- Participants were more willing to volunteer to construct a hiking trail if they had agreed to address envelopes for an environmental group than if they had not acceded to the initial request (Dillard, 1990a).
- Individuals were more likely to volunteer a large amount of time for a children's social skill project if they had initially assisted a child with a small request—helping an 8-year-old get candy from a candy machine (Rittle, 1981).

Emboldened by results like these, researchers have conducted over 100 studies of the FITD strategy. Meta-analytic, statistically based reviews of the research show that the effect is reliable and occurs more frequently than would be expected by chance (e.g., Dillard, Hunter, & Burgoon, 1984). Given its utility, professional persuaders—ranging from telemarketers to university alumni fundraisers—frequently employ FITD.

## Why Does It Work?

There are several reasons why the foot-in-the-door technique produces compliance (Burger, 1999). The first explanation calls on Bem's self-perception theory, described in Chapter 9. According to this view, individuals who perform a small favor for someone look at their behavior and infer that they are helpful, cooperative people. They become, in their own eyes, the kinds of people who do these sorts of things, go along with requests made by strangers, and cooperate with worthwhile causes (Freedman & Fraser, 1966, p. 201). Having formed this self-perception, they naturally accede to the second, larger request.

A second interpretation emphasizes consistency needs. Recalling that they agreed to the first request, individuals find it dissonant to reject the second, target request. Perhaps having formed the perception that they are helpful people, they feel motivated to behave in a way that is consistent with their newly formed view of themselves. In a sense, they may feel more committed to the requester or to the goal of helping others.

A third explanation places emphasis on social norms. "Being asked to perform an initial small request makes people more aware of the norm of social responsibility, a norm that prescribes that one should help those who are in need," William DeJong explains (1979, p. 2236).

## When Does It Work?

The FITD technique does not always produce compliance. It is particularly likely to work when the request concerns a pro-social issue, such as asking for a donation to charity or requesting favors from strangers. Self-perceptions, consistency needs, and social norms are likely to kick in under these circumstances. Foot-in-the-door is also more apt to succeed when the second query is "a continuation," or logical outgrowth, of the initial request, and when people actually perform the requested behavior (Burger, 1999; Dillard et al., 1984).

FITD is not so likely to succeed if the same persuader asks for a second favor immediately after having hit up people for a first request. The bang-bang, request-upon-request approach may create resentment, leading people to say no just to reassert their independence (Chartrand, Pinckert, & Burger, 1999).

Next time you do a favor for someone and are tempted to accede to a second, larger request, check to see if the facilitating factors operating in the situation match those just described. If they do, you may be more apt to go along with the request, and it may be one that you would rather decline.

## DOOR-IN-THE-FACE

This technique undoubtedly gets the award for the most memorable name in the Persuasion Tactics Hall of Fame. It occurs when a persuader makes a large request that is almost certain to be denied. After being turned down, the persuader returns with a smaller request, the target request the communicator had in mind at the beginning. Door-in-the-face (DITF) is exactly the opposite of foot-in-the-door. Foot-in-the-door starts with a small request and moves to a larger one. DITF begins with a large request and scales down to an appropriately modest request. Researchers study the technique by asking experimental group participants to comply with a large request, one certain to be denied. When they refuse, participants are asked if they would mind going along with a smaller, second request. Control group subjects receive only the second request.

The DITF technique has been tested in dozens of studies. It emerges reliably and dependably, meta-analytic studies tell us (O'Keefe & Hale, 1998). Consider the following supportive findings:

■ A volunteer, supposedly working for a local blood services organization, asked students if they would donate a unit of blood once every 2 months for a period of at least 3 years. Everyone declined this outlandish request. The volunteer then asked experimental group subjects if they would donate just one unit of blood between 8:00 a.m. and 3:30 p.m. the next day. Control group participants were asked the same question. Of those who rejected the first request, 49 percent agreed to donate blood, compared with 32 percent of those in the control group (Cialdini & Ascani, 1976).

■ An experimenter working with a boys and girls club asked students if they would mind spending about 15 hours a week tutoring children. When this request was declined, the experimenter asked if students would be willing to spend an afternoon taking kids to a museum or the movies. Students who turned down the initial request were more likely to agree to spend an afternoon with children than those who only heard the second request (O'Keefe & Figgé, 1999).

■ An individual claiming to represent a Californian company asked respondents if they would be willing to spend 2 hours answering survey questions on home or dorm safety. After the request was declined, the experimenter asked if individuals would mind taking 15 minutes to complete a small portion of the survey. Control group participants were asked only the second request. Of those who refused the first request, 44 percent agreed to partake in the shorter survey. By contrast, only 25 percent of control group subjects complied with the second request (Mowen & Cialdini, 1980).

## Why Does It Work?

Several rather interesting explanations for the DITF strategy have been advanced. One view emphasizes a powerful psychological factor akin to dissonance but more emotion packed: guilt. Individuals feel guilty about turning down the first request. To reduce guilt, an unpleasant feeling, they go along with the second request (O'Keefe & Figgé, 1999). There is some evidence that guilt helps explain DITF effects.

Another view emphasizes reciprocal concessions. As a persuader (deliberately) scales down his request, he is seen as having made a concession. This leads the persuadee to invoke the social rule that "you should make concessions to those who make concessions to you" or "you should meet the other fellow halfway." As a result, the persuadee yields and goes along with the second request (Cialdini, Vincent, Lewis, Catalan, Wheeler, & Darby, 1975; Rhoads & Cialdini, 2002; Turner, Tamborini, Limon, & Zuckerman-Hyman, 2007; see also Box 10.1).

Social judgment processes also operate in the DITF situation. The extreme first request functions as an anchor against which the second request is compared. After having heard the outrageous initial request, the second offer seems less costly and severe. However, control group participants who are asked to comply only with the smaller request do not have this anchor available to them. Thus, experimental group participants are more apt than control group subjects to go along with the target request.

Self-presentation concerns may also intervene. People fear that the persuader will evaluate them negatively for turning down the first request. Not realizing that the whole gambit has been staged, they accede to the second request to make themselves look good in the persuader's eyes.

## Box 10.1 | YOU SCRATCH MY WALLET AND I'LL FATTEN YOURS

One of the most venerable principles of interpersonal persuasion is social exchange. The idea is simple and familiar. Person A provides Person B with a tangible, material, or psychological reward. In exchange, when Person A approaches B with a request, B complies. Scholars discuss this under different conceptual umbrellas, such as reciprocation (Cialdini, 2001) and distributive justice (Homans, 1961), and self-interest satisfaction (West & Turner, 2010).

Although social exchange can produce positive outcomes, as when one person returns a favor spontaneously performed by another, it can also lead to exploitation and chicanery. Examples are numerous and run the gamut from radio payola to medical marketing. Consider:

In a case that ultimately attracted the attention of New York's attorney general, Sony BMG Music Entertainment arranged a series of payoffs to radio stations. Some years back, Sony purchased gifts for radio disc jockeys and paid stations for frequent airplay. The company gave the program director of a Greenville, North Carolina, radio station PlayStation 2 games and an out-of-town trip with his girlfriend. A blatant e-mail message from a Sony employee proclaimed, "We ordered a laptop for Donnie Micheals at WFLY in Albany. He has since moved to WHYI in Miami. We need to change the shipping address." One Sony executive considered a proposal to promote a song, "A.D.I.D.A.S" by Killer Mike, by sending radio DJs one Adidas sneaker; the second shoe would arrive when the station played the song 10 times! Sony's gambit was clear: by buying radio personalities computer games, sneakers, and laptops, the company hoped to persuade them to play their records more frequently (Leeds & Story, 2005, p. C4).

Other unseemly cases of social exchange have occurred in medical marketing. The drug maker Schering-Plough paid doctors large sums of money to prescribe the company's drug for hepatitis C. Schering threatened to remove any doctor from its consulting program if the physician wrote prescriptions for competing drugs or spoke favorably about competitors' treatments. Schering's tactics attracted the interest of federal prosecutors, who suspected that it was using payoffs to convince doctors to prescribe drugs that patients did not need (Harris, 2004).

In other cases, companies prefer the carrot to the stick. The drug companies Merck, Novartis, and Sankyo gave $700,000 to a medical society that used the money on a series of dinner lectures at Ruth's Chris Steak Houses. The main theme of the lectures was an expanded notion of high blood pressure that could increase the number of patients buying the companies' drugs. The lecturers argued for a new category of Stage 1 hypertension or incipient high blood pressure that could require the prescription of medications not uncoincidentally produced by the drug companies. A number of doctors saw through the drug companies' ploys and said so publicly. Yet the companies clearly hoped that both the dinner lectures and expanded definition of high blood pressure (developed by doctors who received grants from the firms) would expand the market for their medications (Saul, 2006).

## Box 10.1

"It's not quite brainwashing, but they have a way of influencing your thinking," a doctor said of drug companies' attempts to promote new drugs in another area of medicine (Santora, 2006, p. A13). "You're making (a doctor) money in several ways," explained one former sales manager at Merck, a major drug company. "You're paying him for the talk. You're increasing his referral base so he's getting more patients. And you're helping to develop his name. The hope in all this is that a silent quid quo pro is created. I've done so much for you, the only thing I need from you is that you write more of my products" (Harris & Roberts, 2007, p. A18).

In still another case, the Food and Drug Administration asked a group of medical experts whether they recommended banning several pain pills—Bextra, Celebrex, and Vioxx—that have been linked to life-threatening illnesses like heart attacks and strokes. The advisory panel recommended against banning the drugs. Yet 10 members of the group had received lucrative research grants from the drug companies. If these individuals had not cast their votes in favor of the drug companies, the panel would have recommended withdrawing the drugs from the market (Harris & Berenson, 2005).

Social exchange is powerful for two reasons. First, it capitalizes on the reciprocity norm—the notion that it is socially appropriate to return a favor that someone has bestowed upon you (Cialdini, 2001). Drug companies hope that doctors who have received free lunches, dinners, or consulting contracts will feel obligated to return the favor by prescribing the company's brand-name drugs. In other cases—such as the radio payola example—more nefarious motives are involved. This brings up the second factor underlying social exchange effects: a desire for rewards like money and status. By playing Sony's records, radio DJs received laptops and computer games. They went along to fatten their wallets, one of the oldest motives known to humankind. Social exchange thus lies at the borderline between persuasion and coercion because, in some instances, influence agents use thinly veiled threats, take advantage of their greater power over the other party, or impinge on the other individual's freedom of choice.

You may ask, "What is wrong with a little quid pro quo or the old I'll scratch your back if you scratch mine?" There is nothing wrong with this if opportunities for social exchange are equally available to all and no harm is done. But wealthier communicators have more resources at their disposal than poorer ones. Big record companies like Sony can throw money at disc jockeys; independent record producers don't have this luxury. Social exchanges also become morally suspect when participants violate the trust that observers place in the integrity of the exchange. Radio listeners reasonably presume that DJs select songs or doctors choose medications based on their merits, not on how much they are getting paid as a consulting fee. In such cases, exchange amounts to bribery and unravels the social fabric upon which ethical persuasion is based.

Unfortunately, these benefits have not been lost on unsavory marketers in business and politics, where influence-peddling scandals, kickback schemes, and corruption investigations reach into the highest levels of government.

## When Does It Work?

Like other persuasion factors discussed, the door-in-the-face technique is sensitive to contextual factors (Fern, Monroe, & Avila, 1986; O'Keefe & Hale, 1998). DITF works particularly well when the request concerns pro-social issues. People may feel guilty about turning down a charitable organization's request for a large donation or time expenditure. They can make things right by agreeing to the second request.

Door-in-the-face effects also emerge when the same individual makes both requests. People may feel an obligation to reciprocate a concession if they note that the person who asked for too much is scaling down her request. If two different people make the requests, the feeling that "you should make concessions to those who make concessions to you" may not kick in.

The DITF strategy is also more apt to work if there is only a short delay between the first and second requests. If too long a time passes between requests, the persuadee's guilt might possibly dissipate. In addition, the more time that passes between requests, the less salient is the contrast between the extreme first request and the seemingly more reasonable second request.

## APPLICATIONS

The foot-in-the-door and door-in-the-face techniques are regularly used by compliance professionals. Noting that you gave $25 to a charity last year, a volunteer asks if you might increase your gift to $50. A representative from the local newspaper calls and asks if you would like to take out a daily subscription. When you tell her you don't have time to read the paper every day, she asks, "How about Sunday?" Or the bank loan officer wonders if you can afford a $100 monthly payment on your student loan. When you decline, he asks if you can pay $50 each month, exactly the amount he had in mind from the beginning.

FITD and DITF, like all persuasion techniques, can be used for unethical, as well as morally acceptable, purposes. Unsavory telemarketers or front organizations posing as charities can manipulate people into donating money through adroit use of these tactics. At the same time, pro-social groups can employ these techniques to achieve worth-while goals. For example, a volunteer from MADD might use foot-in-the-door to induce bar patrons to sign a petition against drunk driving. Sometime later in the evening, the volunteer could ask patrons if they would agree to let a taxi take them home (Taylor & Booth-Butterfield, 1993). In the same fashion, charitable organizations such as the Red Cross or Purple Heart might employ door-in-the-face gently to arouse guilt that inevitably follows refusal of the initial request.

## OTHER COMPLIANCE TECHNIQUES

The foot-in-the-door and door-in-the-face strategies have generated the most research, and we know the most about when they work and why. Several other compliance tactics have been explored, and reviewing them offers insights into the canny ways that persuaders use communication to achieve their goals.

The first technique is *low-balling*. This gets its name from the observation that persuaders—typically car salespeople—try to secure compliance by "throwing the customer a low ball." In persuasion scholarship, low-balling has a precise meaning. It occurs when a persuader induces someone to comply with a request and then "ups the ante" by increasing the cost of compliance. Having made the initial decision to comply, individuals experience dissonance at the thought that they may have to back away from their commitment. Once individuals have committed themselves to a decision, they are loath to change their minds, even when the cost of a decision is raised significantly and unfairly (Cialdini, Cacioppo, Bassett, & Miller, 1978).

Low-balling is similar to foot-in-the-door in that the persuader begins with a small request and follows it up with a more grandiose alternative. In low-balling, though, the action initially requested is the target behavior; what changes is the cost associated with performing the target action. In the case of FITD, the behavior that the persuader asks the person to initially perform is a setup to induce the individual to comply with the larger, critical request.

Robert B. Cialdini and colleagues have conducted experiments demonstrating that low-balling can increase compliance. Their findings shed light on sales practices in the ever colorful, always controversial business of selling cars. As the authors explain:

> The critical component of the procedure is for the salesperson to induce the customer to make an *active decision* to buy one of the dealership's cars by offering an extremely good price, perhaps as much as $300 below competitors' prices. Once the customer has made the decision for a specific car (and has even begun completing the appropriate forms), the salesperson removes the price advantage in one of a variety of ways. For example, the customer may be told that the originally cited price did not include an expensive option that the customer had assumed was part of the offer. More frequently, however, the initial price offer is rescinded when the sales-person "checks with the boss," who does not allow the deal because "we'd be losing money." . . . In each instance, the result is the same: the reason that the customer made a favorable purchase decision is removed, and the performance of the target behavior (i.e., buying that specific automobile) is rendered more costly. The increased cost is such that the final price is equivalent to, or sometimes slightly above, that of the dealer's competitors. Yet, car dealership lore has it that more customers will remain with their decision to purchase the automobile, even at the adjusted figure, than would have bought it had the full price been revealed before a purchase decision had been obtained.

> (1978, p. 464; see Figure 10.1)

Another tactic that borrows from persuasion practitioners is the *"that's-not-all"* *technique*. You have probably heard TV announcers make claims like, "And that's not all—if you call now and place an order for this one-time only collection of sixties oldies, we'll throw in an extra rock and roll CD—so call right away!" Researcher Jerry M. Burger

**FIGURE 10.1** | Car salesmen have been known to use low-balling and a host of other interpersonal gambits to make a sale.

Photograph by William C. Rieter

capitalized on such real-life observations. He conceptualized and tested the effectiveness of the that's-not-all technique. In theory, Burger explained:

> The salesperson presents a product and a price but does not allow the buyer to respond immediately. Instead, after a few seconds of mulling over the price, the buyer is told "that's not all"; that is, there is an additional small product that goes along with the larger item, or that "just for you" or perhaps "today only" the price is lower than that originally cited. The seller, of course, had planned to sell the items together or at the lower price all along but allows the buyer to think about the possibility of buying the single item or the higher priced item first. Supposedly, this approach is more effective than presenting the eventual deal to the customer in the beginning.
>
> (1986, p. 277)

Burger demonstrated that the that's-not-all tactic can influence compliance. In one experiment, two researchers sat at tables that had a sign promoting the university psychology club's bake sale. Cupcakes were featured at the table. Individuals who wandered by sometimes expressed interest in the cupcakes, curious how much they cost. Those assigned to the experimental group were told that cupcakes cost 75¢ each. After listening to a seemingly impromptu conversation between the two experimenters, these individuals were told that the price included two medium-sized cookies. By contrast, subjects in the control group were shown the cookies when they inquired about the cost of the cupcakes. They were told that the package cost 75¢. Even though people got the same products for the identical cost in both conditions, more experimental group subjects purchased sweets (73 percent) than did control group subjects (40 percent).

Like door-in-the-face, that's-not-all works in part because of the reciprocity norm. We learn from an early age that when someone does a favor for us, we should do one in return. Participants in Burger's experimental group naively assumed the persuader had done them a favor by throwing in two cookies. Not knowing that this was part of the gambit, they acquiesced.

Yet another sequential influence tactic that is sometimes used is called fear-then-relief. This is somewhat different from the other techniques in that, in this case, the persuader deliberately places the recipient in a state of fear. Suddenly and abruptly, the persuader eliminates the threat, replaces fear with kind words, and asks the recipient to comply with a request. The ensuing relief pushes the persuadee to acquiesce.

Dolinski and Nawrat (1998) demonstrated fear-then-relief in several clever experiments. In one study, they arranged for jaywalking pedestrians to hear a policeman's whistle (actually produced by an experimenter hidden from view). People glanced nervously and walked quickly, fearing they had done something wrong. Twenty seconds later, they were approached by an experimenter who asked them if they would spend 10 minutes filling out a survey. These individuals were more likely to comply than those who did not hear the whistle. In another experiment, the researchers placed a piece of paper that resembled a parking ticket behind a car's windshield wiper. When drivers arrived at their cars, they experienced that telltale feeling of fear on noticing what looked to be a parking ticket. In fact, the paper was a leaflet that contained an appeal for blood donations. As drivers' anxiety was replaced with reassurance, an experimenter asked them if they would mind taking 15 minutes to complete a questionnaire. Sixty-eight percent of experimental group subjects complied with the request, compared with 36 percent of control group participants.

Fear-then-relief works for two reasons. First, the relief experienced when the threat is removed is reinforcing. It becomes associated with the second request, leading to more compliance. Second, the ensuing relief places people in a state of "temporary mindlessness." Preoccupied with the danger they nearly fell into and their own supposed carelessness, individuals are distracted. They are less attentive and more susceptible to the persuader's request.

The technique has interesting implications for a powerful domain of persuasion, yet one infrequently discussed—interrogation of prisoners. We often think that compliance with captors results from the induction of terror and fear. Fear-then-relief suggests that a more subtle, self-persuasion dynamic is in operation. Captors initially scream at a prisoner, threaten him or her with torture, and begin to hurt the prisoner physically. Suddenly, the abuse ends and is replaced by a softer tone and a nice voice. In some cases, "the sudden withdrawal of the source of anxiety intensifies compliance" (Dolinski & Nawrat, 1998, p. 27; Schein, 1961).

Fear-then-relief is used in peacetime situations too—by parents, teachers, and other authority figures who replace the stick quickly with a carrot. Like other tactics (e.g., Aune & Basil, 1994) it capitalizes on the element of surprise, which succeeds in disrupting people's normal defenses. Surprise is the key in an additional technique that psychologists have studied, one no doubt used by compliance professionals. Known as the *pique technique*, it involves "making the request in an unusual and atypical manner so that the target's interest is piqued, the refusal script is disrupted, and the target is induced to think positively about compliance" (Santos, Leve, & Pratkanis, 1994, p. 756). In an experimental demonstration of the technique, Santos and colleagues reported that students posing as panhandlers received more money from passersby when they asked, "Can you spare 17¢ (or 37¢)?" than when they asked if the people could spare a quarter or any change. When was the last time that a panhandler asked you for 37¢? Never happened, right? Therein lies the ingenuity—and potential lure—of the pique technique.

The pique procedure works because it disrupts our normal routine. It engages and consumes the conscious mind, thereby diverting it from the resistance that typically follows a persuader's request. Disruption of conscious modes of thought plays a critical role in acquiescence to persuasion, in the view of psychologist Eric S. Knowles and colleagues (2001). Knowles emphasizes that persuaders succeed when they devise clever, subtle ways to break down our resistance (see Box 10.2). He and his colleagues have shown that persuaders can disrupt resistance by subtly changing the wording of requests. Employing what they call the *disrupt-then-reframe technique*, Knowles and his colleagues have shown that they can dramatically increase compliance by first mildly disrupting "the ongoing script of a persuasive request" and then reframing the request or encouraging the listener to "understand the issue in a new way" (Knowles, Butler, & Linn, 2001, p. 50).

In the bold tradition of interpersonal persuasion research, the researchers went door to door selling Christmas cards. They explained that money from the sales would go—as indeed it did—to a nonprofit center that helps developmentally disabled children and adults. The experimenters told some residents that the price of a Christmas card package was $3. They informed others that the price was $3 and then added, "It's a bargain." In the key disrupt-then-reframe condition, the experimenter stated, "This package of cards sells for 300 pennies" (thereby shaking up the normal script for a door-to-door request). She then added, after pausing, "That's $3. It's a bargain" (reframe). Of respondents who purchased cards, 65 percent were in the disrupt-then-reframe treatment, compared to 35 percent in the other groups. Other experiments obtained similar findings, demonstrating that a small, but subtle, variation in a persuasive request can produce dramatic differences in compliance (Davis & Knowles, 1999).

## Summary

All the techniques discussed in this section play on what Freedman and Fraser called "compliance without pressure." They are soft-sell, not hardball, tactics that worm their way through consumers' defenses, capitalizing on social norms, emotions, and sly

## Box 10.2 | RESISTANCE AND COMPLIANCE

This chapter has focused on how communicators convince other people to comply with their requests. Another way of looking at this is to ask: How can communicators overcome others' resistance to their persuasive requests? Knowles and colleagues (2001) argue that resistance plays a key role in persuasion. They point out that most interpersonal persuasion research has focused on devising ways to make a message more appealing rather than on the obverse: figuring out how best to overcome people's resistance to persuasive messages. By understanding why individuals resist messages, researchers can do a better job of helping them go along with socially beneficial communications. (What goes around comes around. This approach bears resemblance to Lewin's (1951) attitude change model of "unfreezing, change, and refreezing." First, people "unfreeze" an attitude, opening themselves up to persuasion. Next they change the attitude and finally they "refreeze" or internalize the new attitude on the topic. See also Saxe & Chazan, 2008.)

There are many aspects to resistance. One issue is how people resist messages: Do they systematically think through all the weak points of the message, or does resistance operate more peripherally, as when someone simply refuses to listen to a speaker because of religious or ethnic differences? Are some people more resistant to persuasion than others—that is, more inclined to reject a position, regardless of the merits of the arguments (Briñol, Rucker, Tormala, & Petty, 2004). What are the most effective ways to overcome resistance?

Scholarly research suggests that persuaders can neutralize resistance in several ways, including: (a) framing the message to minimize resistance, (b) acknowledging and confronting resistance head-on, (c) reframing the message, and (d) disrupting resistance to the message (Knowles & Linn, 2004). These ideas have practical applications. Consider once again the case of an adolescent who wants to practice safe sex, but is afraid to request it, for fear the suggestion will spark resistance from his or her partner. The traditional approach is to suggest message arguments, cues, and source characteristics that would change the partner's mind. The resistance perspective takes a different tack, making use of the following strategies and appeals:

**Strategy**

- Framing the message to minimize resistance
- Acknowledging and confronting resistance to condoms
- Reframing the message
- Disrupting and distracting resistance (through humor)

**Safe Sex Appeal**

- "Please do this for me. I'd feel more comfortable and secure if we'd use condoms tonight."
- "You say you don't want to talk about condoms. But we've always valued talking and being open about how we feel. Let's talk about this." "You say using condoms turns

**Box 10.2** |

you off. But think how free and unrestrained we'll feel with no worries about sex or pregnancy."

■ "I have these condoms that a friend of mine sent me from Tijuana that have those Goodyear radial ribs on them that will drive you wild."

Comments adapted from Adelman, M. B., 1992. In T. Edgar, M. A. Fitzpatrick, & V. S. Freimuth (Eds.), *AIDS: A communication perspective* (p. 82). Hillsdale, NJ: Lawrence Erlbaum Associates; and Kelly, J. A., 1995. *Changing HIV risk behavior: Practical strategies* (p. 99). New York: Guilford.

Safe sex is not the only example of persuasion overcoming resistance. The resistance approach can be applied to numerous social contexts. While working on this chapter, I ran into an older man I knew. We began talking and, knowing I was an educator, he told me of a discussion between a high school teacher and his student, a teenage girl. The male teacher thought the girl, who dressed scantily showing a lot of flesh, should attend school in more dignified outfits. He called her into his office and asked if she would dress more appropriately for his sake. He explained that it would please him a great deal—make him very happy—if she dressed more suitably. Would she do this? It would make such a difference to him. The next time the teacher saw the girl, he observed that she was dressed in a more appropriate manner. Had he approached the issue directly—criticized her outfits and explained why she must dress more formally—she would have dismissed him as an old-fashioned teacher out of step with the times. But by sidestepping resistance and redefining the relationship as between two human beings—not teacher and student— he neutralized resistance, helped her see the issue from a different light, and changed her behavior.

disruption of ordinary routines. Used adroitly by canny professionals, they can be remarkably effective. Just ask anyone who is still kicking himself or herself for yielding to a series of requests that sounded innocent at the time, but ended up costing the person a pretty penny.

## COMPLIANCE-GAINING

You want to dine out with someone, but you disagree about which restaurant it is going to be; someone in the department must do an unpleasant job, but you want to make sure that in any case it will not be you; you want to make new work arrangements, but you are afraid your boss will not agree; you want to get your partner to come with you to that tedious family party, but you suspect that he or she does not want to come along.

(van Knippenberg, van Knippenberg, Blaauw, & Vermunt, 1999, p. 806)

Add to these more serious requests for compliance: an effort to convince a close friend to return to school after having dropped out for a couple of years, a doctor's attempt to persuade a seriously overweight patient to pursue an exercise program, a lover's effort to persuade a partner to practice safe sex. Such requests, initiatives, and serious attempts to influence behavior are pervasive in everyday life. They speak to the strong interest human beings have in getting their way—that is, in persuading others to comply with their requests and pleas. This section of the chapter moves from an exploration of how professional persuaders achieve their goals to an examination of us—how we try to gain compliance in everyday life. The area of research is appropriately called compliance-gaining.

Compliance-gaining is defined as "any interaction in which a message source attempts to induce a target individual to perform some desired behavior that the target otherwise might not perform" (Wilson, 2002, p. 4). Notice that the focus of compliance-gaining is on communication. It examines not only the psychology of the individual's request for compliance, but also the broader interaction, the dyadic (one-on-one) conversation between people, or among individuals. This is important because it calls attention to the dynamic interpersonal dance that characterizes so much of everyday persuasion. Interpersonal communication scholars, who have pioneered research in this area, have sought to understand how individuals try to get others to go along with their requests in social situations. They have probed the strategies people use, the impact of context on compliance-gaining strategies, and the goals individuals pursue to gain compliance from others.

One of the daunting issues researchers face is how to study so broad an area as compliance-gaining empirically. They could devise experiments of the sort conducted by psychologists researching foot-in-the-door and door-in-the-face. Although these would allow researchers to test hypotheses, they would not tell them how compliance-gaining works in the real world that lies outside the experimenter's laboratory. Scholars could observe people trying to gain compliance—on the job, at school, or in social settings like bars (that might be fun!). However, this would provide an endless amount of data, too much to code meaningfully. Dissatisfied with these methodologies, scholars hit on the idea of conducting surveys that ask people how they would gain compliance, either in situations suggested by the researcher or in an open-ended manner, in the individuals' own words.

The first survey method is *closed ended* in that it provides individuals with hypothetical situations and asks them to choose among various strategies for compliance. For example, researchers have asked participants to imagine that they have been carrying on a close relationship with a person of the opposite sex for 2 years. Unexpectedly, an old acquaintance happens to be in town one evening. Desirous of getting together with their old friend, but mindful that their current boyfriend or girlfriend is counting on getting together that night, respondents are asked to indicate how they would try to convince their current steady to let them visit their former acquaintance (Miller, Boster, Roloff, & Seibold, 1977). Subjects have also been asked to imagine that their neighbors, whom they do not know very well, own a dog who barks almost all night. This in turn incites the other local canines to do the same. Students are asked how they would attempt to convince the neighbors to curb their dog's nighttime antics (Cody, McLaughlin, & Jordan, 1980). Individuals are provided with a list of strategies, such as friendly appeals, moral arguments, manipulative tactics, and threats. They are asked to indicate on a Likert scale how likely they would be to use these techniques.

A second method is *open ended.* Research participants are asked to write a short essay on how they get their way. Invited to be frank and honest, they describe in their own words how they try to gain compliance from others (Falbo, 1977).

Each technique has benefits and drawbacks. The closed-ended selection technique provides an efficient way to gather information. It also provides insights on how people try to gain compliance in representative life situations. Its drawback is that people frequently give socially desirable responses to closed-ended surveys. They are reluctant to admit that they sometimes use brutish, socially inappropriate tactics to get their way (Burleson, Wilson, Waltman, Goering, Ely, & Whaley, 1988).

The strength of the open-ended method is that it allows people to indicate, in their own words, how they get compliance; there is no speculation about hypothetical behavior in artificial situations. A drawback is that researchers must make sense of—and categorize—subjects' responses. This can be difficult and time consuming. Scholars may not fully capture or appreciate the individuals' thought processes.

Despite their limitations, when taken together, open- and closed-ended questionnaires have provided useful insights about compliance-gaining. Researchers, using both types of procedures, have devised a variety of typologies to map out the techniques people use to gain compliance. These typologies have yielded insights about the major strategies individuals (at least on American college campuses) use to influence others. Strategies can be classified according to whether they are:

1. *Direct versus indirect.* Direct techniques include assertion (voicing one's wishes loudly) and persistence (reiterating one's point). Indirect tactics include "emotion-target" (putting the other person in a good mood) and thought manipulation (trying to get your way by making the other person feel it is his idea) (Falbo, 1977; see also Dillard, Kinney, & Cruz, 1996).
2. *Rational versus nonrational.* Rational techniques include reason (arguing logically) and exchange of favors (for a detailed discussion, see Cialdini, 2001). Nonrational tactics include deceit (fast talking and lying) and threat (telling her I will never speak to her again if she doesn't do what I want) (Falbo, 1977).
3. *Hard versus soft.* Hard tactics include yelling, demanding, and verbal aggression. Soft techniques include kindness, flattery, and flirting (Kipnis & Schmidt, 1996).
4. *Dominance-based versus non-dominance-based.* Dominance-oriented strategies emphasize the power the communicator has over the target, while the latter employ a more egalitarian, conciliatory approach (Dillard, Wilson, Tusing, & Kinney, 1997).
5. *External versus internal.* Tactics can be externally focused, such as rewards or punishments. To motivate a child to study, a parent could use a carrot, like promise ("I'll raise your allowance if you study more"), or a stick, like aversive stimulation ("You're banned from driving until you hit the books"). Techniques can also be

internally focused—that is, self-persuasion-type appeals directed at the message recipient's psyche. These include positive self-feeling ("You'll feel good about yourself if you study a lot") and negative self-feeling ("You'll be disappointed with yourself in the long run if you don't study more"; see Marwell & Schmitt, 1967; Miller & Parks, 1982).

Notice that the same techniques can be categorized in several ways. Threat could be direct, nonrational, hard, and external. Positive self-feeling could be indirect, rational, and soft, as well as internal. This cross-categorization occurs because there is not one but a variety of compliance-gaining taxonomies, constructed by different scholars, for different purposes. Nonetheless, these five sets of labels provide a useful way of categorizing compliance-gaining behavior.

## Contextual Influences

People are complex creatures. They use different techniques to gain compliance, depending on the situation. In one situation, a person may use reason; in another she may scream and yell, employing verbal aggression. We are all chameleons to a degree. Which situations are the most critical determinants of compliance-gaining? Scholars have studied this issue, delineating a host of important contextual influences on strategy selection. The following factors are especially important.

**Intimacy**. Contexts differ in the degree to which they involve intimate associations between persuader and persuadee. As you move along the continuum from stranger to acquaintance to friend to lover or family member, you find that the same individual can behave very differently, depending on which of these "others" the person is trying to influence. In an old but still engaging study, Fitzpatrick and Winke (1979) reported that level of intimacy predicted use of conflict-reducing strategies. Focusing on people casually involved in romantic relationships, those in serious relationships, and married partners, the investigators found that married persons were especially likely to employ emotional appeals or personal rejections ("withholding affection and acting cold until he or she gives in") to resolve differences.

"You always hurt the one you love," Fitzpatrick and Winke observed. They explained:

> Individuals in a more committed relationship generally have less concern about the strengths of the relational bonds. Consequently, they employ more spontaneous and emotionally toned strategies in their relational conflicts . . . In the less committed relationships, the cohesiveness of the partners is still being negotiated . . . Undoubtedly, it would be too risky for them to employ the more open conflict strategies of the firmly committed.
>
> (1979, p. 10)

This is not to say that everyone uses more emotional or highly manipulative tactics in intimate settings than in everyday interpersonal encounters. These findings emerged from one study, conducted at one point in time. However, research indicates that intimacy exerts an important impact on compliance-gaining behavior (Cody & McLaughlin, 1980).

**Dependency**. We use different strategies to gain compliance, depending on whether we are dependent on the person we are trying to influence. People are more reluctant to use hard tactics when the other has control over important outcomes in their lives (van Knippenberg et al., 1999). Graduate teaching assistants who say they "dominate arguments" and "argue insistently" with disgruntled undergraduate students acknowledge that they prefer to use nonconfrontational techniques, even sidestepping disagreements, when discussing job-related conflicts with the professor (Putnam & Wilson, 1982). It is only natural to be more careful when trying to gain compliance from those who have control over important outcomes in your life. Thus, when people lack power, they are more likely to employ rational and indirect tactics "because no other power base is available to them" (Cody & McLaughlin, 1985).

**Rights**. People employ different tactics to get their way, depending on whether they believe they have the right to pursue a particular option. If they do not feel they have the moral right to make a request, they may use soft tactics. However, if they believe they have the right to make a request, or if they feel they have been treated unfairly, they are more apt to employ hard rather than soft techniques (van Knippenberg et al., 1999). Consider the marked change in tactics employed by people trying to convince smokers to quit smoking in public places. Decades ago, individuals who objected to smokers polluting public space said little, afraid they would offend smokers. Nowadays, nonsmokers, redefining the meaning of public space and feeling they have the right to insist that smokers not puff in public, frequently use uncompromising, even nonrational, tactics to induce smokers to put out a cigarette. This change in compliance-gaining strategies resulted from years of social protest against smoking. Protests against problematic social norms, and subsequent changes in the law, can empower ordinary people, encouraging them to use feistier techniques to get their way.

**Other situational factors**. Situations also vary in the degree to which (a) the compliance benefits the persuader, (b) the influence attempt has consequences for the relationship between persuader and persuadee, and (c) the target resists the influence attempt (Cody & McLaughlin, 1980). Resistance is particularly important, as people frequently reject persuaders' appeals. Persuaders must adjust their strategy to take resistance into account, although inexperienced communicators are often flummoxed by the recipient's refusal to go along with their request.

## Individual Differences

In addition to situations, personality and individual difference factors influence compliance-gaining. Individuals differ dramatically in how they go about trying to get their way. Some people are direct; others are shy. Some individuals worry a great deal about hurting others' feelings; other individuals care not a whit. Some people respect social conventions; other people disregard them. Consider, for example, how sharply people differ on the rather pedestrian matter of inducing someone to repay a loan. Min-Sun Kim and Steven R. Wilson (1994), in a theoretical study of interpersonal persuasion, listed ways that different individuals might formulate this request. They include:

> I have run out of cash.
>
> I could use the money I loaned you.
>
> Can I ask you to repay the loan?
>
> Would you mind repaying the loan?
>
> You'll repay the loan, won't you?
>
> I'd like you to repay the loan.
>
> You must repay the loan.
>
> Repay the loan.
>
> (Kim & Wilson, pp. 214–215)

If individuals differ in their compliance-gaining strategies, can research elucidate or specify the differences? You bet! Scholars have focused on three factors that reliably produce individual differences in compliance-gaining: *culture, gender, and self-monitoring.*

One important aspect of culture is the degree to which the society emphasizes individualism or collectivism. Individualism stresses independence, self-determination, and pursuit of one's self-interest. Collectivism emphasizes concern with group harmony, maintaining positive interpersonal relationships, and a "we" rather than "I" identification. Western nations like the United States are individualistic, while Asian societies, such as South Korea and Japan, tend to be more collectivist.

In intriguing studies, Min-Sun Kim and colleagues have found that culture influences choice of compliance-gaining strategies. When asked to identify the most important determinants of whether a request is effective, South Korean students emphasized the degree to which the request is sensitive to the other individual's feelings and does not create disapproval. By contrast, U.S. students maintained that a request is more effective when it is made as clearly and directly as possible. South Korean students regard an indirect strategy like hinting as relatively effective for gaining compliance, while American students put a higher premium on direct statements (Kim & Bresnahan, 1994; Kim & Wilson, 1994). Naturally, there are additional differences within Western and Asian cultures that complicate matters. Regardless of country of origin, students whose self-concepts revolve around independence place more emphasis on being direct. Students whose self-concepts center on group harmony put a higher premium on not hurting the other individual's feelings (Kim & Sharkey, 1995).

Gender also influences compliance-gaining. Largely due to socialization and enculturation, women are more likely than men to use polite tactics and to employ powerless speech (Baxter, 1984; Timmerman, 2002). As noted in Chapter 7, these can reduce persuasive effectiveness. In addition, men use more competitive strategies to settle conflict; women rely more on compromise (Gayle, Preiss, & Allen, 1994). But these between-gender differences are not large. Important as gender differences are, it is important to remember that there are also differences within gender: some men are extremely sensitive to another's feelings, while others are brutish; women vary greatly in the degree to which they are aggressive or reticent to intrude on another's face.

A third factor that influences compliance-gaining is the personality factor, self-monitoring. High self-monitors, attuned as they are to the requirements of the situation, tend to adapt their strategy to fit the person they are trying to influence (Caldwell & Burger, 1997). Low self-monitors are more apt to use the same technique with different people. High self-monitors are more likely to develop elaborate strategic plans prior to the actual influence attempt (Jordan & Roloff, 1997). In keeping with their concern with image management, high self-monitors are more apt than low self-monitors to include in their plans a consideration of how they could manipulate their personal impression to achieve their goals.

## Complications

The roles that situational and individual difference factors play in compliance-gaining are interesting and complex. People have multiple, sometimes conflicting, goals they want to accomplish in a particular situation (Dillard, 1990b). What's more, people are always balancing various aspects of the intrapersonal and interpersonal context: they want to maintain their autonomy, yet need approval from others (Brown & Levinson, 1987). They want to get their way, but recognize that this can threaten another's image, autonomy, or "face" (Wilson, Aleman, & Leatham, 1998). They don't want to hurt the other's feelings, but recognize that if they are too nice they may kill the clarity of their request with politeness and ambiguity.

Individuals frequently must balance their desire to achieve a *primary goal*—influencing the target's behavior—with an attempt to meet a *secondary goal* also, such as maintaining a good public impression, not damaging a friendship, or doing the morally right thing (Dillard, Segrin, & Harden, 1989; Wilson, 2002). There is a yin and yang between primary goals, which push the persuader toward action, and secondary goals, which pull or constrain the individual from going too far. We all have been in situations where we want to get our way, but realize that if we are too argumentative or dismissive of the other person's feelings, we will destroy a valued relationship.

Scholars have studied how people process these matters and go about balancing conflicting needs. Their models emphasize that people have elaborate cognitive structures regarding compliance-gaining and ways to achieve their goals (Wilson, 1999). This is fascinating because we all go about the business of trying to get our way, but rarely give any thought to how we think about trying to gain compliance or how we process, in our own minds, "all that stuff going on in the situation." Interpersonal communication models and research shed light on such issues.

Researchers find that when people possess incompatible goals—such as trying to convince a target to do something she most definitely does not want to do, while at the same time not hurting her feelings in the slightest—they pause more and don't communicate as effectively (Greene, McDaniel, Buksa, & Ravizza, 1993). The incongruity of goals puts stress on the mental system. For example, students sometimes are required to do group projects in which individuals' grades are based in part or entirely on the group grade on the project. One student in the group invariably does not pull his weight, and other members of the group must balance their desire to demand that the slacker do his job against a politeness norm. Should they tell the slacker off and risk offending him? Should they say nothing but put their own grade in jeopardy? The context involves conflicting goals and cross-pressures. If they opt to say something, they worry about offending the other person. Yet, if they strive to balance bluntness with politeness, they fear they may become tongue-tied. There is a lot going on interpersonally here, and communication scholars have explored the dynamics of situations like this. Research suggests that in America where directness norms operate, group members will be more effective if they come directly to the point, rather than beating around the bush.

Other studies also pinpoint ways to increase interpersonal persuasive effectiveness. Research on successful influence agents indicates that these individuals typically have greater knowledge of the strategies that are most likely to produce compliance, and are also capable of quickly adjusting their behavior to accommodate the changing needs of others (Jordan & Roloff, 1997). They also plan their strategies in advance, consider the obstacles they may face, and figure out how they can overcome them. Taking a chapter from high self-monitors' playbook, they even visualize the personal impressions they want to convey to their audience.

Effective persuaders bring a rich storehouse of cognitive information to the encounter. They employ many psychological dimensions when explaining others' actions, appreciate the perspective of the person they are trying to influence, and simultaneously consider multiple, even conflicting, goals (see Wilson, 2002). They vary their strategies to fit the individual and situation, much as the long-distance runner adjusts his or her stride to fit the peaks and valleys of a particular terrain.

## Summary, Criticisms, and Applications

Compliance-gaining is a fascinating area to explore. One of its most interesting dimensions is the display of diverse tactics people use to get their way. Ask a group of friends how they get their way some time, and you will find that some people say they use logic, persistently explaining why their point of view is better, while others are emotional persuaders, making the other person feel guilty or putting on a sad face to pull on the persuadee's heartstrings. And then there are the rhetorical barracudas, who use every argument they can or irritate the other person until he yields out of utter exhaustion. By studying compliance-gaining, we can gain insights into our own influence techniques, as well as those of others.

Research has helped to identify generic compliance-gaining strategies, pinpointed the role situations play, and called attention to how personality, gender, and culture influence the choice of compliance-gaining techniques. Like any academic area, compliance-gaining studies can be criticized on various grounds. To their credit, inter-personal communication scholars have been particularly assertive in pointing out key limitations in this research. They have lamented that compliance-gaining strategies are frequently defined ambiguously, inconsistently, or so specifically that it is difficult to know what the strategies mean (Kellermann & Cole, 1994; see also Wilson, 2002). Critics have also noted that much of the research involves responses to hypothetical situations, rather than actual compliance-gaining behavior. In addition, compliance-gaining offers few theoretical predictions to explain or predict communicative choices.

The compliance-gaining glass is not all empty, however. This line of research has provided a needed corrective to social psychological experiments, such as foot-in-the-door, that examine persuasion practitioners. Compliance-gaining research delightfully and importantly focuses on how ordinary people gain compliance in everyday life. Studies also explore the interpersonal unit rather than the individual or the cognitions of the indi-vidual persuader. Finally, compliance-gaining research has generated insights on a variety of intriguing or socially significant problems. These run the gamut from the amusing— how individuals try to convince police not to give them traffic tickets (see Box 10.3) —to the serious: communication between airline pilots about how to navigate bad weather (see Box 10.4). What's more, compliance-gaining research distinguishes itself by sug-gesting implications for health, including how doctors can improve their style of communicating medical information (Burgoon, Parrott, Burgoon, Birk, Pfau, & Coker, 1989) and how young people can secure compliance in the dicey realm of safe sex.

The last domain is particularly relevant in the wake of evidence that many otherwise cautious young people are reluctant to use condoms (Perloff, 2001). College students admit that once a relationship gets serious, condom use seems to drop off. Young people incorrectly believe that a monogamous relationship is safe, and they are concerned that initiating safer-sex behavior might threaten trust or intimacy. Women are sometimes reluctant to propose condom use because they fear it will reduce their attractiveness or trigger angry responses from guys. Men fear that broaching the condom topic will make them seem less "macho" in women's eyes or will give women a chance to reject their sexual advances (Bryan, Aiken, & West, 1999). Safe sex is clearly a context in which people must balance multiple goals, including convincing a partner to use a condom, showing respect for the other person, and not damaging the relationship. These conversa-tions occur in a situation laden with emotion and sexual arousal.

Research offers some clues about how to help young people better navigate the arousing, yet treacherous, domain of safer sex. One intriguing study of students' condom use concluded that "all one needs to do is to bring up the topic of AIDS or condoms in order to get a partner to use a condom" (Reel & Thompson, 1994, p. 137; see also Motley & Reeder, 1995). Other researchers—noting that for many women unsafe sex allows them to enjoy a myth that theirs will always be a faithful, monogamous relationship—suggest that "condoms could be represented as symbolic of the true and loving relationships that many women strive for rather than as necessary armor to protect against partners who will surely cheat" (Sobo, 1995, p. 185).

## Box 10.3 | COMPLIANCE AND THE COPS

You're driving home one evening, speeding a little because you've got to get ready for a party later that night. The radio's blaring and you're feeling good as you tap your fingers and sing the words of a song you've heard many times before. Out of the corner of your eye you see a couple of lights, but ignore them until you see them again—the telltale flashing light of a police car. Your heart skips a beat as you realize the police car is following you. The siren is sounding now and you get that terrible sinking feeling and agonizing fear that something bad is going to happen.

At this point, many of us faced with the impending possibility of a speeding ticket search our minds ferociously for an excuse, an extenuating reason, a white or black lie, a rhetorical rabbit we can pull out of the hat to convince the officer not to give us a ticket. Of course, in an ideal world, if one ran afoul of the law, he or she would admit it and graciously take responsibility for the mistake. But this is not an ideal world, and most of us are probably more willing to shade the truth a little than to come clean and suffer the indemnity of a fine and points on our record. Thus, many people try to persuade the police officer not to ticket them, relying on a variety of compliance-gaining techniques.

How do people try to secure compliance from a police officer when they are stopped for traffic violations? Jennifer Preisler and Todd Pinetti, students in a communication class some years back, explored this issue by talking with many young people who had found themselves in this predicament.

Their research, along with my own explorations, uncovered some interesting findings, including the following responses from young people regarding how they have tried to persuade a police officer not to ticket them:

■ "I will be extra nice and respectful to the officer. I will apologize for my negligence and error. I tell them about the police officers I know."

■ "I flirt my way out of it, smile a lot. [Or I say] 'My speedometer is broken. Honestly, it hasn't worked since August.'"

■ "When I am stopped for speeding, I usually do not try to persuade the officer to not give me a ticket. He has the proof that I was speeding, so I don't try to insult his intelligence by making up some stupid excuse. I do try to look very pathetic and innocent, hoping maybe he will feel bad for me and not give me a ticket."

■ "I turn on the dome light and turn off the ignition, roll down the window no matter how cold it is outside. I put my keys, driver's license, and proof of insurance on the dashboard, and put my hands at 10 and 2 on the wheel. I do all this before the officer gets to the window. I am honest and hope for the best. I have tried three times and all three were successful."

■ "The officer said, 'I've been waiting for an idiot like you [who he could pull over for speeding] all night.' I told him, 'Yeah, I got here as fast as I could.' He laughed for about two minutes straight and let us go."

**Box 10.3** |

■ "I gain compliance by smiling [big] and saying, 'Officer, what seems to be the problem? I'm on my way to church.'"

■ "The line that I have used to get out of a ticket is 'My wife's in labor.'"

■ "My technique is when I am getting pulled over, I reach into my glove compartment and spray a dab of hair spray onto my finger. Then I put it in my eyes and I start to cry. I have gotten pulled over about 15 to 20 times and I have only gotten one ticket."

Many people suspect that sex intervenes—that is, male police officers are more forgiving of females than of males who violate a traffic law. Research bears this out. Male police officers issued a greater percentage of citations to male drivers than did female police officers. In a similar fashion, female police officers issued a greater percentage of their traffic citations to female drivers than did male officers (Koehler & Willis, 1994). Police officers may be more lenient with opposite-sex than same-sex offenders; they may find the arguments provided by opposite-sex individuals to be more persuasive because they are attracted sexually to the drivers. Or they may be less apt to believe excuses offered by members of their own gender.

# ETHICAL ISSUES

"Communication is founded on a presumption of truth," two scholars aptly note (Buller & Burgoon, 1996, p. 203). Yet persuasion commonly involves some shading of truth, a tinting that is rationalized by persuaders and lamented by message receivers. Interpersonal persuasion—from the sequential influence techniques discussed earlier in the chapter to the endless variety of compliance-gaining tactics just described—sometimes seems to put a premium on distorting communication in the service of social influence. Distorting communication in the service of social influence? A blunter, more accurate way to describe this is "lying."

Lying is remarkably common in everyday life. In two diary studies, college students reported that they told two lies a day. They admitted they lied in one of every three of their social interactions (DePaulo, Kashy, Kirkendol, Wyer, & Epstein, 1996). To be sure, some of these lies were told to protect other people from embarrassment, loss of face, or having their feelings hurt. However, other lies were told to enhance the psychological state of the liars—for example, to make the liars appear better than they were, to protect them from looking bad, or to protect their privacy. Many of these were white lies that we have told ourselves; others were darker distortions, outright falsehoods (DePaulo et al., 1996).

Persuasion—from sequential influence tactics to compliance gaining—is fraught with lies. Even flattery involves a certain amount of shading of truth, a convention that many people admittedly enjoy and cherish (Stengel, 2000). All this has stimulated

## Box 10.4 | COMPLIANCE-GAINING IN THE SKIES

Employing hypothetical scenarios, a methodology familiar to compliance-gaining researchers, two researchers asked airplane pilots to imagine that the weather radar showed heavy precipitation ahead and that the plane had encountered moderate turbulence (cf. Gladwell, 2008). Pilots were asked how they would communicate this information to a fellow pilot to make sure he or she switches course and avoids the bad weather conditions. Would they be direct, issuing a command ("Turn 30 degrees right.")? Or would they use a softer approach like a query ("Which direction would you like to deviate?")? Or would they be even more indirect, going with a hint ("That return at 25 miles looks mean.")?

Pilots and subordinates communicated in dramatically different ways, in line with research on relational power (Cody & McLaughlin, 1985). Captains, the pilots in charge, said they would use a command. Speaking to subordinates, they had no concern about coming off frank or blunt. The second-in-command pilots, recognizing that they were speaking to their superiors, chose the weakest alternative: the hint (Gladwell, 2008). What is disturbing about this, writer Malcolm Gladwell observes, is that "a hint is the hardest kind of request to decode and the easiest to refuse" (p. 195). He recalls a tragic 1982 crash near Washington D.C., in which the subordinate pilot attempted on three occasions to inform the captain that there was a dangerous amount of ice on the wings of the plane. The black box recording sadly showed that the subordinate used only the mildest of requests: three hints.

> *Subordinate Pilot*: Look how the ice is just hanging on his, ah, back, back there, see that? . . . See all those icicles on the back there and everything? . . . Boy, this is a, this is a losing battle here on trying to de-ice those things, it (gives) you a false feeling of security, that's all that does . . .

> The last thing the subordinate pilot says to the captain, just before the plane plunges into the Potomac River, is not a hint, a suggestion, or a command. It's a simple statement of fact—and this time the captain agrees with him.

> *Subordinate Pilot*: Larry, we're going down, Larry.

> *Captain*: I know it.

> (Adapted from Gladwell, 2008, p. 196)

By choosing to be unassertive and employing only the mildest of compliance-gaining tactics, the subordinate failed to alert the senior pilot of a danger that could have been avoided. A solution, according to researchers who have studied this phenomenon, is to offer more assiduous crew management training: Compliance-Gaining 101. The results have been positive. Aviation safety experts believe that the training regimen accounts for the large decline in airplane accidents over the past decade.

considerable debate among philosophers over the years. As discussed in Chapter 1, utili-
tarians argue that a lie must be evaluated in terms of its consequences:

Did it produce more negative than positive consequences? More generally, does the
institution of lying generate more costs than benefits for society? Deontological thinkers
tend to disapprove of lies in principle because they distort truth. Related approaches
emphasize that what matters is the motivation of the liar—a lie told for a good, virtuous
end may be permissible under some circumstances (Gass & Seiter, 2003).

We cannot resolve this debate. In my view, social discourse—and the warp and woof
of social influence—contain much truth, shading of truth, and lies. They also contain
certain corrective mechanisms. Those who lie habitually run the risk of earning others'
disapproval, or finding that even their truthful statements are disbelieved. Social norms
operate to discourage chronic lying. So too do psychodynamic mechanisms that have
evolved over human history. Guilt and internalized ethical rules help regulate people's
desire to regularly stretch the truth.

However, a certain amount of lying is inevitable, indeed permissible in everyday
interpersonal communication. Social influence—and persuasive communication—are
human endeavors, part of the drama of everyday life, in which people are free to pursue
their own ends, restrained by internalized moral values and social conventions (Scheibe,
2000). Democratic, civilized society enshrines people's freedom to pursue their own
interests and celebrates those who can exert influence over others. The "downside" of this
is that some people will abuse their freedom and seek to manipulate others, distorting truth
and using deceitful tactics. Human evolution has not yet evolved to the point that ethics
totally trumps (or at least restrains) self-interest, and perhaps it never will. The best hope
is education: increased self-understanding, development of humane values, and (trite as
it may sound) application of the time-honored, but always relevant, Golden Rule.

## CONCLUSIONS

This chapter has examined interpersonal persuasion—the many techniques individuals
use to influence one another in dyadic or one-on-one interactions. Social psychological
research has documented that gambits like foot-in-the-door and door-in-the-face can be
especially effective in securing compliance. Make no mistake: these tactics do not always
work, and many consumers have learned to resist them. However, they are used regularly
in sales and pro-social charity work; under certain conditions, for various psychological
reasons, they can work handily. Other tactics employed by professional persuaders—social
exchange, low-balling, that's-not-all, fear-then-relief, pique, and disrupt-then-reframe—
can also influence compliance. An alternative approach is to devise strategies to overcome
people's resistance to persuasion. By sidestepping resistance, redefining the situation, or
disrupting people's normal reaction to a message, persuaders can nudge people into
complying with requests.

In everyday life, we employ a variety of tactics to get our way. Interpersonal communication scholars have developed typologies to categorize these techniques. Strategies
vary in their directness, rationality, and emphasis on self-persuasion. Different strategies

are used in different situations, and the same person may use a direct approach in one setting and a cautious, indirect technique in another. There are also individual differences in compliance-gaining; culture, gender, and self-monitoring have emerged as important factors predicting tactics people will use.

Interpersonal persuasion is complex and dynamic. Cognitions about appropriate and effective compliance-gaining techniques, goals, and affect toward the other person influence strategy selection. One-on-one persuasive communication includes many different elements—concern about the relationship, desire to accomplish a goal, and concern about preserving face. These elements intersect and interact complexly and emotionally. Given the central role interpersonal persuasion plays in everyday life and in socio-economic transactions, it behooves us to understand and master it. One way to do this is to study approaches employed by highly effective persuaders. Successful persuaders recognize that persuasion requires give-and-take, flexibility, and ability to see things from the other party's point of view (Cody & Seiter, 2001; Delia, Kline, & Burleson, 1979; Waldron & Applegate, 1998). "Effective persuaders have a strong and accurate sense of their audience's emotional state, and they adjust the tone of their arguments accordingly," says Jay A. Conger (1998, p. 93), who notes that they plan arguments and self-presentational strategies in advance and "enter the persuasion process prepared to adjust their viewpoints and incorporate others' ideas. That approach to persuasion is, interestingly, highly persuasive in itself" (p. 87).

*Part Three*

# Persuasion in American Society

# Chapter 11

# Advertising

Y OU'VE seen it in hundreds of commercials and on all types of clothing—shirts, jackets, and hats. It's an oversized check mark, a smoker's pipe that juts outward, a "curvy, speedy-looking blur" (Hartley, 2000). Take a look below. It's the Nike "swoosh"—the symbol of Nike products, promoted by celebrity athletes; an emblem of Nike's television advertising campaigns; and, to many, the embodiment of speed, grace, mobility, and cool. It's a major reason why Nike is the major player in the sneaker market, and a testament to the success of commercial advertising (Goldman & Papson, 1996).

Advertising. That's a topic we know something about, though if you asked, we would probably politely suggest that it's everyone else who's influenced. Yet if each of us is immune to advertising's impact, how come so many people can correctly match the following slogans with the advertised products?

- ■ Whazzup?
- ■ Less filling, tastes great.
- ■ Obey your thirst.
- ■ Good to the last drop.
- ■ Where's the beef?
- ■ Like a rock.
- ■ Do the Dew.
- ■ There are some things money can't buy. For everything else, there's . . .

*Answers:* Budweiser; Miller Lite; Sprite; Maxwell House coffee; Wendy's; Chevy trucks; Mountain Dew; MasterCard.

Advertising—the genre we love to hate, the ultimate symbol of American society, a representation of some of the best, and most manipulative, aspects of U.S. culture—is showcased every day on television and each time we log onto Internet Web sites and catch banner spots. It's on buses and billboards, in ball parks and elementary school classrooms, and increasingly on cell phones. It is on subway turnstiles, which bear messages for Geico car insurance; Chinese food cartons that advertise Continental Airlines; and in bus shelters, where "Got milk?" billboards emit the smell of chocolate chip cookies (Story, 2007). It's the most real of communications, for it promotes tangible objects—things, stuff, and goods. It's also the most surrealistic, most unreal of mass communications. It shows us "a world where normal social and physical arrangements simply do not hold," critic Sut Jhally (1998) observes. "A simple shampoo brings intense sexual pleasure, nerdy young men on the beach, through the wonders of video rewind, can constantly call up beautiful women walking by, old women become magically young, offering both sex and beer to young men," he notes.

Advertising has been universally praised and condemned. It has been cheered by those who view it as emblematic of the American Dream—the notion that anyone with money and moxie can promote a product to masses of consumers, along with the promise, cherished by immigrants, that an escape from brutal poverty can be found through purchase of products and services not available in more oppressive economies. Advertising has been roundly condemned by those who despise its attack on our senses; its appropriation of language for use in a misty world located somewhere between truth and falsehood; and its relentless, shameless exploitation of cultural icons and values to sell goods and services (Cross, 1996, p. 2; Schudson, 1986).

Advertising, the focus of this chapter, is a complex, colorful arena that encompasses television commercials, billboards, and posters placed strategically behind home plate in baseball stadiums. It is paid materialist speech—messages for which companies pay to shape, reinforce, and change attitudes. (And they pay handsomely for these messages, to the tune of over $2.5 million per 30-second ad during the Super Bowl.) Advertising operates on a micro level, subtly influencing consumer behavior. It also works on the macro level, serving as the vehicle by which capitalist society communicates and promotes goods to masses of consumers. To appreciate advertising's effects, we need to look at both micro level effects on individuals and macro level cultural issues.

This chapter and the one that follows build on previous chapters by looking at how commercial and large-scale communication campaigns influence individuals and society. This chapter covers a lot of territory. I begin by debunking a common myth of advertising; move on to discuss the key psychological effects of advertising on attitudes, applying theories described earlier in the book; and conclude with a look at the complex ethical conundrums of contemporary advertising.

## THE SUBLIMINAL MYTH

It began, appropriately enough, in the 1950s, a decade in which post-World War II Americans were bewildered by all manner of things, ranging from reports of flying saucers to the successful Soviet launching of a space satellite. In 1957, the same year the Soviets sent up Sputnik, an enterprising marketer named James Vicary reported an equally jarring set of facts. He arranged for a drive-in movie theater in Fort Lee, New Jersey, a suburb of New York City, to beam the words "Drink Coca-Cola" and "Eat popcorn" for less than a millisecond during the romantic movie, *Picnic*. Vicary immediately proclaimed success. He claimed an 18 percent rise in Coke sales and a 58 percent increase in popcorn purchases, compared to an earlier period.

The nation's media were shocked, *shocked*. Minds have been "broken and entered," *The New Yorker* declared on September 21, 1957. The National Association of Broadcasters forbade its members from using subliminal ads. One writer, convinced that subliminal messages had dangerous effects, wrote several best-selling books on the subject. Wilson Bryan Key claimed that subliminal stimuli were everywhere! "You cannot pick up a newspaper, magazine, or pamphlet, hear radio, or view television anywhere in North America without being assaulted subliminally," Key announced (1974, p. 5). He claimed that advertisements for cigarettes, liquor, and perfume contained embedded erotic pictures that caused people to march off and buy these products, like brainwashed automatons from the old film *Coma*.

You yourself may have heard the term *subliminal* or *subliminal advertising*. It's easy to locate the words on the Web. There are dozens of Web sites with names like "Subliminal Ads—Brainwashing Consumers?" and "The Top 13 Subliminal Messages in Presidential Campaign Ads." Reflecting this belief in the power of subliminal ads, over 70 percent of respondents in scientific surveys maintain that subliminal advertisements are widely used and are successful in promoting products (Rogers & Smith, 1993; Zanot, Pincus, & Lamp, 1983). In a similar fashion, many people believe that subliminal messages in rock songs manipulate listeners. Some years back, parents of two men who committed suicide charged that the rock group Judas Priest had induced their sons to kill themselves. The parents claimed that Judas Priest had subliminally inserted the words "Do it, do it" underneath the lyrics in a morbid song called "Beyond the Realms of Death." (The parents lost the case.)

Beliefs are powerful entities. In the case of subliminal advertising, they can drive fears and influence emotions. Researchers, curious about subliminal message effects, have long studied the impact of subliminally embedded words and pictures. Their conclusion: *there is little evidence to support the claim that subliminal ads influence attitudes or behavior*. To appreciate how scholars arrived at this judgment and what it tells us about the psychology of advertising, we need to briefly examine the research on this issue.

## Definition

In the popular view, subliminal advertising means powerful advertising that appeals to emotional, even unconscious, needs. Given this broad definition, it is not surprising that many people believe advertising is subliminal. Scholars define "subliminal" differently— and far more precisely. Subliminal perception occurs when stimuli are "discriminated by the senses," yet are transmitted in such a way "that they cannot reach conscious awareness, even if attention is directed to them" (Dijksterhuis, Aarts, & Smit, 2005, pp. 80–81).

More simply, subliminal perception is perception without awareness of the object being perceived. It is "sublimen," or below the "limen" or threshold of conscious awareness. Making matters more complicated, the limen is a hypothetical construct, not one that is always easy to pinpoint.

Applying this perceptual concept to advertising is not a simple matter and is far more complicated than glib commentators like Key assume. But if one struggles to apply it to advertising, in order to put popular ideas to the test, we could say that *a subliminal advertisement is one that includes a brief, specific message (picture, words, or sounds) that cannot be perceived at a normal level of conscious awareness.* This definition excludes many appeals commonly associated with subliminal ads. Commercials that contain sexy models, erotic images, vibrant colors, haunting images, or throbbing music are not, in themselves, subliminal. Why? Because the erotic or colorful image appeal is right there —you see it or hear it and, if someone asks, you could tell her what you saw or heard. Product images that have been strategically placed in movies are not necessarily or inherently subliminal because advertisers hope viewers will spot and remember the products. (See Box 11.1.) A subliminal ad—or, more precisely, one that contains a message that eludes conscious awareness—is a very different animal.

Subliminally embedded messages exist though. The key question is: How common are they? A study of advertising executives found that few, if any, advertising agencies strive to develop subliminal ads (Rogers & Seiler, 1994). In view of the powerful impact that ordinary ads exert, it doesn't make much sense for advertisers to rack their brains to embed subliminal messages in commercials. Besides, if the news media ever found out—and, in the United States, they eventually would—that an agency had slipped a subliminal spot into an ad, the bad press the advertiser would receive would overwhelm any potential benefits of the subliminal message.

Does this mean there are no subliminals anywhere in the media? Not quite. In a country as big as the United States, with so many creative, ambitious, and slippery characters, it seems likely that a handful of advertising practitioners subliminally embed sexy messages in ads. (They could do this by airbrushing or using high-powered video editing techniques to insert subliminals in ads, including those that pop up on the Internet). What's more, a tiny minority of other communications—rock songs and motivational audiotapes—contain brief messages that lie below thresholds of conscious awareness. Thus, the major question is: What impact do subliminal messages have on consumers' attitudes or behavior?

## Effects

It is important to distinguish between subliminal perception in theory and subliminal perception in the reality of advertising. People can perceive information on a subliminal level and, under certain circumstances, stimuli processed subliminally can affect judgments (Bargh & Pietromonaco, 1982; Bornstein, 1992). But just because something can happen in a rarefied laboratory setting does not mean it does or is likely to happen in the noisy, cluttered world of advertising. Let's review the research.

## Box 11.1 | PRODUCT PLACEMENTS

Placement of products into movies, television shows, and video games has become so commonplace it's difficult to imagine an era in which anyone raised eyebrows about the practice.

Director Steven Spielberg helped popularize the craze when he inserted Reese Pieces into *E.T.* A later Spielberg movie, *Minority Report*, was jam-packed with brands, including Lexus, Gap, Reebok, and American Express. Episodes of the television show *The Apprentice* have revolved around a particular brand, with aspiring corporate executives promoting a Mars candy bar or creating a new toy for Mattel. Products are placed increasingly into video games and music, as when rapper Ms. Jade drove a Hummer in a "Ching Ching" video some years back. The heroine in a young adult novel even talked about wearing a "killer coat of Lipslicks." Lipslicks just happens to be a lip gloss made by Cover Girl, which developed a marketing arrangement with the book publisher (Rich, 2006). Spending on product placement stretches into the billions, with some $3 billion spent on the practice annually.

Product placement is defined as a paid communication about a product that is designed to influence audience attitudes about the brand through the deliberate and subtle insertion of a product into media entertainment programming. Product placements are similar to advertisements in that they are paid attempts to influence consumers. However, unlike advertising, which identifies the sponsor explicitly, product placements do not indicate that a sponsor has paid for the placement of a product into the media program. Because product placements disguise the attempt of a persuader to influence attitudes, they are regarded by some scholars as less ethical than advertising (Nebenzahl & Jaffe, 1998), and advertising is a medium that has not exactly been free of ethical condemnation.

The issue of disguised attempts to influence raises the question of whether product placements are subliminal messages. This is a thorny issue. One could argue that product placements are so incidental to the plot that they are processed on a subliminal level. But recall that subliminal perception occurs when stimuli are detected by the senses but fail to reach conscious awareness, even when attention is directed at them. Product placements are transmitted above the threshold of conscious awareness, and people are ordinarily aware they saw a branded candy bar or automobile that was inserted into a movie. It is possible that a product placement could be perceived at a subliminal level, and it is an interesting question for future research. A more durable concern than subliminal versus conscious perception is the likelihood that product placements are processed differently than advertising or even publicity because they are integrated into the plot or dramatic theme of the movie, television show, or entertainment content (McCarty, 2004).

Researchers have begun to explore these notions. Moonhee Yang and David R. Roskos-Ewoldsen (2007) noted that a product could be placed in different ways in a commercial. The product could be connected to the storyline, as when it helps a protagonist deal with a problem in the movie. It could be used by one of the main characters in a particular

**Box 11.1** |

situation, or, alternatively, the product could merely be shown with one of the characters, but not used by him or her. Applying cognitive psychological principles, the investigators reasoned that viewers should engage in greater semantic activation of products connected to the plot and therefore remember them best. In a study of placements of beverage and candy products in several movies (e.g., *The Client, Legally Blonde*), they found that viewers recognized the brand more when it was central to the story or was used by the main character than when it was shown in the background. Thus, marketers whose goal is to increase audience recognition of their product will want to build the product into the storyline or have the brand used by a main character.

Inspired by findings like these or marketer's intuitions, entertainment agencies are increasingly weaving product placements into the plots of television shows. For example, an entertainment agency representing Staples, the office supply store, approached the producers of NBC's "The Office" to promote the store's new paper shredding device on the program. In one show, a character, Kevin Malone, was assigned the job of shredding paper with the new device. To emphasize that the shredder was sturdy, Kevin shredded not just paper but a credit card. To show the device could be purchased only at Staples, the entertainment agency worked with writers to end the episode with a humorous reference to the store. Kevin was shown shredding lettuce and putting it into a salad. When a colleague queried where he got the salad, he replied, "Staples" (Clifford, 2008).

Product placements like these raise ethical questions. Critics, noting that the entertainment agency sought to approve the final script before it aired, view this as an unwanted intrusion of advertising into the creative process. They have a point. However, such intrusions are not illegal and are dismissed by television executives who need advertisers to pay for their creative products.

Alas, ethical considerations will play second fiddle to the marketplace. Product placements offer specific benefits to advertisers. They eliminate zapping, where viewers avoid commercials by using a remote control device. They also help advertisers target specific demographic groups that seek out a particular movie, video game, or book.

The first evidence of subliminal advertising effects came in Vicary's report on the effects of "Drink Coca-Cola" and "Eat popcorn" messages. At the time, his study seemed to suggest that subliminals could potently shape human behavior. But when scholars peered beneath the surface, they discovered that his research had serious flaws. In the first place, there was no control group, an essential requirement of a scientific experiment. Thus, there is no way of knowing whether moviegoers bought more popcorn and Cokes because they happened to be hungry and thirsty that particular day. It is even possible that the movie itself stimulated sales; it was named "Picnic" and showed scenes of people enjoying food and drinks!

More seriously, Vicary never released his data or published his study. Publication and open inspection of data are basic principles in scientific research, and Vicary's reluctance to do so casts doubt on the validity of his results. Shortly after Vicary's findings were revealed, a respected psychological firm tried to replicate his study under controlled conditions. Using more rigorous procedures, the psychologists reported no increase in purchases of either Coke or popcorn. In 1958, a Canadian broadcast network subliminally transmitted the message "Phone now" 352 times during a Sunday night TV show. Telephone calls did not rise during this period, and no one called the station (Pratkanis, 1998).

Although these results cast doubt on the subliminal thesis, they do not disprove it. We're talking about only a couple of studies here. A more rigorous test involves evaluating results from dozens of carefully conducted experiments. Researchers have designed and conducted such studies, embedding messages in ads at levels that elude conscious awareness. They have compared the responses of experimental group participants who receive the subliminal stimuli with control group subjects who view a similar message without subliminals. The findings have stimulated lively debate among scholars. Although a handful of researchers make the case for subliminal advertising effects, they frequently confuse subliminal perception with subliminal persuasion or ignore the preponderance of data that show subliminal messages have few effects on attitudes or behavior (Theus, 1994; Trappey, 1996). According to one scholar, the impact of subliminal advertising on consumers' decision-making is roughly the same as "the relationship between alcohol abuse and a tour of duty in Vietnam"—in other words, negligible or nonexistent (Trappey, p. 517).

This may seem surprising in view of what you may have read on this topic over the years. However, it makes good psychological sense. Indeed, there are several reasons why one should not expect subliminally transmitted messages to influence consumer attitudes or behavior:

- *People have different thresholds for conscious awareness of stimuli.* To influence a mass audience, a subliminal message would have to be so discretely beamed that it reached those with normal thresholds of awareness without catching the "attention" of those who are exquisitely sensitive to such stimuli. This would be difficult, perhaps impossible, to achieve using contemporary media.
- *There is no guarantee that consumers "see" or interpret the message in the manner that advertisers intend.* (For example, "Drink Coca-Cola" and "Eat popcorn" moved so quickly across the screen that some moviegoers may have seen "Stink Coke" or "Beat popcorn." This could have had the opposite impact on some viewers.)
- *For a subliminal message to influence attitudes, it must, at the very least, command the viewer's absolute attention.* This can happen in the experimenter's laboratory (Cooper & Cooper, 2002), but is not so likely to occur in the real world. People are frequently distracted or doing other things when they watch TV or come across magazine advertisements.
- Let me be clear: it *is* possible that a subliminal message could be perceived on a subconscious level. A sexy picture might "enter" a subterranean portion of the mind. Big deal. *For soon after the picture is processed, it is apt to be overwhelmed by the*

*more powerful images or sounds depicted in the advertisement—the luscious features of the model that can be processed instantly on a conscious level, the obvious beauty of a mountain scene or jingle-jangle of the advertiser's song.* These attention-grabbing pictures and sounds will swamp the subliminal embed. Just because a message is "in" an ad does not mean it gets "inside" consumers for very long—or at all. If it were that easy, everyone who works for advertising agencies would be very rich.

## Self-Fulfilling Prophecies and Beyond

Research makes abundantly clear that subliminally transmitted messages do not influence consumer attitudes or behavior. But could the belief that subliminals are powerful influence one's attitudes toward an issue? Anthony G. Greenwald and colleagues suspected that it could. As true-blue social scientists, they decided to test their intuition. They focused attention on a different kind of persuasive communication: therapeutic self-help tapes that claim subliminally embedded messages can help listeners solve personal problems.

Greenwald and his associates observed that some self-help tapes promise to enhance self-esteem by subliminally beaming messages like "I have high self-worth and high self-esteem" (Greenwald, Spangenberg, Pratkanis, & Eskenazi, 1991). Others attempt to improve memory skill by subliminally transmitting messages like "My ability to remember and recall is increasing daily." These words might be embedded underneath sounds, like waves lapping against a shore. Knowing the research as they did, Greenwald and colleagues doubted that such subliminals would have any impact. However, they suspected that consumers' expectations that the subliminals were effective might strongly influence beliefs.

In an elaborate study using careful scientific procedures, Greenwald and his associates (1991) obtained strong support for their hypothesis. Individuals who heard an audiotape that contained the subliminal message, "I have high self-worth," did not exhibit any increase in self-esteem. In addition, those who listened to the tape that contained the "My ability to remember is increasing" message did not display improvements in memory. But the belief in subliminals' impact exerted a significant effect. Subjects who thought they had been listening to a tape designed to improve self-esteem (regardless of whether they actually had) believed their self-esteem had improved. Individuals who thought they had been listening to a memory audiotape (regardless of whether they had) were convinced their memory had gotten better!

The researchers argued that what they had discovered was "an illusory placebo effect—placebo, because it was based on expectations; illusory, because it wasn't real" (Pratkanis, 1998, p. 248). Their findings could also be viewed as another demonstration of the power of self-fulfilling prophecy. This is the idea that if you expect something to occur, sometimes it will—not because of the objective event itself, but rather because you altered your thoughts; the alterations in cognitive structure then lead to changes in behavior.

Notice that a self-fulfilling prophecy operates on the conscious level, not the secretive, subconscious level at which subliminal ads are supposed to work. And, ironically, it is the conscious level at which subliminal ads may have their greatest impact. Actually, it is not the ads that exert the impact, but rather the *perceptions* of their effects that are influential.

During the 2000 presidential election campaign, Democratic presidential candidate Al Gore charged that his Republican opponent, George W. Bush, had subliminally implanted the word "rats" in a television advertisement. The Bush spot criticized Gore's position on providing prescription drugs for senior citizens. It showed Gore's image, followed by the words "bureaucrats decide." The word "rats" flickered briefly on the screen before the word "bureaucrats" appeared. Gore's aides charged the ad was a deliberate attempt to influence voters subliminally. A Bush advertising manager said he chose to fade the word in to make the ad more visually compelling, and the fact that the last four letters of "bureaucrats" spelled "rats" was coincidental. There was no evidence viewers could see the word "rats" or that the ad had any effect. Indeed, it was lifted soon after it appeared. But perceptions were everything. No doubt knowing that subliminal ads have virtually no impact but are perceived to be harmful, the Gore campaign seized the moment, exploiting the charge that Bush had deliberately tried to manipulate voters' unconscious minds. Gore's aides hoped that the widespread *belief* that subliminal ads have a negative impact might lead voters to view Bush unfavorably.

Students sometimes argue that marketers might want to suggest that a particular message has subliminal effects simply to stimulate interest in the product. (One thinks of the grilled cheese sandwich purportedly bearing the image of the Virgin Mary that sold for $28,000 on eBay.) The problem with this strategy is that it could easily backfire. Many consumers might simply reject a product, casting aspersions on a manufacturer who would deliberately insert subliminals in an advertisement. Thus, while *perceptions* of subliminal advertising impact are more consequential than *actual* effects (see Andsager & White, 2007), a campaign that deliberately tried to convince consumers that a particular ad exerted subliminal effects in hopes of arousing interest in the product could fail, thereby costing the marketer more in bad public relations than was gained from over-the-counter sales.

In view of the exaggerated notions of subliminal message effects, the interesting question for many researchers is not the objective impact of subliminal stimuli, but the subjective issue. Why are so many people convinced that these short, psychologically vacuous messages have so great an impact on attitudes? Laura A. Brannon and Timothy C. Brock put forth several explanations for the persistence in belief in subliminal communications, including the assumption that "if something exists it must be having an effect" (1994, p. 289). People also yearn for simple explanations of complex phenomena like advertising, and the subliminal thesis gives them a foolproof, conspiracy-type theory that seems to explain all of advertising's powerful influences on consumers.

With all this in mind, perhaps next time you read that liquor ads contain subliminally embedded faces or bikini-clad women, you might step back a moment and ask yourself a few questions. First, what evidence is there that these faces or scantily dressed women are actually in the ads, rather than a figment of the writer's sexually active imagination? Second, even if they are "there," what evidence exists that they influence perceptions? Third, assuming that the stimuli influence perceptions (a large "if"), how realistic is it to assume that they influence consumers' attitudes or behavior? By approaching advertising this way, you will quickly recognize that the mad search for subliminals takes you down the wrong trail in the quest to understand advertising effects. To comprehend the effects of advertising, we need to appreciate the emotional power of ads, but must take a more sophisticated approach.

# THE PSYCHOLOGY OF LOW INVOLVEMENT

A good way to appreciate the many effects of advertising is to dust off the ELM discussed in Chapter 5 and review its applications to commercial persuasion. Recall that the ELM tells us that people process information differently under high and low involvement, and this has important implications for persuasion strategies. Can you think of products that are personally important, mean a lot to you, and fulfill key psychological functions? These are high-involvement purchases. You are highly involved in the consumption of these products, probably thinking about them a lot or reckoning that you have something to lose if you make the wrong choice (Mittal, 1995). For most people, these products include cars, computers, and houses. Now consider the other side of the coin—products that you purchase that are of little personal concern, don't matter much to you, are mundane, and don't stimulate much thought. These are low-involvement purchases. They include soft drinks, countless grocery store products, and convenience goods like paper towels, tissue paper, and toothpaste (see Figure 11.1).

The ELM emphasizes that people process messages peripherally under low involvement and are, therefore, susceptible to simple appeals. Under high involvement, individuals think more centrally and deeply, taking into account the merits of the product and values stimulated by the ad. Advertising for high-involvement products cogently describes tangible benefits associated with the products. Ads also attempt to connect products with deep-seated values. The ELM has many interesting implications for advertising effects, suggesting, as it does, that we look separately at low- and high-involving advertising appeals. The next sections explore this approach.

## Mere Exposure

According to the mere exposure thesis, simple exposure to communications can influence attitudes. Merely seeing a message repeated over and over again leads to liking (Zajonc, 1968). This is a familiar experience. The longer you gaze at a painting in a museum, the more times you hear a hip-hop song on your iPod, and the more frequently you see an advertisement on TV, the more you come to like these stimuli.

Mere exposure is a strong, robust persuasion phenomenon. It works! Research conducted over the past decades provides strong support for the theory (Bornstein, 1989). Psychologists are not sure exactly why repetition leads to liking. Some argue that messages are easier to process and encode when they have been seen or heard before (Bornstein, 1992). Others proffer a more complex explanation. They suggest that consumers infer that advertisements that come more quickly to mind as a result of mere exposure are ones they

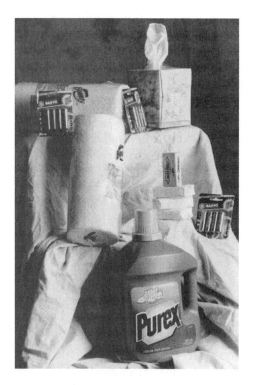

**FIGURE 11.1** | Advertisers use a host of peripheral appeals to promote low-involvement products like these.
Photograph by William C. Rieter.

like a lot. Still other scholars focus on other processes (Fang, Singh, & Ahluwalia, 2007), including the pleasures that come from increased familiarity with an advertisement. The first time television viewers saw the old Taco Bell ad in which the little Chihuahua utters, "Yo quiero Taco Bell" ("I want Taco Bell"), they probably were a little confused by the phrase and put off by the presence of a smirking, talking dog in an ad for a fast-food franchise. But with repetition, they got used to the ad, adjusted to the smug little dog, and developed a sense of what would occur as the quirky ad unfolded. The more they saw the ad, the more comfortable they felt and the more they liked it.

A similar process occurred for the "Can you hear me now?" ads for Verizon cell phones; MasterCard's cute, but incessant, repetition of "For everything else, there's MasterCard"; and McDonald's "I'm lovin' it." (The latter has been parodied on Web sites because the anagram for "I am loving it" is "ailing vomit"!) In all these cases, the more people saw the ads, the more comfortable they felt, and the more they resonated to the products. Indeed, repetition can have such positive effects that it can cause products or companies to become part of the language, as in "Get me some *Kleenex*"; "Make me a *Xerox*"; and "I'll *Google* that."

Mere exposure places more importance on form than content. It is the format—repeated exposure to a neutral stimulus—that matters, not the content of the ad. In early research on the topic, psychologists asked people to pronounce a variety of nonsense words—for example, *afworbu*, *civrada*, and *nansoma*. The words had no inherent meaning or semantic significance. Yet the more frequently individuals were exposed to the words, the more favorably they evaluated them (Zajonc, 1968). In the same fashion, the more we hear advertising slogans like the now-classic "Whazzup?" (Budweiser) or the time-honored "Double your pleasure, double your fun" (Doublemint gum), or see goofy animals (the Energizer bunny), the more favorably we evaluate these ads and the products. People made fun of the old Charmin toilet paper ads ("Please don't squeeze the Charmin"). However, the ads apparently worked as Charmin, never known to consumers before, captured a significant share of the market after its nonstop advertising campaigns.

Is repetition a panacea, a factor that always works? No way! Mere exposure is most effective under certain conditions. First, it works best for neutral products and issues—those to which we have not yet developed a strong attitude. It explains how advertising forms attitudes toward products, not how it *changes* them. Second, once people have developed an especially negative attitude toward a product, company, or politician, repetition cannot change the attitude. In fact, it may have the opposite effect, producing more negative affect toward the issue as people ruminate about how much they hate the fast-food product, big corporation, or obnoxious politician (Tesser, 1978).

Republican presidential candidate Mitt Romney seems to have suffered this fate in 2008. Romney spent over $30 million of his money, hoping that the more people saw his message the more they would like him. But Romney proved to be unpopular with the Republican base. Conservatives questioned the sincerity of his pro-life position, in light of his earlier support of abortion rights as governor of liberal Massachusetts. Despite heavy advertising, he won few primaries and dropped out of the race. Mere exposure will not change voters' attitudes once they have made up their minds they do not like a political candidate.

Mere exposure only works up to a certain point. After a certain number of exposures, repetition leads to boredom, tedium, and irritation. A phenomenon known as *wear-out* occurs (Bornstein, 1989; Solomon, 1999). Early in the mere exposure curve, repetition is a positive experience, reducing uncertainty, inducing calm, and bringing on a certain amount of pleasure. After a certain point, repetition has the opposite effect, and people become annoyed with the ad. Repetition ceases to lead to positive affect and can induce negative feelings toward the ad or product (see Figure 11.2). This is one reason why companies like McDonald's and Coke frequently switch slogans and change advertising agencies. They want to prevent wear-out and preserve the effect of a novel campaign slogan.

## The Magic of Association

There is a marvelous McDonald's ad I have shown in class over the years. It never fails to bring forth smiles and to elicit positive reactions from students who view it. The ad begins with a football coach lecturing a team of 8-year-old boys. He intones, "A great

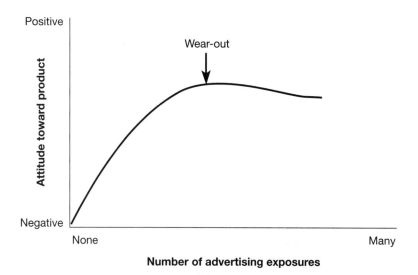

**FIGURE 11.2** | Repetition, advertising, and wear-out. After a certain number of repetitions, advertising can lead to wear-out.

man once said, 'Winning, gentlemen, isn't everything, it's the only thing.'" Suddenly we hear one of the boys, obviously oblivious to the coach's serious tone, shout, "Look, a grasshopper." All the youngsters jump up to take a look. The coach throws down his hat in mock despair. Another coach, kneeling down, says seriously to one of the boys,

"I-formation, 34 sweep, on 2. Got it?" When the boy, doing his best to understand but obviously bewildered, shakes his head, the coach says, "Just give the ball to Matt. Tell him to run for his daddy, okay?" The boy nods happily.

As the camera pans the oh-so-cute boys in their blue uniforms; shows us the misty, but picture-perfect, football day; and lets us watch the players do push-ups while fathers feverishly peer through video cameras to record their sons' every movement, we hear the narrator say, "It starts every September with teams like the Turkey Creek Hawks and the Bronx Eagles." Alas, these September days are about more than just winning football games, the narrator goes on to suggest; they're about dads and sons, good times, and—now the pitch—where you go after the game. Soft, sentimental music builds as the scene slowly shifts to what must be a later point in time—the boys smiling and enjoying themselves at McDonald's, no doubt chomping down burgers and fries. And so, the narrator intones, the scene moving back to football, McDonald's would like to salute the players, coaches, and team spirit that are part of these fall September days. The visual then profiles a boy, looking up at the "winning isn't everything" coach. "Can we go to McDonald's now, Coach?" he asks. Patiently, kindly, but firmly, the coach notes, "Sit down, Lenny. It's only halftime." The music, playing softly in the background, trails off and fades, as the ad gently comes to a close.

The advertisement illustrates the principle of association. It associates the good feelings produced by football, boys playing pigskin on weekend afternoons, and autumn with the fast-food franchise, McDonald's. It has linked these images seamlessly, though obviously, using an indirect strategy to promote McDonald's. McDonald's has not told us the reasons why its hamburgers are tasty (that might be a hard sell, given what we know about fast-food diets!). It has not provided cogent arguments that dining at McDonald's is a healthy, useful activity for budding athletes. In fact, the ad has provided neither argument nor logic. Instead, it has employed the rich language of emotion, telling us a story, associating McDonald's with positive, pleasant images that are peripheral to the purchase decision. If you tried the same technique in a job that required you to provide arguments why clients should purchase your product, trying to associate your product with good times while humming a sentimental tune, you would be fired! Yet McDonald's succeeds because the world of advertising is not purely or primarily rational. It invariably prefers emotion to syllogistic logic. It frequently favors Aristotle's pathos to his deductive logos.

There are countless examples of the use of association in advertising. The most noteworthy example is sex. Displays of nudity, sexual allusions, sexual behavior, and physical attractiveness are . . . everywhere, it seems—in ads on television, in magazines, and on the Internet, the latter employing virtual models (Lambiase, 2003; Reichert, 2003). Perfume ads famously show beautiful women, frequently objectified. Ads for men's cologne display explicit sexual images or tickle the imagination. One magazine ad for a men's fragrance pictured a man and woman in bed with the caption, "Sometimes she recalled his scent so vividly, she would lie there aroused by her own imaginings." Although sex in advertising works on multiple levels, the intent is to transfer the arousal elicited by the imagery to the cologne, perfume, blue jeans, shampoo, etc.

Association is used for other products as well. Shoe companies like Adidas and Nike frequently associate sneakers with athletic success. No longer content to promote linkages between their products and American athletes, these companies have branched out to the international stage. With more than 5 billion viewers expected to watch the World Cup soccer tournament in Germany, Adidas installed a massive poster of a German goalkeeper at the Munich airport and Nike sponsored eight qualifying teams.

Association is also used in more nefarious ways, as when advertisers pair cigarettes with relaxing images or link drugs like Vioxx (thought to cause heart attacks) with idyllic, happy times. The advertised images contrast sharply with the wretched effects these products exert on the body. (See Box 11.2 for a discussion of cigarette marketing.)

Association is perhaps the most important reason why advertising succeeds. It explains why things—material objects with no inherent value—acquire powerful meanings (near-magical auras) in consumers' eyes. Scholars have advanced several theories to explain how association works. They include *classical conditioning, semiotics,* and *accessibility.*

**Classical conditioning**. The granddaddy of association concepts, conditioning, dates back to Pavlov. "Does the name Pavlov ring a bell?" Cialdini (2001) asks humorously, reminding us of the Russian psychologist's century-old study that paired an unconditioned stimulus (food) with a conditioned stimulus (bell) to produce a conditioned response (salivation to the bell). Psychologists have applied classical conditioning to social learning, particularly attitude acquisition. In a study conducted in a post-World War II era preoccupied with understanding how Nazi-type prejudice could have developed, Staats and Staats (1958) showed that individuals could acquire negative attitudes toward the word "Dutch" simply by hearing it paired with words that had negative connotations ("ugly," "failure"). In a similar fashion, consumer-behavior scholars have shown that attitudes toward products can be classically conditioned through association with pleasant images (Grossman & Till, 1998; Stuart, Shimp, & Engle, 1987).

Classical conditioning processes help us understand how people develop favorable attitudes toward products. However, conditioning is a rather primitive model that does not take into account: (a) people's symbolic representations of objects in their minds, and (b) how they mentally link images with products. Consequently, we need to examine other views of association in advertising.

**Semiotics**. Semiotics is the study of signs and symbols. It helps us understand how signs—visual objects or geometric shapes with no inherent meaning—take on a rich tapestry of social and cultural meaning. A symbol is a sign with substance—a sign that bursts with value and emotional signification. Viewed as it might have been prior to Nazi Germany, the swastika is merely a strange, twisted shape. Yet, merged with Hitler's rhetoric and German atrocities, it becomes a symbol of hate, anti-Semitism, and crimes against humanity. The Cross and Star of David are shapes, but as symbols they are much more. The Cross symbolizes Jesus' crucifixion and redemption—an emblem of Christian love. The Star of David, a six-pointed star formed by superimposing two equilateral triangles, is a symbol of Judaism, Jewish culture, and the state of Israel.

Advertising—like religion and politics—thrives on signs. It transforms signs into symbols that give a product its meaning or "zip" (Goldman & Papson, 1996). Take a look at the signs in Figure 11.3 on p. 305. Glance first at Coca-Cola, closing your eyes to gain a clearer fix on the image. Do the same for McDonald's, the Nike swoosh, and iPod. What comes to mind? Images, feelings, pictures, people? I'd be willing to bet they did, even if you don't like the products or purchase them. Such is the power of advertising. It attempts to fill commodity signs with meaning, to give value to brands, and to stamp imagery onto products that differ only trivially from their competitors. Consider that classic entry in the sneaker wars, the Nike swoosh. Robert Goldman and Stephen Papson offer an historical perspective:

> Once upon a time, the Nike swoosh symbol possessed no intrinsic value as a sign, but value was added to the sign by drawing on the name and image value of celebrity superstars like Michael Jordan. Michael Jordan possesses value in his own right—the better his performances, the higher his value. The sign of Nike acquired additional value when it joined itself to the image of Jordan. Similarly, when Nike introduced a new shoe line named "Air Huarache" and wanted to distinguish its sign from those of other shoe lines, Nike adopted John Lennon's song "Instant Karma," as a starting point for the shoe's sign value. Nike justified drawing on Lennon's classic song by insisting that it was chosen because it dovetailed with Nike's own message of "self-improvement: making yourself better."
>
> (1996, p. 10)

## Box 11.2 | CIGARETTE MARKETING

An antismoking videotape shown in college classrooms offers an intriguing insight into the strategies tobacco companies use to market cigarettes. The video begins as magazine ads and billboards depict attractive young people smiling and relaxing while smoking a Kool or Virginia Slims. Smoke wafts up from a lit cigarette, as a guitar plays and a gentle male voice sings:

> If you want some real contentment to live life at its best,
> You can buy these dried tobacco leaves to breathe into your chest.
> And then look up at the billboard while all the promises come true . . . for you.
> You'll feel alive with pleasure, playful as a child
> You've come to where the freedom is.
> You're cool and mild . . .
> So look up at the billboard, see her smile and sexy intent
> But the only one who's laughing is the advertising man.
>
> (Kilbourne & Pollay, 1992)

Cigarette marketing, a multibillion dollar business around the globe, exploits psychological strategies to hook young people into smoking or to convince satisfied customers to stick with their brands. Ads have associated cigarettes with the pristine outdoors, sexuality, and rugged independence (as in the American icon, the Marlboro Man). Appeals geared to young women play on the psychological functions cigarettes serve, like independence and autonomy. The copy in a Virginia Slims ad says, "I always take the driver's seat. That way I'm never taken for a ride." Because cigarettes cannot be advertised on radio or TV in the United States, advertisers have relied on a variety of other techniques to promote their product, including billboards, magazine ads, event sponsorship, and linking their logos with athletic contests and rock concerts, a practice known as brand-stretching (Campbell, Martin, & Fabos, 2002). Movies like *Basic Instinct, Pulp Fiction, Titanic, Slumdog Millionaire,* and *Revolutionary Road* have depicted characters smoking, with apparent enjoyment. Indeed, actors in films smoke almost as frequently today as they did in the 1950s (Walsh-Childers & Brown, 2009). In some cases tobacco companies have paid movie producers to place cigarettes in their films (Basil, 1997). In an effort to reach the burgeoning youth market, multinational cigarette companies have distributed tobacco-branded clothing abroad and, in the United States, have plastered cigarette logos on candy and children's toys.

Perhaps the most famous mass-marketing technique is Old Joe, the cigarette-puffing cartoon character promoting Camels. Several studies reported that Old Joe is recognized by more than 91% of children (e.g., Brandt, 2007; Fischer, Schwartz, Richards, Goldstein, & Rojas, 1991; Horovitz & Wells, 1997). However, now that cigarette advertising cannot be displayed on large billboards, in sports arenas, or other public places, tobacco companies have taken their graphic, hedonistic images to another venue: the World Wide Web. The Web is a potential gold mine for cigarette advertising. Marketers can deliver moving images and interactive features to a captive audience of kids who love to surf the

## Box 11.2 |

Net and delight in playing "grown-up" by revealing consumer information to companies. One study found that cigarettes are a "pervasive presence" on the Web, especially on sites that sell products or feature hobbies and recreation. Sites associate smoking with glamorous lifestyles and with thin, physically appealing women (Hong & Cody, 2001).

In light of increases in teen smoking, evidence that more than one third of high school students smoke, and statistics showing that 90 percent of smokers begin during adolescence, there has been much concern about the effects of such marketing on children (Brown & Walsh-Childers, 2002). Yet so many factors influence smoking behavior—including parental smoking and having siblings who smoke—that it is difficult to parcel out the unique contribution advertising makes. Researchers are not of one mind on this subject. Some scholars are quick to point out that kids may recognize Joe Camel, but have no intention of lighting up a Camel, or any other cigarette for that matter (McDonald, 1993).

Even so, the scholarly consensus is that cigarette marketing predicts increased consumption of cigarettes, and that ads increase the symbolic attractiveness of cigarettes, particularly among young people (Andrews & Franke, 1991; Pierce, Choi, Gilpin, Farkas, & Berry, 1998; Schooler, Feighery, & Flora, 1996). Teenagers are by nature triers and product experimenters. Searching for ways to gain belonging and independence, some adolescents are attracted to cigarettes, and advertising enhances their appeal as badges of youthful identity—products some teens "wear," along with clothing, earrings, and tattoos (Pollay, 1997, p. 62).

What's more, a related marketing strategy—point-of-purchase cigarette marketing—appears to be highly effective. With mass-media advertising being phased out in the wake of the legal agreement between the state attorneys general and the tobacco industry, the industry is spending close to $3 billion on aggressively marketing cigarettes in retail establishments like convenience stores. Convenience stores are a prime location, as many young people frequently shop there. In some stores, more than 20 tobacco ads greet customers. The ads, positioned so that they catch young people's attention, have marked effects on adolescents' perceptions of tobacco. One study found that in-store promotions significantly enhanced eighth- and ninth-graders' perceptions of the accessibility and popularity of cigarettes, factors that increase the chances that young people will begin smoking (Henriksen, Flora, Feighery, & Fortmann, 2002). Tobacco executives are not stupid. They recognize that, even if point-of-purchase and other marketing strategies generate cigarette sales, smoking has become a cultural taboo, a behavior that is widely (and accurately) associated with disease and death in the United States. As a consequence, tobacco companies have increasingly begun marketing their product abroad, directing campaigns at psychologically vulnerable children and adolescents in some low-income developing countries. Nearly a fourth of all smokers world-wide started smoking before the age of 10, and as many as 20 percent of adolescents said they owned clothing that showed a cigarette brand logo (McNeil, 2008). "Just at the moment that the cigarette was

> **Box 11.2** |
>
> losing its glamour, sophistication, and sexual allure in the West, the companies sought to recreate these connotations of smoking in developing countries," historian Allan M. Brandt (2007) observes (p. 455).
>
> All of this raises important ethical questions. Cigarette marketing unquestionably pushes the ethical envelope of persuasion to its limits. Yet even its fiercest critics acknowledge that tobacco marketing—and advertising in particular—is not coercive. People are free to accept or reject advertising's deceptive appeals. Ads are not threatening individuals with sanctions if they don't light up. More broadly, cigarette consumption is legal, and companies have a right to promote their products through the mass media. And yet advertisers associate cigarettes with benefits (sex appeal, ruggedness, independence) that are unlikely to materialize in reality, while saying nothing about the dirty, addictive aspects of the product. Such ads surely must be criticized by those who value honesty and truth telling, particularly to young, vulnerable members of the audience. Legal scholars have noted that cigarette marketing is protected under the First Amendment; yet this does not make it ethically permissible or worthy of endorsement on moral grounds.
>
> It is a complex debate, the question of cigarette advertising—and tobacco marketing more generally. Defenders point to the value of individual liberty and the need to preserve a society in which media can promote any product that consumers desire, even those that can kill them. Critics point to the sham of advertisers spending millions of dollars to come up with ever more clever ways to hook people into depending psychologically on a life-threatening product. "Is this the kind of society we want?" they retort.
>
> Particularly problematic are tobacco companies' blatant attempts to hook young people into smoking. "The clearest statement [of this]," reporter Philip J. Hilts discovered, after extensively studying cigarette marketing, "came in a question and answer period at a regional [R. J. Reynolds Company] sales meeting. Someone asked exactly who the young people were that were being targeted, junior high school kids, or even younger?
>
> "The reply came back 'They got lips? We want 'em'" (Hilts, 1996, p. 98).

This was the Nike "advertising sign machine" of the late 1980s and 1990s, featuring associations between its swoosh and Jordan, Bo ("Bo knows") Jackson, and Spike Lee. Since then, Nike has embarked on numerous ad campaigns, including ones that feature commercials resembling MTV videos—brilliant, but blatant, attempts to associate the swoosh with images resonant with a younger market. Nike, like other advertisers, strives constantly to redefine its image in the eyes of a new market niche through ever inventive ways of combining signs with in-vogue celebrities, trends, and images.

Yet for all of its insights, semiotics does not explain how advertising creeps into the minds of consumers. It is a theory of message content, not message effects. To understand associative advertising impact, we must turn to cognitive psychological concepts. Consider that advertising shapes attitudes toward products by helping forge an association between

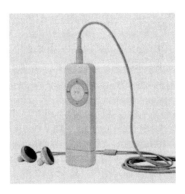

**FIGURE 11.3** | Well-known signs and symbols in American advertising (see also Goldman & Papson, 1996).

the product and a pleasant, memorable image. Once the attitude is formed, it must be retrieved or accessed, particularly at the moment when consumers are making a product decision.

**Accessibility**. The extent to which people can "call up" an attitude from memory, comes to the fore when discussing advertising's effects on attitudes. Research discussed in Chapter 2 suggests that the more exposure consumers have to advertisements that plant the association between a product and image, the more they can quickly get in touch with their attitude when they are trying to decide which soft drink, fast food, or sneaker to purchase. Advertisers recognize this and try to influence the extent to which people can activate product attitudes from memory.

Thus, McDonald's ads try to induce consumers who are in the mood for fast food to call up the feelings they had when they watched an ad like the one described earlier. Coke tries to access years of internalized associations between its product and positive images. These include mid-twentieth-century linkages between Coca-Cola and patriotic appeals that call to mind artist Norman Rockwell; the classic 1971 song that associated Coke with global, ethnic diversity ("I'd like to buy the world a Coke and keep it company. It's the real thing"); and current multicultural campaigns that span Egypt, Saudi Arabia, and South Africa (see Box 11.3). In the view of some observers, Coke may have even built and activated associations between its soft drink and the Christian religion! A minister once told a Coca-Cola bottler, "I see a strange connection between your slogan, 'The pause that refreshes,' and Christ's own words, 'Come unto me all ye that travail, and I will refresh you'" (Martin, 2000). In these ways, Coke ads give powerful meanings to a "mixture of water, carbon dioxide, sugar, flavorings, and colorings" (Myers, 1999, p. 7).

Other advertisements employ similar strategies. Ads for Levi's 501 jeans, particularly outside the United States, attempt to call up connections between jeans and such positive values as youth, rebelliousness, and the United States. The American commercial icon, Campbell's soup, spent much of the twentieth century building powerful linkages between its product and down-home days with Mom and Dad (albeit of the White variety). Campbell's ads seemingly left an imprint, as one consumer acknowledged:

> Campbell's tomato soup is the only one that will do. It's like a cozy, comforting thing. It tastes good mainly because you associate it with what it did for you when you were a kid. Maybe it doesn't even taste that good, but somehow it works on a level beyond just your taste buds.
>
> (Langer, 1997, p. 61)

Association appeals can even succeed in convincing consumers to buy products that have no distinctive qualities. Case in point: bottled water. Blind taste tests reveal that most people cannot tell the difference between bottled and tap water. One researcher arrayed ten bottles of water on a table, including one filled with water from the tap. He asked participants in his informal study to rate samples from each bottle for flavor, aftertaste, feel, and appearance. The majority could not discriminate among the group; indeed, they could not correctly identify the bottle that contained tap water (Standage, 2005). If taste is not the reason why millions buy Aquafina, Evian, Fiji, and other brands,

## Box 11.3 | SELLING GOD, COUNTRY, AND COKE

How did a drink composed of sugar, caramel, caffeine, lime juice, and kola nuts become a multibillion dollar seller? How, in short, did Coke become "the real thing"? In two words: "advertising" and "marketing," conclude authors like Mark Pendergrast, who wrote the book, *For God, Country and Coca-Cola* (2000). Based on his research, Pendergrast offers a number of suggestions on how to market products like Coke through mass media. They include the following:

1.  Sell a good product. And if it contains a small dose of an addictive drug or two, all the better.

2.  Develop a mystique. An air of mystery, with a touch of sin, sells.

3.  Sell a cheaply produced item. Coca-Cola has always cost only a fraction of a cent per drink to produce.

4.  Make your product widely available.

5.  Use celebrity endorsements wisely—but sparingly.

6.  Get 'em young. Obviously, if you can achieve loyalty among youthful consumers, you've possibly fostered lifelong consumption.

7.  Develop cultural sensitivity. If you intend to sell your product around the world, do not trap yourself in an "ugly American" image.

8.  Be flexible enough to change.

9.  Pay attention to the bottom line.

10. Advertise an image, not a product. As one Coke advertiser liked to remind his creative staff, "We're selling smoke. They're drinking the image, not the product."

(pp. 461–465)

why has bottled water become so popular? A major reason is that bottled water has become fashionable, linked with purity, cleanliness, and good health. "Advertisers used words (*pure*, *natural*) and imagery (waterfalls, mountains) to imply that bottled water tasted better and was healthier than tap," notes writer Elizabeth Royte (2008, p. 34). Royte believes the American public was sold a (bottled) bill of goods. The Food and Drug Administration permits the same amount of pesticides, heavy metals, and radioactive substances in bottled water that the Environmental Protection Agency allows in tap. Until recently, bottled water did not contain any fluoride, putting children at greater risk for cavities. No matter. Water, Royte observed, had become "a social—not just a physical—resource. Ordering imported water was classy; it improved the tone of a dinner party. Once that idea took hold in America, there was no going back" (p. 33).

Similar branding occurred with iPod. Imbued with a sleek design, iPod gained in stature and coolness as a result of Apple's advertising campaigns. In each commercial, writer Steven Levy notes:

A hot young person—his or her face not seen but often featuring a touchstone of hip minority status, like dreadlocks—would be going absolutely bananas to a wild rock or hip-hop song, typically a brand-new tune by a band that your kid has heard of but you haven't . . . Finally, the dancer would vanish and on the screen, in Apple's familiar bold Garamond font, would appear all the words you needed to know: "iPod, Mac or PC." And then the Apple logo.

(2006, pp. 63–64)

The ads portrayed iPod as the apotheosis of coolness and spontaneity. The product also became a prized prop—an icon of "techno-chic"—in television shows ranging from *Scrubs* to *Queer Eye for the Straight Guy* (Levy, p. 67).

In all these ways, marketing subtly builds associations into signs, products, and brands. It transforms things into symbols of hope, desire, and status (Langrehr & Caywood, 1995; McCracken, 1986). An iPod is not a mere MP3 player; instead, it is a life-line, a connection with worlds more musically majestic than everyday life. Nike shoes are not sneakers, but rather emblems of excellence, pronouncements of athletic ability. Objects gain this majesty through associational appeals in advertising and the projections of consumers. Although ads do not always exert this impact—the floors in advertising agencies are littered with footage from unsuccessful media campaigns—ads can potently influence affect toward products. In light of advertising's widely recognized ability to shape product attitudes, it is little wonder that people unschooled in advertising effects leapt onto the subliminal seduction bandwagon.

## Peripheral Processing

The ELM's emphasis on peripheral processes complements discussion of association and mere exposure. When consumers are in a low-involvement mode—as most are when they encounter ads for soft drink, lip balm, paper towel, and toothpaste products—they process ads through the peripheral route. Repeated exposure and associations serve as peripheral cues, as do celebrity source factors.

Celebrity product endorsements account for 10 percent of TV advertising spending and more than a billion dollars in ad expenditures (Till, Stanley, & Priluck, 2008). Psychologically, celebrities transfer meaning from their cultural identity to the product. As researcher Grant McCracken observed, calling on classic ads from an earlier time:

No mere model could bring to Baly-Matrix the properties that Cher delivers, nor could any model have summoned the impatient, time-tested integrity, John Houseman gave the Smith-Barney line "We make money the old-fashioned way, we earn it." Only a man playing Houseman's roles in the way Houseman played them could empower the slogan as Houseman did. Celebrities have particular configurations of meaning that cannot be found elsewhere.

(1989, p. 315)

A marketing expert put it more concretely. "The reality is people want a piece of something they can't be. They live vicariously through the products and services that those celebrities are tied to. Years from now, our descendants may look at us and say, 'God, these were the most gullible people who ever lived'" (Creswell, 2008, p. C8).

Celebrities are particularly apt to enhance consumer attitudes when their characteristics "match up with" or are relevant to the product being promoted (Chew, Mehta, & Oldfather, 1994; Lynch & Schuler, 1994; Till et al., 2008; see also Lee & Thorson, 2008). For example, when Michael Jordan and, more recently, LeBron James promoted Nike, their athletic expertise was salient. It served as a simple "click–whirr" reason to prefer Nike sneakers (Cialdini, 2001).

Celebrity characteristics do not always match product attributes, however. Former professional football quarterback Joe Montana promoted Diet Pepsi. Pop singers Britney Spears and Shakira endorsed Pepsi. The rap star Diddy ordered a whopper in a Burger King ad on the YouTube home page. In these cases, the celebrities' fame bonded to the products, enhancing their sign value. Celebrity endorsers can net advertisers millions, but they also can be persuasive liabilities, as Pepsi discovered years ago when Madonna created controversy for her "Like a Prayer" video. Pepsi pulled the ad. In a similar fashion, Christian Dior dumped super-model Kate Moss from its ads when Moss was caught on film snorting cocaine. When actress Sharon Stone made a cruel, insensitive remark about the Chinese earthquake, Dior removed her ads for face cream in China (Horyn, 2008). And when reports of Tiger Woods' extramarital affairs attracted worldwide publicity, major companies dropped him as a celebrity spokesman. Prior to the scandal, an ad for Accenture, a consulting firm, had featured the golfer looking into the distance, with ominous clouds on the horizon. The advertisement said that is it "tougher than ever to be Tiger." The words took on a totally different meaning after allegations of marital infidelities surfaced.

At the same time, ads can also work peripherally simply by putting low-involved consumers in a positive frame of mind. Just being in a good mood can influence positive affect toward products, without impacting beliefs in the slightest (see Petty, Schumann, Richman, & Strathman, 1993). Pleasant music, goofy gimmicks (Budweiser's frogs), and incongruous, humorous situations can put people in a good mood. This can increase memory and liking of the ad, which can influence brand attitudes (Muehling & McCann, 1993).

The same consumer psychology applies when people process Internet advertising under low-involvement conditions. When cruising the Net in a low-involved state or glancing over banner ads for products that don't touch on important needs, consumers are apt to be swayed by attention-grabbing cues, like the size, color, and dynamic animation of banner ads (Cho, 1999).

## HIGH INVOLVEMENT

Another category of advertising concerns high-involvement products—those that are important to us personally; touch on our self-concepts; or are big-ticket, expensive items (see Figure 11.4). When consumers are in the market for an ordinarily high-involvement product, like a car, jewelry, computer, or even clothing, they process ads centrally. The ELM emphasizes that, under high-involvement conditions, people consider the merits of the product, connect the product to core values, and systematically process product commercials (Andrews & Shimp, 1990; Roehm & Haugtvedt, 1999). They carefully process factual

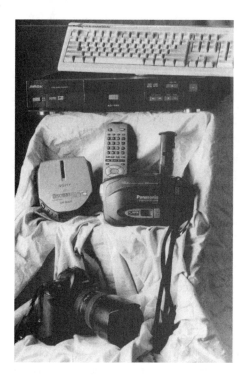

**FIGURE 11.4** | To many consumers, computer, photographic, and electronic products are highly involving. Advertisers use factual, social, and value-based appeals to promote these products.

Photograph by William C. Rieter.

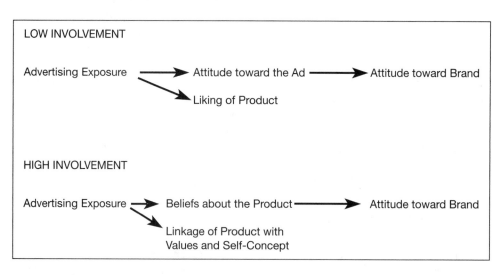

**FIGURE 11.5** | Involvement and brand attitudes.

Based on the ELM, and Mitchell, A. A. (1986). Effects of visual and verbal components of advertisements on brand attitudes. *Journal of Consumer Research, 13,* 12–24.

information like price and consider the material benefits of the purchase (see Figure 11.5). When they are online and come across banner ads for high-involvement products like cars, consumers may be uninfluenced by the ads' size or color. Instead, they may be especially likely to click the ads to request more information about the product (Cho, 1999). As a general rule, strong, cogent arguments on behalf of the product should carry the day.

But what constitutes a strong, cogent argument on behalf of a product? On this point, our ordinarily useful ELM lets us down. It doesn't tell us the specific arguments that are likely to be most compelling under high consumer involvement. To identify the types of messages that are apt to resonate with people purchasing personally important products, we need to turn to another persuasion theory. Functional theory, discussed in Chapter 3, helps bridge consumer attitudes and persuasion. You may recall that the functional approach says that attitudes serve specific psychological functions or needs for individuals. Messages are most likely to influence attitudes if they target the function the attitude serves. Let's see how this works in the case of advertising.

Some attitudes serve a *utilitarian* function. People purchase products to gain specific, tangible rewards (Shavitt & Nelson, 2000). Parents who need a minivan to transport their kids, pets, or groceries have utilitarian reasons for purchasing a car. Ads targeted at these parents commonly emphasize the passenger space and roominess of, say, a Chevy Suburban or Honda Odyssey.

People buy products for reasons other than tangible benefits. They buy to fulfill ambitions, dreams, and fantasies. Thus, product attitudes serve symbolic, as well as material, functions. For example, some attitudes serve a social-adjustive function. People purchase products to gain acceptance from peers. One mother confessed:

> In my neighborhood, if you don't have a brand name bicycle, the kids rib you. We had to go out and buy [my son] a $300 bike so the kids would leave him alone. He was getting harassed because he had a cheaper bike.
>
> (Langer, 1997, p. 64)

Another mother confessed that she tried to get away with buying her 14-year-old daughter an MP3 player that was $100 cheaper than the most popular brand in her daughter's peer group. "I was in the biggest dog box," she said. Her daughter "went to school, and everyone else had got an iPod for Christmas. It was like, 'How come everyone else got one, and you couldn't buy me an iPod?' So we got one for her birthday two months later" (Williams, 2005, p. 1).

Although the mothers' comments might seem silly or petty or worse, they do reflect a common perspective toward products. Advertising designed to reach these mothers would be advised to hype the most expensive, branded products.

Product attitudes also serve a *social identity* function. Consumers purchase cars, jewelry, and other highly involving goods to enhance their identities—to set them apart from others. People buy big-ticket items to gain status, look cool, show off an identity to others, or express love. Ads appeal to these needs, using pictures, images, and the syntax of advertising to suggest that owning products makes you happy. "May promote feelings of superiority," a tag line for a Nissan car unabashedly stated.

Advertisements for highly involving products also employ associational appeals, but they invite deeper processing than do association-based appeals for low-involving products. As Paul Messaris notes:

> In the single category of automotive ads, one can encounter analogies to lions (Toyota), tigers (Exxon), cheetahs (BMW), military aircraft (Dodge, Honda, Jaguar, etc.), and Fabergé eggs (Lincoln) ... If the creator of an ad wants to make the point that a certain car is powerful, the verbal text can convey this message explicitly, through such words as "dynamic," "breathtaking," "supercharged," or, indeed, "powerful." When it comes to the ad's pictorial content, though, this aspect of verbal syntax, the adjective–noun relationship, has no direct visual counterpart. One alternative, then, is simply to show an image of the car accelerating rapidly and trust the viewer to make the appropriate inference ... Showing the car next to some other object or entity that also possesses power increases the likelihood that the viewer will get the point, not so much because of the doubling of powerful objects as because the juxtaposition should lead the viewer to intuit what it is that they have in common.
>
> (1997, pp. 191, 193)

Consumer attitudes also serve a *value-expressive* function. Individuals purchase products to express deep-seated values. People with strong environmental attitudes steer clear of things that damage the environment and seek out products that are environmentally friendly. Advertisers target environmentally conscious consumers by playing up concern for ecology in their ads. The Body Shop plays up its opposition to scientific testing of animals. L. L. Bean advertises its "durable, practical products for men and women who love the outdoors" (Goldman & Papson, 1996, p. 194). Advertisers take code words like recycling and green and cleverly associate them with their products. In these ways they try to convince Baby Boomers, Gen Xers, and Millennials to shop till they drop, while at the same time purchasing products that are oh-so environmentally correct. These strategies can work. BP, the mammoth British Petroleum company, enhanced its brand value by $3 billion by calling itself the environmentally conscious "Beyond Petroleum" company (Zogby, 2008).

Value-based appeals have long been a staple of advertising. In fact, advertising agencies have developed elaborate strategies to measure consumers' values and lifestyle choices, hoping to tailor ads to match the values of particular audience segments. Automobile companies, hoping to solidify their niche in the competitive car market, have been particularly concerned with tapping into consumers' values. Some years back they discovered that minivan buyers sought out cars for reasons different from those of sport-utility customers. Summarizing market research on the topic, a reporter noted that "minivan buyers tend to be more comfortable than sport utility buyers with being married; sport utility buyers are more commonly concerned with still feeling sexy, and like the idea that they could use their vehicles to start dating again" (Bradsher, 2000, p. A1). Minivan buyers are more apt to participate in family gatherings and in conversations with friends. The more restless, self-focused sport-utility owners prefer to dine at fine restaurants, go to sporting events, or physically work out.

Advertisers have exploited these findings. Ads for Ford's Windstar minivan feature a dozen mothers and their kids arrayed around a Windstar. The ads note that the moms are all Ford employees who worked together to redesign the van. In contrast, a TV ad for Jeep Grand Cherokee Limited depicts a driver who had to climb a pile of rocks that blocked access to his mansion. Automobile designers also take advantage of value-based marketing studies. They design SUVs so that they are masculine and aggressive, "often with hoods that resemble those on 18-wheel trucks [and] vertical metal slats across the grilles to give the appearance of a jungle cat's teeth . . . By contrast . . . sedans and station wagons have open grilles that look toothless" (Bradsher, p. A16).

## Summary

Advertisers centrally process high-involved consumers, just as highly involved viewers centrally scrutinize ads. Advertising executives like to stay one step ahead of the consumer, using market research to devise ads that match the functions products serve for individuals in a given culture (Han & Shavitt, 1994).

In addition to functional theory, the ELM provides a framework to appreciate the effects of advertising. When people are highly involved in a product decision, they systematically process product information. Recognizing this, advertisers are currently developing a host of interactive advertising campaigns tailored to consumers' product preferences. For example, EchoStar's Dish Network devised a 30-second spot for the Mercedes M-Class that features a prompt on the screen asking viewers if they want more information. If they say they do, they are taken to an interactive channel on the network, where they can request a brochure, set up an appointment at the dealer, or watch a short video of the automobile on a home shopping network (Manly, 2005). Other marketers are customizing Web sites to match high-involved consumers' profiles, obtained from codes called cookies placed on a hard drive. Under low involvement, consumers are susceptible to peripheral appeals, increasingly adapted to the interactive high-tech media environment. Complicating matters is the fact that involvement is not a static variable in the world of advertising. Advertising frequently tries to convince people that a low-involving product (sneakers) is of deep, personal importance. In this way, it builds brand loyalty and sells products.

More generally, one can argue that advertising is in the business of creating meanings, of stimulating people to imagine that their futures will be brighter if they buy the product. Ads work on the imagination by melding visual images and verbal text, creating metaphors. For example, an ad for the Army shows pictures of soldiers running together on a tarmac, riding motorcycles in the fog, and parachuting from an airplane. Although the literal message is that joining the Army will teach you these skills, the metaphor is conveyed by the juxtaposition of the words and pictures. "Are you ready," the narrator asks, "to find yourself, to prove yourself, to learn how to fly . . . to be all that you can be?" Recognizing that young people join the Army to gain structure and meaning in their lives, the ad deploys pictures and words to convey the message that the Army is a place where the individual can grow, find out more about himself or herself, and gain self-understanding (Wiggin & Miller, 2003). These images highlight the rewarding aspects of the military, while conveniently downplaying the dangers.

## THE ROLE OF PERSONALITY

Before leaving this exploration of advertising, it is useful to discuss an additional factor that enters into the psychology of advertising effects: personality. Individuals differ in their perceptions and evaluations of advertising. Advertisers take this into account when they devise ads that appeal to different personality types or audience niches. The personality factor that has generated the most attention is one discussed earlier in this book —self-monitoring. You may recall that image-conscious, high self-monitors differ in a variety of ways from the relentlessly "Be yourself" low self-monitors. High self-monitors adopt attitudes for social-adjustive purposes, to help them fit into social situations. Low self-monitors hold attitudes for value-expressive reasons, to assist them in expressing their core views toward life.

Psychologist Kenneth G. DeBono argued that these differences in the functional basis of attitudes have interesting implications for advertising. High self-monitors, he suspected, should be especially responsive to advertising messages that help one adjust one's image to fit a particular situation. Low self-monitors, by contrast, should be more influenced by ads that call attention to the intrinsic value or performance of the product.

DeBono tested his ideas in a series of intriguing experiments. As he suspected, high self-monitors were especially influenced by "soft-sell" appeals that called attention to the image one could project by purchasing the product. Low self-monitors were swayed more by "hard-sell" ads that highlighted the quality or durability of the product (DeBono, 2000; Snyder & DeBono, 1985). These findings can be easily applied to advertising campaigns in the mainstream media and on Web sites (Yates & Noyes, 2007). Advertisements frequently highlight the image associated with owning a product. Such ads should be more effective with high self-monitors than with low self-monitors. For example, this classic, a savvy Sprite ad of a few years back geared to a female market, should be particularly influential with high self-monitoring women:

You're a woman of the '90s.

Bold, self-assured and empowered.

Climbing the ladder of success at work and the Stairmaster at the gym.

You're socially aware and politically correct.

But you probably know all this already because every ad and magazine has told you a zillion times.

No wonder you're thirsty.

(Goldman & Papson, 1996, p. 264)

On the other hand, this MasterCard ad, exploiting the desire for authenticity, should appeal more to low self-monitors. The ad shows a guy sitting on top of a hill overlooking a lovely Mediterranean town. As he gazes into the distance, the narrator remarks:

> Alright [sic], brace yourselves. Your credit line has nothing to do with your value as a person, OK? You could have a shiny Gold MasterCard with a credit line of at least $5000, I don't care. It doesn't make you a better person. (He pauses, and shifting his tone of voice he wonders aloud:) Well, I don't know, maybe it does? I mean if knowing that the Master Assist Plan can refer you to a good doctor or lawyer anywhere in the world, let you relax and stop being so uptight and just have fun and be yourself—then, yeah, I suppose a Gold MasterCard could have some effect.
> (Goldman & Papson, pp. 143–144)

Keep in mind that these are general predictions. There is not one type of low self-monitoring consumer, nor one kind of high self-monitoring buyer (Slama & Singley, 1996). High self-monitors like jazzy products, and low self-monitors don't want products that will break once they buy them. Nonetheless, research on self-monitoring reminds us that one size does not fit all when it comes to advertising, and that advertising is more apt to be effective when it targets the needs that products fulfill.

## ADVERTISING ETHICS

It is a lot easier to document advertising effects than to arrive at universally accepted conclusions about its ethics. Long before the arrival of Old Joe Camel and the Budweiser frogs, critics debated the ethics of advertising. (One advertising genre that makes many people particularly uneasy is negative advertising. See Box 11.4 for a discussion.) Adopting a deontological approach (see Chapter 1), critics have argued that the test of ethical communication is whether it treats people as an end, not a means—or, more practically, whether the communicators' motives are honorable or decent. Viewed in this way, advertising can fall drastically short of an ethical ideal. Advertisers develop ads that make promises they know products can't deliver. Cigarettes don't offer hedonistic pleasure; cars don't make you rich or famous; and making pancakes for your kids on Saturday won't assuage your guilt about neglecting them all week, despite the plaintive plea of a Bisquik pancake commercial.

Advertisers want consumers to project fantasies onto products in order to hook individuals on the image of the brand. Viewed from a deontological perspective, advertising is not ethical because advertisers are not truthful. If the decency of the communicators' motives is the criterion for ethical communication, advertising fails. Advertisers deliberately construct fantasies to serve their clients' needs, not to aid the customer in living a healthier, happier life.

Responding to these criticisms, defenders of advertising note that consumers recognize that advertising creates untruths. They do not expect ads to tell them "the way things really are in society," Messaris notes. "Almost by definition," he says, "the

## Box 11.4 | NEGATIVE POLITICAL ADVERTISING

Going negative is a time-honored way to persuade voters that the other candidate is not worth a vote.

In the early nineteenth century, Thomas Jefferson's pamphleteer alleged that Jefferson's opponent, President John Adams, was endowed with a "hideous hermaphroditical character" and was "mentally deranged" (Vitello, 2008). Negative messages continued apace during the nineteenth century, with verbal attacks hurled at such storied political figures as Grover Cleveland, Andrew Jackson, and Abraham Lincoln. In the twentieth century, with the advent of television, candidates paid TV stations to broadcast political commercials, and a new art form—the attack ad—was born.

Both political parties have exploited negative advertising to their advantage. For example, in 1964, Democratic President Lyndon Johnson used a negative ad to disingenuously imply that his opponent would start a nuclear war. In 1988, Republican George Bush repeatedly questioned his opponent's patriotism. Over the course of the past decades, political advertisements have become increasingly negative (Geer, 2006).

In 2004, attack ads descended to such a nadir of negativity that they spawned a new term in the lexicon: "swift boating." In the 2004 election, an independent political action group, Swift Boat Veterans for Truth, ran advertisements against Democratic nominee John Kerry, claiming that he had lied about his Vietnam War record. As a Navy lieutenant, Kerry commanded operations of swift boats, aluminum patrol boats, and received several medals for his valor. Kerry later became disenchanted with the war and threw away his medals in a public demonstration. Angered by what they regarded as his disrespectful and unpatriotic actions, some of the Swift Boaters devised ads that accused Kerry of fabricating his military accomplishments. The charges had no basis in fact. However, the ads were effective in undermining support for Kerry during the 2004 election. As a result, reporter Kate Zernike (2008) quipped, "the term 'swift boat' has become a political verb, a synonym for the kind of attack that helped destroy the presidential campaign of Senator John Kerry in 2004."

Vowing not to be "swift boated," and determined to rebut their opponent's criticisms, candidates Barack Obama and John McCain seized the offense in 2008. They e-mailed their spin to reporters soon after an opponent's ad aired, placed video clips of attack ads on YouTube, and used sophisticated marketing techniques to strategically produce television commercials geared to battleground states. Obama even placed ads on online video games. Both campaigns "sliced and diced" the electorate, precisely the strategy that Obama had deplored in his 2004 speech to the Democratic convention.

One of the ironies of negative spots is that people profess to dislike them, but they have demonstrable effects on public opinion. As Democratic consultant Jill Buckley said, "people say they hate negative advertising, but it works. They hate it and remember it at the same time" (Johnson-Cartee & Copeland, 1991, p.15). Communication studies bear this out.

**Box 11.4**

Negative ads work for several reasons. Voters remember them better than positive spots (Perloff, 1998). Expecting events to be positive, people may be more attentive to images that violate optimistic expectations. Negative ads are also effective because they are repeated endlessly on the news and receive thousands of hits on YouTube. The imprimatur of news lends credibility to an advertisement, and its appearance on YouTube can bestow an aura that an infrequently-viewed commercial would not otherwise receive.

Negative ads are particularly likely to succeed when they resonate with concerns already present in voters' minds. In theory of reasoned action terms, advertisements are especially effective when they connect with salient beliefs and feelings. In 2008, McCain drew early blood with this strategy, playing on voters' feeling that Obama was all show and no substance, a celebrated speaker out of touch with economic woes.

A television ad showed Obama speaking to large crowds in Europe. As the voiceover intoned, "He's the biggest celebrity in the world," images of Paris Hilton and Britney Spears appeared on the screen. "But is he ready to lead?" the announcer asked, proceeding to unmask the celebrity Obama by suggesting he was insensitive to voters' concerns about rising gas prices and taxes. The ad, which aired frequently in the summer, seemed to move the poll numbers in McCain's direction.

It also generated a parody spot on YouTube, produced by the celebrity herself, Paris Hilton. It began, "He's the oldest celebrity in the world—like super-old, old enough to remember when dancing was a sin. But is he ready to lead? Hey America, I'm Paris Hilton and I'm a celebrity too. Only I'm not from the olden days and I'm not promising change like that other guy. I'm just hot."

Negative ads frequently call on associational principles, tarring the opponent by linking him or her with a negatively-valued person or issue. The advertisement seeks to access or "put the voter in touch" with emotionally-charged feelings that are part of a strong attitude. Both presidential candidates developed a barrage of associational negative ads in the 2008 election. Some were misleading.

In a Spanish-language ad targeted at Hispanic voters, Obama linked McCain with Rush Limbaugh, whose picture was shown along with a phrase attributed to him, "stupid, unskilled Mexicans." The ad suggested that McCain "made immigration reform fail," even though he had sponsored a compromise bill with Senator Edward Kennedy. The ad attempted to tarnish McCain by linking him with Limbaugh, presumably seen as prejudiced in the Hispanic community. It implied that McCain was anti-Hispanic, when he had spoken positively of Hispanic achievements. Experts viewed Obama's ad as misleading (Rohter, 2008).

Negative ads frequently call on ELM principles. They access association-based peripheral cues, such as those discussed above, for low involved voters. Ads employ issue arguments or nasty candidate attacks for highly involved voters.

**Box 11.4** |

Although negative ads can be effective and are viewed by critics as political propaganda, they are not magic bullets. When they are perceived to be too strident or irrelevant to individuals' material concerns, they are not likely to persuade targeted voters.

Negative ads raise broad ethical issues. Are candidate attacks morally acceptable? Do they cross an ethical line? Or are they legitimate weapons of political discourse?

Few would disagree that attack messages are unethical when the communicator deliberately transmits false information. But most ads are more nuanced. They can be literally true, but contain information that is misleading or invites false inferences (Jamieson, 1992). These ads are morally unacceptable on deontological grounds. Complicating matters, utilitarian scholars make a strong case that negative campaigning can advance democratic goals. Negative ads contain more issue information than positive spots (Geer, 2006). Positive advertisements, frequently lauded, can puff up a candidate in ways that are as deceptive as negative ads. Moreover, voters have a right to know the shortcomings of an incumbent's record or the weaknesses in a candidate's positions. Negative advertisements put this information directly before the electorate, helping them make a more informed voting choice. The system also has a way of righting itself. When negative ads are perceived as too strident, voters ignore them.

portrayals of the good life presented in ads carry with them the implicit understanding that they are idealizations, not documentary reports" (1997, p. 268). In effect, advertising defenders say, "Don't worry; be happy." Advertising is capitalism's playful communication, an effort to give people an outlet for universal human fantasies.

In the end, the verdict on advertising depends on the criteria we use to judge it. Judged in terms of consequences on society, advertising's effects are ambiguous. Exposure to beautiful people or unimaginable wealth may cause dissatisfaction in some consumers (Richins, 1991), but can lead others to reach for loftier goals. Judged strictly on truth-telling criteria, advertising rarely makes product claims that are demonstrably false. However, it almost always exaggerates, puffs up products, and links products with intangible rewards. "All advertising tells lies," Leslie Savan says. Yet she notes that "there are little lies and there are big lies. Little lie: This beer tastes great. Big lie: This beer makes you great" (1994, p. 7).

In the final analysis, advertising will remain an ethically problematic, but necessary, part of capitalist society. Needed to differentiate and promote products that (truth be told) differ only trivially from one another, advertising keeps the engines of the free market economy rolling. It increases demand and allows companies to sell products, prosper, and employ managers and workers. On the macroeconomic level, advertising plays an essential, critical role in contemporary capitalism. From an ethical perspective, advertising remains, as Schudson put it, an "uneasy persuasion" (1986).

# CONCLUSIONS

We all assume we're not affected in the slightest by advertising. We can see through those ploys, we tell ourselves; it's everyone else—the audience, the unwashed masses who are vulnerable. But this is a fallacy, an illusion (Sagarin, Cialdini, Rice, & Serna, 2002). If you are right that other people are influenced by advertisements, then it certainly stands to reason that you, too, should be swayed. On the other hand, if you are correct that you are not influenced and everyone else presumably claims the same lack of influence, then you exaggerate the effects of advertising on others (Perloff, 2008). "In either case," James Tiedge and colleagues note, "most people appear to be willing to subscribe to the logical inconsistency inherent in maintaining that the mass media influence others considerably more than themselves" (Tiedge, Silverblatt, Havice, & Rosenfeld, 1991, p. 152). (Communication researchers call this the third-person effect: the notion that persuasive media do not affect "you" or "me"—but, rather, "them"—the third persons. See Box 11.5 for a discussion.)

The reality is that, of course, we are influenced by advertising—sometimes subtly, other times quite directly. Indeed, advertising is such a pervasive part of American culture that it is difficult to conjure up mental images of products that have not been formed through advertising. If you were asked to free-associate about Coca-Cola, Budweiser, Nike, Herbal Essences, or cars running the gamut from Mustangs to minivans, your mental images would undoubtedly contain ideas and pictures gleaned from commercials. It is physically difficult, if not impossible, to call to mind an advertising-free image of products. This is because advertising plays a critical role in shaping, reinforcing, and even changing attitudes toward products.

Little wonder that critics have charged that advertising's power comes from subliminally embedded messages that elude conscious awareness. Research finds that subliminal communications exert virtually no impact on attitudes. However, the conscious belief that a message contains a subliminal message can influence attitudes. The subliminal notion is more hoax than reality, but it persists because people cling to simplistic ideas about how advertising works.

As suggested by the ELM, advertising works through different pathways under low and high involvement. When viewing ads for low-involvement products, consumers process information peripherally. Repetition, associational appeals, and celebrity source endorsements are influential. Association, whose theoretical foundations run the gamut from classical conditioning to accessibility, is a potent weapon in advertising campaigns.

When thinking about more personally consequential purchases, consumers process ads centrally, taking into account the benefits that products offer and the psychological functions that products serve. When directing ads at highly involved consumers, advertisers use factual messages and symbolic appeals targeted to particular attitude functions. Advertising frequently invites consumers to imagine that their futures will be brighter if they purchase the product or join the organization the ad is promoting.

Although advertising is pervasive, it does not magically alter attitudes. As social judgment theory reminds us, advertising will not mold deep-seated attitudes toward products. It is not apt to change attitudes on the spot. And, of course, some ads fail to

## Box 11.5 | ADVERTISING AND THE POWER OF PERCEPTION

A new product is advertised. It could be for the latest MP3 player, video game, perfume, beer, or sports car. What happens when people watch commercials like these? Well, many things. They enjoy the ad, remark to themselves the ad is cool (or cheesy), think about the product, decide they don't like it, or alternatively fantasize about partaking in the activities displayed in the ad. But something else happens too. Viewers make a judgment that the ad is going to influence others. This may not be a centrally-processed judgment, but people invariably presume that an advertisement will have an impact. And this perception—this belief about the advertisement's impact—has ripple effects that are very interesting and, in some cases, consequential.

This is a somewhat different arena of persuasive effects than has been discussed up to this point. The focus has been on direct effects of sources, messages, and advertising on attitudes. But this is an indirect influence, and it revolves around perception. We observe this when a consumer assumes that advertisements for a product—like Nintendo Wii sometime ago—will cause others to want to buy the product. Based on this perception, our consumer decides he better rush to the mall to get his Nintendo Wii before everyone else does, or opts to order the game equipment online in the wee (no pun intended!) hours of the morning when everyone else is still asleep. The interesting thing is that advertising may not have this effect at all, but it has, through the power of perception, produced a self-fulfilling prophecy.

This notion flows from the third-person effect, or what communication researcher Albert C. Gunther calls the presumed influence hypothesis. Gunther has examined consequences of simply *presuming* media influence others. In one study, Gunther and colleagues focused on pre-teens, who tend to be very concerned with their perceptions of others and end up behaving in ways they believe will be popular with peers. These perceptions are especially influential in the case of cigarette smoking. Perceived peer smoking, or believing your friends light up, has a greater impact on smoking than whether or not friends actually do.

Gunther, Bolt, Borzekowski, Liebhart, and Dillard (2006) asked sixth and seventh graders to indicate how much exposure they had to prosmoking advertisements in magazines, the Internet, and stores, as well as to actors smoking on TV and in movies. They also asked students to estimate peer exposure to smoking ads (how often they thought their peers had seen or heard prosmoking messages) and assessed perceptions of smoking prevalence (an estimate of how many students their age smoke cigarettes at least once a week), and attitudes toward cigarette smoking.

The ads had intriguing effects. The more exposure students had to smoking messages, the more they thought their peers saw these messages. Perceived peer exposure in turn led students to assume that smoking was prevalent. Importantly, perceiving their peers smoked cigarettes led students to develop more positive personal attitudes toward smoking. Notice that the ads did not influence smoking attitudes directly. Instead, the

**Box 11.5** |

ads—indirectly and subtly—led students to infer that their peers were influenced by prosmoking messages and had therefore decided to light up. Presumably, a desire to fit in with a perceived climate of smoking pushed students to evaluate smoking more favorably themselves. This raises intriguing questions. If blame is to be assigned, is advertising at fault? Or is this a stretch if pre-teens are themselves attributing effects to the ads? Or is it a subtle combination of advertising content and psychological perceptions?

Whatever the causal chain, there is little doubt that many persuasive messages work in this manner. Teenage girls acknowledge that televised images of thin bodies are unrealistic. However, if they perceive that girls in their peer group buy into these televised images, they may think it is cool to accept these images themselves (Park, 2005). It's a fascinating alternative approach to media, this emphasis on perceived effects. You can see that it might suggest different ways of altering attitudes than standard psychological models. For example, if perceptions are the key, then communicators need to counter the mistaken perception that smoking is prevalent or that prosmoking ads influence everybody (Gunther et al., 2006; see also Paek, 2009 for an interesting study of perceived peer influence).

This general approach has been adopted in campaigns designed to alter attitudes toward binge drinking, a topic discussed in Chapter 12. The perceptual approach has become very popular because of the powerful role communication-induced perceptions play in convincing college students to drink. It offers an insightful approach to altering drinking attitudes, but like all approaches ends up raising new questions, as well as eliciting criticisms.

The fascinating thing is that advertisements appear to influence people not just by altering attitudes toward products, but by affecting attitudes about what other people think about the advertisements. And when people begin to behave based on these perceptions, then perception has become reality and advertising has exerted an impact that seems almost magical but, of course, is quite real and in some cases rather disturbing.

resonate with consumers at all. As a general rule, advertising works gradually and with repetition as it creates meanings, arouses emotions, and meshes with consumers' values, lifestyles, and even fantasies about products.

Like other aspects of contemporary communications, advertising is in the midst of change. The 30-second advertisement no longer reigns supreme in an era when viewers with TiVos can zap through commercials, and millions of people have become accustomed to getting entertainment for free on Web sites like YouTube. Advertising increasingly must struggle to get its message heard in a noisy, cluttered world (Thaler & Koval, 2003). Advertisers are adapting their psychological appeals, targeting more nonlinear communications on the Internet and cell phones to those who are used to clicking from icon to icon and symbol to symbol. They are involving consumers in the creation of brands by sponsoring contests on the Internet that invite enthusiasts to submit broadcast-quality ads. Some companies are doing experiential marketing that capitalizes on consumers' proclivity to snap pictures of products and post them on the Internet. Other companies like Nike and Sony are blurring the line between entertainment and advertising by posting videos on YouTube that look genuine but are actually commercial messages. Others are melding their marketing to the format of the Web (Weber, 2007). They are communicating interactively, focusing less on designing pre-packaged messages and more on creating communities. These communities promote social networking with virtual friends, generating and sharing content, and (advertisers hope) psychological identification with the product or service. With techniques like these, advertisers are devising new tricks in an old game.

Critics worry about ethical consequences. They note that new communication technologies offer advertisers a treasure trove of opportunities to invade consumers' privacy. Wireless companies that place ads for clients on mobile sites can have as many as 20 units of data about a cell phone customer who has spent time at the site or played with a network application (Clifford, 2009). An advertiser may know the user's gender, age, favorite sports team and, thanks to global position system technology, the individual's travel patterns. These devices can help advertisers develop ads exquisitely targeted at particular cell phone consumers, a trend that concerns consumer privacy advocates.

Ever controversial, advertising has been condemned by those who see in it a ready way to manipulate Americans into buying products they don't need. Critics argue that advertising inculcates a strange philosophy of life that puts great faith in the ability of products to satisfy universal human desires. Yet even those who criticize advertising ethics acknowledge that people seem to have a need for the "things" advertisers promote.

Whether due to human nature, contemporary capitalism, or a complex combination of both, "things are in the saddle," critic Twitchell notes. But, he adds, "We put them there. If some of us want to think that things are riding us, that's fine. The rest of us know better" (1999, p. 19).

# Chapter 12

# Communication Campaigns

$B$ILL Alcott and Sy Graham were horrified. They were aghast at what people did to their bodies, day after day shoveling unhealthy, even dangerous, food into their mouths. Didn't people know the damage that meat, fried foods, and butter did to the stomach and heart? Convinced that Americans needed to change their diets, Alcott and Graham organized a health food store that supplied fresh fruits and vegetables. A proper diet, in their view, consisted of wheat bread, grains, vegetables, fruits, and nuts. By eating healthy food and avoiding anything that harmed the body, Graham and Alcott emphasized, people could live longer, healthier lives.

Sound familiar? Another example of contemporary activists trying to convince consumers to give up junk food? Well—not exactly. Alcott and Graham were committed health reformers, but they communicated their message some time ago. More than 150 years ago, to be precise! William Alcott and Sylvester Graham, born in the late 1700s, promoted their nutrition reform campaign in the 1830s. They were early advocates of health education, pioneers in a clean-living movement that began in the United States in the 1800s and continues to this day. Alcott's writings can be found in scattered libraries across the country. Graham—or at least his name—is known worldwide through his Graham cracker (Engs, 2000).

Long before it became fashionable to tout one's opposition to smoking or drugs, activists were pounding the pavement, preaching and proselytizing. Campaigns to improve the public health date back to the early 1800s, with Alcott and Graham's vegetarianism, health reformers' condemnation of the "evil, deadly" tobacco, and the Temperance Movement's efforts to promote abstinence from alcohol. Clean-living movements, as Ruth Clifford Engs (2000) calls them, took on special urgency during the 1830s and 1840s, with the outbreak of cholera, an infectious disease that spread through filthy water, a common problem during a time when drainage systems were poor or nonexistent and pigs roamed the streets feeding on uncollected garbage. Although the causes of cholera could be traced to the social environment, cholera (like AIDS a century and a half later) was viewed as "God's punishment for vice, sin, and moral flaws" (Rushing, 1995, p. 168).

The cholera epidemic led to massive changes in sanitation. It also catalyzed the public-health movement in the United States. Over the course of the nineteenth and twentieth centuries, in response to infectious diseases and public-health problems, reformers launched campaign after campaign. These included promotion of "do-it-yourself," herb-based cures for disease, religious revivalist efforts in the 1880s that linked physical fitness to moral fitness, and venereal disease education movements that began in the early twentieth century and continue apace in the twenty-first.

Public campaigns have not focused exclusively on health. Some of the most potent campaigns in the United States have centered on political issues. The Revolutionary Generation—Washington, Jefferson, Adams, and Revere—used newspapers and symbolic protests like the Boston Tea Party to convince their peers to revolt against England. The nineteenth century witnessed the growth of antislavery abolitionists, the Women's Suffrage (Right to Vote) Movement, and—unfortunately—crusades to prevent "undesirable" people (such as Irish Catholics) from emigrating to the United States (Engs, 2000; Pfau & Parrott, 1993).

Political and health campaigns flourished in the twentieth century, with the proliferation of television and realization that activists could change institutions through a combination of persuasion and protest. In the public-health arena, we have continuing campaigns to convince people to quit smoking, stop boozing, reject drugs, and practice safe sex. In the political arena, campaigns are ubiquitous. Presidential elections, local elections, crime prevention, gun control, abortion, stem cell research, the war on terrorism —these are all arenas that have witnessed intensive communication campaigns.

Campaigns reflect this nation's cultivation of the art of persuasion. They rely on argumentation, sloganeering, and emotional appeals in an effort to mold public attitudes. They are not always pretty or logical. They can cross into coercion, as when antismoking groups push for bans on smoking in the workplace. They are conducted to shape public policy, as well as attitudes.

Campaigns—colorful, vibrant, controversial, and American in their smell and taste— are the focus of this final chapter. The chapter is organized into several sections. The first describes the nature of campaigns. The second reviews major theories of campaign effects. In the third section, I summarize knowledge of key campaign effects. The fourth section touches on ethical issues surrounding campaigns, and the final portion looks briefly at campaigns waged in the political arena.

## THINKING ABOUT CAMPAIGNS

This is your brain on drugs . . . Parents: The antidrug . . . Welcome to Loserville. Population: You . . . Friends don't let friends drive drunk.

These are some of the most famous emblems of public information campaigns in the United States. However, campaigns involve more than clever slogans. They are systematic, organized efforts to mold health or social attitudes through the use of communication. Or, to be more specific, campaigns can be defined broadly as:

(1) purposive attempts (2) to inform, persuade, or motivate behavior changes (3) in a relatively well-defined and large audience (4) generally for noncommercial benefits to the individuals and/or society at large (5) typically within a given time period (6) by means of organized communication activities involving mass media and (7) often complemented by interpersonal support.

(Rice & Atkin, 2009, p. 436)

People don't devise campaigns with the flick of a wrist. Campaigns require time and effort. Typically, activists or professional organizations hatch a campaign concept. They sculpt the idea, working with marketing and communication specialists; pretest messages; and take their communications to the real world in the hope they will influence behavior.

Like advertising, information campaigns apply theories to practical problems. However, advertising campaigns differ from their public information counterparts in a variety of ways:

■ Commercial advertising is designed to make a profit for companies. Information campaigns are not purely capitalistic undertakings. They are designed to promote social ideas or improve public health. Typically, pro-social projects have smaller budgets than advertising campaigns. This can limit their effectiveness. What's more, advertising can work at cross-purposes with health campaigns. Campaigns designed to promote healthy eating are thwarted by glitzy advertisements that hype junk food.

■ News plays a greater role in information campaigns than it does in advertising. Advertising involves paid commercial messages. Campaigns utilize ads, but they also attempt to relay messages through the "nonpaid media": news. For example, health education planners have worked with journalists to produce stories that discuss dangers of cigarette smoking and a high-cholesterol diet (Flora, 2001).

■ Interpersonal and organizational communication plays a more important role in campaigns than in advertising. The McGruff "Take a bite out of crime" campaign supplemented media messages with supportive communication from community groups, businesses, and local police forces (O'Keefe, Rosenbaum, Lavrakas, Reid, & Botta, 1996). The Stanford cardiovascular risk reduction project involved multiple communication efforts, including hundreds of educational sessions and distribution of thousands of nutrition tip sheets to grocery stores. The D.A.R.E. (Drug Abuse Resistance Education) campaign developed an elaborate school curriculum, with police officers teaching children ways to say no to drugs.

■ Ad campaigns try to induce people to do something, like buying a six-pack of beer or soft drinks. Information campaigns often try to convince consumers not to perform a particular activity (not to smoke, litter, or drive after imbibing).

■ Information campaigns invariably face more daunting obstacles than commercial efforts do. It is usually easier to convince someone to buy a commercial product than to "buy into" the idea that she should quit smoking or consuming junk food.

■ Campaigns frequently target their messages at the 15 percent of the population that is least likely to change its behavior (Harris, 1999). These may be the poorest, least educated members of society, or the most down-and-out intravenous drug users who continue to share HIV-infected needles. By contrast, commercial campaigns focus on the mainstream—on those who are shopping for a product or a dream.

■ Information campaigns involve more highly charged political issues than do commercial efforts. Campaigns frequently encounter strong opposition from powerful industries, such as tobacco companies, beer distributors, oil companies, or gun manufacturers. Antitobacco campaigns, for example, have become embroiled in the politics and economics of tobacco production.

■ Campaigns are more controversial than ads. Even critics acknowledge that advertising is humorous, fun, and clever. Campaigns touch more directly on values, prejudices, or self-interested positions. They can elicit strong sentiments. For example, gun-control campaigns pit the value of social responsibility (gun companies should not sell products that endanger citizens) against the equally important value of individual liberty (people have a right to arm themselves to protect their property and families).

## Locating Effects

What impact do campaigns and media have on public health? That's a big question; thus, you need big ideas to help you grapple with it. Communication scholars Kim Walsh-Childers and Jane D. Brown (2009) developed a framework to help explain media influences on personal and public health. They proposed that mass media effects fall into three categories: (a) intention of the message communicator (intended/unintended), (b) level of influence (personal/public), and (c) outcome (positive/negative). An effect can be intended, as when health communicators develop campaigns to reduce binge drinking, or unintended, as when a reader is affected by a news story that reports on an accident caused by a drunk driver. The bulk of effects discussed in this chapter are intended, since they emanate from campaigns designed to influence attitudes.

A campaign effect can occur at the personal level (a public service ad convinces parents to buy a new child safety seat to protect their infant) or at the public level (Americans learn from news stories that properly installed child seats can reduce the risk of injury to young kids, or a legislator decides, after watching campaign ads, to introduce a bill requiring that all new cars have a special anchoring device to keep the safety seat in place). Finally, effects can be positive or negative.

Viewed in this way, campaigns are multifaceted phenomena. They are complex events that can be examined from different points of view. A good way to begin this examination is to look at theories articulated to explain campaign effects.

## THEORETICAL PERSPECTIVES

Three major models of campaigns have been developed. The first is a psychological, individual-level perspective. The other two approaches focus on the bigger picture, viewing campaigns from a macro, community-level orientation.

The psychological approach emphasizes that you can't expect a campaign to change behavior instantly, lickety-split. Instead, change occurs gradually, in stages, in line with the ancient Chinese proverb that "a journey of a thousand miles begins with a single step." For example, J. O. Prochaska and colleagues note that people progress through different stages of change, including pre-contemplation, during which they are not aware they have a psychological problem, to contemplation, in which they begin considering how to make a change in behavior, to action, in which they actually modify risky behaviors (Prochaska, DiClemente, & Norcross, 1992). Persuasive communications are tailored to the needs of people at a particular stage. Messages directed at pre-contemplators try to convince them that their behaviors (chain-smoking) put them and loved ones at risk, while communications geared to contemplators encourage them to consider substituting a new behavior for the risky behavior (chewing Nicorette gum instead of smoking Newports). There is some evidence that an affective message is more likely to jar pre-contemplators into changing dietary attitudes. A cognitive message is more effective with contemplators, who are motivated to centrally process information (Hampton, Brinberg, Peter, & Corus, 2009).

A second approach combines stages of change with persuasive communication theory. According to McGuire (1989), persuasion can be viewed as a series of input and output steps. In Figure 12.1, the input column labels refer to standard persuasion variables out of which messages can be constructed. The output row headings correspond to the steps that individuals must be persuaded to take if the message is to have its intended impact.

As the figure shows, a message must clear many hurdles if it is to successfully influence attitudes and behavior. An antidrug campaign may not clear the first hurdle—exposure—because it never reaches the target audience, or alternatively because receivers, finding the message threatening, tune it out as soon as they view it. Or the message may pass the first few steps, but get knocked out of the box when it threatens deeper values or psychological needs.

The input–output matrix has an optimistic side. It says that campaigns can succeed even if they don't lead to major changes in behavior. Indeed, such changes aren't always reasonable to expect, based only on short-term exposure to communications. Campaigns can be regarded as successful if they get people to remember an antidrug ad (Step 4) or if they teach them how to say no to attractive drug-using peers (Step 5). Over time, through subsequent interventions, people can be persuaded to make long-term behavioral changes (Steps 10–12).

Stage-based psychological models are useful. However, they ignore the larger context—the community and society in which campaigns take place. The next two theories address these issues.

## Diffusion Theory

Developed by Everett Rogers (1995), this approach examines the processes by which innovations diffuse, or spread through, society. Campaigns are viewed as large-scale attempts to communicate innovative ideas and practices through mass media and interpersonal communication. The following can be regarded as innovations:

- seat belts
- child safety seats

- bicycle helmets
- designated drivers
- jogging
- low-cholesterol diets
- sunscreen lotion
- latex condom use
- pooper scoopers.

| INPUT: Independent (Communication) Variables / OUTPUT: Dependent Variables (Response Steps Mediating Persuasion) | SOURCE<br>number<br>unanimity<br>demographics<br>attractiveness<br>credibility • • | MESSAGE<br>type of appeal<br>type of information<br>inclusion/omission<br>organization<br>repetitiveness • • | CHANNEL<br>modality<br>directness<br>context • • | RECEIVER<br>demographics<br>ability<br>personality<br>lifestyle • • | DESTIN-ATION<br>immediacy/delay<br>prevention/cessation<br>direct/immunization • • |
|---|---|---|---|---|---|
| 1. Exposure to the communication | | | | | |
| 2. Attending to it | | | | | |
| 3. Liking, becoming interested in it | | | | | |
| 4. Comprehending it (learning what) | | | | | |
| 5. Skill acquisition (learning how) | | | | | |
| 6. Yielding to it (attitude change) | | | | | |
| 7. Memory storage of content and/or agreement | | | | | |
| 8. Information search and retrieval | | | | | |
| 9. Deciding on basis of retrieval | | | | | |
| 10. Behaving in accord with decision | | | | | |
| 11. Reinforcement of desired acts | | | | | |
| 12. Post-behavioral consolidating | | | | | |

**FIGURE 12.1** | Persuasion and campaign stages.

From McGuire, W. J. (1989). Theoretical foundations of campaigns. In R. E. Rice & C. K. Atkin (Eds.), *Public communication campaigns* (2nd ed., pp. 43–65). Thousand Oaks, CA: Sage. Reprinted by permission of Sage.

Diffusion theory identifies a number of factors that influence the adoption of innovations. An important variable is the *characteristic of the innovation*. The more compatible an innovation is with people's values and cultural norms, the more likely it is to diffuse rapidly in society. Conversely, the less congruent an innovation is with prevailing values, the less rapidly it is accepted. Environmental recycling and dropping litter in trash cans did not take hold in the 1960s because they diverged from the dominant ideologies: "Bigger is better" and "Commercial growth trumps all." Two decades later, when environmental preservation had emerged as a major cultural value, these practices were more widely adopted.

Another attribute of an innovation is the degree to which it promises a clear, salient reward to the individual. A barrier to condom use is that condoms do not offer an immediate reward. The advantage condoms offer—preventing pregnancy or HIV infection—is not visible immediately after the consummation of sex. As Rogers notes, "The unwanted event that is avoided . . . is difficult to perceive because it is a non-event, the absence of something that otherwise might have happened" (1995, p. 217). Partly because the benefits of condom use are not readily apparent, safer-sex practices have not always been a quick, easy sell. In a similar fashion, Americans have been reluctant to adopt a "green mind-set" (Gertner, 2009), in part because of the absence of rewards for adopting pro-environmental behaviors. Global warming does not viscerally scare many Americans —its effects are more abstract and distant. Diffusion theory suggests that campaigns designed to persuade people to adopt pro-environmental behaviors should either present salient rewards (such as money saved on gas from buying a Prius) or powerfully illustrate symbolic benefits of such actions.

Communication plays a critical role in the spread of innovations. Diffusion theory asserts that mass media are most influential in enhancing knowledge of the innovation, while interpersonal communication is more effective in changing attitudes toward the innovation. Newspapers, television, and the Internet have played a major role in informing people of unhealthy lifestyles. Why do you think so many people know that smoking causes cancer, buckling up can save your life, or unprotected, risky sex can lead to AIDS? Why do so many of us know you can reduce your cancer risk by quitting smoking, that physical exercise can promote longevity, or condoms can prevent HIV? The media have told us these things. Although the media are frequently criticized, they deserve credit for providing information about unhealthy lifestyles and ways to live a healthier life.

Such information comes from both news and entertainment media. News stories frequently set the agenda, or influence people's beliefs about what constitute the most important problems facing society (McCombs & Reynolds, 2002). Entertainment programming can also have an innovation-diffusing or agenda-setting impact (Singhal, Cody, Rogers, & Sabido, 2004). Spurred by activist groups, television producers have increasingly included discussion of such innovations as designated drivers, rape hotlines, and birth-control pills in their programs. One study reported a 17 percent increase in viewers' knowledge of emergency contraception after *ER* showed a victim of date rape being treated with a morning-after pill (Brown & Walsh-Childers, 2002). Spurred by findings like these, writers for *ER*, as well as *House* and *Grey's Anatomy* increasingly highlight important health issues in the programs. During the finale of *ER*,

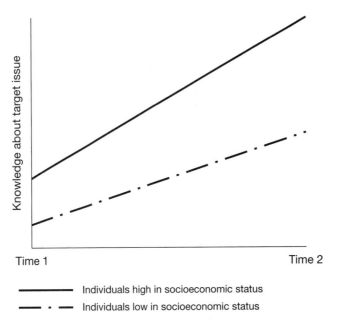

**FIGURE 12.2** | Schematic diagram of the knowledge gap. Communication occurs between Time 1 and Time 2.

Dr. Archie Morris was told that he would require angioplasty if he continued consuming meat pizza.

It is not all blue skies and rosy fields when it comes to media and campaigns. Consider that poor people or those with little education frequently know less about health issues than people who are wealthier or have more education under their belts (Freimuth, 1990). One objective of campaigns is to narrow the gap between the advantaged and disadvantaged members of society. Unfortunately, just the opposite can occur. Campaigns can widen the disparity so that, by the end of the campaign, the rich and better-educated people are even more knowledgeable of the problem than their poorer, less-educated counterparts (Gaziano, 1983; Viswanath & Finnegan, 1996). (This is known as the *knowledge gap*; see Figure 12.2.) There are a number of reasons why such knowledge gaps occur. One key reason is that the health information is less likely to reach, or be mentally accepted by, disadvantaged individuals. Those who have been disadvantaged by society may be so preoccupied with tangible survival needs that they neglect to focus on health issues that are of long-term personal importance.

In a related vein, those most at risk for a particular problem may be least likely to receive the campaign message. Healthy-eating campaigns that deliver messages during television news and through print media are most likely to reach individuals who are already eating nutritional foods (see Dutta-Bergman, 2004b). People with unhealthy eating habits, who are heavy users of TV sports and entertainment Web sites, may not receive the message. As a result, nutritional knowledge gaps between the rich and poor become larger.

Diffusion research suggests ways to reach low-income, low-educated individuals. The news media can publicize health innovations through special programming (Chew & Palmer, 1994). Healthy-eating campaigns could buy time on sports programs or place messages on Web sites frequented by unhealthy eaters. More generally, campaign specialists can supplement media coverage with intensive interpersonal efforts in the community. The similarity principle comes into play here (see Chapter 6). Individuals are typically more receptive to communications delivered by those who are perceived as sharing their values and background. As a staff member in an AIDS prevention program geared to gay Native Americans remarked:

> I think this is pretty basic for us, the philosophy of Natives helping Natives, and we got 100% Native staff, 100% Native board, most of our volunteers are Native, and it's really about hearing the information coming from another Native gay man.
>
> (Dearing, Rogers, Meyer, Casey, Rao, Campo,
> & Henderson, 1996, p. 357)

Of course, in an ideal world it wouldn't matter a whit whether the communicator was Native or gay—just whether the individual knew his stuff and cared about those he sought to influence (the basics of credibility). However, this is a real world, and people are frequently more apt to listen to someone whom they perceive to be similar to themselves, particularly when the topic is a stressful one.

Diffusion theory, in sum, tells us a great deal about how communications can publicize and promote innovations. However, it neglects the hard-nosed, savvy world of media marketing, a key element in today's campaigns. This is the focus of a second, macro approach to campaigns that applies marketing principles to health.

## Social Marketing

Social marketing is defined as "a process of designing, implementing, and controlling programs to increase the acceptability of a pro-social idea among population segments of consumers" (Dearing et al., 1996, p. 345). Social marketing is an intriguing concept. It says, in effect: "You know all those great ideas developed to sell products? You can use them to sell people on taking better care of their health. But to do that, you must understand marketing principles." There are five strategic steps in a social marketing campaign: (a) planning, (b) theory, (c) communication analysis, (d) implementation, and (e) evaluation and reorientation (Maibach, Kreps, & Bonaguro, 1993; see Figure 12.3).

**Planning**. During this first phase, campaigners make the tough choices. They select campaign goals. They decide whether to focus on creating cognitions or changing existing ones. They deliberate about whether to target attitudes or behavior.

**Theory**. Models, concepts, and theories are the backbone of campaigns (Slater, 2006). You cannot wage a campaign without some idea of what you want to achieve and how best to attain your objectives. The central issue is whether your idea is sound, based on concepts, and of sufficient breadth so as to suggest specific hypotheses. Ideas may be cheap, but good

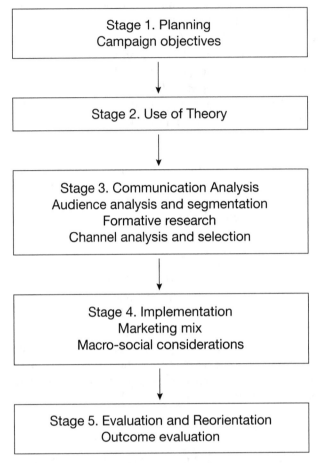

Stage 1. Planning
Campaign objectives

Stage 2. Use of Theory

Stage 3. Communication Analysis
Audience analysis and segmentation
Formative research
Channel analysis and selection

Stage 4. Implementation
Marketing mix
Macro-social considerations

Stage 5. Evaluation and Reorientation
Outcome evaluation

**FIGURE 12.3** | A strategic health communication campaign model.

Adapted from Maibach, E. W., Kreps, G. L., & Bonaguro, E. W. (1993). Developing strategic communication campaigns for HIV/AIDS prevention. In S. Ratzan (Ed.), *AIDS: Effective health communication for the 90s* (pp. 15–35).Washington, DC: Taylor & Francis.

ideas are invaluable. One thing that differentiates effective and ineffective campaigns is that the former reflect painstaking application of theoretical principles; the latter are based on "seat of the pants" intuitions. Theories suggest a host of specific campaign strategies, appeals, and ways to modify projects that aren't meeting stated objectives. Campaigns have employed behavioral theories, affective approaches, and cognitive models (Cappella, Fishbein, Hornik, Ahern, & Sayeed, 2001; Witte, Stokols, Ituarte, & Schneider, 1993). These frequently apply principles of commercial marketing—association, semiotics, mere exposure—and harness them for pro-social purposes. For example, campaigns to reduce prejudice have associated the minority group with positive images, used persuasive metaphors, and repeated messages emphasizing tolerance many times.

**Communication analysis**. After suitable theory and concept are selected, they must be aptly applied to the context. This occurs during the down-to-earth communication analysis phase of the campaign. Early on, campaign specialists conduct formative research to probe audience perceptions (Atkin & Freimuth, 2001). If you were devising a campaign to persuade children not to try cigarettes, you would want to know the negative consequences that kids associate with cigarettes (Bauman, Brown, Bryan, Fisher, Padgett, & Sweeney, 1988; Morrison, Gillmore, & Baker, 1995). You would discover that children don't worry about dying from smoking; they're more concerned about bad breath or becoming unpopular. Armed with these facts, you would develop messages that creatively played up these negative consequences. You would pretest your advertising spots to see which ones worked best, edit them, and ship them to local media for airing at appropriate times of the day.

**Implementation**. During this phase, the campaign is designed, finalized, and launched. Marketing principles play a critical role here. Of particular importance are the four Ps of marketing: product, price, placement, and promotion.

Product? Most of us do not associate products with health campaigns. Yet products can be pro-social, as well as commercial. Products marketed in health campaigns include Neighborhood Crime Watch posters, child safety seats, gun trigger locks, and Don't Drink and Drive pledge cards.

Products come with a price. The price can be monetary or psychological. In the AIDS context, planners debate whether to charge a price for condoms (dispensing them free of charge saves people money, but it also can make the product seem "cheap" or "unworthy"). Psychologically, the price of using condoms may be less pleasurable sex or fear of offending a partner. Campaigns devise messages to convince people that these costs are more than offset by the benefits that safer sex provides.

Placement involves deciding where to transmit the message. This is critically important, as correct placement can ensure reaching the target audience; incorrect placement can mean that a good message misses its target. The favorite weapon in communication campaigns is the public service advertisement (PSA), a promotional message placed in news, entertainment, or interactive media. Once novel, PSAs are now part of the media landscape—informational sound bites that savvy young people have come to enjoy or ignore. Clever, informative PSAs get noticed and can shatter illusions of invulnerability; dull—or obnoxious—ones are mentally discarded. Thus, market research and creative concept development play important roles in sculpting effective PSAs.

The channel—for example, television or Internet—is a key factor in placement decisions. Television allows campaigners to reach lots of people and to arouse emotions through evocative messages. However, it is very expensive. Interactive media offer several advantages. They are usually cheaper than other media, permit upgrading of messages, and allow campaigns to tailor messages to audience subgroups (Kreuter, Farrell, Olevitch, & Brennan, 2000).

Numerous Web sites and CD-ROMs impart health information, and these modalities are particularly likely to engage adolescents and college students. Researchers, who have pondered ways of most effectively using interactive media to influence young audiences, have noted that interactive media are likely to be especially effective when they use age-appropriate role models, promote online discussion, and involve learning by doing (Lieberman, 2001). Engaging, interactive techniques are especially appropriate in campaigns that revolve around video games. For example, one game, *Packy & Marlon*, teaches diabetic children self-management skills by simulating a diabetic character's blood sugar levels. Players can win the game if the food and insulin choices they make for the character allow his blood sugar to stay at normal, healthy levels. They lose if they make choices that push the character's blood sugar to such low or high levels that he cannot function. The game has produced improvements in diabetic children's self-management behaviors. Kids who regularly played the game experienced a 77 percent reduction in emergency room visits (Lieberman, 2001).

Complementing these trends, online and digital campaigns have become increasingly popular. Rice and Atkin (2009) describe a host of such campaigns—a pastiche of interactive games, jazzy Web sites with avatars, and even a memorable viral anti-smoking intervention that allows users to send smokers' coughs, calibrated by dryness and duration to individuals to help them kick the habit. Increasingly, campaigns on issues ranging from childhood obesity to drinking and driving are migrating to the Web, as well as to social networking sites that can build camaraderie through creation of online communities (Elliott, 2007).

Promotion, the final marketing P, flows out of the planning process. Promotion involves persuasion—application of theories discussed in this book and implemented in a campaign setting.

**Evaluation and reorientation**. This is the final phase of the campaign—the point at which planners discover if the campaign worked. Unlike campaigns of the nineteenth and early twentieth centuries, today's projects can be empirically assessed. Effects can be studied at the *individual level*, as when researchers compare those who saw many campaign messages with those who did not. If the campaign worked, individuals who saw many PSAs should change their attitudes more in the intended direction than those who saw relatively few.

Researchers also evaluate campaigns at the *community level*. One town is randomly assigned to be the treatment group; its citizens receive promotional materials—for example, on seat belt use. An equivalent community serves as the control—its residents are not exposed to campaign messages. Researchers then compare the communities—for instance by having police officers stand on street corners counting the number of drivers wearing safety belts. If a higher proportion of drivers in the treatment community wear safety belts than in the control town, the campaign is declared a success (Roberts & Geller, 1994).

Campaigns can also be assessed at the *state* level. Let's assume that the number of traffic accidents drop in Indiana shortly after the conclusion of a media campaign promoting seat belt use in the Hoosier state. Let's also assume that accidents in Iowa, a state that shares some demographic features with Indiana, do not decline over a similar time period. These data give us confidence that the Indiana campaign exerted a causal impact on seat belt behavior.

Evaluation is critical because it indicates whether campaign objectives have been met. It's not a perfect science. In surveys, one never knows for sure whether those who saw campaign messages were the same in all other ways as those who did not happen to view the campaign. In community evaluations, researchers can never be 100 percent certain that the treatment and control towns are exactly alike. If the treatment community in the safety belt study had more drivers who were older (and therefore more safety conscious) than the control community, the older age of drivers, rather than the campaign, could have produced the observed effects. In a similar fashion, if the Indiana news media extensively covered an automobile accident that involved the governor's wife, the news coverage—not the campaign—could have caused the concomitant decline in traffic accidents. Researchers take precautions to factor in these extraneous variables, quantifying their contributions in statistical tests.

Online media campaigns pose a different set of procedural problems. It can be difficult to convince individuals, who are randomly assigned to a particular intervention, to attend to a Web-based campaign. Sites that house campaigns can disappear or change without warning, and different subgroups in a particular sample may answer different portions of the questionnaire (Rice & Atkin, 2009). Hopefully, as researchers gain more experience assessing online campaigns, they will come to grips with these problems.

These difficulties notwithstanding, evaluation research offers a valuable way to assess campaign impact. It gives campaigners useful feedback for future campaigns. It also serves an important political function. Private and public groups spend hundreds of thousands of dollars on campaigns. They are entitled to know if they have gotten their money's worth. When government spends taxpayer money on antismoking or antidrug campaigns, the public has a right to know if socially valuable goals—reducing smoking or drug use—have actually been achieved.

There is one last point to be made about social marketing. Campaigns may be based on theory, planned according to marketing principles, and evaluated through high-powered statistics. However, they take place in the real world, with its rough edges, cultural norms, and political constraints. Societal norms and macrosocial factors influence campaigns in a variety of ways. Antismoking campaigns had little chance of changing attitudes so long as most Americans trusted the tobacco companies or doubted that smoking caused cancer. As Americans learned that tobacco companies withheld knowledge that smoking was addictive and accepted evidence of the causal impact of smoking on cancer as fact, antismoking campaigns faced a more receptive audience to their messages. Even so (and not surprisingly), antismoking campaigns attempting to increase public support for regulation of the tobacco industry have faced daunting opposition from the tobacco industry, as the gripping, factually based movie *The Insider* documented.

In a similar vein, AIDS prevention campaigns have been influenced by macrosocial and cultural factors. Americans' discomfort with homosexuality has impeded—indeed, doomed to failure—activists' efforts to persuade television networks to broadcast PSAs that talk frankly about safer sex among gay men (Perloff, 2001). On the other side of the cultural divide, gay political leaders in cities like San Francisco have sometimes stridently opposed public-health campaigns to clean up or close city bathhouses. Their resistance has stemmed from a strong libertarian desire to pursue private (but sometimes dangerous) pleasures and activities, as well as fears of being stigmatized by social institutions (Rotello, 1997). Thousands of miles away, in AIDS-infected Africa where tens of millions are expected to die in the first decade of the twenty-first century, campaigns are hampered by pro-sex cultural norms. In many African societies, sex is viewed 100 percent positively, as an essential form of recreation between lovers, casual friends, and even adulterers. Polygamy is widespread and sanctioned (Rushing, 1995). In addition, African prostitutes, who would like their clients to use condoms, are hindered by cultural norms that put sex in men's control. "We are women, we are weak and shy, we cannot ask them to use condoms," one prostitute acknowledged (Cameron, Witte, & Nzyuko, 1999, p. 153).

All these factors affect the design and implementation of social marketing campaigns. When we take theory into the real world, with all its politics, values, and emotional messiness, we find that life is more complex and campaigns are inseparable from the culture in which they take place.

## CAMPAIGN EFFECTS

Do campaigns work? Do they influence targeted attitudes and behaviors? What do you think? What's your best guess?

There is little question that campaigns face an up-hill battle. As McGuire's input–output matrix notes, interventions must first attract the target audience and capture its attention. This can be difficult. For a variety of psychological reasons, Caroline Schooler and colleagues note, "Those whom a campaign most seeks to reach with health information are the least motivated to pay attention to it" (1998, p. 414). The last thing addicted smokers, drug users, or gamblers want to do is pay attention to moralistic messages that tell them to stop doing what makes them happy.

Not only do campaigns not always succeed in reaching difficult-to-influence audiences, but they also turn them off with preachy messages or communications that aren't in sync with audience needs. Today's teenagers have grown up with health campaigns and have been lectured and hectored by well-meaning, but sometimes-overbearing, adults. When a media campaign tells them that they are engaging in unhealthy behavior, they can become resistant and reactive. The message may evoke a threat to their freedom, leading them to embrace the unhealthy behavior that the communicator proscribes (Burgoon, Alvaro, Grandpre, & Voulodakis, 2002; Dillard & Shen, 2005). *Psychological reactance theory* suggests that an overly-moralistic health message can threaten an individual's freedom and self-determination, causing the individual to do precisely the opposite of what the communicator recommends (Brehm, 1966). (As parents sang in a song from the musical, *The Fantasticks*: "Why did the kids put beans in their ears? No one can hear with beans in their ears. After a while the reason appears. They did it cause we said no!" Or as a character in the movie, *Hudson Hawk*, said, "I hated cigarettes until I saw my first No Smoking sign!")

Reactance is not the only barrier to campaign success. Even campaigns with creative messages may fail because planners lack money to repeat the message enough times to guarantee an effect. Effects produced by a campaign also may not persist over time. Knowledge of emergency contraception obtained from watching the *ER* episode mentioned earlier dropped significantly at a follow-up measurement (Brown & Walsh-Childers, 2002). Thus, there is no guarantee a campaign will work. It may fail, and many do.

Okay—but I wouldn't be devoting an entire chapter to this topic if campaigns failed consistently and repeatedly! In fact, a half-century of research indicates that if practitioners know their stuff, apply theory deftly, and utilize principles of social marketing, they can wage effective campaigns (Noar, 2006). Campaigns can and have changed health-related attitdes. They are particularly likely to succeed when practitioners:

1. Understand the audience and tailor messages so they congeal with the audience needs and preexisting attitudes. Messages are more likely to succeed if they *resonate with* or *fit* the psychological needs of audience members (Wan, 2008; Cesario Grant, & Higgins, 2004).
2. Segment the audience into different subgroups, fitting messages ever more exquisitely to the orientations of specialized groups.
3. Refine messages so that they are relevant, cogent (based on principles discussed in this book), and of high production value; this is particularly important when targeting young people, who have grown up with savvy, interactive media.
4. Coordinate efforts across media, and repeat messages over time and in different media and interpersonal channels.
5. Choose media channels (PSAs, news, entertainment TV, Internet) that are viewed by members of the target audience.
6. Use entertaining characters, visuals, and themes that weave together different messages (O'Keefe et al., 1996; Parrott, 1995).
7. Supplement media materials as much as possible with community contacts (McAlister & Fernandez, 2002; Rice & Atkin, 2002).
8. Appreciate that it is frequently easier to promote a new behavior (fruit and vegetable consumption) than to convince people to stop a dysfunctional behavior, such as unsafe sex (Snyder, 2001).
9. Try, whenever possible, to build enforcement into the campaign (Snyder & Hamilton, 2002); for example, seat belt campaigns emphasizing that police will enforce seat belt laws have been especially effective in promoting seat belt use.
10. Involve the community by building community participation into campaign conceptualization and design (Rice & Atkin, 2009). A campaign to reduce racial inequities in health care is more likely to succeed if it works with community organizations, like a Black church, to develop culturally relevant messages than if it assumes communications will work because theory says so.
11. Avoid overly-moralistic messages that threaten an individual's freedom and arouse reactance.
12. Adopt a realistic approach. Keep in mind how difficult it is to change deep-seated attitudes and well-learned behaviors. "Set realistic expectations of success . . ., be prepared for a long haul . . ., [and] give more emphasis to relatively attainable impacts, by aiming at more receptive segments of the audience and by creating or promoting more palatable positive products" (Atkin, 2002, p. 37).

With these factors in mind, it is time to turn to specific applications of campaign principles. The next sections review communication campaigns in context.

## THE McGRUFF CRIME PREVENTION PROJECT

Some years back, there was considerable concern about rising crime rates and rampant drug abuse. During the 1980s and 1990s, many people worried they would be mugged if they walked outside at night; inner-city neighborhoods were like war zones, terrorized by drug dealers; and there was little cooperation between neighborhood residents and police. In hopes of changing things for the better, the National Crime Prevention Council sponsored a public communication campaign designed to teach crime and drug prevention behaviors and to encourage citizens to take steps to protect themselves, their families, and their neighborhoods (O'Keefe et al., 1996).

The campaign, produced by the Advertising Council and widely disseminated in the media, centered on a series of entertaining public service announcements. The PSAs attempted to arouse fear about crime, while also generating anger at drug dealers and criminals. The centerpiece of the media campaign was an animated trench-coated dog named McGruff who urged viewers to take concrete steps "to take a bite out of crime," such as by locking doors and windows and participating in neighborhood crime watch programs (see Figure 12.4). Over time, the campaign branched out. Children and teens became a target audience, with PSAs focusing on missing children, drug abuse, and resisting peer pressure to take drugs.

McGruff, as the campaign is sometimes called, is generally regarded as a classic, textbook case of how to run an effective communication campaign. The project was well funded, repeated messages in different media using different motifs (thereby capitalizing on *mere exposure* principles), and promoted cognitive learning by employing an entertaining character (the McGruff dog). It also supplemented media by employing extensive community activities.

Garrett J. O'Keefe and colleagues systematically evaluated the project. Their findings include (O'Keefe, 1985):

- Eighty percent of a sample of U.S. adults recalled having seen or heard McGruff PSAs.
- Nearly 9 in 10 respondents said they believed the ads had increased children's awareness of neighborhood drug abuse. About a quarter of individuals exposed to the campaign said they had taken specific crime prevention precautions as a result of having viewed the PSAs.
- The decade-long campaign coincided with sharp increases in the number of people who used outdoor security lights and special locks on doors or windows.
- Exposure to the campaign led to significant increases in crime prevention behaviors, including reporting suspicious activities to the police and joining with others to prevent crime.

**FIGURE 12.4** | A McGruff "Take the bite out of crime" ad.
Reprinted with permission of the National Crime Prevention Council.

Successful as the campaign was, it is possible that it exerted several unanticipated negative effects. It might have led to increases in accidents by stimulating people untrained in gun use to purchase guns for self-protection. By encouraging people to report suspicious activities to the police, it may have unwittingly increased mistrust or suspicion of unorthodox, but hardly criminal, individuals. Campaigns frequently have unintended effects, and campaigners must hope that the benefits (crime reduction and increased citizen participation in community policing) exceed the costs. In the case of McGruff, the pluses far exceeded the minuses.

# ANTISMOKING AND CARDIOVASCULAR RISK REDUCTION CAMPAIGNS

These are probably the most famous public information campaigns in America. Many of us recall seeing PSAs that associate cigarettes with ugly, despicable images or suggest that no one cool smokes anymore ("Welcome to Loserville. Population: You"). Where do the ideas for these campaigns come from?

In a word, theory! Antismoking campaigns have been among the most theory driven of all public communication interventions. Campaigns have applied *cognitive, affective,* and *behavioral* concepts to the development of campaigns (Ohme, 2000).

Cognitively based campaigns have targeted children's beliefs about smoking and the types of people who smoke. Guided by the theory of reasoned action (see Chapter 3), researchers identify perceived drawbacks of smoking. "It's a gross habit, it smells . . . Even just being around people who smoke, you know, my eyes start to water and burn," children told researchers Laura A. Peracchio and David Luna, who used this information to devise antismoking messages (1998, p. 51). Based on findings that short-term negative consequences of smoking (bad smell and harm to eyes) are of central importance to kids, the researchers developed print ads that played on these themes:

> One of the ads, "Sock," depicts a dirty, grimy sweatsock with the caption, "Gross," next to an ashtray full of cigarette butts with the caption, "Really gross" . . . [A second] ad, "Tailpipe," reads, "Inhale a lethal dose of carbon monoxide and it's called suicide. Inhale a smaller amount and it's called smoking. Believe it or not, cigarette smoke contains the same poisonous gas as automobile exhaust. So if you wouldn't consider sucking on a tailpipe, why would you want to smoke?"
>
> (Peracchio & Luna, p. 53)

The first ad was simple and concrete; it worked well with 7- and 8-year-olds. The second was more complex and resonated more with 11-year-olds.

A more elaborate intervention, devised by Michael Pfau and his associates, succeeded in stiffening adolescents' resistance to experimenting with cigarettes. Pfau drew on inoculation theory, a cognitive approach discussed in Chapter 5. Persuaders employing inoculation deliberately expose people to a message they want them to reject, then follow up this initial treatment with a dose of powerful arguments refuting the message. Applying inoculation to antismoking, Pfau and Van Bockern (1994) told seventh-grade students that peer pressure would cause some of them to modify their opposition to smoking and begin to smoke. This was subsequently followed by statements that smoking was cool or won't affect "me," coupled with *refutations* of these arguments. The inoculation treatment intensified negative attitudes toward smoking.

A cautionary note: cognitive campaigns directed at young people should start before high school. Around the end of middle school, as pressures to be popular mount and self-esteem frequently plummets, teenagers look to smoking as a way to be cool or to enhance their identities (e.g., Pfau & Van Bockern, 1994). Researchers recommend that inoculation campaigns commence in seventh grade—or before.

Affectively oriented campaigns focus on feelings associated with smoking. Tobacco advertising has succeeded in linking smoking with relaxation, pleasant affect, and popularity (Romer & Jamieson, 2001). To counter this, campaigns apply classical conditioning and associative network ideas discussed earlier in this book. They explicitly associate ads with negative images. For example:

> In one ad . . . a young male is chewing tobacco and spitting it from time to time into a soft drink paper cup. His female friend, whose attention is absorbed by the movie they are watching, mechanically grabs the cup and reaches it to her mouth without looking inside. A scream is then heard, suggesting that the friend was horrified and disgusted when she tasted the liquid and, by extension, was also horrified and disgusted by her friend's behavior . . . [In another ad], a beautiful girl is smoking a cigarette, but each time she inhales her face is covered with more and more nicotine and tar. This ad creates a huge aesthetic dissonance and shows that, regardless of how attractive you are, smoking makes you repulsive.
>
> (Ohme, 2000, p. 315)

Other affectively oriented ads play cleverly on fear appeals, walking the razor-thin line between not scaring teens enough and scaring them too much. One TV spot developed by the American Legacy Foundation parodies a soft-drink ad. Three young people bungee jump off a bridge to save cans of fictional Splode soda. Two of the jumpers grab a can and are yanked back to the safety of the bridge. The third jumper's can explodes as he opens it, and he disappears in a burst of flames. On the screen appear the words, "Only one product actually kills a third of the people who use it. Tobacco." There is strong evidence that American Legacy's "truth" campaign led to a decline in smoking among adolescents (Farrelly, Davis, Haviland, Healton, & Messeri, 2005).

The third category of antismoking campaigns—behavioral interventions—draws on social learning theory, a model developed by Albert Bandura. Noting that people do not have to be rewarded, like rats or pigeons, to learn new behaviors, Bandura (1977) has called attention to the powerful role that observing role models plays in social influence. Theorists have adapted his ideas to public health. Using mass media, interpersonal instruction, and behavior modification techniques, they have detailed the dangers of smoking and of maintaining a high-cholesterol diet. At the same time, campaigns have taught people the cognitive skills necessary to quit smoking and adopt a healthier lifestyle.

The classic and most elaborate of these interventions were developed at Stanford University. The campaigns included TV spots, radio PSAs, and a weekly doctor's column that appeared in Spanish-language newspapers. School curricula, workplace classes, and intensive interpersonal instruction supplemented the media messages. During interpersonal sessions, counselors used behavior modification techniques, encouraging smokers to substitute sugar-free lozenges and asking others to keep track of the healthy food they ate each week.

Researchers dreamed up a nifty way to evaluate the campaigns. They chose several small Californian cities with comparable demographic characteristics. Certain cities were assigned to the media treatments; others served as controls. Researchers then compared respondents in the treatment and control cities on several indices, including health knowledge, smoking reduction, and decreases in cholesterol level.

The campaigns had modest effects, smaller than some anticipated, but practically significant (Hornik, 2002). The Stanford communications increased knowledge of healthy eating, diet, and exercise. What's more, communities that received the campaign displayed significant decreases in cholesterol level and blood pressure. At-risk individuals who received interpersonal instruction dramatically reduced the number of cigarettes they smoked a day (Farquhar, Fortmann, Flora, Taylor, Haskell, Williams, Maccoby, & Wood, 1990; Maccoby & Farquhar, 1975).

## State Antismoking Campaigns

Emboldened by Stanford's efforts but determined to do better, campaign planners in several states have mounted impressive antismoking interventions. Using state funds and monies available from the legal settlement with the tobacco companies, states have blitzed the airwaves with antismoking messages. Armed with as much as $90 million, campaigners have enlisted help from creative advertising agencies, developing ads like one aired in California. The advertisement "used actual footage from a congressional hearing, during which the chief executives of each of the major tobacco companies denied, under oath, that nicotine was addictive. The advertisement culminated with the question, 'Do they think we're stupid?'" (Pierce, Emery, & Gilpin, 2002, p. 100).

Campaigns in California, Arizona, Massachusetts, and elsewhere in the United States have significantly influenced smoking attitudes and behavior (Burgoon, Hendriks, & Alvaro, 2001; Pierce et al., 2002; Siegel & Biener, 2002). A multimillion dollar, decade-long campaign seems to have produced a sharp decline in cigarette consumption in California (see Figure 12.5). An Arizona media campaign that endlessly repeated the hip phrase, "*Tobacco: Tumor-causing, teeth-staining, smelly, puking habit*," pushed young people to evaluate smoking more negatively. In addition, media PSAs, coupled with school-based smoking prevention programs, reduced smoking by 35 percent in portions of the U.S. Northeast and Northwest (Worden & Flynn, 2002).

## Macrosocial Picture

One of the critical hard-fact realities of antismoking campaigns is that they take place in a heavily politicized environment, in which well-funded public-health groups battle billion-dollar tobacco companies, who in turn heavily lobby state legislators who control the purse strings for these campaigns. In California, the fighting has been particularly vicious. When the campaign aired its "Do they think we're stupid?" spot, the tobacco industry issued a legal threat to the network TV stations in California. Under political pressure, state campaign planners dumped the ad (Pierce et al., 2002).

In spite of these obstacles, the California campaign succeeded. It did so because the tobacco control program had significant grass-roots support; its messages also contained emotional arguments that smokers found persuasive. Antismoking campaigns have had similar success elsewhere in the country (and abroad as well). Yet, at the outset, few believed that tobacco education stood much of a chance, in light of the political and

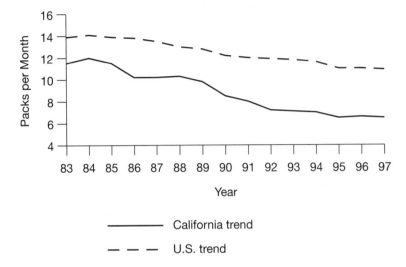

**Capita Consumption for Cigarettes
California vs. U.S.**

———— California trend

— — — U.S. trend

**FIGURE 12.5** | Seasonally adjusted trend of per-capita cigarette consumption, California versus the United States.

Note: Smoking dropped in the United States and California from 1983 to 1997, but the rate of decline increased dramatically in California after the state's smoking campaign began in 1989. In the rest of the United States, it did not. Smoking consumption in California was also below that of the rest of the United States.

From Pierce, J. P., Emery, S., & Gilpin, E. (2002). The California tobacco control program: A long-term health communication project. In R. Hornik (Ed.), *Public health communication: Evidence for behavior change* (pp. 97–114). Mahwah, NJ: Lawrence Erlbaum Associates.

economic power wielded by cigarette companies. However, media campaigns have succeeded in changing attitudes toward smoking, promoting bans on secondhand smoke, and creating a public opinion climate that has made it easier for attorneys to sue tobacco companies successfully for damages. By riding the wave of a contemporary public-health movement, seizing on antipathy to Big Tobacco, appealing to American values of self-improvement, and helping to pass election referenda to ban smoking in public places, the David of anticigarette marketing has successfully battled the Goliath of American tobacco companies. While many Americans smoke—and they always will, as long as cigarettes are legal—the contemporary antismoking movement will long be remembered for helping create a cleaner, smoke-free environment in the United States.

## ANTIDRINKING CAMPAIGNS

The school year over, Carla Wagner and her friend Claudia Valdes enjoyed a leisurely lunch at the Green Street Café in Miami's Coconut Grove. After Wagner, then 17, paid the tab with her credit card, the two hopped into her 2000 Audi A4 and headed to a girlfriend's house, stopping en route to pick up a $25 bottle of tequila using a bogus ID. There Wagner and Valdes drank several shots, passed around two pipefuls of pot and watched TV . . . Wagner jumped back into her car with Valdes, then 18, taking the passenger seat . . . Racing home, Wagner rounded one curve at more than 50 mph . . . A few moments afterward, as Wagner tried to dial a cell phone, the car hit gravel and fishtailed out of control. Valdes, who sustained a broken pelvis and lacerated liver, recalled later, "I think I saw an image walking or Rollerblading or whatever she was doing."

That shadow was Helen Marie Witty, 16, out for an early-evening skate. But the Audi, doing 60 mph in a 30-mph zone, had left the northbound lane and veered onto the bike path, hitting Witty and tossing her 30 ft. before the car wrapped itself, like a giant C, around a tree . . .

As for Witty, "She still looked like an angel, her eyes open" [says a motorist who saw the crash and realized she was dead]. "She looked peaceful and angelic."
(Charles, Trischitta, & Morrissey, 2001, pp. 67–68)

Stories like these are all too common. Some 16,000 Americans are killed in alcohol-related car crashes each year, accounting for 40 percent of all traffic deaths (Webb, 2001). Excessive drinking has other negative consequences. It can cause liver disease and cancer, and induce severe memory loss. Given the gravity of these effects, social activists have launched a variety of anti-alcohol campaigns.

The public service advertisement has been a major weapon in media campaigns. PSAs run the gamut from the famous "friends don't let friends drive drunk" to ads that question the popular image that drinking equals fun by depicting a young woman vomiting after drinking beer (Andsager, Austin, & Pinkleton, 2001). It is tempting to assume that these campaigns work; after all, they are produced by advertising specialists and appear on national television. However, as noted throughout this chapter, such an assumption is unwarranted. Young people frequently complain that popular antidrinking PSAs are corny, cheesy, and preachy (Andsager et al., 2001; see also Slater, Karan, Rouner, Murphy, & Beauvais, 1998). Some PSAs fail to provide a realistic discussion of drinking. By focusing on "generic peers," they neglect to consider the important role that same-sex friends and parents play in decisions about whether to drink (Austin & Meili, 1994; Trost, Langan, & Kellar-Guenther, 1999). Still other campaigns fail to create messages powerful enough to undo the effects of sexy, slick pro-drinking commercial spots.

The news is not all bad. Campaign interventions, with solid foundations in social marketing principles, have helped to reduce alcohol abuse.

## The Designated Driver Campaign

The designated driver is such a simple, potentially effective innovation you would think it would have been invented soon after the first reports of traffic fatalities surfaced. The notion that a group of friends selects one person to abstain from drinking that evening is intuitive and appealing. However, social change takes time, and it took years for the innovation to diffuse. Now, it is commonly accepted, thanks to campaigns organized by activist groups, including the Harvard School of Public Health (Winsten & DeJong, 2001).

Working with Hollywood production studios and TV networks, campaigners succeeded in placing dialogue or messages in 160 entertainment programs, including such classics as *Beverly Hills 90210*, *Growing Pains*, and *Cheers*. PSAs have appeared widely, with some featuring appearances from U.S. presidents.

The campaigns seemed to have influenced beliefs and behaviors. Years ago people used to joke about driving when under the influence. In 1964, President Lyndon B. Johnson gave reporters a tour of his Texas ranch, driving 90 miles per hour and sipping a cup of beer. As late as 1988, 2 months before the campaign began, just 62 percent of respondents said they and their friends designated a driver all or most of the time. Following the campaign, the proportion shot up significantly to 72 percent and is undoubtedly higher today.

The belief that people should not be allowed to drink when they drive has reached such high levels it can be regarded as a social norm. Although the campaign cannot take credit for all this success, it certainly has helped to legitimize the use of designated drivers in the United States.

Public-health experts Jay A. Winsten and William DeJong argue that the campaign succeeded because: (a) it had support from powerful Hollywood insiders; (b) the designated driver message (which places responsibility on the individual, not beer companies) allows the networks to do something positive about drinking, while not alienating the alcohol industry, on whom they depend for much of their advertising; and (c) the message could be easily sandwiched into programs (all a character need ask is, "Who's the designated driver tonight?"). In contrast, teen pregnancy and AIDS prevention appeals are more controversial and more difficult to incorporate into program scripts.

## Social-Norms Marketing

It isn't clear whether Leslie Baltz, who was in her fourth year [at the University of Virginia], wanted to drink that much. The 21-year-old honor student, who had a double major in art history and studio art, liked to paint and sketch. Once, at the age of 11, she wrote 31 poems for her mother, one for each day of the month, about love, dreams, and impermanence.

At a party that Saturday, Ms. Baltz drank enough booze-spiked punch that she decided to lie down at a friend's house while her buddies went out. When they returned that night after U. Va.'s 34–20 upset of Virginia Tech, they found her unconscious at the foot of a stairway. Ms. Baltz's blood-alcohol level was 0.27%, more than triple the state's legal limit for drivers, but probably survivable if not for her fall . . . She was declared dead of head injuries. Thus, Ms. Baltz became the fifth Virginia college student to die of alcohol-related causes that autumn, and the 18th at U. Va. since 1990.

(Murray & Gruley, 2000, p. A10)

Unfortunately, Leslie is not the only student to die as a result of alcohol abuse. Accidents due to drinking claim too many students' lives each year. Drinking, of course, is common on campus. Over 90 percent of students have tried alcohol, close to 25 percent display symptoms of problem drinkers, and others report experiences such as these over the course of a year (Murray & Gruley, 2000):

- Had a hangover: 62.8 percent
- Got nauseated or vomited: 53.8 percent
- Drove a car while under the influence: 31.3 percent
- Were taken advantage of sexually: 12.2 percent
- Took advantage of someone else sexually: 5.1 percent.

Still others can be defined as "binge drinkers"—men who consume at least five, and women who drink four or more, drinks in one sitting (see Figure 12.6).

For years, universities used a pastiche of antidrinking appeals, ranging from scare tactics to pictures of cars destroyed by drunk drivers. Convinced that these did not work and searching for something new, they recently perfected a technique based on communication and social marketing. Called social-norms marketing, it targets students' perception that other people drink a lot. The idea is that students overestimate how much

**FIGURE 12.6** | Binge drinking is a major problem on college campuses. Universities have employed a variety of strategies to curbe binge drinking, with varying success. Photograph by William C. Rieter.

alcohol their peers consume. Believing that everyone else drinks a lot and wanting to fit into the dominant college culture, they drink more than they would like. The solution follows logically: *"If students' drinking practices are fostered, or at least maintained, by the erroneous perception that other students feel more positively toward these practices than they do,"* two scholars noted, *"then correcting this misperception should lower their alcohol consumption"* (Schroeder & Prentice, 1998, p. 2153).

A number of universities have adopted this approach in an effort to curb alcohol abuse. The University of Virginia placed posters in the blue and orange school colors in freshman dorms. "Most U. Va. 1st years have 0 to 4 drinks per week," posters declared. "Zero to 3," stated frisbees distributed at Cornell University, making reference to the number of drinks most students consume when at a party. A Rutgers University "RU SURE?" campaign devised messages listing the top 10 misperceptions on campus, ranging from the humorous ("It's easy to find a parking place on campus") to the critical ("Everyone who parties gets wasted"). The latter was followed with the answer that two thirds of Rutgers students stop at three or fewer drinks (Lederman, Stewart, Barr, Powell, Laitman, & Goodhart, 2001). At Washington State University, Project Culture Change blanketed the campus with posters that said, "Heavy drinking at WSU has decreased every year for the past five years" (see Box 12.1).

What's the verdict? Does social-norming work? The evidence is mixed. Northern Illinois University implemented a social-norms campaign in an attempt to reduce the number of students who thought binge drinking was the campus norm. Prior to the campaign, 70 percent of the students believed binge drinking was common practice. By the campaign's conclusion, the percentage had dropped to 51 percent. Self-reported binge drinking decreased by nearly 9 percent during this period (Haines & Spear, 1996). Other studies, using more fine-tuned scientific methods, have reported similar findings (Godbold & Pfau, 2000; Perkins & Craig, 2003; Schroeder & Prentice, 1998).

These results have intrigued scholars, but raised questions. Some wonder whether students genuinely changed their views or were just saying they had, in order to comply with the norm of pleasing the faculty investigator. Other scholars doubt that simply providing correct information is sufficient to overcome the more emotional reasons why people choose to drink (Austin & Chen, 1999). Lindsey Polonec and colleagues (2006) raised more serious questions. In a study of Penn State undergraduates' perceptions of social norms, they discovered that over 70 percent of respondents did not believe that most students drank "0 to 4" drinks when they partied. If the social norm is not credible with students, the message will not persuade them. The researchers also found that social-norms messages are singularly ineffective in reaching an important target of the campaign: hard-core drinkers. Other carefully conducted studies have also cast doubt on the effectiveness of various university-based social-norms campaigns (Cameron & Campo, 2006; Campo & Cameron, 2006; Russell, Clapp, & DeJong, 2005; Yanovitzky, Stewart, & Lederman, 2006).

One other potential dilemma of social-norms marketing has also surfaced, pointing to the role social context plays in communication campaigns. Which industry do you think might like the idea of encouraging students to drink, if only modestly? That's right: the beer industry! Anheuser-Busch Brewers funded the University of Virginia social-norms campaign to the tune of $150,000. Coors and Miller gave the University of Wyoming and Georgetown University thousands of dollars for similar campaigns. Anheuser made

## Box 12.1 | PROBING PERCEPTIONS OF AN ANTIDRINKING CAMPAIGN

How do researchers conduct formative research and probe audience perceptions of campaign messages? How do planners of a social-norm antidrinking campaign adjust their strategies to fit students' points of view? These questions were on the minds of a group of communication researchers when they evaluated a campus social-norming project (Hansen, Kossman, Wilbrecht, & Andsager, 2000). The researchers conducted in-depth interviews with a variety of Washington State University (WSU) freshmen, asking them pointed questions about binge drinking and campaign messages. Here is some of what they found:

*Moderator:* Some of you say that 16 to 17 drinks is binge drinking. Do you think, on average, that's what a lot of people do?

*A.C.* (a student): Well, for guys and girls, it's, like, different.

*Kelly* (a student): It depends on the girl.

*Moderator:* On average, how many drinks do you think the average person has when they go out?

*A.C.:* It depends on what you do.

*Zach* (a student): Yeah, it depends on what kind of party you go to.

*A.C.:* If you're drinking to get drunk, then you will have a lot, but if you're drinking to socialize and, like, meet some girls or something like that, then you just want to be buzzed so you're just like sort of loose, and you don't have inhibitions or anything like that.

*Moderator:* Do you think drinking is a problem on the WSU campus?

*A.C.:* We drink a lot more than some of the other college campuses I have been on.

*Lisa* (a student): I think everybody knows about it because Pullman is out in the middle of nowhere. What else is there to do but go out and party?

*A.C.:* We should form a drinking team (laughter from the group).

*Moderator:* So at what point do you think that drinking is out of control?

*A.C.:* I think if you're passing out every time you drink.

*Kelly:* I think puking. If you pass out or, like, puke and pass out, that's bad. You shouldn't drink that much to puke.

*Lisa:* I think it's either passing out or just blacking out. If you do that every single time you drink, then maybe that's out of control.

*Moderator:* Okay, we're going to show you some ads that have been developed to kind of dispel any misconceptions about how much drinking there is, and then we're going to talk about them a little bit.

(Moderator presents an ad with a picture of three students smiling and standing arm in arm. The tag line is: "Most WSU students drink moderately. 65% of WSU students have 4 or fewer drinks when they socialize.")

**Box 12.1 |**

*Zach*: It doesn't look like they're drinking. I don't think they were drinking at all. I think he just randomly got some picture. If they had like keg cups and stuff, that would be a rocking picture. (Later.) See, there's, like, a number of people on campus who just don't drink at all and they bring down that mark by a whole lot.

*Moderator*: So you should separate them out into those who drink on campus [and those who don't]?

*Kelly*: It could be true for girls to have four drinks and be buzzed and good to go. But for guys, I think it's totally different. I think there should be a difference for guys and girls.

*Moderator*: (Presents an ad with students rock climbing. The copy reads: "Most WSU students drink moderately. Heavy drinking at WSU has decreased every year for the past five years.") Okay, what do you guys think of this one?

*Zach*: What's with the people climbing?

*A.C.*: Most people don't drink when they're rock climbing. As that would be very dangerous.

*Moderator*: Do you think the ad would be more effective if there were people with alcohol in the pictures? Basically, are you saying that the message in the ad just isn't believable?

*Kelly*: Well, the message is maybe okay, but the pictures just really don't go.

*Zach*: That's a believable message though.

*Kelly*: It's very believable—but just different pictures.

(Excerpts adapted from Hansen et al., 2000)

*Note:* The interviewers' questions were folksy and tapped into students' beliefs. To their credit, students responded openly and genuinely. Based on the interviews, the researchers concluded that university freshmen were not educated about binge drinking (they defined binge drinking as having 16 drinks or puking, when in fact binging involves having 4 to 5 drinks on a single occasion). Researchers concluded that messages should emphasize the impact of drinking on students' lives. Ads, they suggested, should contain pictures that relate more to the message. This type of formative research provides useful insights into students' perceptions, suggesting more effective ways to appeal to the target audience.

certain that the ads displayed its corporate logo. This raises ethical questions. Did beer industry sponsorship inhibit campaigners, causing them to shy away from developing hard-hitting antidrinking ads? Did the association of moderate drinking and the beer company logo actually strengthen pro-boozing attitudes (see Smith, Atkin, & Roznowski, 2006)?

Thus, we glimpse the complex issues surrounding social-norms marketing. It is an engaging idea, one that creatively plays on young people's desire to fit in with the majority. For this reason, social-norms interventions represent a promising approach. Consider, for example, a social-norms campaign to change attitudes toward sexual promiscuity on campus. Many college men believe that 80 percent of guys have sex on any given weekend. Yet one survey indicates that the actual percentage of men who have sex on any particular weekend is between 5 and 10 percent (Kimmel, 2008). College men—and probably women too—harbor a distorted belief about the prevalence of sex on campus, a belief that can propel them to engage in sex when they would prefer to abstain. A carefully-conducted social-norms campaign could change beliefs about sexual prevalence, perhaps reducing unwanted sexual hook-ups.

## DRUG PREVENTION CAMPAIGNS

"The facts are these," researchers Jason T. Siegel and Judee K. Burgoon observe:

> Almost half of all high school students surveyed used marijuana on at least one occasion, and more than 25% of high school students who were questioned reported using marijuana 30 days prior to being surveyed. Illicit drug use costs taxpayers upward of $110 billion a year. In addition to impairing cognitive functioning, marijuana use is associated with increased risk of dropping out of high school, driving under the influence, engaging in crime, and destroying property . . . The goal is simple: Persuade people not to do drugs. Seems easy enough in principle. Unfortunately, even with $3 billion being spent by the Partnership for a Drug-Free America on media time alone, the amount of people who use illegal substances is not decreasing.
>
> (2002, p. 163)

Modern antidrug campaigns date back to First Lady Nancy Reagan, who famously urged a generation of young people tempted by crack cocaine and other 1980s-style substances to "just say no to drugs." Her advice got a lot of bad press at the time. However, it had a simplicity to it, based, as it appeared to be, on Nike's Zen-oriented "Just do it" advertising of the era. The 1980s campaign and a more recent project launched by the U.S. government's Office of National Drug Control Policy have centered on PSAs. These have included the world-famous "this is your brain on drugs" ad and a host of recent spots, including ones in which teens criticize their parents for controlling their behavior when they were younger, but at the end, each says "thanks" to the parents for keeping him or her drug free.

Judging by the number of people who can remember these ads, you might think the campaigns were phenomenal successes. However, recall does not equal attitude change or signal a motivation to alter an intention to experiment with drugs. The campaigns raised awareness, a necessary step in motivating people to change problematic behaviors. However, some ads came off as controlling or condescending, a kiss of death in campaigns directed at naturally rebellious adolescents (see Burgoon, Alvaro, Grandpre, & Voulodakis, 2002). In order to change young people's attitudes toward drugs, campaigns must consider communication principles such as these:

■ *Pretest, target, and tailor.* Antidrug campaigns are more apt to succeed if they identify young people's salient beliefs and target them in compelling messages

(Fishbein, Cappella, Hornik, Sayeed, Yzer, & Ahern, 2002). Formative research tells us that teenagers, who believe they will live forever, are not particularly impressed by the argument that drugs can kill you. More intimidating is the prospect that drugs will ruin a relationship. One successful antidrug campaign put this insight to use in message design, featuring an ad in which a teenage girl complains that, since her boyfriend started smoking marijuana "he just lays around and is forgetting things." She complains that he avoids her like he avoids all his other "problems," and she walks out, slamming the door. A message board reads, "Marijuana: it's messed up a lot of relationships." (Palmgreen, Donohew, Lorch, Hoyle, & Stephenson, 2002, p. 40)

■  *Segment the audience.* Social marketing emphasizes that campaigns should devise different appeals to fit different subgroups. A key factor that has emerged in drug prevention research is the personality variable of sensation seeking. People who are high in sensation seeking (you may be one or know someone who is) enjoy thrills and adventures, like bungee jumping and parachuting. They prefer a nonconformist lifestyle (characterized by unconventional music and art), and seek out a variety of stimulating social and sexual experiences (Zuckerman, 1979). They also derive psychological and physical gratification from drugs and are more apt to use drugs than people who are low in sensation seeking (Donohew, Palmgreen, & Lorch, 1994). Given the many ways that high sensation seekers differ from low sensation seekers, it makes sense that drug prevention communications targeting highs should employ different appeals than those geared to lows. This viewpoint has been articulated and elaborately tested by Lewis Donohew, Philip Palmgreen, and their associates (Donohew, Palmgreen, Lorch, Zimmerman, & Harrington, 2002; Palmgreen et al., 2002; Stephenson, 2003). Far from arguing that the same message fits all potential drug users, Palmgreen and Donohew suggest that communications should be tailored to fit high and low sensation seekers' different needs. In order to reach high sensation seekers, messages should be novel, exciting, graphic, and emotionally strong. Communications targeted at low sensation seekers should be familiar, easygoing, and less intense. However, as a general rule, given that so many drug users are high in sensation seeking, campaigners with a fixed budget are advised to develop PSAs that point out exciting alternatives to drug dependence.

■  *Use multiple formats and channels.* Media PSAs can create awareness and help people recognize they have a drug problem. To help people move from mental to behavioral change, PSAs must be supplemented by news stories mentioning celebrities who have maintained a drug-free lifestyle, as well as by extensive community activities to help people talk with counselors or stay in treatment programs.

# INTERVENTIONS TO REDUCE HEALTH-CARE DISPARITIES

"Racial and ethnic minorities tend to receive a lower quality of health care than non-minorities, even when access-related factors, such as patients' insurance status and income, are controlled," concluded the authors of a major book on the topic (Smedley,

Stith, & Nelson, 2003, p. 1). The disparities are particularly disturbing in the case of African-Americans. Blacks have the highest mortality rate of any U.S. racial or ethnic group, approximately 1.6 times higher than that of Whites. Blacks have the highest incidence of cancer, diabetes, and infant mortality of any U.S. racial or ethnic group (Kreps, 2006).

Health communication expert Gary Kreps (2006), while recognizing that poverty, low education, and prejudice contribute to racial disparities in health, notes that "there are many other significant behavioral contributing factors that can be addressed through health communication interventions" (p. 762). Over the past decade, many communication campaigns have attempted to change African-Americans' health behaviors, in some cases with striking success.

Recognizing the impact of similarity and personalized appeals that hit home to respondents, campaign specialists have tailored messages to fit individuals' particular needs and values. In some cases, communications address an individual by name, offering feedback on the person's diet and offering healthy food alternatives to fatty foods. In other instances, messages target the beliefs of the larger social group. For instance, a middle-aged African-American woman who was particularly proud of her ethnic identity might receive a message suggesting that making dietary changes could reduce disparities that unfairly affect Blacks. A young African-American man who is deeply committed to his church might receive a heart-felt message from the pastor, rather than a dispassionate expert (Campbell & Quintiliani, 2006; Kreuter & Haughton, 2006).

Media materials tailored to meet individuals' values have strongly influenced health behavior. Noting that her African-American respondents held abiding religious values and trusted members of their community, Marci Campbell and colleagues developed personalized newsletters that included relevant passages from the Scriptures and health-related testimonials authored by community members, as well as videotapes that demonstrated how to prepare healthy fruit- and vegetable-based meals. She found that a tailored intervention significantly improved consumption of fruits and vegetables and recreational exercise; it also increased participants' colorectal cancer screening (see Campbell & Quintiliani, 2006).

Positive as these findings are, there remain persistent structural barriers to campaign success. A campaign may change attitudes, reduce time-honored patient distrust of doctors, or convince patients that they can exert more control over their health (see, for instance, Smith-McLallen & Fishbein, 2009). However, the intervention may not produce long-term change in behavior because poor minority individuals lack health insurance or transportation to take them to a doctor for a regular check-up. Hence, attitudes cannot influence behavior. Yet defeatism is not warranted. Campaign-induced attitude change can influence behavior for individuals who do have some health insurance, own a car, or regularly take a bus to their doctor. Campaigns can also influence a behavior, like diet, over which people may have more actual and perceived control. While campaigns cannot relieve structural impediments, they can help individuals re-think their resistance to altering dysfunctional dietary behaviors. This in turn can lead to incremental change in health behaviors that over the long haul may contribute to a reduction in racial disparities in health care.

# COMPLICATING FACTORS

Health campaigns are not magic pills that inject a cure into anesthetized audience members. As discussed, campaigns work in concert with interpersonal, institutional, and cultural forces. In describing the effects of a national campaign to raise awareness about high blood pressure, Robert Hornik suggests that the process of change might work in the following way:

> A person sees some public service announcement and a local TV health reporter's feature telling her about the symptomless disease of hypertension. She checks her blood pressure in a newly accessible shopping mall machine and those results suggest a problem; she tells her spouse (who has also seen the ads) and he encourages her to have it checked. She goes to a physician, who confirms the presence of hypertension, encourages her to change her diet and then return for monitoring. Meanwhile, the physician has become more sensitive to the issue of hypertension because of a recent [*Journal of the American Medical Association*] article, and some recommendations from a specialist society . . . The patient talks with friends at work or family members about her experience; they also increase their concern and go to have their own pressure checked . . . The patient is ready to comply because all the sources around her—personal, professional and mediated—are telling her that she should.
>
> (2002, pp. 11–12)

The campaign modified behavior, but not via exposure to a single series of messages. Instead, the campaign succeeded in changing the public environment. It altered the perspectives of the medical specialist association; influenced owners of suburban malls, who viewed the addition of blood pressure machines as a way to lure shoppers; changed the nature of discussion in the press; and placed blood pressure on the interpersonal agenda in friendship networks (Hornik, 2002). Slowly, but surely, the campaign influenced behavior. But the effects were not direct. Instead, they came as a result of changes in public opinion, interpersonal discussion, and increased belief that high blood pressure was a serious health problem.

The campaign to increase awareness of high blood pressure provides another example of the positive impact that health campaigns can exert on public attitudes. In a similar fashion, campaigns have produced decrements in drunken driving fatalities and teenage drug use (Brooks, 2005; Butterfield, 2002). Campaigns succeed when they are based in theory, implement social marketing principles, and have mechanisms in place to change course if messages fail. But—and this remains an important point—there is no guarantee. As examples from recent AIDS prevention efforts illustrate, campaigns fail when they face daunting social or political obstacles.

AIDS campaigns conducted in the 1980s and 1990s changed attitudes toward HIV/AIDS and the stigma associated with the disease. Significant inroads were made in the gay community as a result of aggressive interventions to promote safe sex. Recently, though, problems have surfaced. Some of the individuals most at risk to get AIDS in the United States—gay men who are sexually active—are not having sex using condoms, a behavior that puts them at even greater risk to contract the disease (Jacobs, 2005; Perloff, 2001). Safe sex interventions directed at these men have run up against the psychological functions that unbridled sex provides (Signorile, 1997), the perception "AIDS can't happen to me," and the illusory belief that new wonder drugs can prevent the ravages of AIDS.

In other instances AIDS prevention campaigns failed because messages were thoughtless or culturally insensitive. Speaking about campaigns directed at low-income African-Americans, one community leader bluntly observed:

> We've had the wrong people delivering the wrong kind of message. The usual prevention message for all these years can be interpreted as saying: "Gee, we're sorry about racism. We're sorry about homophobia in your homes and churches. We're sorry that urban schools are crappy. We're sorry that you can't find a good job . . . We're sorry about all these things, but you really need to start using condoms, because if you don't, you could get infected tomorrow, or next year, or some point during the next decade, and if you do get infected, at some point, you could get sick and die."
>
> (Denizet-Lewis, 2003, p. 53)

In Africa and Southeast Asia, where the HIV infection rate is as high as 35 percent, the problem is more severe. Twenty million people have died of AIDS, the majority in Africa. Polygamy, prostitution, and failure of governments to provide access to condoms have hampered campaigns' effectiveness. Campaigns cannot succeed if there are serious political and sociological obstacles in their path.

Yet human beings' empathy and resilience provides grounds for optimism. Recent AIDS prevention campaigns in Africa have begun to unravel resistance to safer sex. A case in point is a remarkably successful program in South Africa. Aptly called "loveLife," it focuses on teenagers, many of whom know how AIDS is transmitted but do not apply this knowledge to themselves (Rosenberg, 2006). Eschewing a moralistic fear-based approach, campaign organizers adopted a more positive line, calling on social marketing principles and branding loveLife as optimistic and fun. The campaign has programs in many high schools and community organizations in which 18- to 25-year-olds talk about sex and call on their own personal histories to persuade young people to abstain from sex or use condoms. As one participant observed, "These were people the same age as me. It wasn't a celebrity telling me their story living in a million-dollar house. It was another young person from the same township as me" (Rosenberg, p. 59).

## VALUES AND ETHICS

You know the old game "Where's Waldo?" that you played when you were a kid? You would try to spot the cagey character, Waldo, who was hiding somewhere in the house or outdoors. He was always there; you just had to locate his whereabouts. So it is with values and ethical aspects of campaigns, an issue touched on but not directly broached in this chapter. Noted one ethicist, "They are always there, the value judgments: the choices in policy decisions. There are always choices made" (Guttman, 2000, p. 70).

It's nice to think of campaigns as these objective entities, planned by scientifically minded behavioral engineers, implemented by marketing specialists, and evaluated by statisticians. Although campaigns have measurable effects to be sure, they take place in real-world contexts. Social-structural factors, political complexities, and value judgments necessarily intervene. You can appreciate this by considering the following questions. They appear simple at first blush but are actually tinged with value issues:

- *What is the problem the campaign hopes to solve?* A healthy-eating campaign may be designed to change attitudes toward eating high-cholesterol food, or to slowly pressure city restaurants to reduce their use of trans fats. A gun-control campaign may focus on teaching gun owners to take safety precautions when loading a gun, or on intensifying public opinion pressure on legislators to support legal suits against the gun industry like those brought against Big Tobacco.
- *What is the locus of the dilemma?* Campaigners may perceive that the roots of a health problem are psychological—for example, personal shortcomings of drug abusers. Alternatively, they may take a more macro view, arguing that the problem is rooted in social conditions: a billion-dollar global drug industry, indirectly backed by the U.S. government, that preys on vulnerable youth. Planners of a childhood-obesity campaign may feel it is hopeless to try to convince kids not to eat junk food when it is served at restaurants all over the city. Instead, they may decide to focus their energies on convincing the city board of health to ban the use of trans fats in restaurant cooking. Thus, the perceived locus of the problem will influence campaign strategies and choice of social marketing techniques (Dutta, 2006; Dutta-Bergman, 2005).
- If the goal is to benefit the public good, is the campaign designed to do more good for certain members of the public than for others? There is no absolute definition of "public good." Instead, the definition inevitably reflects value judgments. Should good be defined in utilitarian terms—a cardiovascular risk reduction campaign designed to reach the greatest number of people? Or should it be viewed in a more deonto-logical fashion, emphasizing values like justice—as when planners of a blood pressure screening campaign, acknowledging that poverty produces great psychological stress, choose to focus only on poor people? Similarly, as Nurit Guttman puts it, "Should campaign resources be devoted to target populations believed to be particularly needy or those who are more likely to adopt its recommendations?" (1997, p. 181). It is more difficult to reach needy individuals, as well as the hard core that is at greatest risk for disease. By opting for reachable goals—trying to do the greatest good for the greatest number—are campaigns copping out at the get-go, favoring the advantaged over the disenfranchised?
- *How are values implicated in the solutions campaigners recommend?* An AIDS prevention campaign that urges people to practice safer sex has opted not to communicate the values of abstinence or waiting to have sex until you are married.

Social-norm-based antidrinking campaigns advocate moderate drinking, an option that some parents oppose.

■ *How do values influence criteria used to proclaim success?* Evaluators must devise benchmarks that can be used to determine if a campaign has succeeded. Values come into play here. For example, an intervention to promote breast cancer screening could be deemed successful if it increased the number of women who had mammograms yearly. However, given that those most likely to get mammograms are women with insurance that covers the procedure, the criterion for success excludes poor women (Guttman, 2000). The evaluator may reason that a campaign cannot do everything and note that increases in mammography, even among those with insurance policies, is an achievement. That may be a reasonable call, but it reflects a certain set of value judgments.

■ Finally, although different values shape campaigns, all campaigns are based on a core assumption: *the world will be a better place if social interventions try to change individual behavior.* Campaigns assume that social marketing interventions to change individual behavior and improve the public health are worthwhile ventures. This puts communication campaigns at odds with a strict libertarianism that regards individual liberty as an unshakable first principle. However, in some cases campaigns launched with good intentions may have unintended effects. Consider the case of campaigns to increase awareness of prostate cancer. These campaigns have caused false alarms, leading people to overestimate their chances of dying from cancer, in turn creating unnecessary anxiety (Singer, 2009). What's more, on a philosophical level, campaigns can be at odds with a strict libertarianism that regards individual liberty as an unshakeable first principle. Libertarians would question why we need campaigns since people know that smoking causes cancer but choose to smoke, or know all about the risks of HIV but prefer to practice unsafe sex because it's fun. Don't people have a right to make their own choices and live life according to their own rules, even those that strike others as self-destructive?

It is a good question, one that philosophers have been asking in one fashion or another for centuries. Campaigns must necessarily balance individual liberties and the public good. Both are important values. Clearly, when your liberty (to smoke) threatens my good health by exposing me to secondhand smoke, it's a no-brainer for many people. But how far should you go in infringing on smokers for the sake of the larger whole? Is it right to finance public service projects by increasing the tax on cigarettes rather than on other products like candy, salt, or butter, which also cause adverse health outcomes? Should schools become the food police, banning even the most innocuous fatty food from children's diets? Where do we draw the line?

## CONCLUSIONS

Communication campaigns are vital activities that use mass media and interpersonal support to improve social conditions. They have a long, proud history in this country.

Contemporary campaigns are creatures of the current era, with its technological marvels and cultural diversity. Campaigns are persuasion writ large, applications of persuasion principles to society as a whole. They are guided by social psychological approaches, such as stage-oriented perspectives, diffusion theory, and social marketing. Campaigns are more likely to succeed if they are based on theory, harness social marketing principles, are aesthetically appealing, and build in corrective evaluation mechanisms to change course in midstream. Values and ethics are inextricable from campaigns and remind us that campaigns should call on a humane ethical perspective.

Campaigns are ever changing. The mass media-based antismoking campaigns of the 1980s have given way to new interventions, focused on fatty fast food, obesity, and bullying. With more interventions going online, targeted at ever-more specialized audiences, one wonders if the age of the mass mediated campaign, focused on a broad heterogeneous audience, has finally passed. The form and content of campaigns will undoubtedly change dramatically in the years to come. However, the challenge of developing mediated messages that can alter well-learned health attitudes is not going away. Contemporary theoretical and methodological approaches continue to offer general guidelines for how to design effective pro-social interventions.

Tempting as it is to see campaigns as all powerful, they are not. Campaigns take place in a larger political structure and can fail if opposed by powerful interest groups. Social and cultural mores also play a role in campaign effectiveness. What works in one culture will not succeed in another. Campaign organizers can have brilliant ideas, but if they don't congeal with cultural norms or lack the support of prominent opinion leaders, they are unlikely to succeed. And yet research has made it abundantly clear that well-conceptualized, well-executed campaigns can convince people to rethink their resistance to innovation and adopt healthier lifestyles.

This chapter and the book as a whole have argued that if we understand how people think and feel about communication, we have a pretty good chance of changing their views in socially constructive ways. Stated somewhat differently, the more communicators understand the dynamics of the mind, the better their chances of constructing attitude-altering messages. As we have seen, if communicators understand the structure, functions, and strength of attitudes, processing routes, consistency needs, and interpersonal relational dynamics, their chances of influencing attitudes are enhanced. This is a centerpiece of contemporary persuasion scholarship and seems to have a great deal of empirical support. Yet it is always worth playing devil's advocate with oneself and noting that there are people whose attitudes you can't change. There are people who will smoke, no matter how many times they are exposed to an antismoking message, and others who will abuse drugs even after you tell them they can get busted, precisely because they enjoy the thrill of testing the law. Still others will practice unsafe sex, knowing full well that they are HIV-positive.

Persuasive communication, like all forces in life, has limits, a point emphasized at various times in this text (see Box 12.2 for a research perspective). Yet the fact that communication has limits does not mean it is powerless or ineffectual or necessarily plays into the hands of the rich or corrupt. Persuasion can have these effects, of course, but it can also be an instrument of self-insight, healing, and social change. Persuasive

## Box 12.2 | KNOWING WHAT WE DON'T KNOW

There is a great deal about persuasion that we do not know.

This may seem heretical or surprising, given that this is a scholarly textbook that examines the knowledge base in the field of persuasive communication. But it is true.

To be sure, knowledge of persuasion has grown exponentially in the last half-century, and scholarship reviewed in this book has enlarged our understanding of persuasion and attitudes. Yet important gaps in knowledge remain. A persuasion book should describe not only what we know about persuasion, but also what we do not yet comprehend.

First, there remains much to be learned about *how* and *why* people change their attitudes. For instance, what exactly happens psychologically when someone changes her mind? Is the change primarily cognitive or emotional? How do these different processes interact? What role does physiology play in psychological change? Why does one person change attitudes and another doesn't? What psychological and communication forces lead people to rethink their approaches to life?

Second, what makes a communicator persuasive? We know that credible sources can promote attitude change, but we don't know precisely what it is about certain credible individuals that enable them to connect with audience members verbally and nonverbally.

Communicators who empathize with audience members can be influential, harnessing persuasion for positive purposes, as in the case of an empathic family doctor, and with negative effects, as exemplified by cult leaders and charismatic despots. Just *how* does the communicator's display of empathic concern plant the persuasive seeds, inducing individuals to put trust in a beneficent or malevolent communicator?

Third, despite more than 50 years of painstaking studies, we still need to know more about how to construct compelling persuasive messages. What makes a message persuasive? How can persuaders combine logic, warrants, and arguments to influence message receivers? What makes stirring political oratory so powerful? Which types of message arguments are most effective on individuals in a particular motivational state?

Fourth, there remain gaps in knowledge of real-world persuasion effects. Experimental studies of ELM and EPPM phenomena are wonderful and immensely valuable. However, the dynamics of persuasion are very different in the actual worlds of advertising, politics, and health campaigns than in experimental studies. We have known for years that experimentally-produced results are more nuanced in the real world or are qualified by intersection with other variables. Before accepting results of experiments as fact, researchers need to test hypotheses in real-world settings, reframing hypotheses so they take into account contextual features.

Fifth, as you probably know, the overwhelming majority of persuasion studies test hypotheses on American adults, frequently college students, many of whom are White. These studies do advance knowledge, and to the extent that research participants are

**Box 12.2** |

similar to others from different classes and ethnic groups, the knowledge generalizes. But we know that class and ethnicity profoundly influence behavior. We need to examine persuasion theories in other contexts—in poorer American subcultures, in different countries, and in cultures with distinctive religious and anthropological rituals.

Sixth, we need to know more about the influences of campaign messages on individuals and society. How do political communications—from advertising to blogs—form, reinforce, and change political attitudes? Just how do primordial symbols in advertising, such as Nike's legendary swoosh, access feelings and influence buying behavior? What types of health campaigns reduce racial disparities in health care? More generally, we know a great deal about why people do not take care of their health, but much less about how to plug in these factors to wage effective health campaigns.

Finally, scholars must gain more understanding of how persuasion changes with advances in technology. Do social networking sites that combine intimacy with immediacy reduce barriers to perceived self-influence? What are the influences of persuasive messages relayed through virtual environments or via avatars that offer digital representations of the self (Nick & Bailenson, 2009)? Do time-honored processes, like peripheral/central mechanisms, and communicator characteristics, such as similarity and attractiveness, function differently in these arenas?

In order to answer these questions, we will need new theories, building on classic concepts. We also need increased appreciation of the social context of persuasion and the willingness to test hypotheses in gritty real-world settings. New ideas and research designs can advance persuasion knowledge. They can also generate findings that can help human beings. A new generation of persuasion scholars, some of whom may be reading this book, can take up the mantle. Standing on the hefty intellectual shoulders of their predecessors, they can create new theories and elevate persuasion discourse.

communication, when used in innovative and ethical ways, can alter unhealthy behaviors and change institutions.

George Bernard Shaw once noted, "The reasonable man adapts himself to the world. The unreasonable one persists in trying to adapt the world to himself. Therefore, all progress depends on the unreasonable man" (Power, 2002). Persuasion practitioners are all too accustomed to reasonably adapting their messages to the world. Amelioration of our numerous problems depends on their joining the legions of the unreasonable.

# References

Abelson, R. P. (1959). Modes of resolution of belief dilemmas. *Journal of Conflict Resolution*, 343–352.

Abelson, R. P. (1982). Three modes of attitude–behavior consistency. In M. P. Zanna, E. T. Higgins, & C. P. Herman (Eds.), *Consistency in social behavior: The Ontario symposium* (Vol. 2, pp. 131–146). Hillsdale, NJ: Lawrence Erlbaum Associates.

Aberson, C. L., & McVean, A. D. W. (2008). Contact and anxiety as predictors of bias toward the homeless. *Journal of Applied Social Psychology, 38*, 3009–3035.

Abramson, P. R., Aldrich, J. H., & Rohde, D. W. (1994). *Change and continuity in the 1992 elections*. Washington, DC: CQ Press.

Adelman, M. B. (1992). Healthy passions: Safer sex as play. In T. Edgar, M. A. Fitzpatrick, & V. S. Freimuth (Eds.), *AIDS: A communication perspective* (pp. 69–89). Hillsdale, NJ: Lawrence Erlbaum Associates.

Adkins, M., & Brashers, D. E. (1995). The power of language in computer-mediated groups. *Management Communication Quarterly, 8*, 289–322.

Adler, J. (1999, November 29). Living canvas. *Newsweek*, 75–76.

Ajzen, I. (1991). The theory of planned behavior. *Organizational Behavior and Human Decision Processes, 50*, 179–211.

Ajzen, I., & Fishbein, M. (1977). Attitude–behavior relations: A theoretical analysis and review of empirical research. *Psychological Bulletin, 84*, 888–918.

Ajzen, I., & Fishbein, M. (1980). *Understanding attitudes and predicting social behavior*. Englewood Cliffs, NJ: Prentice-Hall.

Ajzen, I., & Fishbein, M. (2005). The influence of attitudes on behavior. In D. Albarracín, B. T. Johnson, & M. P. Zanna (Eds.), *The handbook of attitudes* (pp. 173–221). Mahwah, NJ: Lawrence Erlbaum Associates.

Ajzen, I., & Fishbein, M. (2008). Scaling and testing multiplicative combinations in the expectancy-value model of attitude. *Journal of Applied Social Psychology, 38*, 2222–2247.

Albarracín, D., Johnson, B. T., & Zanna, M. P. (2005). Preface. In D. Albarracín, B. T. Johnson, & M. P. Zanna (Eds.), *The handbook of attitudes* (pp. vii–ix). Mahwah, NJ: Lawrence Erlbaum Associates.

Alexander, J. E., & Tate, M. A. (1999). *Web wisdom: How to evaluate and create information quality on the Web*. Mahwah, NJ: Lawrence Erlbaum Associates.

Allen, M. (1998). Comparing the persuasive effectiveness of one and two sided messages. In M. Allen & R. W. Preiss (Eds.), *Persuasion: Advances through metaanalysis* (pp. 87–98). Cresskill, NJ: Hampton Press.

Allen, M., Bruflat, R., Fucilla, R., Kramer, M., McKellips, S., Ryan, D. J., & Spiegelhoff, M. (2000). Testing the persuasiveness of evidence: Combining narrative and statistical forms. *Communication Research Reports, 17*, 331–336.

Allen, M., & Preiss, R. (1997a). Persuasion, public address, and progression in the sciences: Where we are at what we do. In G. A. Barnett & F. J. Boster (Eds.), *Progress in communication sciences* (Vol. 13, pp. 107–131). Greenwich, CT: Ablex.

Allen, M., & Preiss, R. W. (1997b). Comparing the persuasiveness of narrative and statistical evidence using meta-analysis. *Communication Research Reports, 14,* 125–131.

Allen, M., & Stiff, J. B. (1998). An analysis of the sleeper effect. In M. Allen & R. W. Preiss (Eds.), *Persuasion: Advances through meta-analysis* (pp. 175–188). Cresskill, NJ: Hampton Press.

Allport, G. W. (1935). Attitudes. In C. Murchison (Ed.), *A handbook of social psychology* (Vol. 2, pp. 798–844). Worcester, MA: Clark University Press.

Allport, G. W. (1945). The psychology of participation. *Psychological Review, 53,* 117–132.

Ambah, F. S. (2006, July 24). The would-be terrorist's explosive tell-all tale. *The Washington Post,* C1, C4.

Andersen, K. (1971). *Persuasion: Theory and practice.* Boston: Allyn & Bacon.

Anderson, R. B., & McMillion, P. Y. (1995). Effects of similar and diversified modeling on African American women's efficacy expectations and intentions to perform breast self-examination. *Health Communication, 7,* 324–343.

Andrews, J. C., & Shimp, T. A. (1990). Effects of involvement, argument strength, and source characteristics on central and peripheral processing in advertising. *Psychology & Marketing, 7,* 195–214.

Andrews, R. L., & Franke, G. R. (1991). The determinants of cigarette consumption: A meta-analysis. *Journal of Public Policy & Marketing, 10,* 81–100.

Andsager, J. L., Austin, E. W., & Pinkleton, B. E. (2001). Questioning the value of realism: Young adults' processing of messages in alcohol-related public service announcements and advertising. *Journal of Communication, 51*(1), 121–142.

Andsager, J. L., & White, H. A. (2007). *Self versus others: Media, messages, and the third-person effect.* Mahwah, NJ: Lawrence Erlbaum Associates.

Angier, N. (2000a, November 7). Cell phone or pheromone? New props for the mating game. *The New York Times,* D5.

Angier, N. (2000b, November 7). Who is fat? It depends on culture. *The New York Times,* D1–D2.

Angier, N. (2008, December 23). A highly involved propensity for deceit. *The New York Times,* D1, D4.

Ansolabehere, S., & Iyengar, S. (1995). *Going negative: How attack ads shrink and polarize the electorate.* New York: Free Press.

Ariely, D. (2008). *Predictably irrational: The hidden forces that shape our decisions.* New York: HarperCollins.

Arkes, H. R. & Tetlock, P. E. (2004). Attributions of implicit prejudice, or "Would Jesse Jackson 'fail' the Implicit Association Test?" *Psychological Inquiry, 15,* 257–278.

Armitage, C. J., & Conner, M. (2000). Attitudinal ambivalence: A test of three key hypotheses. *Personality and Social Psychology Bulletin, 26,* 1421–1432.

Aron, A., & Aron, E. N. (1989). *The heart of social psychology: A backstage view of a passionate science* (2nd ed.). Lexington, MA: Lexington Books.

Aronson, E. (1968). Dissonance theory: Progress and problems. In R. P. Abelson, E. Aronson, W. J. McGuire, T. M. Newcomb, M. J. Rosenberg, & P. H. Tannenbaum (Eds.), *Theories of cognitive consistency: A sourcebook* (pp. 5–27). Chicago: Rand McNally.

Aronson, E. (1999). Dissonance, hypocrisy, and the self-concept. In E. Harmon-Jones & J. Mills (Eds.), *Cognitive dissonance: Progress on a pivotal theory in social psychology* (pp. 103–126). Washington, DC: American Psychological Association.

Aronson, E., & Mills, J. (1959). The effect of severity of initiation on liking for a group. *Journal of Abnormal and Social Psychology, 59,* 177–181.

Aronson, J., Cohen, G., & Nail, P. R. (1999). Self-affirmation theory: An update and appraisal. In E. Harmon-Jones & J. Mills (Eds.), *Cognitive dissonance: Progress on a pivotal theory in social psychology* (pp. 127–147). Washington, DC: American Psychological Association.

*References*

Atkin, C. (2002). Promising strategies for media health campaigns. In W. D. Crano & M. Burgoon (Eds.), *Mass media and drug prevention: Classic and contemporary theories and research* (pp. 35–64). Mahwah, NJ: Lawrence Erlbaum Associates.

Atkin, C. K., & Freimuth, V. S. (2001). Formative evaluation research in campaign design. In R. E. Rice & C. K. Atkin (Eds.), *Public communication campaigns* (3rd ed., pp. 125–145). Thousand Oaks, CA: Sage.

Atkinson, M. (2004). Tattooing and civilizing processes: Body modification as self-control. *Canadian Review of Sociology & Anthropology, 41,* 125–146.

Atlas, D., Dodd, J., Lang, A., Bane, V., & Levy, D. S. (2008, April 28). Life in the cult. *People,* 62–67.

Atwood, R. W., & Howell, R. J. (1971). Pupilometric and personality test score differences of female aggressing pedophiliacs and normals. *Psychonomic Science, 22,* 115–116.

Aune, R. K., & Basil, M. D. (1994). A relational obligations approach to the foot-in-the-mouth effect. *Journal of Applied Social Psychology, 24,* 546–556.

Aune, R. K., & Reynolds, R. A. (1994). The empirical development of the normative message processing scale. *Communication Monographs, 61,* 135–160.

Austin, E. W., & Chen, Y. J. (1999, August). *The relationship of parental reinforcement of media messages to college students' alcohol-related behaviors.* Paper presented to the annual convention of the Association for Education in Journalism and Mass Communication, New Orleans.

Austin, E. W., & Meili, H. K. (1994). Effects of interpretation of televised alcohol portrayals on children's alcohol beliefs. *Journal of Broadcasting & Electronic Media, 38,* 417–435.

Baesler, E. J., & Burgoon, J. K. (1994). The temporal effects of story and statistical evidence on belief change. *Communication Research, 21,* 582–602.

Bakker, A. B. (1999). Persuasive communication about AIDS prevention: Need for cognition determines the impact of message format. *AIDS Education and Prevention, 11,* 150–162.

Bandura, A. (1977). *Social learning theory.* Englewood Cliffs, NJ: Prentice Hall.

Barden, J., & Petty, R. E. (2008). The mere perception of elaboration creates attitude certainty: Exploring the thoughtfulness heuristic. *Journal of Personality and Social Psychology, 95,* 489–509.

Bargh, J. A., & Pietromonaco, P. (1982). Automatic information processing and social perception: The influence of trait information presented outside of conscious awareness on impression formation. *Journal of Personality and Social Psychology, 43,* 437–449.

Baron, A. S., & Banaji, M. R. (2006). The development of implicit attitudes: Evidence of race evaluations from ages 6 and 10 and adulthood. *Psychological Science, 17,* 53–58.

Barstow, D., & Stein, R. (2005, March 13). Is it news or public relations? Under Bush, lines are blurry. *The New York Times,* 1, 18–19.

Bartholet, J., & Breslau, K. The apostle of Alaska. *Newsweek,* online (September 7).

Bartsch, K., & London, K. (2000). Children's use of mental state information in selecting persuasive arguments. *Developmental Psychology, 36,* 352–365.

Basil, D. Z., Ridgway, N. M., & Basil, M. D. (2006). Guilt appeals: The mediating effect of responsibility. *Psychology & Marketing, 23,* 1035–1054.

Basil, D. Z., Ridgway, N. M., & Basil, M. D. (2008). Guilt and giving: A process model of empathy and efficacy. *Psychology & Marketing, 25,* 1–23.

Basil, M. D. (1997). The danger of cigarette "special placements" in film and television. *Health Communication, 9,* 191–198.

Bassili, J. N. (1995). Response latency and the accessibility of voting intentions: What contributes to accessibility and how it affects vote choice. *Personality and Social Psychology Bulletin, 21,* 686–695.

Bauman, K. E., Brown, J. D., Bryan, E. S., Fisher, L. A., Padgett, C. A., & Sweeney, J. M. (1988). Three mass media campaigns to prevent adolescent cigarette smoking. *Preventive Medicine, 17,* 510–530.

Baumrind, D. (1964). Some thoughts on ethics of research: After reading Milgram's "Behavioral study of obedience." *American Psychologist, 19,* 421–423.

Baxter, L. A. (1984). An investigation of compliance-gaining as politeness. *Human Communication Research, 10,* 427–456.

Bellafante, G. (2000, October 8). Read my tie: No more scandals. *The New York Times,* 9–1, 9–9.

Belluck, P. (2009, April 26). Yes, looks do matter. *The New York Times* (Sunday Styles), 1., 8.

Bem, D. J. (1970). *Beliefs, attitudes, and human affairs.* Belmont, CA: Brooks/Cole.

Bem, D. J. (1972). Self-perception theory. In L. Berkowitz (Ed.), *Advances in experimental social psychology* (Vol. 6, pp. 1–62). New York: Academic Press.

Bennett, W. J. (1998). *The death of outrage: Bill Clinton and the assault on American ideals.* New York: Free Press.

Benoit, W. L. (1991). Two tests of the mechanism of inoculation theory. *Southern Communication Journal, 56,* 219–229.

Benoit, W. L. (1998). Forewarning and persuasion. In M. Allen & R. W. Preiss (Eds.), *Persuasion: Advances through meta-analysis* (pp. 139–154). Cresskill, NJ: Hampton Press.

Bentler, P. M., & Speckhart, G. (1979). Models of attitude–behavior relations. *Psychological Review, 86,* 452–464.

Berke, R. L., & Elder, J. (2000, November 30). Public splits on party lines over vote and long delay. *The New York Times,* 1, A30.

Berke, R. L., & Elder, J. (2001, September 16). Strong backing for using force is found in poll. *The New York Times,* 1, 4.

Berlo, D. K., Lemert, J. B., & Mertz, R. J. (1969). Dimensions for evaluating the acceptability of message sources. *Public Opinion Quarterly, 33,* 563–576.

Berscheid, E. (1966). Opinion change and communicator–communicatee similarity and dissimilarity. *Journal of Personality and Social Psychology, 4,* 670–680.

Bettinghaus, E. P., & Cody, M. J. (1987). *Persuasive communication* (4th ed.). New York: Holt, Rinehart & Winston.

Bishop, B. (with R. G. Cushing). (2008). *The big sort: Why the clustering of like-minded America is tearing us apart.* Boston: Houghton-Mifflin.

Bishop, G. F., Tuchfarber, A. J., & Oldendick, R. W. (1986). Opinions on fictitious issues: The pressure to answer survey questions. *Public Opinion Quarterly, 50,* 240–250.

Bishop, G. W. (2005). *The illusion of public opinion: Fact and artifact in American public opinion polls.* Lanham, MD: Rowman & Littlefield.

Blakeslee, S. (1998, October 13). Placebos prove so powerful even experts are surprised. *The New York Times,* D1, D4.

Blass, T. (1992). The social psychology of Stanley Milgram. In M. P. Zanna (Ed.), *Advances in experimental social psychology* (Vol. 25, pp. 277–329). San Diego: Academic Press.

Blass, T. (1999). The Milgram paradigm after 35 years: Some things we now know about obedience to authority. *Journal of Applied Social Psychology, 29,* 955–978.

Blumenthal, R. (2006, March 30). A preacher's credo: Eliminate the negative, accentuate prosperity. *The New York Times,* B1, B7.

Boninger, D. S., Brock, T. C., Cook, T. D., Gruder, C. L., & Romer, D. (1990). Discovery of a reliable attitude change persistence resulting from a transmitter tuning set. *Psychological Science, 1,* 268–271.

Boninger, D. S., Krosnick, J. A., Berent, M. K., & Fabrigar, L. R. (1995). The causes and consequences of attitude importance. In R. E. Petty & J. A. Krosnick (Eds.), *Attitude strength: Antecedents and consequences* (pp. 159–189). Hillsdale, NJ: Lawrence Erlbaum Associates.

Booth-Butterfield, S., & Welbourne, J. (2002). The Elaboration Likelihood Model: Its impact on persuasion theory and research. In J. P. Dillard & M. Pfau (Eds.), *The persuasion handbook: Developments in theory and practice* (pp. 155–173). Thousand Oaks, CA: Sage.

Borchert, D. M., & Stewart, D. (1986). *Exploring ethics.* New York: Macmillan.

*References*

Bornstein, R. F. (1989). Exposure and affect: Overview and meta-analysis of research, 1968–1987. *Psychological Bulletin, 106,* 265–289.

Bornstein, R. F. (1992). Subliminal mere exposure effects. In R. F. Bornstein & T. S. Pittman (Eds.), *Perception without awareness: Cognitive, clinical, and social perspectives* (pp. 191–210). New York: Guilford.

Boster, F. J., & Mongeau, P. (1984). Fear-arousing persuasive messages. In R. N. Bostrom (Ed.), *Communication yearbook 8* (pp. 330–375). Beverly Hills: Sage.

Bowers, J. W. (1964). Some correlates of language intensity. *Quarterly Journal of Speech, 50,* 415–420.

Boxer, S. (2005, September 24). Art of the Internet: A protest song, reloaded. *The New York Times,* A17.

Boyer, M. S. (2006, August 13). Close ties to far east. *The Plain Dealer,* C1, 10.

Bradley, P. H. (1981). The folk linguistics of women's speech: An empirical examination. *Communication Monographs, 48,* 73–90.

Bradsher, K. (2000, July 17). Was Freud a minivan or S.U.V. kind of guy? *The New York Times,* A1, A16.

Brandt, A. M. (2007). *The cigarette century: The rise, fall, and deadly persistence of the product that defined America.* New York: Basic Books.

Brannon, L. A., & Brock, T. C. (1994). The subliminal persuasion controversy: Reality, enduring fable, and Polonius's weasel. In S. Shavitt & T. C. Brock (Eds.), *Persuasion: Psychological insights and perspectives* (pp. 279–293). Needham Heights, MA: Allyn & Bacon.

Braverman, J. (2008). Testimonials versus informational persuasive messages: The moderating effect of delivery mode and personal involvement. *Communication Research, 35,* 666–694.

Breckler, S. J. (1984). Empirical validation of affect, behavior, and cognition as distinct components of attitude. *Journal of Personality and Social Psychology, 47,* 1191–1205.

Brehm, J. W. (1966). *A theory of psychological reactance.* New York: Academic Press.

Brewer, P. R., & Wilcox, C. (2005). Trends: Same-sex marriage and civil unions. *Public Opinion Quarterly, 69,* 599–616.

Briggs, S. R., & Cheek, J. M. (1988). On the nature of self-monitoring: Problems with assessment, problems with validity. *Journal of Personality and Social Psychology, 54,* 663–678.

Brinberg, D., & Durand, J. (1983). Eating at fast-food restaurants: An analysis using two behavioral intention models. *Journal of Applied Social Psychology, 13,* 459–472.

Briñol, P., & Petty, R. E. (2005). Individual differences in attitude change. In D. Albarracín, B. T. Johnson, & M. P. Zanna (Eds.), *The handbook of attitudes* (pp. 575–615). Mawhah, NJ: Lawrence Erlbaum Associates.

Briñol, P., Rucker, D. D., Tormala, Z. L., & Petty, R. E. (2004). Individual differences in resistance to persuasion: The role of beliefs and meta-beliefs. In E. S. Knowles & J. A. Linn (Eds.), *Resistance and persuasion* (pp. 83–104). Mawhah, NJ: Lawrence Erlbaum Associates.

Broad, W. J., & Shane, S. (2008, August 10). For suspects, anthrax case had big costs. *The New York Times,* 1, 17.

Brock, T. C. (1965). Communicator–recipient similarity and decision change. *Journal of Personality and Social Psychology, 1,* 650–654.

Brock, T. C. (1967). Communication discrepancy and intent to persuade as determinants of counterargument production. *Journal of Experimental Social Psychology, 3,* 296–309.

Brock, T. C., Strange, J. J., & Green, M. C. (2002). Power beyond reckoning: An introduction to narrative impact. In M. C. Green, J. J. Strange, & T. C. Brock (Eds.), *Narrative impact: Social and cognitive foundations* (pp. 1–15). Mahwah, NJ: Lawrence Erlbaum Associates.

Brody, J. E. (2000, April 4). Fresh warnings on the perils of piercing. *The New York Times,* D8.

Brooke, J. (2000, January 3). A Cassandra with no regrets, and besides, it is not over yet. *The New York Times,* A16.

Brooks, D. (2004, June 29). Age of political segregation. *The New York Times,* A27.

Brooks, D. (2005, August 7). The virtues of virtue. *The New York Times,* Week in Review, 12.

Brown, J. D., & Walsh-Childers, K. (2002). Effects of media on personal and public health. In J. Bryant & D. Zillmann (Eds.), *Media effects: Advances in theory and research* (2nd ed., pp. 453–488). Mahwah, NJ: Lawrence Erlbaum Associates.

Brown, P., & Levinson, S. C. (1987). *Politeness: Some universals in language usage.* Cambridge, UK: Cambridge University Press.

Bryan, A. D., Aiken, L. S., & West, S. G. (1999). The impact of males proposing condom use on perceptions of an initial sexual encounter. *Personality and Social Psychology Bulletin, 25,* 275–286.

Budesheim, T. L., & DePaola, S. J. (1994). Beauty or the beast? The effects of appearance, personality, and issue information on evaluations of political candidates. *Personality and Social Psychology Bulletin, 20,* 339–348.

Buller, D. B., & Burgoon, J. K. (1996). Interpersonal deception theory. *Communication Theory, 6,* 203–242.

Buller, D. B., & Hall, J. R. (1998). The effects of distraction during persuasion. In M. Allen & R. W. Preiss (Eds.), *Persuasion: Advances through meta-analysis* (pp. 155–173). Cresskill, NJ: Hampton Press.

Buller, D. B., LePoire, B. A., Aune, R. K., & Eloy, S. V. (1992). Social perceptions as mediators of the effect of speech rate similarity on compliance. *Human Communication Research, 19,* 286–311.

Bumiller, E., & Zeleny, J. (2008, September 6). With themes set, both campaigns begin a 60-day dash to election day. *The New York Times,* A11.

Burger, J. M. (1986). Increasing compliance by improving the deal: The that's not all technique. *Journal of Personality and Social Psychology, 51,* 277–283.

Burger, J. M. (1999). The foot-in-the-door compliance procedure: A multiple process analysis and review. *Personality and Social Psychology Review, 3,* 303–325.

Burger, J. M. (2009). Replicating Milgram: Would people still obey today? *American Psychologist, 64,* 1–11.

Burgoon, J. K. (1994). Nonverbal signals. In M. L. Knapp & G. R. Miller (Eds.), *Handbook of interpersonal communication* (2nd ed., pp. 229–285). Thousand Oaks, CA: Sage.

Burgoon, M. (1989). Messages and persuasive effects. In J. J. Bradac (Ed.), *Message effects in communication science* (pp. 129–164). Newbury Park, CA: Sage.

Burgoon, M., Alvaro, E., Grandpre, J., & Voulodakis, M. (2002). Revisiting the theory of psychological reactance: Communicating threats to attitudinal freedom. In J. P. Dillard & M. Pfau (Eds.), *The persuasion handbook: Developments in theory and practice* (pp. 213–232). Thousand Oaks, CA: Sage.

Burgoon, M., Denning, V. P., & Roberts, L. (2002). Language expectancy theory. In J. P. Dillard & M. Pfau (Eds.), *The persuasion handbook: Developments in theory and practice* (pp. 117–136). Thousand Oaks, CA: Sage.

Burgoon, M., Hendriks, A., & Alvaro, E. (2001, May). *Tobacco prevention and cessation: Effectiveness of the Arizona tobacco education and prevention media campaign.* Paper presented to the annual convention of the International Communication Association, Washington, DC.

Burgoon, M., Parrott, R., Burgoon, J., Birk, T., Pfau, M., & Coker, R. (1989). Primary care physicians' selection of verbal compliance-gaining strategies. *Health Communication, 2,* 13–27.

Burke, K. (1950). *A rhetoric of motives.* New York: Prentice Hall.

Burleigh, M. (2000). *The Third Reich: A new history.* New York: Hill and Wang.

Burleson, B. R., Wilson, S. R., Waltman, M. S., Goering, E. M., Ely, T. K., & Whaley, B. B. (1988). Item desirability effects in compliance gaining research: Seven studies documenting artifacts in the strategy selection procedure. *Human Communication Research, 14,* 429–486.

Burrell, N. A., & Koper, R. J. (1998). The efficacy of powerful/powerless language on attitudes and source credibility. In M. Allen & R. W. Preiss (Eds.), *Persuasion: Advances through meta-analysis* (pp. 203–215). Cresskill, NJ: Hampton Press.

Buss, D. M., & Kenrick, D. T. (1998). Evolutionary social psychology. In D. T. Gilbert, S. T. Fiske, & G. Lindzey (Eds.), *The handbook of social psychology* (4th ed., Vol. 2, pp. 982–1026). Boston: McGraw-Hill.

Butterfield, F. (2002, December 17). Teenage drug use is dropping, a study finds. *The New York Times,* A23.

Cacioppo, J. T., Harkins, S. G., & Petty, R. E. (1981). The nature of attitudes and cognitive responses and their relationships to behavior. In R. E. Petty, T. M. Ostrom, & T. C. Brock (Eds.), *Cognitive responses in persuasion* (pp. 31–54). Hillsdale, NJ: Lawrence Erlbaum Associates.

Cacioppo, J. T., & Petty, R. E. (1982). The need for cognition. *Journal of Personality and Social Psychology, 42,* 116–131.

*References*

Cacioppo, J. T., Petty, R. E., Feinstein, J. A., & Jarvis, W. B. G. (1996). Dispositional differences in cognitive motivation: The life and times of individuals varying in need for cognition. *Psychological Bulletin, 119,* 197–253.

Cacioppo, J. T., Petty, R. E., & Kao, C. F. (1984). The efficient assessment of need for cognition. *Journal of Personality Assessment, 48,* 306–307.

Cacioppo, J. T., Petty, R. E., & Marshall-Goodell, B. (1984). Electromyographic specificity during simple physical and attitudinal tasks: Location and topographical features of integrated EMG responses. *Biological Psychology, 18,* 85–121.

Cacioppo, J. T., Priester, J. R., & Berntson, G. G. (1993). Rudimentary determinants of attitudes. II: Arm flexion and extension have differential effects on attitudes. *Journal of Personality and Social Psychology, 65,* 5–17.

Caldwell, D. F., & Burger, J. M. (1997). Personality and social influence strategies in the workplace. *Personality and Social Psychology Bulletin, 23,* 1003–1012.

Calmes, J., & Thee, M. (2008, November 5). Polls find Obama built broader base than past nominees. *The New York Times,* P1, P10.

Cameron, K. A., & Campo, S. (2006). Stepping back from social norms campaigns: Comparing normative influences to other predictors of health behaviors. *Health Communication, 20,* 277–288.

Cameron, K. A., Witte, K., & Nzyuko, S. (1999). Perceptions of condoms and barriers to condom use along the Trans-Africa Highway in Kenya. In W. N. Elwood (Ed.), *Power in the blood: A handbook on AIDS, politics, and communication* (pp. 149–163). Mahwah, NJ: Lawrence Erlbaum Associates.

Campbell, K. K. (1989). *Man cannot speak for her: A critical study of early feminist rhetoric* (Vol. 1). New York: Greenwood.

Campbell, M. K, & Quintiliani, L. M. (2006). Tailored interventions in public health: Where does tailoring fit in interventions to reduce health disparities? (Communication and racial disparities in health care, R. M. Perloff, Ed.), *American Behavioral Scientist, 49,* 775–793.

Campbell, R., Martin, C. R., & Fabos, B. (2002). *Media & culture: An introduction to mass communication* (3rd ed.). Boston: Bedford/St. Martin's.

Campo, S., & Cameron, K. A. (2006). Differential effects of exposure to social norms campaigns: A cause for concern. *Health Communication, 19,* 209–219.

Cappella, J. N., Fishbein, M., Hornik, R., Ahern, R. K., & Sayeed, S. (2001). Using theory to select messages in antidrug media campaigns: Reasoned action and media priming. In R. E. Rice & C. K. Atkin (Eds.), *Public communication campaigns* (3rd ed., pp. 214–230). Thousand Oaks, CA: Sage.

Carr, D. (2006, January 30). Oprahness trumps truthiness. *The New York Times,* C1, C5.

Cave, D. (2005a, March 27). For recruiters, a hard toll from a hard sell. *The New York Times,* 1, 21.

Cave, D. (2005b, June 3). Growing problem for military recruiters: Parents. *The New York Times,* 1, 23.

CBS News Polls (2004, November 22). Poll: Creationism trumps evolution. Online: www.cbsnews.com/stories/2004/11/22/opinion/polls/.

Cesario, J., Grant, H., & Higgins, E.T. (2004). Regulatory fit and persuasion: Transfer from "feeling right." *Journal of Personality and Social Psychology, 86,* 388–404.

Chaiken, S. (1979). Communicator's physical attractiveness and persuasion. *Journal of Personality and Social Psychology, 37,* 1387–1397.

Chaiken, S., Liberman, A., & Eagly, A. H. (1989). Heuristic and systematic information processing within and beyond the persuasion context. In J. S. Uleman & J. A. Bargh (Eds.), *Unintended thought: Limits of awareness, intention, and control* (pp. 212–252). New York: Guilford.

Chaiken, S., Wood, W., & Eagly, A. H. (1996). Principles of persuasion. In E. T. Higgins & A. W. Kruglanski (Eds.), *Social psychology: Handbook of basic principles* (pp. 702–742). New York: Guilford Press.

Chapanis, N. P., & Chapanis, A. C. (1964). Cognitive dissonance: Five years later. *Psychological Bulletin, 61,* 1–22.

Chappell, T. (1998). Platonism. In R. Chadwick(Ed.), *Encyclopedia of applied ethics* (Vol. 3, pp. 511–523). San Diego: Academic Press.

Charles, N., Trischitta, L., & Morrissey, S. (2001, August 13). End of the party. *People*, pp. 67–68, 70.

Chartrand, T., Pinckert, S., & Burger, J. M. (1999). When manipulation backfires: The effects of time delay and requester on the foot-in-the-door technique. *Journal of Applied Social Psychology, 29*, 211–221.

Chen, D. W. (2006, October 26). New Jersey court backs full rights for gay couples. *The New York Times*, A1, A24.

Chen, S., & Chaiken, S. (1999). The Heuristic–Systematic Model in its broader context. In S. Chaiken & Y. Trope (Eds.), *Dual-process theories in social psychology* (pp. 73–96). New York: Guilford.

Chew, F., Mehta, A., & Oldfather, A. (1994). Applying concept mapping to assess the influence of celebrity message dynamics on communication effectiveness. In K. W. King (Ed.), *Proceedings of the 1994 Conference of the American Academy of Advertising* (pp. 26–39). New York: American Academy of Advertising.

Chew, F., & Palmer, S. (1994). Interest, the knowledge gap, and television programming. *Journal of Broadcasting & Electronic Media, 38*, 271–287.

Cho, C. H. (1999). How advertising works on the WWW: Modified Elaboration Likelihood Model. *Journal of Current Issues and Research in Advertising, 21*, 33–50.

Cho, H., & Boster, F. J. (2008). Effects of gain versus loss frame antidrug ads on adolescents. *Journal of Communication, 58*, 428–446.

Cho, H., & Salmon, C. T. (2006). Fear appeals for individuals in different stages of change: Intended and unintended effects and implications on public health campaigns. *Health Communication, 20*, 91–99.

Cialdini, R. B. (2001). *Influence: Science and practice* (4th ed.). Boston: Allyn & Bacon.

Cialdini, R. B., & Ascani, K. (1976). Test of a concession procedure for inducing verbal, behavioral, and further compliance with a request to give blood. *Journal of Applied Psychology, 61*, 295–300.

Cialdini, R. B., Cacioppo, J. T., Bassett, R., & Miller, J. A. (1978). Low-ball procedure for producing compliance: Commitment then cost. *Journal of Personality and Social Psychology, 36*, 463–476.

Cialdini, R. B., Trost, M. R., & Newsom, J. T. (1995). Preference for consistency: The development of a valid measure and the discovery of surprising behavioral implications. *Journal of Personality and Social Psychology, 69*, 318–328.

Cialdini, R. B., Vincent, J. E., Lewis, S. K., Catalan, J., Wheeler, D., & Darby B. L. (1975). Reciprocal concessions procedure for inducing compliance: The door-in-the-face technique. *Journal of Personality and Social Psychology, 31*, 206–215.

Clary, E. G., Snyder, M., Ridge, R. D., Miene, P. K., & Haugen, J. A. (1994). Matching messages to motives in persuasion: A functional approach to promoting volunteerism. *Journal of Applied Social Psychology, 24*, 1129–1149.

Clifford, S. (2008, July 14). Product placements acquire a life of their own on shows. *The New York Times*, C1, C6.

Clifford, S. (2009, March 11). Advertisers get a trove of clues in Smartphones. *The New York Times*, A1, A14.

Clines, F. X. (2001, October 21). In uneasy time, seeking comfort in the familiar frights of Halloween. *The New York Times*, B8.

Cody, M. J., & McLaughlin, M. L. (1980). Perceptions of compliance-gaining situations: A dimensional analysis. *Communication Monographs, 47*, 132–148.

Cody, M. J., & McLaughlin, M. L. (1985). The situation as a construct in interpersonal communication research. In M. L. Knapp & G. R. Miller (Eds.), *Handbook of interpersonal communication* (pp. 263–312). Beverly Hills, CA: Sage.

Cody, M. J., McLaughlin, M. L., & Jordan, W. J. (1980). A multidimensional scaling of three sets of compliance-gaining strategies. *Communication Quarterly, 28*, 34–46.

Cody, M. J., & Seiter, J. S. (2001). Compliance principles in retail sales in the United States. In W. Wosinska, R. B. Cialdini, D. W. Barrett, & J. Reykowski (Eds.), *The practice of social influence in multiple cultures* (pp. 325–341). Mahwah, NJ: Lawrence Erlbaum Associates.

Cohen, A. R., Stotland, E., & Wolfe, D. M. (1955). An experimental investigation of need for cognition. *Journal of Abnormal and Social Psychology, 51*, 291–294.

*References*

Cohen, C., & Regan, T. (2001).*The animal rights debate*. Lanham, MD: Rowman & Littlefield.

Cohen, R. (1999, August 13). Why? New Eichmann notes try to explain. *The New York Times*, A1, A3.

Collins, F. S. (2006). *The language of God: A scientist presents evidence for belief*. New York: Free Press.

Condit, C. M. (1990). *Decoding abortion rhetoric: Communicating social change*. Urbana: University of Illinois Press.

Conger, J. A. (1998, May–June). The necessary art of persuasion. *Harvard Business Review, 76*, 84–95.

Connelly, M. (2009, October 29). Framing the debate. *The New York Times*, p. A17.

Conner, M., & Armitage, C. J. (1998). Extending the theory of planned behavior: A review and avenues for further research. *Journal of Applied Social Psychology, 28*, 1429–1464.

Conover, P. J., & Feldman, S. (1984). How people organize the political world: A schematic model. *American Journal of Political Science, 28*, 95–126.

Cooper, B. (1998). "The White–Black fault line": Relevancy of race and racism in spectators' experiences of Spike Lee's Do the Right Thing. *Howard Journal of Communications, 9*, 205–228.

Cooper, J., & Axsom, D. (1982). Effort justification in psychotherapy. In G. Weary & H. L. Mirels (Eds.), *Integrations of clinical and social psychology* (pp. 214–230). New York: Oxford Press.

Cooper, J., & Cooper, G. (2002). Subliminal motivation: A story revisited. *Journal of Applied Social Psychology, 32*, 2213–2227.

Cooper, J., & Fazio, R. H. (1984). A new look at dissonance theory. In L. Berkowitz (Ed.), *Advances in experimental social psychology* (Vol. 17, pp. 229–266). Orlando, FL: Academic Press.

Cooper, J., & Scher, S. J. (1994). When do our actions affect our attitudes? In S. Shavitt & T. C. Brock (Eds.), *Persuasion: Psychological insights and perspectives* (pp. 95–111). Boston: Allyn and Bacon.

Cooper, M. D., & Nothstine, W. L. (1998). *Power persuasion: Moving an ancient art into the media age* (2nd ed.). Greenwood, IN: Educational Video Group.

Coyne, M. (2000). Paper prepared for course on persuasion and attitude change, Cleveland State University, Cleveland, OH.

Creswell, J. (2008, June 22). Nothing sells like celebrity: The boom in human billboards. *The New York Times*, C1, C8.

Crites, S. L., Jr., Fabrigar, L. R., & Petty, R. E. (1994). Measuring the affective and cognitive properties of attitudes: Conceptual and methodological issues. *Personality and Social Psychological Bulletin, 20*, 619–634.

Cronkhite, G., & Liska, J. (1976). A critique of factor analytic approaches to the study of credibility. *Communication Monographs, 43*, 91–107.

Cross, M. (1996). Reading television texts: The postmodern language of advertising. In M. Cross (Ed.), *Advertising and culture: Theoretical perspectives* (pp. 1–10). Westport, CT: Praeger.

Crossen, C. (1991, November 14). Studies galore support products and positions, but are they reliable? *The Wall Street Journal*, A1, A7.

Crusco, A. H., & Wetzel, C. G. (1984). The Midas touch: The effects of interpersonal touch on restaurant tipping. *Personality and Social Psychology Bulletin, 10*, 512–517.

Cruz, M. G. (1998). Explicit and implicit conclusions in persuasive messages. In M. Allen & R. W. Preiss (Eds.), *Persuasion: Advances through meta-analysis* (pp. 217–230). Cresskill, NJ: Hampton Press.

Czopp, A. M., Monteith, M. J., & Mark, A. Y. (2006). Standing up for a change: Reducing bias through interpersonal confrontation. *Journal of Personality and Social Psychology, 90*, 784–803.

Davidson, E. (1977). *The making of Adolf Hitler*. New York: Macmillan.

Davies, M. F. (1998). Dogmatism and belief formation: Output interference in the processing of supporting and contradictory cognitions. *Journal of Personality and Social Psychology, 75*, 456–466.

Davis, B. P., & Knowles, E. S. (1999). A disrupt-then-reframe technique of social influence. *Journal of Personality and Social Psychology, 76*, 192–199.

Davis, D. (2008, September 13). Do voters want passion, policy or both? *The New York Times* (Letter to the Editor), A28.

Dawes, R. M., & Smith, T. L. (1985). Attitude and opinion measurement. In G. L. Lindzey & E. A. Aronson (Eds.), *Handbook of social psychology* (3rd ed., Vol. 1, pp. 509–566). New York: Random House.

Dearing, J. W., Rogers, E. M., Meyer, G., Casey, M. K., Rao, N., Campo, S., & Henderson, G. M. (1996). Social marketing and diffusion-based strategies for communicating with unique populations: HIV prevention in San Francisco. *Journal of Health Communication, 1*, 343–363.

DeBono, K. G. (1987). Investigating the social-adjustive and value-expressive functions of attitudes: Implications for persuasion processes. *Journal of Personality and Social Psychology, 52*, 279–287.

DeBono, K. G. (2000). Attitude functions and consumer psychology: Understanding perceptions of product quality. In G. R. Maio & J. M. Olson (Eds.), *Why we evaluate: Functions of attitudes* (pp. 195–221). Mahwah, NJ: Lawrence Erlbaum Associates.

DeBono, K. G., & Harnish, R. J. (1988). Source expertise, source attractiveness, and the processing of persuasive information: A functional approach. *Journal of Personality and Social Psychology, 55*, 541–546.

DeBono, K. G., & Klein, C. (1993). Source expertise and persuasion: The moderating role of recipient dogmatism. *Personality and Social Psychology Bulletin, 19*, 167–173.

de Botton, A. (2000). *The consolations of philosophy*. New York: Pantheon.

Deci, E. L. (1975). *Intrinsic motivation*. New York: Plenum Press.

DeJong, W. (1979). An examination of self-perception mediation of the foot-in-the-door effect. *Journal of Personality and Social Psychology, 37*, 2221–2239.

Delia, J. G., Kline, S. L., & Burleson, B. R. (1979). The development of persuasive communication strategies in kindergartners through twelfth graders. *Communication Monographs, 46*, 241–256.

Denizet-Lewis, B. (2003, August 3). Double lives on the down low. *The New York Times Magazine*, 28–33, 48, 52–53.

Dennett, D. C. (2005, August 28). Show me the science. *The New York Times* [Week in Review], 11.

Denton, R. E., Jr. (Ed.) (1994). *The 1992 presidential campaign: A communication perspective*. Westport, CT: Praeger.

DePaulo, B. M., Kashy, D. A., Kirkendol, S. E., Wyer, M. M., & Epstein, J. A. (1996). Lying in everyday life. *Journal of Personality and Social Psychology, 70*, 979–995.

de Waal, F. (1982). *Chimpanzee politics: Power and sex among apes*. London: Jonathan Cape Ltd.

Dewan, S., & Goodstein, L. (2005, March 16). Hostage's past may have helped win captor's trust. *The New York Times*, A11.

DiClemente, R. J. (Ed.). (1992). *Adolescents and AIDS: A generation in jeopardy*. Thousand Oaks, CA: Sage.

Dijksterhuis, A., Aarts, H., & Smith, P.K. (2005). The power of the subliminal: On subliminal persuasion and other potential applications. In R. R. Hassin, J. S. Uleman, & J. A. Bargh (Eds.), *The new unconscious* (pp. 77–106). New York: Oxford University Press.

Dillard, J. P. (1990a). Self-inference and the foot-in-the-door technique: Quantity of behavior and attitudinal mediation. *Human Communication Research, 16*, 422–447.

Dillard, J. P. (1990b). A goal-driven model of interpersonal influence. In J. P. Dillard (Ed.), *Seeking compliance: The production of interpersonal influence messages* (pp. 41–56). Scottsdale, AZ: Gorsuch-Scarisbrick.

Dillard, J. P. (1993). Persuasion past and present: Attitudes aren't what they used to be. *Communication Monographs, 60*, 90–97.

Dillard, J. P. (1994). Rethinking the study of fear appeals: An emotional perspective. *Communication Theory, 4*, 295–323.

Dillard, J. P., & Anderson, J. W. (2004). The role of fear in persuasion. *Psychology & Marketing, 21*, 909–926.

Dillard, J. P., Hunter, J. E., & Burgoon, M. (1984). Sequential request persuasive strategies: Meta-analysis of foot-in-the-door and door-in-the-face. *Human Communication Research, 10*, 461–488.

Dillard, J. P., Kinney, T. A., & Cruz, M. G. (1996). Influence, appraisals, and emotions in close relationships. *Communication Monographs, 63*, 105–130.

Dillard, J. P., Segrin, C., & Harden, J. M. (1989). Primary and secondary goals in the production of interpersonal influence messages. *Communication Monographs, 56*, 19–38.

*References*

Dillard, J. P., & Shen, L. (2005). On the nature of reactance and its role in persuasive health communication. *Communication Monographs, 72,* 144–168.

Dillard, J. P., Wilson, S. R., Tusing, K. J., & Kinney, T. A. (1997). Politeness judgments in personal relationships. *Journal of Language and Psychology, 16,* 297–325.

Dolinski, D., & Nawrat, R. (1998). "Fear-then-relief" procedure for producing compliance: Beware when the danger is over. *Journal of Experimental Social Psychology, 34,* 27–50.

Doll, J., & Ajzen, I. (1992). Accessibility and stability of predictors in the theory of planned behavior. *Journal of Personality and Social Psychology, 63,* 754–765.

Donohew, L., Palmgreen, P., & Lorch, E. P. (1994). Attention, need for sensation, and health communication campaigns. *American Behavioral Scientist, 38,* 310–322.

Donohew, L., Palmgreen, P., Lorch, E., Zimmerman, R., & Harrington, N. (2002). Attention, persuasive communication, and prevention. In W. D. Crano & M. Burgoon (Eds.), *Mass media and drug prevention: Classic and contemporary theories and research* (pp. 119–143). Mahwah, NJ: Lawrence Erlbaum Associates.

Doppelt, J. C. & Shearer, E. (1999). *Nonvoters: America's no-shows.* Thousand Oaks, CA: Sage.

Dowd, M. (2006a, June 3). Teaching remedial decency. *The New York Times,* A23.

Dowd, M. (2006b, May 3). The captors become the captives. *The New York Times,* A27.

Dudczak, C. A. (2001, January). *Comments on the Dynamics of Persuasion.* Prepared for Lawrence Erlbaum Associates.

Dutta, M. J. (2006). Theoretical approaches to entertainment education campaigns: A subaltern critique. *Health Communication, 20,* 221–231.

Dutta-Bergman, M. J. (2004a). The impact of completeness and Web use motivation on the credibility of e-health information. *Journal of Communication, 54,* 337–354.

Dutta-Bergman, M. J. (2004b). Reaching unhealthy eaters: Applying a strategic approach to media vehicle choice. *Health Communication, 16,* 493–506.

Dutta-Bergman, M. J. (2005). Theory and practice in health communication campaigns: A critical interrogation. *Health Communication, 18,* 103–122.

Dyson, M. E. (2001, January 22). Moral leaders need not be flawless. *The New York Times,* A23.

Dyson, M. E. (2005). *Is Bill Cosby right? Or has the Black middle class lost its mind?* New York: Basic Civitas Books.

Eagly, A. H. (1978). Sex differences in influenceability. *Psychological Bulletin, 85,* 86–116.

Eagly, A. H., & Carli, L. L. (1981). Sex of researchers and sex-typed communications as determinants of sex differences in influenceability: A meta-analysis of social influence studies. *Psychological Bulletin, 90,* 1–20.

Eagly, A. H., & Chaiken, S. (1993). *The psychology of attitudes.* Fort Worth, TX: Harcourt, Brace, Jovanovich.

Eagly, A. H., & Chaiken, S. (1995). Attitude strength, attitude structure, and resistance to change. In R. E. Petty & J. A. Krosnick (Eds.), *Attitude strength: Antecedents and consequences* (pp. 413–432). Hillsdale, NJ: Lawrence Erlbaum Associates.

Eagly, A. H., & Chaiken, S. (1998). Attitude structure and function. In D. T. Gilbert, S. T. Fiske, & G. Lindzey (Eds.), *Handbook of social psychology* (4th ed., Vol. 1, pp. 269–322). Boston: McGraw–Hill.

Eagly, A. H., Chen, S., Chaiken, S., & Shaw-Barnes, K. (1999). The impact of attitudes on memory: An affair to remember. *Psychological Bulletin, 125,* 64–89.

Eagly, A. H., Kulesa, P., Chen, S., & Chaiken, S. (2001). Do attitudes affect memory? Tests of the congeniality hypothesis. *Current Directions in Psychological Science, 10,* 5–9.

Eagly, A. H., Mladinic, A., & Otto, S. (1994). Cognitive and affective bases of attitudes toward social groups and social policies. *Journal of Experimental Social Psychology, 30,* 113–137.

Eagly, A. H., Wood, W., & Chaiken, S. (1978). Causal inferences about communicators and their effect on opinion change. *Journal of Personality and Social Psychology, 36,* 424–435.

Easterbrook, G. (2006, May 24). Finally feeling the heat. *The New York Times,* A27.

Edwards, K., & Smith, E. E. (1996). A disconfirmation bias in the evaluation of arguments. *Journal of Personality and Social Psychology, 71,* 5–24.

Eisenstadt, D., Leippe, M. R., Stambush, M. A., Rauch, S. M., & Rivers, J. A. (2005). Dissonance and prejudice: Personal costs, choice, and change in attitudes and racial beliefs following counterattitudinal advocacy that benefits a minority. *Basic and Applied Social Psychology, 27,* 127–141.

Elkin, R. A., & Leippe, M. R. (1986). Physiological arousal, dissonance, and attitude change: Evidence for a dissonance–arousal link and a "don't remind me" effect. *Journal of Personality and Social Psychology, 51,* 55–65.

Elliot, A. J., & Devine, P. G. (1994). On the motivational nature of cognitive dissonance: Dissonance as psychological discomfort. *Journal of Personality and Social Psychology, 67,* 382–394.

Elliott, S. (2007, November 28). Pro bono efforts follow targets to the Web. *The New York Times,* C5.

Elliott, S. (2008, June 18). Crude? So what? These characters still find work in ads. *The New York Times,* C9.

Engs, R. C. (2000). *Clean living movements: American cycles of health reform.* Westport, CT: Praeger.

Erickson, B., Lind, E. A., Johnson, B. C., & O'Barr, W. M. (1978). Speech style and impression formation in a court setting: The effects of "powerful" and "powerless" speech. *Journal of Experimental Social Psychology, 14,* 266–279.

Falbo, T. (1977). Multidimensional scaling of power strategies. *Journal of Personality and Social Psychology, 35,* 537–547.

Fallon, A. (1990). Culture in the mirror: Sociocultural determinants of body image. In T. F. Cash & T. Pruzinsky (Eds.), *Body images: Development, deviance, and change* (pp. 80–109). New York: Guilford.

Fang, X., Singh, S., & Ahluwalia, R. (2007). An examination of different explanations for the mere exposure effect. *Journal of Consumer Research, 34,* 97–103.

Farquhar, J. W., Fortmann, S. P., Flora, J. A., Taylor, C. B., Haskell, W. L., Williams, P. T., Maccoby, N., & Wood, P. D. (1990). Effects of community-wide education on cardiovascular disease risk factors: The Stanford Five City Project. *Journal of the American Medical Association, 264,* 359–365.

Farrelly, M. C., Davis, K. C., Haviland, M. L., Healton, C. G., & Messeri, P. (2005). Evidence of a dose-response relationship between "truth" antismoking ads and youth smoking prevalence. *American Journal of Public Health, 95,* 425–431.

Fazio, R. H. (1989). On the power and functionality of attitudes: The role of attitude accessibility. In A. R. Pratkanis, S. J. Breckler, & A. G. Greenwald (Eds.), *Attitude structure and function* (pp. 153–179). Hillsdale, NJ: Lawrence Erlbaum Associates.

Fazio, R. H. (1990). Multiple processes by which attitudes guide behavior: The MODE model as an integrative framework. In M. P. Zanna (Ed.), *Advances in experimental social psychology* (Vol. 23, pp. 75–109). San Diego: Academic Press.

Fazio, R. H. (1995). Attitudes as object-evaluation associations: Determinants, consequences, and correlates of attitude accessibility. In R. E. Petty & J. A. Krosnick (Eds.), *Attitude strength: Antecedents and consequences* (pp. 247–282). Hillsdale, NJ: Lawrence Erlbaum Associates.

Fazio, R. H. (2000). Accessible attitudes as tools for object appraisal: Their costs and benefits. In G. R. Maio & J. M. Olson (Eds.), *Why we evaluate: Functions of attitudes* (pp. 1–36). Mahwah, NJ: Lawrence Erlbaum Associates.

Fazio, R. H., Powell, M. C., & Williams, C. J. (1989). The role of attitude accessibility in the attitude-to-behavior process. *Journal of Consumer Research, 16,* 280–288.

Fazio, R. H., & Roskos-Ewoldsen, D. R. (1994). Acting as we feel: When and how attitudes guide behavior. In S. Shavitt & T. C. Brock (Eds.), *Persuasion: Psychological insights and perspectives* (pp. 71–93). Boston: Allyn and Bacon.

Fazio, R. H., & Williams, C. J. (1986). Attitude accessibility as a moderator of the attitude–perception and attitude–behavior relations: An investigation of the 1984 presidential election. *Journal of Personality and Social Psychology, 51,* 505–514.

Fazio, R. H., & Zanna, M. P. (1978). Attitudinal qualities relating to the strength of the attitude–behavior relationship. *Journal of Experimental Social Psychology, 14,* 398–408.

Fazio, R. H., & Zanna, M. P. (1981). Direct experience and attitude–behavior consistency. In L. Berkowitz (Ed.), *Advances in experimental social psychology* (Vol. 14, pp. 162–202). New York: Academic Press.

*References*

Feinberg, J. (1998). Coercion. In E. Craig (Ed.), *Routledge encyclopedia of philosophy* (pp. 387–390). London: Routledge.

Fern, E. F., Monroe, K. B., & Avila, R. A. (1986). Effectiveness of multiple request strategies: A synthesis of research results. *Journal of Marketing Research, 23,* 144–152.

Festinger, L. (1957). *A theory of cognitive dissonance.* Stanford, CA: Stanford University Press.

Festinger, L., & Carlsmith, J. M. (1959). Cognitive consequences of forced compliance. *Journal of Abnormal and Social Psychology, 58,* 203–210.

Festinger, L., & Maccoby, N. (1964). On resistance to persuasive communications. *Journal of Abnormal and Social Psychology, 68,* 359–366.

Finckenauer, J. O. (1982). *Scared straight and the panacea phenomenon.* Englewood Cliffs, NJ: Prentice Hall.

Fischer, P. M., Schwartz, M. P., Richards, J. W., Jr., Goldstein, A. O., & Rojas, T. H. (1991). Brand logo recognition by children aged 3 to 6 years. *Journal of American Medical Association, 266,* 3145–3148.

Fishbein, M. (2000). The role of theory in HIV prevention. *AIDS Care, 12,* 273–278.

Fishbein, M., & Ajzen, I. (1974). Attitudes toward objects as predictors of single and multiple behavioral criteria. *Psychological Review, 81,* 59–74.

Fishbein, M., & Ajzen, I. (1975). *Belief, attitude, intention and behavior: An introduction to theory and research.* Reading, MA: Addison–Wesley.

Fishbein, M., Cappella, J., Hornik, R., Sayeed, S., Yzer, M., & Ahern, R. K. (2002). The role of theory in developing effective antidrug public service announcements. In W. D. Crano & M. Burgoon (Eds.), *Mass media and drug prevention: Classic and contemporary theories and research* (pp. 89–117). Mahwah, NJ: Lawrence Erlbaum Associates.

Fitzpatrick, C. (2000, May 18). A new era of male attractiveness? *Plain Dealer,* 5-F.

Fitzpatrick, M. A., & Winke, J. (1979). You always hurt the one you love: Strategies and tactics in interpersonal conflict. *Communication Quarterly, 27,* 1–11.

Flora, J. A. (2001). The Stanford community studies: Campaigns to reduce cardiovascular disease. In R. E. Rice & C. K. Atkin (Eds.), *Public communication campaigns* (3rd ed., pp. 193–213). Thousand Oaks, CA: Sage.

Fountain, H. (2006, October 31). Observatory: The elephant in the mirror. *The New York Times,* D3.

Fox, R. M., & DeMarco, J. P. (1990). *Moral reasoning: A philosophic approach to applied ethics.* Ft. Worth, TX: Holt, Rinehart & Winston.

Frankena, W. (1963). *Ethics.* Englewood Cliffs, NJ: Prentice Hall.

Freedman, J. L., & Fraser, S. C. (1966). Compliance without pressure: The foot-in-the-door technique. *Journal of Personality and Social Psychology, 4,* 195–202.

Freimuth, V. (1990). The chronically uninformed: Closing the knowledge gap in health. In E. B. Ray & L. Donohew (Eds.), *Communication and health: Systems and applications* (pp. 171–186). Hillsdale, NJ: Lawrence Erlbaum Associates.

Frey, D. (1986). Recent research on selective exposure to information. In L. Berkowitz (Ed.), *Advances in experimental social psychology* (Vol. 19, pp. 41–80). Orlando, FL: Academic Press.

Frey, K. P., & Eagly, A. H. (1993). Vividness can undermine the persuasiveness of messages. *Journal of Personality and Social Psychology, 65,* 32–44.

Friedman, T. L. (2006, March 1). Who's afraid of a gas tax? *The New York Times,* A25.

Frymier, A. B., & Nadler, M. K. (2007). *Persuasion: Integrating theory, research, and practice.* Dubuque, Iowa: Kendall/Hunt.

Gamson, W. A. (1989). News as framing: Comments on Graber. *American Behavorial Scientist, 33,* 157–161.

Gardner, H. (1993). *Multiple intelligences: The theory in practice.* New York: Basic Books.

Garland, H. (1990). Throwing good money after bad: The effect of sunk costs on the decision to escalate commitment to an ongoing project. *Journal of Applied Psychology, 75,* 728–731.

Garst, J., & Bodenhausen, G. V. (1996). "Family values" and political persuasion: Impact of kin-related rhetoric on reactions to political campaigns. *Journal of Applied Social Psychology, 26,* 1119–1137.

Gass, R. H., & Seiter, J. S. (2003). *Persuasion, social influence, and compliance gaining* (2nd ed.). Boston: Allyn & Bacon.

Gayle, B. M., Preiss, R. W., & Allen, M. (1994). Gender differences and the use of conflict strategies. In L. H. Turner & H. M. Sterk (Eds.), *Differences that make a difference: Examining the assumptions in gender research* (pp. 13–26). Westport, CT: Bergin & Garvey.

Gaziano, C. (1983). The knowledge gap: An analytical review of media effects. *Communication Research, 10,* 447–486.

Geer, J. G. (2006). *In defense of negativity: Attack ads in presidential campaigns.* Chicago: University of Chicago Press.

Gerard, H. B., & Mathewson, G. C. (1966). The effect of severity of initiation on liking for a group: A replication. *Journal of Experimental Social Psychology, 2,* 278–287.

Gerrig, R. J. (1993). *Experiencing narrative worlds: On the psychological activities of reading.* New Haven, CT: Yale University Press.

Gerth, J., & Shane, S. (2005, December 1). U.S. is said to pay to plant articles in Iraq papers. *The New York Times,* A1, A18.

Gertner, J. (2009, April 19). Why isn't the brain green? *The New York Times Magazine,* 36–43.

Giles, H., & Street, R. L., Jr. (1994). Communicator characteristics and behavior. In M. L. Knapp & G. R. Miller (Eds.), *Handbook of interpersonal communication* (2nd ed., pp. 103–161). Thousand Oaks, CA: Sage.

Gladwell, M. (2008). *Outliers: The story of success.* New York: Little Brown.

Gladwell, M. (2005). *Blink: The power of thinking without thinking.* New York: Little, Brown.

Glick, P., & Fiske, S. T. (1996). The ambivalent sexism inventory: Differentiating hostile and benevolent sexism. *Journal of Personality and Social Psychology, 70,* 491–512.

Glynn, C. J., Herbst, S., O'Keefe, G. J., & Shapiro, R. Y. (1999). *Public opinion.* Boulder, CO: Westview Press.

Godbold, L. C., & Pfau, M. (2000). Conferring resistance to peer pressure among adolescents: Using inoculation theory to discourage alcohol use. *Communication Research, 27,* 411–437.

Goethals, G. R., & Nelson, R. E. (1973). Similarity in the influence process: The belief–value distinction. *Journal of Personality and Social Psychology, 25,* 117–122.

Goldberg, J. (2000, June 25). The education of a holy warrior. *The New York Times Magazine,* 32–37, 53, 63–64, 70–71.

Golden, J. L., Berquist, G. F., & Coleman, W. E. (2000). *The rhetoric of Western thought* (7th ed.). Dubuque, IA: Kendall/Hunt.

Goldman, R., & Papson, S. (1996). *Sign wars: The cluttered landscape of advertising.* New York: Guilford Press.

Goodstein L. (1997, April 7). No one put a gun to their heads. *The Washington Post National Weekly Edition,* 32.

Gore, A. (2006). *An inconvenient truth: The planetary emergency of global warming and what we can do about it.* Emmaus, PA: Rodale.

Gore, T. D., & Bracken, C. C. (2005). Testing the theoretical design of a health risk message: Reexamining the major tenets of the Extended Parallel Process Model. *Health Education & Behavior, 32,* 27–41.

Granberg, D. (1993). Political perception. In S. Iyengar & W. J. McGuire (Eds.), *Explorations in political psychology* (pp. 70–112). Durham, NC: Duke University Press.

Granberg, D., & Seidel, J. (1976). Social judgments of the urban and Vietnam issues in 1968 and 1972. *Social Forces, 55,* 1–15.

Green, M. C., Kass, S., Carrey, J., Herzig, B., Feeney, R., & Sabini, J. (2008). Transportation across media: Repeated exposure to print and film. *Media Psychology, 11,* 512–539.

Green, M. C., & Brock, T. C. (2000). The role of transportation in the persuasiveness of public narratives. *Journal of Personality and Social Psychology, 79,* 701–721.

Green, M. C., & Brock, T. C. (2002). In the mind's eye: Transportation-imagery model of narrative persuasion. In M. C. Green, J. J. Strange, & T. C. Brock (Eds.), *Narrative impact: Social and cognitive foundations* (pp. 315–341). Mahwah, NJ: Lawrence Erlbaum Associates.

*References*

Green, M. C., & Brock, T. C. (2005). Persuasiveness of narratives. In T. C. Brock & M. C. Green (Eds.), *Persuasion: Psychological insights and perspectives* (pp. 117–142). Thousand Oaks, CA: Sage.

Goodman, P. S., & Morgenson, G. (2008, December 28). Saying yes to anyone, WaMu built empire on shaky loans. *The New York Times*, 1, 21.

Greenberg, B. S., & Miller, G. R. (1966). The effects of low-credible sources on message acceptance. *Speech Monographs*, *33*, 127–136.

Greene, J. O., McDaniel, T. L., Buksa, K., & Ravizza, S. M. (1993). Cognitive processes in the production of multiple-goal messages: Evidence from the temporal characteristics of speech. *Western Journal of Communication*, *57*, 65–86.

Greenhouse, L. (1999, September 29). Managed care challenge to be heard by high court. *The New York Times*, A22.

Greenwald, A. G. (1968). Cognitive learning, cognitive response to persuasion, and attitude change. In A. G. Greenwald, T. C. Brock, & T. M. Ostrom (Eds.), *Psychological foundations of attitudes* (pp. 147–170). New York: Academic Press.

Greenwald, A. G., McGhee, D. E., & Schwartz, J. L. K. (1998). Measuring individual differences in implicit cognition: The Implicit Association Test. *Journal of Personality and Social Psychology*, *74*, 1464–1480.

Greenwald, A. G., Spangenberg, E. R., Pratkanis, A. R., & Eskenazi, J. (1991). Double-blind tests of subliminal self-help audiotapes. *Psychological Science*, *2*, 119–122.

Grimes, W. (2005, November 18). Winnowing the field of America to one representative. *The New York Times*, B42.

Grossman, R. P., & Till, B. D. (1998). The persistence of classically conditioned brand attitudes. *Journal of Advertising*, *27*, 23–31.

Gruder, C. L., Cook, T. D., Hennigan, K. M., Flay, B. R., Alessis, C., & Halamaj, J. (1978). Empirical tests of the absolute sleeper effect predicted from the discounting cue hypothesis. *Journal of Personality and Social Psychology*, *36*, 1061–1074.

Grush, J. E., McKeough, K. L., & Ahlering, R. F. (1978). Extrapolating laboratory exposure research to actual political elections. *Journal of Personality and Social Psychology*, *36*, 257–270.

Gunther, A. C., Bolt, D., Borzekowski, D. L. G., Liebhart, J. L., & Dillard, J. P. (2006). Presumed influence on peer norms: How mass media indirectly affect adolescent smoking. *Journal of Communication*, *56*, 52–68.

Guttman, L. (1944). A basis for scaling qualitative data. *American Sociological Review*, *9*, 139–150.

Guttman, N. (1997). Ethical dilemmas in health campaigns. *Health Communication*, *9*, 155–190.

Guttman, N. (2000). *Public health communication interventions: Values and ethical dilemmas*. Thousand Oaks, CA: Sage

Haines, M., & Spear, S. F. (1996). Changing the perception of the norm: A strategy to decrease binge drinking among college students. *Journal of American College Health*, *45*, 134–140.

Hale, J. L., Householder, B. J., & Greene, K. L. (2002). The theory of reasoned action. In J. P. Dillard & M. Pfau (Eds.), *The persuasion handbook: Developments in theory and practice* (pp. 259–286). Thousand Oaks, CA: Sage.

Haleta, L. L. (1996). Student perceptions of teachers' use of language: The effects of powerful and powerless language on impression formation and uncertainty. *Communication Education*, *45*, 16–28.

Hamilton, M. A., & Hunter, J. E. (1998). The effect of language intensity on receiver evaluations of message, source, and topic. In M. Allen & R. W. Preiss (Eds.), *Persuasion: Advances through meta-analysis* (pp. 99–138). Cresskill, NJ: Hampton Press.

Hampton, B., Brinberg, D., Peter, P., & Corus, C. (2009). Integrating the unified theory and stages of change to create targeted health messages. *Journal of Applied Social Psychology*, *39*, 449–471.

Han, S.P., & Shavitt, S. (1994). Persuasion and culture: Advertising appeals in individualistic and collectivistic societies. Journal of Experimental *Social Psychology*, *30*, 326–350.

Hannah, D. B., & Sternthal, B. (1984). Detecting and explaining the sleeper effect. *Journal of Consumer Research*, *11*, 632–642.

Hansen, M., Kossman, C., Wilbrecht, K., & Andsager, J. (2000). *Culture change on campus.* Unpublished paper, Washington State University, Pullman.

Harmon, A. (2004, June 20). In new tests for fetal defects, agonizing choices for parents. *The New York Times,* 1, 19.

Harmon, A. (2005, November 16). Young, assured and playing pharmacist to friends. *The New York Times,* A1, A17.

Harmon-Jones, E. (2002). A cognitive dissonance theory perspective on persuasion. In J. P. Dillard & M. Pfau (Eds.), *The persuasion handbook: Developments in theory and practice* (pp. 99–116). Thousand Oaks, CA: Sage.

Harmon-Jones, E., Brehm, J. W., Greenberg, J., Simon, L., & Nelson, D. E. (1996). Evidence that the production of aversive consequences is not necessary to create cognitive dissonance. *Journal of Personality and Social Psychology, 70,* 5–16.

Harmon-Jones, E., & Mills, J. (1999). An introduction to cognitive dissonance theory and an overview of current perspectives on the theory. In E. Harmon-Jones & J. Mills (Eds.), *Cognitive dissonance: Progress on a pivotal theory in social psychology* (pp. 3–21). Washington, DC: American Psychological Association.

Harres, A. (1998). "But basically you're feeling well, are you?" Tag questions in medical consultations. *Health Communication, 10,* 111–123.

Harris, G. (2004, June 27). As doctors write prescriptions, drug companies write checks. *The New York Times,* A1, 19.

Harris, G., & Berenson, A. (2005, February 25). 10 advisers voting on pain pills' sale have industry ties. *The New York Times,* A1, A16.

Harris, G. R., & Roberts, J. (2007, March 21). A state's files put doctors' ties to drug makers on close view. *The New York Times,* A1, A18.

Harris, R. J. (1999). *A cognitive psychology of mass communication* (3rd. ed.). Mahwah, NJ: Lawrence Erlbaum Associates.

Harrison, K., & Cantor, J. (1997). The relationship between media consumption and eating disorders. *Journal of Communication, 47*(1), 40–67.

Hart, R. P. (1984). *Verbal style and the presidency: A computer-based analysis.* Orlando, FL: Academic Press.

Hart, R. P., Friedrich, G. W., & Brummett, B. (1983). *Public communication* (2nd ed.). New York: Harper & Row.

Hartley, R. E. (2000). *Marketing mistakes* (8th ed.). New York: Wiley.

Hastorf, A., & Cantril, H. (1954). They saw a game: A case study. *Journal of Abnormal and Social Psychology, 49,* 129–134.

Haugtvedt, C. P., Petty, R. E., & Cacioppo, J. T. (1992). Need for cognition and advertising: Understanding the role of personality variables in consumer behavior. *Journal of Consumer Psychology, 1,* 239–260.

Haugtvedt, C. P., & Wegener, D. T. (1994). Message order effects in persuasion: An attitude strength perspective. *Journal of Consumer Research, 21,* 205–218.

Hazlett, R. L., & Hazlett, S. Y. (1999). Emotional response to television commercials: Facial EMG vs. self-report. *Journal of Advertising Research, 39*(2), 7–23.

Healy, P. (2008, January 10). Her message, and moment, won the day. *The New York Times,* A1, A22.

Heider, F. (1958). *The psychology of interpersonal relations.* New York: Wiley.

Henneberger, M. (1999, February 7). Cool refusal to take on damsel role. *The New York Times,* 1, 26.

Henriksen, L., Flora, J. A., Feighery, E., & Fortmann, S. P. (2002). Effects on youth of exposure to retail tobacco advertising. *Journal of Applied Social Psychology, 32,* 1771–1789.

Henriques, D. B., & Bergman, L. (2000, March 15). Profiting from fine print with Wall Street's help, *The New York Times,* A1, C12–C13.

Herbert, B. (2005a, June 16). Uncle Sam really wants you. *The New York Times,* A29.

Herbert, B. (2005b, August, 22). Truth in recruiting. *The New York Times,* A17.

Hernandez, R. (2006, February 13). At the lectern, critics and admirers agree, Hillary Clinton is no Bill Clinton. *The New York Times,* A19.

*References*

Hewitt, B., Fields-Meyer, T., Frankel, B., Jewel, D., Lambert, P., O'Neill, A. M., & Plummer, W. (1997, April 14). Who they were. *People*, 40–56.

Hilts, P. J. (1996). *Smokescreen: The truth behind the tobacco industry cover-up*. Reading, MA: Addison–Wesley.

Hippler, H. J., Schwarz, N., & Sudman, S. (Eds.). (1987). *Social information processing and survey methodology*. New York: Springer–Verlag.

Holbert, R. L., & Hansen, G. J. (2006). Fahrenheit 9–11, need for closure, and the priming of affective ambivalence: An assessment of intra-affective structures by party identification. *Human Communication Research, 32*, 109–129.

Holbrook, A. L., Berent, M. K., Krosnick, J. A., Visser, P. S. & Boninger, D. S. (2005). Attitude importance and the accumulation of attitude-relevant knowledge in memory. *Journal of Personality and Social Psychology, 88*, 749–769.

Holmes, S. A. (1998, November 20). Klan case transcends racial divide. *The New York Times*, A14.

Holt, J. (2006, December 3). The new, soft paternalism. *The New York Times Magazine*, 15–17.

Holtgraves, T., & Lasky, B. (1999). Linguistic power and persuasion. *Journal of Language and Social Psychology, 18*, 196–205.

Homans, G. C. (1961). *Social behavior: Its elementary forms*. New York: Harcourt, Brace.

Hong, T., & Cody, M. J. (2001, May). Presence of pro-tobacco messages on the Web. Paper presented to the annual convention of the International Communication Association, Washington, DC.

Hornik, R. (2002). Public health communication: Making sense of contradictory evidence. In R. Hornik (Ed.), *Public health communication: Evidence for behavior change* (pp. 1–19). Mahwah, NJ: Lawrence Erlbaum Associates.

Horovitz, B., & Wells, M. (1997, January 31–February 2). How ad images shape habits. *USA Today*, 1A–2A.

Horyn, C. (2008, June 1). Insensitive, yes. But sorry? Well . . . *The New York Times*, Sunday Styles, 2.

Hosman, L. A. (1989). The evaluative consequences of hedges, hesitations, and intensifiers: Powerful and powerless speech styles. *Human Communication Research, 15*, 383–406.

Hosman, L. A. (2002). Language and persuasion. In J. P. Dillard & M. Pfau (Eds.), *The persuasion handbook: Developments in theory and practice*. (pp. 371–390). Thousand Oaks, CA: Sage.

Hovland, C. I. (1959). Reconciling conflicting results derived from experimental and survey studies of attitude change. *American Psychologist, 14*, 8–17.

Hovland, C. I., Harvey, O. J., & Sherif, M. (1957). Assimilation and contrast effects in reactions to communication and attitude change. *Journal of Abnormal and Social Psychology, 55*, 244–252.

Hovland, C. I., Janis, I. L., & Kelley, H. H. (1953). *Communication and persuasion: Psychological studies of opinion change*. New Haven, CT: Yale University Press.

Hovland, C. I., Lumsdaine, A. A., & Sheffield, F. D. (1949). *Experiments on mass communication*. Princeton, NJ: Princeton University Press.

Huff, D. (1954). *How to lie with statistics*. New York: Norton.

Hullett, C. R. (2004). Using functional theory to promote sexually transmitted disease (STD) testing: The impact of value-expressive messages and guilt. *Communication Research, 31*, 363–396.

Hullett, C. R. (2006). Using functional theory to promote HIV testing: The impact of value-expressive messages, uncertainty, and fear. *Health Communication, 20*, 57–67.

Infante, D. A., & Rancer, A. S. (1982). A conceptualization and measure of argumentativeness. *Journal of Personality Assessment, 46*, 72–80.

Infante, D. A., & Rancer, A. S. (1996). Argumentativeness and verbal aggressiveness: A review of recent theory and research. In B. Burleson (Ed.), *Communication yearbook 19* (pp. 319–351). Thousand Oaks, CA: Sage.

Infante, D. A., & Wigley, C. J., III (1986). Verbal aggressiveness: An interpersonal model and measure. *Communication Monographs, 53*, 61–69.

Iyengar, S., & Hahn, K. S. (2009). Red media, blue media: Evidence of ideological selectivity in media use. *Journal of Communication, 59*, 19–39.

Jacobs, A. (2005, February 15). Gays debate radical steps to curb unsafe sex. *The New York Times*, A1, A21.

Jaggar, A. M. (2000). Feminist ethics. In H. LaFollette (Ed.), *The Blackwell guide to ethical theory* (pp. 348–374). Malden, MA: Blackwell.

Jamieson, K. H. (1992). *Dirty politics: Deception, distraction, and democracy.* New York: Oxford University Press.

Jamieson, K. H. (1995). *Beyond the double bind: Women and leadership.* New York: Oxford Press.

Jarvis, W. B. G., & Petty, R. E. (1996). The need to evaluate. *Journal of Personality and Social Psychology, 70,* 172–194.

Jhally, S. (1998). *Advertising and the end of the world* (video). Northampton, MA: Media Education Foundation.

Johnson, B. T., & Eagly, A. H. (1989). Effects of involvement on persuasion: A meta-analysis. *Psychological Bulletin, 106,* 290–314.

Johnson, B. T., Maio, G. R., & Smith-McLallen, A. (2005). Communication and attitude change: Causes, processes, and effects. In D. Albarracín, B. T. Johnson, & M. P. Zanna (Eds.), *The handbook of attitudes* (pp. 617–669). Mahwah, NJ: Lawrence Erlbaum Associates.

Johnson, D. (2000, May 21). No executions in Illinois until system is repaired. *The New York Times,* 14.

Johnson-Cartee, K. S., & Copeland, G. A. (1991). *Negative political advertising: Coming of age.* Hillsdale, NJ: Erlbaum Associates.

Johnston, D. C. (2001, February 14). Dozens of rich Americans join in fight to retain the estate tax. *The New York Times,* A1, A18.

Jordan, J. M., & Roloff, M. E. (1997). Planning skills and negotiator goal accomplishment: The relationship between self-monitoring and plan generation, plan enactment, and plan consequences. *Communication Research, 24,* 31–63.

Julka, D. L., & Marsh, K. L. (2005). An attitude functions approach to increasing organ-donation participation. *Journal of Applied Social Psychology, 35,* 821–849.

Kahle, L. R. (1996). Social values and consumer behavior: Research from the list of values. In C. Seligman, J. M. Olson, & M. P. Zanna (Eds.), *The psychology of values: The Ontario symposium,* (Vol. 8, pp. 135–151). Mahwah, NJ: Lawrence Erlbaum Associates.

Kahle, L. R., & Homer, P. M. (1985). Physical attractiveness of the celebrity endorser: A social adaptation perspective. *Journal of Consumer Research, 11,* 954–961.

Kalichman, S. C., & Coley, B. (1995). Context framing to enhance HIV-antibody testing messages targeted to African American women. *Health Psychology, 14,* 247–254.

Kaplowitz, S. A., & Fink, E. L. (1997). Message discrepancy and persuasion. In G. A. Barnett & F. J. Boster (Eds.), *Progress in communication sciences* (Vol. 13, pp. 75–106). Greenwich, CT: Ablex.

Kassan, L. D. (1999). *Second opinions: Sixty psychotherapy patients evaluate their therapists.* Northvale, NJ: Jason Aronson Press.

Katz, D. (1960). The functional approach to the study of attitudes. *Public Opinion Quarterly, 24,* 163–204.

Kaufman, D. Q., Stasson, M. F., & Hart, J. W. (1999). Are the tabloids always wrong or is that just what we think?: Need for cognition and perceptions of articles in print media. *Journal of Applied Social Psychology, 29,* 1984–1997.

Kaufman, L. (2000, September 17). And now, a few more words about breasts. *The New York Times,* [Week in Review], 3.

Kazoleas, D. C. (1993). A comparison of the persuasive effectiveness of qualitative versus quantitative evidence: A test of explanatory hypotheses. *Communication Quarterly, 41,* 40–50.

Kellermann, K., & Cole, T. (1994). Classifying compliance gaining messages: Taxonomic disorder and strategic confusion. *Communication Theory, 4,* 3–60.

Kelly, J. A. (1995). *Changing HIV risk behavior: Practical strategies.* New York: Guilford.

Kelman, H. C. (1958). Compliance, identification, and internalization: Three processes of attitude change. *Journal of Conflict Resolution, 2,* 51–60.

Kelman, H. C., & Hamilton, V. L. (1989). *Crimes of obedience: Toward a social psychology of authority and responsibility.* New Haven: Yale University Press.

Kennedy, G. (1963). *The art of persuasion in Greece.* Princeton, NJ: Princeton University Press.

Key, W. B. (1974). *Subliminal seduction.* New York: Signet Books.

*References*

Kiesler, C. A., Collins, B. E., & Miller, N. (1969). *Attitude change: A critical analysis of theoretical approaches.* New York: Wiley.

Kilbourne, J., & Pollay, R. (1992). *Pack of lies: The advertising of tobacco* (videotape). Northampton, MA: Foundation for Media Education.

Kim, M. S., & Bresnahan, M. (1994). A process model of request tactic evaluation. *Discourse Processes, 18,* 317–344.

Kim, M. S., & Hunter, J. E. (1993). Attitude–behavior relations: A meta-analysis of attitudinal relevance and topic. *Journal of Communication, 43*(1), 101–142.

Kim, M. S., & Sharkey, W. F. (1995). Independent and interdependent construals of self: Explaining cultural patterns of interpersonal communication in multicultural organizational settings. *Communication Quarterly, 43,* 20–38.

Kim, M. S., & Wilson, S. R. (1994). A cross-cultural comparison of implicit theories of requesting. *Communication Monographs, 61,* 210–235.

Kim, S. S., Kaplowitz, S., & Johnston, M. V. (2004). The effects of physician empathy on patient satisfaction and compliance. *Evaluation & the Health Professions, 27,* 237–251.

Kimmel, M. (2008). *Guyland: The perilous world where boys become men.* New York: HarperCollins.

Kincaid, D. L. (2002). Drama, emotion, and cultural convergence. *Communication Theory, 12,* 136–152.

Kinder, D. R., & Sanders, L. M. (1990). Mimicking political debate with survey questions: The case of White opinion on affirmative action for Blacks. *Social Cognition, 8,* 73–103.

King, C. S. (1969). *My life with Martin Luther King, Jr.* New York: Holt, Rinehart & Winston.

King, S. W., Minami, Y., & Samovar, L. A. (1985). A comparison of Japanese and American perceptions of source credibility. *Communication Research Reports, 2,* 76–79.

Kipnis, D., & Schmidt, S. (1996). The language of persuasion. In E. J. Coats & R. S. Feldman (Eds.), *Classic and contemporary readings in social psychology* (pp. 184–188). Upper Saddle River, NJ: Prentice Hall.

Kleinfield, N. R. (1999, November 15). For three interns, fatigue and healing at top speed. *The New York Times,* A1, A28.

Kleinfield, N. R. (2000, October 19). It's root, root, root, but for which team? *The New York Times,* A1, C27.

Kline, S. L., & Clinton, B. L. (1998). Developments in children's persuasive message practices. *Communication Education, 47,* 120–136.

Kluckhohn, C. (1951). Values and value-orientations in the theory of action: An exploration in definition and classification. In T. Parsons & E. A. Shils (Eds.), *Toward a general theory of action* (pp. 388–433). Cambridge, MA: Harvard University Press.

Klusendorf, S. (2001). Why pro-life advocates should use graphic visual aids. Online: www.str.org/free/bioethics/visuals.htm.

Knowles, E. S., Butler, S., & Linn, J. A. (2001). Increasing compliance by reducing resistance. In J. P. Forgas & K. D. Williams (Eds.), *Social influence: Direct and indirect processes* (pp. 41–60). Philadelphia: Taylor & Francis.

Knowles, E. S., & Linn, J. A. (2004). Approach-avoidance model of persuasion: Alpha and omega strategies for change. In E. S. Knowles & J. A. Linn (Eds.), *Resistance and persuasion* (pp. 117–148). Mahwah, NJ: Lawrence Erlbaum Associates.

Koehler, S. P., & Willis, F. N. (1994). Traffic citations in relation to gender. *Journal of Applied Social Psychology, 24,* 1919–1926.

Kolata, G. (2001, May 24). Placebo effect is more myth than science, a study says. *The New York Times,* A1, A19.

Kopfman, J. E., Smith, S. W., Ah Yun, J. K., & Hodges, A. (1998). Affective and cognitive reactions to narrative versus statistical evidence organ donation messages. *Journal of Applied Communication Research, 26,* 279–300.

Kovach, G. C. (2008, June 6). A sect's families reunite, and start to come home. *The New York Times* (online, www.nytimes.com/2008/06/06/us/06polygamy.htlm).

379

*References*

Kraus, S. J. (1995). Attitudes and the prediction of behavior: A meta-analysis of the empirical literature. *Personality and Social Psychology Bulletin, 21,* 58–75.

Kreps, G. L. (2006). Communication and racial inequities in health care. (Communication and racial disparities in health care, R. M. Perloff, Ed.), *American Behavioral Scientist, 49,* 760–774.

Kreuter, M. W., & Haughton, L. T. (2006). Integrating culture into health information for African American women. (Communication and racial disparities in health care, R. M. Perloff, Ed.), *American Behavioral Scientist, 49,* 794–811.

Kreuter, M., Farrell, D., Olevitch, L., & Brennan, L. (2000). *Tailoring health messages: Customizing communication with computer technology.* Mahwah, NJ: Lawrence Erlbaum Associates.

Kristof, N. D. (2008, September 21). The push to "otherize" Obama. *The New York Times* (Week in Review), 9.

Krosnick, J. A., Boninger, D. S., Chuang, Y. C., Berent, M. K., & Carnot, C. G. (1993). Attitude strength: One construct or many related constructs? *Journal of Personality and Social Psychology, 65,* 1132–1151.

Krosnick, J. A., Judd, C. M., & Wittenbrink, B. (2005). The measurement of attitudes. In D. Albarracin, B. T. Johnson, & M. P. Zanna (Eds.), *The handbook of attitudes* (pp. 21–76). Mahwah, NJ: Lawrence Erlbaum Associates.

Krosnick, J. A., & Petty, R. E. (1995). Attitude strength: An overview. In R. E. Petty & J. A. Krosnick (Eds.), *Attitude strength: Antecedents and consequences* (pp. 1–24). Hillsdale, NJ: Lawrence Erlbaum Associates.

Kruglanski, A. W., & Thompson, E. P. (1999). Persuasion by a single route: A view from the unimodel. *Psychological Inquiry, 10,* 83–109.

Kruglanski, A. W., Thompson, E. P., & Spiegel, S. (1999). Separate or equal? Bimodal notions of persuasion and a single-process "unimodel." In S. Chaiken & Y. Trope (Eds.), *Dual-process theories in social psychology* (pp. 293–313). New York: Guilford.

Krugman, P. (2008, September 5). The resentment stategy. *The New York Times,* A27.

Kuczynski, A. (2006). *Beauty junkies: Inside our $15 billion obsession with cosmetic surgery.* New York: Doubleday.

Kull, S., Ramsay, C., & Lewis, E. (2003). Misperceptions, the media, and the Iraq war. *Political Science Quarterly, 118,* 569–598.

Kumkale, G. T., & Albarracín, D. (2004). The sleeper effect in persuasion: A meta-analytic review. *Psychological Bulletin, 130,* 143–172.

LaBarbera, P. A., & Tucciarone, J. D. (1995). GSR reconsidered: A behavior-based approach to evaluating and improving the sales potency of advertising. *Journal of Advertising Research, 35(5),* 33–53.

LaFeber, W. (1999). *Michael Jordan and the new global capitalism.* New York: Norton.

Lakoff, G. (1996). *Moral politics: What conservatives know that liberals don't.* Chicago: University of Chicago Press.

Lakoff, G. (2004). *Don't think of an elephant! Know your values and frame the debate.* White River Junction, VT: Chelsea Green Publishing.

Lambiase, J. J. (2003). Sex—Online and in Internet advertising. In T. Reichert & J. Lambiase (Eds.), *Sex in advertising: Perspectives on the erotic appeal* (pp. 247–269). Mahwah, NJ: Lawrence Erlbaum Associates.

Langer, J. (1997). What consumers wish brand managers knew. *Journal of Advertising Research, 37(6),* 60–65.

Langrehr, F. W., & Caywood, C. L. (1995). A semiotic approach to determining the sins and virtues portrayed in advertising. *Journal of Current Issues and Research in Advertising, 17,* 33–47.

LaPiere, R. T. (1934). *Attitudes vs. action.* Social Forces, 13, 230–237.

Lavin, M. (2001). *Clean new world: Culture, politics, and graphic design.* Cambridge, MA: MIT Press.

Lavine, H., Thomsen, C. J., & Gonzales, M. T. (1997). The development of inter-attitudinal consistency: The shared-consequences model. *Journal of Personality and Social Psychology, 72,* 735–749.

Lavine, H., Thomsen, C. J., Zanna, M. P., & Borgida, E. (1998). On the primacy of affect in the determination of attitudes and behavior: The moderating role of affective–cognitive ambivalence. *Journal of Experimental Social Psychology, 34,* 398–421.

Leave No Sales Pitch Behind (2005, January 4). *The New York Times* [Editorial], A22.

*References*

Lederman, L. C., Stewart, L. P., Barr, S. L., Powell, R. L., Laitman, L., & Goodhart, F. W. (2001). RU SURE? Using communication theory to reduce dangerous drinking on a college campus. In R. E. Rice & C. K. Atkin (Eds.), *Public communication campaigns* (3rd ed., pp. 295–299). Thousand Oaks, CA: Sage.

Lee, J. G., & Thorson, E. (2008). The impact of celebrity-product incongruence on the effectiveness of product endorsement. *Journal of Advertising Research, 48,* 433–449.

Leeds, J., & Story, L. (2005, July 26). Radio payoffs are described as Sony settles. *The New York Times,* A1, C4.

Leippe, M. R., & Eisenstadt, D. (1994). Generalization of dissonance reduction: Decreasing prejudice through induced compliance. *Journal of Personality and Social Psychology, 67,* 395–413.

Leippe, M. R., & Elkin, R. A. (1987). When motives clash: Issue involvement and response involvement as determinants of persuasion. *Journal of Personality and Social Psychology, 52,* 269–278.

Leland, J. (2005, September 18). Under din of abortion debate, an experience shared quietly. *The New York Times,* 1, 29.

Leodoro, G., & Lynn, M. (2007). The effect of server posture on the tips of Whites and Blacks. *Journal of Applied Social Psychology, 37,* 201–209.

Lewin, K. (1951). *Field theory in social science.* New York: Harper and Row.

Levasseur, D., & Dean, K. W. (1996). The use of evidence in presidential debates: A study of evidence levels and types from 1960 to 1988. *Argumentation and Advocacy, 32,* 129–142.

Levine, J. M., & Valle, R. S. (1975). The convert as a credible communicator. *Social Behavior and Personality, 3,* 81–90.

Levy, N. (2005, May 3). Private England pleads guilty to abuses. *The New York Times,* A8.

Levy, S. (2006). *The perfect thing: How the iPod shuffles commerce, culture, and coolness.* New York: Simon & Schuster.

Lieberman, D. A. (2001). Using interactive media in communication campaigns for children and adolescents. In R. E. Rice & C. K. Atkin (Eds.), *Public communication campaigns* (3rd ed., pp. 373–388). Thousand Oaks, CA: Sage.

Lifton, R. J. (2003). Foreword. In M. T. Singer, *Cults in our midst* (Rev. ed., pp. xi–xiii). San Francisco: Jossey-Bass.

Likert, R. (1932). A technique for the measurement of attitudes. *Archives of Psychology, 140,* 1–55.

Lim, J. S., & Ki, E. J. (2007). Resistance to ethically suspicious parody video on YouTube: A test of inoculation theory. *Journalism and Mass Communication Quarterly, 84,* 713–728.

Linz, D. G., & Penrod, S. (1984). Increasing attorney persuasiveness in the courtroom. *Law and Psychology Review, 8,* 1–47.

Lord, C. G., Desforges, D. M., Fein, S., Pugh, M. A., & Lepper, M. R. (1994). Typicality effects in attitude toward social policies: A concept-mapping approach. *Journal of Personality and Social Psychology, 66,* 658–673.

Lord, C. G., Lepper, M. R., & Mackie, D. (1984). Attitude prototypes as determinants of attitude–behavior consistency. *Journal of Personality and Social Psychology, 46,* 1254–1266.

Lord, C. G., Ross, L., & Lepper, M. R. (1979). Biased assimilation and attitude polarization: The effects of prior theories on subsequently considered evidence. *Journal of Personality and Social Psychology, 37,* 2098–2109.

Lynch, J., & Schuler, D. (1994). The matchup effect of spokesperson and product congruency: A schema theory interpretation. *Psychology & Marketing, 11,* 417–445.

Lynn, M., & Mynier, K. (1993). Effect of server posture on restaurant tipping. *Journal of Applied Social Psychology, 23,* 678–685.

Maccoby, N., & Farquhar, J. W. (1975). Communication for health: Unselling heart disease. *Journal of Communication, 25,* 114–126.

Mahler, J. (2005, March 27). The soul of the new exurb. *The New York Times Magazine,* 30–37, 46, 50, 54, 57.

Maibach, E. W., Kreps, G. L., & Bonaguro, E. W. (1993). Developing strategic communication campaigns for HIV/AIDS prevention. In S. Ratzan (Ed.), *AIDS: Effective health communication for the 90s* (pp. 15–35). Washington, DC: Taylor & Francis.

Mailer, N. (1999). Ego. In D. Halberstam (Ed.), *The best American sports writing of the century* (pp. 713–737). Boston: Houghton Mifflin.

Maio, G. R., & Esses, V. M. (2001). The need for affect: Individual differences in the motivation to approach or avoid emotions. *Journal of Personality, 69,* 583–614.

Maio, G. R., & Olson, J. M. (1998). Values as truisms: Evidence and implications. *Journal of Personality and Social Psychology, 74,* 294–311.

Maio, G. R., & Olson, J. M. (Eds.) (2000a). *Why we evaluate: Functions of attitudes.* Mahwah, NJ: Lawrence Erlbaum Associates.

Maio, G. R., & Olson, J. M. (2000b). What is a "value-expressive" attitude? In G. R. Maio & J. M. Olson (Eds.), *Why we evaluate: Functions of attitudes* (pp. 249–269). Mahwah, NJ: Lawrence Erlbaum Associates.

Manly, L. (2005, March 27). The future of the 30-second spot. *The New York Times* (Sunday Business), 1, 4.

Manstead, A. S. R., Proffitt, C., & Smart, J. L. (1983). Predicting and understanding mothers' infant-feeding intentions and behavior: Testing the theory of reasoned action. *Journal of Personality and Social Psychology, 44,* 657–671.

Marcus, E. N. (2006, November 21). When young doctors strut too much of their stuff. *The New York Times,* D5.

Marklein, M. B. (2000, October 11). Ugly truths about hazing. *USA Today,* 6D.

Martin, D. (2000, January 9). What's in a name: The allure of labels. *The New York Times,* 4–2.

Martin, M. (2001, March 30). Man sentenced to educate himself. *Plain Dealer,* 1-B, 5-B.

Marwell, G., & Schmitt, D. R. (1967). Dimensions of compliance-gaining behavior: An empirical analysis. *Sociometry, 30,* 350–364.

Max, D. T. (1999, December 26). The Oprah effect. *The New York Times Magazine,* 36–41.

McAlister, A. L., & Fernandez, M. (2002). "Behavioral journalism" accelerates diffusion of healthy innovations. In R. Hornik (Ed.), *Public health communication: Evidence for behavior change* (pp. 315–326). Mahwah, NJ: Lawrence Erlbaum Associates.

McBane, D.A. (1995). Empathy and the salesperson: A multidimensional perspective. *Psychology and Marketing, 12,* 349–369.

McCarty, J. A. (2004). Product placement: The nature of the practice and potential avenues of inquiry. In L. J. Shrum (Ed.), *The psychology of entertainment media: Blurring the lines between entertainment and persuasion* (pp. 45–61). Mahwah, NJ: Lawrence Erlbaum Associates.

McCombs, M., & Reynolds, A. (2002). News influence on our pictures of the world. In J. Bryant & D. Zillmann (Eds.), *Media effects: Advances in theory and research* (2nd ed., pp. 1–18). Mahwah, NJ: Lawrence Erlbaum Associates.

McConahay, J. B. (1986). Modern racism, ambivalence, and the Modern Racism scale. In J. F. Dovidio & S. L. Gaertner (Eds.), *Prejudice, discrimination, and racism* (pp. 91–125). Orlando, FL: Academic Press.

McCracken, G. (1986). Culture and consumption: A theoretical account of the structure and movement of the cultural meaning of consumer goods. *Journal of Consumer Research, 13,* 71–84.

McCracken, G. (1989). Who is the celebrity endorser? Cultural foundations of the endorsement process. *Journal of Consumer Research, 16,* 310–321.

McCroskey, J. C. (1969). A summary of experimental research on the effects of evidence in persuasive communication. *Quarterly Journal of Speech, 55,* 169–176.

McCroskey, J. C. (1972). *An introduction to rhetorical communication.* Englewood Cliffs, NJ: Prentice Hall.

McCroskey, J. C. (1997). *An introduction to rhetorical communication* (7th ed.). Boston: Allyn and Bacon.

McCroskey, J. C., & Teven, J. J. (1999). Goodwill: A reexamination of the construct and its measurement. *Communication Monographs, 66,* 90–103.

*References*

McCroskey, J. C., & Young, T. J. (1981). Ethos and credibility: The construct and its measurement after three decades. *Central States Speech Journal, 32*, 24–34.

McDonald, C. (1993). Children, smoking and advertising: What does the research really tell us? *International Journal of Advertising, 12*, 279–287.

McGuire, W. J. (1968). Personality and susceptibility to social influence. In E. F. Borgatta & W. W. Lambert (Eds.), *Handbook of personality theory and research*, (pp. 1130–1187). Chicago: Rand McNally.

McGuire, W. J. (1969). The nature of attitudes and attitude change. In G. Lindzey & E. Aronson (Eds.), *Handbook of social psychology* (2nd ed., Vol. 3, pp. 136–314). Reading, MA: Addison-Wesley.

McGuire, W. J. (1970, February). A vaccine for brainwash. *Psychology Today*, pp. 36–39, 63–64.

McGuire, W. J. (1989). Theoretical foundations of campaigns. In R. E. Rice & C. K. Atkin (Eds.), *Public communication campaigns* (2nd ed., pp. 43–65). Thousand Oaks, CA: Sage.

McGuire, W. J., & Papageorgis, D. (1961). The relative efficacy of various types of prior belief-defense in producing immunity against persuasion. *Journal of Abnormal and Social Psychology, 62*, 327–337.

McKelvey, T. (2007). *Monstering: Inside America's policy of secret interrogations and torture in the terror war.* New York: Carroll & Graf.

McLuhan, M. (1967). *The medium is the massage.* New York: Random House.

McNeil, Jr., D. G. (2008, June 3). Global update. *The New York Times*, D6.

Meeus, W. H. J., & Raaijmakers, Q. A. W. (1986). Administrative obedience: Carrying out orders to use psychological-administrative violence. *European Journal of Social Psychology, 16*, 311–324.

Messaris, P. (1997). *Visual persuasion: The role of images in advertising.* Thousand Oaks, CA: Sage.

Messud, C. (2008, September 1). Some like it cool. *Newsweek*, 46–50.

Metzger, M. J., Flanagin, A. J., Eyal, K., Lemus, D. R, & McCann, R. M. (2003). Credibility for the 21st century: Integrating perspectives on source, message, and media credibility in the contemporary media environment. In P. J. Kalbfleisch (Ed.), *Communication yearbook 27* (pp. 293–335). Mahwah, NJ: Lawrence Erlbaum Associates.

Meyerowitz, B. E., & Chaiken, S. (1987). The effect of message framing on breast self-examination attitudes, intentions, and behavior. *Journal of Personality and Social Psychology, 52*, 500–510.

Middlebrook, P. N. (1974). *Social psychology and modern life.* New York: Knopf.

Milburn, M. A. (1991). *Persuasion and politics: The social psychology of public opinion.* Pacific Grove, CA: Brooks/Cole.

Miles, H. L. (1993). Language and the orangutan: The old "person" of the forest. In P. Cavalieri & P. Singer (Eds.), *The great ape project: Equality beyond humanity* (pp. 42–57). New York: St. Martin's Griffin.

Milgram, S. (1963). Behavioral study of obedience. *Journal of Abnormal and Social Psychology, 67*, 371–378.

Milgram, S. (1974). *Obedience to authority: An experimental view.* New York: Harper & Row.

Millar, M. G., & Millar, K. U. (1996). The effects of direct and indirect experience on affective and cognitive responses and the attitude–behavior relation. *Journal of Experimental Social Psychology, 32*, 561–579.

Miller, A. G. (1986). *The obedience experiments: A case study of controversy in social science.* New York: Praeger.

Miller, A. G., Collins, B. E., & Brief, D. E. (1995). Perspectives on obedience to authority: The legacy of the Milgram experiments. *Journal of Social Issues, 51*, 1–19.

Miller, A. G., McHoskey, J. W., Bane, C. M., & Dowd, T. G. (1993). The attitude polarization phenomenon: Role of response measure, attitude extremity, and behavioral consequences of reported attitude change. *Journal of Personality and Social Psychology, 64*, 561–574.

Miller, G. R. (1980). On being persuaded: Some basic distinctions. In M. E. Roloff & G. R. Miller (Eds.), *Persuasion: New directions in theory and research* (pp. 11–28). Beverly Hills, CA: Sage.

Miller, G. R., Boster, F., Roloff, M., & Seibold, D. (1977). Compliance-gaining message strategies: A typology and some findings concerning effects of situational differences. *Communication Monographs, 44*, 37–51.

Miller, G. R., & Parks, M. R. (1982). Communication in dissolving relationships. In S. Duck (Ed.), *Personal relationships 4: Dissolving relationships* (pp. 127–154). Orlando, FL: Academic Press.

Miller, K. D. (1992). *Voice of deliverance: The language of Martin Luther King, Jr. and its sources*. New York: Free Press.

Miller, N., Maruyama, G., Beaber, R. J., & Valone, K. (1976). Speed of speech and persuasion. *Journal of Personality and Social Psychology, 34*, 615–624.

Mills, J. (1999). Improving the 1957 version of dissonance theory. In E. Harmon-Jones & J. Mills (Eds.), *Cognitive dissonance: Progress on a pivotal theory in social psychology* (pp. 25–42). Washington, DC: American Psychological Association.

Mitchell, A. A. (1986). Effects of visual and verbal components of advertisements on brand attitudes. *Journal of Consumer Research, 13*, 12–24.

Mittal, B. (1995). A comparative analysis of four scales of consumer involvement. *Psychology & Marketing, 12*, 663–682.

Mongeau, P. A. (1998). Another look at fear-arousing persuasive appeals. In M. Allen & R. W. Preiss (Eds.), *Persuasion: Advances through meta-analysis* (pp. 53–68). Cresskill, NJ: Hampton Press.

Moore, M. T. (1993, June 15). Visual overload: Fleeing ad images catch viewers. *USA Today*, B1.

Morin, R. (1997, September 1). The worst of the worst. *The Washington Post National Weekly Edition*, 35.

Morley, D. D., & Walker, K. B. (1987). The role of importance, novelty, and plausibility in producing belief change. *Communication Monographs, 54*, 436–442.

Morris, K. A., & Swann, W. B., Jr. (1996). Denial and the AIDS crisis: On wishing away the threat of AIDS. In S. Oskamp & S. C. Thompson (Eds.), *Understanding and preventing HIV risk behavior: Safer sex and drug use* (pp. 57–79). Thousand Oaks, CA: Sage.

Morrison, D. M., Gillmore, M. R., & Baker, S. A. (1995). Determinants of condom use among high-risk heterosexual adults: A test of the theory of reasoned action. *Journal of Applied Social Psychology, 25*, 651–676.

Morrison, D. M., Gillmore, M. R., Simpson, E. E., Wells, E. A., & Hoppe, M. J. (1996). Children's decisions about substance use: An application and extension of the theory of reasoned action. *Journal of Applied Social Psychology, 26*, 1658–1679.

Motley, M. T., & Reeder, H. M. (1995). Unwanted escalation of sexual intimacy: Male and female perceptions of connotations and relational consequences of resistance messages. *Communication Monographs, 62*, 355–379.

Mowen, J. C., & Cialdini, R. B. (1980). On implementing the door-in-the-face compliance technique in a business context. *Journal of Marketing Research, 17*, 253–258.

Muehling, D. D., & McCann, M. (1993). Attitude toward the ad: A review. *Journal of Current Issues and Research in Advertising, 15*, 25–58.

Murray, S., & Gruley, B. (2000, November 2). On many campuses, big brewers play a role in new alcohol policies. *The Wall Street Journal*, A1, A10.

Muthusamy, M., Levine, T. R., & Weber, R. (2009). Scaring the already scared: Some problems with HIV/AIDS fear appeals in Namibia. *Journal of Communication, 59*, 317–344.

Mutz, D.C. (2006). *Hearing the other side: Deliberative versus participatory democracy*. Cambridge, England: Cambridge University Press.

Myers, G. (1999). *Ad worlds: Brands, media, audiences*. London: Arnold.

Nabi, R. L. (2002). Anger, fear, uncertainty, and attitudes: A test of the cognitive-functional model. *Communication Monographs, 69*, 204–216.

Nabi, R. L., Moyer-Guse, E., & Byrne, S. (2007). All joking aside: A serious investigation into the persuasive effect of funny social issue messages. *Communication Monographs, 74*, 29–54.

Nagourney, A. (2008, September 2). In political realm, "family problem" emerges as test and distraction. *The New York Times*, A18.

Nan, X. (2007). The relative persuasive effect of gain- versus loss-framed messages: Exploring the moderating role of the desirability of end-states. *Journalism and Mass Communication Quarterly, 84*, 509–524.

*References*

Nebenzahl, I. D., & Jaffe, E. D. (1998). Ethical dimensions of advertising executions. *Journal of Business Ethics, 17,* 805–815.

Nelson, T. E., Oxley, Z. M., & Clawson, R. A. (1997). Toward a psychology of framing. *Political Behavior, 19,* 221–245.

Newman, L. S., Duff, K., Schnopp-Wyatt, N., Brock, B., & Hoffman, Y. (1997). Reactions to the O. J. Simpson verdict: "Mindless tribalism" or motivated inference processes? *Journal of Social Issues, 53,* 547–562.

Nick, Y., & Bailenson, J. N. (2009). The difference between being and seeing: The relative contribution of self-perception and priming to behavioral changes via digital self-representation. *Media Psychology, 12,* 195–209.

Nienhuis, A. E., Manstead, A. S. R., & Spears, R. (2001). Multiple motives and persuasive communication: Creating elaboration as a result of impression motivation and accuracy motivation. *Personality and Social Psychology Bulletin, 27,* 118–132.

Nilsen, T. R. (1974). *Ethics of speech communication* (2nd ed.). Indianapolis: Bobbs–Merrill.

Nisbett, R. E., Borgida, E., Crandall, R., & Reed, H. (1976). Popular induction: Information is not necessarily informative. In J. S. Carroll & J. W. Payne (Eds.), *Cognition and social behavior* (pp. 113–133). Hillsdale, NJ: Lawrence Erlbaum Associates.

Nitze, S. P. (2001, April 8). How to be an impostor. *The New York Times Magazine,* 38–40.

Noar, S. M. (2006). A 10-year retrospective of research in health mass media campaigns: Where do we go from here? *Journal of Health Communication, 11,* 21–42.

O'Brien, T. L. (2005, September 25). Madison Avenue wants you: How to pitch the military when a war drags on? *The New York Times* [Sunday Business], Section 3; 1, 8).

Ohme, R. K. (2000). Social influence in media: Culture and antismoking advertising. In W. Wosinka, R. B. Cialdini, D. W. Barrett, & J. Reykowski (Eds.), *The practice of social influence in multiple cultures* (pp. 309–324). Mahwah, NJ: Lawrence Erlbaum Associates.

O'Keefe, D.J. (2002). Guilt as a mechanism of persuasion. In J. P. Dillard & M. Pfau (Eds.), *The persuasion handbook: Developments in theory and practice* (pp. 329–344). Thousand Oaks, CA: Sage.

O'Keefe, D. J. (1990). *Persuasion: Theory and research.* Newbury Park, CA: Sage.

O'Keefe, D. J. (1997). Standpoint explicitness and persuasive effect: A meta-analytic review of the effects of varying conclusion articulation in persuasive messages. *Argumentation and Advocacy, 34,* 1–12.

O'Keefe, D. J. (1999). How to handle opposing arguments in persuasive messages: A meta-analytic review of the effects of one-sided and two-sided messages. In M. E. Roloff (Ed.), *Communication yearbook 22,* 209–249.

O'Keefe, D. J. (2000). Guilt and social influence. In M. E. Roloff (Ed.), *Communication yearbook 23* (pp. 67–101). Thousand Oaks, CA: Sage.

O'Keefe, D. J. (2003). Message properties, mediating states, and manipulation checks: Claims, evidence, and data analysis in experimental persuasive message effects research. *Communication Theory, 13,* 251–274.

O'Keefe, D. J., & Figgé, M. (1999). Guilt and expected guilt in the door-in-the-face technique. *Communication Monographs, 66,* 312–324.

O'Keefe, D. J., & Hale, S. L. (1998). The door-in-the-face influence strategy: A random-effects meta-analytic review. In M. E. Roloff (Ed.), *Communication yearbook 21* (pp. 1–33). Thousand Oaks, CA: Sage.

O'Keefe, D. J., & Jensen, J. D. (2006). The advantages of compliance or the disadvantages of noncompliance?: A meta-analytic review of the relative persuasive effectiveness of gain-framed and loss-framed messages. In C. S. Beck (Ed.), *Communication yearbook 30* (Mahwah, NJ: Erlbaum Associates),1–43.

O'Keefe, D. J., & Jensen, J. D. (2009). The relative persuasiveness of gain-framed and loss-framed messages for encouraging disease detection behaviors: A meta-analytic review. *Journal of Communication, 59,* 296–316.

O'Keefe, G. J. (1985). "Taking a bite out of crime": The impact of a public information campaign. *Communication Research, 12,* 147–178.

O'Keefe, G. J., Rosenbaum, D. P., Lavrakas, P. J., Reid, K., & Botta, R. A. (1996). *Taking a bite out of crime: The impact of the National Citizens' Crime Prevention Media Campaign.* Thousand Oaks, CA: Sage.

Olney, B. (2000, July 9). Hitters vs. pitchers. *The New York Times Magazine*, 38–41.

Olson, M. A. & Fazio, R. H. (2004). Reducing the influence of extrapersonal associations on the Implicit Association Test: Personalizing the IAT. *Journal of Personality and Social Psychology, 86,* 653–667.

Orenstein, P. (2000). *Flux: Women on sex, work, kids, love, and life in a half-changed world.* New York: Doubleday.

Orne, M. T., & Holland, C. H. (1968). On the ecological validity of laboratory deceptions. *International Journal of Psychiatry, 6,* 282–293.

Osgood, C. E. (1974). Probing subjective culture/Part I: Cross linguistic tool making. *Journal of Communication, 24*(1), 21–35.

Osgood, C. E., Suci, G. J., & Tannenbaum, P. H. (1957). *The measurement of meaning.* Urbana: University of Illinois Press.

Osterhouse, R. A., & Brock, T. C. (1970). Distraction increases yielding to propaganda by inhibiting counterarguing. *Journal of Personality and Social Psychology, 15,* 344–358.

Ostrom, T. M., Bond, C. F., Jr., Krosnick, J. A., & Sedikides, C. (1994). Attitude scales: How we measure the unmeasurable. In S. Shavitt & T. C. Brock (Eds.), *Persuasion: Psychological insights and perspectives* (pp. 15–42). Boston: Allyn and Bacon.

O'Sullivan, C. S., Chen, A., Mohapatra, S., Sigelman, L., & Lewis, E. (1988). Voting in ignorance: The politics of smooth-sounding names. *Journal of Applied Social Psychology, 18,* 1094–1106.

Paek, H-J. (2009). Differential effects of different peers: Further evidence of the peer proximity thesis in perceived peer influence on college students' smoking. *Journal of Communication, 59,* 434–455.

Palmgreen, P., Donohew, L., Lorch, E. P., Hoyle, R. H., & Stephenson, M. T. (2002). Television campaigns and sensation seeking targeting of adolescent marijuana use: A controlled time series approach. In R. Hornik (Ed.), *Public health communication: Evidence for behavior change* (pp. 35–56). Mahwah, NJ: Lawrence Erlbaum Associates.

Park, H. S., Levine, T. R., Kingsley Westerman, C. Y., Orfgen, T., & Foregger, S. (2007). The effects of argument quality and involvement type on attitude formation and attitude change: A test of dual-process and social judgment predictions. *Human Communication Research, 33,* 81–102.

Park, S. Y. (2005). The influence of presumed media influence on women's desire to be thin. *Communication Research, 32,* 594–614.

Parker, D., Stradling, S. G., & Manstead, A. S. R. (1996). Modifying beliefs and attitudes to exceeding the speed limit: An intervention study based on the theory of planned behavior. *Journal of Applied Social Psychology, 26,* 1–19.

Parrott, R. L. (1995). Motivation to attend to health messages: Presentation of content and linguistic considerations. In E. Maibach & R. L. Parrott (Eds.), *Designing health messages: Approaches from communication theory and public health practice* (pp. 7–23). Thousand Oaks, CA: Sage.

Parrott, R., Silk, K., Dorgan, K., Condit, C., & Harris, T. (2005). Risk comprehension and judgments of statistical evidentiary appeals: When a picture is not worth a thousand words. *Human Communication Research, 31,* 423–452.

Pendergrast, M. (2000). *For God, country and Coca-Cola: The definitive history of the great American soft drink and the company that makes it.* New York: Basic Books.

Peplau, L. A., Hill, C. T., & Rubin, Z. (1993). Sex role attitudes in dating and marriage: A 15-year follow-up of the Boston couples study. *Journal of Social Issues, 49*(3), 31–52.

Peracchio, L. A., & Luna, D. (1998). The development of an advertising campaign to discourage smoking initiation among children and youth. *Journal of Advertising, 27,* 49–56.

Perkins, H. W., & Craig, D. W. (2003). The Hobart and William Smith Colleges experiment: A synergistic social norms approach using print, electronic media, and curriculum infusion to reduce collegiate problem drinking. In H. W. Perkins (Ed.), *The social norms approach to preventing school and college age*

*References*                 *substance abuse: A handbook for educators, counselors, and clinicians* (pp. 35–64). San Francisco: Jossey–Bass.

Perloff, R. (1971). Caught up in the dreams of revolution. In C. R. Reaske & R. F. Willson, Jr. (Eds.), *Student voices one* (pp. 24–25). New York: Random House.

Perloff, R. M. (1996). Perceptions and conceptions of political media impact: The third-person effect and beyond. In A. N. Crigler (Ed.), *The psychology of political communication* (pp. 177–197). Ann Arbor: University of Michigan Press.

Perloff, R. M. (1998). *Political communication: Politics, press, and public in America.* Mahwah, NJ: Lawrence Erlbaum Associates.

Perloff, R. M. (2001). *Persuading people to have safer sex: Applications of social science to the AIDS crisis.* Mahwah, NJ: Lawrence Erlbaum Associates.

Perloff, R. M. (2008). Mass media, social perception, and the third-person effect. In J. Bryant & M. B. Oliver (Eds.), *Media effects: Advances in theory and research* (3rd ed., pp. 252–268). New York: Taylor & Francis.

Perloff, R. M., & Brock, T. C. (1980). "And thinking makes it so": Cognitive responses to persuasion. In M. E. Roloff & G. R. Miller (Eds.), *Persuasion: New directions in theory and research* (pp. 67–99). Beverly Hills, CA: Sage.

Petrocelli, J. V., Tormala, Z. L., & Rucker, D. D. (2007). Unpacking attitude certainty: Attitude clarity and attitude correctness. *Journal of Personality and Social Psychology, 92,* 30–41.

Petty, R. E., & Cacioppo, J. T. (1977). Forewarning, cognitive responding, and resistance to persuasion. *Journal of Personality and Social Psychology, 35,* 645–655.

Petty, R. E., & Cacioppo, J. T. (1984). The effects of involvement on responses to argument quantity and quality: Central and peripheral routes to persuasion. *Journal of Personality and Social Psychology, 46,* 69–81.

Petty, R. E., & Cacioppo, J. T. (1986). The Elaboration Likelihood Model of persuasion. In L. Berkowitz (Ed.), *Advances in experimental social psychology* (Vol. 19, pp. 123–205). New York: Academic Press.

Petty, R. E., Cacioppo, J. T., & Goldman, R. (1981). Personal involvement as a determinant of argument-based persuasion. *Journal of Personality and Social Psychology, 41,* 847–855.

Petty, R. E., Cacioppo, J. T., Kasmer, J. A., & Haugtvedt, C. P. (1987). A reply to Stiff and Boster. *Communication Monographs, 54,* 257–263.

Petty, R. E., Cacioppo, J. T., Strathman, A. J., & Priester, J. R. (1994). To think or not to think: Exploring two routes to persuasion. In S. Shavitt & T. C. Brock (Eds.), *Persuasion: Psychological insights and perspectives* (pp. 113–147). Boston: Allyn and Bacon.

Petty, R. E., Haugtvedt, C. P., & Smith, S. M. (1995). Elaboration as a determinant of attitude strength: Creating attitudes that are persistent, resistant, and predictive of behavior. In R. E. Petty & J. A. Krosnick (Eds.), *Attitude strength: Antecedents and consequences* (pp. 93–130). Hillsdale, NJ: Lawrence Erlbaum Associates.

Petty, R. E., Ostrom, T. M., & Brock, T. C. (1981a). Historical foundations of the cognitive response approach to attitudes and persuasion. In R. E. Petty, T. M. Ostrom, & T. C. Brock (Eds.), *Cognitive responses in persuasion* (pp. 5–29). Hillsdale, NJ: Lawrence Erlbaum Associates.

Petty, R. E., Ostrom, T. M., & Brock, T. C. (Eds.) (1981b). *Cognitive responses in persuasion.* Hillsdale, NJ: Lawrence Erlbaum Associates.

Petty, R. E., Schumann, D. W., Richman, S. A., & Strathman, A. J. (1993). Positive mood and persuasion: Different roles for affect under high- and low-elaboration conditions. *Journal of Personality and Social Psychology, 64,* 5–20.

Petty, R. E., & Wegener, D. T. (1998). Matching versus mismatching attitude functions: Implications for scrutiny of persuasive messages. *Personality and Social Psychology Bulletin, 24,* 227–240.

Petty, R. E., & Wegener, D. T. (1999). The Elaboration Likelihood Model: Current status and controversies. In S. Chaiken & Y. Trope (Eds.), *Dual-process theories in social psychology* (pp. 41–72). New York: Guilford.

Petty, R. E., Wegener, D. T., Fabrigar, L. R., Priester, J. R., & Cacioppo, J. T. (1993). Conceptual and methodological issues in the Elaboration Likelihood Model of persuasion: A reply to the Michigan State critics. *Communication Theory, 3,* 336–363.

Petty, R. E., Wells, G. L., & Brock, T. C. (1976). Distraction can enhance or reduce yielding to propaganda: Thought disruption versus effort justification. *Journal of Personality and Social Psychology, 34,* 874–884.

Petty, R. E., Wheeler, S. C., & Tormala, Z. L. (2003). Persuasion and attitude change. In T. Millon & M. J. Lerner (Eds.), *Handbook of psychology* (Vol. 5, pp. 353–382). Hoboken, NJ: Wiley.

Pew Forum on Religion and Public Life (2008, June). *U.S. religious landscape survey. Religious beliefs and practices: Diverse and politically relevant,* Online.

Peyser, M. (2006, February 13). The truthiness teller. Retrieved from: www.msnbc.msn.com/id/1182033/site/*Newsweek.*

Pfau, M. (1997). The inoculation model of resistance to influence. In G. A. Barnett & F. J. Boster (Eds.), *Progress in communication sciences* (Vol. 13, pp. 133–171). Greenwich, CT: Ablex.

Pfau, M., & Burgoon, M. (1988). Inoculation in political campaign communication. Human *Communication Research, 15,* 91–111.

Pfau, M., Ivanov, B., Houston, B., Haigh, M., Sims, J., Gilchrist, E., Russell, J., Wigley, S., Eckstein, J., & Richert, N. (2005). Inoculation and mental processing: The instrumental role of associative networks in the process of resistance to counterattitudinal influence. *Communication Monographs, 72,* 414–441.

Pfau, M., & Kenski, H. C. (1990). *Attack politics: Strategy and defense.* New York: Praeger.

Pfau, M., & Parrott, R. (1993). *Persuasive communication campaigns.* Boston: Allyn and Bacon.

Pfau, M., Roskos-Ewoldsen, D., Wood, M., Yin, S., Cho, J., Lu, K. H., & Shen, L. (2003). Attitude accessibility as an alternative explanation for how inoculation confers resistance. *Communication Monographs, 70,* 39–51.

Pfau, M., & Van Bockern, S. (1994). The persistence of inoculation in conferring resistance to smoking initiation among adolescents: The second year. *Human Communication Research, 20,* 413–430.

Pfau, M., Van Bockern, S., & Kang, J. G. (1992). Use of inoculation to promote resistance to smoking initiation among adolescents. *Communication Monographs, 59,* 213–230.

Pharnor, A. (1999, May). Breaking the code. *The Source,* p. 72.

Phillips, A. (1998, October 2). How much does monogamy tell us? *The New York Times,* A27.

Pierce, J. P., Choi, W., Gilpin, E. A., Farkas, A. J., & Berry, C. C. (1998). Tobacco industry promotion of cigarettes and adolescent smoking. *Journal of the American Medical Association, 279,* 511–515.

Pierce, J. P., Emery, S., & Gilpin, E. (2002). The California tobacco control program: A long-term health communication project. In R. Hornik (Ed.), *Public health communication: Evidence for behavior change* (pp. 97–114). Mahwah, NJ: Lawrence Erlbaum Associates.

Pigilito (2006, June 1). *Animal testing is good and proper.* Online: http://pigilito.blogspot.com/2006/06/animal-testing-is-good-and-proper.html.

Pollay, R. W. (1997). Hacks, flacks, and counter-attacks: Cigarette advertising, sponsored research, and controversies. *Journal of Social Issues, 53,* 53–74.

Polonec, L. D., Major, A. M., & Atwood, L. E. (2006). Evaluating the believability and effectiveness of the social norms message "Most students drink 0 to 4 drinks when they party." *Health Communication, 20,* 23–34.

Power, S. (2002). *A problem from hell: America and the age of genocide.* New York: Basic Books.

Pratkanis, A. R. (1989). The cognitive representation of attitudes. In A. R. Pratkanis, S. J. Breckler, & A. G. Greenwald (Eds.), *Attitude structure and function* (pp. 71–98). Hillsdale, NJ: Lawrence Erlbaum Associates.

Pratkanis, A. R. (1998). Myths of subliminal persuasion: The cargo-cult science of subliminal persuasion. In K. Frazier (Ed.), *Encounters with the paranormal: Science, knowledge, and belief* (pp. 240–252). Amherst, NY: Prometheus Books.

Pratkanis, A. R., & Aronson, E. (1992). *Age of propaganda: The everyday use and abuse of persuasion.* New York: W. H. Freeman.

Preiss, R. W., & Allen, M. (1998). Performing counterattitudinal advocacy: The persuasive impact of incentives. In M. Allen & R. W. Preiss (Eds.), *Persuasion: Advances through meta-analysis* (pp. 231–242). Cresskill, NJ: Hampton Press.

*References*

President Bush Waffles. (2001, August 10). *The New York Times* [Editorial], A22.

Priester, J., & Petty, R.E. (1995). Source attributions and persuasion: Perceived honesty as a determinant of message scrutiny. *Personality and Social Psychology Bulletin, 21,* 637–654.

Priester, J., Wegener, D., Petty, R., & Fabrigar, L. (1999). Examining the psychological process underlying the sleeper effect: The Elaboration Likelihood Model explanation. *Media Psychology, 1,* 27–48.

Prochaska, J. O., DiClemente, C. C., & Norcross, J. C. (1992). In search of how people change: Applications to addictive behaviors. *American Psychologist, 47,* 1102–1114.

Prochaska, J. O., Redding, C. A., Harlow, L. L., Rossi, J. S., & Velicer, W. F. (1994). The transtheoretical model of change and HIV prevention: A review. *Health Education Quarterly, 21,* 471–486.

Pryor, J. B., & Reeder, G. D. (1993). Collective and individual representations of HIV/AIDS stigma. In J. B. Pryor & G. D. Reeder (Eds.), *The social psychology of HIV infection* (pp. 263–286). Hillsdale, NJ: Lawrence Erlbaum Associates.

Puente, M. (1999, September 7). Casual clothes hit sour note with some. *USA Today,* 1D–2D.

Putnam, L. L., & Wilson, C. E. (1982). Communicative strategies in organizational conflicts: Reliability and validity of a measurement scale. In M. Burgoon (Ed.), *Communication yearbook 6* (pp. 629–652). Beverly Hills, CA: Sage.

Quinn, J. M., & Wood, W. (2004). Forewarnings of influence appeals: Inducing resistance and acceptance. In E. S. Knowles & J. A. Linn (Eds.), *Resistance and persuasion* (pp. 193–213). Mahwah, NJ: Lawrence Erlbaum Associates.

Rancer, A. S. (1998). Argumentativeness. In J. C. McCroskey, J. A. Daly, M. M. Martin, & M. J. Beatty (Eds.), *Communication and personality: Trait perspectives* (pp. 149–170). Cresskill, NJ: Hampton Press.

Rancer, A. S., Whitecap, V. G., Kosberg, R. L., & Avtgis, T. A. (1997). Testing the efficacy of a communication training program to increase argumentativeness and argumentative behavior in adolescents. *Communication Education, 46,* 273–286.

Rankin, B., & Plummer, D. (2005, March 15). "God brought him to my door." *Plain Dealer,* A1–2.

Ratcliff, C. D., Czuchry, M., Scarberry, N. C., Thomas, J. C., Dansereau, D. F., & Lord, C. G. (1999). Effects of directed thinking on intentions to engage in beneficial activity: Actions versus reasons. *Journal of Applied Social Psychology, 29,* 994–1009.

Ray, G. B., Ray, E. B., & Zahn, C. J. (1991). Speech behavior and social evaluation: An examination of medical messages. *Communication Quarterly, 39,* 119–129.

Reardon, K. K. (1991). Persuasion in practice. Newbury Park, CA: Sage. Redford, R. (2001, May 23). Bush vs. the American landscape. *The New York Times,* A29.

Reel, B. W., & Thompson, T. L. (1994). A test of the effectiveness of strategies for talking about AIDS and condom use. *Journal of Applied Communication Research, 22,* 127–140.

Reichert, T. (2003). What is sex in advertising? Perspectives from consumer behavior and social science research. In T. Reichert & J. Lambiase (Eds.), *Sex in advertising: Perspectives on the erotic appeal* (pp. 11–38). Mahwah, NJ: Lawrence Erlbaum Associates.

Reinard, J. C. (1988). The empirical study of the persuasive effects of evidence: The status after fifty years of research. *Human Communication Research, 15,* 3–59.

Reinard, J. C. (1991). *Foundations of argument: Effective communication for critical thinking.* Dubuque, IA: Wm. C. Brown.

Reinhart, A. M., Marshall, H. M., Feeley, T. H., & Tutzauer, F. (2007). The persuasive effects of message framing in organ donation: The mediating role of psychological reactance. *Communication Monographs, 74,* 229–255.

Remnick, D. (2005, October 3). Letter from Louisiana: High water. *The New Yorker,* pp. 48–57.

Reynolds, R. A., & Reynolds, J. L. (2002). Evidence. In J. E. Dillard & M. Pfau (Eds.), *The persuasion handbook: Developments in theory and practice* (pp. 427–444). Thousand Oaks, CA: Sage.

Rhoads, K. (1997). Everyday influence. In *Working psychology: Introduction to influence.* Retrieved from: www.workingpsychology.com/evryinfl.html.

Rhoads, K. V. L., & Cialdini, R. B. (2002). The business of influence: Principles that lead to success in commercial settings. In J. P. Dillard & M. Pfau (Eds.), *The persuasion handbook: Developments in theory and practice* (pp. 513–542). Thousand Oaks, CA: Sage.

Rhodes, N., & Wood, W. (1992). Self-esteem and intelligence affect influenceability: The mediating role of message reception. *Psychological Bulletin, 111,* 156–171.

Rice, R. E., & Atkin, C. K. (2009). Public communication campaigns: Theoretical principles and practical applications. In J. Bryant & M. B. Oliver (Eds.), *Media effects: Advances in theory and research* (3rd ed., pp. 436–468). New York: Routledge.

Rice, R. E., & Atkin, C. K. (2002). Communication campaigns: Theory, design, implementation, and evaluation. In J. Bryant & D. Zillmann (Eds.), *Media effects: Advances in theory and research* (2nd ed., pp. 427–451). Mahwah, NJ: Lawrence Erlbaum Associates.

Rich, M. (2006, June 12). Product placement deals make leap from film to books. *The New York Times,* C1, C5.

Richardson, L. (2006). *What terrorists want: Understanding the enemy, containing the threat.* New York: Random House.

Richins, M. L. (1991). Social comparison and the idealized images of advertising. *Journal of Consumer Research, 18,* 71–83.

Richtel, M. (2009, July 19). Dismissing the risks of a deadly habit. *The New York Times,* 1, 18–19.

Riggio, R. E. (1987). *The charisma quotient: What it is, how to get it, how to use it.* New York: Dodd, Mead.

Rimal, R. N., & Real, K. (2003). Perceived risk and efficacy beliefs as motivators of change: Use of the Risk Perception Attitude (RPA) framework to understand health behaviors. *Human Communication Research, 29,* 370–399.

Rind, B., & Bordia, P. (1995). Effect of server's "thank you" and personalization on restaurant tipping. *Journal of Applied Social Psychology, 25,* 745–751.

Rind, B., & Bordia, P. (1996). Effect on restaurant tipping of male and female servers drawing a happy, smiling face on the backs of customers' checks. *Journal of Applied Social Psychology, 26,* 218–225.

Ritter, K., & Henry, D. (1994). *The 1980 Reagan–Carter presidential debate.* In R. V. Friedenberg (Ed.), *Rhetorical studies of national political debates, 1960–1992* (2nd ed., pp. 69–93). Westport, CT: Praeger.

Rittle, R. H. (1981). Changes in helping behavior: Self-versus situational perceptions as mediators of the foot-in-the-door effect. *Personality and Social Psychology Bulletin, 7,* 431–437.

Roberto, A. J., Meyer, G., Johnson, A. J., & Atkin, C. K. (2000). Using the Extended Parallel Process Model to prevent firearm injury and death: Field experiment results of a video-based intervention. *Journal of Communication, 50*(4), 157–175.

Roberts, D. S., & Geller, E. S. (1994). A statewide intervention to increase safety belt use: Adding to the impact of a belt use law. *American Journal of Health Promotion, 8,* 172–174.

Robertson, L. S., Kelley, A. B., O'Neill, B., Wixom, C. W., Eiswirth, R. S. & Haddon, W., Jr. (1974). A controlled study of the effect of television messages on safety belt use. *American Journal of Public Health, 64,* 1071–1080.

Robinson, J. P., Shaver, P. R., & Wrightsman, L. S. (Eds.). (1999). *Measures of political attitudes.* San Diego: Academic Press.

Robinson, W. G. (1998). Heaven's Gate: The end? *Journal of Computer Mediated Communication.* Retrieved from: www.ascusc.org/jcmc/vol3/issue3/robinson.html.

Roehm, H. A., & Haugtvedt, C. P. (1999). Understanding interactivity of cyberspace advertising. In D. W. Schumann & E. Thorson (Eds.), *Advertising and the World Wide Web* (pp. 27–39). Mahwah, NJ: Lawrence Erlbaum Associates.

Rogers, E. M. (1995). *Diffusion of innovations* (4th ed.). New York: Free Press.

Rogers, M., & Seiler, C. A. (1994). The answer is no: A national survey of advertising industry practitioners and their clients about whether they use subliminal advertising. *Journal of Advertising Research, 34,* 2, 36–45.

*References*

Rogers, M., & Smith, K. H. (1993, March–April). Public perceptions of subliminal advertising: Why practitioners shouldn't ignore this issue. *Journal of Advertising Research, 33*, 10–18.

Rogers, R. W. (1975). A protection motivation theory of fear appeals and attitude change. *Journal of Psychology, 91*, 93–114.

Rogers, R. W., & Mewborn, C. R. (1976). Fear appeals and attitude change: Effects of a threat's noxiousness, probability of occurrence, and the efficacy of coping responses. *Journal of Personality and Social Psychology, 34*, 54–61.

Rohter, L. (2007, January 14). In the land of bold beauty, a trusted mirror cracks. *The New York Times*, [Week in Review], 1, 3.

Rohter, L. (2008, September 19). Obama attacks McCain in a bid to attract Hispanic voters. *The New York Times*, A13.

Rokeach, M. (1960). *The open and closed mind.* New York: Basic Books.

Rokeach, M. (1973). *The nature of human values.* New York: Free Press.

Romano, L. (1998, October 19). Boss, you want me to do WHAT? *The Washington Post National Weekly Edition*, 29.

Romer, D., & Jamieson, P. (2001). Advertising, smoker imagery, and the diffusion of smoking behavior. In P. Slovic (Ed.), *Smoking: Risk, perception, & policy* (pp. 127–155). Thousand Oaks, CA: Sage.

Rook, K. S. (1987). Effects of case history versus abstract information on health attitudes and behaviors. *Journal of Applied Social Psychology, 17*, 533–553.

Root-Bernstein, R. S. (1993). *Rethinking AIDS: The tragic cost of premature consensus.* New York: Free Press.

Rosenbaum, A. S. (1986). *Coercion and autonomy: Philosophical foundations, issues, and practices.* Westport, CT: Greenwood.

Rosenberg, S. W., & McCafferty, P. (1987). The image and the vote: Manipulating voters' preferences. *Public Opinion Quarterly, 51*, 31–47.

Rosenberg, T. (2006, August 6). When a pill is not enough. *The New York Times Magazine*, 40–45, 52, 58–59.

Rosenthal, E. (2008, August 20). Drug makers' push leads to vaccines' fast rise. *The New York Times*, A1, A18, A19.

Roskos-Ewoldsen, D. R. (1997a). Implicit theories of persuasion. *Human Communication Research, 24*, 31–63.

Roskos-Ewoldsen, D. R. (1997b). Attitude accessibility and persuasion: Review and a transactive model. In B. R. Burleson (Ed.), *Communication Yearbook, 20*, 185–225.

Roskos-Ewoldsen, D. R., Arpan-Ralstin, L., & St. Pierre, J. (2002). Attitude accessibility and persuasion: The quick and the strong. In J. P. Dillard & M. Pfau (Eds.), *The persuasion handbook: Developments in theory and practice* (pp. 39–61). Sage: Thousand Oaks, CA: Sage.

Roskos-Ewoldsen, D. R., & Fazio, R. H. (1992). On the orienting value of attitudes: Attitude accessibility as a determinant of an object's attraction of visual attention. *Journal of Personality and Social Psychology, 63*, 198–211.

Roskos-Ewoldsen, D. R., Yu, H. J., & Rhodes, N. (2004). Fear appeal messages affect accessibility of attitudes toward the threat and adaptive behaviors. *Communication Monographs, 71*, 49–69.

Rotello, G. (1997). *Sexual ecology: AIDS and the destiny of gay men.* New York: Dutton.

Rothman, A. J., Salovey, P., Antone, C., Keough, K., & Martin, C. D. (1993). The influence of message framing on intentions to perform health behaviors. *Journal of Experimental Social Psychology, 29*, 408–433.

Rousseau, F. L., Vallerand, R. J., Ratelle, C. F., Mageau, G. A., & Provencher, P. J. (2002). Passion and gambling: On the validation of the gambling passion scale (GPS). *Journal of Gambling Studies, 18*, 45–66.

Royte, E. (2008). *Bottlemania: How water went on sale and why we bought it.* New York: Bloomsbury.

Rubin, R. B., Palmgreen, P., & Sypher, H. E. (Eds.). (1994). *Communication research measures: A sourcebook.* New York: Guilford.

Rudman, L. A., & Kilianski, S. E. (2000). Implicit and explicit attitudes toward female authority. *Personality and Social Psychology Bulletin, 26*, 1315–1328.

Rushing, W. A. (1995). *The AIDS epidemic: Social dimensions of an infectious disease*. Boulder, CO: Westview.

Russell, C. A., Clapp, J. D., & DeJong, W. (2005). Done 4: Analysis of a failed social norms marketing campaign. *Health Communication, 17*, 57–65.

Rydell, R. J., & McConnell, A. R. (2006). Understanding implicit and explicit attitude change: A systems of reasoning analysis. *Journal of Personality and Social Psychology, 91*, 995–1008.

Sabato, L. J., & Simpson, G. R. (1996). *Dirty little secrets: The persistence of corruption in American politics*. New York: Times Books.

Sagarin, B. J., Cialdini, R. B., Rice, W. E., & Serna, S. B. (2002). Dispelling the illusion of invulnerability: The motivations and mechanisms of resistance to persuasion. *Journal of Personality and Social Psychology, 83*, 526–541.

Salovey, P., Schneider, T. R., & Apanovitch, A. M. (2002). Message framing in the prevention and early detection of illness. In J. P. Dillard & M. Pfau (Eds.), *The persuasion handbook: Developments in theory and practice* (pp. 391–406). Thousand Oaks, CA: Sage.

Salovey, P., & Wegener, D. T. (2002). Communicating about health: Message framing, persuasion, and health behavior. In J. Suls & K. Wallston (Eds.), *Social psychological foundations of health and illness*. Oxford: Blackwell.

Santora, M. (2006, November 25). In diabetes fight, raising cash and keeping trust. *The New York Times*, A1, A13.

Santos, M. D., Leve, C., & Pratkanis, A. R. (1994). Hey buddy, can you spare seventeen cents? Mindful persuasion and the pique technique. *Journal of Applied Social Psychology, 24*, 755–764.

Saul, S. (2005, November 28). Gimme an Rx! Cheerleaders pep up drug sales. *The New York Times*, A1, A16.

Saul, S. (2006, May 20). Unease on industry's role in hypertension debate. *The New York Times*, A1, B9.

Savan, L. (1994). *The sponsored life: Ads, TV, and American culture*. Philadelphia: Temple University Press.

Saxe, L., & Chazan, B. (2008). *Ten days of Birthright Israel: A journey in young adult identity*. Waltham, MA: Brandeis University Press.

Scheibe, K. E. (2000). *The drama of everyday life*. Cambridge, MA: Harvard University Press.

Schein, E. H. (1961). *Coercive persuasion: A socio-psychological analysis of the "brainwashing" of the American civilian prisoners by the Chinese communists*. New York: W. W. Norton.

Schell, J. (1982). *The fate of the earth*. New York: Knopf.

Scher, S. J., & Cooper, J. (1989). Motivational basis of dissonance: The singular role of behavioral consequences. *Journal of Personality and Social Psychology, 56*, 899–906.

Schmermund, A., Sellers, R., Mueller, B., & Crosby, F. (2001). Attitudes toward affirmative action as a function of racial identity among African American college students. *Political Psychology, 22*, 759–774.

Schmierbach, M., Xu, Q., Bellur-Thandaveshwara, S., Ash, E., Oeldorf-Hirsch, A., & Kegerise, A. (2009). *What do your friends say about you?: Activist group evaluations in a social networking context*. Paper presented to the annual convention of the Association for Education in Journalism and Mass Communication, Boston, August.

Schmitt, E. (2004, August 26). Abuses at prison tied to officers in intelligence. *The New York Times*, A1, A10.

Schooler, C., Chaffee, S. H., Flora, J. A., & Roser, C. (1998). Health campaign channels: Tradeoffs among reach, specificity, and impact. *Human Communication Research, 24*, 410–432.

Schooler, C., Feighery, E., & Flora, J. A. (1996). Seventh graders' self-reported exposure to cigarette marketing and its relationship to their smoking behavior. *American Journal of Public Health, 86*, 1216–1221.

Schott, B. (2008, December 20). The way we were, 1968. *The New York Times*, A21.

Schroeder, C. M., & Prentice, D. A. (1998). Exposing pluralistic ignorance to reduce alcohol use among college students. *Journal of Applied Social Psychology, 28*, 2150–2180.

Schudson, M. (1986). *Advertising, the uneasy persuasion*. New York: Basic Books.

Schuman, H., & Presser, S. (1981). *Questions and answers in attitude surveys: Experiments on question form, wording, and context*. Orlando, FL: Academic Press.

*References*

Schwartz, S. (1996). Value priorities and behavior: Applying a theory of integrated value systems. In C. Seligman, J. M. Olson, & M. P. Zanna (Eds.), *The psychology of values: The Ontario symposium* (Vol. 8, pp. 1–24). Mahwah, NJ: Lawrence Erlbaum Associates.

Schwartz, S. H., & Bilsky, W. (1987). Toward a universal psychological structure of human values. *Journal of Personality and Social Psychology, 53,* 550–562.

Schwartz, T. (1973). *The responsive chord.* Garden City, NJ: Anchor Press.

Schwarz, N. (1999). Self-reports: How the questions shape the answers. *American Psychologist, 54,* 93–105.

Schwarz, N., & Bless, H. (1992). Scandals and the public's trust in politicians: Assimilation and contrast effects. *Personality and Social Psychology Bulletin, 18,* 574–579.

Scott, E. C. (2004). *Evolution vs. creationism: An introduction.* Berkeley, CA: University of California Press.

Sears, D. O., & Funk, C. L. (1991). The role of self-interest in social and political attitudes. In M. P. Zanna (Ed.), *Advances in experimental social psychology* (Vol. 24, pp. 1–91). San Diego: Academic Press.

Sears, D. O., Henry, P. J., & Kosterman, R. (2000). Egalitarian values and contemporary racial politics. In D. O. Sears, J. Sidanius, & L. Bobo (Eds.), *Racialized politics: The debate about racism in America* (pp. 75–117). Chicago: University of Chicago Press.

Sears, D. O., Lau, R. R., Tyler, T. R., & Allen, H. M., Jr. (1980). The self-interest vs. symbolic politics in policy attitudes and presidential voting. *American Political Science Review, 74,* 670–684.

Seelye, K. Q. (2008, August 21). Obama shifts message to everyday concerns. *The New York Times,* A16.

Segrin, C. (1993). The effects of nonverbal behavior on outcomes of compliance gaining attempts. *Communication Studies, 44,* 169–189.

Seibold, D. R., Cantrill, J. G., & Meyers, R. A. (1994). Communication and interpersonal influence. In M. L. Knapp & G. R. Miller (Eds.), *Handbook of interpersonal communication* (2nd ed., pp. 542–588). Thousand Oaks, CA: Sage.

Seligman, C., & Katz, A. N. (1996). The dynamics of value systems. In C. Seligman, J. M. Olson, & M. P. Zanna (Eds.), *The psychology of values: The Ontario symposium* (Vol. 8, pp. 53–75). Mahwah, NJ: Lawrence Erlbaum Associates.

Sharma, A. (1999). Does the salesperson like customers? A conceptual and empirical examination of the persuasive effect of perceptions of the salesperson's affect toward customers. *Psychology and Marketing, 16,* 141–162.

Shavitt, S., & Nelson, M. R. (2000). The social-identity function in person perception: Communicated meanings of product preferences. In G. R. Maio & J. M. Olson (Eds.), *Why we evaluate: Functions of attitudes* (pp. 37–57). Mahwah, NJ: Lawrence Erlbaum Associates.

Sheeran, P., Abraham, C., & Orbell, S. (1999). Psychosocial correlates of heterosexual condom use: A meta-analysis. *Psychological Bulletin, 125,* 90–132.

Sherif, C. W., Sherif, M., & Nebergall, R. E. (1965). *Attitude and attitude change: The social judgment-involvement approach.* Philadelphia: W. B. Saunders.

Sherif, M. (1967). Introduction. In C. W. Sherif & M. Sherif (Eds.), Attitude, ego-involvement, and change (pp. 1–5). New York: Wiley.

Sherif, M., & Sherif, C. W. (1967). Attitude as the individual's own categories: The social judgment-involvement approach to attitude and attitude change. In C. W. Sherif & M. Sherif (Eds.), *Attitude, ego-involvement, and change* (pp. 105–139). New York: Wiley.

Siebert, F. S., Peterson, T., & Schramm. W. (1956). *Four theories of the press: The authoritarian, libertarian, social responsibility, and Soviet communist concepts of what the press should be and do.* Urbana: University of Illinois Press.

Siegel, J. T., & Burgoon, J. K. (2002). Expectancy theory approaches to prevention: Violating adolescent expectations to increase the effectiveness of public service announcements. In W. D. Crano & M. Burgoon (Eds.), *Mass media and drug prevention: Classic and contemporary theories and research* (pp. 163–186). Mahwah, NJ: Lawrence Erlbaum Associates.

Siegel, M., & Biener, L. (2002). The impact of antismoking media campaigns on progression to established smoking: Results of a longitudinal youth study in Massachusetts. In R. Hornik (Ed.), *Public health communication: Evidence for behavior change* (pp. 115–130). Mahwah, NJ: Lawrence Erlbaum Associates.

Signorile, M. (1997). *Life outside: The Signorile report on gay men: Sex, drugs, muscles, and the passages of life.* New York: HarperCollins.

Simon, A. F., & Jerit, J. (2007). Toward a theory relating political discourse, media, and public opinion. *Journal of Communication, 57, 2,* 254–271.

Simon, L., Greenberg, J., & Brehm, J. (1995). Trivialization: The forgotten mode of dissonance reduction. *Journal of Personality and Social Psychology, 68,* 247–260.

Singer, N. (2009, July 17). In push for cancer screening, limited benefits. *The New York Times,* A1, A15.

Singhal, A., Cody, M. J., Rogers, E. M., & Sabido, M. (Eds.). (2004). *Entertainment-education and social change: History, research and practice.* Mahwah, NJ: Erlbaum Associates.

Skalski, P., Tamborini, R., Glazer, E., & Smith, S. (2009). Effects of humor on presence and recall of persuasive messages. *Communication Quarterly, 57,* 136–163.

Slama, M. E., & Singley, R. B. (1996). Self-monitoring and value-expressive vs. utilitarian ad effectiveness: Why the mixed findings? *Journal of Current Issues and Research in Advertising, 18,* 39–52.

Slater, M. (2002). Involvement as goal-directed strategic processing: Extending the Elaboration Likelihood Model. In J. P. Dillard & M. Pfau (Eds.), *The persuasion handbook: Developments in theory and practice* (pp. 175–194). Thousand Oaks, CA: Sage.

Slater, M. D. (2002). Entertainment education and the persuasive impact of narratives. In M. C. Green, J. J. Strange, & T. C. Brock (Eds.), *Narrative impact: Social and cognitive foundations* (pp.157–181). Mahwah, NJ: Lawrence Erlbaum Associates.

Slater, M. D. (2006). Specification and misspecification of theoretical foundations and logic models for health communication campaigns. *Health Communication, 20,* 149–157.

Slater, M. D., Karan, D., Rouner, D., Murphy, K., & Beauvais, F. (1998). Developing and assessing alcohol warning content: Responses to quantitative information and behavioral recommendations in warnings with television beer advertisements. *Journal of Public Policy & Marketing, 17,* 48–60.

Slater, M. D., & Rouner, D. (1996). Value-affirmative and value-protective processing of alcohol education messages that include statistical evidence or anecdotes. *Communication Research, 23,* 210–235.

Smedley, B. D., Stith, A.Y., & Nelson, A. R. (Eds.) (2003). *Unequal treatment: Confronting racial and ethnic disparities in health care.* Washington, DC: National Academies Press.

Smith, B. L., Lasswell, H. D., & Casey. R. D. (1946). *Propaganda, communication, and public opinion.* Princeton, NJ: Princeton University Press.

Smith, M. B., Bruner, J. B., & White, R. S. (1956). *Opinions and personality.* New York: Wiley.

Smith, M. J. (1982). *Persuasion and human action: A review and critique of social influence theories.* Belmont, CA: Wadsworth.

Smith, R.A., Downs, E., & Witte, K. (2007). Drama theory and entertainment education: Exploring the effects of a radio drama on behavioral intentions to limit HIV transmission in Ethiopia. *Communication Monographs, 74,* 133–153.

Smith, R. D. (1993). Psychological type and public relations: Theory, research, and applications. *Journal of Public Relations Research, 5,* 177–199.

Smith, S. M., & Shaffer, D. R. (1995). Speed of speech and persuasion: Evidence for multiple effects. *Personality and Social Psychology Bulletin, 21,* 1051–1060.

Smith, S. W., Atkin, C. K., & Roznowski, J. (2006). Are "Drink Responsibly" alcohol campaigns strategically ambiguous? *Health Communication, 20,* 1–11.

Smith, T. W. (1995). Review: The Holocaust denial controversy. *Public Opinion Quarterly, 59,* 269–295.

Smith-McLallen, A., & Fishbein, M. (2008). Predictors of intentions to perform six cancer-related behaviors: Roles for injunctive and descriptive norms. *Psychology, Health & Medicine, 13,* 389–401.

*References*

Smith-McLallen, A., & Fishbein, M. (2009). Predicting intentions to engage in cancer prevention and detection behaviors: Examining differences between Black and White adults. *Psychology, Health & Medicine, 14,* 180–189.

Smythe, T. W. (1999). Moral responsibility. *Journal of Value Inquiry, 33,* 493–506.

Snyder, L. B. (2001). How effective are mediated health campaigns? In R. E. Rice & C. K. Atkin (Eds.), *Public communication campaigns* (3rd ed., pp. 181–190). Thousand Oaks, CA: Sage.

Snyder, L. B., & Hamilton, M. A. (2002). A meta-analysis of U.S. health campaign effects on behavior: Emphasize enforcement, exposure, and new information, and beware the secular trend. In R. Hornik (Ed.), *Public health communication: Evidence for behavior change* (pp. 357–383). Mahwah, NJ: Lawrence Erlbaum Associates.

Snyder, M. (1974). Self-monitoring of expressive behavior. *Journal of Personality and Social Psychology, 30,* 526–537.

Snyder, M. (1987). *Public appearances/private realities: The psychology of self-monitoring.* New York: W. H. Freeman.

Snyder, M., Clary, E. G., & Stukas, A. A. (2000). The functional approach to volunteerism. In G. R. Maio & J. M. Olson (Eds.), *Why we evaluate: Functions of attitudes* (pp. 365–393). Mahwah, NJ: Lawrence Erlbaum Associates.

Snyder, M., & DeBono, K. G. (1985). Appeals to image and claims about quality: Understanding the psychology of advertising. *Journal of Personality and Social Psychology, 49,* 586–597.

Snyder, M., & Kendzierski, D. (1982). Acting on one's attitudes: Procedures for linking attitude and behavior. *Journal of Experimental Social Psychology, 18,* 165–183.

Snyder, M., & Tanke, E. D. (1976). Behavior and attitude: Some people are more consistent than others. *Journal of Personality, 44,* 510–517.

Sobo, E. J. (1995). *Choosing unsafe sex: AIDS-risk denial among disadvantaged women.* Philadelphia: University of Pennsylvania Press.

Soldat, A. S., Sinclair, R. C., & Mark, M. M. (1997). Color as an environmental processing cue: External affective cues can directly affect processing strategy without affecting mood. *Social Cognition, 15,* 55–71.

Solomon, M. R. (1999). *Consumer behavior: Buying, having, and being* (4th ed.) Boston: Allyn & Bacon.

Sopory, P., & Dillard, J. P. (2002). Figurative language and persuasion. In J. P. Dillard & M. Pfau (Eds.), *The persuasion handbook: Developments in theory and practice* (pp. 407–426). Thousand Oaks, CA: Sage.

Sparks, J. R., & Areni, C. S. (2008). Style versus substance: Multiple roles of language power in persuasion. *Journal of Applied Social Psychology, 38,* 37–60.

Spence, J. T., Helmreich, R., & Stapp, J. (1973). A short version of the Attitudes Toward Women Scale (AWS). *Bulletin of the Psychonomic Society, 2,* 219–220.

Sperber, B. M., Fishbein, M., & Ajzen, I. (1980). Predicting and understanding women's occupational orientations: Factors underlying choice intentions. In I. Ajzen & M. Fishbein (Eds.), *Understanding attitudes and predicting social behavior* (pp. 113–129). Englewood Cliffs, NJ: Prentice Hall.

Staats, A. W., & Staats, C. K. (1958). Attitudes established by classical conditioning. *Journal of Abnormal and Social Psychology, 57,* 37–40.

Standage, T. (2005, August 1). Bad to the last drop. *The New York Times,* A17.

Steele, C. M. (1988). The psychology of self-affirmation: Sustaining the integrity of the self. In L. Berkowtiz (Ed.), *Advances in experimental social psychology* (Vol. 21, pp. 261–302). San Diego: Academic Press.

Stengel, R. (2000). *You're too kind: A brief history of flattery.* New York: Simon & Schuster.

Stephenson, M. T. (2003). Examining adolescents' responses to antimarijuana PSAs. *Human Communication Research, 29,* 343–369.

Stevens, S. S. (1950). Mathematics, measurement, and psychophysics. In S. S. Stevens (Ed.), *Handbook of experimental psychology* (pp. 1–49). New York: Wiley.

Stiff, J. B. (1994). *Persuasive communication.* New York: Guilford.

Stiff, J. B., & Boster, F. J. (1987). Cognitive processing: Additional thoughts and a reply to Petty, Kasmer, Haugtvedt, and Cacioppo. *Communication Monographs, 54,* 250–256.

Stolberg, S. G. (1998, March 9). U.S. awakes to epidemic of sexual diseases. *The New York Times,* A1, A14.

Stolberg, S. G. (2001, August 10). A science in its infancy, but with great expectations for its adolescence. *The New York Times,* A17.

Stone, J., Aronson, E., Crain, A. L., Winslow, M. P., & Fried, C. B. (1994). Inducing hypocrisy as a means of encouraging young adults to use condoms. *Personality and Social Psychology Bulletin, 20,* 116–128.

Stone, J., Wiegand, A. W., Cooper, J., & Aronson, E. (1997). When exemplification fails: Hypocrisy and the motive for self-integrity. *Journal of Personality and Social Psychology, 72,* 54–65.

Story, L. (2007, January 15). Anywhere the eye can see, it's now likely to see an ad. *The New York Times,* A1, A14.

Street, R. L., Jr., & Brady, R. M. (1982). Speech rate acceptance ranges as a function of evaluative domain, listener speech rate, and communication context. *Communication Monographs, 49,* 290–308.

Stroud, N. J. (2007). Media effects, selective exposure, and *Fahrenheit 9/11. Political Communication, 24,* 415–432.

Stuart, E. W., Shimp, T. A., & Engle, R. W. (1987). Classical conditioning of consumer attitudes: Four experiments in an advertising context. *Journal of Consumer Research, 14,* 334–349.

Sudman, S., & Bradburn, N. M. (1982). *Asking questions.* San Francisco: Jossey-Bass.

Sunstein C. R. (2003). *Why societies need dissent.* Cambridge: Harvard University Press.

Sutton, S. (1998). Predicting and explaining intentions and behavior: How well are we doing? *Journal of Applied Social Psychology, 28,* 1317–1338.

Swim, J. K., Aikin, K. J., Hall, W. S., & Hunter, B. A. (1995). Sexism and racism: Old-fashioned and modern prejudices. *Journal of Personality and Social Psychology, 68,* 199–214.

Szabo, E. A., & Pfau, M. (2002). Nuances in inoculation: Theory and applications. In J. P. Dillard & M. Pfau (Eds.), *The persuasion handbook: Developments in theory and practice* (pp. 233–258). Thousand Oaks, CA: Sage.

Talbot, M. (2000, January 9). The placebo prescription. *The New York Times Magazine,* 34–39, 44, 58–60.

Tannen, D. (1990). *You just don't understand: Women and men in conversation.* New York: William Morrow.

Takaku, S. (2006). Reducing road rage: An application of the dissonance-attribution model of interpersonal forgiveness. *Journal of Applied Social Psychology, 36,* 2362–2378.

Tavris, C., & Aronson, E. (2007). *Mistakes were made (but not by me): Why we justify foolish beliefs, bad decisions, and hurtful acts.* Orlando, FLA: Harcourt, Inc.

Taylor, S. E. (1981). The interface of cognitive and social psychology. In J. H. Harvey (Ed.), *Cognition, social behavior, and the environment* (pp. 189–211). Hillsdale, NJ: Lawrence Erlbaum Associates.

Taylor, S. E., & Thompson, S. C. (1982). Stalking the elusive "vividness" effect. *Psychological Review, 89,* 155–181.

Taylor, T., & Booth-Butterfield, S. (1993). Getting a foot in the door with drinking and driving: A field study of healthy influence. *Communication Research Reports, 10,* 95–101.

Tedeschi, J. T., Schlenker, B. R., & Bonoma, T. V. (1971). Cognitive dissonance: Private ratiocination or public spectacle? *American Psychologist, 26,* 685–695.

Tesser, A. (1978). Self-generated attitude change. In L. Berkowitz (Ed.), *Advances in experimental social psychology* (Vol. 11, pp. 181–227). New York: Academic Press.

Tesser, A. (1993). The importance of heritability in psychological research: The case of attitudes. *Psychological Review, 100,* 129–142.

Tetlock, P. E., & Arkes, H. R. (2004). The implicit prejudice exchange: Islands of consensus in a sea of controversy. *Psychological Inquiry, 15,* 311–321.

Tetlock, P. E., Peterson, R. S., & Lerner, J. S. (1996). Revising the value pluralism model: Incorporating social content and context postulates. In C. Seligman, J. M. Olson, & M. P. Zanna (Eds.), *The psychology of values: The Ontario symposium* (Vol. 8, pp. 25–51). Mahwah, NJ: Lawrence Erlbaum Associates.

*References*

Thaler, L. K., & Koval, R. (2003). *Bang! Getting your message heard in a noisy world.* New York: Currency/Doubleday.

Thaler, R. H., & Sunstein, C. R. (2008). *Nudge: Improving decisions about health, wealth, and happiness.* New Haven: Yale University Press.

Thernstrom, S., & Thernstrom, A. (1997). *America in black and white: One nation, indivisible.* New York: Simon & Schuster.

Theus, K. T. (1994). Subliminal advertising and the psychology of processing unconscious stimuli: A review of research. *Psychology & Marketing, 11,* 271–290.

Thompson, L. (1995). "They saw a negotiation": Partisanship and involvement. *Journal of Personality and Social Psychology, 68,* 839–853.

Thompson, M. M., Zanna, M. P., & Griffin, D. W. (1995). Let's not be indifferent about (attitudinal) ambivalence. In R. E. Petty & J. A. Krosnick (Eds.), *Attitude strength: Antecedents and consequences* (pp. 361–386). Hillsdale, NJ: Lawrence Erlbaum Associates.

Thompson, S. C., Anderson, K., Freedman, D., & Swan, J. (1996). Illusions of safety in a risky world: A study of college students' condom use. *Journal of Applied Social Psychology, 26,* 189–210.

Thurstone, L. L. (1928). Attitudes can be measured. *American Journal of Sociology, 33,* 529–544.

Tiedge, J. T., Silverblatt, A., Havice, M. J., & Rosenfeld, R. (1991). Discrepancy between perceived first-person and perceived third-person mass media effects. *Journalism Quarterly, 68,* 141–154.

Tierney, J. (2009, August 25). Guilt and atonement on the path to adulthood. *The New York Times,* D1, D3.

Till, B. D., Stanley S. M., & Priluck, R. (2008). Classical conditioning and celebrity endorsers: An examination of belongingness and resistance to extinction. *Psychology & Marketing, 25,* 179–196.

Timmerman, L. M. (2002). Comparing the production of power in language on the basis of sex. In M. Allen, R. W. Preiss, B. M. Gayle, & N. A. Burrell (Eds.), *Interpersonal communication research: Advances through meta-analysis* (pp. 73–87). Mahwah, NJ: Lawrence Erlbaum Associates.

Todorov, A., Chaiken, S., & Henderson, M. D. (2002). The Heuristic-Systematic Model of social information processing. In J. P. Dillard & M. Pfau (Eds.), *The persuasion handbook: Developments in theory and practice* (pp. 195–211). Thousand Oaks, CA: Sage.

Toulmin, S. (1958). *The uses of argument.* New York: Cambridge University Press.

Tourangeau, R., & Rasinski, K. A. (1988). Cognitive processes underlying context effects in attitude measurement. *Psychological Bulletin, 103,* 299–314.

Trappey, C. (1996). A meta-analysis of consumer choice and subliminal advertising. *Psychology & Marketing, 13,* 517–530.

Trost, M. R., Langan, E. J., & Kellar-Guenther, Y. (1999). Not everyone listens when you "just say no": Drug resistance in relational context. *Journal of Applied Communication Research, 27,* 120–138.

Turner, M. M., Tamborini, R., Limon, M. S., & Zuckerman-Hyman, C. (2007). The moderators and mediators of door-in-the-face requests: Is it a negotiation or a helping experience? *Communication Monographs, 74,* 333–356.

Tuttle, S. (2006, December 4). The elusive hunter. *Newsweek,* pp. 50–53.

Twitchell, J. B. (1999). *Lead us into temptation: The triumph of American materialism.* New York: Columbia University Press.

van Knippenberg, B., van Knippenberg, D., Blaauw, E., & Vermunt, R. (1999). Relational considerations in the use of influence tactics. *Journal of Applied Social Psychology, 29,* 806–819.

Verhovek, S. H. (1997, December 14). In poll, Americans reject means but not ends of racial diversity. *The New York Times,* 1, 18.

Vidrine, J. I., Simmons, V. N., & Brandon, T. H. (2007). Construction of smoking relevant risk perceptions among college students. The influence of need for cognition and message content. *Journal of Applied Social Psychology, 37,* 91–114.

Viswanath, K., & Finnegan, J. R., Jr. (1996). The knowledge gap hypothesis: Twenty-five years later. In B. R. Burleson (Ed.), *Communication yearbook 19* (pp. 187–227). Thousand Oaks, CA: Sage.

Vitello, P. (2008, August 17). How to erase that smea . . . *The New York Times* (Week in Review), 3.

Waggenspack, B. (2000). Women's role in rhetorical traditions. In J. L. Golden, G. F. Berquist, & W. E. Coleman (Eds.), *The rhetoric of Western thought* (7th ed., pp. 340–370). Dubuque, IA: Kendall/Hunt.

Waldron, V. R., & Applegate, J. L. (1998). Person-centered tactics during verbal disagreements: Effects on student perceptions of persuasiveness and social attraction. *Communication Education, 47*, 53–66.

Wallace, D. S., Paulson, R. M., Lord, C. G., & Bond, C. F., Jr. (2005). Which behaviors do attitudes predict? Meta-analyzing the effects of social pressure and perceived difficulty. *Review of General Psychology, 9*, 214–227.

Wallace, K. R. (1967). An ethical basis of communication. In R. L. Johannesen (Ed.), *Ethics and persuasion: Selected readings* (pp. 41–56). New York: Random House.

Walsh-Childers, K., & Brown, J. D. (2009). Effects of media on personal and public health. In J. Bryant & M. B. Oliver (Eds.), *Media effects: Advances in theory and research* (3rd ed., pp. 469–489). New York: Routledge.

Wan, H-H. (2008). Resonance as a mediating factor accounting for the message effect in tailored communication—Examining crisis communication in a tourism context. *Journal of Communication, 58*, 472–489.

Wang Erber, M., Hodges, S. D., & Wilson T. D. (1995). Attitude strength, attitude stability, and the effects of analyzing reasons. In R. E. Petty & J. A. Krosnick (Eds.), *Attitude strength: Antecedents and consequences* (pp. 433–454). Hillsdale, NJ: Lawrence Erlbaum Associates.

Waxman, S. (2004, July 13). Two Americas of "Fahrenheit" and "Passion." *The New York Times*, B1.

Weaver, R. M. (1953). *The ethics of rhetoric.* Chicago: Henry Regnery.

Webb, E. J., Campbell, D. T., Schwartz, R. D., & Sechrest, L. (1966). *Unobtrusive measures: Nonreactive research in the social sciences.* Chicago: Rand McNally.

Webb, M. I. (2001, November 26–December 2). MADD: Strategies for safer streets. Advertisement supplement to *The Washington Post National Weekly Edition*, 1.

Weber, L. (2007). *Marketing to the social web: How digital consumer communities build your business.* Hoboken, NJ: Wiley.

Weber, M. (1968). *On charisma and institution building.* Chicago: University of Chicago Press.

Webster, D. M., & Kruglanski, A. W. (1994). Individual differences in need for cognitive closure. *Journal of Personality and Social Psychology, 67*, 1049–1062.

Wegner, D. M., Schneider, D. J., Carter, S. R., III, & White, T. L. (1987). Paradoxical effects of thought suppression. *Journal of Personality and Social Psychology, 53*, 5–13.

Weigel, R. H., & Newman, L. S. (1976). Increasing attitude–behavior correspondence by broadening the scope of the behavioral measure. *Journal of Personality and Social Psychology, 33*, 793–802.

Weinstein, N. D. (1980). Unrealistic optimism about future life events. *Journal of Personality and Social Psychology, 39*, 806–820.

Weinstein, N. D. (1993). Testing four competing theories of health-protective behavior. *Health Psychology, 12*, 324–333.

West, D. M. (1997). *Air wars: Television advertising in election campaigns, 1952–1996* (2nd ed.). Washington, DC: Congressional Quarterly Press.

West, R., & Turner, L. H. (2010). *Introducing communication theory: Analysis and application* (4th ed.). Boston: McGraw-Hill Higher Education.

Westen, D., Blagov, P.S., Harenski, K., Kilts, C., & Hamann, S. (2006). Neural bases of motivated reasoning: An fMRI study of emotional constraints on partisan political judgment in the 2004 U.S. presidential election. *Journal of Cognitive Neuroscience, 18*, 1947–1958.

Whalen, D. J. (1996). *I see what you mean: Persuasive business communication.* Thousand Oaks, CA: Sage.

Wicker, A. W. (1969). Attitudes vs. actions: The relationship of verbal and overt behavioral responses to attitude objects. *Journal of Social Issues, 25*, 41–78.

Wicklund, R. A., & Brehm, J. W. (1976). *Perspectives on cognitive dissonance.* Hillsdale, NJ: Lawrence Erlbaum Associates.

*References*

Wiggin, A. A., & Miller, C. M. (2003). "Uncle Sam wants you!" Exploring verbal– visual juxtapositions in television advertising. In L. M. Scott & R. Batra (Eds.), *Persuasive imagery: A consumer response perspective* (pp. 267–295). Mahwah, NJ: Lawrence Erlbaum Associates.

Wigley, C. J., III. (1998). Verbal aggressiveness. In J. C. McCroskey, J. A. Daly, M. M. Martin, & M. J. Beatty (Eds.), *Communication and personality: Trait perspectives* (pp. 191–214). Cresskill, NJ: Hampton Press.

Williams, A. (2005, May 29). "But I neeeeeed it!'" she suggested. *The New York Times*, [Sunday Styles], 1, 6.

Williams, A. (2008, August 17). I was there. Just ask Photoshop. *The New York Times*, [Sunday styles], 1, 12.

Williams, K. D., & Dolnik, L. (2001). Revealing the worst first: Stealing thunder as a social influence strategy. In J. P. Forgas & K. D. Williams (Eds.), *Social influence: Direct and indirect processes* (pp. 213–231). Philadelphia: Taylor & Francis.

Williams-Piehota, P., Schneider, T. R., Pizarro, J., Mowad, L., & Salovey, P. (2003). Matching health messages to information-processing styles: Need for cognition and mammography utilization. *Health Communication, 15*, 375–392.

Wilson, S. R. (1999). Developing theories of persuasive message production: The next generation. In J. O. Greene (Ed.), *Message production* (pp. 15–44). Mahwah, NJ: Lawrence Erlbaum Associates.

Wilson, S. R. (2002). *Seeking and resisting compliance: Why people say what they do when trying to influence others*. Thousand Oaks, CA: Sage.

Wilson, S. R., Aleman, C. G., & Leatham, G. B. (1998). Identity implications of influence goals: A revised analysis of face-threatening acts and application to seeking compliance with same-sex friends. *Human Communication Research, 25*, 64–96.

Wilson, T. D., LaFleur, S. J., & Anderson, D. E. (1996). The validity and consequences of verbal reports about attitudes. In N. Schwarz & S. Sudman (Eds.), *Answering questions: Methodology for determining cognitive and communicative processes in survey research* (pp. 91–114). San Francisco: Jossey–Bass.

Wilson, T. D., Lindsey, S., & Schooler, T. Y. (2000). A model of dual attitudes. *Psychological Review, 107*, 101–126.

Winfield, B. (1994). *FDR and the news media*. New York: Columbia University Press.

Winsten, J. A., & DeJong, W. (2001). The designated driver campaign. In R. E. Rice & C. K. Atkin (Eds.), *Public communication campaigns* (3rd ed., pp. 290–294). Thousand Oaks, CA: Sage.

Without-Feathers.com. *Why animal testing is unethical*. Online.

Witte, K. (1997). Preventing teen pregnancy through persuasive communications: Realities, myths, and the hard-fact truths. *Journal of Community Health, 22*, 137–154.

Witte, K. (1998). Fear as motivator, fear as inhibitor: Using the Extended Parallel Process Model to explain fear appeal successes and failures. In P. A. Andersen & L. K. Guerrero (Eds.), *Handbook of communication and emotion: Research, theory, applications, and contexts* (pp. 423–450). San Diego: Academic Press.

Witte, K., & Allen, M. (2000). A meta-analysis of fear appeals: Implications for effective public health campaigns. *Health Education & Behavior, 27*, 591–615.

Witte, K., Meyer, G., & Martell, D. (2001). *Effective health risk messages: A step-by-step guide*. Thousand Oaks, CA: Sage.

Witte, K., Stokols, D., Ituarte, P., & Schneider, M. (1993). Testing the health belief model in a field study to promote bicycle safety helmets. *Communication Research, 20*, 564–586.

Wong, N. C. H., & Cappella, J. N. (2009). Antismoking threat and efficacy appeals: Effects on smoking cessation intentions for smokers with low and high readiness to quit. *Journal of Applied Communication Research, 37*, 1–20.

Wood, W., Kallgren, C. A., & Preisler, R. M. (1985). Access to attitude-relevant information in memory as a determinant of persuasion: The role of message attributes. *Journal of Experimental Social Psychology, 21*, 73–85.

Wood, W., Rhodes, N., & Biek, M. (1995). Working knowledge and attitude strength: An information-processing analysis. In R. E. Petty & J. A. Krosnick (Eds.), *Attitude strength: Antecedents and consequences* (pp. 283–313). Hillsdale, NJ: Lawrence Erlbaum Associates.

Worden, J. K., & Flynn, B. S. (2002). Using mass media to prevent cigarette smoking. In R. Hornik (Ed.), *Public health communication: Evidence for behavior change* (pp. 23–33). Mahwah, NJ: Lawrence Erlbaum Associates.

Yang, M., & Roskos-Ewoldsen, D.R. (2007). The effectiveness of brand placements in the movies: Levels of placements, explicit and implicit memory, and brand-choice behavior. *Journal of Communication, 57*, 469–489.

Yanovitzky, I., Stewart, L. P., & Lederman, L. C. (2006). Social distance, perceived drinking by peers, and alcohol use by college students. *Health Communication, 19*, 1–10.

Yates, R. A., & Noyes, J. M. (2007). Web site design, self-monitoring style, and consumer preference. *Journal of Applied Social Psychology, 37*, 1341–1362.

Yousef, F. S. (1982). North Americans in the Middle East: Aspects of the roles of friendliness, religion, and women in cross-cultural relations. In L. A. Samovar & R. E. Porter (Eds.), *Intercultural communication: A reader* (3rd ed., pp. 91–99). Belmont, CA: Wadsworth.

Zajonc, R. B. (1968). Attitudinal effects of mere exposure. *Journal of Personality and Social Psychology Monographs Supplement, 9* (2, Pt. 2), 1–27.

Zakaria, F. (2001, October 15). Why do they hate us? *Newsweek*, pp. 22–30, 32–38, 40.

Zaller, J. R. (1992). *The nature and origins of mass opinion.* New York: Cambridge University Press.

Zanna, M. P., & Fazio, R. H. (1982). The attitude–behavior relation: Moving toward a third generation of research. In M. P. Zanna, E. T. Higgins, & C. P. Herman (Eds.), *Consistency in social behavior: The Ontario symposium* (Vol. 2, pp. 283–301). Hillsdale, NJ: Lawrence Erlbaum Associates.

Zanna, M. P., & Rempel, J. K. (1988). Attitudes: A new look at an old concept. In D. Bar-Tal & A. Kruglanski (Eds.), *The social psychology of knowledge* (pp. 315–334). New York: Cambridge University Press.

Zanot, E. J., Pincus, J. D., & Lamp, E. J. (1983). Public perceptions of subliminal advertising. *Journal of Advertising, 12*, 39–45.

Zernike, K. (2008, June 22). Veterans rebut "swift boat" charges against Kerry in answer to challenge. *The New York Times*, Online.

Zimbardo, P. (2007). *The Lucifer effect: Understanding how good people turn evil.* New York: Random House.

Ziv, L. (1998, February). "I gave him my love, he gave me HIV." *Cosmopolitan*, pp. 240–243.

Zogby, J. (2008). *The way we'll be: The Zogby report on the transformation of the American dream.* New York: Random House.

Zuckerman, M. (1979). *Sensation-seeking: Beyond the optimal level of arousal.* Hillsdale, NJ: Lawrence Erlbaum Associates.

# Subject Index

# Author Index

# Communication Research Methods II

## Rebecca B. Rubin, Alan M. Rubin, Elizabeth E. Graham, Elizabeth M. Perse, David R. Seibold

### ROUTLEDGE COMMUNICATION SERIES

Expanding and building on the measures included in the original 1994 volume, *Communication Research Measures II: A Sourcebook* provides new measures in mass, interpersonal, instructional, and group/organizational communication areas, and highlights work in newer subdisciplines in communication, including intercultural, family, and health. It also includes measures from outside the communication discipline that have been employed in communication research.

The measures profiled here are "the best of the best" from the early 1990s through today. They are models for future scale development as well as tools for the trade, and they constitute the main tools that researchers can use for self-administered measurement of people's attitudes, conceptions of themselves, and perceptions of others. The focus is on up-to-date measures and the most recent scales and indexes used to assess communication variables.

Providing suggestions for measurement of concepts of interest to researchers; inspiring students to consider research directions not considered previously; and supplying models for scale developers to follow in terms of the work necessary to produce a valid and reliable measurement instrument in the discipline, the authors of this key resource have developed a significant contribution toward improving measurement and providing measures for better science.

ISBN13 hbk 978–0–8058–5132–8
ISBN13 pbk 978–0–8058–5133–5

*For ordering and further information please visit:*
www.routledge.com

# Handbook of Mass Media Ethics

## Edited by

## Lee Wilkins and Clifford G. Christians

### ROUTLEDGE COMMUNICATION SERIES

*The Handbook of Mass Media Ethics* brings together the intellectual history of mass media ethics over the past 25 years. Each chapter includes a section that summarizes current understandings and research in the field. Contributions come from many of the best minds in the field, including international scholars. Many have worked as journalists, public relations professionals, or advertising practitioners.

The volumes coverage provides:

- Foundations, sets out to define the boundaries of the intellectual work that follows
- Professional practice that cross many professional boundaries
- Concrete issues, such as privacy and justice
- Institutional perspectives

Key features of the Handbook include:

- Up-to-date and comprehensive coverage of media ethics, one of the hottest topics in the media community
- "One-stop shopping" for historical and current research in media ethics
- Experienced, top-tier editors, advisory board, and contributors

Taken in total, *The Handbook of Mass Media Ethics* provides an examination of the depth and the breadth of current thinking on media ethics. For students and professionals who seek to understand and do the best work possible, this book will provide both insight and direction. Readers wanting to learn what scholars believe they know will find in this book a good grounding from which to begin more in-depth and individualized explorations, and the extensive bibliographies for each chapter will aid that process. Standing apart in its comprehensive and in-depth coverage, the Handbook is required reading for scholars, graduate students, and researchers in media, mass communication, journalism, ethics, and related areas.

**Lee Wilkins**, University of Missouri
**Clifford G. Christians**, University of Illinois, Urbana-Champaign

ISBN13 hbk 978–0–8058–6191–4
ISBN13 pbk 978–0–8058–6192–1

*For ordering and further information please visit:*
www.routledge.com

# The Interplay of Truth and Deception

### Edited by

## Matthew S. McGlone and Mark L. Knapp

### NEW AGENDA IN COMMUNICATION SERIES

During the past 30 years, there have been a steadily increasing number of scientific and popular publications dealing with lying and deception. Questions about the extent to which public officials are deceptive are standard fare in current magazines and newspapers. This volume aims to present on a more precise conceptualization of this phenomenon, manifested in some well-known constructions like spin, hype, doublespeak, equivocation, and contextomy (quoting out of context).

The contents of the volume have been generated for the New Agendas symposium at the University of Texas College of Communication, and all the authors are young, leading-edge researchers offering innovative perspectives and explorations of lying and deception in various contexts.

This volume will appeal to scholars, researchers, and advanced/graduate students in communication, media, and psychology. It is written to the level of advanced undergraduates, and it is appropriate for use in courses covering lying and deception.

**Matthew S. McGlone**, University of Texas at Austin
**Mark L. Knapp**, University of Texas at Austin

ISBN13 hbk 978–0–415–99566–5
ISBN13 pbk 978–0–415–99567–2

*For ordering and further information please visit:*
www.routledge.com